# The American Family in Social-Historical Perspective

## Second Edition

# The American Family in Social-Historical Perspective

*Second Edition*

MICHAEL GORDON, Editor
*The University of Connecticut*

NEW YORK   ST. MARTIN'S PRESS

# ACKNOWLEDGMENTS

## I  FAMILY AND HOUSEHOLD

"Family Structure in Seventeenth-Century Andover, Massachusetts" by Philip J. Greven, Jr. First published in *William and Mary Quarterly*, 23 (1966), 234–256. A revised and expanded version of this article has been incorporated in Mr. Greven's book *Four Generations: Population, Land, and Family in Colonial Andover, Massachusetts* (Ithaca, N.Y.: Cornell University Press, 1970). Reprinted by permission.

"Family, Household, and the Industrial Revolution" by Michael Anderson. Reprinted by permission of the author and publisher from Peter Laslett (ed.), *Household and Family in Past Time* (Cambridge: Cambridge University Press, 1972). Revised by author.

"Urbanization and the Malleable Household: An Examination of Boarding and Lodging in American Families" by John Modell and Tamara K. Hareven. Reprinted from *Journal of Marriage and the Family*, 35 (August 1973), 467–479. Copyright 1973 by the National Council on Family Relations. Reprinted by permission.

"The Fall in Household Size and the Rise of the Primary Individual in the United States" by Frances Kobrin. Reprinted by permission of the author and publisher from *Demography*, 13 (February 1976), 127–138. Copyright 1976 by *Population Association of America*.

Acknowledgments and copyrights continue on pages 567–568, which constitute an extension of the copyright page.

# PREFACE

It is with considerable pleasure that I have undertaken the second edition of *The American Family in Social-Historical Perspective*. My aim in the first edition was to convey to both scholars and their students the important implications for teaching and research of the work being done by what was then a small band of social historians and historically minded sociologists. I would like to think that the first edition in some way contributed to making family history a more central concern in the sociology of the family. Although still only a minority of family sociologists see family history as their chief interest, a continually growing number recognize how vital a historical perspective is for a full understanding of the family in today's world.

The second edition differs from the first in several important ways. For one, it is larger, as befits a book dealing with a field that has grown rapidly in the intervening period. Two new sections have been added, one dealing with life stages and another dealing with marriage. A second major difference is that most of the twenty-six selections are new, only seven having been retained from the first edition. This is not because only a handful have withstood the test of time, but rather because I have found other articles that better provide the coverage a book of this kind should have in order to function successfully as a text as well as a reference book.

A third important difference between the two editions is that there are more selections dealing with women in the present volume. Not only has the number of articles in the section on women been increased from three to four, but four articles in other sections (those by Cott, Barker-Benfield, Degler, and Pleck) focus on issues that relate directly to women. The reason for this emphasis is my belief that if one is to understand the changes in the American family, or the family in any Western nation, during the last three centuries, perhaps the most fundamental way of doing so is through an appreciation of alterations in the roles and relationships of women.

Although a number of historians have commented that they would have preferred to have the selections in the first edition organized by time period rather than by subject matter, I have chosen to retain the topical organization, which lends itself better to the type of courses taught in the sociology of the family. Individual instructors will, of course, take up the readings in whatever sequence suits their purposes; but it seems somewhat easier for instructors to impose a chronological sequence on a topically arranged collection than a topical order on one chronologically arranged.

In the preface to the first edition I acknowledged the courage of St. Martin's Press in publishing what was then seen by others as a "risky" project because of the esoteric quality of the material being anthologized. As it happened their judgment was vindicated by the positive reception accorded the book. Nevertheless, I would like to express my thanks to Thomas Broadbent, Bertrand W. Lummus, and Anita Samen, all of St. Martin's Press, for facilitating the publication of the second edition.

MICHAEL GORDON
Storrs, Connecticut

# CONTENTS

# The American Family in Social-Historical Perspective

*Second Edition*

# INTRODUCTION

Until fairly recently American sociology had been remarkably ahistorical, but now a concern with long-term trends is increasingly evident in many areas, especially the family. There are several reasons why sociologists have developed a new respect for the past, but predominant among them are the changes that have occurred within the discipline of history during the last two decades.

It used to be said that historians were concerned with the lives of important people and the course of great events. While historians have hardly abandoned such concerns, there is a developing interest in the way in which the hoi polloi conducted their everyday affairs, with the result that social history has grown at an unprecedented rate since the 1960s. Because a new breed of social historians were studying topics such as marriage, migration, and mobility, an affinity was created with issues that sociologists, from their much narrower time perspective, were also considering. However, it was not subject matter alone that brought sociologists into the historical camp: they were also interested in the way in which the subject matter was being investigated.

There used to—and to some extent still does—exist within the sociological community a certain skepticism about the research of historians which, because of its traditional reliance on literary sources, was seen as "soft," if not "impressionistic." Social historians often ran into problems when attempting to find source material for their new areas of interest. The poor, often being illiterate, seldom kept diaries; and their lives were not seen as worthy of the attention of the chroniclers of their time. When the lives of common people did find their way into literary sources, they were generally given a less than sympathetic or "objective" treatment. In order to overcome the problems posed by the scarcity of traditional sources, historians turned to materials of a kind they had earlier neglected or discounted. More specifically, they began to investigate various local and national statistical sources, censuses, commission reports, and other compilations of data. In the process historians found that these sources lent themselves to the quantitative techniques that had long been used by social scientists. Thus a social-historical focus, in combination with "hard" data sources and methods of analysis, gave the historians' work a credibility in the eyes of certain sociologists, a credibility that traditional historiography had never achieved.

This convergence of sociological and historical interests has not been all one-sided. Historians appear to have done their sociological homework, perhaps more diligently than the converse is true among sociologists. Sociological concepts are now almost commonplace in social-historical literature. In fact, the degree of similarity between some social-historical work and some historical sociology is so great that it is often difficult to tell if the author of an article in an interdisciplinary journal is a sociologist or a historian. Moreover, collaborative efforts among sociologists and historians are beginning to emerge, and that is, perhaps, the best indicator of how far the convergence has progressed.

Probably no area of sociology has reaped greater benefits from the new social history than the family. Until the 1960s, sociologists had only a handful of sources to turn to if their interests centered on the American family, or the family in any society for that matter. There were two rather ambitious studies published during opening decades of this century. George Elliott Howard's *A History of Matrimonial Customs*[1] looked at the history of marriage in England and the United States largely from a legalistic perspective—Howard was a specialist in constitutional law. The discussion of legislation is filled, however, with rich detail concerning actual matrimonial practice. For example, in considering divorce Howard provides us with abundant information on the issues involved in the large group of seventeenth-century Massachusetts cases he was able to locate; similarly, in discussing adultery Howard deals not only with the laws but also with the conditions under which they were enforced and the treatment received by those charged with this offense. It is surprising that the historically minded family sociologists failed to recognize the richness of this work; perhaps they were intimidated by what they saw as a legal tome.

Arthur W. Calhoun's *A Social History of the American Family*[2] received a somewhat more favorable response from the sociological community. Calhoun's work was a bold attempt to look at the American family in all parts of the country from the days of first settlement to the post–Civil War period. The ambitiousness of this effort is remarkable in view of its modest origins. The study began as a project in a graduate seminar given before World War I at the University of Wisconsin by E. A. Ross, one of the founders of American sociology. "The result was a huge term paper, but I had so much material I couldn't bear to waste that I went on and on (1911-1919)."[3] Given its scope and the limited sources available to Calhoun, it is not surprising that time has been unkind to this study; but for half a century it existed as scripture for sociologists interested in the history of the American family.

Only a minute number of scholarly works on the American family, other than Howard and Calhoun, was produced before the 1960s, and those that were published tended to be limited in scope.[4] Perhaps the only truly outstanding work among them is Edmund Morgan's *The Puritan Family*.[5] This is traditional historiography and relies largely on literary sources; it continues to be read and cited by historians even though sociologists have made relatively little use of it in their writings. What accounts for the durability of this work is that it not only describes various aspects of family life but also attempts to explain them in terms of an overriding interpretation of Puritan ideology and culture. The fact that an essay by Morgan is the only pre-1960 work included in this volume is an indication of the special place held by his work.

Given the low level of interest in the history of the American family, how can one account for the outburst of activity in the 1960s? Part of it was due to the general growth of social history mentioned earlier, but there was also a special element involved, namely, the methodological innovations of a group of French demographers working in the early 1950s. They undertook the *reconstitution* of family patterns in a number of different eighteenth-century French parishes, with a primary focus on fertility patterns. Louis Henry, one of the key figures in this movement, reports:

> I am not a historian, and I came to historical demography because I needed information on natural fertility (fertility unlimited by birth control). Because historical demography furnished this information, it was possible to advance the study of biological factors in fertility and to construct a model that could serve as a guide to biologists in certain studies of the physiology of reproduction. As a demographer, I also know that modern statistics do not furnish so much diverse information as can be collected from the study of rural families of the eighteenth century.[6]

Thus historical demography arose as much because of problems in studying current phenomena as it did because of any intrinsic interest in historical phenomena. The technique of reconstitution used by Henry and other French demographers is nothing new; what is new is its application to a large population rather than a family. Reconstitution is essentially what genealogists do when they are compiling a family history: they check available records and study patterns of marriage, birth, and death in particular families over specified time periods. Why the French were in the vanguard here is partly a matter of the resourcefulness of their demographers, but it also has something to do with the kind of data they had available to them.

The taking of national censuses (as we understand that term) is a relatively modern phenomenon, going back to the end of the eighteenth- and the beginning of the nineteenth-centuries. To be sure, there were censuses undertaken in England and on the Continent, as well as in various colonies, before that time, but they generally fail to meet modern standards in terms of their scope or their accuracy, and demographers have been reluctant to use them to do longitudinal analysis.[7] Despite the absence of census-data statistics before the nineteenth century, many countries do have good local historical-demographic statistics, and France is especially well endowed in this respect. In the diocese of Nantes, for example, the formal registration of vital events in the form of burials and baptisms (rather than births and deaths) as well as marriages goes back to the early 1400s, and by the end of that century this practice had spread to several other dioceses. In sixteenth-, seventeenth-, and eighteenth-century France various papal and royal edicts reinforced such record keeping throughout the country, resulting in a situation which gives today's historical demographer vital records dating back several centuries. After 1792, mayors rather than priests were given the responsibility for record keeping, and many of the earlier church records were transferred to town halls, where they remain today. These local records were rich sources for the French demographers in their early reconstitution studies of premodern fertility.[8]

As one might expect, news of the work being done in France reached the United States via the demographic rather than the historical community. As early as 1964, the Office of Population Research at Princeton undertook a large-scale study known as the "European Fertility Project," which was an attempt to investigate fertility patterns in several hundred European provinces over the past century. While this work owes an acknowledged debt to the research of French demographers, it is based largely on census material and employs little in the way of reconstitution techniques.[9]

For most historians, we suspect, the news of the developments in France probably came via England, or more specifically, by means of Peter Laslett's *The World We Have Lost*, first published here in 1965.[10] This book is often thought to be the first publication produced by the Cambridge Group for the History of Population and Social Structure, which Laslett founded and currently directs. However, the book was an independent effort of Laslett's and was begun before the Cambridge Group became involved with its ambitious study of English parishes between 1574 and 1821. As social history the implications of the *The World We Have Lost* are wide ranging. It is much more than family history, though this is one of its central points. It considers various aspects of everyday life in preindustrial England: village structure, social stratification, diet, and, of course, demographic patterns. While Laslett did employ family reconstitution studies in this book it relies more heavily on the technique of *aggregate analysis*. (This is, essentially, a snapshot approach which looks at demographic and familial events at one point in time. Reconstitution, in contrast, looks at the same events in specific groups of families over time.) A preference for aggregate analysis continues to characterize the work of the Cambridge Group and its associates. Laslett's book captured the imagination of a group of American historians and inspired some of them to begin work of a similar nature in this country.

As was the case in France and England, the new family history in this country took shape around what were essentially community studies based on parish and civil records. If we look at the influential early studies, we see that Lockridge's *A New England Town*[11] dealt with Dedham, Massachusetts; Greven's *Four Generations . . . .*,[12] with Andover, Massachusetts; and Demos's *A Little Commonwealth: Family Life in the Plymouth Colony*[13] with, of course, Plymouth. Two of these studies began as doctoral dissertations: the first at Princeton, the second at Harvard; the last study took form while its author was a graduate student at Harvard. Although each of these books was first published in 1970, articles based on the research reported in them were appearing as early as 1965.[14] All three books focus on Massachusetts communities during the first century or so of their existence and use the techniques of the new historical demography; nevertheless, each study is distinctive. Lockridge's is most clearly a community study in the sense in which sociologists understand the term. It is concerned with the way in which Dedham was transformed as a political and social entity from somewhat Utopian beginnings in 1636 to its status a century later. In the process of considering the religious and political structure of the community, Lockridge employs reconstitution techniques to consider such issues as the geographic mobility of the town's population and inheritance patterns, but he never directly considers the family. The focus of Greven's book is much more demographic. Its central theme is, as its subtitle indicates, *Population, Land and Family in Colonial Andover, Massachusetts.* In it we are given information not only on household composition and family size but also on patterns of land transfer and their familial implications. Of the three, Demos's book is most directly concerned with the family. It contrasts nicely with and complements Morgan's work on the same topic.[15] While Morgan depended largely on literary sources and thus had somewhat of a patrician bias, Demos's demographic data are more revealing of the life of the common men and women in Plymouth. What gives the book its real strength is that Demos fleshes out the demographic data with material drawn from traditional historiographic sources, resulting in a much fuller picture than either demographic records or literary sources by themselves could provide.

While the work of Demos, Lockridge, and Greven does not encompass the totality of the new history of the American family as it took shape in the latter part of the 1960s, these men clearly were the most influential figures. The community focus and the demographic and behavioral approaches of their studies, rather than their literary approaches, set the tone of what was to come. (Although one might argue that the community focus was as much a result of the form in which data were available, that is, on a community basis, as anything else.) Much of the work that followed responded to these initial studies by criticizing, questioning, and refining them.

As an example of the continuing re-evaluation of the earlier studies, the Australian historian J. R. Prest has recently taken both Greven and Lockridge to task for arguing that seventeenth-century Andover and Dedham were more stable in terms of population movement than their English counterparts.[16] While other American studies (e.g., Breen and Foster and Bissel[17]) have shown greater mobility than that found in either of these Massachusetts communities, their authors are committed to Lockridge's and Greven's view that the contemporary English village was a more fluid place in terms of migration.

The nature of Prest's criticism is interesting because it conveys the way in which the field is changing. Lockridge's assumptions of the relative stability of New England settlements is based on comparisons with Laslett and Harrison's data on two seventeenth-century Midland English villages: Clayworth and Cogenhoe.[18] Prest points out that the Dedham lists which Lockridge used were tax lists and thus included only adult male taxpayers, most of whom were married men. The parochial censuses used by Laslett and Harrison, on the other hand, included women and children as well.

Moreover, Prest notes that the population-turnover rate of 61.8 percent in Clayworth between 1677 and 1688 is based on turnover from death and birth as well as migration. Prest then proceeds to limit his analysis to English household heads in Clayworth during this period in order to make the relevant comparisons with their American counterparts as studied by Lockridge. His data seem to indicate that when the samples are refined so as to make them as comparable as possible from this point in time, Dedham in 1640 to 1700 still shows a higher household-head persistence rate than Clayworth in 1676 to 1688. The difference is, however, a function of mortality rates rather than geographic mobility with the exception of the last twenty years of the century, and this may be a function of under-recording at that time. Thus it no longer seems as clear that geographic mobility in seventeenth-century America was higher than in seventeenth-century England. What we have, then, in Prest's work is not a startling transformation of perspective springing from a methodological innovation; rather it is a more precise analysis of the same data, resulting in some of the original conclusions no longer seeming tenable.

The growth of American family history in the 1970s has occurred not just as the result of the replication, extension, and refinement of first-generation studies. It has also been the result of the expansion and elaboration of certain subareas, among which the black family and women in the family immediately come to mind. When the first edition of this book was published relatively little research existed about either of these two areas. Articles on blacks were beginning to appear, but virtually no reconstitution, or even aggregate analysis, had done for slaves during the antebellum period.[19] Now there are several major studies available,[20] as well as several less broad-ranging, but by no means inconsequential, ones.[21] This new body of literature has broadened our knowledge of the black family during and after slavery, and, more importantly, it has raised serious questions about traditional images of the slave family.

The older, more literary histories argued that since slaves had no legal rights, they could not marry, and the unions that they did form were thus rendered unstable.[22] Moreover, this instability was contributed to by the frequency with which slaves were sold to other plantation owners and the extent to which slave women were sexually abused by their masters.

Through the use of plantation records, slave-market registers, and even oral history, the research of the 1970s has shown that blacks under slavery were able to maintain an extraordinary amount of nuclear-family integrity and develop important extended kinship patterns because of their own resourcefulness and because the prevalence of the insidious practices mentioned above may have been exaggerated in earlier historical studies. Thus, new studies are challenging those who would place the blame for today's relatively high incidence of single-parent families among blacks at the doorstep of slavery. Similarly, during the Reconstruction era and the years immediately after, black families maintained themselves with both parents present. To be sure, by the last decades of the nineteenth century we can see the roots of twentieth-century patterns of higher rates of single-parent households emerging as blacks encounter racism in the cities to which they are moving. Considerable debate has raged among the historians involved in this research over the interpretation and generalization permitted by each other's findings, but this has simply added to the excitement of reading this new literature.[23]

The enormous growth of women's history during the past ten years is treated as part of family history because of the extent to which such research is concerned with the role of women in the family.[24] Work being done in this area is of the demographic and literary variety. As in the case of black history, it, too, seems to have its controversies, though the debates have not been quite as heated.

The question that looms largest for historians dealing with women in the family is the effect of industrialization on women's place in and out of the home. Traditional wisdom held that the growth of the factory quickly resulted in married women staying home while their husbands and, to a lesser extent, their children went out to work. It does appear that throughout the nineteenth century the number of married women in the external work force was inconsequential. What is being questioned by historians today is both what it meant to be a housewife during this time (especially for working-class women) and what sort of work (of an income-generating kind) was performed in the home.[25] In other words, did staying home equal being "unproductive" in any meaningful sense? As evidence of how far such work has progressed, we are beginning to see not only studies that are concerned with international differences in the role and position of women during the early industrial period,[26] but also others which look at differences between groups in American society.[27] An example of the latter is Elizabeth H. Pleck's fine study, "A Mother's Wages: Income Earning Among Italian and Black Women, 1896–1911," in part six of this book.

The field of family history has also been enhanced by the development of new perspectives; an important example of this is the concern with the family life cycle. The first edition of this book included an article by Lutz Berkner in which he took issue with Laslett's claim that the nuclear family has long been the primary household unit in the West.[27] Drawing upon his research dealing with peasants in a section of eighteenth-century Austria, Berkner points out that there commonly was a period (between when the father retired and allowed a son to start his own family and take over the farm and when the elderly parents died) during which households were of the three-generation extended variety. Whether or not a family went through such a phase, or for how long, was largely a matter of parental longevity; but when parents did not die prematurely it was a typical pattern. Laslett did not recognize this period because, Berkner maintains, England may have had less land in the hands of its peasantry, and because Laslett used aggregate analysis. Since the latter gives a picture of one point in time, only a small number of families will be in an extended phase; thus the true prevalence of the three-generation pattern will be underestimated.

Other scholars have investigated the way in which household composition has varied over the life cycle. For example, the article "Urbanization and the Malleable Household: An Examination of Boarding and Lodging in American Families" by John Modell and Tamara K. Hareven reveals that boarders and lodgers tended to be young adults, and those who took them in were older people whose children had already left home, leaving both physical space and financial need.[28] The realization that the household is a dynamic entity which responds to change in the biological and social status of family and nonfamily members is really only the beginning of an appreciation of life cycle as an important variable.[29] In the work of Glen H. Elder, Jr., the life cycle is treated in a manner that has wide-ranging implications. Drawing upon the Oakland Growth study, Elder was able to analyze a cohort of working- and middle-class Californians from their childhood years in the early 1930s to the formation of their own families in the postwar decades.[30] He was primarily concerned with assessing the effects of the Depression—or, more specifically, the degree to which the respondents' families felt the effects of it—as a subsequent influence on the vocational and familial activities of these people. The importance of this study is that it not only follows individuals through various phases of the life cycle but attempts to relate the way in which a great event (the normal concern of the historians) impinged on their lives. At the same time it reveals how social class served to insulate some people from certain problems—not by providing an economic buffer, since many of the middle-class families lost as much (relatively speaking) as the working-class—but in terms of the provision of nonmaterial factors. In Elder's words: "Problem-solving resources and support for adaptive responses tend to increase with class position."[31] Elder's work probably represents the most sophisticated application of the life-cycle or life-course perspective in the field of family history to date, but this approach offers considerable potential for other equally provocative studies.

Scholarly fields grow not only through the search for new forms of data, innovations in modes of analyzing data, and the creation of interest in certain issues but also through the development of theory. In fact, theory often serves as catalyst for all of these. In the first edition of this book we spoke of modernization as a unifying theme and then proceeded to discuss the meaning of this concept. We still believe that modernization remains the key concept in the study of change in the family. However, criticism directed at this concept in the intervening years demands that we follow any discussion of modernization with some commentary on the scholarly debate in this area.

Since this book of readings has been prepared primarily as an introduction to family history for sociologists, it is necessary to review some of the relevant sociological literature. This will provide a backdrop against which the findings presented can be viewed.

A theme that runs through the sociological literature on the family is the impact of modernization on this institution. Here, the term *modernization* encompasses much more than the replacement of cottage industry by the factory system of production; it involves profound and revolutionary changes that took place in Europe during the eighteenth and nineteenth centuries and that affected all aspects of society, from the types of community in which people lived to the way in which they viewed the world. An informative scheme for exploring the nature and meaning of these changes is provided by Robert Nisbet in his important book, *The Sociological Tradition.*[32] This book essentially presents the emergence of sociology as a discipline during the nineteenth century; but it is Nisbet's thesis that sociology arose as a new way of seeing the world in response to the changes brought about by the resounding impact of what E. J. Hobsbawm has called the "dual revolution": the simultaneous occurrence of the French Revolution and the Industrial Revolution.[33] Nisbet believes that the five basic concepts, or "unit-ideas," of the discipline get to the core of these changes; these concepts are: community, authority, status, the sacred, and alienation. Each concept focuses on an aspect of social structure or culture that was in a state of flux during the nineteenth century. Together they provide a composite picture of the alterations in Western society that have variously been referred to as the movement from *Gemeinschaft* to *Gesellschaft*—from organic to mechanical solidarity—or, later, the movement from folk to urban society, or, perhaps most appropriately, as modernization. Whatever the phrase employed, the basic issue is still dramatic social change, social change that both directly and indirectly affected the family. Let us look at each of these unit-ideas in some detail.

The concept of *community* as it figured in the writings of sociology's "founding fathers" dealt with the quality of the individual's relationships with other people through group and associational involvement. Obviously, then, an important determinant of community becomes the degree to which a society is urbanized. While cities did exist long before industrial growth took place, they were scattered centers containing only a small proportion of the population. As markets grew and factories multiplied, the escalated need for labor created a veritable urban explosion. Referring to England's industrial midlands, Michael Anderson points out that "the population of Preston in 1851 was 5.7 [times] what it had been in 1801 and Burnley, Ashton, Blackburn, Stockport, Rochdale, Bolton, and Bury had all grown by more than three times. The population of Preston, and also of Burnley, more than doubled between 1831 and 1851."[34] The sociological implications of such dramatic shifts in population are far-ranging indeed. Most obviously—and this touches the heart of the so-called Industrial Revolution—these shifts meant that for the first time in history, agriculture and husbandry were dethroned as the major sources of production and social position. From the individual's point of view, it meant that the relatively insulated social existence possible in farm and village was now out of the question. Almost by definition, urban life involved what Richard Sennett has aptly called "contact points."[35] It is tempting, though dangerous, as Michael Anderson shows us, to play down the maintenance of extended kin ties in an urban setting; but it does seem evident that the likelihood of living near nonkin was greater and that people were required to leave their homes to obtain services and items previously provided by the domestic unit. In short, these new rural migrants were forced to interact with strangers in settings that were alien to them. Yet, at the very center of the urban experience and, perhaps, overriding all other factors was a phenomenon that William Goode, with his usual acuity, describes so well: 'The city became the carrier of new ideologies, thus giving a moral validation to these alterations in social patterns. Thus, the urban-rural differences begin to decline, since the thinking of those who live in rural areas is shaped by the forces that urbanize the nation."[36] The meaning of this quotation will become clearer as we consider the other unit-ideas.

By directing our attention to concepts of *authority*, Nisbet is referring not only to change in government but also to more fundamental changes in the legitimation of power within the community. Quite correctly, he is going beyond the replacement of monarchies by legislative forms of government and considering more subtle and wide-ranging alterations.

In traditional society authority is hardly recognized as having separate or even distinguishable identity. How could it be? Deeply embedded in social functions, an inalienable part of the inner order of family, neighborhood, parish, and guild, ritualized at every turn, authority is so closely woven into the fabric of tradition and morality as to be scarcely more noticeable than the air men breathe. Even in the hands of the king, authority in such a society tends to maintain this diffuse and indirect character. Such is the tendency of monarchial power to become submerged in the whole ethos of patriarchalism that the power of the king seems to its subjects as but little different from that exercised by fathers over sons, priests over communicants, and masters over apprentices. The entire weight of morality—which is typically the morality of duty and allegiance—makes authority an undifferentiated aspect of the social order, the government hardly more than a symbolic superstructure.[37]

Not surprisingly, then, the coming of new forms of national authority was associated with the questioning of authority in other spheres of life, and the family did not remain unscathed. Paternal authority, a relevant example, resided not only in the broad legitimating sources described by Nisbet but also in the basic control that a father could exercise over his son's vocational life chances. Where we find the intergenerational transmission of land intact, as in peasant societies, we find paternal authority to be strong; but in industrial societies a son no longer required—at least not to the same extent—the good offices of his father to obtain work. Thus he could assert his autonomy at the expense of his father's authority. To be sure, the effects of this liberating process were not equally felt in all segments of society. Among the wealthy, even after industrialization, the intergenerational transmission of wealth and opportunity resulted in the maintenance of parental control over children and a dulling of industrialization's impact; yet here, too, the new ideology of equalitarianism ultimately weakened paternal dominance.

The weakening of paternal authority through the emergence of a broader division of labor is related in a fundamental way to questions of social stratification. In focusing on the unit-idea of *status*, Nisbet directs our attention to the preoccupation with the question of social class that is found in the writings of Marx, Weber, Tocqueville, and other early sociological lights. Clearly, the previously held picture of a continuous hierarchy was no longer adequate to describe social reality, and a debate now raged over the shape of the new stratification system. From the present point of view, the question of whether "class" or "status group" best describes it is not as significant as the fact that such issues were beginning to gain importance. In terms of the family, what is most relevant is that the new stratification—whether status group or class—permitted much more social mobility.

Stratification systems vary in the degree to which they permit mobility between strata. Estate systems such as that which characterized medieval Europe (i.e., the nobility, clergy, and commons) are generally thought of as allowing little interstrata movement, while current class or status systems are seen as more permeable. Industrialization not only undermined agriculture as the primary vocational activity and source of social placement, but, as part of a broader institutional differentiation that was occurring in society, it created a multiplicity of jobs, that is, a division of labor much greater than anything that had previously existed. This meant that although a man might not move out of the stratum into which he was born during his own lifetime (vertical mobility), he might still move into a job which would involve a different occupational subculture and work surroundings while in the same stratum as his father. This is horizontal mobility. What we must keep in mind is that such intergenerational discontinuity in the realm of work adds one more nail to the coffin of traditional society because of the potential for societal diversity in outlook and life style that it introduces.

Since, as Nisbet so eloquently argues, sociology arose in the nineteenth century as a response to developments that some saw as crises in the realms of societal integration and social control, it is not surprising to find that there was a considerable amount of interest evidenced in religion. This concern with *the sacred* reflects what early sociologists saw as the increasing secularization of European society. Secularization refers less to such things as church attendance than to the extent to which everyday life is infused with religious significance and the degree to which religious proscriptions and prescriptions affect behavior. Many nineteenth-century intellectuals—sociologists as well as nonsociologists—saw religion rapidly slipping into insignificance and in the process creating a situation of moral crisis, a theme which echoes and reechoes in their writings. In terms of its immediate relevance for the family, we see this concern with the loss of God and purity, and the spread of prostitution, pornography, and so forth. In a sense we might say that the family, viewed as the cornerstone of society, was held to be the institution most vulnerable to the floodgates of irreligion that were apparently opening.

To this point, the four unit-ideas we have discussed (community, authority, status, and the sacred) deal more with the societal consequences of modernization than with the impact on the individual of these dramatic changes. Given current perspectives it may be difficult to imagine just how profoundly social life was changed in the nineteenth century. For some, this change resulted in feelings of being cut off from the "self" and from a world that was rapidly undergoing modification before their eyes. Marx's early writings, for example, deal explicitly with what might be called "personal alienation" arising from man's being cut off from the products of his own labor. We should not emphasize solely the economic aspects of alienation. In even simpler terms, the growth in societal scale, with its concomitant impersonality and remoteness, fosters the feeling of isolation and detachment that we have come to identify as *alienation*. Yet, one must also remember that modernization is associated with the appearance of a degree of personal freedom never previously experienced by most people; perhaps freedom and alienation are best seen as opposite sides of the same coin.

When we look at the composite social picture of the concepts of community, authority, status, the sacred, and alienation, we can see how fundamental were the changes brought about by the two revolutions with which Nisbet deals. Obviously, the impact of these revolutions was not felt at all places at the same time. This country, for example, experienced its major industrial growth almost a century after England.[38] The later the modernization, the greater the ideological factor becomes—that is, whether these changes are regarded as right, proper, and even desirable. There are, of course, important and basic differences between a nation now emerging out of a colonial system of government and a primary economic system and England in the second half of the eighteenth century. Still, comparisons are not without value, and the historical data may provide considerable insights into present events.

The criticism that has been directed at modernization theory comes from a number of different quarters and has centered on a number of different themes.[39] Essentially, the criticism can be summarized in two points: (1) there is no such thing as modernization theory, and (2) theory or not, modernization is a model based on the Western experience and has limited generality there, much less to Third World countries today. Each of these points requires our separate consideration.

The point of whether or not something called modernization theory exists is perhaps of greater interest to philosophers of science than it is to people working in the field of family history. It is our impression that most practitioners have looked at modernization as more of a diagram than a theory. In other words, they have considered certain general changes in the structure of Western society and the impact these changes have had on the life-style and thinking of people, and have said, perhaps too hastily, that this template will fit all societies undergoing similar processes. As a result, critics point to the countries which have failed to fulfill the prophecies based on the experiences of England, France, and Germany. As an illustration of this let us consider some demographic phenomena.

In the past demographers relied heavily on the demographic transition theory to explain the impact of modernization and industrialization upon populations.[40] Stated simply, the theory posits: in the premodern era both fertility and mortality existed at high levels, in effect neutralizing each other. The result was that, with the exception of periods of war, famine, or some other catastrophe, populations remained fairly constant. The improved agricultural production associated with the early stages of industrialization, as well as later improvements in sanitation and health care, created a declining mortality rate in the face of a continued high level of fertility, and population thus grew. Slowly, and for a variety of reasons which are still not completely understood, fertility also began to decline, returning population growth to a level of stability not unlike that which existed while both rates were neutralizing each other at high levels. The fact that many third world countries have continued to manifest very high rates of fertility despite the rapid decline in death rates has been cited as an example of the inability of demographic transition theory (and, by implication, modernization as theory) to deal with the realities of Third World nations as they "modernize." One could, of course, respond by saying that the time scale being applied is much more compressed than the one used historically. England's fertility, some too readily forget, did not fall until almost a century after the onset of industrialization. Given the facts that death rates have only recently fallen in the Third World and many of these countries are still in several respects traditional, the so-called failure of the demographic transition model should be kept in perspective.

Still, the criticism that has been directed at modernization as a theory has proven useful because it has sensitized researchers to an issue which they might have otherwise ignored. Patricia Branca, for example, has shown in a recent article how the patterns of female employment during the nineteenth century have been discussed as though they were the same in all industrializing European countries; but, in fact, the model that has been used is much more applicable to the Anglo-American situation than it is to the Continental-European one.[41] In the latter women did not move into the factories in large numbers but worked in agriculture and domestic industry; moreover, Branca reminds us that in Continental Europe, as well as in England and America, domestic service was the most prevalent occupation among single women. Branca's work makes us aware of important aspects of modernization; namely, it presents problems in dealing with change at different points in time, but it also must be used in a way that does not blur the differences between the experiences of the European countries, which modernized more or less contemporaneously.

Despite the criticism that has been directed at modernization as a theory, it continues to be a useful tool for studying the family over time. To be sure, in using it we must be aware of the problems it poses and the traps it presents, but with this in mind modernization still serves to illuminate and make coherent various aspects of the social history of the family in the West.

We have in this introductory essay attempted to consider both the development of the field of family history and the direction that work in the area has taken since the first edition of this book was published. Given limitations of space, this review has by necessity been abbreviated and only the more salient developments have been touched upon. Similarly, in choosing readings we have attempted to provide examples of some of the best recent work, but we have also attempted to assemble articles that touch upon a wide area of family-related subjects. This has resulted in our having to exclude several first-rate articles. In order to compensate for this, a selected bibliography has been appended to this essay as well as to the end of each section.

## NOTES

1. George E. Howard, *A History of Matrimonial Institutions*, 3 vols. (Chicago: University of Chicago Press, 1904).

2. Arthur W. Calhoun, *A Social History of the American Family*, first published 1917 (New York: Barnes & Noble, 1945).

3. Letter from Calhoun, August 4, 1973.

4. See, for example, Levin L. Schücking, *Die Puritanische Familie* (Leipzig: B. G. Teubner Verlag, 1929), and Charles E. Ironside, *The Family in Colonial New York* (New York: Columbia University Press, 1942).

5. Edmund S. Morgan, *The Puritan Family* (Boston: Boston Public Library, 1944).

6. Louis Henry, "Historical Demography," *Daedalus*, 97 (1968), 385–396.

7. An interesting example of how these early censuses can be used is found in Robert V. Wells, *The Population of the British Colonies in America Before 1776* (Princeton: Princeton University Press, 1975).

8. Henry, "Historical Demography," p. 386.

9. Ansley J. Coale, Foreword to Etienne Van De Walle, *The Female Population of France in the Nineteenth Century* (Princeton: Princeton University Press, 1974).

10. Peter Laslett, *The World We Have Lost*, 2nd ed. (New York: Scribner, 1973).

11. Kenneth A. Lockridge, *A New England Town: The First Hundred Years.* (New York: Norton, 1970).

12. Philip J. Greven, Jr., *Four Generations: Population, Land, and Family in Colonial Andover, Massachusetts.* (Ithaca, N.Y.: Cornell University Press, 1970).

13. John Demos, *A Little Commonwealth: Family Life in the Plymouth Colony* (New York: Oxford University Press, 1970).

14. Kenneth A. Lockridge, "The Population of Dedham, Massachusetts, 1636–1736," *Economic History Review*, 19 (1966), 318–344; Philip J. Greven, Jr., "Family Structure in Seventeenth-Century Andover, Massachusetts," *William and Mary Quarterly*, 23 (1955), 234–256; John Demos, "Notes on Life in Plymouth Colony," *William and Mary Quarterly*, 22 (1965), 264–286.

15. Morgan, *The Puritan Family*.

16. W. R. Prest, "Stability and Change in Old and New England: Clayworth and Dedham," *Journal of Interdisciplinary History*, 6 (1976), 359–374.

17. T. H. Breen and Stephen Foster, "Moving to the New World: The Character of Early Massachusetts Immigration," *William and Mary Quarterly*, 30 (1973), 243–254; L. A. Bissell, "From One Generation to Another: Mobility in Seventeenth-Century Windsor, Connecticut," *William and Mary Quarterly*, 31 (1974), 79–110.

18. Peter Laslett and John Harrison, "Clayworth and Cogenhoe," in *Historical Essays Prescribed to David Ogg*, ed. H. E. Bill and R. L. Ollard (New York: Barnes & Noble, 1963), pp. 147–184.

19. Theodore Hershberg, "Free Blacks in Ante-Bellum Philadelphia, *Journal of Social History*, 5 (1971–1972), 183–209; Elizabeth H. Pleck, "The Two-Parent Household: Black Family Structure in Late Nineteenth Century Boston," *Journal of Social History*, 6 (1972), 1–31.

20. Robert W. Fogel and Stanley L. Engerman, *Time on the Cross* (Boston: Little, Brown, 1974); Eugene V. Genovese, *Roll, Jordan, Roll* (New York: Pantheon, 1974); Herbert G. Gutman, *The Black Family in Slavery and Freedom,* (New York: Pantheon, 1976).

21. Paul J. Lammermeier, "The Urban Black Family of the Nineteenth Century: A Study of Black Family Structure in the Ohio Valley, 1850–1880," *Journal of Marriage and the Family*, 31 (1969), 145–152; Frank F. Furstenberg, Jr., Theodore Hershberg, and John Modell, "The Origins of the Female-Headed Black Family: The Impact of the Urban Experience," *Journal of Interdisciplinary History*, 6 (1975), 24–33; Crandall A. Shifflett, "The Household Composition of Rural Black Families: Louisa County, Virginia, 1880." *Journal of Interdisciplinary History*, 6 (1975), 235–260.

22. See, for example, Frank Tannenbaum, *Slave and Citizen* (New York: Knopf, 1946).

23. Herbert G. Gutman, *Slavery and the Numbers Game* (Urbana: University of Illinois Press, 1975).

24. For a sampling of this literature see the bibliography that follows the introduction to section four, "Women: Roles and Relationships."

25. See, for example, Susan J. Kleinberg, "Technology and Women's Work: The Lines of Working Class Women in Pittsburgh, 1870–1900," *Labor History*, 17 (1976), 58–72.

26. See, for example, Patricia Branca, "A New Perspective on Women's Work: A Comparative Typology," *Journal of Social History*, 9 (1975) 129–153.

27. Laslett, *The World We Have Lost*, and Lutz K. Berkner, "The Stem Family and the Developmental Cycle: An 18th-Century Austrian Example," *American Historical Review*, 77 (1972), 398–414.

28. Included in part one, "Family and Household," of this book.

29. A useful discussion of the life cycle as a variable is found in Maris A. Vinovskis, "From Household Size to the Life Course: Some Observations on Recent Trends in Family History," *American Behavioral Scientist* (forthcoming).

30. Glen H. Elder, Jr. *Children of the Great Depression*. (Chicago: University of Chicago Press, 1974).

31. Ibid., p. 277.

32. Robert A. Nisbet, *The Sociological Tradition* (New York: Basic Books, 1966).

33. E. J. Hobsbawm, *The Age of Revolution, 1789–1848* (New York: Mentor Books, 1964).

34. Michael Anderson, *Family Structure in Nineteenth-Century Lancashire* (Cambridge: Cambridge University Press, 1971), p. 33.

35. Richard Sennett, *The User of Disorder* (New York: Knopf, 1970).

36. William J. Goode, *World Revolutions and Family Patterns* (New York: The Free Press, 1963), p. 375.

37. Nisbet, *Sociological Tradition*, p. 108.

38. For a discussion of modernization in the United States, see Richard D. Brown, *Modernization, The Transformation of American Life 1600–1865* (New York: Hill & Wang, 1976).

39. See, for example, Dean C. Tipps, "Modernization Theory and the Comparative Study of Societies," *Comparative Studies in Society and History*, 15 (1973), 199–226, and Christopher Lasch, "The Family and History," *New York Review of Books*, 22 (November 13, 1975), 33–38.

40. See, for example, Frank W. Notestein, "Population: The Long View, in *Food for the World*, ed. T. W. Schultz (Chicago: University of Chicago Press, 1945), pp. 36–57.

41. Branca, "A New Perspective."

# SELECTED READINGS FOR THE INTRODUCTION

ANDERSON, MICHAEL *Family Structure in Nineteenth-Century Lancashire*. Cambridge, Eng.: Cambridge University Press, 1971.

CALHOUN, ARTHUR W. *A Social History of the American Family*. 1917. Reprint. New York: Barnes & Noble, 1945.

DEMOS, JOHN. *A Little Commonwealth: Family Life in the Plymouth Colony*. New York: Oxford University Press, 1970.

FARBER, BERNARD. *Guardians of Virtue: Salem Families in 1800*. New York: Basic Books, 1972.

GREVEN, PHILIP J., JR. *Four Generations: Population Land, and Family in Colonial Andover, Massachusetts*. Ithaca, N.Y.: Cornell University Press, 1970.

HAREVEN, TAMARA K., ed. *Family and Kin in Urban Communities, 1700-1930*. New York: New Viewpoints, 1977.

HOWARD, GEORGE E. *A History of Matrimonial Institutions*. 3 vols. Chicago: University of Chicago Press, 1904.

KATZ, MICHAEL B. *The People of Hamilton, Canada West*. Cambridge: Harvard University Press, 1975.

LASCH, CHRISTOPHER. *Haven in a Heartless World*. New York: Basic Books, 1977.

LASLETT, PETER. *The World We Have Lost*. 2nd ed. New York: Scribner, 1973.

MORGAN, EDMUND. *The Puritan Family*. 1944. Reprint. New York: Harper & Row, 1966.

RABB, THEODORE K., AND ROBERT I. ROTBERG, eds. *The Family in History*. New York: Harper & Row, 1973.

ROSENBERG, CHARLES, ed. *The Family in History*. Philadelphia: University of Pennsylvania Press, 1975.

SHORTER, EDWARD. *The Making of the Modern Family*. New York: Basic Books, 1975.

STONE, LAWRENCE. *The Family, Sex and Marriage in England, 1500 1800*. New York: Harper & Row, 1977.

# PART ONE |

# FAMILY AND HOUSEHOLD

The opening section of this book is devoted to the family and the household structure, with special emphasis on the latter. It might be argued that the first issue explored by the emerging field of family history was whether and how household size and composition had changed over the last few centuries. One of the fruits of this effort was the realization of the need to differentiate between family and household in discussing change over time, with the result that the focus of family history is now generally on the household unit. A recent summary of the work of the Cambridge Group for the History of Population and Social Structure (Laslett, 1977)* as well as related research indicates that Laslett still firmly believes that the nuclear family has been the primary residential unit in England and Western Europe for as far before industrialization as current research is able to ascertain. However, this point continues to be debated (Goubert, 1977). Although we know more now than we did at the beginning of the 1970s, considerably more research must be done in Western and non-Western settings before we can have an accurate reading of the early residential structure of family life and the factors that have acted upon it.

Philip J. Greven's article "Family Structure in Seventeenth-Century Andover, Massachusetts" has earned a place as a classic in the field of American family history. From it we can picture key aspects of domestic life during the early years of settlement in a Massachusetts village. The crux of the paper is the relationship between fathers and sons, that is, between those who settled the community and their male offspring. By current standards the extent of paternal control over a young man as he reached maturity was truly extraordinary. In order for him to start a family of his own, he first had to obtain land on which to build a home and farm, and the most direct avenue for achieving it was through a paternal gift. It appears that most fathers were fairly generous, having often received an abundant supply of property in the early divisions of the town land. However, they insisted on exercising a good degree of control over their sons' lives by maintaining formal ownership of the land until their own deaths. Thus Greven quite correctly characterizes the situation as standing some-

*Complete citations for works referred to are in the selected readings on p. 82.

17

where between a nuclear family and an extended family, which he appropriately describes as a "modified extended family." The extension resides both in the proximity of the first-generation married sons to their fathers and in the persistence of paternal dominance even after marriage. Most discussions of the extended family regrettably neglect this element of family authority and mistakenly focus only on household structure. It is interesting to compare Greven's description of seventeenth-century Andover with Young and Willmott's of a working-class section of London in the 1950s (Young and Wilmott, 1962). In the latter, the modified extended family focuses on the mother and the emotional and social support she provides, but from a structural point of view it is remarkably similar to Greven's Andover.

Michael Anderson's paper "Family, Household, and the Industrial Revolution" is the only one in this section that does not focus on the United States. It has been included because of its excellence and because similar research for the early industrial period in this country has not yet been carried out. Especially intriguing are Anderson's findings which question the relationship between industrialization and small household size. Contrary to what once passed as conventional sociological wisdom, he discovered that in 1851 there were more households with kin in residence in Preston, an industrial city, than in households in the British preindustrial communities studied by the Cambridge Group. To some extent, of course, this represents the "piling up" typical of rapidly growing industrial cities. When making the move from an outlying rural region to an industrial city, who could help more than kin? Yet, the reason for a higher incidence of three-generation families (involving older, often widowed, parents) in Preston than in rural and urban areas was also to be found, Anderson feels, in the service these persons performed for the family. In fact, Anderson argues that kin were an economic asset rather than the drain they might have been in another setting. For example, an aged grandmother could free her daughter from child care and thus allow her to do other work. Anderson's argument draws upon what sociologists call "exchange theory." His interpretation assumes that kin ties and kin contacts, to a large extent, will be maintained only where kin can perform *reciprocal* services. Household composition during the beginning stages of industrialization, then, may represent a distinctive transitional stage rather than a full-blown picture of later industrial patterns.

Anderson does discuss the phenomenon of boarding and lodging, but it is not a central concern of his paper. John Modell and Tamara K. Hareven, however, deal exclusively with this most interesting household type in "Urbanization and the Malleable Household: An Examination of Boarding and Lodging in American Families." Lodging involves renting part of one's residence, sometimes a room, at other times a bed in a corner; boarding involves lodging as well as the provision of one or more meals for the lodger. Like Michael Anderson, Modell and Hareven interpret boarding and lodging as an outgrowth of the early stages of industrialization. For young people in search of work—from either the rural countryside or another country—who came to a rapidly expanding industrial city where they had no kin, boarding and lodging were important adaptive devices. Not only did they provide young people with a place to stay when the cost of an individual residence was beyond their means, but they also gave them a socializing experience, a way of learning the ins and outs of urban life. By taking up residence with people whose offspring were already self-supporting, the newcomers could benefit from the counsel of these people while at the same time providing them with income that they lost when their children went out into the world.

Boarding/lodging is an aspect of family history that typifies the danger of taking a bipolar view of modernization and/or industrialization. If we were to compare preindustrial America or England with their situations today, we would miss boarding/lodging since it was associated largely with the early stages of industrialization.

In "The Fall in Household Size and the Rise of the Primary Individual in the United States" Frances E. Kobrin brings us up to date on the American household and points to an area that frequently gets insufficient attention in discussions of the ways in which the household has changed in modern societies. When the sociologists of the 1950s and 1960s seriously questioned the concept that modern families were not the isolated and atomized nuclear units that an earlier generation of sociologists had maintained, and when, later, historians began to show that the nuclear family had been the most common residential form for several centuries in the West, some were tempted to ignore differences over time. Kobrin points out that while the nuclear family may not be a more common residential unit now than it was in the nineteenth century, there has been a movement, nonetheless, toward a stricter adherence to the nuclear-family pattern. Not only have the servants commonly encountered during the seventeenth and eighteenth centuries vanished, as well as the boarders and lodgers of the late nineteenth and early twentieth centuries, but unmarried adult children and the widowed parents are also leaving the nuclear family. Thus, in the twentieth century, single-person households have grown more rapidly than any other category, especially since World War II. While this trend is a reflection of a growing affluence that enables people to maintain expensive forms of residence, it is also, we would argue, a reflection of a value system that emphasizes independence and privacy.

This section allows the reader to consider various aspects of American family life, and especially the household, over a three-hundred-year period. It shows how important the transmission of family land was in the first centuries of American history and how this consideration receded as we moved from being a nation of agriculturists to one of city dwellers. It is noteworthy that the nuclear family has continued to be the most prevalent residential unit even though there has been a departure of various ancillary personnel—kin and nonkin alike—who, in the past, provided variety in household form.

# 1 | FAMILY STRUCTURE IN SEVENTEENTH-CENTURY ANDOVER, MASSACHUSETTS

## PHILIP J. GREVEN, JR.

Surprisingly little is known at present about family life and family structure in the seventeenth-century American colonies. The generalizations about colonial family life embedded in textbooks are seldom the result of studies of the extant source materials, which historians until recently have tended to ignore.[1] Genealogists long have been using records preserved in county archives, town halls, churches, and graveyards as well as personal documents to compile detailed information on successive generations of early American families. In addition to the work of local genealogists, many communities possess probate records and deeds for the colonial period. A study of these last testaments and deeds, together with the vital statistics of family genealogies, can provide the answers to such questions as how many children people had, how long people lived, at what ages did they marry, how much control did fathers have over their children, and to what extent and under what conditions did children remain in their parents' community. The answers to such questions enable an historian to reconstruct to some extent the basic characteristics of family life for specific families in specific communities. This essay is a study of a single seventeenth-century New England town, Andover, Massachusetts, during the lifetimes of its first and second generations—the pioneers who carved the community out of the wilderness, and their children who settled upon the lands which their fathers had acquired. A consideration of their births, marriages, and deaths, together with the disposition of land and property within the town from one generation to the next, reveals some of the most important aspects of family life and family structure in early Andover.

The development of a particular type of family structure in seventeenth-century Andover was dependent in part upon the economic development of the community during the same period. Andover, settled by a group of about eighteen men during the early 1640s and incorporated in 1646, was patterned at the outset after the English open field villages familiar to many of the early settlers. The inhabitants resided on house lots adjacent to each other in the village center, with their individual holdings of land being distributed in small plots within two large fields beyond the village center. House lots ranged in size from four to twenty acres, and subse-

Mr. Greven is a member of the Department of History, Rutgers University.

quent divisions of land within the town were proportionate to the size of the house lots. By the early 1660s, about forty-two men had arrived to settle in Andover, of whom thirty-six became permanent residents. During the first decade and a half, four major divisions of the arable land in the town were granted. The first two divisions established two open fields, in which land was granted to the inhabitants on the basis of one acre of land for each acre of house lot. The third division, which provided four acres of land for each acre of house lot, evidently did not form another open field but was scattered about the town. The fourth and final division of land during the seventeenth century occurred in 1662 and gave land to the householders at the rate of twenty acres for each acre of their house lots. Each householder thus obtained a minimum division allotment of about eighty acres and a maximum allotment of about four hundred acres. Cumulatively, these four successive divisions of town land, together with additional divisions of meadow and swampland, provided each of the inhabitants with at least one hundred acres of land for farming and as much as six hundred acres. During the years following these substantial grants of land, many of the families in the town removed their habitations from the house lots in the town center onto their distant, and extensive, farm lands, thus altering the character of the community through the establishment of independent family farms and scattered residences. By the 1680s, more than half the families in Andover lived outside the original center of the town on their own ample farms. The transformation of the earlier open field village effectively recast the basis for family life within the community.[2]

An examination of the number of children whose births are recorded in the Andover town records between 1651 and 1699 reveals a steady increase in the number of children being born throughout the period. (See Table 1.[3]) Between 1651 and 1654, 28 births are recorded, followed by 32 between 1655 and 1659, 43 between 1660 and 1664, 44 between 1665 and 1669, 78 between 1670 and 1674, and 90 between 1675 and 1679. After 1680 the figures rise to more than one hundred births every five years. The entire picture of population growth in Andover, however, cannot be formed from a study of the town records alone since these records do not reflect the pattern of generations within the town. Looked at from the point of view of the births of the children of the first generation of settlers who arrived in Andover between the first settlement in the mid-1640s and 1660, a very different picture emerges, hidden within the entries of the town records and genealogies.[4] The majority of the second-generation children were born during the two decades of the 1650s and the 1660s. The births of 159 second-generation children were distributed in decades as follows: 10 were born during the 1630s, either in England or in the towns along the Massachusetts coast where their parents first settled; 28 were born during the 1640s; 49 were born during the 1650s; 43 were born during the 1660s; declining to 21 during the 1670s, and falling to only 8 during the 1680s. Because of this pattern of births, the second generation of Andover children, born largely during the 1650s and the 1660s, would mature during the late 1670s and the 1680s. Many of the developments of the second

**Table 1**  THE NUMBER OF SONS AND DAUGHTERS LIVING AT THE AGE OF 21 IN TWENTY-NINE FIRST-GENERATION FAMILIES

| Sons | 0 | 1 | 2 | 3 | 4 | 5 | 6 | 7 | 8 | 9 | 10 |
|---|---|---|---|---|---|---|---|---|---|---|---|
| Families | 1 | 2 | 7 | 1 | 6 | 6 | 3 | 3 | 0 | 0 | 0 |
| Daughters | 0 | 1 | 2 | 3 | 4 | 5 | 6 | 7 | 8 | 9 | 10 |
| Families | 0 | 2 | 7 | 6 | 11 | 2 | 0 | 0 | 0 | 1 | 0 |

half of the seventeenth century in Andover, both within the town itself and within the families residing there, were the result of the problems posed by a maturing second generation.

From the records which remain, it is not possible to determine the size of the first-generation family with complete accuracy, since a number of children were undoubtedly stillborn or died almost immediately after birth without ever being recorded in the town records. It is possible, however, to determine the number of children surviving childhood and adolescence with considerable accuracy, in part because of the greater likelihood of their names being recorded among the children born in the town, and in part because other records, such as church records, marriage records, tax lists, and wills, also note their presence. Evidence from all of these sources indicates that the families of Andover's first settlers were large, even without taking into account the numbers of children who may have been born but died unrecorded. An examination of the families of twenty-nine men who settled in Andover between 1645 and 1660 reveals that a total of 247 children are known to have been born to these particular families. Of these 247 children whose births may be ascertained, thirty-nine, or 15.7 percent, are known to have died before reaching the age of 21 years.[5] A total of 208 children, or 84.3 percent of the number of children known to be born, thus reached the age of 21 years, having survived the hazards both of infancy and of adolescence. This suggests that the number of deaths among children and adolescents during the middle of the seventeenth century in Andover was lower than might have been expected.

In terms of their actual sizes, the twenty-nine first-generation families varied considerably, as one might expect. Ten of these twenty-nine families had between 0 and 3 sons who survived to the age of 21 years; twelve families had either 4 or 5 sons surviving, and six families had either 6 or 7 sons living to be 21. Eighteen of these families thus had four or more sons to provide with land or a trade when they reached maturity and wished to marry, a fact of considerable significance in terms of the development of family life in Andover during the years prior to 1690. Fewer of these twenty-nine families had large numbers of daughters. Fifteen families had between 0 and 3 daughters who reached adulthood, eleven families had 4 daughters surviving, and three families had 5 or more daughters reaching the age of 21. In terms of the total number of their children born and surviving to the age of 21 or more, four of these twenty-nine first-generation families had between 2 and 4 children (13.8 percent), eleven families had between 5 and 7 children (37.9 percent), and fourteen families had between 8 and 11 children (48.3 percent). Well over half of the first-generation families thus had 6 or more children who are known to have survived adolescence and to have reached the age of 21. The average number of children known to have been born to these twenty-nine first-generation families was 8.5, with an average of 7.2 children in these families being known to have reached the age of 21 years.[6] The size of the family, and particularly the number of sons who survived adolescence, was a matter of great importance in terms of the problems which would arise later over the settlement of the second generation upon land in Andover and the division of the estates of the first generation among their surviving children. The development of a particular type of family structure within Andover during the first two generations depended in part upon the number of children born and surviving in particular families.

Longevity was a second factor of considerable importance in the development of the family in Andover. For the first forty years following the settlement of the town in 1645, relatively few deaths were recorded among the inhabitants of the town. Unlike Boston, which evidently suffered from smallpox epidemics throughout the seventeenth century, there is no evidence to suggest the presence of smallpox or other epidemical diseases in Andover prior to 1690. With relatively few people, many of whom by the 1670s were scattered about the town upon their own farms, Andover appears to have been a remarkably healthy community during its early years. Lacking virulent epidemics, the principal hazards to health and to life were birth, accidents, non-epidemical diseases, and Indians. Death, consequently, visited relatively few of Andover's inhabitants during the first four decades following its settlement. This is evident in the fact that the first generation of Andover's settlers were very long lived. Prior to 1680, only five of the original settlers who came to Andover before 1660 and established permanent residence there had died; in 1690, fifteen of the first settlers (more than half of the original group) were still alive, forty-five years after the establishment of their town. The age at death of thirty men who settled in Andover prior to 1660 can be determined with a relative degree of accuracy. Their average age at the time of their deaths was 71.8 years. Six of the thirty settlers died while in their fifties, 11 in their sixties, 3 in their seventies, 6 in their eighties, 3 in their nineties, and 1 at the advanced age of 106 years.[7] The longevity of the first-generation fathers was to have great influence on the lives of their children, for the authority of the first generation was maintained far longer than would have been possible if death had struck them down at an early age. The second generation, in turn, was almost as long lived as the first generation had been. The average age of 138 second-generation men at the time of their deaths was 65.2 years, and the average age of sixty-six second-generation women at the time of their deaths was 64.0 years. (See Table 2.[8]) Of the 138 second-generation men who reached the age of 21 years and whose lifespan is known, only twenty-five, or 18.1 percent, died between the ages of 20 and 49. Forty-two (30.3 percent) of these 138 men died between the ages of 50 and 69; seventy-one (51.6 percent) died after reaching the age of 70. Twenty-five second-generation men died in their eighties, and four died in their nineties. Longevity was characteristic of men living in seventeenth-century Andover.

The age of marriage often provides significant clues to circumstances affecting family life and to patterns of family relationships which might otherwise remain elusive.[9] Since marriages throughout the seventeenth century and the early part of the eighteenth century were rarely fortuitous, parental authority and concern, family interests, and economic considerations played into the decisions determining when particular men and women could and would marry for the first time. And during the seventeenth century in Andover, factors such as these frequently dictated delays of appreciable duration before young men, especially, might marry. The age of marriage both of men and of women in the second generation proved to be much higher than most historians hitherto have suspected.[10]

**Table 2** SECOND-GENERATION AGES AT DEATH

| | Males | | Females | |
|---|---|---|---|---|
| AGES | NUMBERS | PERCENTAGES | NUMBERS | PERCENTAGES |
| 20–29 | 10 | 7.3 | 4 | 6.1 |
| 30–39 | 9 | 6.5 | 4 | 6.1 |
| 40–49 | 6 | 4.3 | 6 | 9.1 |
| 50–59 | 16 | 11.5 | 10 | 15.2 |
| 60–69 | 26 | 18.8 | 13 | 19.7 |
| 70–79 | 42 | 30.4 | 16 | 24.2 |
| 80–89 | 25 | 18.1 | 8 | 12.1 |
| 90–99 | 4 | 3.1 | 5 | 7.5 |
| Total | 138 | 100.0% | 66 | 100.0% |

Traditionally in America women have married younger than men, and this was generally true for the second generation in Andover. Although the assertion is sometimes made that daughters of colonial families frequently married while in their early teens, the average age of sixty-six second-generation daughters of Andover families at the time of their first marriage was 22.8 years. (See Table 3.) Only two girls are known to have married at 14 years, none at 15, and two more at 16. Four married at the age of 17, with a total of twenty-two of the sixty-six girls marrying before attaining the age of 21 years (33.3 percent). The largest percentage of women married between the ages of 21 and 24, with twenty-four or 36.4 percent being married during these years, making a total of 69.7 percent of the second-generation daughters married before reaching the age of 25. Between the ages of 25 and 29 years, fourteen women (21.2 percent) mar-

**Table 3** SECOND-GENERATION FEMALE MARRIAGE AGES

| Age | Numbers | Percentages | | |
|---|---|---|---|---|
| Under 21 | 22 | 33.3 | 24 & under | = 69.7% |
| 21–24 | 24 | 36.4 | 25 & over | = 30.3% |
| 25–29 | 14 | 21.2 | 29 & under | = 90.9% |
| 30–34 | 4 | 6.1 | 30 & over | = 9.1% |
| 35–39 | 1 | 1.5 | | |
| 40 & over | 1 | 1.5 | | |
| | 66 | 100.0% | Average age | = 22.8 years |

ried, with six others marrying at the age of 30 or more (9.1 percent). Relatively few second-generation women thus married before the age of 17, and nearly 70 percent married before the age of 25. They were not as young in most instances as one might have expected if very early marriages had prevailed, but they were relatively young nonetheless.

The age of marriage for second-generation men reveals a very different picture, for instead of marrying young, as they so often are said to have done, they frequently married quite late. (See Table 4.) The average age for ninety-four second-generation sons of Andover families at the time of their first marriages was 27.1 years. No son is known to have married before the age of 18, and only one actually married then. None of the ninety-four second-generation men whose marriage ages could be determined married at the age of 19, and only three married at the age of 20.

**Table 4**    SECOND-GENERATION MALE MARRIAGE AGES

| Age | Numbers | Percentages | | |
|---|---|---|---|---|
| Under 21 | 4 | 4.3 | 24 & under | = 39.4% |
| 21–24 | 33 | 35.1 | 25 & over | = 60.6% |
| 25–29 | 34 | 36.2 | 29 & under | = 75.6% |
| 30–34 | 16 | 17.2 | 30 & over | = 24.4% |
| 35–39 | 4 | 4.3 | | |
| 40 & over | 3 | 2.9 | | |
| | 94 | 100.0% | Average age = 27.1 years | |

The contrast with the marriages of the women of the same generation is evident, since only 4.3 percent of the men married before the age of 21 compared to 33.3 percent of the women. The majority of second-generation men married while in their twenties, with thirty-three of the ninety-four men marrying between the ages of 21 and 24 (35.1 percent), and thirty-four men marrying between the ages of 25 and 29 (36.2 percent). Nearly one quarter of the second-generation men married at the age of 30 or later, however, since twenty-three men or 24.4 percent delayed their marriages until after their thirtieth year. In sharp contrast with the women of this generation, an appreciable majority of the second- generation men married at the age of 25 or more, with 60.6 percent marrying after that age. This tendency to delay marriages by men until after the age of 25, with the average age being about 27 years, proved to be characteristic of male marriage ages in Andover throughout the seventeenth century.

Averages can sometimes obscure significant variations in patterns of behavior, and it is worth noting that in the second generation the age at which particular sons might marry depended in part upon which son was being married. Eldest sons tended to marry earlier than younger sons in many families, which suggests variations in their roles within their families, and differences in the attitudes of their fathers towards them compared to their younger brothers. For twenty-six eldest second- generation sons, the average age at their first marriage was 25.6 years. Second sons in the family often met with greater difficulties and married at an average age of 27.5 years, roughly two years later than their elder brothers. Youngest sons tended to marry later still, with the average age of twenty-two youngest sons being 27.9 years. In their marriages as in their inheritances, eldest sons often proved to be favored by their families; and family interests and paternal wishes were major factors in deciding which son should marry and when. More often than not, a son's marriage depended upon the willingness of his father to allow it and the ability of his father to provide the means for the couple's economic independence. Until a second-generation son had been given the means to support a wife—which in Andover during the seventeenth century generally meant land—marriage was virtually impossible.

Marriage negotiations between the parents of couples proposing marriage and the frequent agreement by the father of a suitor to provide a house and land for the settlement of his son and new bride are familiar facts.[11] But the significance of this seventeenth-century custom is much greater than is sometimes realized. It generally meant that the marriages of the second generation were dependent upon their fathers' willingness to let them leave their families and to establish themselves in separate households elsewhere. The late age at which so many sons married during this period indicates that the majority of first-generation parents were unwilling to see their sons married and settled in their own families until long after they had passed the age of 21. The usual age of adulthood, marked by marriage and the establishment of another family, was often 24 or later. Since 60 percent of the second-generation sons were 25 or over at the time of their marriage and nearly one quarter of them were 30 or over, one wonders what made the first generation so reluctant to part with its sons?

At least part of the answer seems to lie in the fact that Andover was largely a farming community during the seventeenth century, structured, by the time that the second generation was maturing, around the family farm which stood isolated from its neighbors and which functioned independently. The family farm required all the labor it could obtain from its own members, and the sons evidently were expected to assist their fathers on their family farms as long as their fathers felt that it was necessary for them to provide their labor. In return for this essential, but prolonged, contribution to their family's economic security, the sons must have been promised land by their fathers when they married, established their own families, and wished to begin their own farms. But this meant that the sons were fully dependent upon their fathers as long as they remained at home. Even if they wanted to leave, they still needed paternal assistance and money in order to purchase land elsewhere. The delayed marriages of second-generation men thus indicate their prolonged attachment to their families, and the continuation of paternal authority over second-generation sons until they had reached their mid-twenties, at least. In effect, it appears, the maturity of this generation was appreciably later than has been suspected hitherto. The psychological consequences of this prolonged dependence of sons are difficult to assess, but they must have been significant.

Even more significant of the type of family relationships emerging with the maturing of the second generation than their late age of marriage is the fact that paternal authority over sons did not cease with marriage. In this

community, at least, paternal authority was exercised by the first generation not only prior to their sons' marriages, while the second generation
continued to reside under the same roof with their parents and to work on
the family farm, and not only at the time of marriage, when fathers generally provided the economic means for their sons' establishment in separate
households, but also *after* marriage, by the further step of the father's
withholding legal control of the land from the sons who had settled upon
it.[12] The majority of first-generation fathers continued to own the land
which they settled their sons upon from the time the older men received it
from the town to the day of their deaths. All of the first-generation fathers
were willing to allow their sons to build houses upon their land, and to live
apart from the paternal house after their marriage, but few were willing to
permit their sons to become fully independent as long as they were still
alive. By withholding deeds to the land which they had settled their sons
upon, and which presumably would be theirs to inherit someday, the first
generation successfully assured the continuity of their authority over their
families long after their sons had become adults and had gained a nominal
independence.[13] Since the second generation, with a few exceptions,
lacked clear legal titles to the land which they lived upon and farmed, they
were prohibited from selling the land which their fathers had settled them
upon, or from alienating the land in any other way without the consent of
their fathers, who continued to own it. Being unable to sell the land which
they expected to inherit, second-generation sons could not even depart
from Andover without their fathers' consent, since few had sufficient capital of their own with which to purchase land for themselves outside of Andover. The family thus was held together not only by settling sons upon
family land in Andover but also by refusing to relinquish control of the
land until long after the second generation had established a nominal independence following their marriages and the establishment of separate
households. In a majority of cases, the dependence of the second-generation sons continued until the deaths of their fathers. And most of the first
generation of settlers was very long lived.

The first generation's reluctance to hand over the control of their property to their second-generation sons is evident in their actions.[14] Only
three first-generation fathers divided their land among all of their sons before their deaths and gave them deeds of gift for their portions of the paternal estate. All three, however, waited until late in their lives to give their
sons legal title to their portions of the family lands. Eleven first-generation
fathers settled all of their sons upon their family estates in Andover but
gave a deed of gift for the land to only one of their sons; the rest of their
sons had to await their fathers' deaths before inheriting the land which
they had been settled upon. Ten of the settlers retained the title to all of
their land until their deaths, handing over control to their sons only by
means of their last wills and testaments. For the great majority of the second generation, inheritances constituted the principal means of trans-
ferring the ownership of land from one generation to the next.[15] The use of
partible inheritances in Andover is evident in the division of the estates of
the first generation.[16] Twenty-one of twenty-two first-generation families
which had two or more sons divided all of their land among all of their

surviving sons. Out of seventy-seven sons who were alive at the time their fathers either wrote their wills or gave them deeds to the land, seventy-two sons received some land from their fathers. Out of a total of sixty-six sons whose inheritances can be determined from their fathers' wills, sixty-one or 92.4 percent received land from their fathers' estates in Andover. Often the land bequeathed to them by will was already in their possession but without legal conveyances having been given. Thus although the great majority of second-generation sons were settled upon their fathers' lands while their fathers were still alive, few actually owned the land which they lived upon until after their fathers' deaths. With their inheritances came ownership, and with ownership came independence. Many waited a long time.

The characteristic delays in the handing over of control of the land from the first to the second generation may be illustrated by the lives and actions of several Andover families. Like most of the men who wrested their farms and their community from the wilderness, William Ballard was reluctant to part with the control over his land. When Ballard died intestate in 1689, aged about 72 years, his three sons, Joseph, William, and John, agreed to divide their father's estate among themselves "as Equally as they could."[17] They also agreed to give their elderly mother, Grace Ballard, a room in their father's house and to care for her as long as she remained a widow, thus adhering voluntarily to a common practice for the provision of the widow. The eldest son, Joseph, had married in 1665/6, almost certainly a rather young man, whereas his two brothers did not marry until the early 1680s, when their father was in his mid-sixties. William, Jr., must have been well over 30 by then, and John was 28. Both Joseph and William received as part of their division of their father's estate in Andover the land where their houses already stood, as well as more than 75 acres of land apiece. The youngest son, John, got all the housing, land, and meadow "his father lived upon except the land and meadow his father gave William Blunt upon the marriage with his daughter," which had taken place in 1668. It is unclear whether John lived with his wife and their four children in the same house as his parents, but there is a strong likelihood that this was the case in view of his assuming control of it after his father's death. His two older brothers had been given land to build upon by their father before his death, but no deeds of gift had been granted to them, thus preventing their full independence so long as he remained alive. Their family remained closely knit both by their establishment of residences near their paternal home on family land and by the prolonged control by William Ballard over the land he had received as one of the first settlers in Andover. It was a pattern repeated in many families.

There were variations, however, such as those exemplified by the Holt family, one of the most prominent in Andover during the seventeenth century. Nicholas Holt, originally a tanner by trade, had settled in Newbury, Massachusetts, for nearly a decade before joining the group of men planning the new town of Andover during the 1640s. Once established in the wilderness community, Holt ranked third among the householders, with an estate which eventually included at least 400 acres of land in Andover as a result of successive divisions of the common land.[18] At some time prior to 1675, he removed his family from the village, where all the original house lots had been located, and built a dwelling house on his third division of land. Although a small portion of his land still lay to the north and west of the old village center, the greatest part of his estate lay in a reasonably compact farm south of his new house. Holt owned no land outside of Andover, and he acquired very little besides the original division grants from the town. It was upon this land that he eventually settled all his sons. In 1662, however, when Nicholas Holt received the fourth division grant of 300 acres from the town, his eldest son, Samuel, was 21 years old, and his three other sons were 18, 15, and 11. The fifth son was yet unborn. His four sons were thus still adolescents, and at ages at which they could provide the physical labor needed to cultivate the land already cleared about the house and to clear and break up the land which their father had just received. The family probably provided most of the labor, since there is no evidence to indicate that servants or hired laborers were numerous in Andover at the time. With the exception of two daughters who married in the late 1650s, the Holt family remained together on their farm until 1669, when the two oldest sons and the eldest daughter married.

By 1669, when Holt's eldest son, Samuel, finally married at the age of 28, the only possible means of obtaining land to settle upon from the town was to purchase one of the twenty-acre lots which were offered for sale. House-lot grants with accommodation land had long since been abandoned by the town, and Samuel's marriage and independence therefore depended upon his father's willingness to provide him with sufficient land to build upon and to farm for himself. Evidently his father had proved unwilling for many years, but when Samuel did at last marry, he was allowed to build a house for himself and his wife upon his father's "Threescore Acres of upland," known otherwise as his third division.[19] Soon afterwards, his second brother, Henry, married and also was given land to build upon in the third division. Neither Samuel nor Henry was given a deed to their land by their father at the time they settled upon it. Their marriages and their establishment of separate households left their three younger brothers still living with their aging father and stepmother. Five years passed before the next son married. James, the fourth of the five sons, married in 1675, at the age of 24, whereupon he, too, was provided with a part of his father's farm to build a house upon.[20] The third son, Nicholas, Jr., continued to live with his father, waiting until 1680 to marry at the late age of 32. His willingness to delay even a token independence so long suggests that personal factors must have played an important part in his continued assistance to his father, who was then about 77 years old.[21] John Holt, the youngest of the sons, married at the age of 21, shortly before his father's death.

For Nicholas Holt's four oldest sons, full economic independence was delayed for many years. Although all had withdrawn from their father's house and had established separate residences of their own, they nonetheless were settled upon their father's land not too far distant from their family homestead, and none had yet been given a legal title to the land where he lived. Until Nicholas Holt was willing to give his sons deeds of gift for the lands where he had allowed them to build and to farm, he retained all legal rights to his estate and could still dispose of it in any way he chose. Without his consent, therefore, none of his sons could sell or mortgage the land where he lived since none of them owned it. In the Holt family, paternal authority rested upon firm economic foundations, a situation characteristic of the majority of Andover families of this period and these two generations.

Eventually, Nicholas Holt decided to relinquish his control over his Andover property by giving to his sons, after many years, legal titles to the lands which they lived upon. In a deed of gift, dated February 14, 1680/1, he conveyed to his eldest son, Samuel, who had been married almost twelve years, one-half of his third division land, "the Said land on which the said Samuels House now Stands," which had the land of his brother, Henry, adjoining on the west, as well as an additional 130 acres of upland from the fourth division of land, several parcels of meadow, and all privileges accompanying these grants of land.[22] In return for this gift, Samuel, then forty years old, promised to pay his father for his maintenance so long as his "naturall life Shall Continue," the sum of twenty shillings a year. Ten months later, December 15, 1681, Nicholas Holt conveyed almost exactly the same amount of land to his second son, Henry, and also obligated him to pay twenty shillings yearly for his maintenance.[23] Prior to this gift, Nicholas had given his fourth son, James, his portion, which consisted of one-third part of "my farme" including "the land where his house now stands," some upland, a third of the great meadow, and other small parcels. In return, James promised to pay his father three pounds a year for life (three times the sum his two elder brothers were to pay), and to pay his mother-in-law forty shillings a year when she should become a widow.[24] The farm which James received was shared by his two other brothers, Nicholas and John, as well. Nicholas, in a deed of June 16, 1682, received "one third part of the farme where he now dwells," some meadow, and, most importantly, his father's own dwelling house, including the cellar, orchard, and barn, which constituted the principal homestead and house of Nicholas Holt, Sr.[25] In "consideration of this my fathers gift . . . to me his sone," Nicholas, Junior, wrote, "I doe promise and engage to pay yearly" the sum of three pounds for his father's maintenance. Thus Nicholas, Junior, in return for his labors and sacrifices as a son who stayed with his father until the age of 32, received not only a share in the family farm equal to that of his two younger brothers but, in addition, received the paternal house and homestead. The youngest of the five Holt sons, John, was the only one to receive his inheritance from his father by deed prior to his marriage. On June 19, 1685, Nicholas Holt, Sr., at the age of 83, gave his "Lovinge" son a parcel of land lying on the easterly side of "my now Dwelling house," some meadow, and fifteen acres of upland "as yett unlaid out."[26] One month later, John married, having already built himself a house upon the land which his father promised to give him. Unlike his older brothers, John Holt thus gained his complete independence as an exceptionally young man. His brothers, however, still were not completely free from obligations to their father since each had agreed to the yearly payment of money to their father in return for full ownership of their farms. Not until Nicholas Holt's death at the end of January 1685/6 could his sons consider themselves fully independent of their aged father. He must have died content in the knowledge that all of his sons had been established on farms fashioned out of his own ample estate in Andover, all enjoying as a result of his patriarchal hand the rewards of his venture into the wilderness.[27]

Some Andover families were less reluctant than Nicholas Holt to let their sons marry early and to establish separate households, although the control of the land in most instances still rested in the father's hands. The Lovejoy family, with seven sons, enabled the four oldest sons to marry at the ages of 22 and 23. John Lovejoy, Sr., who originally emigrated from England as a young indentured servant, acquired a seven-acre house lot after his settlement in Andover during the mid-1640s and eventually possessed an estate of over 200 acres in the town.[28] At his death in 1690, at the age of 68, he left an estate worth a total of £327.11.6, with housing and land valued at £260.00.0, a substantial sum at the time.[29] Although he himself had waited until the age of 29 to marry, his sons married earlier. His eldest son, John, Jr., married on March 23, 1677/8, aged 22, and built a house and began to raise crops on land which his father gave him for that purpose. He did not receive a deed of gift for his land, however; his inventory, taken in 1680 after his premature death, showed his major possessions to consist of "one house and a crope of corn" worth only twenty pounds. His entire estate, both real and personal, was valued at only £45.15.0, and was encumbered with £29.14.7 in debts.[30] Three years later, on April 6, 1683, the land which he had farmed without owning was given to his three-year-old son by his father, John Lovejoy, Sr. In a deed of gift, the elder Lovejoy gave his grandson, as a token of the love and affection he felt for his deceased son, the land which John, Jr., had had, consisting of fifty acres of upland, a piece of meadow, and a small parcel of another meadow, all of which lay in Andover.[31] Of the surviving Lovejoy sons only the second, William, received a deed of gift from the elder Lovejoy for the land which he had given them.[32] The others had to await their inheritances to come into full possession of their land. In his will dated September 1, 1690, shortly before his death, Lovejoy distributed his estate among his five surviving sons: Christopher received thirty acres together with other unstated amounts of land, and Nathaniel received the land which his father had originally intended to give to his brother, Benjamin, who had been killed in 1689. Benjamin was 25 years old and unmarried at the time of his death, and left an estate worth only £1.02.8, his wages as a soldier.[33] Without their father's land, sons were penniless. The youngest of the Lovejoy sons, Ebenezer, received his father's homestead, with the house and lands, in return for fulfilling his father's wish that his mother should "be made comfortable while she Continues in this world."[34] His mother inherited the east end of the house, and elaborate provisions in the will ensured her comfort. With all the surviving sons settled upon their father's land in Andover, with the residence of the widow in the son's house, and with the fact that only one of the sons actually received a deed for his land during their father's lifetime, the Lovejoys also epitomized some of the principal characteristics of family life in seventeenth-century Andover.

Exceptions to the general pattern of prolonged paternal control over sons were rare. The actions taken by Edmund Faulkner to settle his eldest son in Andover are instructive precisely because they were so exceptional. The first sign that Faulkner was planning ahead for his son came with his purchase of a twenty-acre lot from the town at the annual town meeting of March 22, 1669/70.[35] He was the only first-generation settler to purchase such a lot, all of the other purchasers being either second-generation sons or newcomers, and it was evident that he did not buy it for himself since he already had a six-acre house lot and more than one hundred acres of land in Andover.[36] The town voted that "in case the said Edmund shall at any time put such to live upon it as the town shall approve, or have no just matter against them, he is to be admitted to be a townsman." The eldest of his two sons, Francis, was then a youth of about nineteen years. Five years later, January 4, 1674/5, Francis was admitted as a townsman of Andover "upon the account of the land he now enjoyeth," almost certainly his father's twenty acres.[37] The following October, aged about 24, Francis married the minister's daughter. A year and a half later, in a deed dated February 1, 1676/7, Edmund Faulkner freely gave his eldest son "one halfe of my Living here at home" to be "Equally Divided between us both."[38] Francis was to pay the town rates on his half and was to have half the barn, half the orchard, and half the land about his father's house, and both he and his father were to divide the meadows. Significantly, Edmund added that "all my Sixscore acres over Shawshinne river I wholly give unto him," thus handing over, at the relatively young age of 52, most of his upland and half of the remainder of his estate to his eldest son. The control of most of his estate thereby was transferred legally and completely from the first to the second generation; Edmund's second and youngest son, John, was still unmarried at the time Francis received his gift and waited until 1682 before marrying at the age of 28. Eventually he received some land by his father's will, but his inheritance was small compared to his brother's. Edmund Faulkner's eagerness to hand over the control of his estate to his eldest son is notable for its rarity and accentuates the fact that almost none of his friends and neighbors chose to do likewise.[39] It is just possible that Faulkner, himself a younger son of an English gentry family, sought to preserve most of his Andover estate intact by giving it to his eldest son. If so, it would only emphasize his distinctiveness from his neighbors. For the great majority of the first-generation settlers in Andover, partible inheritances and delayed control by the first generation over the land were the rule. Faulkner was the exception which proved it.

Embedded in the reconstructions of particular family histories is a general pattern of family structure unlike any which are known or suspected to have existed either in England or its American colonies during the seventeenth century. It is evident that the family structure which developed during the lifetimes of the first two generations in Andover cannot be classified satisfactorily according to any of the more recent definitions applied to types of family life in the seventeenth century. It was not simply a "patrilineal group of extended kinship gathered into a single household,"[40] nor was it simply a "nuclear independent family, that is man, wife, and children living apart from relatives."[41] The characteristic family structure which emerged in Andover with the maturing of the second generation during the 1670s and 1680s was a combination of both the classical extended family and the nuclear family. This distinctive form of family structure is best described as a *modified extended family*—defined as a kinship group of two or more generations living within a single community in which the dependence of the children upon their parents continues after the children have married and are living under a separate roof. This family structure is a *modified* extended family because all members of the family are not "gathered into a single household," but it is still an *extended* family because the newly created conjugal unit of husband and wife live in separate households in close proximity to their parents and siblings and continue to be economically dependent in some respects upon their parents. And because of the continuing dependence of the second generation upon their first-generation fathers, who continued to own most of the family land throughout the better part of their lives, the family in seventeenth-century Andover was *patriarchal* as well. The men who first settled the town long remained the dominant figures both in their families and their community. It was their decisions and their actions which produced the family characteristic of seventeenth-century Andover.

One of the most significant consequences of the development of the modified extended family characteristic of Andover during this period was the fact that remarkably few second-generation sons moved away from their families and their community. More than four-fifths of the second-generation sons lived their entire lives in the town which their fathers had wrested from the wilderness.[42] The first generation evidently was intent upon guaranteeing the future of the community and of their families within it through the settlement of all of their sons upon the lands originally granted to them by the town. Since it was quite true that the second generation could not expect to acquire as much land by staying in Andover as their fathers had by undergoing the perils of founding a new town on the frontier, it is quite possible that their reluctance to hand over the control of the land to their sons when young is not only a reflection of their patriarchalism, justified both by custom and by theology, but also of the fact that they could not be sure that their sons would stay, given a free choice. Through a series of delays, however, particularly those involving marriages and economic independence, the second generation continued to be closely tied to their paternal families. By keeping their sons in positions of prolonged dependence, the first generation successfully managed to keep them in Andover during those years in which their youth and energy might have led them to seek their fortunes elsewhere. Later generations achieved their independence earlier and moved more. It remains to be seen to what extent the family life characteristic of seventeenth-century Andover was the exception or the rule in the American colonies.

## NOTES

1. Two notable exceptions to this generalization are Edmund S. Morgan, *The Puritan Family* . . . (Boston, 1956), and John Demos, "Notes on Life in Plymouth Colony," *William and Mary Quarterly*, 3d Ser., XXII (1965), 264–286.

2. For a full discussion of the transformation of seventeenth-century Andover, see my article, "Old Patterns in the New World: The Distribution of Land in 17th Century Andover," *Essex Institute Historical Collections.* CI (April 1965), 133–148. See also the study of Sudbury, Mass., in Summer Chilton Powell, *Puritan Village: The Formation of a New England Town* (Middletown, Conn. 1963).

3. The figures in Table I were compiled from the first MS book of Andover vital records, A Record of Births, Deaths, and Marriages, Begun 1651 Ended 1700, located in the vault of the Town Clerk's office, Town Hall, Andover, Mass. For a suggestive comparison of population growth in a small village, see W. G. Hoskins. "The Population of an English Village, 1086–1801: A Study of Wigston Magna," *Provincial England: Essays in Social and Economic History* (London, 1963), 195–200.

4. The most important collection of unpublished genealogies of early Andover families are the typed MSS of Charlotte Helen Abbott, which are located in the Memorial Library, Andover. The two vols. of *Vital Records of Andover, Massachusetts, to the End of the Year 1849* (Topsfield, Mass., 1912) provide an invaluable and exceptionally reliable reference for vital statistics of births, marriages, and deaths.

5. While this figure is low, it should not be discounted entirely. Thomas Jefferson Wertenbaker, *The First Americans, 1607–1690* (New York, 1929), 185–186, found that, "Of the eight hundred and eight children of Harvard graduates for the years from 1658 to 1690, one hundred and sixty-two died before maturity. This gives a recorded child mortality among this selected group of *twenty* percent." Italics added.

6. Comparative figures for the size of families in other rural New England villages are very rare. Wertenbaker, *First Americans,* 182–185, suggested that families were extremely large, with 10 to 20 children being common, but his data for Hingham, Mass., where he found that 105 women had "five or more children," with a total of 818 children "giving an average of 7.8 for each family," is in line with the data for Andover. The figures for seventeenth-century Plymouth are also remarkably similar. See Demos, "Notes on Life in Plymouth Colony," 270–271.

7. The town of Hingham, according to the evidence in Wertenbaker, *First Americans,* 181–186, was remarkably similar to Andover, since the life expectancy of its inhabitants during the seventeenth century was very high. "Of the eight hundred and twenty-seven persons mentioned as belonging to this period [seventeenth century] and whose length of life is recorded, one hundred and five reached the age of eighty or over, nineteen lived to be ninety or over and three . . . attained the century mark."

8. Since the size of the sample for the age of women at the time of their death is only half that of the sample for men, the average age of 64.0 may not be too reliable. However, the evidence for Hingham does suggest that the figures for Andover ought not to be dismissed too lightly. "The average life of the married women of Hingham during the seventeenth century," Wertenbaker noted, "seems to have been 61.4 years." He also found that for their 818 children, the average age at the time of death was 65.5 years. "These figures," he added, "apply to one little town only, and cannot be accepted as conclusive for conditions throughout the colonies, yet they permit of the strong presumption that much which has been written concerning the short expectation of life for women of large families is based upon insufficient evidence." Ibid. 184. The observation remains cogent. For the longevity of Plymouth's settlers, see Demos, "Notes on Life in Plymouth Colony," 271.

9. The most sophisticated analyses of marriage ages and their relationship to the social structure, family life, and economic conditions of various communities have been made by sociologists. Two exceptionally useful models are the studies of two contemporary English villages by W. M. Williams: *Gosforth: The Sociology of an English Village* (Glencoe, Ill., 1956), esp. pp. 45–49, and *A West Country Village, Ashworthy: Family, Kinship, and Land* (London, 1963), esp. pp. 85–91. Another useful study is Conrad M. Arensberg and Solon T. Kimball, *Family and Community in Ireland* (Cambridge, Mass., 1940). For the fullest statistical and historiographical account of marriage ages in the United States, see Thomas P. Monahan, *The Pattern of Age at Marriage in the United States,* 2 vols. (Philadelphia, 1951).

10. In Plymouth colony during the seventeenth century, the age of marriage also was higher than expected. See Demos, "Notes on Life in Plymouth Colony," 275. For a discussion of various historians' views on marriage ages during the colonial period, see Monahan, *Pattern of Age at Marriage,* 1, 99–104.

11. See especially Morgan, *Puritan Family*, 39–44. For one example of marriage negotiations in Andover during this period, see the agreement between widow Hannah Osgood of Andover and Samuel Archard, Sr., of Salem, about 1660 in the *Records and Files of the Quarterly Courts of Essex County, Massachusetts* (Salem, 1012–1021),3, 463, cited hereafter as *Essex Quarterly Court*. Also see the negotiations of Simon Bradstreet of Andover and Nathaniel Wade of Ipswich, *New England Historical and Genealogical Register*, XIII, 204, quoted in Morgan, *Puritan Family*, 41.

12. Similar delays in the handing over of control of the land from one generation to the next are discussed by W. M. Williams in his study of Ashworthy, *West Country Village*, 84–98. Williams noted (p. 91) that "the length of time which the transference of control takes is broadly a reflection of the degree of patriarchalism within the family: the more authoritarian the father, the longer the son has to wait to become master."

13. The use of inheritances as a covert threat by the older generation to control the younger generation is revealed only occasionally in their wills but must have been a factor in their authority over their sons. One suggestive example of a threat to cut off children from their anticipated inheritances is to be found in the will of George Abbot, Sr., who died in 1681, about 64 years old. Prior to his death, his two eldest sons and one daughter had married, leaving at home five unmarried sons and two unmarried daughters with his widow after his death. Abbot left his entire estate to his wife except for the land which he had already given to his eldest son. At her death, he instructed, his wife was to divide the estate with the advice of her sons and friends, and all the children, except the eldest, who had already received a double portion, were to be treated equally unless "by their disobedient carige" towards her "there be rasen to cut them short." Widow Abbot thus had an effective means for controlling her children, the oldest of whom was 24 in 1681. George Abbot, MS will, Dec. 12, 1681, Probate File 43, Probate Record Office, Registry of Deeds and Probate Court Building, Salem, Mass.

14. For deeds of gift of first generation Andover fathers to their second-generation sons, see the following deeds, located in the MSS volumes of Essex Deeds, Registry of Deeds and Probate Court Building, Salem, Mass.: Richard Barker, v. 29, pp. 115–116; Hannah Dane (widow of George Abbot), v. 94, pp. 140–141; Edmund Faulkner, v. 39, p. 250; John Frye, v. 9, pp. 287–288; Nicholas Holt, v. 6, pp. 722–723, 814–821; v. 7, pp. 292–296; v. 9, p. 12; v. 32, pp. 130–131; v. 34, pp. 255–256; Henry Ingalls, v. 14, pp. 40–41; John Lovejoy, v. 33, pp. 40–41.

15. The intimate relationship between inheritance patterns and family structure has been noted and examined by several historians and numerous sociologists. George C. Homans, in his study of *English Villagers of the Thirteenth Century* (New York, 1960), 26, pointed out that "differences in customs of inheritance are sensitive signs of differences in traditional types of family organization." See Homans' discussions of inheritance in England, chs. VIII and IX. H. J. Habakkuk, in his article, "Family Structure and Economic Change in Nineteenth-Century Europe," *The Journal of Economic History*, XV (1955), 4, wrote that "inheritance systems exerted an influence on the structure of the family, that is, on the size of the family, on the relations of parents to children and between the children. . . ." Very little, however, has been written about the role of inheritance in American life, or of its impact upon the development of the American family. One of the few observers to perceive the importance and impact of inheritance customs upon American family life was the shrewd visitor, Alexis de Tocqueville. See, for instance, his discussion of partible inheritance in *Democracy in America*, ed. Phillips Bradley (New York, 1956), I, 47–51.

16. For further details, see the following wills: George Abbot, Probate File 43; Andrew Allen, Probate File 370; John Aslett, *Essex Quarterly Court*, IV, 409; William Ballard, Administration of Estate, Probate Record, Old Series, Book 4, vol. 304, pp. 388–389; Richard Barker, Probate File 1708; Samuel Blanchard, Probate File 2612; William Blunt, Probate File 2658; Thomas Chandler, Probate File 4974; William Chandler, Probate File 4979; Rev. Francis Dane, Probate File 7086; John Farnum, Probate File 9244; Thomas Farnum, Probate File 9254; Edmund Faulkner, Probate File 9305; Andrew Foster, Probate Record, Old Series, Book 2, vol. 302, pp. 136–137 (photostat copy); John Frye, Probate File 10301; Henry Ingalls, Probate File 14505; John Lovejoy, Probate File 17068; John Marston, Probate File 17847; Joseph Parker, *Essex Quarterly Court*, VII, 142–144; Andrew Peters, Probate File 21550; Daniel Poor, Probate Record, vol. 302, pp. 196–197; John Russ, Probate File 24365;

John Stevens, *Essex Quarterly Court* II, 414–416; and Walter Wright, Probate File 30733. The Probate Files of manuscript wills, inventories, and administrations of estates, and the bound Probate Records, are located in the Probate Record Office, Registry of Deeds and Probate Court Building, Salem, Mass.

17. MS Articles of Agreement, Oct. 23, 1689, Probate Records, Old Series, Book 4, vol. 304, pp. 388–389 (photostat copy). For genealogical details of the Ballard family, see Abbott's Ballard genealogy, typed MSS, in the Memorial Library, Andover.

18. For Nicholas Holt's land grants in Andover, see the MS volume, A Record of Town Roads and Town Bounds, 18–19, located in the vault of the Town Clerk's office, Andover, Mass. For genealogical information on the Holt family, see Daniel S. Durrie, *A Genealogical History of the Holt Family in the United States. . . .* (Albany, N. Y., 1864), 9–16.

19. Essex Deeds, v. 32, p. 130.

20. Ibid., v. 7, pp. 292–296.

21. See ibid., v. 6, pp. 814–815.

22. Ibid., v. 32, pp. 130–131.

23. Ibid., v. 34, pp. 255–256.

24. Ibid., v. 7, pp. 292–296.

25. Ibid., v. 6, pp. 814–816.

26. Ibid., v. 9, p. 12.

27. For an example of a first-generation father who gave a deed of gift to his eldest son only, letting his five younger sons inherit their land, see the MS will of Richard Barker, dated Apr. 27, 1688, Probate File 1708. The deed to his eldest son is found in the Essex Deeds, v. 29, pp. 115–116. All of Barker's sons married late (27, 31, 35, 28, 28, and 25), and all but the eldest continued to be under the control of their father during his long life.

28. For John Lovejoy's Andover land grants, see the MS volume, A Record of Town Roads and Town Bounds, 96–98.

29. See John Lovejoy's MS inventory in Probate File 17068.

30. For the inventory of the estate of John Lovejoy, Jr., see *Essex Quarterly Court*, VIII, 56.

31. Essex Deeds, v. 33, pp. 40–41.

32. This deed from John Lovejoy, Sr., to his son, William, is not recorded in the Essex Deeds at the Registry of Deeds, Salem, Mass. The deed, however, is mentioned in his will, Probate File 17068, wherein he bequeathed to William the lands which he already had conveyed to his son by deed. It was customary for such deeds to be mentioned in wills, since they usually represented much or all of a son's portion of a father's estate.

33. For the inventory to Benjamin Lovejoy's estate, see the Probate File 17048.

34. Ibid., 17068. Provision for the widow was customary and is to be found in all the wills of first-generation settlers who left their wives still alive. Generally, the son who inherited the paternal homestead was obligated to fulfill most of the necessary services for his mother, usually including the provision of firewood and other essentials of daily living. Provision also was made in most instances for the mother to reside in one or two rooms of the paternal house, or to have one end of the house, sometimes with a garden attached. Accommodations thus were written into wills to ensure that the mother would be cared for in her old age and would retain legal grounds for demanding such provisions.

35. Andover, MS volume of Ancient Town Records, located in the Town Clerk's office, Andover.

36. For Edmund Faulkner's land grants in Andover, see the MS Record of Town Roads and Town Bounds, 52–53.

37. Town meeting of Jan. 4, 1674/5, Andover, Ancient Town Records.

38. Essex Deeds, v. 39, p. 250. Only one other instance of the copartnership of father and son is to be found in the wills of seventeenth-century Andover but not among the men who founded the town. See the MS will of Andrew Peters, Probate File 21550.

39. The only instance of impartible inheritance, or primogeniture, to be found in the first

generation of Andover's settlers occurred within the first decade of its settlement, before the extensive land grants of 1662 had been voted by the town. See John Osgood's will, dated Apr. 12, 1650, in *Essex Quarterly Court*, I, 239. Osgood left his entire Andover estate to the eldest of his two sons.

40. Bernard Bailyn, *Education in the Forming of American Society: Needs and Opportunities for Study* (Chapel Hill, 1960), 15–16. "Besides children, who often remained in the home well into maturity," Bailyn adds, the family "included a wide range of other dependents: nieces and nephews, cousins, and, except for families at the lowest rung of society, servants in filial discipline. In the Elizabethan family the conjugal unit was only the nucleus of a broad kinship community whose outer edges merge almost imperceptibly into the society at large." For further discussions of the extended family in England, see Peter Laslett, "The Gentry of Kent in 1640," *Cambridge Historical Journal*, IX (1948), 148–164; and Peter Laslett's introduction to his edition of *Patriarcha and Other Political Works of Sir Robert Filmer* (Oxford, 1949), esp. 22–26.

41. Peter Laslett and John Harrison, "Clayworth and Cogenhoe," in H. E. Bell and R. L. Ollard, eds., *Historical Essays, 1660–1750, Presented to David Ogg* (London, 1963), 168. See also H. J. Habakkuk, "Population Growth and Economic Development," in *Lectures on Economic Development* (Istanbul, 1958), 23, who asserts that "from very early in European history, the social unit was the nuclear family—the husband and wife and their children—as opposed to the extended family or kinship group." See also Robin M. Williams, Jr., *American Society: A Sociological Interpretation*, 2d ed. rev. (New York, 1963), 50–57. For a contrasting interpretation of family structure in other seventeenth-century New England towns, see Demos, "Notes on Life in Plymouth Colony," 279–280.

42. Out of a total of 103 second-generation sons whose residences are known, only seventeen, or 16.5 percent, departed from Andover. Five left before 1690, and twelve left after 1690. The majority of families in seventeenth-century Andover remained closely knit and remarkably immobile.

# 2 | FAMILY, HOUSEHOLD, AND THE INDUSTRIAL REVOLUTION

## MICHAEL ANDERSON

### AIMS OF THE PAPER

The Lancashire cotton towns in the middle of the nineteenth century were in many ways a halfway house between a predominantly rural preindustrial England and the predominantly urban-industrial/commercial postcapitalist society of the present day. Communities like Preston, the town I shall be most concerned with here, had between a quarter and a third of their adult male population directly involved in factory industry. Because of the extensive use of child labor, however, a considerably higher proportion of the population were at one time or another of their lives employed in the dominant cotton textile industry. The domestic handloom sector still survived, but it was of ever-shrinking size. Of those not employed in industry, hardly any had agricultural occupations. The prosperity of the mass of the population of almost 70,000 was firmly linked to the cotton textile industry.

These communities were, then, firmly a part of the urban-industrial order, oases in the midst of a predominantly rural nation. In them were to be found all the problems which beset capitalist societies—cyclical unemployment, overcrowding, large families struggling on low wages, factory-working wives and mothers, and large immigrant populations. But this was still an early stage in the transition to the more integrated advanced industrial society we know today. The problems had emerged with full force, but the social changes which were to ameliorate or remove them had not yet appeared. Thus bureaucratically organized social security provision for the old, the sick, the unemployed, the pregnant mother, and the large family was minimal and only given at great social and psychological cost to the recipient. Bureaucratically organized community social welfare services were almost nonexistent. Fertility control was only just beginning, and mortality was as high or higher than ever. Wages were low, primary poverty widespread, housing appalling and relatively expensive.

Obviously, these communities have particular interest to the social historian and the sociologist. By investigating their family and household structure, we can perhaps get clues which will help us resolve the many paradoxes which appear when we compare preindustrial England with the present day. Here I want to concentrate particularly on one of these.

Why, contrary to all that one might be led to expect by the predictions of the cruder, and even of many of the more sophisticated, proponents of the thesis of convergence of family structures with industrialization towards a conjugal type, has there apparently been a massive *increase* over the past two centuries in coresidence of married couples and their parents, and precisely how and when did it come about?

The remainder of this paper falls into two parts. The first presents some (necessarily selective) data on various aspects of household and family structure in Preston in 1851, and contrasts it, on the one hand, with some of the figures which Laslett has at various times made public from his investigations on preindustrial England (e.g., Laslett, 1969), and, on the other, with recent data on British family structure, notably from the 1966 sample census and from Rosser and Harris's study of Swansea.[1] I have also included for comparison some figures for 1851 from my own data on the Lancashire agricultural villages where many of the migrants to Preston had been born. This area was, however, unlike most of the rest of rural England where the agriculture was based on large farms and outdoor day laborers. In rural Lancashire there was much more of an almost peasant-type subsistence family farm system, where what employed labor there was was mainly the indoor farm servant, marriage was late, many never married, and children remained at home into their twenties in the expectation of an inheritance of the farm or of a portion of the family estate (cf. Anderson, 1971, a, chapter 7).

The second part offers an interpretation of the trends which the first reveals. Many of these interpretations are necessarily rather speculative. We still do not have nearly enough studies of the family structure of factory towns in the nineteenth, let alone in the early twentieth, century to be able to make firm generalizations about the impact of the various facets of urban-industrial life. Nor do we have adequate descriptive data for preindustrial rural England to support our crude data on coresidence. What data we have, however, seem compatible with the interpretations offered here.

The Preston data are taken from a 10 percent sample of houses from the enumerators' books of the 1851 census. The rural sample is not representative of any finite population. It was drawn with the object of comparing the family structure of those persons who had migrated to Preston from villages where more than half the 1831 population had been employed in agriculture, with the family types which were found in the villages from which they had come. A variable fraction stratified sample was therefore drawn so that the percentage of sample households taken from any one village was proportional to the percentage of all the migrants who had come from that village. Since, however, the family and household structure of these migrants turned out to be little different from that of the population as a whole, I shall here, for convenience, use it for comparisons with the whole Preston population.

Households are taken as "census families." Doubtful cases follow the rules outlined elsewhere (Anderson, 1972, c).

## HISTORICAL DATA

Table 1 shows the extent to which households were likely, at different points in the past, to contain persons outside the nuclear family of the head.[2]

**Table 1** PERCENTAGE OF HOUSEHOLDS WITH KIN, LODGERS, AND SERVANTS FOR VARIOUS COMMUNITIES

|  | Kin | Lodgers | Servants * |
|---|---|---|---|
| England and Wales 1966 (approx.) | 10 | † | 0 |
| Swansea 1960 (approx.) | 10–13 | <3 | 3 |
| Preston 1851 | 23 | 23 | 10 |
| Rural 1851 | 27 | 10 | 28 |
| Laslett 1564–1821 | 10 | <1 | 29 |

*Servants include apprentices in Preston and the rural samples.
†Figures not available.

The most marked differences which seem to emerge here are:

1. When compared with preindustrial England, the larger proportion of households with kin in both 1851 samples, to a level well above the modern figure. This figure, indeed, approximates to that for preindustrial England. The Lancashire rural sample is probably not typical of England as a whole, though Professor Williams's Ashworthy figure (between 31 percent and 34 percent) is actually higher (Williams, 1963, p. 218). Both Ashworthy and North Lancashire had a predominance of family farms and few farm laborers, and it was above all on these family farms that kin, particularly married children coresiding with parents, were to be found.[3]

2. The far larger number of households with lodgers in Preston, compared both with preindustrial England and with Swansea. In Preston, lodgers made up 12 percent of the sample and over 20 percent of the twenty to twenty-four age group. The married couples in lodgings were largely young and with small families, and inmigrants were over-represented in their number (cf. Anderson, 1971, a, chapter 5).

3. Servants in Preston in 1851 already show signs of the ultimate decline to which this class was destined. Employment in the factories was, of course, not conditional on coresidence, and the opportunities it offered to the young made it difficult to recruit suitable children to service. Servants and apprentices made up 3 percent of the population.

In the rural sample servants made up 16 percent of the sample population aged over fifteen. By contrast with the towns, the number of men more or less equalled the number of women, and the 225 farm servants who were aged over fifteen made up 43 percent of the paid agricultural labor force in these age groups.

Table 2 turns attention to the structure of the families of household heads.

The markedly higher present-day figures for both Swansea and England and Wales as a whole are obviously the most striking features of this table.

Little difference appears in Table 2 in the proportion living without any relative in their household. The different distribution of childless couples compared with couples with unmarried children mainly reflects the fall in family size and the older age distribution of the Swansea population.

Other highly significant differences appear in the remaining rows.

**Table 2**  STRUCTURE OF THE FAMILIES OF HOUSEHOLD HEADS[4]

| Family Type | England & Wales 1966 (approx.) | Swansea 1960 (approx.) | Preston 1851 | Rural 1851 | Laslett 1564–1821 |
|---|---|---|---|---|---|
| No related person | 17 | 10+ | 4 | 5 | |
| Married couple only | 24 | 22+ | 10 | 12 | 90 |
| Parent(s) and unmarried child(ren) only | 49 | 54+ | 63 | 56 | |
| Parent(s) and married child(ren) but no other kin | 5 | 9+ | 9 | 6 | 10 |
| Parent(s) and married child(ren) with other kin | 0 | <5* | 1 | 0 | |
| Other combinations of kin | 4 | | 13 | 21 | |
| All (percentage) | 99 | 100 | 100 | 100 | 100 |
| N= | 1,533,954 | 1958 | 1240 | 855 | — |

*Some of this group are here because they have coresiding nonkin, since the figures for Swansea are for household structure, not structure of the families of the household heads.

Laslett's communities have very few parent/married child households indeed (Laslett, 1969). By contrast, in Preston, 10 percent of all families were of this type, and Rosser and Harris's modern figures are at about the Preston level, though the figures for England and Wales as a whole are lower. Foster also found a 10 percent figure for Oldham (1967, p. 314). The urban-industrial revolution, then, seems, contrary surely to all expectations ten years ago, to have been associated with a considerable increase in coresidence of parents and married children. However, Foster's (1967) finding[5] that the comparable 1851 figures for Northampton and South Shields, both industrial towns, were only 5 percent and 4 percent respectively suggests that the issue is not as simple as it might at first appear. Further discussion of this issue appears below.

The other main point to emerge from Table 2 is the way in which "other kin" family types maintained or even increased their proportion in the urban industrial society and only fell away in the past 100 years. This issue too is best discussed below. Suffice to note here that Foster found these "other kin" in 12 percent of Northampton families, 16 percent of Oldham families, and 11 percent of South Shields families (1967, p. 314). Certainly this family type was a widespread phenomenon.

Just who these coresiding kin were is explored further in Table 3.

By far the most remarkable thing to modern eyes about both columns of Table 3 is the immense number of "parentless" children, 28 percent of all kin in Preston and 42 percent in the rural sample. I have been unable to find any comparable tables for present-day communities, but a glance at the first column of Table 2 suggests that the figure is well under 5 percent. By contrast the proportion for preindustrial England may well have been higher still and can certainly have been little lower.

**Table 3**  RELATIONSHIP OF KIN TO HOUSEHOLD HEAD (PERCENTAGE OF ALL KIN)

| | Preston 1851 | | Rural 1851 | |
|---|---|---|---|---|
| Father or father-in-law | 3.3* | | 3.2† | |
| Mother or mother-in-law | 5.7* | | 4.0† | |
| Married/widowed son or son-in-law | 11.1 | | 6.9 | |
| Married/widowed daughter or daughter-in-law | 12.3 | | 5.9 | |
| Grandchild with parents | 13.7 | | 10.9 | |
| "Stem" family members | | 46.1 | | 30.9 |
| Unmarried siblings (married head) | 9.1 | | 8.4 | |
| Unmarried siblings (unmarried head) | 5.0 | | 8.6 | |
| Unmarried members of family of orientation | | 14.1 | | 17.0 |
| Married or widowed siblings or siblings-in-law | 5.1 | | 4.0 | |
| Nieces/nephews with parents | 4.3 | | 2.2 | |
| Married siblings and family | | 9.4 | | 6.2 |
| Nieces/nephews without parents | 15.0 | | 11.9 | |
| Grandchildren without parents | 13.3 | | 30.2 | |
| "Parentless" children | | 28.3 | | 42.1 |
| Uncles, aunts, and cousins | 1.4 | 1.4 | 2.0 | 2.0 |
| Others | 0.8‡ | 0.8 | 1.7§ | 1.7 |
| All (percentage) | 100.1 | 100.1 | 99.9 | 99.9 |
| N= | 513 | 513 | 404 | 404 |

*All widowed.
†All but one widowed.
‡Son-in-law's father, son-in-law's brother, grandmother, great nephew.
§Five not specified (probably nieces/nephews, siblings-in-law, or cousins) great-niece, and her illegitimate child.

Thus in Preston, while there were also still large numbers of this "parentless" group so rare today, there was also a much larger number of the "new," "twentieth-century" group of one or two grandparents, or one or two married children and their families, and married siblings and their families. We appear, therefore, to have in Preston something of a halfway stage in the transition, with both preindustrial and modern types of kinship superimposed.

Before trying to analyze just who these various groups were and why they were coresiding, attention is perhaps usefully turned to Tables 4 and 5. Aggregate tables on family structure, such as Tables 2 and 3, can be rather misleading in a comparative perspective because, given the typical English pattern where coresidence of married children and parents is mainly confined to the first years of marriage, and to the old age (particularly the widowhood) of the parents, such tables are highly sensitive to varying population age structures. Before proceeding further, then, it is instructive to look briefly at some tables where age or life-cycle stage are controlled.

Table 4 shows the coresidence patterns of the section of the community aged over sixty-five. The "Britain" figures are from the old people in a three industrial societies study (Stehouwer, 1965, p. 146).

The marked pattern of coresidence with children in Preston is particularly to be noted. Rather few old people there lived apart from a relative. Indeed, when the proportion of old people who could have had a child

**Table 4** HOUSEHOLD COMPOSITION OF THE OVER SIXTY-FIVES (PERCENTAGE) LISTING IN PRIORITY ORDER

| | Married | | | Widowed, single, and separated | | |
|---|---|---|---|---|---|---|
| | BRITAIN 1962 | PRESTON 1851 | RURAL 1851 | BRITAIN 1962 | PRESTON 1851 | RURAL 1851 |
| Living with: | | | | | | |
| Married child(ren) | 6 | 16 | 13 | 27 | 41 | 26 |
| Unmarried child(ren) | 26 | 47 | 36 | 27 | 29 | 21 |
| Spouse only | 68 | 37 | 50 | — | — | — |
| Other kin only | — | — | — | 4 | 8 | 18 |
| No related person | — | — | — | 42 | 22 | 35 |
| All (percentage) | 100 | 100 | 99 | 100 | 100 | 100 |
| N= | 1022 | 70 | 143 | 889 | 124 | 106 |

alive at all is estimated (and this figure is considerably below that for modern Britain and probably below the rural figure), it is obvious that well over 80 percent of those old people who had a child alive were, in Preston in 1851, in fact living with one or other of their children.[6]

Table 5 shows the residence patterns of the young childless couples.[7]

In Preston, as in Swansea, only just over half of all childless younger couples lived in households of their own and apart from their parents. In contrast to Swansea, however, where most of the rest lived with parents, over half of this group in Preston lived as lodgers in another household. (None in Preston coresided in a household headed by a kinsman other than a parent.) Part of this difference may be due to the rather different criteria by which households are distinguished in the two studies, but there is no doubt that many of these lodger couples did, in fact, share a common table and would therefore have been classified as lodgers even by Rosser and Harris. Compared with Laslett's figures, in contrast, even the 16 percent who lived with parents are probably a very numerous body indeed.

Thus it seems likely that urban-industrial life of the cotton-town type markedly increased the proportion of wage-earner families in which parents and married children coresided. It also markedly increased the alternative form of residence for the young married couple, living as lodgers with another family. Compared with preindustrial England, however, the proportion of "parentless" children did not decline and may even have increased somewhat. Twentieth-century urban life saw a marked reduction in this latter group but some considerable further increase in the

**Table 5** RESIDENCE PATTERNS OF CHILDLESS COUPLES WHERE THE WIFE WAS AGED UNDER FORTY-FIVE (PERCENTAGE)

| | Swansea 1960 | Preston 1851 | Rural 1851 |
|---|---|---|---|
| Percentage living: | | | |
| In own household | 57 | 58 | 80 |
| Coresiding with parents | 40 | 16 | 13 |
| Other | 3 | 26 | 7 |
| All (percentage) | 100 | 100 | 100 |
| N= | 97 | 158 | 46 |

coresidence of young married children and their parents, probably to some extent at the expense of the lodger group. But, in spite of this increase, more old people live alone today than in nineteenth-century Preston; possibly more do so than did in preindustrial England.

## INTERPRETATION OF DATA

I have argued elsewhere (Anderson, 1971, a, especially chapter 2) that, if we are to understand variations and changes in patterns of kinship relationships, the only worthwhile approach is consciously and explicitly to investigate the manifold advantages and disadvantages that any actor can obtain from maintaining one relational pattern rather than another, and I have outlined what I see as the main considerations which must be taken into account in any such approach. Here I want to go further and suggest, that, in the case of *coresidence*, a very special set of hypotheses, which consider only economic advantages and disadvantages, may be appropriate. In short, I am suggesting that any significant proportion of one group of actors in a society (say young married men) will generally only be found *coresiding* with another given class of kin (say widowed parents) if:

1. The time discounted, average life-span, economic advantages to most of them of doing so (bearing in mind that coresidence will normally imply some sharing of resources and support if necessary) outweigh or at least are not greatly exceeded by the economic disadvantages which they would suffer either directly from the kinsman, or from third parties, if they did not do so: and
2. If most of the other party would also receive net advantages calculated in the same way.

Conscious calculation of these advantages is seen in this approach as only occurring under rather special conditions;[8] generally norms develop to set a seal on conduct which is in line with these economic pressures. In highly stable and fairly prosperous societies (which the societies we are concerned with here were not), where the future is reasonably predictable, it can be shown, on the premises used, that norms would logically develop as a kind of insurance policy to provide at least for all who have relatives some minimum standard of living provided by kin except if assistance at this minimal level were seen as obtainable from some other outside agency.

There is no space to go further into this matter in this paper. Here I am mainly concerned with the principle as a conceptual framework which may help us to understand changes and differences in patterns of coresidence. To this detailed problem I now return.

**"Parentless" Children**  Firstly, then, who were these parentless children who seem to have been present in a sizeable proportion of households over most of rural and urban England?

Some of the odd grandchildren were undoubtedly illegitimate sons and daughters of coresiding daughters or, indeed, of daughters who had left home to marry or for other reasons.[9] It is now impossible except by reconstitution techniques to ascertain what this proportion might have been, but it does seem as if this was a fairly standard behavior pattern. A second group were children of orphaned parents, children who had lost one parent (particularly the mother), and also children of mothers who had remarried. In all these cases it seems to have been normal for relatives to take over the children, assisted often by a small parish allowance in return (Anderson, 1971, a, chapter 10). Children in this class undoubtedly make up a not inconsiderable proportion of the group as a whole. A third, and probably small, group are those who, though they had parents alive and living in the community, lived with aunts, uncles, or grandparents to relieve the overcrowding in their own households or, possibly, to provide aged grandparents with some company and help around the house or in a small shop. Several cases which look very much like this cropped up during the work on enumerators' books, and the phenomenon of "lending a child" is not unknown in modern working-class communities (cf., e.g., Young and Willmott, 1957, p. 38).

Certainly, for one reason or another, widows and single women were more than twice as likely to have such "parentless" kin in their households as were the rest of the population. Most of these young men and women were already earning and would thus be already keeping themselves and, indeed, probably making some useful contribution towards the family finances (about 80 percent were over ten years of age). Many more would soon be doing so in a society where child labor was the norm (and many of those who were sent out to work very young do, indeed, seem to have been being cared for by kin; cf., eg., Parliamentary Papers, PP. 1833, XX, DI, 34, and see also Anderson, 1971, a, chapter 11). Many of the rest would have been the children of coresiding daughters who more than paid for their keep.

To this social welfare function, however, one must also add an important economic function of kinship which both overlapped with the first and also made its own independent contribution to the figures. In the nineteenth century it was above all through the agency of kin that one got a job.[10] Where one had a kinsman who had his own business or farm he might frequently offer a job directly, particularly to the sons of siblings who had fallen on hard times, and this would frequently involve coresidence (Anderson, 1971, a, chapters 9 and 10). Some of these kin are described in the occupation columns of the schedules as servants, while many so-called servants were almost certainly kin. Their status in the household was probably often little different from that of the nonrelative who would otherwise have been given the place. The net cost, therefore, was probably minimal; the system meant that orphans and the children of destitute kin were provided for, and kin were probably easier to sanction, less likely to leave their jobs, and probably, therefore, more reliable.

In the towns, of course, most of the population were employees, but recruitment to jobs in the factories or in the laboring gangs was similarly influenced by kinship considerations. "Asking for" a job for kin was normal in the factory towns, and the employers used the kinship system to recruit labor from the country (Anderson, 1971, a, chapter 9). This process of drawing in kin from rural areas continued in London to the end of the nineteenth century at least.[11] Most of these kin were single, being especially siblings, and nieces and nephews. When they got to the town to the job their kinsman found for them, they had nowhere to live, so they normally lodged with him. This, then, is the second major source of "parentless" kin. It is also, surely, the reason why inmigrant couples (except significantly those from other factory towns) had almost as many siblings, nieces and nephews, and cousins in their households as did the Preston born (for details, see Anderson, 1971, a, chapter 10), and also, surely, the reason why it was above all the better paid factory workers—overseers and spinners and the like—who had these relatives in their homes (Anderson, 1971, a, chapter 10). These were the men with the greatest influence over factory recruitment.

In sum, then, in industrializing England, men continued to be able and, indeed, possibly became more able to perform functions for their kin which were to these kin a considerable economic advantage. They could, moreover, do this at minimum cost to themselves, except sometimes in the rather short run. The twentieth century, by contrast, reduced the control of kin over jobs, and reduced the scale of migration of young single persons. At the same time orphanage decreased and the Welfare State cushioned the poor from the worst ravages of crises. In consequence this class of kin largely disappeared from British homes.

**Parents and Married Children** To explain the coresidence of parents and married children in larger proportions in Preston and Oldham than in both preindustrial England and other nineteenth-century towns so far studied is a considerably more difficult problem. By contrast with the situation among the better-off farmers in rural Lancashire, a fairly simple economic explanation based on economic cooperation in a family enterprise and the promise of future rewards from it is clearly unsuitable (Anderson, 1971, a, chapter 7); by far the larger proportion of the population of Preston were employees, and, anyway, there was no clear association between socio-economic group, and parent/married child coresidence.

Rather, as I have argued at greater length elsewhere (Anderson, 1971, a, especially chapters 10–12), my interpretation requires that attention be turned to other aspects of urban-social life. In most working-class communities before the coming of the Welfare State, if someone survived to old age (and many did not), then he could look forward to a life of poverty. This was particularly true, perhaps, in the towns where the cost of living and also rents were higher. It seems probable then that old people, particularly widows, would in general have been best off if they could coreside with married children. They would thus save on rent and participate in the economies of scale of the common table. Young married couples, too, might benefit from sharing, because they, too, would save on rent. But, and this is the crucial point, nineteenth-century society and the society which preceded it were, in general, poor societies, societies where after one had done one's best for one's own nuclear family, there was little left for anyone else unless that someone else could contribute to the family's resources in return. And, if one was young and newly married, to take an old person into one's household or to join the household of that old person meant that this person could not but be given some of these scarce resources now and also in the future when one's family was larger and poverty loomed at the door; the old persons would probably need some help even if they were receiving a parish pittance. If one refused to take them in, the Guardians would usually make sure they did not die of want; indeed, their standard of living would probably be little if at all lower. Usually, moreover, this person could not give much of use in return. This, I would argue, explains the reluctance of the population of most nineteenth-century towns, and probably also of nineteenth-century and indeed pre-industrial rural areas, to share with old people even when soon after marriage they could for a while afford to do so. It is much more difficult to eject someone than never to take them in.

In the cotton towns, however, the situation was different. Here, though poverty was widespread, it was a little less biting than elsewhere, and it lasted for a shorter part of the life cycle (cf. Foster, 1967). The drain of a nonproductive relative was thus anyway somewhat less severe. But, and this may have been the crucial issue, the relative could also substantially *increase the family income*, not usually by seeking employment in the labor market, but by caring for the children and home while the mother worked in the factory. In this way the mother could have child and home looked after better, and probably more cheaply, than by hiring someone to do so, and the income she brought in kept the relative and gave a considerable surplus to the family budget.

Thus, in these communities, the old person could be valuable, not a drain on family resources. Even if the wife did not work, the old person could frequently earn her keep by performing similar services for a neighbor who did. It is, then, perhaps not surprising that few old people lived alone.

By contrast, however, not all young married couples had parents alive, and many were inmigrants whose parents lived elsewhere. It was migrants in particular who lived in lodgings rather than with kin, though some actually brought their parents in to join them. Some others had many siblings still living at home, so here considerations of overcrowding prevented their coresiding, though many lived near by. It would thus seem that only a minority of young married couples, even in Preston, were physically able to coreside.

One may then perhaps suggest more speculatively that in the later nineteenth and early twentieth centuries these advantages of coresidence continued in Lancashire and gradually spread elsewhere. The advantages to young married couples of coresidence if anything increased as housing continued to be in short supply. At the same time the decline in family poverty meant that, proportionally, the cash disadvantages to them of taking in dependent kin declined. At the same time family size began to fall. More space thus became available at home, and fewer other married siblings were competing for the right to coreside. More people had parents available too, because inmigrants came to be a smaller proportion of the total population, and some decline in adult mortality set in.

On the other hand, this very stabilization of communities, together with the old-age pension, changed the situation for the old. They could live near their children, not with them,[12] and more and more could afford to pay rent for a home of their own. Their children anyway were younger and most had left home for a while before widowhood struck.

Thus, while more and more couples came to coreside for a few years after marriage, the proportion of old people who wished to coreside probably began to fall. Some detailed investigations of household structure in the early twentieth century are necessary before we can understand the full situation here. The changes brought about by the introduction of the old-age pension in 1908 may well have been particularly significant.

What evidence is there in support of this interpretation?

Firstly, it is possible to show that in Preston it was only those in more affluent states who took in kin who could not support themselves. In Preston, of all households whose family standard of living was estimated as being within 4s. of the primary poverty line, only 2 percent contained kin none of whom had a recorded means of support; of those with a standard of living 20s. and more above, the figure was 11 percent. By contrast 9 percent of the first group and 12 percent of the second contained kin at least one of whom was self-supporting.[13]

There is also considerable contemporary comment by members of the working class that the possibility of assistance to kin was severely circumscribed by the costs which it incurred, unless such kin could either bring in some income through employment, or unless the Poor Law authorities were prepared to pay them some relief (see Anderson, 1971, a, chapters 10 and 11). The Poor Law Commissioners of 1834 found a similar attitude to support of parents to be prevalent in many parts of rural England (e.g., PP 1834 XXVII, especially 54). In addition, calculating reactions of this kind to assistance to kin in situations of extreme poverty have been pointed out by my own research on prefamine rural Ireland (Anderson, 1971, a, chapter 7), by Banfield in Italy (1958, especially p. 121), and by Sahlins as typical of primitive societies (1965, especially p. 165).

Secondly, there is also supporting evidence for the special interpretation which has been offered for the cotton towns. Just such an explanation was offered for the low Lancashire poor rates by the special commissioner sent to inquire into the state of Stockport in 1842 (PP 1842 XXXV, 7 and 77). Households with children under ten where the wife worked were three times as likely to have had a coresiding grandmother (Anderson, 1971, a). Some married couples actually took unrelated old people into their households rent free and all found to provide just such a service (cf., eg., Waugh, 1881, p. 85; cited in Anderson, 1972, a, chapter 11), and others brought their parents in from the country (PP 1836 XXXIV, 25, 69; PP 1859 Ses 2, VII, 116; PP 1837–1838 XIX, 309; and sample data). Booth's (1894) data on poor relief for the elderly, compiled at the end of the century, show markedly fewer old people in receipt of relief in areas where married women habitually worked.

Obviously, at this stage, such an interpretation remains speculative, but it does seem to offer considerable scope for future research. The problem is a complex one, and many factors are obviously involved which we are only gradually coming to understand.

# NOTES

1. General Register Office (1968); Rosser and Harris (1965). Neither of these sources present data in quite the form required for the purpose at hand, so some estimates have had to be made. The data based on these two sources are, therefore, only approximate. For a fuller discussion of this point see the original version of this paper.

2. The figures for England and Wales are from General Register Office (1968, pp. 1–2). Those for Swansea are derived from Rosser and Harris (1965, p. 148). The figures in the original are for household, not family composition, and contain a 4 percent "other" category, which includes both coresiding nonkin, and families with kin other than married children and their children, and siblings. The figures for preindustrial England are from Laslett (1969), except for the lodger figure which is from Armstrong (1968, p. 72).

3. For a fuller discussion and explanation, see Anderson (1971, a) chapters 3 and 7.

4. For comment on the Swansea figures see footnote 2. The preindustrial figures are derived from Laslett (1969).

5. Firth (1964, p. 74) found that only 16 percent of his Highgate sample (though 30 percent of the middle class [Crozier, 1965, p. 17]) had coresiding kin, which suggests that in London, too, this family type was not as predominant as it was in Lancashire.

6. For details of the estimate, see Anderson (1972).

7. For Swansea, from Rosser and Harris (1965, p. 167).

8. These problems, together with those raised by the next sentence, and such problems as the determinants of rates of time discount, are discussed at some length in Anderson 1971, a).

9. For the detailed references in support of this statement see Anderson (1971, a, chapter 10).

10. For a detailed discussion see Anderson (1971, a, chapter 9).

11. Perhaps the classic discussion of this kin-based migration and occupational recruitment service is in Booth (1892, pp. 132–135).

12. For a similar observation on modern communities, cf. Willmott and Young (1960, p. 43).

13. Cf. Anderson (1971, a, especially chapter 11). The method of calculating the standard of living is set out in Anderson (1972, b).

# REFERENCES

ANDERSON, M. (1971, a), *Family Structure in Nineteenth-Century Lancashire*, Cambridge University Press.

———. (1972, b), "Sources and techniques for the study of family structure in nineteenth-century Britain" in E.A. Wrigley (ed.) *Nineteenth-Century Society*, Cambridge University Press.

———. (1972, c), "Standard tabulation procedures for houses, households and other groups of residents, in the enumeration books of the censuses of 1851 to 1891," in E. A. Wrigley (ed.), *Nineteenth-Century Society*. Cambridge University Press.

ARMSTRONG, W. A. (1968), "The interpretation of the census enumerators' books for Victorian towns" in H. J. Dyos (ed.), *The Study of Urban History*, Edward Arnold.

BANFIELD, E. C. (1958), *The Moral Basis of a Backward Society*, Free Press.

BOOTH, C. (ed.) (1892), *Life and Labour of the People in London*, vol. 3, Macmillan.

BOOTH, C. (1894), *The Aged Poor in England and Wales*, Macmillan.

CROZIER, D. (1965), "Kinship and occupational succession," *Sociological Review*, new series, vol. 13, pp. 15–43.

FIRTH, R. (1964), "Family and kinship in industrial society," in P. Halmos (ed.), "The development of industrial societies," *Sociological Review Monograph*, no. 8, Keele.

FOSTER, J. O. (1967), "Capitalism and class consciousness in earlier nineteenth-century Oldham," Ph.D. thesis, University of Cambridge.

GENERAL REGISTER OFFICE (1968), *Sample Census, 1966. Household Composition Tables*, H.M.S.O.

LASLETT, T. P. R. (1969), "Size and structure of the household in England over three centuries: mean household size in England since the sixteenth century," *Population Studies*, vol. 23, pp. 199–223.

ROSSER, C. AND HARRIS, C. C. (1965), *The Family and Social Change*. Routledge & Kegan Paul.

SAHLINS, M. D. (1965), "On the sociology of primitive exchange," in M. Banton (ed.), *The Relevance of Models for Social Anthropology*, Tavistock.

STEHOUWER, J. (1965), "Relations between generations and the three generation household in Denmark," in E. Shanas and G. F. Streib (eds.), *Social Structure and the Family: Generational Relations*. Prentice-Hall.

WAUGH, E. (1881), *Factory Folk During the Cotton Famine: in Works*, Haywood, vol. 2.

WILLIAMS, W. M. (1963), *A West Country Village: Family Kinship and Land*, Routledge & Kegan Paul.

WILLMOTT, P., AND YOUNG, M. (1960), *Family and Class in a London Suburb*, Routledge & Kegan Paul.

YOUNG, M. AND WILMOTT, P. (1957), *Family and Kinship in East London*, Routledge & Kegan Paul; Penguin Books, 1962.

PARLIAMENTARY PAPERS:

1833 XX *First report of the . . . Commissioners . . .* [on] *the employment of children in factories . . . with minutes of evidence . . .*

1834 XXVII *Report from His Majesty's Commissioners for inquiring into the administration and practical operation of the Poor Laws.*

1836 XXXIV *Poor inquiry, Ireland: Appendix G. Report on the state of the Irish poor in Great Britain.*

1837–1838 XIX *Report by the Select Committee of the House of Lords . . .* [on] *. . . several cases . . .* [arising from] *. . . the operation of the Poor Law Amendment Act. . . . with minutes of evidence.*

1842 XXXV *. . . Evidence taken, and report made, by the Assistant Poor Law Commissioner sent to inquire into the state of the population of Stockport.*

1859 Ses 2 VII *Minutes of evidence taken before the Select Committee on irremoveable poor.*

# 3 | URBANIZATION AND THE MALLEABLE HOUSEHOLD: AN EXAMINATION OF BOARDING AND LODGING IN AMERICAN FAMILIES

## JOHN MODELL and TAMARA K. HAREVEN

The challenges to traditional values posed by the urbanization of American society included by the late nineteenth century a new and widespread doubt that the family was capable of withstanding the pressures to which it was exposed. One aspect of family life upon which this lack of faith focused was the common practice of taking into the household boarders or lodgers.[1] What once had seemed a genial practice, a way of providing at once temporary accommodation and a family setting for those who lacked their own menage, now seemed a threat to the institution of the family itself. James Quayle Dealey expressed the setting of the anxiety nicely in 1912, when his *Family in Its Sociological Aspects* likened even the modern urban family (biologically defined) to "a temporary meeting place for boarding and lodging," where strangers entered while family members passed large portions of their time on the streets or in other company (Dealey, 1912:90–91). By this time, however, boarding and lodging within the family had been under attack for a quarter of a century, and a somewhat diffuse but nevertheless damning bill of particulars had been drawn up against it. The present paper seeks to suggest the social and economic significance of this transit of values, while exploring the extent and functions of the institution of boarding within the family.[2]

Family governance was the lynchpin of the Puritan theory of social control, as it was in less dramatic form of the whole English tradition carried over into the American republic (Morgan, 1944; Demos, 1970; Farber, 1972: ch. 2; Flaherty, 1972: ch. 2). In its multiple functions as a workshop, a church, an asylum, and a reformatory, the Colonial family included boarders as well as servants and apprentices and dependent strangers. The presence of strangers in the household was accepted as a normal part of

Modell wishes to thank Winifred Bolin, whose student work on lodgers has contributed insight into their importance. Hareven is grateful to Stuart Blumin, Maris Vinovskis, Richard Jensen, Stephen Shedd, and Randolph Langenbach for their advice and expert help. Research on the Boston data in this essay was supported in part by the Clark University Graduate Research Fund, and the Clark Computer Fund.

family organization. Town governments customarily boarded the home-less, poor, or juveniles with families for a fee. The first federal census, taken in 1790, showed a very small proportion of persons living alone (3.7 percent of households were of one person only, as compared with nearly 20 percent in 1970). Even a frontier state in 1820, peopled almost entirely by newcomers to the region, saw all but 2.7 percent of its white households with two or more living together (Rossiter, 1909; U.S. Bureau of the Census, 1972; Modell, 1971).

Inspection of census enumerators' manuscripts from 1850 onward reveals large numbers of persons recorded as "lodgers" in established households of otherwise predominantly nuclear structure, who were either juveniles, distant relatives, apparently unrelated persons of similar village origin or from the same foreign land, or young men sharing a trade with the household head. Occasionally they constituted an entire family group in the household. Studies now in progress for rural and urban com-munities in the decade before the Civil War show around one in five families with lodgers. Blumin has found an average of 17 to 20 percent of all households augmented by one or more nonkin members in three Hudson Valley communities—Troy, Marlborough, and Kingston—while Glasco has found that about 21 percent of all native households and 15 percent of all Irish households in Buffalo in the 1850s were augmented by strangers. A figure of 15.7 percent has been computed for Detroit in 1880 (Blumin, 1972:19–20; Glasco, 1972:28–31; Bloomberg et al., 1971:39). Boston neighborhoods in the same period show from 10 to 30 percent of households containing strangers in the family.

The nineteenth-century American family was an accommodating and flexible institution, as had been its eighteenth- and seventeenth-century predecessors.[3] Lodging was one major rubric under which its biologically-defined limits were breached, by an instrumental relationship based on economic and service exchange.

Yet by the end of the nineteenth century such Progressive moralists as Lawrence Veiller, the housing reformer, had created both a new name for the old practice—"the lodger evil"—and a behavioral measure for it: "room overcrowding as we know it in America," Veiller wrote, "is almost entirely wrapped up with the lodger evil" (Veiller, 1912:60). In matter of fact, Veiller was quite wrong; but in any case, the lodger evil could not *really* be measured spatially. A speaker at the 1910 biennial session of the National Conference of Jewish Charities revealed this neatly when he argued that "above all the keeping of lodgers, other than those related by blood ties to the family, should be prohibited absolutely," and went on to explain the dangers of overcrowding just as though biologically related persons required less space than unrelated individuals (Bremner, 1971: II, first part, p. 355). Social, not physical space, was the question.

It was a matter of privacy, and middle-class definitions of privacy were tightening. Carol Aronovici, another housing reformer, spoke with horror of "this widespread practice of exposing the private life of the heads of the family and that of the young girls to the presence of men in no way con-nected by blood relationships with the members of the household" (Aron-ovici, 1911:5). Still another reformer saw fit to record the statements made to her by "little girls" that "the men (boarders) are nasty and lift up our skirts" (Von Wagner, 1914:10). For (according to a government report), when strangers become members of the household

> . . . the close quarters often destroy all privacy, and the lodger or boarder be-
> comes practically a member of the family. . . . While such conditions, through
> custom and long usage, lose the startling effect they would have to one unused
> to them, they cannot help but blunt a girl's sense of proper relations with the
> other sex and foster standards which are not acceptable in this country. [U.S.
> Bureau of Labor, 1910: V, p. 62]

Sexuality rampant, or potentially so when and if the family failed to so-
cialize its young properly, that was the fear.[4] The context of this fear of
family breakdown was that which underlay so many middle-class fears of
the period: that the conditions of rapid urbanization were making life on
its traditional basis impossible, an anxiety visible (again with sexual over-
tones) as well in the literature of the period dealing with women's work,
the tragic end of the prostitute, and the vast library of progressive discussion of the immigrant.

Veiller's rich fantasy about what went on in the teeming immigrant tene-
ments need hardly be rehearsed here, but it is significant that it surfaced
(among other places) in his appeal for widely expanded police powers to
stamp out "the lodger evil" which he mainly identified with immigrants.
Aronovici was so convinced of this linkage that she contradicted her own
empirical findings in her study of Saint Paul, Minnesota, housing conditions (which found that in "striking contrast to the ordinary conception of
the lodger evil," foreign-born residents were not particularly disposed to
taking in lodgers) to assert that "the main reasons for the lodger evil are to
be found in the gregarious habits of the foreign elements" (Aronovici,
1917:51, 52).

The fear expressed by social workers and reformers, of family deterioration and breakdown under the impact of lodging and boarding, was closely associated with a general fear of the disintegration of traditional
primary groups under the pressures of urban life. While earlier the guardians of social norms had used boarding as a safety valve, they had come
to view it as a manifestation of social breakdown in the urban environment. This association of the practice of boarding with the social
deterioration of the city was reinforced in reformers' minds by the actual
transformations in housing patterns which they were witnessing in their
own environment. In Boston, for example, the South End was changing
from an elegant bay-front town house neighborhood into a boarding and
lodging and tenement district through the subdivision of three- to five-
story row houses and their conversion into multiple-family apartments, or
into one-family houses with lodgers and boarders on the top floors. Aside
from its impact on the family, lodging and boarding was clearly associated
with the decline of neighborhoods and with social disorder.

By the early twentieth century, thus, the ideal of the lodger-free household was associated in the minds of social workers and reformers with that
of the upright, decent working girl, that of the acculturated immigrant
family, and indeed with the whole set of values encompassing the well-

ordered family, the wisely-budgeted household, and the child protected from the most corrupting of life's threats. Since progressives believed that the future belonged to the young and acted accordingly, they turned their reforming attention to the family, bewailing its imminent demise. In part their approach was surgical: to cut out from the family those strangers whose presence apparently placed its integrity, cohesion, and socializing values under strain.

Yet families—even native-born families—did not on the whole conform to the reformers' prescription for nearly half a century. From a wide variety of sources, one gets the impression that for half a century and probably more the proportion of urban households which *at any particular point in time* had boarders or lodgers was between 15 and 20 percent. For 1920 we find for such varied cities as Chicago, Wilkes-Barre, Passaic, and Rochester figures at roughly this level. When in 1930 the Census Bureau first published uniform statistics on lodging in large cities, the proportion of urban American families who kept boarders was 11.4 percent. At this date, Chicago's percentage had increased during the decade, while Rochester's had declined (Monroe, 1932:154, 191–199; Nienburg, 1923:25; U.S. Department of Labor, Women's Bureau, 1922:25; 1925:57–58; U.S. Bureau of the Census, 1933:25, 67).[5]

Lodging in families was on the decline by the 1930s, despite the fact that in the short run the Depression worked to increase the tendency of established families to take in boarders. The 11.4 percent overall figure for 1930 was down to 9.0 percent for 1940. By 1970, even a city with a very "high" incidence of boarding in families, like San Francisco, had a shade under 4.5 percent of families with boarders, with most cities considerably under this figure (U.S. Bureau of the Census, 1943:28; Lee et al., 1971–1972, passim). The institution of boarding in families was, at last, disappearing.

We have already implied our point of view about boarders and lodgers in the family: that the practice was, like cityward migration itself, one institutionalized mode of the "social equalization of the size of the family," in Irene B. Taeuber's felicitous phrase (Taeuber, 1969:5). From this perspective, change-over-time figures for the incidence of boarding pose two questions. First, in view of the middle-class opposition to the practice, why did this vehicle for family equalization persist as long as it did and as late as it did, given the ample opportunities for institutional alternatives to have developed? And second, why did the ultimate decline of boarding and lodging come when at last it did?

In its urban, nineteenth-century manifestation, boarding in families was an adaptation of a traditional middle-class practice[6] to a situation in which large numbers of new urbanites, both foreign and native-born, usually young and with shallow resources, were thrown into a chaotic housing market. Confusion, economic considerations, and the need for socialization into the ways of the city all made a quasifamilial setting a very attractive proposition to the newcomer, the more so when he had in common with the family in which he would temporarily settle origin, ethnicity, occupation, or kinship.

We can look at the Rhode Island state censuses of 1885 and 1895 for some insight into the local conditions conducive to boarding in the family.

To do so we will have to shift our focus momentarily from the family itself, for the "boarders and lodgers" figure on the Rhode Island censuses included lodgers under the same head, whether they were living in families or in boarding houses. This, however, is not troublesome if we allow that these two categories (from the point of view of the lodger) essentially competed within a single market, that is, were substitutable goods. The town-to-town range of boarders enumerated per household was tremendous: a firm minimum was found in the declining agricultural town of Foster, whose ratio of lodgers to families implied that perhaps 3 percent of Foster families took in these strangers in 1885 and perhaps 4 percent in 1895. The maximum figures are a bit less certain, because in each year one town (each on the seacoast) had what seem quite inflated figures for boarders. If we exclude these, we find maxima of 44 and 43 lodgers per 100 families for the two years, implying that about 25 or 30 percent of families in the two years had boarders at the time of the census, if the usual quota of lodgers per household (about 1.5 as a mean) obtained in Barrington, the locus of the maxima. Barrington posed quite a contrast to Foster: its steadily growing population was engaged during this period in a changeover from a fairly agricultural setting to one which was very substantially industrial.

Looking systematically at the Rhode Island town figures, we find strong and significant positive correlations between the lodging ratio and such characteristic aspects of industrial urbanization as five-year population gain, proportion of manufacturing employees in the local labor force, and proportion of the local population born in foreign countries. The last mentioned is the strongest of the three, highly significant in both years, accounting for about half the town-to-town variation in 1885 and about a quarter in 1895.[7] The correlation observed in the Rhode Island materials can and should be explained quite simply: the kind of town the foreign-born came to was the same kind of town potential lodgers both foreign and native came to.

Statewide data for Massachusetts in 1885 (Massachusetts, 1887: 470–485) permit us to refine these clues somewhat, by computing the ratios by age, sex, and nativity, between boarders and lodgers, and those living in households as nonlineal kin (brothers or sisters, uncles or aunts, nephews or nieces, and cousins)—roughly as a measure of "taste" for living as boarders rather than as extended family members. Having had relatively less time in which to develop kinship networks, the foreign-born of both sexes had higher ratios of boarders to extended-family relationships, overall, but taking this into consideration, the patterns are age- and sex-specific, rather than varying by nativity.

For both native- and foreign-born males, there was a broad peak of preference for boarding extending from the 20 to 29 category through the 40 to 49 category, peaking slightly among those 30 to 39; ratios are about 4.5 times as many boarders as extended kin for the native-born, about 5.75 times for the foreign-born. Among women, the peak is in the 20 to 29 group, and it is a sharp peak, declining quickly on either side, with the peak ratio about three times for the native-born but only 2.1 for the foreign-born. The overall lower ratios for females than for males speaks eloquently of a lingering societal preference for family governance for women, while the sharp peak ratio for the women is no doubt parallel to their brief exposure to "independent" existence in the labor force. Among males of both nativities, both the height and the breadth of the peak of preference for lodging points to the extent to which an economic relationship served instead of a possibly traditional familial one for all but those at the opposite ends of the age continuum. The young and the old, of course, included high proportions of the dependent, for whom familiar relationships were evidently considered preferable. That the age- and sex-specific patterns were parallel for the native- and the foreign-born indicates yet again how thoroughly by 1885 the institution of boarding had become part of the American social structure.

When we turn from aggregate data for the state to individual data for Boston, we discover that in boarding as in many other areas, America was a multilayered society. An analysis of family and household structure and residential patterns in select Boston neighborhoods in 1880 corroborates the general patterns found in the state data but also reveals significant differences.[8]

The Boston data show conclusively that boarding with families was far more pervasively a native American phenomenon than an immigrant practice. The Irish, Boston's largest immigrant group, included the lowest percentage of boarders in the neighborhoods studied. The highest concentration of boarders was among natives of Massachusetts (38 percent) and among natives of Maine, New Hampshire, and Vermont, many of whom were recent arrivals to the city (19.3 percent). In Boston's South End, where the Irish comprised about 31 percent of the entire population studied, Irish boarders made up only 10 percent of all boarders sampled. The Boston data support our hypothesis that boarding was a *migrant* rather than a foreign immigrant practice: individuals who showed the highest tendency to board were newest to the city. Immigrants from abroad, however, resorted to boarding as a temporary measure until they settled in their own households in other parts of the city or in other towns. For native Americans, on the other hand, lodging was a regular and long-term alternative to the nuclear or extended family. (In the South End, 30 percent of all households studied had boarders. Only 15 percent included extended kin.)

Whether a temporary measure or a longer-lasting arrangement, boarding was a function of the life cycle. It was most prevalent among unmarried men and women, most of whom were employed in the central downtown area. About 37 percent of all boarders in the entire Boston sample studied were in the age group 20 to 29, and about 27.5 percent in the age group 30 to 39—a significantly higher concentration than in the rest of the population sample, where these age groups comprised 22 percent and 19 percent respectively. There were no significant differences in age grouping between men and women. While the largest part of this group boarded in the interim between their departure from their parents' households to the establishment of a household of their own, others continued to board through their thirties and forties. Children under 14 and teenagers were least represented in the boarding population (6.5 percent for those below 14, and 8.2 percent for the age group 14 to 19). Where they appeared as boarders, they were generally members of an entire family which boarded in the household. Such families consisted generally of parents in their late twenties or thirties with one or more children or, more frequently, of widows or single women with their children. This type of boarding was most common among the Irish in the group studied (Irish boarders included 12 percent children under 14), which suggests their tendency to board in family clusters, no doubt in part a function of the higher mortality of Irish males.

A comparison of the age distribution of boarders and lodgers with that of the heads of households with whom they boarded shows a marked decline in the tendency of individuals in their forties to board. The data reveal, in fact, a role reversal at this stage. Rather than board or live with extended kin, men and women in their forties tended to head their own households and to take in boarders. One-third of all boarders studied were living with household heads in their forties. This practice appears to be particularly widespread in the South End which housed the highest concentration of female-headed households in the neighborhoods studied, as well as the highest number of widows over forty. Female-headed households constituted 28 percent of all households studied in the South End. Of these, 39 percent took in boarders, in contrast to male-headed households, of which only 26.5 percent took in boarders.

A correlation of individuals with the heads of households with whom they boarded showed a clear pattern of bunching by age groups. While the largest proportion of boarders, regardless of age, lived with heads of households in the 40 to 50 age group, there was generally a "generation gap" between boarders and their heads. Most boarders under 35 tended to live in households headed by individuals who were their seniors by 15 years or more. This age pattern clearly suggests that the practice of boarding and of taking in boarders was a function of the life cycle. A conservative estimate would suggest that at least one-third to one-half of all individuals were likely to experience both—boarding in their early adulthood and taking in boarders at a later stage of life.

The desire for independence from family ties was no doubt a major factor in the decision of boarders to pay rent rather than live with their kin in extended household arrangements. Young men and women in their twenties, employed in semiskilled or skilled jobs, preferred boarding with a strange family, over their own, because the exchange of rent and services was defined in strict economic terms. Boarding offered the advantages of a family setting, without the affective and lasting obligations that are woven into family relationships.[9] It also often placed them into a peer-group relationship with fellow boarders, an association which they sometimes carried over from their place of employment. Location in the city was an equally important consideration. In Boston, boarders and lodgers constituted 25 percent of the entire population of the centrally-located South End, which had become by then the city's primary boarding and lodging center. By contrast, in South Boston, a predominantly Irish section removed from the center of the city and thus inconvenient to the location of most jobs held by newcomers, only five percent of the groups studied were lodgers and boarders.

Boarding and lodging patterns in the South End reveal a distinct tendency toward ethnic clustering and a lesser though nevertheless significant tendency toward occupational clustering. A comparison of each of about 700 boarders in Boston's South End with the head of household with whom he boarded suggests strong connections between the boarders' places of origin and those of their household heads. Table 1 presents these data in the form of a comparison between the matchings observed in the Boston data and those which would have been "expected" had boarders from different origins simply placed themselves at random in the homes of those offering space. The highest ratio of observed to expected frequencies is seen— understandably enough—in the category "same foreign country," in which nearly four times the number of exact matches was found as one would expect by chance alone. Among foreign nationalities, the highest concentrations of matches appeared among the Irish and the Canadians (principally from the Maritimes). Of Irish boarders, nearly six in ten were found living in households with Irish heads. Yet Irish-headed households with boarders had fellow Irishmen as boarders in only 35 percent of the cases, a number which contrasts sharply with a 60 percent figure for Canadian-headed homes with boarders sharing their nativity. But only 38 percent of Canadian boarders were lodged in Canadian-headed homes. The orderly quality of this rather complicated pattern is attested to by noting that Irish-headed families tended most often (40 percent of the time) to take in Massachusetts-born persons, no doubt often second-generation Irishmen, while Canadian boarders apparently had little trouble in situating themselves in the homes of the New-England-born, whom they evidently sufficiently resembled to make fitting boarders.

**Table 1** OBSERVED FREQUENCY OF SELECTED ETHNIC MATCHES, BOSTON, (SOUTH END) BOARDERS WITH THEIR HOUSEHOLD HEADS, COMPARED WITH "EXPECTED" FREQUENCY OF MATCHES, 1880 (N = 645)

|  | Same US state category* | Same foreign country | Different US state category | Different foreign country | Boarder US head FB | Boarder FB, head US |
|---|---|---|---|---|---|---|
|  | % | % | % | % | % | % |
| Observed | 22.3 | 13.5 | 27.4 | 4.5 | 17.8 | 14.5 |
| "Expected" | 15.7 | 3.5 | 27.7 | 8.1 | 24.2 | 20.8 |
| Ratio, observed: "expected" | 1.43:1 | 3.81:1 | 0.99:1 | 0.56:1 | 0.74:1 | 0.70:1 |

*State categories are: Massachusetts; Maine-Vermont-New Hampshire: Connecticut-Rhode Island; rest of United States.

Table 1 shows, too, a distinct clustering pattern by state and a distinct avoidance pattern for three combinations. Of these, matches of different foreign nativity groups were the rarest, while foreigners mingled with the New-England-born at roughly three-fourths the "expected" rate, both for foreign boarders in native households and native boarders in foreign households. The intensity of ethnic clustering is revealed not only in the comparison of boarders to their heads of households but also among fellow boarders. In households containing several boarders, all boarders were frequently from the same place of origin, even if the head of household was not.

Occupational clustering (based upon data excluding all matches in which either boarder or household head had no occupation listed) was weaker, but reasonably convincing, especially in view of the broad occupational categories employed (professional; semiprofessional; white collar; skilled; semiskilled; and unskilled). Exact occupational matches occurred 1.14 times as frequently as would be expected by chance, while nearmatches (between adjacent occupational categories) appeared 1.06 times the "expected" frequency. Among those where matching was more distant, surprisingly, it was slightly more likely that boarders would *exceed* their household head in status (0.92 times the chance likelihood) than would *be exceeded by* the head (0.87 times chance likelihood). The differences here are slight but suggestive: boarders and their households sought out appropriate matches, no doubt utilizing the pricing mechanism as well as outright rejection. A perfect occupational match was seemingly optimal, but a near match would also serve without being offensive to either party. Where no match or near match was achieved (as in about 45 percent of the cases) boarders more frequently accepted accommodations with a less well-placed family than the reverse.[10]

By the beginning of the twentieth century Boston's South End was christened by one of its dedicated social workers as "The City Wilderness." As a tenement and lodging-house section in the commercial and entertainment center of the city, the South End already showed most of its "wilderness" characteristics by 1880. It was a polyglot section, a depository for most newly arrived immigrants, an area containing a patchwork of ethnic enclaves, highly populated by unskilled and semiskilled workers, and showing the highest proportion of unmarried and widowed persons in the city. It also housed the city's highest concentration of boarders and lodgers. This neighborhood can serve, therefore, as an excellent test for the stigma of social breakdown and anomie attached to boarding. Yet boarders in the South End were representative of the entire population groups studied, differing only in age and in marital status. They included a higher proportion of individuals in their twenties and thirties, and, in this age group, they were more frequently unmarried than the rest of the population studied. The overall occupational distribution for the South End lodgers is not substantially different from that of the neighborhood as a whole. The persistence of lodgers in the city parallels that of heads of households studied, and their lodging pattern is not random; it gives every impression of a sensible and orderly accommodation to urban life.

Families took in boarders primarily for economic considerations, which, in turn, depended in part on the characteristics of the housing market and in part on the uncertainties of income in a period of high morbidity and mortality and oppressive cyclical unemployment. Families which were prepared to accept lodgers: (1) were able to receive a "brokerage fee" for adapting the predominantly large dwelling units to the needs of usually single immigrants, usually from their own social level and of a similar standard of living; (2) realized income for work performed by the wife *within the home*, varying with the amount of effort the housewife wished to devote, reflected in the quantity, "quality," and duration of accommodations offered,[11] (3) benefited by a gain in flexibility in terms of their potential family income, available even in times of sickness or unemployment; (4) were in a position to stabilize their income through the family life cycle by moving a paying guest into the room once inhabited by a son or daughter who had left the home; (5) afforded widows and single women in their forties, fifties, and sixties an opportunity to maintain their own households rather than to live with their kin.

**Figure 1.** PROPORTION OF NATIVE-BORN MASSACHUSETTS RESIDENTS WHO ARE LIVING AS BOARDERS OR LODGERS, 1885, BY SEX AND AGE: AND PROPORTION OF NATIVE WORKING-CLASS FAMILIES WHICH HAVE BOARDERS OR LODGERS, 1890, BY AGE OF MALE HOUSEHOLD HEAD AND BY AGE OF OLDEST CHILD IN THE FAMILY[a]

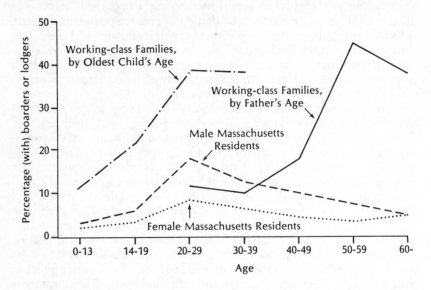

[a]Source: Massachusetts, Bureau of the Statistics of Labor (1887); U.S. Bureau of Labor (1892), and see text footnote 13. The 1895 Massachusetts state census gives substantially similar patterns. The working-class family sample excludes those families with no children in the household.

In an industrializing, rapidly urbanizing society, however, boarding was so widespread as to be reasonably considered indispensable: it was, in fact, far more common than the aggregate momentary estimate of 15 to 20 percent would suggest. For in nineteenth-century cities the practice of boarding in families was closely articulated to the life cycles both of the boarders and of the families which took them in. Figure 1 is admittedly based upon two entirely different and strictly noncomparable sets of data, one of which suffers from unrepresentative sampling techniques, the other of which suffers from a too-broad definition of the variable "boarder." Nevertheless, if the exact figures the graph suggests are imperfect, its implications are unmistakable and of great importance: boarding in families in industrial America in the late nineteenth century was the province of young men of an age just to have left their parents' homes and was an arrangement entered into and provided by household heads who were of an age to have just lost a son from the residential family to an independent residence. It was *plausibly* a surrogate family—in the psychological sense. But in terms of an economic calculus, it was *almost precisely this.* Or rather, in Taeuber's terms, it was a social equalization of the family which operated *directly* by the exchange of a young-adult person and a portion of his young-adult income from his family of orientation to what might be called his family of reorientation—reorientation to the city, to a job, to a new neighborhood, to independence. It was a transfer from a family (often rural, whether domestic or foreign) with excess sons or daughters (or insufficient economic base) to one (usually urban) with excess room (or present or anticipated economic need). And often both the excess room and the present or anticipated economic need can have come from the departure from the household of a newly independent son.[12]

The *economic* logic of boarding for the family life cycle can be examined by manipulating the household budget materials collected by the Commissioner of Labor in his 1890 study of the standard of living in working-class families.[13] The central fact of this economic logic was that while taking the sample of working-class families *as a whole*, family expenses varied somewhat less widely than did fathers' incomes, *over the life cycle* average expenses changed markedly without corresponding changes in fathers' incomes (see Table 2). Families thus suffered a double economic squeeze: a

**Table 2.** ECONOMIC CHARACTERISTICS ASSOCIATED WITH STAGES IN THE LIFE CYCLE, NATIVE WORKING-CLASS FAMILIES IN THE INDUSTRIAL NORTH, 1890[a]

|  | Childless[b] | Young bearing[b] | Middle bearing[b] | Middle stopped bearing[b] | Older bearing[b] | Older stopped bearing[b] |
|---|---|---|---|---|---|---|
| Mean family expenses (only nuclear families here) | $480 | $576 | $580 | $635 | $661 | $641 |
| Mean fathers' incomes (all families with fathers) | $484 | $409 | $494 | $504 | $475 | $421 |
| Implied deficit | $ 4 | $167 | $ 86 | $131 | $186 | $220 |
| Mean income from children | 0 | 0 | $ 21 | $ 88 | $185 | $249 |
| Mean income from wife | $ 43 | $ 26 | $ 15 | $ 34 | $ 11 | $ 10 |
| Proportion of families with paying lodgers | 10.9% | 20.0% | 9.8% | 10.6% | 35.2% | 35.6% |
| N | 137 | 30 | 511 | 132 | 75 | 129 |

[a]Commissioner of Labor household budget sample, described in text footnote 13.
[b]The life-cycle categories are based upon the age of the youngest child of the household ("bearing" when a child younger than five years is present) and the age of the male household head ("young" is under 25 years, "middle" 25–44, "older" 45 years or older).

relatively mild one from the greater "chance" variability of income as compared with expenditures; and a severe and regular one, from the tendency for costs to outstrip fathers' incomes as families passed through their life cycles.

Mean fathers' incomes varied less than $100 over the life cycle, while expenses even for families of nuclear composition varied almost $200. And the cyclical developments did not match in direction! The problem of the mismatch of income to outgo was no doubt a daily concern to the working classes, a potent motive for family decisions.[14] One answer to this mismatch was occupational mobility (excluded, of course, from these data as from all cross-sectional samples though of obvious theoretical relevance); another was age-graded pay scales (demonstrably rare in nineteenth-century industrial employment); another common answer was the early employment of youth; women's work was equally logical but less common. Taking in a boarder was still another response, from an economic point of view not largely different from sending a child out to work, as Table 2 suggests.

With the data at hand we are in a position to make a rough partitioning of the "causes" of boarding (from the viewpoint of families taking in boarders) into those enforced by immediate economic need, and those brought about either by anticipated needs or as a product of culture directly. Table 3 seeks to supply some insight into the mix of immediate economic motives, and other motives, by examining the proportion of working-class families with lodgers at various life-cycle stages, holding the current gap between father's income and family expenses constant. Cases in many of the cells of the table are admittedly rather few, but the story is clear nonetheless: the logic of the life cycle dominates, and though the economic squeeze is still of some influence, it plays *directly* a relatively minor role, even as it intervenes potently (as Table 2 suggested) between the life-cycle stage and household malleability.

Why did families more advanced in the life cycle show by far the greatest tendency to take in boarders and lodgers, even when they did not have immediate budgetary reasons for doing so? Figure 1 provided one clue. Another may be seen by noting that as families passed through their

**Table 3.** PROPORTION OF NATIVE WORKING-CLASS FAMILIES WITH BOARDERS BY LIFE CYCLE AND RELATION OF FATHER'S INCOME TO FAMILY EXPENSES (EXCLUDING ESTIMATED EXPENSES FOR BOARDER), 1890 (PERCENT SHOWN IS BASED ON NUMBER OF CASES IN CELL, SHOWN IN PARENTHESES)

| | Childless | Young bearing | Middle bearing | Middle stopped bearing | Older bearing | Older stopped bearing |
|---|---|---|---|---|---|---|
| | % | % | % | % | % | % |
| Deficit of $100 or more | 18.2 (22) | 12.5 (8) | 13.6 (118) | 10.4 (48) | 39.5 (43) | 42.1 (88) |
| Deficit of $99 to surplus of $99 | 11.8 (76) | 21.0 (19) | 9.6 (322) | 14.3 (63) | 29.6 (27) | 25.9 (27) |
| Surplus of $100 or more | 5.1 (39) | 33.3 (3) | 4.2 (71) | 0.0 (21) | 25.0 (4) | 14.3 (14) |

life cycle, they also tended to acquire their own houses, rising from a base level of around 10 percent at the earlier stages to 15 and 21 percent homeowners at the final two life-cycle stages. Thernstrom (1964) has suggested the meaning of this tendency for an earlier period, and his reasoning would seem to apply for turn-of-the-century workingmen as well. He documented the agonizingly slow accumulative process leading up to the purchase of a house, and the modicum of security it offered in a highly insecure industrial environment, despite the obligations it entailed. Since mortgage costs considerably exceeded rentals at this time (U.S. Bureau of Labor, 1903), such security was clearly at a substantial premium. Aging— the life cycle—was a dynamic development, in which foresignt and anxiety no less than calculation played a part, to which the family's function and composition had to bend.

By the 1930s, most of the conditions which had made boarding in families an arrangement of widespread functionality had at last begun to disappear. The depression decade, for one thing, interrupted the flow of both foreign and domestic migrants to cities. A sharp decline in demand for urban housing thus followed sharply a changed supply situation, for in the prosperity of the 1920s urban housing construction began to catch up with demand, which had outrun it for many decades (Gottlieb, 1964:chs. 2–4; Campbell, 1966).

The later 1930s and the subsequent decades saw the elaboration of the welfare state, among the consequences of which was to remove some of the need for just such a source of supplementary family income as boarding offered. Cyclical unemployment, sickness, and old age all had at least partial answers in the new provisions. So, too (though for different reasons), covert women's work became needless, as profitable and honorable jobs outside the home opened up during and after World War II. Correspondingly, added duties within the home seemed increasingly onerous to housewives.

At the same time, privacy, both within and without the family, was being redefined, partly but only partly in ways congruent with the hopes of the urban progressives decades earlier, due more than anything to the previously unimagined prosperity which reached down to the level of the workingman. Seeley, Sim, and Loosely (1956), for example, point to the extraordinary demands for *individual* privacy within the household. The arrangements of such ideal households, urban as well as suburban, hardly left room—social or physical—for a lodger. And the concurrently changing definition of permissible sexuality—permissible, however, only as highly private acts—called for a great deal of apartness, most especially for the unmarried young adult—formerly the most typical lodger. As one-person households became the ideal for this stage in the life cycle, prosperity made the maintenance of such settings possible. As from the supply side, so from the demand side, boarding and lodging in the family became obsolete.

We began this excursion into the workings of an almost forgotten family institution by looking at middle-class reformers' criticisms directed toward it, and at the quantitative spatial metaphor—room overcrowding—which they employed in condemning it. We are now in a position to contemplate the literal justness of this aspect of the criticism, again basing our discussion on the 1890 Bureau of Labor Statistics data, which included an item on number of rooms occupied by each renter family. With these we are able to compute, for each life-cycle stage, a room-to-person quotient for each family, subdivided into those families consisting only of heads and their children and those who had lodgers. The findings are unequivocal. For *all but one life-cycle stage*, families who had lodgers had *more* rooms per person when we exclude their lodgers from the calculation than families without lodgers. But when the lodgers are included in our divisors, then the *nonlodger* families had more room in all but one life-cycle stage.[15] In other words, though the progressives were correct in asserting that some crowding was a concomitant of taking in lodgers, they did not recognize that lodgers were on the whole taken in where there was some "excess" room in being.[16]

Accepting a lodger into the family was not evidence of incipient family disorganization, as reformers feared, nor a helter-skelter piling of individuals upon one another without regard to privacy. The largest discrepancy between families with and without lodgers in rooms-per-person (with lodgers counted) in *any* life-cycle stage was 31 percent, for younger families just in the childbearing stage. Yet this discrepancy was scarcely greater than that found *between* life-cycle stages, *for nonboarder families*, even if we exclude the spatially plush childless stage. The median additional crowding in lodger families was only 16 percent; there was a tradeoff, to be sure, but a narrow one. Lodging in the family was a vehicle by which urban Americans gained control of their environment, not one by which they lost it.

Although the hostility and anxiety expressed by reformers towards lodging and boarding was misplaced, their fears were a response to major historical changes in the role of the institution and its relationship to the family, which had taken place over an entire century. Under the impact of urbanization in the nineteenth century, the functions of asylum which had previously been assigned to the family by the town authorities were gradually transferred to institutions established specifically for the care of the young, the poor, the dependent, and the delinquent. By mid-nineteenth century the urban family lost its cachet as a rehabilitative haven for "boarded out" poor and dependent strangers.

From 1850, the influx of foreign immigrants and rural migrants into American cities overwhelmed the available housing facilities. Middle-class boarding, a voluntary practice, for individuals in certain stages of the life cycle or in certain occupational groups, was overshadowed by the emergence of lower-class boarding. By the 1880s, family boarding lost both its official use for social control, as well as its middle-class respectability. It became identified exclusively (if erroneously) as a lower-class practice and was attacked in the context of tenement squalor and the poverty of immigrant life.

In this instance the demonology of boarding is characteristic of the entire theory of family breakdown under the impact of industrialization and urbanization. Sociologists who have promoted this thesis have cited the surrender to other institutions in society of functions which had been exclusive to the family as proof for family breakdown. Though by the end of the nineteenth century boarding had, indeed, lost its "formal" poor-relief function, in a society which even at the turn of the century was still familistic, boarding was still chosen (no doubt consciously in many instances) as a family surrogate.

The family was not fragile but malleable. That so many misunderstood this distinction is itself symptomatic, for reformers who bewailed the imminent breakup of the family had displaced their concern from the hardness of life inherent in the industrial system to an institution that not only was a sensible response to industrialization but, in cushioning the shock of urban life for newcomers, was decidedly humane.

## NOTES

1. We shall use the terms "lodger" and "boarder" synonomously in this paper. Although currently their meaning is somewhat distinct—the latter term implying meals as well as bed taken in the family—nineteenth-century usage was less distinct. One distinction that *is* intended here is between boarding (or lodging) *within families*, the subject of the paper, and that in houses specialized for the purpose. The latter is itself a significant development, one of which contemporaries were relatively aware. For an excellent contemporary study see Wolfe (1906).

2. The present paper owes much to John Modell's "Strangers in the Family," an earlier treatment of the boarding and lodging theme delivered at the Clark University Conference on the History of the Family, April, 1972, and to Tamara K. Hareven, "Social Change and Family Patterns in Nineteenth-Century Boston," delivered at the Organization of American Historians, Washington, D.C., April, 1972.

3. "The problems of mutual observation by lodgers and family were neither new nor unusual [in colonial New England]. The most common remedy was for a family gradually to accept a boarder into the intimacy of the family" (Flaherty, 1972:69).

4. Oddly, though the campaign against boarders in the family was waged largely in terms of the effects of the practice on the young, what case history material has come to our attention bears rather upon the sexual relations of the conjugal pair. See, for example, the pathetic *Bintel Brief* quoted in Thomas (1923:13–14), the cases from the Chicago Legal Aid Society printed in Thomas and Znaniecki (1958, II, pp. 1723–1725), and the authors' explanation of why "'boarder' stories [involving sexual infidelity of wives] have become a well-known feature of Polish-American life" (ibid., p. 1741). And see also the odd assertion contained in a social worker's report from the 1920s printed in Shaw (1931:44): "Mrs. Blotzman came into the office and stated that Mr. Blotzman had taken a man into their home as a boarder. She was afraid that Mr. Blotzman was scheming with the boarder to make it appear that she was immoral with this man."

5. We only touch here upon the questions of ethnicity and the relationship of boarding to the socioeconomic integration of the immigrant to native patterns. A few empirical points, however, should be noted. First, several sets of data confirm the absence of a substantial direct correlation between foreign birth and propensity to take in lodgers, when other relevant factors are accounted for. Initial insights into this question are available in the standard-of-living data presented by states in U.S. Bureau of Labor (1904), and in the United States Census of 1930, which shows that in most cities the foreign-born had a lower proportion of families with boarders than native whites. A final tantalizing suggestion arises from the juxtaposition of the Immigration Commission's finding (1911) that (holding city and ethnic group constant) the longer the immigrant had been in America the less likely he was to have a lodger, with that discovered in 1920 census data for Passaic, where the *reverse* pattern obtained (U.S. Department of Labor, Women's Bureau, 1922:34).

6. Strickland (1969:30), for example, reports that the Bronson Alcott family readily (though, in the end, unhappily) resorted to taking in juvenile boarders when the family "was hovering between genteel poverty and outright destitution," and thus remained on the more desirable side of that line.

7. To make much of the problem of multicollinearity in multiple regressions based on such indicators would be fruitless though justified from a statistical point of view. Dependent and independent variables alike are imperfect here and used more for what they suggest than for the assessment of causal relationships.

8. The individual data on boarders and lodgers for Boston are part of a larger study of family and ethnicity in nineteenth-century Boston. The study is based on an analysis of family and residential patterns of approximately 6,000 individuals, selected by household from the manuscript schedules of the 1880 Federal Census. The households were sampled from four distinct neighborhoods, representing a variety of ethnic compositions, different socioeconomic groups, and varying lengths of residence in the city. In the South End, the most ethnically complex neighborhood in the city, the households were chosen by stratified samples, in proportion to the ethnic composition of the neighborhood. The entire sample consisted of 3,363 males and 3,960 females. The total South End population sampled consisted of 3,314 individuals, of which 700 were listed as "boarders." Except where the entire Boston population sample is mentioned specifically, most data on boarders and lodgers cited in this article are based on this group of 700.

The heads of household and individuals sampled from the 1880 census (the only one which designates relationship to the household) were traced backwards and forward through city directories to their earliest as well as most recent listing in the directory. They were also traced back to the censuses of 1870, 1860, and 1850, wherever this was possible. The findings presented in this paper represent data observations rather than the result of statistical manipulation and are among the earlier materials to be derived from this long-range project.

9. There is no doubt that in certain instances, individuals designated as boarders might have been relatives who had entered a boarding relationship. Unfortunately, the census listings provide no systematic clues to such relationships.

10. In this context, we should note that while the *incidence* of boarding was somewhat greater among families of lower socioeconomic strata, this was only relatively true. Absolutely, one can say that boarding was practiced by families at all economic levels (see Monroe, 1932:191, 194).

11. Apparently, it would be an error to assume that, on the whole, families chose whether women would work outside the home *or* take in boarders, since they both could do both and did do so, according to 1930 census data. At that time, it would seem, families with homemakers gainfully employed outside the home were *more* likely to have boarders than the national average (although only slightly more), with especially high proportions of boarders admitted to families where the gainfully employed homemaker was an older woman, a servant or waitress, or a professional worker! (U.S. Women's Bureau, 1936:22)

12. These speculations are obviously just that and call for empirical verification.

13. The data here employed consist of 1,048 family budgets of factory workers, with information on ages, household composition, nativity, and details of income and expenditure. Over 5,000 such budgets—potentially magnificent social documents—are published in U.S. Bureau of Labor (1892). The Commissioner of Labor does not specify his sampling techniques, which we may assume were born of convenience rather than statistical sophistication. In order to obtain as homogeneous a sample as possible—to observe as clearly as possible the workings of family composition, life cycle, and budgetary considerations—we have included 1,048 only American-born workers in major industries living in northern and midwestern states. For present purposes, we have further excluded from analysis families headed by widows.

14. A brilliant exposition of this nineteenth-century dilemma (in an English setting), together with an impressive theoretical framework, is Michael Anderson's *Family and Kinship in Nineteenth-Century Lancashire* (1972). We could cite this volume at many places in this essay but can best suggest our debt to it by urging that our readers avail themselves of it.

15. The formulae treated all household members as requiring the same amount of room, regardless of their age.

16. Note, too, that the exclusion of families which owned houses (but whose rooms were not counted in the data) biases the sample *against* roominess in the boarder families, since in

five of the six life-cycle stages home-owning families were more likely to have boarders than were renters—which makes sense, since they (one imagines) had more room and higher monetary obligations to worry about. (But in Boston's South End, with few exceptions, heads of households taking in boarders did not own the houses they lived in.)

# REFERENCES

ANDERSON, MICHAEL. 1972. Family and Kinship in Nineteenth-Century Lancashire. Cambridge: the University Press.

ARONOVICI, CAROL. 1911. Housing Conditions in Fall River. N.p.: Associated Charities Housing Committee.

———. 1917. Housing Conditions in the City of Saint Paul. Saint Paul: The Housing Commission of the Saint Paul Association.

BLOOMBERG, SUSAN E. et al. 1971. "A census probe into nineteenth-century family history: Southern Michigan, 1850–1880." Journal of Social History 5.

BLUMIN, STUART. 1972. "Families and households in the Hudson Valley, 1800–1860." Manuscript delivered at the Clark University Conference on The Family, Social Structure, and Social Change.

BREMNER, ROBERT H., JOHN BARNARD, TAMARA K. HAREVEN, AND ROBERT MENNELL (eds.). 1971. Children and Youth in America. 2. Cambridge: Harvard University Press.

CAMPBELL, BURNHAM O. 1966. Population Change and Building Cycles. University of Illinois, Bureau of Economic and Business Research, Bulletin series, No. 91. Urbana.

DEALEY, JAMES QUAYLE. 1912. The Family in Its Sociological Aspects. Boston: Houghton, Mifflin.

DEMOS, JOHN. 1970. A Little Commonwealth; Family Life in Plymouth Colony. New York: Oxford University Press.

FARBER, BERNARD. 1972. Guardians of Virtue. Salem Families in 1800. New York: Basic Books.

FLAHERTY, DAVID H. 1972. Privacy in Colonial New England. Charlottesville: University Press of Virginia.

GLASCO, LAWRENCE. 1972. "Ethnicity and family structure in nineteenth-century America: the native-born, Irish and Germans of Buffalo, N.Y. 1855." Manuscript delivered at the Clark University Conference on The Family, Social Structure and Social Change.

GOTTLIEB, MANUEL. 1964. Estimates of Residential Building, United States, 1840–1939. National Bureau of Economic Research, Technical Paper 17.

HAREVEN, TAMARA K. 1972. "Social change and family patterns in nineteenth-century Boston." Manuscript.

LEE, EVERETT S. et al. 1971–1972. Demographic Profiles of the United States. Oak Ridge, Tennessee: Oak Ridge National Laboratory.

MASSACHUSETTS, BUREAU OF THE STATISTICS OF LABOR. 1887. Census of Massachusetts: 1885. Boston: Wright and Potter.

———. 1897. Census of the Commonwealth of Massachusetts: 1895. Boston: Wright and Potter.

MODELL, JOHN. 1971. "Family and fertility on the Indiana frontier: 1820." American Quarterly.

MONROE, DAY. 1932. Chicago Families. Chicago: University of Chicago Press (Social Sciences Series 22).

MORGAN, EDMUND S. 1944. The Puritan Family. Boston: Trustees of the Public Library.

NIENBURG, BERTHA M. 1932. The Woman Home-Maker in the City. Washington: United States Bureau of the Census.

RHODE ISLAND, CENSUS BUREAU. 1887. Rhode Island State Census, 1885. Providence: E. L. Freeman and Sons.

———. 1898. Census of Rhode Island, 1895. Providence: E. L. Freeman and Sons.

ROSSITER, W. S. (compiler). 1909. A Century of Population Growth. Washington: Government Printing Office.

SEELEY, JOHN R., R. ALEXANDER SIM, AND E. W. LOOSELY. 1956. Crestwood Heights: The Culture of Suburban Life. New York: Basic Books.

SHAW, CLIFFORD R. in collaboration with MAURICE E. MOORE. 1931. The Natural History of a Delinquent Career. Chicago: University of Chicago Press.

STRICKLAND, CHARLES. 1969. "A transcendental father: the child-rearing practices of Bronson Alcott." Perspectives in American History 3.

TAEUBER, IRENE B. 1969. "Change and transition in family structures." The Family in Transition (Fogarty International Center Proceedings). Washington: U.S.G.P.O.

THERNSTROM, STEPHAN. 1964. Poverty and Progress. Cambridge: Harvard University Press.

THOMAS, W. I. 1923. The Unadjusted Girl. Boston: Little Brown.

THOMAS, W. I. AND FLORIAN ZNANIECKI. 1958. The Polish Peasant in Europe and America. New York: Dover Publications (reprint).

VEILLER, LAWRENCE. 1912. "Room overcrowding and the lodger evil." Housing Problems in America: Proceedings of the Second National Conference on Housing, Philadelphia.

VON WAGNER, JOHANNA. 1914. Teaching the Tenant (National Housing Association Publications 8, 2nd edition).

U.S. BUREAU OF THE CENSUS. 1933. Fifteenth Census of the United States, Population, VI, Families. Washington: Government Printing Office.

_____. 1943. Sixteenth Census of the United States: 1940, Population and housing. Families, General Characteristics, Washington: U.S.G.P.O.

_____. 1972. Census of Housing: 1970. Detailed Housing Characteristics.

U.S. BUREAU OF LABOR. 1892. Seventh Annual Report of the Commissioner of Labor, 1891, II, part 3. Washington: Government Printing Office.

_____. 1904. Eighteenth Annual Report of the Commissioner of Labor, 1903. Washington: Government Printing Office, 1904.

_____. 1910. Report on Conditions of Women and Child Wage-Earners in the United States. S. Doc. 645, 61st Congress, Second Session.

U.S. DEPARTMENT OF LABOR, WOMEN'S BUREAU. 1922. Bulletin #23: The Family Status of Breadwinning Women. Washington: Government Printing Office.

_____. 1925. Bulletin #41: Family Status of Breadwinning Women in Four Selected Cities. Washington: Government Printing Office.

U.S. IMMIGRATION COMMISSION. 1911. Reports, Immigrants in Cities (vol. 26 of the Commission's Reports). S. Doc. 338, 61st Congress, Second Session.

U.S. WOMEN'S BUREAU. 1936. Bulletin #148. The Employed Woman Homemaker in the United States. Washington: U.S.G.P.O.

# 4 | THE FALL IN HOUSEHOLD SIZE AND THE RISE OF THE PRIMARY INDIVIDUAL IN THE UNITED STATES

FRANCES E. KOBRIN

## THE FALL IN FAMILY AND HOUSEHOLD SIZE: INTRODUCTION

The average size of the household has fallen sharply in every modernized country. In the United States, household size has nearly halved since 1790, dropping from 5.8 persons per household to 3.0 in 1973. Early explanations attributed this fall in size to the breakup of an extended family system which was said to have existed in the past in both the United States and Western Europe. This line of argument has generated considerable controversy (Berkner, 1973, reviews this literature for Western Europe); and the term "extended family" still has no widely agreed-upon meaning. It now appears clear that if the definition of extension requires more than one married pair, no matter how related, neither early rural nor more recent urban populations in the United States give evidence of such a pattern having existed with any great frequency. Married couples, except for brief periods or in unusual circumstances, were expected to maintain a separate household (B. Laslett, 1973).

As a result of these findings, the extended family issue for the United States is now rarely considered, and the fall in household size is viewed as largely the result of the decline in fertility and the removal from the household of unrelated individuals such as boarders, lodgers, and servants. However, if the term "extension" is defined to mean the ordinary inclusion in families of adults who are not currently married—the grown children, siblings, and parents of the married couple—then extension has declined, and thus a process of "nuclearization" has occurred which, in interaction with demographic changes, has contributed greatly to the fall in household size. The fall in fertility has decreased the number of very large units; the fall in mortality has increased the proportion of small units by increasing the length of time couples survive after their children are grown. These factors were important during the earlier stages of the decline in the average size of the household. These demographic changes have also contributed to a shift in the structure of the population, increasing the proportion of the not currently married adult relatives, particularly at the older ages. The changes, along with increased separation and divorce, and the recent rise in the proportion of never married among the young, have led to a rise in the number of very small households where these adults now live. The continuing decline in household size in the most recent period, then, is primarily the result of the increase in the proportion of one-person households.

## LIVING ARRANGEMENTS, CONCEPTS AND DATA

Using census data to study household patterns involves problems of changing definitions, and these changes, in turn, raise the issue of what the meaning of a "household" is and what residential behavior underlies the living arrangements patterns the census records. Table 1 presents data on household size for the United States over the span available from the decennial censuses and the Current Population Survey (1790–1973). A wide variety of definitions of "the household" have been used over this period, although the definitions used for the dates presented are more nearly comparable than for other dates.

The important components of household definitions are *use* (indicated ordinarily by the presence of various items of cooking equipment); *privacy* (the consideration here is usually separate access); and *the number of unrelated persons who are present.* Changes involving the first two aspects of the definition have occurred primarily in the most recent censuses and have so far had relatively little effect on the number and character of households, though future effects could be much more substantial. Of greater consequence for the historical data, however, have been the changes in treatment of what might be called residential aggregations of unrelated individuals, which have varied greatly in prevalence in U.S. history. Hotels, military barracks, college dormitories, and other large institutions have always been excluded from the count of households, but boarding and lodging houses, structures which resemble (and had often been) private dwellings, have been sometimes included and sometimes excluded.

Such shifts, which have occurred between censuses, reflect the fact that the cultural definition of "household" is not very clear, once a residence does not conform to the one-nuclear-family form. The census of 1790 excluded "households of a public or semi-public character" (U.S. Bureau of the Census, 1909), but between then, when such units were relatively uncommon, and 1973, when they were again rare, the society passed through a period of heavy immigration, high population mobility, and rapid urbanization, when it became common for families to take in boarders and lodgers. Proportions of such households ranged from 15 to 20 percent in urban areas (Modell and Hareven, 1973). To have excluded such "semi-public" households would have excluded many families as well, so all the censuses of the period 1850 to 1920 except that of 1900 included them.

More recent changes reveal concerns which no longer involve "public" families (in fact, the 1970 census stopped counting families which are not in households) but revolve instead about private individuals and the minimum size and functioning of the residential units in which are found our increasingly solitary population. The criteria that make a small living space a separate household have been changed between each of the postwar censuses. (For a discussion of the 1950 to 1960 changes, see U.S.

Bureau of the Census, 1964a, p. XII; and Kobrin, 1971, pp. 18–20.) This problem will persist and become more important in later censuses as food preparation continues to be withdrawn from households, and since, as this research indicates, very small units will increase both in number and in proportion of all households. The meaningfulness of the designation "household" will become less and less clear. Table 1, showing changes up to the present, however, is based on reasonably consistent data and reveals major changes in household patterns, whose sources are discussed below.

**Table 1.**    DISTRIBUTION OF HOUSEHOLDS BY SIZE: UNITED STATES 1790–1973[a]

| | 1790[b] | 1900 | 1950 | 1973 | 1790–1900 | 1900–1950 | 1950–1973 |
|---|---|---|---|---|---|---|---|
| Household Size | | | | | | | |
| Total | 100.0 | 100.0 | 100.0 | 100.0 | — | — | — |
| 1 | 3.7 | 5.1 | 9.3 | 18.5 | + 1.4 | + 4.2 | +9.2 |
| 2 | 7.8 | 15.0 | 28.1 | 30.2 | + 7.2 | +13.1 | +2.1 |
| 3–4 | 25.5 | 34.4 | 41.1 | 33.0 | + 8.9 | + 6.7 | - 8.1 |
| 5–6 | 27.1 | 25.1 | 15.7 | 14.2 | - 2.0 | - 9.4 | - 1.5 |
| 7 or more | 35.9 | 20.4 | 5.8 | 4.1 | - 15.5 | - 14.6 | - 1.7 |
| Average Household Size | 5.8 | 4.8 | 3.5 | 3.0 | | | |

Sources: 1790–1950: Taeuber and Taeuber, 1971; 1973: U.S. Bureau of the Census, 1973a.

a All dates exclude those collections of paying, unrelated individuals living in what are variously called "group quarters" (1950 and 1973); "quasihouseholds" (1900); or "households of a public or semipublic character" (1790).
b "Free" population only (U.S. Bureau of the Census, 1909).

## DEMOGRAPHIC CHANGES AND THE FALL IN HOUSEHOLD SIZE

Demographic changes in fertility and mortality have had a major impact in the fall in household size in the past although not always in the way one might expect. The first effect of the aging of the population comes about through a decline in number of children born, which could be called aging at the base of the population pyramid. A fall in fertility contributes to the fall in average household size by reducing the proportion of very large households. Between 1790 and 1900, the percentage of households containing seven or more individuals declined from 35.9 percent to 20.4 percent (Table 1). There was as well a slight decline in households of 5–6 members with consequent increases in the smaller categories. The category of 3–4 person households showed the greatest increase, rising from 25.5 to 34.4 percent of all households. There was almost no increase in the proportion of one-person households during this period.

The declines in fertility and in mortality have additional effects on household size which begin to appear in this first period (1790–1900) but become much more striking in the next (1900–1950). Since the fall in fertility reduces the number of large families, it also serves to lower the age of the parents at the birth of their last child. (Glick and Parke, 1965, show a drop in the median age of mothers at the birth of their last child of about three years between roughly 1915 and 1955 which is attributable primarily to this effect as well as to a drop in age at marriage and closer childspacing.) Further, mortality declines operate to increase the joint survival of couples. The proportion of the population widowed, holding age constant, has dropped continuously during the past century.

Changes in these two "pure" demographic variables—fertility and mortality—then, affect the household distribution not only directly but also indirectly by their effect on the intervening variable of the marriage structure. For example, Ryder (1973, p. 18) presents calculations from stable populations to document his observation that "the so-called 'empty nest' phase of the family life cycle . . . is a unique characteristic of low equilibrium." His calculations suggest that nearly 30 percent of all married couples will be in an "empty nest" stage when low equilibrium is reached. Similarly, Glick and Parke (1965), using the U.S. data referred to above, concluded that "the effect of the increase in survivorship has been to increase greatly the proportion of couples enjoying many years of married life after the last child leaves home." Norton (1974) has reached similar conclusions. The effect of continued fertility and mortality decline on the household distribution, then, is a great increase in the proportion of two-person units. And between 1900 and 1950, while moderate-sized households continued to gain at the expense of larger ones, the biggest gains did not go to the 3–4 person category as they did previously. The two-person household increased its importance from 15 percent in 1900 to 28.1 percent of all households in 1950.

Because of demographic changes operating on the population-marriage structure, then, the proportion of "small-family households," containing 2–4 persons, increased continuously between 1790 and 1950 from one-third to more than two-thirds of all households. At each date, however, the proportion of households containing more than four persons was much larger than the proportion of one-person households. Since 1950 this trend has changed. The proportion of small-family households of 2–4 declined as, for the first time, the percentage of 3–4 person households decreased and the increase in two-person households slowed substantially. Also for the first time, there were more units containing one person than there were with five or more. The proportion of one-person households, which had held at a low level of 4–5 percent through 1900 and increased somewhat by 1950 to 9.3 percent, doubled between 1950 and 1973 to include 18.5 percent of all U.S. households. The continued fall in average household size is due not to a fall in current fertility but to a gain in very, very small units.

The question, at this point, is: can this change, too, be ascribed to changes in demographic variables in a fashion similar to the changes during the preceding period? One-person households are concentrated among the old; the continued aging of the population has greatly increased the proportion of older people; and the increased differential between male and female mortality has slowed the increase in couple survival and enlarged the imbalance of the sexes at the older ages. Are demographic changes again at work?

## THE RISE OF THE PRIMARY INDIVIDUAL

At this point in the discussion it is necessary to switch from concepts based clearly on household size, such as "one-person household," to the terms used by the Bureau of the Census since 1947. The data needed to explore the questions at issue are in this form. A "primary individual" is a household head who lives either alone (and is thus equivalent to a "one-person household") or with unrelated persons. Cross-tabulations of primary individuals by household size are presented by age and sex for very recent dates, but except for only a few other characteristics of primary individuals, one cannot distinguish those living alone from those living with others. However, this does not present a major problem since the proportion of primary individuals living alone is very high. Overall only about 10 percent of primary individuals have boarders, lodgers, servants, or partners living with them. For women aged 45 or older, all except 5 percent live alone.

Data on primary individuals by age and sex for 1950 and 1974 are presented in Table 2. From these data we can discover whether the aging of the population is having an important effect. Does the increase in primary individuals come at the oldest ages as one would predict?

For males the answer clearly is no. Substantial increases in primary individuals occurred during the period 1950–1974 but not in a pattern easily related to the changes associated with the aging of the population. The total number of male primary individuals tripled while the number of young (20–34) primary individuals increased more than eightfold. Although the shape of the age distribution of male primary individuals in 1950 showed concentrations among the old, increases favored the young. By 1974 there were more male primary individuals aged 20–34 than in either of the older age groups.

It would seem that the effect of the aging of the population was unimportant for males. The increase of males in the oldest ages was either less than the gains in survivorship their wives experienced or else obscured by increases in remarriage. (Nine percent of men aged 55–74 were widowed or divorced in 1970 as compared with 34 percent of women.) The increases in living alone for men have come at an early stage of the life cycle. They represent yet another change in behavior associated with that period in life which the historian Katz has described as "semi-autonomy"—the period between leaving one's parents' family and founding another, a stage which has associated with it tangled and fascinating patterns of apprenticeship, boarding, and lodging during various periods in the past (Katz, 1972; Anderson, 1971; and Modell and Hareven, 1973).

For the recent period the well-known drop in age at marriage since 1940 (which partially reversed itself after 1960) is actually only one aspect of a drop in the age of leaving home. Table 3 shows the proportions of males and females aged 18–24 who are living as (1) family heads, (2) family members who are not family heads (and are ordinarily "child of head"), and (3) those who are not living with family. The fall in age at marriage for males is reflected in the increase in family heads from 14.6 percent in

**Table 2.** Components of Change for Primary Individuals by Age and Sex, 1950–1974

| | Total in 1950 | Total in 1974 | Total Increase 1950–1974 (In 1,000's) | Age Distribution of Increase | Increase Resulting from ΔPOPULATION | ΔMS[a] (In 1,000's) | ΔR[b] |
|---|---|---|---|---|---|---|---|
| Total Male Primary Individuals | | | | | | | |
| 20–74 | 1,577 | 4,883 | 3,306 | 100.0 | 538 | −545 | 3,313 |
| 20–34 | 254 | 2,087 | 1,833 | 55.5 | 94 | 5 | 1,734 |
| 35–54 | 555 | 1,372 | 817 | 24.7 | 126 | −79 | 770 |
| 55–74 | 768 | 1,424 | 656 | 19.8 | 318 | −471 | 809 |
| Total Female Primary Individuals | | | | | | | |
| 20–74 | 2,520 | 7,165 | 4,644 | 100.0 | 1,383 | −78 | 3,339 |
| 20–34 | 271 | 1,461 | 1,190 | 25.6 | 96 | 133 | 961 |
| 35–54 | 812 | 1,328 | 516 | 11.1 | 236 | −75 | 355 |
| 55–74 | 1,437 | 4,376 | 2,938 | 63.3 | 1,051 | −136 | 2,023 |

Source: Analysis based on U.S. Bureau of the Census, 1953, Table 1 and 1974, Table 6.

a Changes in marital status distribution of the given age and sex.
b Change in the proportion of primary individuals within a given marital status, sex, and age.

**Table 3.** Living Arrangements of Young Adults, 1940–1970

|  | 1940 | 1950 | 1960 | 1970 |
|---|---|---|---|---|
| Males | | | | |
| 18–24 | 100.00 | 100.00 | 100.0 | 100.0 |
| Family heads | 14.6 | 22.7 | 28.3 | 27.3 |
| Other family members | 69.5[a] | 57.8 | 47.7 | 46.2 |
| Unrelated individuals | 15.9[a] | 19.5 | 24.0 | 26.5 |
| Primary individuals | 0.9 | 1.0 | 2.4 | 4.9 |
| Other unrelated individuals[b] | 15.0 | 18.4 | 21.6 | 21.6 |
| Females | | | | |
| 18–24 | 100.0 | 100.0 | 100.0 | 100.0 |
| Family heads | 33.1 | 44.7 | 50.8 | 44.6 |
| Other family members | 56.1[a] | 44.3 | 36.3 | 38.5 |
| Unrelated individuals | 10.8[a] | 11.0 | 12.9 | 16.9 |
| Primary individuals | 0.8 | 1.1 | 2.2 | 4.2 |
| Other unrelated individuals[b] | 10.0 | 9.9 | 10.7 | 12.7 |

Sources: U.S. Bureau of the Census, 1943, 1953, 1964b, 1973c.

a A conservative adjustment has been made for the different treatment of college students.

b Includes secondary individuals—those who are living in households with nonrelatives and are not the head of that household and those living in group quarters; and inmates of institutions.

1940 to 27.3 percent in 1970, but a similar increase in unrelated individuals occurred as well, from 15.9 percent to 26.5 percent. The fall from 70 to 46 percent in the proportion living as family members, then, was the result not only of young men moving out earlier into families of their own but of moving out earlier to college dorms, military barracks, and most dramatically, to bachelor quarters, as primary individuals. It is the younger, not older, men who are contributing most to the fall in household size.

On the other hand, the data in Tables 2 and 3 suggest that while young women show changes similar to those for young men, the aging of the population has been a much more important variable in the increase of female primary individuals. Of the 4.6 million increase in female primary individuals, 63 percent or nearly 3 million were aged 55–74. The proportion of female primary individuals widowed and divorced increased from 81 percent in 1950 to 84 percent in 1974, suggesting that the growth in the proportion of women in these groups which is accompanying the evolution in population structure may be contributing substantially to the increase.

To discover more directly how the change in population structure has contributed to the increase in female primary individuals, a components of change analysis was performed on data on primary individuals by age, sex, and marital status for 1950 and 1974. Using an average components method (Durand and Holden, 1969), the procedure isolates changes coming from population change (hereafter designated $\Delta P$), changes in the marital status distribution (designated $\Delta MS$), and changes in the proportion of people of a given age and marital status who become primary individuals (designated $\Delta R$, or change in the primary individual headship rate). So, in this case, the numbers of female primary individuals aged 55–74 are affected if the number of females of that age changes; or if the proportions widowed and divorced (which contribute large shares of primary individuals) shift relative to the single, "married, spouse absent," or, "married, spouse present" (which contribute fewer primary individuals); or finally, if the proportions of primary individuals in the various marital statuses change. As a result of the demographic changes discussed, we would predict a large increase from $\Delta P$ because of the growth and aging of the population; and a small decrease from $\Delta MS$ because of the continuing increase in the joint survival of married couples. We have no basis for predicting changes in $\Delta R$; nothing in the logic so far suggests any reason, for example, why the proportion of widowed women who are primary individuals should change.

The results of this analysis appear in the right-hand side of Table 2. As expected, $\Delta P$ was large and positive, and heavily concentrated in ages 55–74. Also, as a result of declines in proportions widowed (although partially offset by increases in the proportions divorced), $\Delta MS$ was negative in the older ages. However, the total contribution of these two factors explains less than one-third of the increase in female primary individuals at these older ages. The largest component by far was $\Delta R$. Two million of the total increase of nearly 3 million female primary individuals occurred because while in 1950 about 30 percent of widowed and divorced women aged 55–74 were primary individuals, in 1974, more than 60 percent were classified as primary individuals.

## CHANGES IN THE PRIMARY INDIVIDUAL HEADSHIP RATE

The behavior of this variable $\Delta R$, then, is crucial to understanding the increase in single-person households. Its behavior is very puzzling because there is substantial evidence that throughout most of U.S. history (as well as for much of the world), household headship rates by age, sex, and marital status have been remarkably stable, only varying over a narrow range. This, of course, is far different from the changes shown above. Twenty-two national projections of household growth have been done holding this proportion constant (United Nations, 1973a). Beresford and Rivlin (1966) present data that suggest little change in this variable occurred in the United States between 1840 and 1950. Furthermore, between 1940 and 1950, changes in population size and marital status proportions accounted for 97 percent of the increases in male household heads in the United States (Kobrin, 1973). So the rapid change in the primary individual headship rate occurring among unmarried people in the United States is a new phenomenon, contributing strongly to the decrease in average size of household. (A similar trend has been recorded recently in England and in Europe, particularly the Scandinavian countries; see Laslett, 1970, and United Nations, 1973a.)

In Figure 1, one can see that the fall in average size of household which followed so closely declines in fertility seems now to be responding to other variables. One frequently suggested variable is increases in income. Beresford and Rivlin (1966) suggest that increasing affluence has allowed Americans to buy privacy. Swedish data show a strong cross-sectional relationship between household headship and income for both sexes, every age group, and each marital status (United Nations, 1973b). But the increase over time is more difficult to explain in this fashion. Gains in income occurred over a much longer period without strongly affecting the headship rate. So although the increase in separate residence for older women followed the advent of the social security system, social security can be no more than a partial explanation for this increase, especially

FIGURE 1. CHANGES IN HOUSEHOLD SIZE, FERTILITY, AND SOME ASPECTS OF POPULATION STRUCTURE: 1890-1973

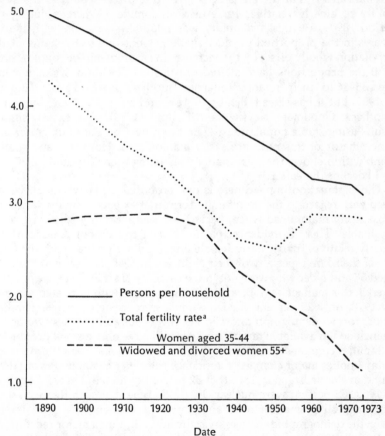

Persons per household

Total fertility rate[a]

Women aged 35-44
Widowed and divorced women 55+

Date

a. Averaged over the preceding twenty years.

Sources: Household size: 1890-1950—Taeuber and Taeuber, 1971; 1960-1973—U.S. Bureau of the Census, 1964a, 1973a, 1973b. Total fertility rate: 1890-1910—Coale and Zelnick, 1963, p. 36; 1920-1973—U.S. Public Health Service, 1970, 1975. Women 35-44 and widowed and divorced women 55+: U.S. Bureau of the Census, 1902, 1913, 1922, 1933, 1943, 1953, 1964a, 1973b, 1974.

when parallel increases for young single people were occurring at the same time.

Consider, instead, reexamining the changes in the age pyramid that have occurred not simply in terms of the changes in absolute shares of the various age groups but in terms of shifts in the *relationships* between various age groups. The period covered by Social Security, 1937–1974, is the same period which has witnessed a remarkable shift in the size of certain categories of the population relative to other categories. Figure 1, which plots persons per household against total fertility, includes as well a measure of "women aged 35–44 per woman aged 55 and over who is widowed or divorced." This measure takes older widowed and divorced women rather than all older women because older couples have rarely lived with their children's families while widowed mothers more often have. Adding single women would alter the measure very little. What this measure indicates is that there has been a rapid and recent shift in the availability of elderly relatives for American families. Whereas during the period 1890–1930 this availability was relatively constant, with the increases in the proportion of older single persons due to the aging of the population wholly offset by the increases in survivorship of couples, since 1930 the proportions have altered drastically. The ratio of "daughters" aged 35–44 to "their" no longer married "mothers" hovered around 2.8 until 1930; but it has since fallen by more than half, to 1.2 "daughters" per "mother." Goodman, Keyfitz, and Pullum (1974) have shown similar results using stable populations. (The age ranges on both numerator and denominator of this ratio are easily manipulated. However, any similar combination shows the same pattern of timing—stability until 1930 and rapid decline thereafter.)

The explanation implied here is one proposed by Levy (1965). He argued with regard to the stem family form that extended family norms are most easily maintained when, because of high mortality, they are rarely attainable. There is evidence that in the not too distant American past elderly relatives, particularly female ones, ordinarily lived with the families of their kin, especially of their children. In 1940, 58 percent of women aged 65 and older who were not in the category "married, spouse present" lived in this manner as opposed to living alone or with unrelated persons. By 1970, only 29 percent of such women were living with their families. Under former demographic conditions, it was possible for these women to be included in available families and yet still have only a small proportion of families contain such relatives. But to find a similarly small proportion today implies major changes in residence rules. For example, Pryor (1972) found in Rhode Island in 1875 that 82 percent of all families were nuclear; in 1960, 85 percent were nuclear. I would argue that such figures, rather than suggesting small or no change in family residence patterns, imply, given the demographic changes over the interval, that a major redefinition of the appropriate family group must have occurred. For while the economic necessity for larger units has decreased, it must also be true that either tolerance for nonnuclear members within the group or the necessity to be a nonnuclear member has greatly declined, or both. Otherwise, a sharp rise in nonnuclear families would have to have occurred in order to absorb the increases in eligibles caused by the shift in population structure.

Under pressure from demographic changes, then, residence norms have changed, resulting in a great increase in the proportion of older females who live alone. Evidence of similar changes in residence norms can be found, actually, in the changes in living patterns shown by young males referred to above. The other great pool of potential additional family members is composed of the grown children of the family heads. Because of sex differences in age at marriage, these individuals are predominantly males. No new income maintenance programs pertain to them, yet the shift in their residence patterns occurred at precisely the same time. The continued decline in household size, then, is a result of a general redefinition of the family toward invariable and perhaps uncompromising nuclearity. While there may never have been an extended family pattern in U.S. history, the evidence so far is that norms have changed to make it less likely, despite demographic pressures, that there ever will be such a pattern in the foreseeable future.

## IMPLICATIONS OF THE FALL IN HOUSEHOLD SIZE FOR THE STUDY OF FAMILY CHANGE

Relying heavily on household data in order to study changes in the family has been criticized sharply (Berkner, 1975). The reification of coresidence and the subsequent neglect of kinship ties that transcend the household, as well as data sources that might provide evidence about such ties—literary sources, wills, and deeds—are research tendencies evident in some recent household analyses, as Berkner points out. Yet in the great shift in household structure which has occurred, several aspects of family change are closely implicated—the fall in fertility and the development of a commonly experienced "empty-nest" stage for marriages are those most commonly cited.

It is true many kin relations exist which are not bound by common residence. Nevertheless, "living together" adds a significantly different element to a relationship; this is recognized by people of every age, although most recent research has been on college students (e.g., Lyness et al., 1972; and Macklin, 1972). Deciding whether or not to live together requires considering desires for independence and dependency, and for privacy and companionship, which are important factors in any relationship.

The data and interpretations discussed here suggest that the fall in household size has had an important effect on the family as a social unit beyond the fertility and "empty-nest" effects. The great increase in persons living separately from families, and the concentration of these people at the youngest and oldest stages of the adult life cycle, indicate two major changes: that a process of age-segregation is going on, and that there is a decreasing tolerance for family forms which include nonnuclear members. Family membership is becoming much less continuous over the life cycle, affecting the relationships between the generations (which are now much less visible to each other) and life-cycle patterns of interaction generally.

That these changes should be clearly associated with the changes in age structure accompanying the transition to low levels of fertility and mortality is the interesting and rather surprising conclusion of this analysis. As the age-sex structure of the population resembles less and less the age-sex composition of the nuclear family, and the population contains more and more adults who are dissociated from such families, the nuclear family as it is now constituted, and is now ordinarily studied, will become a less central social institution. Family membership will occur over a more restricted portion of the life cycle, and, at any given time, perhaps less than a majority of adults will be living in families. The rest, if current trends continue, will live alone.

## ACKNOWLEDGMENT

The research reported here was supported by a grant from the Ford Foundation to the Population Studies and Training Center, Brown University. I wish to thank Professor Sidney Goldstein for his generous support and encouragement for this research. This paper has also benefited from the comments of Paul Glick, Gerry Hendershot, Robert Potter, Jr., Sylvia Wargon, and Basil Zimmer.

## REFERENCES

ANDERSON, MICHAEL S. 1971. Family Structure in Nineteenth Century Lancashire. London: Cambridge University Press.

BERESFORD, J. C., AND A. M. RIVLIN. 1966. Privacy, Poverty, and Old Age. Demography 3:247–258.

BERKNER, L. 1973. Recent Research on the History of the Family in Western Europe. Journal of Marriage and the Family 35:395–405.

———. 1975. The Use and Misuse of Census Data for the Historical Analysis of Family Structure. Journal of Interdisciplinary History 5:721–738.

COALE, ANSLEY J., AND MELVIN ZELNICK. 1963. New Estimates of Fertility and Population in the United States: A Study of Annual White Births from 1855 to 1960 and of Completedness of Enumeration in the Censuses from 1880 to 1960. Princeton: Princeton University Press.

DURAND, JOHN, AND K. C. HOLDEN. 1969. Methods for Analyzing Components of Change in Size and Structure of the Labor Force with Application to Puerto Rico, 1950–1960. University of Pennsylvania, Population Studies Center, Analytical and Technical Reports, No. 8. Philadelphia.

GLICK, P. C., AND R. PARKE, JR. 1965. New Approaches in Studying the Life Cycle of the Family. Demography 2:187–202.

GOODMAN, L. A., N. KEYFITZ, AND T. W. PULLUM. 1974. Family Formation and the Frequency of Various Kinship Relationships. Theoretical Population Biology 5:1–27.

KATZ MICHAEL. 1972. Growing-up in the Nineteenth Century. Working Paper No. 31. Canadian Social History Project.

KOBRIN, FRANCES E. 1971. Components of Change in United States Household Headship: A Cohort Analysis, 1940–1960. Unpublished Ph.D. dissertation. Philadelphia: Graduate School of Arts and Sciences, University of Pennsylvania.

———. 1973. Household Headship and Its Changes in the United States, 1940–1960, 1970. Journal of the American Statistical Association 68:793–800.

LASLETT, B. 1973. The Family as a Public and Private Institution: An Historical Perspective. Journal of Marriage and the Family 35:480–492.

LASLETT, P. 1970. The Decline of the Size of the Domestic Group in England: A Comment on J. W. Nixon's Note. Population Studies 24:449–454.

LEVY, M., JR. 1965. Aspects of the Analysis of Family Structure. Pp. 1–63 in Ansley J. Coale et al., Aspects of the Analysis of Family Structure. Princeton: Princeton University Press.

LYNESS, J. L., M. E. LIPETZ, AND K. E. DAVIS. 1972. Living Together: An Alternative to Marriage. Journal of Marriage and the Family 34:305–311.

MACKLIN, E. D. 1972. Heterosexual Cohabitation Among Unmarried College Students. The Family Coordinator 21:463–472.

MODELL, J., AND T. K. HAREVEN. 1973. Urbanization and the Malleable Household: An Examination of Boarding and Lodging in American Families, Journal of Marriage and the Family 35:467–479.

NORTON, A. J. 1974. The Family Life Cycle Updated: Components and Uses. Pp. 162–169 in Robert F. Winch and Graham B. Sparrier (eds.), Selected Studies in Marriage and the Family, 4th edition. New York: Holt, Rinehart and Winston.

PRYOR, E. T., JR. 1972. Rhode Island Family Structure: 1875 and 1960. Pp. 571–589 in P. Laslett and R. Wall (eds.), Household and Family in Past Time. Cambridge, England: Cambridge University Press.

RYDER, N. B. 1974. Reproductive Behavior and the Family Life Cycle. Symposium on Population and the Family, Honolulu, August 6–15, 1973. New York: United Nations Economic and Social Council, World Population Conference.

TAEUBER, CONRAD, AND IRENE TAEUBER. 1971. People of the United States in the 20th Century. A Census Monograph. Washington, D.C.: U.S. Government Printing Office.

UNITED NATIONS. 1973a. Determinants and Consequences of Population Trends. New York: United Nations.

_____. 1973b. Manual VII: Methods of Projecting Households and Families. New York: United Nations.

U.S. BUREAU OF THE CENSUS. 1909. A Century of Population Growth, 1790–1900. Washington, D.C.: U.S. Government Printing Office.

_____. 1943. Sixteenth Census of the United States: 1940. Population. The Labor Force (Sample Statistics). Employment and Personal Characteristics. Washington, D.C.: U.S. Government Printing Office.

_____. 1953. United States Census of Population: 1950. Vol. IV: Special Reports. Marital Status. Table 1. Washington, D.C.: U.S. Government Printing Office.

_____. 1964a. United States Census of Population: 1960. Vol. II. Subject Reports. Families. Washington, D.C.: U.S. Government Printing Office.

_____. 1964b. United States Census of Population: 1960. Vol. II. Subject Reports. Persons by Family Characteristics. Washington, D.C.: U.S. Government Printing Office.

_____. 1973a. Current Population Reports. Series P-20. Population Characteristics. No. 258. Household and Family Characteristics: March, 1973. Washington, D.C.: U.S. Government Printing Office.

_____. 1973b. 1970 Census of Population: Subject Reports. Family Composition. Table 23. Washington, D.C.: U.S. Government Printing Office.

_____. 1973c. 1970 Census of Population: Subject Reports. Persons by Family Characteristics. Washington, D.C.: U.S. Government Printing Office.

_____. 1974. Current Population Reports. Series P-20. Population Characteristics. No. 271. Marital Status and Living Arrangements: March, 1974. Table 6. Washington, D.C.: U.S. Government Printing Office.

U.S. PUBLIC HEALTH SERVICE. 1970. National Center for Health Statistics, Series 21, No. 19. Natality Statistics Analysis, United States, 1965–1967. Table 2. Washington, D.C.: U.S. Government Printing Office.

_____. 1975. Summary Report: Final Natality Statistics, 1973, Monthly Vital Statistics Report 23: Table 4.

# SELECTED READINGS FOR PART ONE

BERKNER, LUTZ K. "The Stem Family and the Developmental Cycle of the Peasant Household: An 18th-Century Austrian Example." *American Historical Review,* 77 (1972), 398–418.

——. "Recent Research on the History of the Family in Western Europe." *Journal of Marriage and the Family,* 35 (1973), 395–405.

CLARK, CLIFFORD E., JR. "Domestic Architecture as an Index to Social History: The Romantic Revival and the Cult of Domesticity in America, 1840–1870." *Journal of Interdisciplinary History,* 7 (1976), 33–56.

GOUBERT, PIERRE. "Family and Province: A Contribution to the Knowledge of Family Structures in Early Modern France." *Journal of Family History,* 2 (1977), 179–195.

JEFFREY, KIRK. "The Family as Utopian Retreat from the City." *Soundings,* 55 (1972), 21–41.

LASLETT, BARBARA. "The Family as a Public and Private Institution: An Historical Perspective." *Journal of Marriage and the Family,* 35 (1973), 480–494.

——. "Social Change and the Family: Los Angeles, California, 1850–1870." *American Sociological Review,* 42 (1977), 268–291.

LASLETT, PETER. *Family Life and Illicit Love in Earlier Generations.* Cambridge: Cambridge University Press, 1977.

——. ed. *Household and Family in Past Time.* Cambridge: Cambridge University Press, 1972.

MACFARLANE, ALAN. *The Family Life of Ralph Josselin.* Cambridge: Cambridge University Press, 1970.

PARISH, WILLIAM L., JR., and MOSHE SCHWARTZ, "Household Complexity in Nineteenth-Century France." *American Sociological Review,* 37 (1972), 154–172.

PLAKANS, ANDREJS. "Seigneurial Authority and Peasant Family Life: The Baltic Area in the Eighteenth Century." *Journal of Interdisciplinary History,* 4 (1975), 629–654.

STONE, LAWRENCE. *"The Family, Sex and Marriage: In England 1500–1800."* New York: Harper & Row, 1977.

WHEATON, ROBERT. "Family and Kinship in Western Europe: The Problem of the Joint Family Household." *Journal of Interdisciplinary History,* 4 (1975), 601–628.

YOUNG, MICHAEL, and PETER WILLMOTT. *Family and Kinship in East London.* Baltimore: Penguin, 1962.

# PART TWO |

# MARRIAGE: BEGINNINGS AND ENDINGS

Since various aspects of married life are discussed in articles included throughout this volume, this section is limited to those that focus on the initiation of marriage or its civil termination; hence, the title "beginnings and endings."

Daniel Scott Smith's article "Parental Power and Marriage Patterns: An Analysis of Historical Trends in Hingham, Massachusetts" and Peter Dobkin Hall's "Marital Selection and Business in Massachusetts Merchant Families, 1800–1900" complement each other quite nicely, though their concerns are not as similar as one might initially think. Smith is concerned with the question of the exercise of parental authority; more specifically, to what extent mate choice was subject to parental control and what changes, if any, can be observed over time in the exercise of this authority. To some extent, he might be seen as investigating the notion of a movement from a "parent-run" to a "participant-run" courtship system. Smith's procedure reflects how imaginative historians can be in getting the skeletal data contained in demographic records to yield rather meaty findings. He compares the age at first marriage of men whose fathers died before they were twenty-one with those whose fathers were still living, and then he analyzes the wealth of fathers-in-law of first-born sons (who until 1789 received a double share of their father's estate) and the wealth of fathers-in-law of younger sons. Finally, he looks at birth order of daughters in the same family and the order in which they married, the assumption being that when family investment in marriage was great, parents were loathe to have younger daughters marry before their older sisters for fear of casting some doubt on the desirability of the latter. The changes over time that Smith discovers in all three of these patterns provide us with important data on the decline in parental authority and parental involvement in mate choice.

Peter Dobkin Hall studies the question of parental involvement in mate choice from the perspective of family economic enterprise and provides us with data on both American economic history and family history. His central argument is an interesting and important one: parental involvement in mate selection reflected their concern with the maintenance of the family line and the preservation of the family enterprise. In addition, Hall points out, the type of enterprise engaged in by the family posed special problems that required special solutions. For example, in the early decades of the eighteenth century Massachusetts merchants were faced with problems of

83

capital accumulation which were intensified because, rather than adhering to the English custom of primogeniture (whereby the eldest son received virtually all of his father's estate), they divided their estates among all surviving children after a double share had been given to the oldest son. This resulted in their being unable to maintain enough capital over the generations to aggrandize or even stabilize their economic position. However, wealth could remain concentrated in the family by means of advantageous marriages between first cousins, or amalgamated by means of marriages between economic equals or near equals. Hall considers how the patterning of mate selection over time relates to stages in the economic history of Massachusetts. He discovers that kin marriage did appear more common before the creation of business corporations which separated capital from family wealth. In Hall's words, "corporate capital is legally distinct from the personal property of the investors." At the same time he points out that the growth of corporate enterprise paralleled the growth of testamentary trust, which allowed the family wealth to remain intact—though governed by a trustee—while its income could be distributed in a way that satisfied the rule of equal shares. Thus marriage eventually became less useful as a device for the maintenance or the augmentation of capital.

With the expansion of trade following the American Revolution the scale of commercial endeavor and the amount of capital involved, as well as the implications of business decisions, made it imperative for economic considerations to replace familial ones in the management of business; this further contributed to the decline of marriages along kin lines. At this time fewer and fewer sons followed their fathers into mercantile careers. In short, the growth of large-scale economic enterprise seems to require a separation of familial and business concerns.

These two papers, then, offer distinct sets of data which contribute to our understanding of the dynamics of parental involvement in the marriage of their offspring. They seem to indicate that "modern" patterns of courtship, at least in terms of the relative autonomy of young people, first became prevalent during the last quarter of the eighteenth century. Such patterns were part of a more general "modernization" of domestic practices and will be commented on in Nancy F. Cott's article "Divorce and the Changing Status of Women in Eighteenth-Century Massachusetts."

Marital dissolution is a topic which regularly receives more than its share of publicity in the popular press. We read reports of how many of today's marriages will end in divorce and of the enormous increase in divorce rates. To be sure, there has been a great surge in the number of divorces since the mid-1960s, but during the previous century the number had also been rising though not at such a staggering rate. However, two factors are often overlooked by those who bemoan current levels of divorce: (1) it is only recently that the rate of marital dissolution due to both death and divorce has surpassed mid-nineteenth century levels, and (2) most people who divorce today remarry and with remarkable rapidity. The significance of the first factor is that while the causes of marital dissolution have shifted over time so that more marriages end in divorce each year; still the rate of marital dissolution has not changed very much. In the words of Kingsley Davis: "The compensatoriness of the trend may be in part motivational. As the probability of escaping a bad marriage by death approaches zero, the willingness ot consider divorce must surely rise" (Davis, 1972:255).* At the same time the growth of "no fault" divorce laws and more positive attitudes toward the divorced have also contributed their share, not to mention the improved economic position of women. The second factor (remarriage) reveals that persons who seek divorce today do not necessarily do so out of disillusionment with marriage itself but, rather, because they may not have found the fulfillment they feel it should bring and are searching for this in another relationship.

The richness of Nancy Cott's paper on divorce in eighteenth-century Massachusetts lies in its information not only on divorce but also on marriage and relations between the sexes in general. The period covered by Cott is from 1692 to 1786, and she was able to uncover 229 divorce petitions during that time. From the facts of these petitions and their outcomes we learn that the practices of colonial Massachusetts differed from those of England. There, divorce which permitted remarriage, rather than simple separation, was something which only the very wealthy could obtain, while in Massachusetts those who brought suit came from all spheres of society, though those of the middle ranks were most heavily represented. As we move toward the American Revolution we see wives having increasing success in the court, and often they are able to obtain a divorce solely on the grounds of their husbands' adultery. According to Cott, this means that a new concept of marriage emerged, one which rejected the notion of marriage as an indenture served by the wife and which replaced it with an image of marriage as a relationship in which the position of women was improved, if not economically, then at least socially.

A word of caution is in order when reading Cott's paper. One must keep in mind that for a period of almost one hundred years, only 229 petitions were filed. Given the fact that Massachusetts had the greatest concentration of population in the colonies during that period, we must recognize how rare an event divorce was. People petitioned only when extreme circumstances existed. The criteria of "compatibility" and "fulfillment" that operate today would have been alien to the residents of colonial Massachusetts.

If Nancy Cott makes us aware that even in the halcyon days of colonial America divorce existed, William L. O'Neill's paper shows us that the beginnings of divorce as a relatively common occurrence can probably be traced to the Progressive Era. Reliable divorce statistics are not available prior to the Civil War period, but between that time and the end of the century divorce rates more than trebled. They continued to rise steadily—with a brief surge after World War II—until the 1960s, when they soared at an unprecedented rate, something which they have continued to do up until very recently. While the rate of divorce in the seventeenth, eighteenth, and early nineteenth centuries was not sufficient to elicit public

* Complete citations for works referred to are in the selected readings on p. 152.

concern or political activity, by the last quarter of the nineteenth century we notice the start of antidivorce organizations which see the family and society itself being threatened by growing divorce rates.

O'Neill's quotations from the Reverend Dike and George Howard echo what continue to be major themes in American society when divorce is being discussed. On the one hand, we have those who envision all civil order being swept away when people are allowed to couple and uncouple at their will. On the other hand, we have those who believe that the growth in divorce does not reflect moral bankruptcy but rather a new conception of marriage, one which places greater emphasis on personal satisfaction. In any case, this article provides us with insights into the emergence of divorce as a controversial issue requiring public debate, if not governmental intervention, at the turn of the present century.

# 5 | PARENTAL POWER AND MARRIAGE PATTERNS: AN ANALYSIS OF HISTORICAL TRENDS IN HINGHAM, MASSACHUSETTS

DANIEL SCOTT SMITH

Perhaps the central conceptual issue in the sociology of the family is the relationship of modernization to family structure. Paradoxically the theoretical significance of this problem has not engendered an empirical preoccupation with the details of the transition from "traditional" to "modern" family structure. For sociologists, as Abrams (1972:28) puts it, "the point after all was not to know the past but to establish an idea of the past which could be used as a comparative base for the understanding of the present." While historians often implicitly use a conception of the modern family as a baseline for their researches into the past, formally at least they attempt to relate the family to the culture and other institutions of an historical period. Only rarely has either group of scholars actually measured the dimensions of change by analyzing data over a long time interval. Thus the element of change in family structure has been more usually assumed or inferred from casual comparisons of past and present than consciously measured and analyzed. A great chasm persists between the theoretical perspective on the family and modernization (see Smelser, 1966:115–117, for a concise summary) and a limited body of empirical evidence more often qualifying or denying these relationships (for example, Furstenberg, 1966; Lantz et al., 1968; and Laslett and Wall, 1972) than supporting or extending them.

The problem of the connections between modernization and family structure may be conveniently divided into three analytically distinct areas—the relevance of the family for the structuring of other institutions, the role of the family in shaping individual lives, and finally the significance to the individual of the family he is born into (family of orientation) for the one he creates by marriage (family of procreation). Since the historical trends in the first two areas have presumably seemed so obvious, systematic empirical data have not been collected and analyzed to establish the precise dimensions and timing of change. In the first instance the modern family is not as quantitatively important for the organization of other structures—economic, political, and social.[1] What influence the modern family exerts in these areas is indirect, exerted either through early socialization and personality formation or mediated by intervening institutions. Male occupational status in modern America, for example, is related to the family of orientation mainly through the provision of education, not by direct parental placement. Few families today control jobs which can be given to their children (Blau and Duncan, 1967:131–133). Having less of an instrumental role, the family is now a specialized institution providing nurture and affection for both children and adults. Perhaps the best historical study of the transformation in this second area is the impressionistic classic of Aries (1962) which delineates the social separation of the family from the community and the emergence of the psychological centrality of the child in the conjugal family. Since this interpretation now rests on changes in ideals and lacks adequate behavioral support, more historical analysis is required to determine the extent of this shift. It is possible, for example, that emotional or expressive ties between parents and children have been essentially invariant over the course of American history. These affective relationships may appear to have increased historically only because of the separation of instrumental activities from the family.

Although not necessarily more significant than the changes in the first two areas, the relationship between the family of orientation and the family of procreation has often been considered to be the central issue in the modernization of the family. Davis (1949:414–418), in fact, has argued that this distinction is the most adequate key to understanding other variations in family structure. If the family newly created by marriage is dominated by preexisting families of birth, then households are more likely to be extended in structure, marriages are more likely to be arranged and will take place at earlier ages, intrafamilial relationships will tend to be authoritarian, etc. Despite Parsons' later disclaimer that his well-known analysis (Parsons, 1943) was mainly concerned with the isolation of the family from other social structures and his acceptance of the Litwack-Seeman critique as complementary, not contradictory, he was not deterred from elaborating his earlier argument. The substance of the debate on extended kinship in modern American society continues precisely on the quantity and nature of interaction between married couples and their parents (Parsons, 1965). Historians as well have concentrated on this question, usually employing the classic extended-nuclear dichotomy to summarize their findings. Greven (1970) has argued that by withholding land, fathers in seventeenth-century Andover, Massachusetts, were able to exercise considerable power over their adult sons. Once land had become relatively scarce in the early eighteenth century, they found it more difficult or less desirable to do so. More recently an entire volume of papers has been devoted to crushing the proposition that extended *households* ever were a significant element in western society, at least since the Middle Ages (Laslett and Wall, 1972).[2]

## THE HISTORICAL PROBLEM

In a decade review of research on modern American kinship, Adams (1970) has suggested that the most recent work is moving beyond debate and description to the more significant tasks of specification, interrelation, and comparison. This change of emphasis is as important for historical as for contemporary studies, even though an adequate, empirically based, systematic description of the historical evolution of the relationship between the family of orientation and the family of procreation does not presently exist. Despite the fact that it is always easier to decry than to remedy scholarly failures, this absence should be a challenge rather than an obstacle for historians. Much of the critical evidence regarding the extent and kind of interaction between parents and adult children is, of course, unwritten. Despite their interest in the same substantive issues, historians inevitably are forced to employ different methods than sociologists. Yet there are serious problems in the interpretation of historical evidence on the family. While a body of literary comment on ideal family relationships does exist, it becomes progressively more biased toward higher social strata as one moves farther back into the past (Berkner, 1973). Furthermore, the relating of historical information about ideals to actual behavior is not easily accomplished (Goode, 1968:311–313). Since literary sources are available, relatively inexpensive to exploit, and suggestive concerning the more subtle aspects of family interaction, it would be foolish to dismiss them as biased and unreliable. It would be equally risky to base the entire history of the American family on these sources. What appears to be crucial at this point for a reliable descriptive history of the American family is the development of series of quantitative indicators for various aspects of family behavior.

On both theoretical and historical grounds the idea that a shift from the centrality of the family of orientation to the family of procreation has occurred within the time span of American history may be questioned. American history, it is often argued, lacks a "traditional" or "premodern" period. If modernization and the transformation of the family from extended to nuclear are related, one would not expect to find evidence for it within the three and one-half centuries of American history. The classic polarities of sociological theory are often used by historians to contrast America with England or as a literary device to highlight rather small shifts over time. Still, the dominant theme in American historiography is "uniqueness" and this peculiar quality of the American experience is linked to the various characteristics of modernity. Ideal types, of course, describe no particular empirical realities. Since these classic dichotomies emerged from the attempt to understand the transformation of western society in the nineteenth century, their empirical relevance surely ought to be as much in the analysis of the history of western development as in the explanation of cross-cultural differences. If the discussion of historical change in the family is to progress, the selection of terms is less important than the precise specification of the extent of change along the theoretical continuum.

Some important aspects of the nuclear, conjugal, or family-of-procreation-dominant family system, such as neolocal residence, undoubtedly have been dominant since the earliest American settlement in the seventeenth century (Goode, 1970a:xvi). Other significant historical continuities such as the priority given to nuclear as against extended kin (Demos, 1970:181) may also be present. If change is to be detected in an area of known continuity, a specific, well-defined problem and subtle and discriminating measures of change are required. The relative centrality of the family of orientation versus the family of procreation can be examined from various angles. Marriage formation, however, is probably the most crucial since it is the point of transition for the individual. Transitions involving decisions are inevitably problematic. Furthermore, marriages produce records for nearly the entire population, not just for atypical elites. Thus a substantial data base exists for historical analysis. If the American family has undergone substantial historical change, it should be reflected in the conditions of marriage formation. Were, in fact, the marriages of a significant segment of the American population ever controlled by parents at any point in our history? Parents today are, of course, not irrelevant in the courtship and marriage formation process. The earlier, "traditional," pattern of control should be direct rather than indirect, involve material rather than psychological relationships, and involve power exercised by parents in their own interest at the expense of the children.

A shift in the control of marriage formation is clearly to be expected by the sociological theory of family modernization.[3] Confident, if vague, statements exist describing the emergence of a nonparentally controlled, participant-run courtship system within the time span encompassed by American history (Reiss, 1964:57-58; Stone, 1964:181-182).[4] Yet Reiss presumably relies on literary evidence in his broad summary and Stone on the decidedly atypical experience of the English aristocracy. Furthermore, the shift specified is subtle—from a parental choice, child veto system in the seventeenth century to its converse by the late nineteenth or early twentieth century. Given the particularistic relationship between parents and children, choosing and vetoing choices may not be a constitutional system but instead an ongoing process of action and reaction.

## METHOD AND SAMPLE

The dead, of course, cannot be subjected to surveys. The extent of parental power in courtship and marriage formation cannot be directly measured. Inherently the concept has a certain diffuseness and multidimensionality. Parents, for example, could determine the actual choice of spouse, they could determine the age at marriage but not name the partner, or they could merely structure indirectly the range of acceptable spouses. The actual process of decision making and bargaining is forever lost to the historian of ordinary people. If the dead cannot be interviewed, they can be made to answer questions if various consequences of the larger issue of parental control over marriage can be explicitly formulated. This is possible through the construction of long-term series of indices which are logically associated with the operational existence of parental control. Unlike the possibilities available in direct interaction with respondents, these indices inevitably lack meaning in an absolute, substantive sense. Conclusions must rest not just on one measure but on the conformity of various indicators to some pattern. Quantitative measures, whatever their limitations, have the great advantage of providing consistent information about change over time—the great question in the sociological history of the family and the most severe limitation of literary source materials.

Since the expected transition to a participant-run courtship system allegedly occurred between the seventeenth and late nineteenth century, either comparable data sets separated by more than a century or a long continuous series seem appropriate. For sociological purposes the former would be sufficient since a test of the change is all that is required. For historical analysis the time-series approach is better suited since the timing and pace of the transition are equally interesting. If the change did occur, was it gradual or concentrated in a few decades as a result, say, of the American Revolution or the inception of rapid economic growth.

The larger study from which the ensuing data derive covers the social and demographic experience of the population of one Massachusetts town over a quarter-millennium (Smith, 1973). Economically, this period—1635 to 1880—encompasses the shift, mainly after 1800, from agriculture to commerce and industry. Demographically, it includes the transition from a fertility level which was high by west European standards to the below replacement reproduction rates of the mid-nineteenth century (Smith, 1972a; Uhlenberg, 1969). The basic methodological technique of the larger study was family reconstitution—essentially statistical genealogy (Wrigley, 1966). Records of births, deaths, intentions to marry, marriages, and wealth data from tax lists were combined into family units for analysis. Various series of comparable data extending over the two centuries were constructed to measure change in demographic, familial, and social behavior. By examining differences in the timing of changes in these indicators, the history of the evolution of the population and social stucture can be interpreted (Furet, 1971). Every decision about research design necessarily involves a price. Although long-term trends and change can be studied by this approach, the conclusions strictly must be limited to the population of the town of Hingham. Furthermore, primarily because of migration, nearly one-half of the families could not be fully reconstituted. Although wealth is inversely related to outmigration after marriage, this distortion only marginally affects most indicators. Since the wealth-bias is fairly consistent over time, trends are affected to a lesser degree than levels for any particular cohort.

## EVIDENCE

In early New England, as in the preindustrial West generally, marriage was intimately linked to economic independence (Wrigley, 1969:117–118). As a result, age at marriage and proportions never-marrying were higher in western Europe than in other cultural areas (Hajnal, 1965). Since the late marriage pattern tended to reduce fertility, European societies had less of a dependency burden from nonproductive children; the easy mobility of the young, unmarried adult population may also have facilitated the transition to modern economic growth. Arguing in theoretical terms, one historical demographer has suggested that mortality level was also an important mechanism in the determination of marriage age. Higher mortality would open up opportunities for sons who then could marry earlier than if their fathers survived longer. The growth of population was thus controlled by the countervailing forces of mortality and marriage age (Ohlin, 1961).

These central demographic characteristics of west European societies can be used to formulate a test of the extent of paternal economic power. Since newly married sons were not incorporated into the paternal economic or living unit, marriage meant a definite transfer of power intergenerationally. The transfer might be eased by custom, limited by paternal retention of formal title to the land, and moderated by continuing relations along noninstrumental lines. However, fathers inevitably had something to lose—either economic resources or unpaid labor services—by the early marriage of their sons.[5] One might expect, therefore, that sons of men who die early would be able to marry before sons of men who survive into old age. By law male orphans inherited at age twenty-one and were thus economically free to marry. On the other hand, if fathers either could not or would not exercise such control, no differential in marriage age should exist between these two groups of sons.

Over two centuries of the study 60 years was the approximate mean age of fathers at the time of marriage of their sons. For the three cohorts of sons born to marriages up to 1740, Table 1 shows a differential of 1.6, 1.6, and 2.0 years in the predicted direction between sons whose fathers died before age 60 and sons whose fathers survived that age. For sons born to marriages formed after 1740 and especially after 1780, the "paternal power" effect is greatly diminished. While one and one-half to two years may appear to be a small difference, this gap is wider than that between the marriage ages of first and younger sons or between sons of wealthy and less wealthy parents (Smith, 1973). Nor should an extreme differential be expected. Fathers had a cultural obligation to see their children married although it was not in their short-run self-interest. The most meaningful interpretation of the magnitude of the differential depends on comparison with results obtained from reconstitution studies of English population samples.

**Table 1.**    DIFFERENTIAL IN MARRIAGE AGE OF SONS BY AGE AT DEATH OF FATHERS

| Period of Fathers' Marriage Cohort | Age at marriage of sons by age at death of fathers: | | |
| | UNDER 60 | 60 AND OVER | DIFFERENCE |
| --- | --- | --- | --- |
| 1641–1700 | 26.8 ( 64) | 28.4 (142) | +1.6 |
| 1701–1720 | 24.3 ( 30) | 25.9 (130) | +1.6 |
| 1721–1740 | 24.7 ( 38) | 26.7 (104) | +2.0 |
| 1741–1760 | 26.1 ( 43) | 26.5 (145) | +0.4 |
| 1761–1780 | 25.7 ( 42) | 26.8 (143) | +1.1 |
| 1781–1800 | 26.0 ( 71) | 25.8 (150) | −0.2 |
| 1801–1820 | 25.7 ( 93) | 26.5 (190) | +0.8 |
| 1821–1840 | 26.0 ( 42) | 25.9 (126) | −0.1 |
| 1641–1780 | 25.73(217) | 26.89(664) | +1.16 |
| 1781–1840 | 25.86(206) | 26.11(466) | +0.25 |

Note: Sample size of sons whose marriage ages are known in parentheses.

Since the meaning of this differential is inferential, this index cannot by itself confirm the argument that parents significantly controlled the marriage of their sons. An additional aspect of the relative centrality of the family of orientation in a society is a concern for the preservation of the line at the expense of a coexistent desire to provide for all children in the family. Inasmuch as the number and sex composition of surviving children are not completely certain and economic circumstances are not perfectly forecast, this tension is essentially insoluble for individual families (Goode, 1970b:125–126). By favoring only one son, families could help to maintain the social continuity of the family line. Although strict primogeniture did not obtain in Massachusetts, the eldest son was granted a double share in intestacy cases before the egalitarian modification of the law in 1789. Fathers, however, were not legally required to favor the eldest son. They had a free choice between an emphasis on the lineage or giving each child an equal start in life. If common, this limited form of primogeniture should have an influence on the social origins of the spouses of first and younger sons. Having more resources eldest sons should be able, on the average, to marry daughters of wealthier men. In seventeenth-century marriage contracts the wife's parents provided half as much as the husband's for launching the couple into marriage (Morgan, 1966:82). In order to test the influence of birth order on marriage chances, Table 2 compares the quintile wealth status of fathers and fathers-in-law who were living in Hingham at the earlier date to men who were taxed by the town at the later date. While these nonmigratory requirements limit and perhaps bias the sample, the differences are quite dramatic. First sons taxed on the 1680, 1779, and 1810 property lists were roughly twice as likely as younger sons to have a father-in-law who was in a higher wealth quintile than their own father. They were similarly only half as likely as younger sons to have a father-in-law who was poorer than their own father. Birth order was thus an important determinant of the economic status of the future spouse and influential in determining the life chances of men during the colonial period.[6]

A radical change is apparent for men on the town tax lists of 1830 and 1860. Birth order in the nineteenth century exerted no significant effect on the relationship between the relative wealth of father and father-in-law.

**Table 2.** RELATIONSHIP OF WEALTH STATUS OF FATHERS AND FATHERS-IN-LAW OF FIRST AND YOUNGER SONS

| Tax list date for: | | Percentage of men whose fathers-in-law were in: | | | | | |
|---|---|---|---|---|---|---|---|
| FATHERS AND FATHERS-IN-LAW | SONS | SAME QUINTILE AS FATHER | | HIGHER QUINTILE THAN FATHER | | LOWER QUINTILE THAN FATHER | |
| | | 1ST | YOUNGER | 1ST | YOUNGER | 1ST | YOUNGER |
| | | % | % | % | % | % | % | N |
| 1647–1680 | | 25 | 29 | 58 | 29 | 17 | 43 | 26 |
| 1749–1779 | | 30 | 33 | 44 | 26 | 25 | 41 | 94 |
| 1779–1810 | | 26 | 30 | 55 | 27 | 18 | 43 | 117 |
| 1810–1830 | | 36 | 27 | 30 | 36 | 34 | 37 | 139 |
| 1830–1860 | | 34 | 35 | 34 | 30 | 32 | 34 | 138 |

Instead of a gradual dimunition in paternal power, as was apparent in the effect of father's survival on the marriage age of sons, a decisive break is apparent.[7] While the measure in Table 1 involves the operation of paternal power on the individual level, primogeniture reflected in Table 2 is more a social constraint on the "freeness" of marriage choice. Apparently it was easier for all fathers to discriminate automatically against younger sons than it was for individual fathers, after the middle of the eighteenth century, to postpone the age at marriage of their own sons. The change evident in both indicators relating to the marriage process of sons is consistent with the larger hypothesis of a shift away from the dominance of the family of orientation in the family system.

The distinction between individual and social aspects of parental control is also apparent for daughters as well as sons. Traditionally in western society women have been more subject than men to parental control, particularly in the area of sexual behavior. Although penalties for premarital fornication were assessed equally against both parties, colonial New England did not escape this patriarchal bias. As a symbolic example geographically-mixed marriages usually occurred in the hometown of the bride, suggesting that the husband had to receive his wife from her father. Postmarital residence in these cases, however, was more often in the husband's town. Although the Puritan conception of marriage as a free act allowed women veto power over the parental choice of the husband, marriages in the upper social strata were arranged through extensive negotiations by the parents (Morgan, 1966:79–86). In short, the existing evidence points to a pattern intermediate between total control of young women by their parents and substantive premarital autonomy for women. The historical question, once again, is not either-or but how much? Were women, in fact, "married off," and was there any change over time in the incidence of this practice? Direct evidence does not exist to chart a trend, but a hypothetical pattern may be suggested. If parents did decide when their daughters could and should marry, one might expect them to proceed on the basis of the eldest first and so on. Passing over a daughter to allow a younger sister to marry first might advertise some deficiency in the elder and consequently make it more difficult for the parents to find a suitable husband for her. If, on the other hand, women decided on the basis of personal considerations when (and perhaps whom) they should marry, more irregularity in the sequence of sisters' marriages should be expected.

Table 3 demonstrates a marked increase in the proportions of daughters who fail to marry in order of sibling position after the middle of the eighteenth century. Because of the age difference among sisters, most will marry in order of birth. Since women may remain single for reasons independent of parental choice, for example, the unfavorable sex ratio in eastern Massachusetts in the second half of the eighteenth century, the measure which omits these cases (left column of Table 3) is a more precise indicator of the trend. However, the increasing tendency in the eighteenth and particularly the nineteenth century for women to remain permanently single is certainly consistent with an increasing absence of strong parental involvement in the marriage process of their children. More and more women in the late eighteenth and early nineteenth century were obviously not being "married off." Suggesting the obvious point that their marriages

**Table 3.** PERCENTAGE OF DAUGHTERS NOT MARRYING IN BIRTH ORDER IN RELATIONSHIP TO THOSE AT RISK

| Periods when daughters are marriageable | Spinsters excluded | | Spinsters included | |
|---|---|---|---|---|
| | % | N | % | N |
| 1651–1670 to 1691–1710 | 8.1 | 86 | 11.2 | 89 |
| 1701–1720 to 1731–1750 | 11.6 | 138 | 18.4 | 147 |
| 1741–1760 to 1771–1790 | 18.2 | 176 | 25.1 | 191 |
| 1781–1800 to 1811–1830 | 14.9 | 214 | 24.9 | 245 |
| 1821–1840 to 1861–1880 | 18.4 | 298 | 24.7 | 320 |

Note: In a family with n known adult sisters, there are n–1 possibilities for not marrying in birth order, e.g., an only daughter cannot marry out of birth order, two daughters can marry out of order in only one way, etc. The interpretation of this measure is dependent, of course, on the assumption (true until the early nineteenth century) that the mean interval separating living sisters remains constant. With the fall in marital fertility during the nineteenth century, the gap between sisters increases. Since daughters who never marry obviously do not marry in order of birth, the left column excludes and right column includes these women.

were controlled more indirectly through the power fathers had over economic resources, a similar index of sons marrying out of birth order shows no secular trend.

Just as primogeniture relates to the intergenerational transmission of economic resources, so too does the relationship of parental wealth to the marriage age of daughters. If wealth transmission by marriage were important in the society, then parents obviously would have greater direct control over their daughters than if women were expected to provide no resources to their future husbands. If daughters brought economic resources to the marriage, then one would expect that daughters of wealthier men would naturally be sought after by other families as being the more desirable marriage partners for their sons. The higher level of demand should mean that daughters of the wealthier would marry at a younger age than daughters of the less wealthy. If, on the contrary, property transfer and marriage were not intimately connected, then the class pattern of female marriage age would conform to male class career patterns. Market conditions rather than the behavior of individual actors can be assessed by examining the differential by wealth in the female age at first marriage. For daughters born to marriages formed in Hingham between 1721 and 1780 there is a perfect inverse relationship between paternal wealth and marriage age. Once more there is evidence for a significant role of the family of orientation in structuring marriage patterns. This wealth pattern is dramatically reversed for daughters born to marriages between 1781 and 1840. The stability in the mean marriage age (bottom row of Table 4) masks the divergent class trends. Daughters of the wealthy married later in the nineteenth century, while daughters of the less wealthy married at a younger age than before.[8] The slight positive relationship between wealth

**Table 4.**   AGE AT MARRIAGE OF DAUGHTERS BY WEALTH QUINTILE OF FATHERS

| Wealth quintile class of father | Daughters born to marriages of | | | | CHANGE IN MEAN AGE |
| | 1721–1780 | | 1781–1840 | | |
| | AGE | N | AGE | N | |
|---|---|---|---|---|---|
| Richest 20 percent | 23.3 | 99 | 24.5 | 114 | +1.31 |
| Upper-middle 20 percent | 23.5 | 98 | 24.4 | 179 | +0.96 |
| Middle 20 percent | 23.6 | 110 | 22.1 | 172 | −1.47 |
| Lower-middle 20 percent | 24.5 | 92 | 23.1 | 159 | −1.37 |
| Poorest 20 percent | 24.5 | 57 | 22.9 | 135 | −1.63 |
| Fathers not present on extant tax list | 22.7 | 37 | 23.0 | 96 | +0.30 |
| Totals | 23.7 | 493 | 23.3 | 855 | −0.37 |

and male marriage age becomes much stronger during the nineteenth century as well. Nothing could be more suggestive of the severing of direct property considerations from marriage.

During the nineteenth century, then, daughters were not property exchanged between families. Nineteenth-century marriage, in contrast to the preceding two centuries, was between individuals rather than families. Parents, of course, continue to play an important role in structuring the premarital environment of their children (Sussman, 1953). Their role today is presumably more indirect and their influence is more psychological than instrumental. What may be conceded in principle may be denied in practice. The extent of parental resources and the age of the children are key determinants of the efficacy of parental power. One could argue that the historical shift has been not the disappearance of parental power but its limitation to the earlier phases of the life cycle of the child. On the symbolic-ideological level the shift, albeit incomplete, toward the recognition of the child's independence from his family of orientation is apparent in child-naming patterns.[9]

The decline of parental involvement in marriage formation is also suggested by the decrease in the proportion of marriages involving couples who were both residents of the town. One may presume that parents were more knowledgeable about, and hence more influential in, marriages to children of other families in the town. Between 59.6 percent and 71.8 percent of all marriages in decades between 1701–1710 and 1791–1800 involved two residents of Hingham; by 1850–1853, only 48.2 percent of all marriages, by 1900–1902 only 32.0 percent and finally by 1950–1954, a mere 25.8 percent were both residents of the town. Improved transportation and communication in the nineteenth and twentieth centuries, of course, modify the magnitude of this trend. Once again, the shift is in the predicted direction and it occurs at the time—the first half of the nineteenth century—consistent with changes in the other indices.

## CONCLUSIONS

At least in the area of parental control over marriage, significant, documentable historical change has occurred in American family behavior. There are difficulties, of course, in extending the findings of a local study to the entire American population. The trend in the family parameter which has been best-documented on the national level, fertility, is consistent with the more detailed evidence on the families of Hingham. From the early nineteenth century onward American marital fertility has been declining. With a level of fertility lower than the national average in 1800, New England was the leader in the American fertility transition (Grabill et al., 1958:14–16; Yasuba, 1962:50–69). What the sequence of change in the Hingham indicators suggests is an erosion and collapse of traditional family patterns in the middle and late eighteenth century *before* the sharp decline in marital fertility began. In the seventeenth and early eighteenth century there existed a stable, parental-run marriage system, in the nineteenth century a stable, participant-run system. Separating these two eras of stability was a period of change and crisis, manifested most notably in the American Revolution itself—a political upheaval not unconnected to the family (Burrows and Wallace, 1972).[10]

Articles which begin with a capsule or caricature of a theoretical perspective and then proceed to a narrow body of empirical evidence typically conclude that the theory fails to explain the data adequately. Only criticism and revisionism represent *real* scholarly contributions. Only covertly does this study follow that format. Substantively, the empirical measures presented above for the population of Hingham, Massachusetts, confirm, if more precisely define and elaborate, the conclusions and interpretations of Smelser, Goode, Reiss, and Stone. It is perhaps revisionist in the sense that the current state of the field is confused because of the great gap separating a bold and sweeping theory of change and the evidence which would support it. A systematic history of the American family can be reconstructed if sociological theory, long-run series of quantitative data, and historical imagination in devising subtle measures of change are combined. The vulgar notion of a drastic shift from "extended" to "nuclear" families had to be exposed and rejected in order to generate historical research. The equally simple-minded opposite extreme of the historical continuity of the conjugal family is just as fallacious both on historical as well as the better-known sociological grounds. American *households* may always have been overwhelmingly nuclear in structure, but household composition is a measure of family structure—not the structure of the family itself. Historians love complexity—the tension between change and continuity over time. Unravelling this complexity is the particularly challenging task for scholars working in the history of the family.

## NOTES

1. While it is undoubtedly true, for example, that more members of the Virginia House of Burgesses in 1773 had fathers who served in that body than United States Congressmen of 1973 whose fathers were also congressmen, no quantitative evidence exists to determine the magnitude of these changes. Perhaps more importantly, it is not certain how family status "worked" to get men into office in the colonial period—whether through deference to the family name or through arrangement by the class of elite families. Nor has the relative importance of wealth and family status in political recruitment been determined. Determina-

tion of the timing of the shift away from family domination of office would be of considerable historical importance. Trends in this area are not necessarily linear. Harvard students, for example, were ranked by their ability in the seventeenth century, but their family status counted in the eighteenth (Shipton, 1954). The fathers of 16 percent of the U.S. Senators of 1820 had held political office, 8 percent in 1860, 12 percent in 1900 and 19 percent in 1940 (Hoogenbloom, 1968:60). Although the numbers involved are very small to be sure, perhaps the final phase of the system in which office was a concomitant of social prestige and the emergence of politics as a specialized profession is reflected in this cycle. In the economic area nineteenth-century entrepreneurial capitalism may be closer in terms of the linkage between family and property to medieval feudalism than to twentieth-century corporate capitalism (Bell 1961:39–45).

2. The relevance of household composition data to the nuclear-extended dichotomy pertains only to three-generation households. Although servants were an important addition to preindustrial western households and lodgers to nineteenth-century urban-industrial households, these nonkin additions were *in* but not *of* the family. Other kin also resided in households, but their presence is probably chiefly due to demographic failure elsewhere—orphanhood, widowhood, and spinsterhood.

3. According to Smelser (1966:117), for example, "In many traditional settings, marriage is closely regulated by elders; the tastes and sentiments of the couple to be married are relatively unimportant. . . . With the decay of extended kinship ties and the redefinition of parental authority, youth becomes emancipated with respect to choosing a spouse."

4. The necessary imprecision of Reiss' succinct summary reflects the dearth of hard historical evidence: "The seventeenth century saw the working out of a solution. Romantic love had spread to much of the populace (but) almost exclusively among couples who were engaged. . . . The parents were still choosing mates. . . . By the eighteenth century the revolt had secured many adherents and was increasingly successful, so that by the end of the nineteenth century, in many parts of Europe and especially in America, young people were choosing their own mates and love was a key basis for marriage. The revolution had been won!" (Reiss, 1964:57–58).

5. John Winthrop, the leader of the great Puritan migration of 1630, was partially influenced to leave England by his declining economic status resulting from launching three of his sons with substantial gifts of land that cut his own holdings in half (Morgan, 1958:43).

6. This empirical conclusion contradicts the conventional interpretation of the social insignificance of primogeniture in colonial America (Bailyn, 1962:345; Keim, 1968:545–586). Earlier studies, however, have only shown that all sons generally got some property, not *how much* each one actually received. Wills lack a monetary value for the bequests making direct measurement impossible. In Virginia younger sons often received land in less-developed (and presumably land of less value) frontier areas while first sons got the home plantation. More generally historians who have analyzed inequality in colonial America have thought in terms of industrial society and have thus ignored sources of *intrafamilial* inequality. No published studies exist comparing the actual life experiences of first and younger sons in early America. In England, of course, the differential treatment accorded to first and younger sons was of considerable economic, social, and political importance (Thirsk, 1969).

7. The use of primogeniture may actually have increased in the early and mid-eighteenth century as the supply of land within settled areas declined. This trend has been documented for the town of Andover, Massachusetts (Greven, 1970:131–132), and on a broader cross-cultural basis the relationship between land scarcity and impartible inheritance has been suggested (Goldschmidt and Kunkel, 1971).

8. Although the data are unreliable because of an absence of information on the marital status of many daughters, the same shift occurred in the class incidence of permanent spinsterhood. In the eighteenth century the daughters of the wealthier strata were most likely to marry; in the 1781–1840 period, daughters of the wealthier were most likely to remain spinsters.

9. Some 94.4 percent of families formed before 1700 with three or more sons and 98.5 percent with three or more daughters named a child for the parent of the same sex. For families formed between 1841 and 1880 with the same number of boys or girls (to control for declining fertility), the respective figures are 67.8 percent and 53.2 percent. The decline in parent-child name sharing and especially the more rapid decrease in mother-daughter name sharing

reflects the symbolic fact of the ultimate separation of children, especially girls, from their family of birth. The persistence of kin-naming in the nineteenth and twentieth centuries simultaneously confirms the continuing importance of kinship in modern American society. (Rossi, 1966; Smith, 1972b).

10. Trends in premarital pregnancy—very low mid-seventeenth and mid-nineteenth century levels, high mid- and late eighteenth century rates—support this periodization of family change (Smith and Hindus, 1971).

# REFERENCES

ABRAMS, PHILIP. 1972. "The sense of the past and the origins of sociology." Past and Present 55 (May):18–32.

ADAMS, BERT N. 1970. "Isolation, function, and beyond: American kinship in the 1960's." Journal of Marriage and the Family 32 (November):575–597.

ARIES, PHILLIPE. 1962. Centuries of Childhood. A Social History of Family Life. Tr. by Robert Baldwick. New York: Knopf.

BAILYN, BERNARD. 1962. "Political experience and enlightenment ideas in eighteenth-century America." American Historical Review 67 (January): 339–351.

BELL, DANIEL. 1961. "The breakup of family capitalism: on changes of class in America." Pp. 39–45 in Daniel Bell, The End of Ideology. New York: Collier.

BERKNER, LUTZ K. 1973. "Recent research on the history of the family in Western Europe." Journal of Marriage and the Family 35 (August).

BLAU, PETER AND OTIS DUDLEY DUNCAN. 1967. The American Occupational Structure. New York: Wiley.

BURROWS, EDWIN G. AND MICHAEL WALLACE. 1972. "The American Revolution: the ideology and practice of national liberation." Perspectives in American History 6:167–306.

DAVIS, KINGSLEY. 1949. Human Society. New York: Macmillan.

DEMOS, JOHN. 1970. A Little Commonwealth: Family Life in Plymouth Colony. New York: Oxford.

FURET, FRANCOIS. 1971. "Quantitative history." Daedalus 100 (Winter):151–167.

FURSTENBERG, FRANK F., JR. 1966. "Industrialization and the American family: a look backward." American Sociological Review 31 (June):326–337.

GOLDSCHMIDT, WALTER AND EVALYN JACOBSON KUNKEL. 1971. "The structure of the peasant family." American Anthropologist 73 (October): 1058–1076.

GOODE, WILLIAM J. 1968. "The theory and measurement of family change." Pp. 295–348 in Eleanor Bernert Sheldon and Wilbert E. Moore (eds.), Indicators of Social Change. New York: Russell Sage Foundation.

———. 1970a. World Revolution and Family Patterns. New York: Free Press Paperback.

———. 1970b. "Family systems and social mobility." Pp. 120–136 in Reuben Hill and Rene Konig (eds.), Families in East and West. Paris: Mouton.

GRABILL, WILSON H., CLYDE V. KISER, AND PASCAL K. WHELPTON. 1958. The Fertility of American Women. New York: Wiley.

GREVEN, PHILIP J., JR. 1970. Four Generations: Population, Land, and Family in Colonial Andover, Massachusetts. Ithaca: Cornell.

HAJNAL, J. 1965. "European marriage patterns in perspective." Pp. 101–143 in D. V. Glass and D. E. C. Eversley (eds.), Population in History. London: Edward Arnold.

HOOGENBLOOM, ARI. 1968. "Industrialism and political leadership: a case study of the United States Senate," Pp. 49–78 in Frederic Cople Jaher (ed.), The Age of Industrialism in America. New York: Free Press.

KEIM, C. RAY. 1968. "Primogeniture and entail in colonial Virginia." William and Mary Quarterly 25 (October):545–586.

LANTZ, HERMAN R., MARGARET BRITTON, RAYMOND SCHMITT, AND ELOISE C. SNYDER. 1968. "Pre-industrial patterns in the colonial family in America: a content analysis of colonial magazines." American Sociological Review 33 (June):413–426.

LASLETT, PETER AND RICHARD WALL (eds.). 1972. Household and Family in Past Time. Cambridge: Cambridge University Press.

MORGAN, EDMUND S. 1958. The Puritan Dilemma: The Story of John Winthrop. Boston: Little, Brown.

_____. 1966. The Puritan Family: New York: Harper Torchbooks.

OHLIN, G. 1961. "Mortality, marriage, and growth in preindustrial populations." Population Studies 14 (March):190–197.

PARSONS, TALCOTT. 1943. "The kinship system of the contemporary United States." American Anthropologist 45 (January-March):22–38.

_____. 1965. "The normal American family." Pp. 31–50 in Seymour Farber, Piero Mustacchi, and Roger H. Wilson (eds.), Man and Civilization: The Family's Search for Survival. New York: McGraw-Hill.

REISS, IRA L. 1964. Premarital Sexual Standards in America. New York: Free Press Paperback.

ROSSI, ALICE S. 1965. "Naming children in middle class families." American Sociological Review 30 (August):499–513.

SHIPTON, CLIFFORD K. 1954. "Ye mystery of ye ages solved, or, how placing worked at colonial Harvard and Yale." Harvard Alumni Bulletin 57 (December 11): 258–263.

SMELSER, NEIL J. 1966. "The modernization of social relations." Pp. 110–122 in Myron Weiner (ed.), Modernization: The Dynamics of Growth. New York: Basic Books.

SMITH, DANIEL SCOTT. 1972a. "The demographic history of colonial New England." Journal of Economic History 32 (March):165–183.

_____. 1972b. "Child-naming patterns and family structure change: Hingham, Massachusetts, 1640–1880." Unpublished paper presented at the Clark University conference on the family, social structure, and social change.

_____. 1973. "Population, family and society in Hingham, Massachusetts, 1635–1880." Unpublished Ph.D. dissertation, University of California.

SMITH, DANIEL SCOTT AND MICHAEL S. HINDUS. 1971. "Premarital pregnancy in America. 1640–1966: an overview and interpretation." Unpublished paper presented at the annual meeting of the American Historical Association.

STONE, LAWRENCE. 1964. "Marriage among the English nobility." Pp. 153–183 in Rose Laub Coser (ed.), The Family: Its Structure and Functions. New York: St. Martin's Press.

SUSSMAN, M. B. 1953. "Parental participation in mate selection and its effects upon family continuity." Social Forces 32 (October):76–81.

THIRSK, JOAN. 1969. "Younger sons in the seventeenth century." History 54 (October):358–377.

UHLENBERG, PETER R. 1969. "A study of cohort life cycles: cohorts of native born Massachusetts women, 1830–1920." Population Studies 23 (November):407–420.

WRIGLEY, E. A. 1966. "Family reconstitution." Pp. 96–159 in E. A. Wrigley (ed.), An Introduction to English Historical Demography. New York: Basic Books.

_____. 1969. Population and History. New York: McGraw-Hill.

YASUBA, YASUKICHI. 1962. Birth Rates of the White Population of the United States, 1800–1860. Baltimore: Johns Hopkins.

# 6 | MARITAL SELECTION AND BUSINESS IN MASSACHUSETTS MERCHANT FAMILIES, 1700–1900

## PETER DOBKIN HALL

In order to understand the significance of marital selection in Massachusetts merchant families, it is necessary to examine the economic and social context in which marriage took place and the function it had in the relation between family life and business activity.

It is in the area of economic enterprise that the family assumed particular importance. Indeed, it was because of the family's involvement in economic enterprise that it was able to perform that multitude of tasks imposed upon it by the state. In order to understand the significance of this fact it is necessary to recall the two fundamental requirements of economic enterprise: capital and manpower. The family-business nexus supplied both to colonial mercantile enterprises.

New England society before 1780 was a society almost totally lacking in formal organizations for the performance of basic economic and social welfare activities. In the economic realm, there were no banks, no insurance companies, and no corporate enterprises. Nonetheless, business was carried on to so great an extent that the elite in Massachusetts was a *mercantile* elite. In the delivery of social services there were no hospitals, asylums, or orphanages. The church in the eighteenth century had not yet taken up a social gospel mission of performing charitable activities. Nonetheless, orphans were cared for, the sick were healed (within the capacities of eighteenth-century physick), and the poor were not left to starve. There were no organizations responsible for vocational education or the training of professionals. Although Harvard College was an important institution, it provided only an unspecialized classical education. Nonetheless, professionals and artisans were trained in their various fields and skills.

The fact that social and economic activities of a fairly high order could be carried on rested on the integration of family and economic enterprise—together with a civil polity that depended explicitly on the family and "family government" to take on responsibilities that went far beyond simple internal regulation. The family was the unit through which virtually all major social and economic activities were mediated. It provided basic welfare services: not only through caring for kin, however distantly related, but also by caring for those who did not have families. Orphans, widows, the insane, and others in need of care or supervision were lodged by the towns with families. Vocational training, whether professional or manual, took place under a system of apprenticeship. Under this system a trainee took up residence for a number of years with his instructor's family. He became, in effect, a member of that family, learning his profession or trade in exchange for a sum of money and his day-to-day labors. Finally, and most important, the family was almost indistinguishable from economic enterprises and the conduct of economic activities.

Given the absence of formal economic organizations such as banks and insurance companies, colonial merchants had great difficulty in ensuring adequate capital for investment and trading activities. The problem of capital was made more difficult because Massachusetts had, from its foundation, adopted a system of partible inheritance whereby a testator's estate was, after a double portion had been given to the eldest son, divided equally among all children, both male and female. Needless to say, this partition tended to prevent the accumulation of capital and interfered with the ability of Massachusetts merchants to conduct business transgenerationally—as they might have been able to do under a system of primogeniture.[1] Inability to accumulate capital interfered seriously with the carrying on of commercial activities—and certainly tended to inhibit the ability of merchants to build up capital either for purposes of prestige and power or for purposes of more effective trade positions in world markets.

There were two possible ways for merchants to deal with this situation. Since sons tended to be taken into family firms, it was possible to make *inter vivos* transfers of capital from parents to sons in the context of businesses. This was analogous to the practices of Massachusetts farmers during this period as described by Philip Greven in *Four Generations: Population, Land, and Family in Colonial Andover, Massachusetts*.[2] As Greven describes it, a farm would often be given by a parent to one of his sons during his lifetime in exchange for the son's labor and an agreement to care for the father in his old age. This helped prevent the fragmentation of agricultural capital into portions so small that they could no longer sustain economical agriculture—as occurred in France during the eighteenth century. The use of such *inter vivos* transfers of property by merchants to their partner-sons had a similar intent—to circumvent the total partition of family-business capital at a merchant's death and facilitate a rudimentary form of transgenerational capital accumulation.

This arrangement, however, had serious shortcomings. In the first place, it was inherently unfair to children who were not their fathers' business partners, particularly daughters and sons who became partners in firms other than their fathers'. Secondly, a merchant could not afford to transfer too much of his capital during his own lifetime. For to do so would have diminished his control not only over his children but over his business as well. And this would have violated the mandates of patriarchal family government by removing authority from the head of the family to one of its younger members.

There were other possibilities, however, both involving selective intermarriage. The first possibility was the marriage of first cousins. In order to understand the relevance of such kin-marriage to problems of capital accumulation, it is necessary to set forth a model of partible testamentary division and the potential effects of cousin marriage within it. Visualize a family with four children, each of whom married nonkin spouses and each of whom had, at their father's death, two children. In such a situation, the possible divisions of the paternal estate would be four within the generation of the testator's children and eight within the generation of his grandchildren. If two of the grandchildren—first cousins—married, the number of possible testamentary divisions would be reduced from eight to seven— since the shares of the two grandchildren would be recombined. If four grandchildren intermarried, combining first-cousin marriage with sibling exchange, the number of possible divisions of the grandparent's estate would be reduced from eight to six. To put it another way, rather than splitting the grandparental estate into eight portions—each representing 12.5 percent of the whole—a combined cousin-marriage-sibling exchange would reconcentrate four portions, representing 50 percent of the grandparental estate.

The second method of avoiding capital vitiation through kin-marriage would involve sibling exchanges with nonconsanguineous families. Unlike cousin marriage, this kind of alliance would be more directed at *consolidating* and *combining* the fortunes of two unrelated families rather than merely recombining the divided capital of a single one. Visualize two families, each with four children, each child having produced two children at the deaths of their parents. The number of possible estate divisions would be eight in the first generation and sixteen in the second. However, if a sibling exchange took place, with two children from one family marrying two children in the other, the number of possible divisions would be reduced from eight to six within the first generation—double the reduction possible through first-cousin marriage. By the second generation, a sibling exchange would reduce possible divisions from sixteen to fourteen that would be possible with simple first-cousin marriage. Clearly, with partible testamentation, sibling exchange was a more advantageous form of marital exchange than cousin marriage. Not only did it present the possibility of combining two fortunes—one from each set of parents—but it also permitted capital concentration within a much shorter span of time than would be possible through cousin marriage.

If the hypothesis that marital selection served particular purposes of capital concentration is true, one should expect to find two prominent features in the marriages of the Massachusetts merchant families under study. First, kin-marriage, whether of the cousin or the sibling exchange type, should occur with greatest frequency during the periods preceding the introduction of formal credit organizations and corporate business— that is, the periods during which the family would have been the only means of capital concentration. Secondly, one should expect to find a greater incidence of sibling exchange than of first-cousin marriage. This would be so because of the greater capital concentration possible through sibling exchange than through first-cousin marriage.

Table 1 shows the proportion of eligible males and females per birth cohort in a selected group of merchants who married and the percentage of kin-marriage that took place (combining both cousin and sibling exchange). "Eligible" is defined for both men and women as having lived past the age of twenty-one, the age of legal capacity. While this somewhat

**Table 1.** Percentage of Eligible Males and Females Who Married and Kin Marriage in the Amory, Cabot. Codman, Higginson, Jackson, Lawrence, Lee, Lowell, and Peabody Families, 1680–1859, by Birth Cohort and Sex

*Males*

| BIRTH COHORT | N | % OF COHORT MARRIED | % KIN MARRIAGE |
|---|---|---|---|
| 1680–1699 | 4 | 100.0 | 25.0 |
| 1700–1719 | 11 | 91.1 | 30.0 |
| 1720–1739 | 11 | 70.3 | 44.5 |
| 1740–1759 | 22 | 80.2 | 66.6 |
| 1760–1779 | 31 | 77.5 | 40.0 |
| 1780–1799 | 43 | 67.4 | 41.4 |
| 1800–1819 | 83 | 63.5 | 32.1 |
| 1820–1839 | 110 | 68.2 | 26.0 |
| 1840–1859 | 136 | 67.7 | 20.6 |
| N=451 | | | |

*Females*

| BIRTH COHORT | N | % OF COHORT MARRIED | % KIN MARRIAGE |
|---|---|---|---|
| 1680–1699 | 3 | 100.0 | —— |
| 1700–1719 | 13 | 92.3 | 41.7 |
| 1720–1739 | 11 | 91.1 | 20.0 |
| 1740–1759 | 13 | 53.9 | 38.4 |
| 1760–1779 | 25 | 72.0 | 33.3 |
| 1780–1799 | 40 | 67.5 | 33.3 |
| 1800–1819 | 67 | 68.7 | 41.3 |
| 1820–1839 | 81 | 77.8 | 23.8 |
| 1840–1859 | 112 | 52.7 | 21.0 |
| N=365 | | | |

Total Males + Females=816

arbitrary definition of eligibility may distort the figures to a certain extent, it is defensible on the grounds that twenty-one is, almost without exception, the minimum age at which marriage took place in these families regardless of sex and throughout the period 1680–1859.

Table 1, which shows the percentage of kin-marriage among the children of the eight merchant families, reveals three important features. First, kin-marriage occurs with considerable frequency for both males and females throughout the period under study. Second, it occurs with the greatest frequency during the periods in which the family merchant partnership was the primary form of business organization—that is, for the cohorts born before 1800. Third, there appears to be differential between male and female kin-marriage. It is most important for the males born between 1720 and 1799. It is most important for the females born between 1740 and 1819.

The first feature, involving the overall frequency of kin-marriage among the merchant families, cannot be intelligently discussed without examining the other points. For the fact that kin-marriage occurs with considerable frequency in these groups means nothing in itself. A behavior of a certain type can take place for a variety of reasons. Kin-marriage can serve different purposes at different points in time. In order to ascertain the function of kin-marriage at various times between 1680 and 1859, it is necessary to examine it in relation to other behaviors.

The most important assertion about kin-marriage to be proved is that it took place with greatest frequency during the period preceding the broad adoption of corporate enterprise and the creation of forms of testamentation which circumvented the partible division of capital. These two innovations are related. Corporate enterprise involves the separation of capital from immediate family concerns. A corporation must, since it deals in funds invested by nonfamily persons, operate with concerns that are not identical with those of merchant families. Unlike a partnership, in which the business capital is identical with the personal funds of the partners, corporate capital is legally distinct from the personal property of the investors. While investors own their shares in corporate enterprises, they cannot take money from corporate funds for personal or family purposes. Nor can a corporate enterprise be made to serve the social welfare purposes of a family business. Employment takes place according to criteria of competence, not according to criteria of consanguineal obligation. While it is true that the personal concerns of shareholders and administrators may affect employment practices to the extent of hiring personnel from their own families, consanguinity is really a subsidiary factor. For such an employee will only be kept on as long as he performs well.

Historically, the growth of importance of corporate enterprise is parallelled by the growth of testamentary trusts. This latter legal device permits a circumvention of strict partible inheritance while satisfying traditional mandates of sharing family fortunes. Essential to the idea of a trust is the division of ownership of property into two types, legal and equitable.[3] It is possible for these two types of ownership to exist simultaneously and for one person to hold the legal title and for another to hold the equitable title. In testamentation this means that a testator can leave the legal title of his estate to one person, a trustee, and the equitable title to his children. The holder of the legal title can exercise the rights of ownership over the property. He can buy and sell with it, bring suit on behalf of it, and do all the things that an individual can do with a piece of property. However, the equitable title represents a claim on the property by its possessors. It imposes on the holder of the legal title certain personal duties towards the holders of the equitable title. Usually these duties involve the distribution of the income of a piece of property among certain beneficiaries.

In terms of testamentation and capital accumulation, this trust arrangement means that it is possible for an estate to remain intact while the income resulting from it is distributed among a testator's heirs. The result is that capital remains undivided—and separated from the demands of heirs. And in the hands of the trustee it can be allocated into the economic system through investment in corporate enterprises. In terms of families, it means that marriage no longer necessarily serves a capital accumulation function.

Following the American Revolution, pressures were brought to bear on the merchant families to reconsider the close relation between family and business. Freed from the trading restrictions of British mercantilism, Massachusetts merchants were in a position to engage freely in global trade.

To do so, however, required larger amounts of capital than could easily be raised through family means alone. Moreover, global trade greatly increased commercial risk and made insurance much more imperative. Insurance operations required pools of capital sufficient to reimburse merchants for large losses—and such capital pools could not exist as long as capital was too closely tied to family interests. Finally, global trade required expansion of the geographical scope of operations to the point that employees and partners would have to travel abroad and would, as a result, be out of the sphere of control of copartners and family members. Not only did this increase the necessity for responsible commercial decisions on the part of individual businessmen, but it made businesses much more vulnerable to errors in judgment and irresponsibility by firm members. For increased responsibility, it became increasingly necessary to choose employees according to criteria of competence rather than according to the needs of family members for employment.

It was one thing to contemplate the necessity for separating family concerns from business activities and quite another thing to accomplish it. To do so required basic changes in family patterns—particularly in the occupational choices of sons. For if family were to be separated from business, it was necessary to concentrate the activities of family members in fields other than business. While it would obviously be necessary for a portion of family manpower to remain in business—in order to retain control over economic life in the society—it was no longer desirable for businesses to carry on an employment function for merchants' sons. If sons could be directed into nonbusiness pursuits, it would be possible to separate business activities from the familial obligation to care for children. Moreover, if sons could be directed out of business, they would no longer need control of family capital. The capital could remain intact in trust devices which allocated it into business activities, while the personal needs of merchant children were attended to in their roles as trust beneficiaries.

If actions of the sort described above were taken, they should be clearly visible in the occupational choices of merchants' sons. Further, they should be identifiably the product of parental decisions. Table 2 shows the occupational choices of sons in the eight merchant families by birth cohort of fathers.

Table 2 indicates a rather sudden change in occupational choices for sons of fathers born after 1740. The fact that the change is away from business into the professions suggests strongly that these choices were made by parents for their children. For professional education demands a financial commitment that exceeds the resources of sons alone and could only be made by willing fathers. In other words, it would appear that the merchants born after 1740 increasingly determined that not all their sons would enter business—as had been the case in the past, when the percentage of sons entering business ranged between 91.7 to 83.3 percent.

The trend indicated in Table 2 is supported by evidence on the involvement of members of the merchant families in the governance of Harvard College from 1780. In the course of the Revolution there was a takeover of the College's governing board by merchants—several of them from the families under study. This was followed by an alteration in the educa-

**Table 2.** Occupational Choices of Sons of Fathers Born in Birth Cohorts 1680-1839, in the Amory, Cabot, Codman, Higginson, Jackson, Lawrence, Lee, Lowell, and Peabody Families

| Birth Cohorts of Fathers | N | 1680-1699 | 1700-1719 | 1720-1739 | 1740-1759 | 1760-1779 | 1780-1799 | 1800-1819 | 1820-1839 |
|---|---|---|---|---|---|---|---|---|---|
| Business | 221 | 91.7% | 85.6% | 83.3% | 73.2% | 54.9% | 51.6% | 40.5% | 29.5% |
| Law | 55 | — | 14.4% | 8.3% | 11.5% | 9.8% | 11.9% | 12.8% | 18.2% |
| Medicine | 34 | 8.3% | — | — | 1.4% | 11.6% | 6.3% | 11.9% | 8.0% |
| Clergy | 10 | — | — | — | 3.8% | 2.0% | 1.1% | 1.8% | 4.5% |
| Arts | 12 | — | — | — | — | 2.0% | 4.3% | 1.8% | 6.8% |
| Engineering | 6 | — | — | — | — | 3.9% | — | 1.8% | 2.3% |
| Education | 10 | — | — | — | — | — | — | 1.8% | 9.1% |
| Nothing | 46 | — | — | — | 10.1% | 7.8% | 21.5% | 22.9% | 13.7% |
| Misc. | 13 | — | — | 4.2% | — | — | 1.1% | 4.6% | 6.8% |
| Unknown | 8 | — | — | 4.2% | — | 7.8% | 2.2% | — | 1.1% |
| Total % | | 100.0 | 100.0 | 100.0 | 100.0 | 100.0 | 100.0 | 100.0 | 100.0 |
| N | 436 | 12 | 7 | 24 | 52 | 51 | 93 | 109 | 88 |

tional goals of the institution—particularly in the introduction of a medical course in 1782. Complementing the increasing role of Harvard as a credentials-granting institution for the professions was the development of charitable institutions funded with endowments given by merchants and staffed by the latter's sons. These institutions made it possible for merchants to ensure the status and economic security of their nonbusiness sons and to carry on traditional mandates of kin-support. At the same time, such institutions had an economic function very similar to that of trusts. The institutions' endowments were invested and hence reallocated into the economic sector. At the same time, the income yielded by them benefited the children of the donors who served as staff.

If it is true that the merchants acted to disengage families from business in order to free capital for expanded economic activities by altering the occupational choices of their sons, they ought to have behaved in similar manner in regard to marital selection. For if the concentration of capital was to be increasingly achieved through formal organizations—through banks, trusts, insurance companies, and incorporated businesses—*inter vivos* transfers among kin-partners and selective intermarriage would be no longer necessary. Table 3 shows the association between occupational choice and kin-marriage for males born between 1680 and 1859.

Table 3 shows the association between the decline in the entrance of sons of the merchant families into business and the decline in kin-marriage by sons. From 1760 on, both show a steady decline, reflecting the apparent decisions made by merchant parents to separate family concerns from business concerns and to turn to the creation of formal organizations for capital accumulation and entrepreneurial activity.

**Table 3.** OCCUPATIONAL CHOICE AND KIN-MARRIAGE AMONG SONS IN THE AMORY, CABOT, CODMAN, HIGGINSON, JACKSON, LAWRENCE, LEE, LOWELL, AND PEABODY FAMILIES, 1680–1859, BY BIRTH COHORT OF SONS

| Birth Cohorts | % Sons in Business | % Sons Marrying Kin |
|---|---|---|
| 1680–1699 | 100.0 | 25.0 |
| 1700–1719 | 66.6 | 30.0 |
| 1720–1739 | 100.0 | 44.5 |
| 1740–1759 | 90.1 | 66.6 |
| 1760–1779 | 81.2 | 40.0 |
| 1780–1799 | 69.1 | 41.4 |
| 1800–1819 | 57.5 | 32.1 |
| 1820–1839 | 54.2 | 26.0 |
| 1840–1859 | 40.0 | 20.6 |
| N=451 | | |

The preceding discussion has skirted the fundamental question raised by Farber and others with regard to the purposes of kin-marriage. Was it, as Farber asserts, an attempt to build "a single dominating class" based on kinship and motivated by a generalized drive for power in merchant families? Or was it a much more specific and instrumental behavior, oriented to mercantile needs for capital accumulation? If Farber is correct, the pattern of selection in kin-marriage should be towards certain kinds of kin. As Farber writes in *Guardians of Virtue*,

The high sex differentiation and strong sibling solidarity in the Hebraic social structure suggest that in Salem society, which followed the Hebraic model, ties between same-sex siblings would be firmer than those for cross-sex siblings. Accordingly, we would anticipate that in the Salem of 1770–1820, first-cousin marriages would tend to occur more often with father's brother's daughter and with mother's sister's daughter than with children of cross-sex siblings. This strong sibling solidarity also suggests that a major way for exchange to occur between families would be for the two sets of siblings to intermarry with one another. In that manner, alliances could be maintained from one generation to the next with multiple family ties. Thus we would anticipate that not only would marriage between parallel cousins tend to occur, but also marriages denoting sibling exchange.[4]

And, as he continues,

In relating first-cousin marriage to the social structure, it is important to note whether a man marries his cousin on his mother's side or his father's side. The uncle or aunt who provides him with a wife apparently maintains a close tie with his parents. In a society where male kinship ties are emphasized, if the children of two sisters marry, they are in effect tying together the previously unrelated families of the sisters' husbands. Such an arrangement would denote the creation of unstable alliances, which might not persist through future generations. On the other hand, if the children of two brothers married, the marriage would merely multiply previously existing male bonds to perpetuate and strengthen an existing alliance.[5]

Restated somewhat, different kinds of kin-marriage are conducive to different kinds of social integration. If the purpose of kin-marriage is to create a consanguineally cohesive *family* group, one would expect to find a predominance of marriages of sons to their fathers' brothers' daughters. Such marriages would tie together the children of two brothers, reinforcing the bond between the two male siblings. If the purpose of kin-marriage is to create a consanguineally cohesive *group of several families*, one would expect to find a predominance of sons marrying their mothers' brothers' daughters. Such marriages would establish a system of exchange of women between several families which would be highly stable—for every woman ceded by one family in the group would be replaced by a woman from one of the other families in the group. On the other hand, if the purpose of kin-marriage is merely to promote short-term gains—such as capital concentration and partner reliability—one would expect to find first-cousin marriages of various types coexisting without any special emphasis on any type and a high incidence of sibling exchanges. The lack of systematic prescription in such kin-marriages would indicate that the goals of the families did not involve the creation of a kin-defined dominant group—but merely emphasized the more directly instrumental economic capital and manpower needs resulting from the nature of colonial testamentation and business practice.

Table 4 shows the distribution of types of kin-marriage for sons in the merchant families by year of marriage. In this tabulation, "other" denotes all kin-marriages other than sibling exchanges and those within the first degree of consanguinity.

Table 4 would seem to demonstrate that the most favored forms of kin-

**Table 4.** PERCENTAGE OF TYPES OF KIN-MARRIAGE ENGAGED IN BY SONS IN THE AMORY, CABOT, CODMAN, HIGGINSON, JACKSON, LAWRENCE, LEE, LOWELL, AND PEABODY FAMILIES, BY YEAR OF MARRIAGE, 1700-1899

| Year of Marriage | Types of Marriage | | | | | | |
|---|---|---|---|---|---|---|---|
| | FaBroDa | MoBroDa | FaSiDa | MoSiDa | Sib-Ex | Other | N |
| 1700-1719 | — | — | — | — | — | — | 0 |
| 1720-1739 | — | — | — | — | 100.0 | — | 1 |
| 1740-1759 | — | — | — | 25.0 | 25.0 | 50.0 | 4 |
| 1760-1779 | — | 18.2 | 9.1 | 9.1 | 18.2 | 45.5 | 11 |
| 1780-1799 | — | — | — | 40.0 | 20.0 | 40.0 | 5 |
| 1800-1819 | — | 10.1 | — | — | 70.0 | 20.0 | 10 |
| 1820-1839 | 7.1 | 14.2 | 21.4 | — | 14.3 | 41.9 | 14 |
| 1840-1859 | 8.3 | — | 24.9 | — | 16.7 | 50.1 | 12 |
| 1860-1879 | — | 7.1 | — | 7.1 | 14.2 | 71.6 | 14 |
| 1880-1899 | — | 8.3 | — | — | 16.7 | 75.0 | 12 |

N = 84

marriage were those that promoted short-term instrumental alliances— particularly those that provided the economic advantages of capital concentration without the creation of on-going kin-systems. For the period before 1820—which was the period before the broad adoption of corporate business and testamentary trustmaking in Massachusetts—the most consistently favored form of kin-marriage was sibling exchange. These amounted to 13 out of 31 kin-marriages, or 41.9 percent. In the same period, the next most favored form was marriage by sons to their mother's sister's daughters. This type account for 4 of 31 kin-marriages, or 12.9 percent. Of the types of marriage that would tend to promote kin-cohesion of either the family or family-group type, only 3 out of 31, or 9.7 percent.

The data in Table 4 seem to suggest that no effort was made to create the kind of kin-defined elite structures discussed by Farber in *Guardians of Virtue*—at least by the families in this study. Indeed, the only periods in which the types of kin-marriage which Farber considers most conducive to strong kinship structures (FaBroDa and MoBroDa) occur after kin-marriage has been reduced to a very small proportion of the total number of marriages entered into by the merchant families. To say that these data refute Farber would, however, be incorrect. For the two research populations were differently structured. Farber studied all kin-marriages taking place in Salem between 1770 and 1820 and broke them down by SES. In so doing, Farber made no judgments about the ultimate economic or social success of particular families engaging in kin-marriage. He merely studied the range of kin-marriages in high-SES families and concluded that they failed to make the kind of alliances which would have promoted a "single dominating class."

This study took a different approach. It was, at the outset, a study of the development of the Boston Brahmins—the elite which began to form at Boston after the Revolution and which persists to this day. It was thus necessarily a study of a select group—a study of winners, rather than a study of a general population. Fortunately, five of the eight families studied came from Salem and appear to have been included in Farber's study of that area. Thus it is possible to compare the importance of marital selection among the "winners" as against marital selection in the inclusive high-SES group of Salem studied by Farber. Such a comparison yields interesting conclusions about the formation of the Massachusetts mercantile-capitalist elite and the role of marital selection in that process.

Table 5 presents a comparison of Farber's figures on first-cousin marriages by SES in Salem between 1770 and 1820 with cousin marriage among the eight Boston "Brahmin" families during the same period—a period during which five of the eight were in Salem.

If one views the data in Table 5 as presenting the relation between marital selection and ultimate economic success, one sees some rather interesting features. The "Boston Brahmin" category consists exclusively of families who experience ultimate and lasting economic success. The "Salem High SES" category is a mixed group, composed of some families who succeeded economically and became "Boston Brahmins" (such as the Cabots, Ropeses, Higginsons, and Crowninshields) and some who did not (the Sparhawks, Kings, and Pierces). The "Salem Middle SES" category consists of persons whose ultimate economic success or failure is unknown. It is assumed, however, that none joined the Brahmin group.

**Table 5.** COMPARISON OF TYPES OF FIRST-COUSIN MARRIAGES IN GENERAL POPULATION OF SALEM, BY SES DURING THE PERIOD 1770–1820, WITH MARRIAGES IN THE AMORY, CABOT, CODMAN, HIGGINSON, JACKSON, LAWRENCE, LEE, LOWELL, AND PEABODY FAMILIES

| Wife's Relation to Husband | Boston Brahmins | Salem High SES | Salem Middle SES |
|---|---|---|---|
| FaBroDa | 0 ( 0%) | 7 ( 28%) | 9 ( 53%) |
| MoBroDa or FaSiDa | 5 ( 71%) | 8 ( 32%) | 7 ( 41%) |
| MoSiDa | 2 ( 29%) | 10 ( 40%) | 1 ( 6%) |
| Total | 7 (100%) | 25 (100%) | 17 (100%) |

This breakdown of first-cousin marriage would seem to explain why certain families were able to migrate from Salem to Boston and were able to make major alterations in their family lives and business activities during a fairly short period of time. The most successful group, the Boston Brahmins, were the least prone to FaBroDa marriages. Indeed, they did not practice them at all. This meant that when presented with the need for economic change after the Revolution, they were *most* able to make those changes since they were not tied into a closed system of kinship. The moderately successful group, the Salem High SES, engaged in FaBroDa marriages but to a far less extent, than the Salem Middle SES, the least successful group.

The reasons for the relative successfulness of these groups does not lie in the marriages themselves but in the purposes for different types of marriages. The FaBroDa marriage is, as Farber states, the most suited to marginal activities—to mutual aid and support. However, while it helps economically marginal families to survive, it limits their ability to be mobile, for all human resources tend to be reconcentrated into the narrow family group. They tend, in sum, to limit their ability to make alliances with other families by which resources might be combined and expanded—rather than being merely reconcentrated.

The kinds of marriages involving the more successful groups tend to be more conducive to *alliances* rather than to mutual support. While it is true that the Boston group more closely resembles the Salem Middle SES group than the Salem High SES group during the 1770–1820 period, this can probably be accounted for by the fact that Farber mixes his MoBroDa and FaSiDa marriages into a single category. If broken down, the Middle SES group would probably consist primarily of FaSiDa marriages—another form of closed-kin consolidation in which the husband and wife share all four grandparents (a double first-cousin marriage). In the Boston group, however, the MoBroDa-FaSiDa category of cousin marriages consists almost entirely of MoBroDa marriages, the type most conducive to groupings of several families into cohesive groups. The Salem High SES group would probably contain both types.

Finally, the type of first-cousin marriage most conducive to generalized alliances is the MoSiDa type, which links two unrelated husbands. This type is least suited to mutual support but most suited to generalized alliances and to capital combination. Not surprisingly, it occurs least among the Middle SES group. The results for the High SES and Boston Brahmin group are ambiguous. However, Table 4 shows that marriages of this type took place among the Boston group *before* the 1770–1820 period and that, in fact, MoSiDa marriages are the most common type of first-cousin marriage engaged in by the Boston group. This implies that if one expanded the temporal scope of Farber's study, one would find a simple progression in which the Boston group would have most MoSiDa marriages, the High SES the next most frequent, and the Middle SES, the least frequent.

These patterns of marital selection take on great importance when one seeks to understand the composition of the Boston elite—particularly in clarifying why some families were able to effect major alterations in their businesses and families, separating them in order to free capital for corporate investment and large-scale capital pooling. For those families who were most dependent on mutual support through kinship and who concentrated their resources through FaBroDa and FaSiDa marriages would be least able to respond to the economic challenges presented by the post-Revolutionary era. Even if they had not been poor families to begin with, they would have been limited in their ability to grow and become socially and economically mobile because the types of kin-marriage in which they engaged precluded the making of alliances and involved too great a dependence on the reconcentration of family resources. The families who were least dependent on mutual support and most dependent on alliances would be in the best position to face the new economic problems. Because they emphasized short-term and instrumental marital selection—sibling exchanges and MoSiDa first-cousin marriages—they would have a number of important advantages. First, the short-term qualities of their alliances would give them maximum flexibility in the face of challenges. Because the bond of sentiment between two unrelated husbands (MoSiDa) is weaker, it can be broken more easily and with less serious consequences than other bonds. Secondly, the concentration of the more successful groups on sibling exchange would have created a larger concentration of capital in their hands than in the hands of those who had depended primarily on first-cousin bonds. For sibling exchange emphasized capital *combination* rather than mere reconcentration. In sum, the group most likely to make the most successful transition into the post-Revolutionary world was the group whose criteria for marital selection were the least particularistic. The Middle SES group tended to emphasize and depend on particularistic bonds between same sex siblings and to exploit them for mutual support. The high SES and Boston Brahmin groups tended to emphasize more universalistic criteria in regard to mate selection. They married along lines of economic and political advantage rather than placing a value on consanguinity *per se.* As a result, when economic challenges presented themselves that required abandonment of the traditional family-business nexus, these families were in a far better position to do so than other groups.

This approach would appear to explain the patterns of marital selection shown in Table 1—involving both the overall decline in kin-marriage and its continuance at a fairly low level to the end of the nineteenth century. For even after the adoption of corporate business and testamentary trust-making, alliances continued to be important insofar as the elite structure necessarily limited the pool of potential marriage partners. In addition, there were still economic advantages to kin-marriage. Even though testamentary trusts tended to keep family capital intact, the combined incomes of two testamentary trusts were greater than one. Moreover, the adoption of the Rule Against Perpetuities by the Massachusetts courts in the 1830s meant that such concentrated capital would be ultimately distributed among residuary legatees and remaindermen.[6] And it was unquestionably advantageous for these ultimate recipients of their forebears' thrift and luck to become allied. Nonetheless, while such alliances were economically sensible, alliances with other nonrelated wealthy merchant families in Boston were equally or more sensible. So while kin-marriage was still an option which made economic sense, it was an option increasingly less taken.

In conclusion, both marital selection and occupational choice were part of a powerful and compelling social alteration in which dominance in society and in the economy is contingent on the adoption of increasingly universalistic criteria for functioning. Those who are able to adopt those criteria are the most able to survive and continue their dominance. Those who are not are left behind in the Salems, Newburyports, and other minor ports—reminding one of Hawthorne's description of Salem in the middle nineteenth century:

> The pavement round about the above-described edifice—which we may as well name at once as the Custom House of the port—has grass enough growing in its chinks to show that it has not, of late days, been worn by any multitudinous resort of business. In some months of the year, however, there often chances a forenoon when affairs move onward with a livelier tread. Such occasions might remind the elderly citizen of that period before the last war with England, when

Salem was a port by itself; not scorned, as she is now, by her own merchants and shipowners, who permit her wharves to crumble to ruin, while their ventures go to swell, needlessly and imperceptibly, the mighty flood of commerce at New York or Boston. . . . [7]

## NOTES

1. It is difficult to understand the reasons for the adoption of partible inheritance by the Massachusetts Puritans. It may well have involved their hostility to commerce and, by extension, to inherited wealth. After all, if the ability to earn wealth was an evidence of God's grace, it seems sensible that the transference of that grace along with *inherited* wealth would have been something of a travesty. For an interesting discussion of points bearing on this, *vide* Bernard Bailyn, *The New England Merchants in the Seventeenth Century* (Cambridge, 1955).

2. Austin Wakeman Scott, *The Law of Trusts*, 4 vols. (Boston, 1939), 1.0,3.

3. Bernard Farber, *Guardians of Virtue, Salem Families in 1800* (New York, 1972), 124.

4. Ibid., 125.

5. Ibid., 128.

6. *15 Pickering's Reports* 104 (1833).

7. Nathaniel Hawthorne, *The Scarlet Letter* (New York, 1955). 3–4.

# 7 | DIVORCE AND THE CHANGING STATUS OF WOMEN IN EIGHTEENTH-CENTURY MASSACHUSETTS

## NANCY F. COTT

When a neighbor asked John Backus, silversmith of Great Barrington, Massachusetts, in 1784, why he kicked and struck his wife, John replied that "it was Partly owing to his Education for his father often treated his mother in the same manner."[1] John's mother may have tolerated that abuse but his wife did not: she complained of his cruelty, desertion, and adultery, and obtained a divorce.

This epitome of two generations' marital strife, one item in early Massachusetts divorce records, suggests how valuable such records may be to the interpretation of marriage and family life in the past. Divorce proceedings not only elucidate customs and ideals of marriage; they also disclose the marital behavior of the litigants. The history of divorce practice documents sex role expectations, permits comparison between the obligations and freedoms of husbands and of wives, and provides a test of the double standard of sexual morality. Divorce records from provincial Massachusetts are especially interesting because the years they cover are those least explored in studies of marriage and family in New England. Historians have yet to explain the transition from "Puritan" to "Victorian" standards, but current research has begun to suggest that unrest and change in patterns of sexual and familial behavior were conspicuous during the eighteenth century.[2] Records of divorce in provincial Massachusetts illuminate these little-known aspects of individuals' lives.[3]

Massachusetts divorce proceedings between 1692 and 1786 can be fairly readily traced because they took place (with a few notable exceptions) before one body, a "court" composed of the governor and his Council.[4] One hundred twenty-two wives and 101 husbands filed 229 petitions in all (six wives petitioned twice).[5] So far as their occupational and residential characteristics are known, the petitioners included the whole range of types in the population. Slightly more than a quarter of them lived in

Ms. Cott is a member of the Department of History and the American Studies Program at Yale University. She wishes to acknowledge her indebtedness to David H. Flaherty and Hiller B. Zobel for helpful research suggestions, and to Douglas L. Jones for comments on an earlier draft. Shorter versions of this paper were read at the Conference on Women in the Era of the American Revolution, George Washington University, July 1975, and at Princeton University, November 1975.

Boston, the others in all varieties of towns, from the smallest to the largest, the most remote to the most advantageously located.[6] Almost 63 percent of the petitioners disclosed the occupation of the man of the family. Thirty-two percent of these cases involved families of artisans or traders; 22 percent, husbandmen or yeomen; and another 22 percent, mariners or fishermen. About 17 percent originated in families in which the husbands had the more prestigious status of gentlemen, merchants, professionals, ship captains, or militia officers; and the remaining 7 percent involved families at the lower end of the occupational scale—laborers, truckmen, and servants. Although one would need to know the petitioners' wealth to ascertain their economic standing or to judge how accurately they typified the Massachusetts population, it is likely that the great majority—perhaps three-fourths—occupied the "middling ranks."[7] Whether or not they were a representative sample, the group included all varieties of the Massachusetts population, urban and rural dwellers, rich and poor.

The petitioners had an easier time gaining divorce in provincial Massachusetts than they would have had in the mother country.[8] In England marital controversies were judged by the ecclesiastical courts, and these courts applied canon law, under which a valid marriage was regarded as indissoluble. True divorce (*divortium a vinculo matrimonii*), allowing the partners to remarry, was never granted unless a marriage was judged null to begin with, on grounds such as consanguinity, bigamy, or sexual incapacity. Such causes as adultery, desertion, or cruelty warranted only separation from bed and board (*divortium a mensa et thoro*), which sustained the legal obligations of marriage, excepting cohabitation, and did not allow either partner to remarry. At the end of the seventeenth century, in order to relieve the stringency of ecclesiastical rule for noblemen whose wives were adulterous, the House of Lords began to dissolve marriages by private act. Only a select group could take advantage of this avenue to divorce. The cost often amounted to several thousand pounds, because a petitioner was expected to have first obtained a decree of divorce *a mensa* and a civil judgment against the adulterers. The Lords passed only about ninety private acts of divorce between 1697 and 1785, all resting on adultery charges and all awarded to husbands.[9] Divorce *a vinculo* from a valid marriage was more frequent in Massachusetts during the same period. Between 1692 and 1786, 110 divorces were granted in the province on grounds other than those considered legitimate by the English ecclesiastical courts—63 to men, 47 to women— and England and Wales had a population of almost seven million in 1765, when the Massachusetts population was under 250,000.[10]

The authority of the governor and Council over divorce originated in provincial statute. No causes for divorce were codified, however, and their divorce policy combined elements of English practice, Puritan divorce theory, seventeenth-century Massachusetts precedents, and innovation. Opposing canon law, Puritan divorce theory held that marriage was a civil contract which could and should be dissolved for such breaches as adultery, long absence, or irremediable cruelty.[11] In the seventeenth century the civil courts of Massachusetts tried to effect this theoretical position, so far as is shown by the results of forty known petitions between 1639 and 1692. The county courts and the General Court, as well as the Court of Assistants (predecessor to the Council) judged petitions for divorce, even after the Code of 1660 gave jurisdiction to the assistants. They annulled marriages on grounds of consanguinity, bigamy, and sexual incapacity, and dissolved them for long absence and for adultery alone or in combination with desertion, neglect, or cruelty. No clear decrees of separate bed and board have been discovered, but our knowledge of seventeenth-century divorce proceedings is probably incomplete.[12]

When the governor and Council assumed more uniform jurisdiction over divorce after 1692, they granted annulments, divorces (literally, dissolutions of marriage bonds) allowing the innocent party to remarry, and decrees of separate bed and board.[13] The years 1754 to 1757 formed a curious exception. During that period, for reasons not apparent in the historical record, the governor and Council declined to dissolve valid marriages and decreed separate bed and board for petitioners who formerly and subsequently would have been granted divorce.[14] In 1755, 1756 and 1757, six petitioners whose spouses were adulterous sought relief from the General Court and obtained legislative divorces instead of divorce decrees. These legislative divorces were the only ones enacted under the provincial charter of 1691.[15] In passing them the General Court assumed the role of Parliament in England; and in two of the six, the governor and Council filled the role of the English ecclesiastical courts by granting prior decrees of separate bed and board. Since they were legislative acts, these divorces were subject to review by the imperial Board of Trade, as was all colonial legislation. Reporting on the first three in 1758, the board called them "extraordinary" and "liable to great objections." The specific points of disapproval highlighted some of the differences between English and Massachusetts divorce policy. All three suits—two of them brought by women—rested on adultery charges. The divorces granted to the two women were called unprecedented, "the first of their kind . . . in the colonies or elsewhere." Moreover, the proofs of adultery were not clear enough; criminal conviction of the adulterers had not preceded the three divorce bills; and only one was supported by a prior decree of separate bed and board. Beyond these objections, which seemed sufficient grounds for disallowance, doubt existed whether any colonial legislature had the right to assume the parliamentary prerogative of granting divorces. The board referred the matter to the attorney-general and the solicitor-general for a decision whether to disallow the acts or declare them null; but no hearing took place, and these divorce bills and the subsequent three in Massachusetts were apparently allowed to stand.[16]

The interlude of legislative divorce in Massachusetts clarified the advantage the province gained through its usual practice of divorce by decree. If Massachusetts had taken the legislative route, the history of divorce there would probably have been quite different. Legislative divorces might well have been disallowed for lack of conformity to English practice or declared null for invading the authority of Parliament. In fact, between 1769 and 1773 several colonial acts of legislative divorce, passed in Pennsylvania, New Jersey, and New Hampshire, met this fate. The crown's resentment of them resulted in a directive of 1773 to all royal governors to withhold consent from any divorce act passed by a colonial legislature.[17] This order halted divorce in the colonies other than Massachusetts until the Revolution, but in that province both petitions for and grants of divorce continued to multiply. Petitioners no longer resorted to the General Court, for in 1760, after investigating their own precedents for dissolving marriages before 1755, the governor and Council returned to the policy of decreeing divorces *a vinculo*.[18]

Divorce petitions and decrees showed a general pattern of increase during the eighteenth century in Massachusetts. As Table 1 indicates, more than half of the petitions and decrees between 1692 and 1786 occurred after 1764 and more than a third of them after 1774. This striking concentration took place without any change in the laws regarding divorce. What caused it? The population grew but not nearly as rapidly as did the number of petitions. The incidence of petitions per decade increased by 77 percent from 1755–1764 to 1765–1774 and by 61 percent from 1765–1774 to 1775–1784, while the white population grew by approximately 5.7 percent from 1760 to 1770 and by approximately 14 percent from 1770 to 1780.[19]

**Table 1**  NUMBER OF PETITIONS/NUMBER OF FAVORABLE DECREES, BY DECADE

| Petitioners | 1692–1704 | 1705–1714 | 1715–1724 | 1725–1734 | 1735–1744 | 1745–1754 | 1755–1764 | 1765–1774 | 1775–1786 | Total |
|---|---|---|---|---|---|---|---|---|---|---|
| all | 7/5 | 6/5 | 5/2 | 9/4 | 23/15 | 21/11 | 26/16 | 46/24 | 86/61 | 229/143 |
| female | 4/3 | 3/2 | 4/1 | 4/1 | 8/4 | 12/6 | 12/7 | 29/13 | 53/37 | 128/74 |
| male | 3/2 | 3/3 | 1/1 | 5/3 | 15/11 | 9/5 | 14/9 | 18/11 | 33/24 | 101/69 |

Note: Favorable decrees include divorce, annulment, and separate bed and board.

Perhaps the governor and Council became more willing to consider and grant divorces after 1765, thus encouraging larger numbers of petitioners. In these pre-Revolutionary years the Council may have been more assertive in its divorce practice, which opposed England's, just as it became more independent of the royal prerogative in political matters and more sympathetic to the whig leaders in the legislature.[20] Two decrees of the early 1770s in particular indicated that the Council would proceed on its own initiative in divorce actions whether or not the governor agreed. The Council alone declared Abigail Bradstreet separated from her husband in 1771, and James Richardson divorced from his wife in 1772, although Gov. Thomas Hutchinson did not judge these decrees warranted by the evidence and would not sign them.[21]

The chronological coincidence of the concentration of divorce petitions with the War for Independence suggests a causal link. We might suppose that wartime disruption of families led to an increase of petitions, but there is little direct evidence of this. Very few petitions originated from war-related grievances, such as a married man's adultery with a camp-follower or a woman's pregnancy while her husband was absent in military service.[22] Gauged by the evidence of prenuptial pregnancy, premarital sexual relations increased dramatically during the mid- to late eighteenth century—suggesting the possibility of a similar rise in adultery—but that phenomenon antedated the war.[23]

Most likely, divorce petitions increased not because spouses more often had legitimate marital grievances but because they were more often motivated to respond to marital wrongs by seeking divorce. Perhaps, then, the rise in divorce related in a general way to the War for Independence in the sense that a certain personal outlook—one that implied self-assertion and regard for the future, one that we might label more "modern" than "traditional"—may have led a person to seek divorce and also to support American independence.[24] The evidence that aggrieved spouses desired to have their marriages ended officially, rather than taking more traditional measures such as "self-divorce" through desertion, or resigning themselves to the ties of unsatisfactory marriages, suggests a modernization of attitudes.[25] Communication about the granting of divorces may also have had a cumulative effect: the more divorces were allowed, the more likely it became for a discontented spouse to consider the possibility. Especially in small towns, news of divorces being obtained must have encouraged more men and women to petition. The growth in petitions seems to indicate that more individuals were asserting control over the direction of their lives and were refusing to be ruled by unhappy fates—characteristics which are also considered "modern." In the Revolutionary period this kind of self-assertion may have gone along with an enhanced sense of citizenship and legal rights. Not only men claimed the rights of citizens. At least one Boston woman in 1784 and another in 1785 petitioned "as a citizen of this Commonwealth" for a hearing of her case.[26]

More wives than husbands sued for divorce during the period 1692–1786, and the concentration of women's petitions during the Revolutionary years was more marked than that of men's. One can only speculate whether these figures mean that women generally had more marital grievances or that their grievances were growing faster or being more readily voiced. Several variables hindered or encouraged men and women to seek divorce. A man might hesitate because he was shy of the authorities, hated to arouse adverse publicity about his marriage, or could not afford the expense, whatever it was; or because the worth of his wife's domestic service seemed to outweigh her transgressions. Male domination of colonial public life suggests, however, that men were less shy of the authorities than were women, better able to stand adverse publicity about their marriages without risking their entire reputation, significantly more independent economically, and better equipped than women to pay legal expenses. A man could also take the initiative in acquiring a second spouse.

All the feelings that might have kept men from suing for divorce probably affected women even more intensely. Consider the doubts and anguish of Abigail Bailey as she pondered whether to seek divorce from her husband, who had committed incest with their daughter and had also had sexual liaisons with several other women. "Whether it would be consisted [sic] with faithfulness to suffer him to flee, and not be made a monument of civil justice, was my query. The latter looked to me inexpressibly painful. And I persuaded myself, that if he would do what was right, relative to our property, and would go to some distant place, where we should be afflicted with him no more, it might be sufficient; and I might be spared the dreadful scene of prosecuting my husband."[27]

Women apparently expected less success with their petitions than did men. While men always asked for divorce (dissolution of the bonds of marriage), women frequently equivocated; they requested divorce or, if that were not possible, whatever separation the governor and Council were willing to grant.[28] Perhaps other wives who had cause did not even petition because they did not expect to win. According to the most recent study, illiteracy handicapped half or more of the female population in initiating civil actions, compared to 10 or 20 percent of the male population. The female petitioners were distinguished by their literacy: almost three-quarters of them (two-thirds of the non-Boston residents) could sign their names.[29] The high rate of literacy among female petitioners suggests that they may have been a group self-selected by stronger-than-average initiative or education, who did not fully represent the frequency of wives' dissatisfaction in marriage.

Whatever the inhibitions, powerful reasons urged unhappy wives to sue for divorce—reasons that did not so affect husbands. Self-preservation compelled wives whose husbands were physically abusive. A woman whose husband deserted or failed to provide for her gained little advantage from marriage, and the marriage contract hindered her from supporting herself because her property and earnings legally belonged to her husband. Many women pointed this out. In her petition of 1759, for example, Henrietta East Caine of Boston lamented that while her marriage contract lasted, "her Friends will not supply her with Goods to carry on her business as before." Another Boston woman warned that she and her three children would become public charges if she remained subject to her husband, whereas if divorced "she apprehends she shall be able to find Friends that will place her in some business to maintain herself and children." Sarah Backus claimed in 1783 that she "would be content by the most penurious industry to gain a support for herself and Child, but every Idea of comfort is banished from her Breast when she reflects, that by Law her Person is subjected to be controuled by a man possessing no one tender sentiment, but on the contrary under the entire dominion of every criminal and foul pollution."[30]

Sixty-eight percent of the husbands and 58 percent of the wives succeeded in gaining favorable action on their petitions, but 67 percent of the husbands gained freedom to remarry, in contrast to only 45 percent of the wives. Sixteen of the seventeen separations from bed and board granted during the period went to wives. When petitioners failed to obtain favorable action, it was more often because their suits remained unresolved than because they were dismissed. Fewer than 15 percent of the women's and 11 percent of the men's petitions were actually dismissed, but more than 27 percent of the women's and 20 percent of the men's never resulted in decrees. (See Table 2.) It is unclear if the lack of resolution of these cases reflected some aim of the court or the petitioner, or whether the records are faulty or missing. No significant pattern of economic or geographic discrimination, or unusual lack of clarity in the cases, appears to account for the fate of these petitions; but the percentages reveal that women's petitions were slightly more likely than men's to suffer this end.[31]

Analysis of the suits by cause clarifies the comparison of men's and

**Table 2**  PETITION RESULTS

|  | Male Petitions | Female Petitions | All |
|---|---|---|---|
| Divorce | 64 | 51 | 115 |
| Annulment | 4 | 7 | 11 |
| Separate bed and board | 1 | 16 | 17 |
| Dismissed or not granted | 11 | 19 | 30 |
| Unresolved | 21 | 35 | 56 |
| Total | 101 | 128 | 229 |

women's experiences and of the results of their petitions. All suits involved invalidity or breach of the marriage contract. The causes (and the numbers of petitions) can be categorized as follows:[32]

A. sexual incapacity (3 m, 4 f)
B. bigamous or fraudulent marriage (3 m, 12 f)
C. adultery (50 m, 6 f)*
D. adultery and desertion or nonsupport (16 m, 12 f)*
E. adultery, desertion, and cohabitation with another (10 m, 16 f)*
F. desertion and remarriage (i.e., adultery) (3 m, 19 f)*
G. adultery and cruelty (2 m, 19 f)*
H. interracial adultery (4 m, 3 f)*
I. desertion (8 m, 10 f)
J. cruelty (0 m, 23 f)
K. unknown (2 m, 4 f)[33]

The first two causes, sexual incapacity and invalid marriage, warranted annulment, but the governor and Council were not always consistent in wording when they granted petitions on these grounds. Two of the three men's petitions charging their wives with incapacity for coitus were granted after court-appointed "discreet Matrons" confirmed the charges, one by annulment (1739) and the other by dissolution of marriage bonds (1781). This is unremarkable, except that the one husband waited five years after marrying, and the other, eight, before petitioning for divorce.[34] Men fared better than women in this category of suits. None of the three women's petitions to the governor and Council was granted: one was dismissed and the others were left unresolved, although in one of these cases the husband acknowledged his debility. In a unique instance, however, the General Court in 1780 enacted a legislative annulment of a marriage upon proof of the wife's complaint that her husband was impotent.[35]

Twelve female and three male petitioners pursued divorce for the second cause that warranted annulment—bigamous or fraudulent marriage. Two men, in 1762 and 1770, proved their wives to be bigamists, and their marriages were declared null. Another argued that his recent marriage was invalid because he had been tricked into it, while drunk, by kinfolk of a young woman who was pregnant with his child. The governor and Council believed him and ruled the marriage null.[36] Women also had considerable success in ending bigamous marriages. Nine of the twelve wives' peti-

*adultery - inclusive

tions were granted, six by annulment and three by dissolution, while three others remained unresolved.[37] Women's petitions against bigamous husbands revealed some of the vagaries of marriage in eighteenth-century Massachusetts. In only two instances had the husband's prior marriage taken place long before and in another country.[38] In five, the husband's prior marriage occurred in another New England town between two and eight years earlier (and in one other case, fifteen years earlier).[39] Six of the bigamous husbands had also deserted, either to return to their first wives or to marry third wives.[40] These cases, especially when considered together with cases involving desertion, suggest the ease and perhaps the appeal of running away from one partner and finding another—the traditional "self-divorce." Husbands more frequently made such escapes and new starts than did wives. Twelve wives but only three husbands charged bigamy (category B); sixteen wives but only ten husbands complained of their spouses' desertion and adulterous cohabitation with another (E); nineteen wives but only three husbands charged their partners with desertion and remarriage (F); ten wives but eight husbands petitioned on grounds of desertion alone (I). Men moved more easily from place to place, it seems; certainly, according to custom, they, and not women, took the initiative in deciding to marry or remarry.

The bulk of the petitions—84 percent of the husbands', 59 percent of the wives'—included the grievance of adultery. Men had more success than women in adultery-inclusive causes, but both sexes fared better in these causes than in others. (See Table 3.) The comparison between men's and women's experiences in suing on grounds of adultery is especially interesting because it can inform us of the presence of a double standard of sexual morality. Were men's and women's infidelities considered equally cause for divorce? The cultural heritage of Massachusetts contained equivocal answers to this question. Despite the seventh commandment, English tradition enshrined the double standard, forgiving a husband's sexual transgressions but calling a wife's abhorrent. As mentioned earlier, all the parliamentary divorces for adultery in the eighteenth century were awarded to husbands, none to wives. Decorum among the aristocracy required wives to ignore their husbands' extramarital affairs.[41] In Massachusetts, however, Puritan religious values strongly infused the English tradition. Puritan ideology, partially to repudiate aristocratic manners, demanded fidelity of both partners. From the sixteenth century through the eighteenth, Puritan reformers attacked the double standard by advocating chastity before marriage, and fidelity after, for men as well as women.[42]

It is striking that in Massachusetts half of all the men's petitions named

**Table 3** PROPORTION OF PETITIONS RECEIVING FAVORABLE DECREES, 1692–1786

|  | All Causes | Adultery-Inclusive Only | Adultery-Exclusive Only |
| --- | --- | --- | --- |
| male petitioners | 63% | 72% | 50% |
| female petitioners | 58% | 65% | 47% |

Note: Favorable decrees include divorce, annulment, separate bed and board.

adultery as the sole major grievance (C), and that these petitions had a high rate of success: 70 percent resulted in divorce, only 4 percent were dismissed, and the remaining quarter did not result in decrees.[43] To obtain divorce a petitioner had to produce two eyewitnesses to the act of adultery or a confession from the accused spouse, or show record of criminal conviction of the adulterers, or of the failure of the accused to answer the court summons. Alternatively, a male petitioner might show that his wife had become pregnant in his absence. In England prior court conviction of the adulterers was prerequisite to a bill of divorce; but in Massachusetts civil court action only seldom, and randomly, preceded or accompanied divorce suits.[44] Usually the governor and Council themselves determined the justice of the adultery charge. Since a wife's adultery was virtually sure cause for divorce, it was not unknown for a restless husband to "frame" his wife be setting up her seduction or by bribing deponents to testify that they had seen adultery committed. In several cases such plots by the husband were manifest or inferable.[45] The two husbands whose petitions were dismissed brought witnesses who incriminated the accused wives, but the court suspected bribery and believed the wives' contrary testimony.[46]

Clearly, the governor and Council would grant divorce to a man whose spouse committed adultery. Would they grant it to a woman for the same cause? There was no English precedent for such action. Only one suit from seventeenth-century Massachusetts has been found in which a wife sought and received a divorce for the sole cause of adultery—and this decree was subsequently reversed on the husband's appeal.[47] Women in eighteenth-century Massachusetts could be said to have taken a cue from these negative precedents. In contrast to the weight of men's petitions, not a single wife petitioned for the sole grievance of adultery until 1774, and only six did so between 1774 and 1786. Unless we assume that husbands displayed much more virtue than wives, the difference between the numbers of petitions from men and from women in this category (C) suggests a deeply entrenched double standard of marital fidelity. Whether individual women thought that men's adultery warranted divorce remains uncertain; but we can logically conclude that before 1774 women did not expect to obtain divorce for that reason alone and so did not petition.

We can gain an approximation of the governor and Council's response to petitions grounded on husbands' adultery alone, before 1774, by looking at decrees in the other adultery-inclusive categories (D through H). Husbands' suits in these categories, dependent on their substantiation of the adultery charges, had great success. More than four-fifths of their petitions charging adultery and desertion (D), or adultery, desertion, and cohabitation (E), resulted in divorce. Few husbands petitioned on the other adultery-inclusive grounds, and only the ones who proved adultery won their suits. By contrast, the pre-Revolutionary governor and Council gave a woman very little reason to expect divorce for her spouse's infidelity. Seven out of twelve female petitoners before 1774 obtained divorces by proving their partner's desertion, adultery, and remarriage (F), but these decrees took bigamy, as well as adultery, into account.[48] Fourteen women petitioned the governor and Council on other adultery-inclusive grounds prior to 1773. Eight of these received no decrees; one suit with apparent proof of the adultery was dismissed; and three—two of which charged adultery and cruelty—gained decrees of separate bed and board, the same decree which women's petitions charging cruelty alone could obtain.[49] Only two of the fourteen wives won divorces, and their cases were not conclusive on the question of adultery. Sarah Mitchell of Deerfield, who brought suit in 1718 on grounds of her husband's "fornication" with a black woman, obtained a divorce and the return of her marriage portion as well. The uniqueness of the decree suggests that not the adultery, but its interracial nature, was the crucial factor.[50] Hannah Rolfe of Lancaster made the other successful petition, in 1752. Her grievances included desertion, adultery, and cohabitation; her husband Ezra had been jailed for fornicating with a minor and for failing to provide for his bastard child, and he absconded to avoid answering Hannah's petition.[51]

Seventeen hundred and seventy-three was a turning point. In that year, two women who petitioned on the grounds of adultery and cruelty were granted not separate bed and board, but divorce, for the specified cause of adultery. The original notation on Sarah Gould's petition recorded a unanimous decision for separate bed and board, but the formal decree of March 2, 1773, declared her marriage dissolved. Martha Air's petition a few months later resulted in an unequivocal dissolution of marriage bonds on account of Adam Air's adultery.[52] After that, women began to petition for divorce on the sole ground of adultery. The governor and Council (or the Council alone, between 1776 and 1780) granted five out of the six such petitions during the next twelve years. The increasing number of wives who brought other adultery-inclusive charges also obtained divorces, and almost all of these decrees went on to the record as owing specifically to the adultery charge.[53] (See Table 4.)

These decrees were not quite as unprecedented as they may seem at first glance. In the 1750s, during the interval when the governor and Council declined to dissolve marriages, three women obtained bills of divorce from the General Court on adultery-inclusive grounds. The first was Mary Clapham, wife of a gentleman. After obtaining a decree of separate bed and board from the governor and Council because of her husband's desertion and adulterous cohabitation with a woman in Nova Scotia, she petitioned the General Court, "in whom she apprehend[ed] the Power to be vested," to dissolve her marriage and assign her alimony. The court obliged her first request, citing as William Clapham's "Violation of his Marriage Contract" his "leaving the said Mary, cohabiting and committing adultery with Another Woman."[54] The two other women who appealed successfully to the General Court both charged their husbands with adultery and desertion. Mary Parker, also a gentleman's wife, obtained her divorce because, the bill said, "Phineas Parker has for sundry Years pass'd left the said Mary, and stands convict[ed] of committing Adultery with another woman." The act granted at the plea of Lydia Kellogg, wife of a laborer of Sunderland, declared only that "it appears to this court that the said Ephraim [Kellogg] has been guilty of the crime of adultery."[55]

The General Court seems to have been more liberal in granting divorces to women before 1773 than were the governor and Council. In enacting bills of divorce for three wives during the 1750s the court presaged actions

**Table 4** ADULTERY-INCLUSIVE CHARGES:
NUMBER OF PETITIONS/NUMBER OF FAVORABLE DECREES

| | 1692–1704 | 1705–1714 | 1715–1724 | 1725–1734 | 1735–1744 | 1745–1754 | 1755–1764 | 1765–1774 | 1775–1786 | Total |
|---|---|---|---|---|---|---|---|---|---|---|
| **C** | | | | | | | | | | |
| men | 2/1 | 1/1 | | 2/1 | 6/6 | 4/2 | 9/5* | 12/8 | 14/11 | 50/35* |
| women | | | | | | | | 1/1 | 5/4 | 6/5 |
| **D** | | | | | | | | | | |
| men | | | | | 2/2 | 1/1 | 1/1 | 4/2 | 8/6 | 16/12 |
| women | | | | | | 2/0 | 2/2* | 2/0 | 6/5 | 12/7 * |
| **E** | | | | | | | | | | |
| men | 1/1 | | | | | | 2/2* | 1/0 | 6/6 | 10/9 * |
| women | | | | | 1/1 | 2/2* | | 2/0 | 11/8 | 16/11 |
| **F** | | | | | | | | | | |
| men | | 1/1 | | | | 2/0 | | | | 3/1 |
| women | 1/1 | | 3/0 | 2/1 | 1/1 | 1/1 | 1/1 | 3/2 | 7/6 | 19/13 |
| **G** | | | | | | | | | | |
| men | | | | | | | 1/0 | | 1/0 | 2/0 |
| women | | | | | | 1/1** | | 6/3** | 12/7 | 19/11** |
| **H** | | | | | | | | | | |
| men | | | | 1/1 | 1/1 | 2/2 | | | | 4/4 |
| women | | | 1/1 | | | | 1/0 | | 1/1 | 3/2 |

*Includes legislative divorce.
**Includes separate bed and board.

which the Council would take during, but not before, the Revolutionary period.[56] The legislative divorces, viewed together with the Council's decrees after 1773, suggest that the more whiggish and the more representative the authority, the more likely it was to treat male and female adultery equally as cause for divorce. The transformation of the Council's attitude toward male adultery would be simpler to explain if it had occurred in 1776, when the composition of the Council changed radically. Though some new members replaced old ones in 1773, specific changes in membership do not clearly account for the new pattern of decrees beginning in that year.[57]

Divorce actions in Massachusetts may have paralleled larger political struggles, but did changes in divorce policy also move against the double standard and advance equality between the sexes? In several ways the record of petitions and decrees implies an improvement in women's status. The great increase in the number of women's petitions after 1764 suggests that women were becoming less resigned to their circumstances and were taking more initiative to end unsatisfactory marriages. Women's petitions were more concentrated in the period after 1764 than were men's.[58] The proportion of petitions including adultery charges rose for both sexes, but more emphatically for wives. (See Table 5.) The higher the proportion of

**Table 5** PROPORTION OF ALL PETITIONS CONTAINING ADULTERY CHARGE

| | 1692–1764 | 1765–1774 | 1775–1786 |
|---|---|---|---|
| male petitioners | 78% | 94% | 91% |
| female petitioners | 40% | 50% | 79% |

adultery-inclusive petitions, the greater success petitioners were likely to have. In fact, both male and female petitioners fared better between 1765 and 1786 but only on account of decrees made after independence. From 1765 through 1774 an unusually high proportion of suits remained unresolved, reducing petitioners' chances of favorable action. The proportion of unresolved petitions jumped from 23 percent for the years 1692-1764 to 41 percent for 1765-1774, and then dropped to 13 percent for 1775-1786. This noteworthy improvement in efficiency, along with the rise in the proportion of adultery-inclusive petitions, increased petitioners' likelihood of gaining favorable decrees. Because of the added factor of the new treatment of male adultery, wives' rate of success improved dramatically from 49 percent between 1692 and 1774 to 70 percent between 1775 and 1786; husbands' rate of success rose only from 66 percent to 73 percent. Wives' rate of success almost equalled that of husbands' during the decade after independence.

It is tempting to propose from this evidence that the Revolutionary era ushered in a "new deal" that recognized the injustice of the double standard, evened obligations of marital fidelity, and made redress within marriage more accessible to women. To an extent, however small, acceptance of male adultery as grounds for divorce moved in these directions. Motives for the change in the treatment of male adultery probably originated, however, more in men's political intentions than in their desire for sexual justice. Revolutionary rhetoric, in its repudiation of British "vice," "corruption," "extravagance," and "decadence," enshrined ideals of republican virtue—of personal and national simplicity, honesty, frugality, and public spirit. In the view of Revolutionary leaders, republicanism required a moral reformation of the American people as well as a political transformation, because a republic's success depended on the virtue of its citizens. As John Adams wrote to his wife Abigail in July 1776, "the new Governments we are assuming . . . will require a Purification from our Vices, and an Augmentation of our Virtues or they will be no Blessings." Samuel Adams stated in 1777, "We shall succeed if we are virtuous. . . . I am infinitely more apprehensive of the Contagion of Vice than the Power of all other Enemies."[59] The dynamism of the words "virtue" and "vice," in Revolutionary usage, derived at least in part from their sexual connotation.[60] Rejection of British "corruption" implied a critique of the traditionally loose sexual standards for men of the British ruling class. The republican ideology of private as well as public virtue also produced an emphasis on marital fidelity, because it focused on the family as the training ground of future citizens. It was wholly consistent that judges in Massachusetts, where patriotic rhetoric evoked Puritan conceptions of righteousness (and thus Puritan standards of fidelity), no longer saw male adultery as venial but called it sufficient grounds for divorce. Such a change in standards for male conduct may well have produced a divorce policy that had the appearance of improving women's marital status.

Petitioners also brought suits on account of important marital breaches other than adultery—namely, desertion (I) and cruelty (J). Desertion suits were the least successful among all the categories. Of ten wives who

charged desertion—all but one abandoned for more than three years—
only two achieved any favorable result. Five of the petitions were not resolved. Three more were dismissed, suggesting that the governor and
Council regarded a husband's willful desertion in itself as insufficient cause
to dissolve a marriage.[61] One wife who asked only for her conjugal right
to restoration of maintenance, since her husband had deserted long before,
obtained her object. The court formalized the couple's agreement for yearly maintenance payments by the husband.[62] In the other successful suit
Abigail Bradstreet, whose complaints included cruelty as well as desertion, won a decree of separate bed and board with maintenance payments.[63]

Among the eight men who sued because of their wives' desertion, the
earlier petitioners fared better than the later. The court declared John
Emery of Newbury separated from his wife in 1710 on his complaint that
she slandered him and refused to live with him. Two other men obtained
divorces on desertion pleas. John Ferre, a husbandman of Springfield,
petitioned in 1718 and was ordered by the governor and Council to post
notification that if his wife did not return within six months she would be
divorced. Ferre obeyed, his wife did not return, and in 1719 the divorce
was granted. Jonathan Fletcher's petition of 1734 stated that his wife had
departed sixteen years earlier, after two months of marriage. In this case
the governor and Council took the unusual step of declaring both parties
single and free to marry, the marriage portion to be returned.[64] After 1734,
however, men's desertion pleas all failed. The court gave John Williston's
petition in 1737 only a first reading, apparently, and dismissed other petitions in 1739, 1740, 1743, and 1786.[65] These dismissals contradicted the
implication of the Ferre and Fletcher cases, and they force the general conclusion that desertion alone, whether by wife or husband, was not considered sufficient cause for divorce. Why not? Certainly desertion violated
the marriage contract. In Puritan theory desertion warranted divorce.
Under canon law, on the contrary, desertion was not even grounds for
separate bed and board unless it was combined with cruelty.[66] Excepting
the Ferre and Fletcher cases, the governor and Council acted as though
canon law controlled their decisions on desertion.[67] Perhaps the New
World offered too great opportunities for desertion for the court to wish to
establish desertion as reason for divorce.

Canon law rather than Puritan precept appears to have guided the decisions in cruelty cases as well. Puritan divorce theory allowed divorce for
incorrigible enmity between spouses or for dangerous abuse, but canon
law prescribed only separate bed and board. Of the twenty-three Massachusetts petitions entered on grounds of cruelty, nine obtained decrees of
separate bed and board, three more were settled by separations based on
mutual consent, six were dismissed for insufficient evidence, and five were
left unresolved. Not a single one gained divorce. However, not all of these
petitions asked for divorce. All of the petitioners in this category were
women, and almost two-thirds of them requested only separate bed and
board with maintenance. It is difficult to tell whether this reflected their
pragmatism or their personal preference. Divorce was virtually impossible
to obtain for this cause, but separate bed and board was possible. To gain

a separation, with alimony, may have seemed a satisfactory solution to the grievance, expecially for older women who did not foresee marrying again. Yet even separate bed and board was not easy to obtain, as the six dismissals attested. In all but one of these six cases the wives asked only for separation and maintenance, but the governor and council would not grant the plea.[68]

Women who petitioned on grounds of cruelty were significantly more urban—and thus perhaps more sophisticated—than petitioners in general. Fourteen of the twenty-two[69] lived in Boston, three in towns immediately outside Boston, two in other large port towns, and only three in smaller, more remote locations. Perhaps urban women had higher standards for kind treatment in marriage than did rural women, or more readily took official steps to combat physical abuse. Urban women also predominated, though not as strongly, among wives petitioning on grounds of adultery and cruelty (G): ten of the nineteen lived in Boston and three in towns nearby.

The governor and Council usually judged requests for maintenance in cases in which they decreed separate bed and board, although a provincial statute of 1695 located jurisdiction over alimony in the Superior Court of Judicature. Alimony ordinarily took the form of regular cash payments, the amount varying with the husband's wealth.[70] Gentlemen's wives, who married with considerable portions, might ask only for the return or use of their own former property to support themselves. Mary Arthur of Boston did so in 1754 when she sought separation from her husband because of his nine years of abuse. After she obtained the separation, a second petition was required before the Council awarded her her household goods and the income from her Boston real estate.[71] The governor and Council assigned to another Bostonian, in lieu of the alimony she requested, the rent and profit of her own real property, removing it from her husband's control. Yet she was not permitted to sell the lands, which were uncultivated and produced no profit, without petitioning again for that privilege. Upon her plea, the General Court enacted a bill allowing her to sell and convey the lands as though she were single, but the Privy Council disallowed it.[72] These alimony arrangements revealed starkly how the marriage bond circumscribed the legal and economic individuality of women.[73]

In three separate bed and board decrees after 1780 the governor and Council failed to mention alimony, although the Massachusetts constitution of 1780 put the matter under their jurisdiction. They granted *divorce* with alimony to two women petitioners, however—the only two such decrees between 1692 and 1786—although no extraordinary characteristics of the cases explain why.[74] It may be that divorced women had earlier sought alimony from the superior courts. Sarah Griffin (Sarah Gould before her divorce) filed a petition for this purpose with the Superior Court of Judicature of Suffolk County on August 31, 1773, but the court appears to have taken no action.[75]

It is doubtful how well the assignment of alimony worked to provide for separated or divorced wives. In those four cases in which the couple mutually agreed to separation and maintenance no complaints followed.[76] But six of the nine decrees of separate bed and board with alimony were succeeded by further petitions from the wives, because their husbands had not made the required payments.[77] Petitioners who won separate bed and board thus had an ambiguous success, not being allowed to remarry, nor released from the economic constraints of the marriage contract, nor guaranteed current support. The husband's provision of alimony, like his support during marriage, was required by law and enforceable by compulsory process, but his performance actually depended on his own conscientiousness and goodwill.

The records of divorce in Massachusetts are most interesting for what they reveal about men's and women's respective power and advantages within marriage. The alimony petitions emphasize something the divorce suits as a whole suggest, that while marriage was a contract—a covenant, in contemporary language—it was a contract between unequals with disparate obligations. Sexual fidelity and good conduct were expected of both partners, but fidelity was not regularly enforced upon husbands by the threat of divorce until the mid-1770s, and a husband's abusive conduct never warranted divorce. The husband's characteristic obligation was provision of support; the wife's, obedient service. In this, marriage resembled an indenture between master and servant; and, indeed, the marriage relation was only one of a number of dependency relations—such as parent-child and master-servant—in traditional society. The husband's obligation—enhanced by his control over his wife's property and labor—was unequivocal. In a case, for example, in which an aggrieved wife returned to her parents' household, her father sued her husband for the cost of maintaining her during that time, and his view of the husband's responsibility was upheld in court.[78] The wife performed her part in her subjection. Like a servant in relation to a master, she contributed continual service and received support. Besides working in the household (many deponents in divorce cases mentioned the industry of wives), she was expected to use frugally what her husband provided. Amos Bliss of Rehoboth felt he had a valid complaint against his wife Phebe because she "behaved herself unfriendly and unsubjectedly toward him; and . . . had linked herself in friendship with her father's Family against him; who . . . had ocationed a great Deal of Trouble, as well as Loss, to his Interest: and he Represented her to be Very Disloyal towards his person: and wastefull and Careless of his provisions and goods"; but Amos was willing to invite Phebe home again if she would act the good and obedient wife and "be in subjection to him."[79] The indenture-like nature of marriage appeared in the practice of a husband's "advertising" his runaway wife, warning others not to harbor or trust her, and refusing responsibility for her debts. A husband would not be bound to provide for his wife if he could not command her services, and he could compel her services by preventing her from obtaining support elsewhere.

Since marriage resembled an indenture contract, divorce should have been more readily available for varieties of nonperformance such as desertion or cruelty. That it was not suggests, first, that the sexual definition of marriage was its essence, and, second, that English divorce policy had more influence on eighteenth-century Massachusetts than might appear at first glance. Although marriage was regarded as a civil contract, and Massachusetts had no ecclesiastical courts, decisions in desertion and cruelty suits were almost entirely consistent with English application of canon law. On the whole, however, Massachusetts divorce practice diverged significantly from that of England. A much wider range of individuals—a laborer, a poor woman, a black servant—were able to obtain divorce with freedom to remarry, while in England only very rich men had that opportunity. In addition, the procedure was simpler than the parliamentary process. No prior ecclesiastical decree or criminal conviction of the adulterers was necessary in adultery cases, although the latter sufficed to warrant divorce. What was more innovative, women were able to obtain divorce with freedom to remarry and after 1773 did so on approximately the same terms as men. When in 1786 Massachusetts enacted a divorce law to codify the practice that had evolved, it allowed divorce for consanguinity, bigamy, impotency, or adultery *in either partner*, and separate bed and board for extreme cruelty.[80]

Throughout the period 1692–1786 husbands found it easier than wives to obtain divorce—not a surprising circumstance, since men also had the legal and economic independence which married women lacked, occupied all political and religious offices, were more literate than women, exercised greater control over geographic moves and choice of spouse, and by the terms of the marriage covenant could command their wives' obedience. It is more remarkable that the number of women's petitions and their rate of success accelerated during the century, so that in the decade after independence more than half again as many women as men pursued divorce, and their rate of success was almost the same. Divorce pleas by both sexes increased during the Revolutionary period, and efficiency in treating them improved, reflecting modernization of both personal values and bureaucratic procedure. The disproportionate growth in women's petitions suggests that they, even more than men, had rising expectations in marriage; and the changing treatment of their petitions implies that wives' objections were being regarded more seriously—that their status within the family had risen in the eyes of authorities.

The equalization of the consequences of adultery by either spouse, which was unmistakably the reason for the increasing success of women petitioners, may have signified a retreat from hierarchical models and an advance toward ideals of complementarity in the prevailing conception of the marriage relationship. In Hingham, Massachusetts, Daniel Scott Smith has found a consonant change in marriage patterns—a move away from parental control in the direction of individual autonomy in marriage choice—beginning markedly in the Revolutionary years. Smith sees the departure from the stable, parent-run system of selecting spouses as evidence of the "erosion and collapse of traditional family patterns in the middle to late eighteenth century."[81] Furthermore, on the basis of her analysis of New England funeral sermons Lonna Malmsheimer affirms that views of women altered significantly during these years. No longer stressing the rigid subordination of wife to husband as they had done earlier, although still insisting on the importance of the wife's domestic service, the sermons began to focus on friendship, complementarity, and emotional bonds between spouses. The seventeenth-century linkage of woman with moral evil, Eve's legacy, gave way to a new image of woman as a being ruled by conscience and religion.[82] Additionally, writers in contemporary Boston magazines seem to have been preoccupied with the reciprocal obligations and advantages of the sexes. They, too, idealized the complementary nature of men's and women's marital roles: an essayist in the Boston *Gentleman's and Lady's Town and Country Magazine*, for example, of September 1784, described "matrimonial felicity" as the uniting of two congenial souls, "the man all truth, the woman all tenderness; he possessed of cheerful solidity, she of rational gaiety; acknowledging his superior judgment she complies with all his reasonable desires, whilst he, charmed with such repeated instances of superior love, endeavors to suit his requests to her inclinations."[83]

By the last quarter of the eighteenth century both parties were evidently restating the terms of the "indenture" of marriage. The divorce court's reprobation of male adultery newly defined one limit to the marital contract. This indicated an improvement in the position of wives, although it did not change their economic status, the essence of their dependency. By making men culpable for adultery, the court may also have heralded a new ideology of sexual roles—one that would encourage families in the young Republic to produce upright citizens. Stricter standards for men's marital fidelity helped enforce ideals of republican character and counteract British social models. The assumption that men could resist the temptation of adultery also implied a nontraditional view of woman[84]— not the devil-as-woman Eve, whose seductiveness absolved men of their sexual transgressions, but the angel-as-woman Pamela, who upheld and typified sexual virtue.

## NOTES

1. Deposition of William Whiting, Jr., Suffolk Court Files #129846, Suffolk County Court House, Boston, 106.

2. Robert V. Wells, "Quaker Marriage Patterns in a Colonial Perspective," *William and Mary Quarterly*, 3d Ser., XXIX (1972), 415–442; Daniel Scott Smith, "Parental Power and Marriage Patterns: An Analysis of Historical Trends in Hingham, Massachusetts," *Journal of Marriage and the Family*, XXXV (1973), 419–439; Daniel Scott Smith and Michael Hindus, "Premarital Pregnancy in America, 1640–1966," *Journal of Interdisciplinary History*, VI (1975), 537–570.

3. See Nancy F. Cott, "Eighteenth-Century Family and Social Life Revealed in Massachusetts Divorce Records," *Journal of Social History*, 10 (1976), where these documents are used to investigate questions about privacy and community, relations among conjugal-family and extended-family members, and romantic love and sex.

4. In June 1692 the General Court declared that "all controversies concerning marriage and divorce shall be heard and determined by the governor and council." *Acts and Resolves, Public and Private, of the Province of Massachusetts Bay . . .* (Boston, 1869–1922), I, chap. 25, sec. 4, 61. The state constitution of 1780 confirmed this practice, until "An Act for Regulating Marriage and Divorce" of Mar. 16, 1786, located jurisdiction over divorce suits in the Supreme Judicial Court held for each county. *Acts and Resolves of Massachusetts, 1784–1785* (Boston, ca. [1892]), 564–567.

5. The most informative records are the original petitions and depositions preserved for most of the cases between 1739 and 1786 in volumes 793–796 of the Suffolk Court Files. Similar documents from some earlier cases appear in volume IX of the Massachusetts Archives, at the Archives Dept., State House, Boston. A single bound manuscript volume labeled "Divorces, 1760-1786," hereafter cited as "Divorces," located with the Suffolk Files, summarizes most of the divorce petitions and decrees between those dates. Mass. Archives, CXL, contains a fairly complete record of divorces between 1780 and 1786. Additional cases before 1780 have been recovered from the executive records of the Council, also at the Archives Dept., hereafter cited as Council Recs. Surprisingly, the Council Records do not contain the most inclusive recording of petitions and decrees; their completeness varies considerably through the years. The legislative records of the Council, a separate series in the Archives Dept. called Court Records, have been used in those cases that involved legislation.

6. The overrepresentation of Bostonians—for the city held only 6% of the province's population in 1765—was at least partially owing to the requirement that petitioners appear before the governor and Council at their sessions in Boston. The legislation of 1786 shifted jurisdiction over divorce to the superior courts held in each county because of remote petitioners' difficulty in getting to Boston. I have estimated the geographical distribution of petitioners by using the population figures in the 1764–1765 provincial census, obviously not an exact means since the divorce cases span almost a century but the only one available. Place of residence was disclosed in almost 90% of the suits. On the basis of 1764–1765 population figures, 24.6% of petitioners resided in towns of less than 1,000 pop.; 22.6% in towns of 1,000 to 1,999; 15.9% in towns of 2,000 to 2,999; 8.2% in towns of 3,000 to 5,000; and 28.7% in Boston. More than two-fifths of the petitioners lived in the populous counties of Suffolk and Essex; a slightly smaller proportion in the eastern counties of Middlesex, Worcester, Bristol, Plymouth, Barnstable, and Dukes; and the remainder (slightly under a fifth) in the remote and lightly populated counties of Hampshire, Berkshire, Cumberland, Lincoln, and York. See J. H. Benton, *Early Census Making in Massachusetts* (Boston, 1905).

7. There are some interesting differences between the occupational levels of male petitioners and female—the latter judged by their *husbands'* occupations, however. Among the 122 wives, 73 disclosed the occupations of their husbands. Fifteen percent were esquires, gentlemen, or merchants; 4% doctors or officers; 19% husbandmen or yeomen; 16% mariners or fishermen; 37% craftsmen or traders; and 8% laborers, servants, or truckmen. Among the 101 husbands, 67 disclosed their occupations. Only 4.5% were esquires, gentlemen, or merchants; 9% professionals or officers; 25% husbandmen or yeomen; 28% mariners (reflecting the high incidence of adultery on the part of wives whose husbands were at sea for long periods); 27% craftsmen or traders; and 6% the lower occupations.

8. They may have had an even easier time in Connecticut, which had the most liberal divorce policy of all the colonies; both judicial and legislative divorces were granted there. Between 1740 and 1789, 174 superior court divorces were recorded in Hartford County alone. Henry S. Cohn, "Connecticut's Divorce Mechanism: 1636-1969," *American Journal of Legal History*, XIV (1970), 43, n. 39.

9. This discussion of English divorce practice relies on George Elliott Howard, *A History of Matrimonial Institutions, Chiefly in the United States and England* . . . (Chicago, 1904), II, 52-57, 77-85, 92-93, 102-107; Reginald Haw, *The State of Matrimony* (London, 1952), 74-89; Oliver McGregor, *Divorce in England* (London, 1957), 1-12; Joseph W. Madden., *Handbook of the Law of Persons and Domestic Relations* (St. Paul, Minn., 1931), 256-260; and L. Kinvin Wroth and Hiller B. Zobel, eds., *The Legal Papers of John Adams*, I (Cambridge, Mass., 1965), 280-285. The several accounts of divorce in England differ slightly in their estimates of numbers of parliamentary divorces before 1800.

10. The population figure for England and Wales is estimated from a table in J. D. Chambers, *Population, Economy, and Society in Pre-Industrial England* (London, 1972), 108.

11. The document best illustrating Puritan divorce reform theory in England is the *Reformatio Legum Ecclesiasticarum*, authorized by Parliament and drafted by eminent divines in 1552. The *Reformatio* regarded marriage as a civil contract rather than an indissoluble sacred bond, omitted mention of separate bed and board, allowed dissolution of marriage for adultery, desertion, continued absence without news, or unmitigable enmity or cruelty by either spouse—and was never put into effect. Howard, *Matrimonial Institutions*, II, 78-79.

12. Ibid., 331-338; Edmund S. Morgan, *The Puritan Family: Religion and Domestic Rela-*

*tions in Seventeenth-Century New England* (New York, 1966), 35–37; John Demos, *A Little Commonwealth: Family Life in Plymouth Colony* (New York, 1970), 92–97; D. Kelly Weisberg, "Under Greet Temptations Heer: Women and Divorce in Puritan Massachusetts," *Feminist Studies,* II (1975), 183–194. Since Howard's list of divorce suits for the period 1692–1786 is incomplete (he lists only 107 suits), it is likely that his list of 40 for ther period 1639–1692 is similarly fragmentary.

13. Wroth and Zobel, eds., *Legal Papers of Adams,* I, 282, erroneously states that jurisdiction to grant divorce *a vinculo* was ambiguous after 1692 and that the governor and Council did not grant divorces between 1692 and 1760.

14. They did so despite a law enacted by the General Court in 1755, empowering them to enforce their decrees in divorce suits by ordering imprisonment for disobedience. *Acts and Resolves, Mass. Bay,* III, chap. 15, 782.

15. The acts are in ibid., VI, 165, 169, 170, 173, 174, 177, and can be corroborated in Court Recs., XX, 337–338, 346, 351–352, 373, 379, 460, 461, 468, XXI, 97, 157, 161, 329, 497, 500, 517, 540, XXII, 40. Howard, *Matrimonial Institutions,* II, 340, errs in saying that "after 1692 the legislature does not seem to have interfered in divorce suits either on appeal or in the first instance."

16. Report of the Lords of Trade, June 6, 1758. Mass. Arch., XXII, 9–10. See also *Acts and Resolves, Mass. Bay,* VI, vi–vii, and Joseph Henry Smith, *Appeals to the Privy Council from the American Plantations* (New York, 1950), 582–585. Smith points out that in 1741 the Lords disallowed a Jamaica act of legislative divorce passed in 1739.

17. See William Renwick Riddell, "Legislative Divorce in Colonial Pennsylvania," *Pennsylvania Magazine of History and Biography,* LVII (1933), 175–180; Thomas R. Meehan, "'Not Made Out of Levity'. Evolution of Divorce in Early Pennsylvania," ibid., XCII (1968), 441–464; Leonard Woods Labaree, ed., *Royal Instructions to British Colonial Governors, 1670–1776,* I (New York, 1935), 154–155.

18. A bill "for enabling the Governor and Council to grant Divorces from the Bands of Matrimony," passed by the House of Representatives in Aug. 1757, never became law because the Council neglected or declined to concur. Mass. Arch., IX 419; *Journals of the House of Representatives of Massachusetts, 1757,* XXXIV (Meriden, Conn., 1961), 105. On July 30, 1759, the Council appointed four of its members to investigate the precedents of divorce actions before 1756. Why the Council had so short a collective memory—when several members had been on the Council in the early 1750s—is puzzling. The committee reported (accurately) on Nov. 10, 1759, that the Council had decreed seven divorces and one separation between 1747 and 1754. See Mass. Arch. IX, 432–434, and Council Recs., XIV, 122, 134. Another influence leading to the Council's resumption of divorce by decree may have been Gov. Thomas Pownall's message of Feb. 2, 1760, which touched on the Council's power as a divorce court. Josiah Quincy, Jr., *Reports of Cases Argued and Adjudged in the Superior Court of Judicature of the Province of Massachusetts Bay between 1761 and 1772* (Boston, 1865), 573–579.

19. The white population of Massachusetts in 1780 was about five-and-a-half times as large as it had been in 1690, but there were twelve times as many petitions and decrees in the years 1775–1786 as in 1692–1704. Population data are from U.S. Bureau of the Census, *Historical Statistics of the United States: Colonial Times to 1957* (Washington, D.C., 1960).

20. See Francis G. Walett, "The Massachusetts Council, 1766–1774: The Transformation of a Conservative Institution," *WMQ,* 3d Ser., VI (1949), 605–627.

21. Abigail Bradstreet v. Joseph Bradstreet, Suffolk Files #129762. "Divorces," 68–70; James Richardson v. Hannah Richardson, Suffolk Files #129769. "Divorces," 70–72.

22. For example, Chloe Welch v. Luke Welch, Suffolk Files #129790, "Divorces," 122–125, and Andrew Gage v. Elizabeth Gage, Suffolk Files #129829, "Divorces," 192–193; see also Ann Lovell v. John Lovell, Jr., Suffolk Files #129778.

23. See Smith and Hindus, "Premarital Pregnancy," *Jour. Interdisciplinary Hist.,* VI (1975), 537–570.

24. See Kenneth A. Lockridge, "Social Change and the Meaning of the American Revolution," *Jour. Soc. Hist.,* VI (1973), 403–439, for several hypothetical models of "preparedness" for the War for Independence.

25. On modernization in New England see ibid., and two articles by Richard D. Brown:

"Modernization and the Modern Personality in Early America, 1600–1865: A Sketch of a Synthesis," *Jour. Interdisciplinary Hist.*, II (1972), 201–228, and "The Emergence of Urban Society in Rural Massachusetts, 1760–1820," *Journal of American History*, LXI (1974), 29–51. For a typology of the "modern" personality see Alex Inkeles, "Making Men Modern: On the Causes and Consequences of Individual Change in Six Developing Countries," *American Journal of Sociology*, LXXV (1969), 208–225, and "The Modernization of Man," in Myron Weiner, ed., *Modernization: The Dynamics of Growth* (New York, 1966), 138–150.

26. See Sarah Vernon v. William Vernon, Suffolk Files #129840, petition, 78, and Rebecca Simpson v. Ebenezer Simpson, ibid. #129854, petition, 140.

27. *Memoirs of Mrs. Abigail Bailey . . . written by herself . . .* , ed. Ethan Smith (Boston, 1815), 58–59. Mrs. Bailey eventually did petition and obtain a divorce in 1792.

28. For example, Mary Fairservice v. John Fairservice (1767), petition in "Divorces," 40–42; Sarah Gould v. William Gould (1773), Suffolk Files #129772, petition, 56; Sarah Kingsley v. Enoch Kingsley (1771), Suffolk Files #129773, petition, 58; Martha Air v. Adam Air (1773), Suffolk Files #129779, petition, 85.

29. Kenneth A. Lockridge, *Literacy in Colonial New England: An Enquiry into the Social Context of Literacy in the Early Modern West* (New York, 1974), esp. tables on pp. 24 and 41, indicates that Boston women's ability to sign moved from about 40% in 1700 to a peak of 68% in 1758–1762, and then fell to 60% by 1787, while rural women's ability remained below 40% for the whole period; and that Boston men's ability to sign moved from about 75% in 1700 to 80% in 1758–1762, while rural men's ability moved from 65% to 75%. Literacy data (signature or mark) appeared for 96 female divorce petitioners and 56 male petitioners. Sixty-one percent of these female petitioners before 1765 could sign—all of the 9 Boston women, and 8 of the 19 non-Boston women. Seventy-eight percent of the female petitioners between 1765 and 1786 could sign, including 16 of the 20 Boston women and 37 (77%) of the 48 non-Boston women. Among 17 male petitioners before 1765, 94% could sign—that is, all except one black man of Boston, a servant. Of 39 male petitioners between 1765 and 1786, 95% could sign—all of the 8 Boston men and all but two of the 31 non-Boston men. If Lockridge's figures are correct for the general population, both male and female divorce petitioners, as judged by ability to sign, had literacy above the norm. For a control group independent of Lockridge's study, there are the scores of deponents who testified in the divorce cases. They suggest a different norm. The ability to sign of 495 male deponents was 98.4%; it was 100% among the 64 deponents before 1765, and 98.1% among the 431 deponents between 1765 and 1786. The ability to sign of 224 female deponents was 58%; it was 68% among 50 deponents before 1765 and fell to 55.1% among the 174 deponents between 1765 and 1786. Both male and female deponents included large proportions of low-status persons, such as hired laborers and domestic servants, but the male deponents also included many of high status.

30. Henrietta Maria East Caine v. Hugh Caine, Suffolk Files #129736, "Divorces," 2–3; Mary Hunt v. Richard Hunt (1761), "Divorces," 8–9; Sarah Backus v. John Backus, Suffolk Files #129846, 100. See also Sarah Bloget v. John Bloget, Mass. Arch., IX, 211.

31. Ten of the unresolved petitions—seven from women and three from men—show no sign of ever having been read by the Council. If these petitions are removed from the comparison, the difference between the number of men's and the number of women's petitions left unresolved (after at least a first reading) diminishes.

32. In a few cases it is debatable whether the suit should be placed in one category or another: I and J in particular tend to overlap. Any of the adultery causes, C through H, might have included the charge of illegitimate offspring; as a divorce charge, this was included rather as a means of proving adultery than as a separate grievance.

33. The records are so sparse in this category that the charges are not apparent. Rachel Draper won her divorce in 1709, and Joseph Hale's suit was dismissed in 1779; the results of the four others remain as mysterious as the charges. Rachel Draper v. John Draper, Council Recs., V, 124; Mary Parce v. John Parce, ibid., XVIII, 100; Experience Simpson v. husband, ibid., XXIV, 392; Elizabeth Laud v. David Laud, Mass. Arch., CXL, 194; Joseph Hale (or Hail) v. Isabella Hale, Council Recs., XXIII, 64, 76, 414; Thomas Patter v. wife, ibid., XXIII, 64.

34. Jesse Turner v. Grace Turner, Suffolk Files #129727. Council Recs., X, 331, 378; George Sherman v. Phebe Sherman, Suffolk Files #129796, Council Recs., XXIII, 92, XXIV, 206, 301, XXVI, 104, "Divorces," 137–140. Jeremiah Ingraham petitioned for divorce from Mercy Ingraham for this cause in 1733, after 15 years of marriage, but his charge was not substantiated and his petition was dismissed. Council Recs., IX, 464, 533.

35. Sarah Maggin v. William Maggin (dismissed, 1736), Council Recs., X, 47; Elizabeth Bredeen v. Joseph Bredeen (1744), Suffolk Files #129728, Council Recs., XI, 151, 156, 174–175, 184; Judith Walker v. Simeon Walker (1773), Suffolk Files #129777; "An Act for dissolving the Marriage of Philip Turner and Mercy Turner," Acts and Resolves, Mass. Bay, VI, 229.

36. William Davidson v. Hannah Davidson (1762), "Divorces." 16–17; Samuel Lefebvre v. Sarah Lefebvre (1770), Suffolk Files #129758, "Divorces," 57–59; Gill Belcher v. Mary Finney alias Belcher (1739), Suffolk Files #129726. Mass. Arch., IX, 228–229, Council Recs., X, 254–315.

37. Annulled: Susanna T. Kennet v. Edward Kennet (1694), Council Recs., II, 290; Reliance Drew v. John Drew (1737), ibid., X, 79, 122; Elizabeth Eldredge v. Ezekiel Eldredge (1751), Suffolk Files #129730, Mass. Arch., IX, 354–356; Rachel Wormley v. John Wormley (1765), Suffolk Files #129744, "Divorces," 33–34; Mary Bates v. Henry Bates (1771), Suffolk Files #129759, "Divorces," 59–62; Mehetabel Nicholson v. Joshua Nicholson (or Nickerson) (1771), Suffolk Files #129761, "Divorces," 62–64. Marriages dissolved: Rebecca Wansford v. Nicholas Wansford (1698), Council Recs., II, 562; Mary Hamilton alias Arthur v. George Arthur (1756), Mass. Arch., IX, 399–402, Council Recs., XIII, 140; Sibble Babcock v. George Babcock (1784), Suffolk Files #129835, "Divorces," 202–203. Not resolved: Abigail Hamen v. John Hamen (1748), Mass. Arch., IX, 321–323, Council Recs., XII, 46; Henrietta Maria East Caine v. Hugh Caine, Suffolk Files #129736, "Divorces," 2–3; Mary Drinkwater v. William Drinkwater (1771), Suffolk Files #129765

38. Mary Arthur and Henrietta Maria East Caine.

39. Abigail Hamen, Elizabeth Eldredge, Mary Bates, Mehetabel Nicholson, Mary Drinkwater, and Sibble Babcock.

40. Reliance Drew, Abigail Hamen, Mary Arthur, H. M. E. Caine, Rachel Wormley, and Mary Bates. One petitioner, Mary Arthur, had already been granted separate bed and board because of her husband's cruelty. Perhaps wives would not have complained of the bigamy if their husbands had not compounded the insult with other grievances.

41. See Keith Thomas, "The Double Standard," Journal of the History of Ideas, XX (1959), 195–216, and, for an example of such advice, [George Savile], The Lady's New Year's Gift, or, Advice to a Daughter (London, 1688).

42. Thomas, "Double Standard," Jour. Hist. Ideas, XX (1959), 203–205.

43. At least 17 of the 50 adulteries charged in husbands' petitions occurred while the husband was absent at sea or on a military campaign. In almost all of the cases in which bastard offspring were mentioned, the husband had been absent for a year or more. The wives' partners in adultery were neighbors, hired laborers, boarders, or, in a few cases, casual visitors or traveling companions.

44. Only six of the male petitioners in category C gave evidence of prior court actions. Three were actions to punish the adulterers: Benjamin Bucklin v. Rebeccah Bucklin (1737), Council Recs., X, 112, 121; Thomas Gelpin v. Abigail Gelpin (1743), Mass. Arch., IX, 263–267, Council Recs., XI, 65–66, 73–74; George Raynord v. Mary Raynord (1752), Suffolk Files #129729, Council Recs., XII, 268. Three were actions for the husband to collect money damages from the wife's lover: Thomas Hammet v. Abigail Hammet (1767), Suffolk Files #129747, "Divorces," 37–40; James Dougherty v. Mary Dougherty (1768), Suffolk Files #129750, "Divorces," 45–48; Joshua Gay v. Sarah Gay (1778), Suffolk Files #129784, "Divorces," 101–103, Council Recs., XXII, 46, 48.

45. For example, Jacob Brown v. Ruth Brown (1758), Mass. Arch., IX, 420–428, Council Recs., XIII, 350, 354; Russell Knight v. Mary Knight (1766), Suffolk Files #129745, "Divorces," 35–37, Mass. Arch., IX, 446–447; Andrew Shank v. Sarah Shank (or Schenk) (1772), Suffolk Files #129766; James Richardson v. Hannah Richardson (1772), Suffolk Files #129769, "Divorces," 70–72; William Sturgis v. Sarah Sturgis (1778), Suffolk Files #129785,

"Divorces." 104–106, Council Recs., XXII, 256, 320; Samuel Hemenway v. Hannah Hemenway (1782), Suffolk Files #129804. The legal process attendant on a divorce petition was meant to insure justice to the accused spouse: he or she was allowed to be present when depositions to support the petitioner were taken and was able to bring his or her own witnesses.

46. Andrew Shank v. Sarah Shank (1772), Suffolk Files #129766; Samuel Hemenway v. Hannah Hemenway (1782), ibid. #129804.

47. Howard, *Matrimonial Institutions*, II, 334. But John Demos, *Little Commonwealth*, 97, has found in seventeenth-century Plymouth Colony records a divorce and favorable settlement granted to one woman who chiefly complained of her husband's "act of uncleanes" with another woman.

48. "An Act against Adultery and Polygamy," passed June 6, 1794, made polygamy (that is, marrying again while one's first spouse was living) a felony punishable by death. *Acts and Resolves, Mass. Bay*, I, 171–172.

49. Not decided: Ann Hall v. William Hall, category D (1753), Mass. Arch., IX, 370–373; Kezia Downing v. Nathaniel Downing, D. (1765), Suffolk Files #129742; Lydia Sharp v. Boston (a black), D (1773), ibid. #129775; Marcy Robinson v. Leonard Robinson, E (1770), ibid. #129755; Sarah Wheeler v. Valentine Wheeler, E (1772), ibid. #129792; Hannah Medberry v. Ebenezer Medberry, G (1767), ibid. #129746; Eunice Mountfort v. Benjamin Mountfort, G (1771), ibid. #129760; Lucy Foster v. Benjamin Foster, H. (1755), Mass. Arch., IX, 393–395. Dismissed: Elizabeth Shaw v. John Shaw, D (1748), ibid., 324, Council Recs., XII, 57. Separate bed and board: Mary Clapham v. William Clapham, E (1754), Suffolk Files #129733. Council Recs., XII, 349; Eleanor Gray v. Samuel Gray, G (1747), Mass. Arch., IX, 296–311. Council Recs., XII, 12; Mary Fairservice v. John Fairservice, G (1767), Suffolk Files #129749, "Divorces," 40–44.

50. Sarah Mitchell v. Michael Mitchell, Council Recs., VI, 305, 621. The older definition of adultery, incorporating the double standard, hinged on the involvement of a married *woman*. Thus a married man's sexual transgression could still be called fornication, if his partner was single.

51. Hannah Rolfe v. Ezra Rolfe, Mass. Arch., IX, 357–358, Council Recs., XII, 218, 239.

52. Sarah Gould v. William Gould, Suffolk Files #129772, notation on petition, 56; also "Divorces," 78–80. Martha Air v. Adam Air, Suffolk Files #129779. "Divorces," 81–82.

53. Between 1774 and 1786, 5 of the 6 women who charged adultery and desertion, 8 of the 11 who brought suits on account of adultery, desertion and cohabitation, 7 of the 8 who alleged adultery, desertion and remarriage, 7 of the 13 whose grievances were adultery and cruelty, and one whose husband committed interracial adultery all obtained decrees of divorce from the governor and Council. These figures differ slightly from the 1775–1786 column of Table 4 because they include the cases of 1774.

54. Court Recs., Dec. 4, 1754, XX, 337–338; Mass. Arch., IX, 381–382: "An Act to dissolve the Marriage of Mary Clapham with William Clapham and to allow her to marry again," *Acts and Resolves*, Mass. Arch., VI, 165. The Council later awarded Mary her household furniture, worth £100. Council Recs., XII. 386.

55. Mary Parker v. Phineas Parker, Mass. Arch., IX, 374–380, Council Recs., XII, 337, *Acts and Resolves, Mass. Bay*, VI, 169; Lydia Kellogg v. Ephraim Kellogg, Mass. Arch., IX, 403–413, *Acts and Resolves, Mass. Bay*, VI, 173. The Parker and Kellogg divorce acts, and two of the three legislative divorces obtained by male petitioners, were passed without prior decrees of separate bed and board from the governor and Council. Only in the Parker case was prior court conviction of the adulterer mentioned. The men's cases were John Farnum, Jr., v. Elizabeth Farnum, Mass. Arch., IX, 396–398, *Acts and Resolves, Mass. Bay*, VI, 170; Jonah Galusha v. Sarah Galusha, Mass. Arch, IX, 414. *Acts and Resolves, Mass. Bay* VI, 174. Court Recs., XX, 329; and Daniel McCarthy v. Mary McCarthy, Suffolk Files, #129734, Mass. Arch., IX, 418, Council Recs., XIII, 259, 262, *Acts and Resolves, Mass. Bay*, VI, 177. The three cases reviewed by the Board of Trade in 1758 were Clapham's, Parker's, and Farnum's.

56. Between 1760 and 1773 seven women filed adultery-inclusive petitions and none obtained divorce, although Mary Fairservice, with a plea of adultery and cruelty, obtained separate bed and board. See n. 49.

57. "Divorces" list names of Council members present at each decision.

58. See Table 1. Half of all men's but 63% of all women's petitions occurred after 1764.

59. John Adams to Abigail Adams, July 3, 1776, and Samuel Adams to John Langdon, Aug. 7, 1777, in Gordon S. Wood, *The Creation of the American Republic, 1776–1787* (Chapel Hill, N.C., 1972), 123–124.

60. Ian Watt, "The New Woman: Samuel Richardson's *Pamela*," in Rose Laub Coser, ed., *The Family: Its Structure and Functions* (New York, 1964), 281–282., points out that "the eighteenth century [in England] witnessed a temendous narrowing of the ethical scale, a redefinition of virtue in primarily sexual terms. . . . The same tendency can be seen at work on the ethical vocabulary itself: words such as virtue, propriety, decency, modesty, delicacy, purity, came to have the almost exclusively sexual connotation which they have since very largely retained."

61. Howard, *Matrimonial Institutions*, II, 333, lists two late seventeenth-century cases in which women petitioned on account of their husbands' desertion and failure to provide, and the assistants declared the marriages dissolved, but no comparable eighteenth-century women's suits had that result. The presumption of the law was that seven years' absence by one spouse allowed the other to remarry. The "Act against Adultery and Polygamy" of 1694 (*Acts and Resolves, Mass. Bay*, I, 171–172) exempted from its punishments any person whose spouse had been overseas for seven years or absent more than seven years, so perhaps the Council assumed that decrees of divorce were unnecessary. Two suits dismissed, however, involved absences of five and six years.

62. That is, this was a separate bed and board arrangement by mutual consent. Ann Vansise v. Cornelius Vansise, "Divorces," 44–45.

63. Abigail Bradstreet v. Joseph Bradstreet, Suffolk Files #129762, "Divorces." 68–70. Her lawyer, John Adams, argued her case according to canon law. See Wroth and Zobel, eds., *Legal Papers of Adams*, I, 280–285.

64. John Emery v. Abigail Emery, Council Recs., V, 180. (Abigail also petitioned unsuccessfully for divorce from John for cruelty. Mass. Arch., IX, 162–163.) John Ferre v. Elizabeth Ferre, Council Recs., VII, 165; Jonathan Fletcher v. wife, ibid., IX, 552, 565.

65. The duration of the wife's absence is not apparent in these cases, except in the last, John Chapin v. Margaret Chapin, Suffolk Files #129856, in which it was three years. One probable reason why John's suit failed was that Margaret was willing to be divorced. Divorce was an adversary process in Massachusetts; separate bed and board, but never divorce, was decreed on the basis of a couple's mutual agreement. Any apparent collusion on the part of the couple to gain divorce invalidated the suit, so that, ironically, one way for a husband or wife to stop a divorce proceeding was to agree to it. See, for example, Sarah Rust v. Francis Rust (Jan. 1784), Suffolk Files #129833, "Divorces," 199–200; and Sarah Rust v. Francis Rust (June 1784). Suffolk Files #129836, "Divorces," 204–205. Cf. n. 80.

66. Wroth and Zobel, eds., *Legal Papers of Adams*, I, 284; Howard, *Matrimonial Institutions*, II, 52–54.

67. Possibly the change from granting of divorces for wives' desertions before 1735 to dismissing such pleas later represented an "anglicization" of divorce policy. The appearance of separate bed and board decrees during the eighteenth century, when none, according to Howard, was made during the previous century, supports such a theory; but the change in treatment of male adultery in 1773 opposes it. Cf. John Murrin, "Anglicizing an American Colony: The Transformation of Puritan Massachusetts" (Ph.D. diss., Yale University, 1966); Kenneth A. Lockridge, "Land, Population, and the Evolution of New England Society, 1630–1790," *Past and Present*, XXXIX (1968), 62–80; and Kenneth A. Lockridge, *A New England Town, The First Hundred Years: Dedham, Massachusetts, 1636–1736* (New York, 1970), 167–180.

68. The records remaining for five of the six cases are not extensive enough to allow evaluation of the "sufficiency" of the cruelty alleged. One woman whose petition was dismissed sued a second time, however, bringing additional evidence, and then won separate bed and board. Mary Lobb v. George Lobb, Suffolk Files #129800, "Divorces," 145–148. In the sixth case, the wife gave evidence of enormous cruelty, but the governor and Council accepted her husband's promise henceforth to treat her kindly as reason to dismiss her petition. Apparently their judgment was mistaken, for the wife petitioned again less than a year later, indicating that her plight had not improved. Margaret Knodle v. Frederick Knodle (1764), Suffolk Files #129743, "Divorces," 32.

69. There were 23 suits but only 22 petitioners, since Mary Lobb petitioned twice (n. 68).

70. *Acts and Resolves, Mass. Bay*, I, 209. Some of the alimony awards made by the governor and Council in separate bed and board decrees were as follows: Anne Leonard v. Henry Leonard (a turner, of Boston), in 1743, 5s. per week (Mass. Arch., IX, 268–294, Council Recs., XI, 69, 113–114); Eleanor Gray v. Samuel Gray (a yeoman, of Pelham, Hampshire County), 1747, £6 per year (Mass. Arch., IX. 296–311, Council Recs., XII, 12); Mary Fairservice v. John Fairservice (a trader of Boston), 1767, £12 yearly (Suffolk Files #129749, "Divorces," 40–44); Lucy Purnam v. Scipio Purnam (a truckman, of Newburyport), 1768, 6s. per month (Suffolk Files #129751, "Divorces" 48–51). This last was the most bizarre suit on grounds of cruelty. The couple were black; Lucy accused Scipio not only of treating her cruelly but also of attempting to sell her as a slave. Scipio denied the charges and brought witnesses who impugned Lucy's character. Eventually he agreed to the official separation but objected strongly to paying alimony, claiming "she is at least was well able to support herself as he is himself and Family." See Suffolk Files #129751, 124.

71. Mary Arthur v. George Arthur, Suffolk Files #129733b, Council Recs., XII, 371, 385.

72. Mary Hunt v. Richard Hunt, "Divorces," 6–11, Council Recs., XIV, 268, 270, 277; "An Act for enabling Mary Hunt to dispose and Convey her lands and interest in Holden," passed Apr. 24, 1762, disallowed by Privy Council Mar. 16, 1763. *Acts and Resolves, Mass. Bay*, VI, 187–188.

Alexander Keyssar, "Widowhood in Eighteenth-Century Massachusetts: A Problem in the History of the Family," *Perspectives in American History*, VIII (1974), esp. 100–103, 114–118, points out that widows commonly faced similar problems: as dower they received the use and profit of one-third of their husbands' real property but not the right to dispose of it. "Dozens" of widows in eighteenth-century Massachusetts petitioned the General Court to be enabled to dispose of real property because it was not profitable to them. Keyssar's conclusion that "the legal structure aimed at the sustenance, rather than the economic freedom, of widows" (p. 103) could apply to the position of wives separated from their husbands.

73. Under common law all of a woman's personal property and earnings became her husband's upon marriage, and while she retained title to any real estate she owned, her husband gained the right to its use and income. A husband could not liquidate his wife's real property without her consent—this was the root of the quarrel in Bradstreet v. Bradstreet (n. 63)—but neither could she sell it of her own accord.

74. Sarah Wheeler v. Valentine Wheeler, Suffolk Files #129792, "Divorces," 128–131, 144–145, Council Recs., XXV, 181, 400, XXVI, 118; Sarah Sawyer v. Abel Sawyer, Suffolk Files #129827, "Divorces," 188–191. Cf. Sarah Vernon v. William Vernon, Suffolk Files #129849, "Divorces," 216–217, 222–224, for an explicit refusal of alimony after a divorce decree.

75. See Suffolk Files #91716. Her petition is in John Adams's handwriting, according to Worth and Zobel, eds., *Legal Papers of Adams*, I, 285n.

76. Ann McAlpine v. William McAlpine (1763), Suffolk Files #129737—no information on amount of settlement. Ann Vansise v. Cornelius Vansise (1768). "Divorces." 44–45—alimony of £10 yearly. Ann Lovell v. John Lovell (1773). Suffolk Files #129778—wife received her own estate and earnings. Ann Gardner v. David Gardner (1783), ibid., #129813, "Divorces," 168–170—settlement of £40 plus wife's retention of dower rights.

77. See the Bradstreet, Gray, and Purnam cases cited in nn. 63 and 70, and Elizabeth Keith v. Mark Keith, Suffolk Files #129738, "Divorces," 24–27, Mass. Arch., IX, 441–442; Mary Fairservice v. John Fairservice (1770), Suffolk Files #129756, "Divorces," 56–57; Mary Hamilton alias Arthur v. George Arthur (1756). Mass. Arch., IX, 399–492, Council Recs., XIII, 140. Those that did not produce subsequent complaints were Thankfull Winehall's case of 1710, which is very sparsely documented (Council Recs., V, 238); Ann Leonard's settlement of 5s. per week; and Mary Hunt's award of her own property (see nn. 70 and 72).

78. William Sturgis v. Sarah Sturgis, Suffolk Files #129785, "Divorces," 104–106. Council Recs., XXII, 256, 320. See also Burditch v. Sturgis, Suffolk Files #102540.

79. Amos Bliss v. Phebe Bliss, Suffolk Files #129799, depositions of Silvanus Martin and Eleazar Bliss, 49, 43.

80. This law, passed Mar. 16, 1786 (*Acts and Resolves, 1784–1785*, 564–567), also stated that no divorce would be granted if the adultery or cruelty were occasioned by collusion in order to obtain divorce, or if both spouses committed adultery.

81. Smith, "Parental Power and Marriage Patterns," *Jour. Marriage and Family*, XXXV (1973), 426.

82. Lonna Myers Malmsheimer, "New England Funeral Sermons and Changing Attitudes toward Women, 1672–1792" (Ph.D. diss., University of Minnesota, 1973).

83. *Gentleman's and Lady's Town and Country Magazine* (Sept. 1784). 194. See also Herman R. Lantz et al., "Pre-Industrial Patterns in the Colonial Family in America: A Content Analysis of Colonial Magazines," *American Sociological Review*, XXXIII (1968), 413–426.

84. Malmsheimer, "New England Funeral Sermons," finds this kind of shift in ideology in funeral sermons.

# 8 | DIVORCE IN THE PROGRESSIVE ERA

## WILLIAM L. O'NEILL

During the Progressive years the divorce rate, which had been rising steadily since the Civil War, attained critical dimensions. Consequently, Americans of this period took a graver view of the problem than any subsequent generation. Their varied responses proved to be decisive as far as the future of divorce itself was concerned, and they illuminate aspects of the Progressive Era which have received little attention from historians.

The precipitate growth of the divorce rate can be easily demonstrated. In 1880 there was one divorce for every twenty-one marriages; in 1900 there was one divorce for every twelve marriages; in 1909 the ratio dropped to one in ten, and by 1916 it stood at one in nine.[1] Naturally this dramatic increase in the divorce rate stimulated public alarm.

In 1881 the new England Divorce Reform League was established to conduct research on family problems, educate the public and lobby for more effective legislative curbs on divorce.[2] Under the leadership of Samuel Dike, a congregational minister, the league enjoyed a long and useful life, but Dike's reluctance to advance legislative solutions to the divorce problem failed to deter others from resorting to politics.

Efforts to arrest the spread of divorce by legal means took two forms. State campaigns were waged to amend local divorce laws, and repeated attempts were made to achieve uniform marriage and divorce laws either through a constitutional amendment or through the voluntary enactment of uniform codes by the several states.[3] Typical of the many local fights to alter state divorce laws was the successful battle in 1893 to end South Dakota's status as a divorce colony. After their admission to the Union in 1889 North and South Dakota retained Dakota Territory's generous ninety-day residence requirement. Sioux City, largest and most accessible town in the two states, soon developed a substantial divorce trade and gained national fame as a divorce colony. The resulting notoriety provoked local resentment which was mobilized by the return from Japan of the popular Episcopal Bishop William Hobart Hare, who in 1893 led Protestants, Catholics, and Populists in an attack on the ninety-day residence requirement. The state legislature was successfully petitioned to extend the residence requirement to six months and the migratory divorce trade was diverted to North Dakota.[4]

The South Dakota campaign conformed to what was already an established pattern. It was led by conservative clergymen, supported by women's groups, and met little apparent opposition. Although these local campaigns did not succeed anywhere in abolishing divorce, they were part of a widespread tendency toward stricter divorce legislation.[5] When such local crusades failed, it was usually because of public apathy, sometimes coupled with undercover resistance from commercial and legal interests which profited from the divorce trade.

Serious attempts to secure uniform marriage and divorce legislation through a constitutional amendment began in 1892 when James Kyle, the Populist Senator from South Dakota, introduced a joint resolution which read in full: "The Congress shall have the exclusive power to regulate marriage and divorce in the several states, Territories, and the District of Columbia.[6] Senator Kyle's resolution died in committee as did all later resolutions, presumably because of a disinclination on the part of Congress to increase the power of the Federal government at the expense of the states.[7]

More popular, if equally unsuccessful, was the movement to secure voluntary uniformity through the drafting of model statutes which were to be enacted by the states. The most persistent of the organizations dedicated to this goal was the National Conference of Commissioners on Uniform State Laws, which met annually in connection with the American Bar Association. It was established by the Bar Association in 1889 to frame model codes on a wide range of subjects. The Commissioners were usually appointed by their state governors and over the years drafted seven model statutes concerning marriage and divorce.[8] However, few of the states demonstrated an interest in these models, and by 1916 the Commissioners were forced to admit that their approach had been a failure.

If the experience of the National Conference of Commissioners on Uniform State Laws to 1906 had not been conclusive, the fate of the National Divorce Congress in that year was. A national meeting to draft uniform legislation had been talked about for years on the grounds that it would attract sufficient attention to succeed where the more diffident commissioners had failed. In 1906 President Roosevelt was persuaded to request a new census study of marriage and divorce, and the interest aroused by this led Governor Pennypacker of Pennsylvania to call a national conference to draft model uniform legislation on these subjects. The Congress met twice, once in Washington to appoint committees and again in Philadelphia to ratify the proposed statutes. The first meeting was attended by delegates from 42 of the 45 states and consisted largely of clergymen and lawyers, many of the latter having also been members of the NCCUSL. Despite the widespread approval which met their efforts, few states adopted their model statutes.[9]

The antidivorce forces were also active within the established Protestant churches. During the Progressive Era repeated efforts were made in almost all the great Protestant denominations to stiffen their positions on divorce. The Episcopal church, traditionally more hostile to divorce than most Protestant bodies, was in the van of this movement, thanks principally to William Croswell Doane, Bishop of Albany, New York. Doane was perhaps the most vocal and consistent enemy of divorce in the whole country. He favored prohibiting divorce altogether, and his activities within the Episcopal church were directed at the canon which allowed the innocent party in an adultery suit to remarry. This canon was only slightly less severe than the refusal of the Roman Catholic church to allow any divorced person to remarry, but it seemed dangerously lax to Doane and he regularly introduced an amendment which would have denied the sacraments to all divorced persons without exception.

In 1898 the House of Bishops, usually more conservative than the lower House, which included laymen, at the policy-making Triennial Convention, rejected Doane's amendment 31 to 24.[10] In 1901 his amendment was defeated by a narrower margin, but in 1904 it passed the House of Bishops only to fail in the House of Deputies, whose members felt that it was too far removed from the spirit of the country.[11] Thereafter enthusiasm within the Episcopal church for the Doane amendment declined, and while it was reintroduced at later conventions, it failed to pass even in the House of Bishops. Similar efforts were made in the other Protestant denominations with what proved to be an equal lack of success.[12]

American attitudes toward marriage and divorce during the Progressive years must be seen in terms of the widespread fear of divorce demonstrated by these examples. It is not too much to say that there was a national crisis generated by divorce. It was a crisis to begin with because people believed it was. As Daniel Bell has demonstrated in his *The End of Ideology*, it is not necessary for activities seen to be antisocial actually to increase in order to create a crisis atmosphere—it is enough if people simply believe that such activities are increasing.[13]

An even better example perhaps was the white slave panic of 1912–1913. If anything, prostitution was declining, but irrespective of the facts, widespread public alarm over this presumed social evil was triggered by local investigations and newspaper publicity.[14]

However, divorce actually was increasing by leaps and bounds. When one marriage in twelve ended in divorce, there were legitimate grounds for concern. These were crucial years for divorce, finally, because the Progressive period was the last time when public opinion could reasonably have been expected to support genuinely repressive action. With the 1920s and the advent of the revolution in morals, the opportunity to abolish or seriously restrict divorce was lost forever. Some of the antidivorce leaders sensed that time was running out for them, and this awareness gave their strictures an urgent tone which became more shrill with the years.

Although divorce had political, psychological, and other dimensions, the increase of divorce was usually seen as a moral and social problem.[15] It is difficult, if indeed not actually pointless, to try to determine which of these two aspects alarmed critics of divorce the most. The enemies of divorce invariably regarded it as both immoral and antisocial. Since most opponents of divorce were either clergymen or strongly religious people, it seems fair to assume that the moral side of the divorce question was what first engaged their attention, but having once declared divorce to be immoral, there is little more one can say in that direction, and most of the serious attacks on divorce emphasized its antisocial character.[16]

The attack on divorce hinged on the common belief that divorce destroyed the family, which was the foundation of society and civilization. Theodore Schmauk, editor of the *Lutheran Church Review*, President of the Lutheran General Council and a leading theologian, characterized the family as "the great and fundamental institution in social life."[17] *The Cath-*

*olic World* in an attack on H. G. Wells' view of divorce felt that it had demolished his position when it observed that Wells failed to see that the family "was the cradle of civil society."[18] Lyman Abbott, an influential Progressive editor and associate of Theodore Roosevelt, once charged a prominent divorcee with being "the worst type of anarchist" because divorce, like anarchy, threatened to destroy society altogether.[19] President Roosevelt, in addressing Congress on the need for uniform legislation, described marriage as being "at the very foundation of our social organization. . . ."[20] Marriage and the family are, of course, quite different institutions, but the critics of divorce did not usually distinguish between them.

Felix Adler took this contention a step further when he insisted that divorce menaced "the physical and spiritual existence of the human race. . . ."[21] Adler was in some ways a surprising figure to find on this side of the divorce question. The founder of Ethical Culture and a leading advocate of liberal religion, he consistently attacked dogma and orthodoxy and supported a wide variety of social reforms.[22] He had earlier supported divorce but by 1915 had changed his mind and accepted the point, usually advanced by the theologically orthodox, that divorce had to be suppressed as a matter of social survival. His conversion showed how this argument operated independently of its conservative religious base and helps to explain why some enemies of divorce attached such importance to their campaign. One could hardly play for higher stakes.

A related theme which engaged the attention of divorce critics was the role of woman. It was generally believed that the family was woman's special responsibility and its protection her primary concern. Moreover women were thought to be more active than men in securing divorces (and they probably were since about two-thirds of all divorces were awarded to women). *The North American Review* reflected this point of view when it entitled one of its divorce symposiums, "Are Women to Blame?"[23] The *Review*'s female panelists charged women with responsibility for the divorce rate and accused them of being spoiled, romantic, impatient, jealous of men, and usurpers of the male's time-honored functions. Many of these women were successful writers, as was Anna B. Rogers, a popular essayist, who repeated the same charges in her book, *Why American Marriages Fail*, nineteen years later.[24]

While the critics of divorce, especially the men, were inclined to argue that women were really happier when they stayed at home and held the family together, the more tough-minded accepted the fact that the woman's traditional role was often painful and difficult.[25] Few had a clearer picture of what was involved than the respected novelist Margaret Deland. Mrs. Deland was a warm supporter of many Progressive causes and a woman with courage enough to defend the rights of unwed mothers in Victorian Boston. But she believed that civilization "rests on the permanence of marriage."[26] For this reason women dared not turn to divorce, for it would mean the end of everything. "If we let the flame of idealism be quenched in the darkness of the senses," she cried, "our civilization must go upon the rocks."[27] Even adultery was no excuse for giving up the fight, she continued, because men were instinctively promiscuous, and their lapses from grace had to be tolerated for the sake of the greater good.

Implicit in these arguments was the belief that the individual was less important than the group. Most opponents of divorce agreed that divorce was part of an unwholesome tendency toward a "dangerous individualism." Margaret Deland bewailed the absence of team play among women and Professor Lawton called frankly for the "suppression of the individual in favor of the community."[28] Samuel Dike in his Cook Lecture attributed divorce to the rising tide of individualism menacing all progressive societies, while Felix Adler as early as 1890 was tracing the whole ugly business back to Rousseau's "false democratic ideals."[29] Although, as we shall see, most leading sociologists believed in divorce, Charles A. Ellwood did not. This future president of the American Sociological Society, despite his Progressive sympathies, also attributed divorce to excessive individualism.[30] Francis Peabody, an eminent theologian and student of the Higher Criticism, believed that the family's major enemies were scientific socialism and "the reactionary force of self-interested individualism. . . ."[31]

The opponents of divorce were more varied and had much more to say than I have been able to indicate, but the foregoing gives at least some idea of who they were and what they thought. The defenders of divorce, by way of contrast, were fewer in number and easier to locate. Opinion against divorce was so widespread and diffuse that it cannot be attributed to a handful of groups, but the sentiment favoring divorce was largely confined to sociologists, liberal clergymen, and feminists. The defenders of divorce, like its enemies, viewed the problem primarily in moral and social terms. But unlike the critics of divorce, its supporters, who were with few exceptions liberals, were much more interested in the morality of divorce and more inclined to see its moral and social dimensions as too interrelated for separate discussion and analysis.

The case for divorce gained initial momentum in the 1880s and 1890s when a trickle of protest against Victorian marriage began to make itself heard. The plays of Henrik Ibsen, especially A Doll's House (1879) and Ghosts (1881), were affecting English audiences in the late 1880s and American opinion somewhat later. By the 1890s a number of Englishmen were attacking marriage and the views of Mona Caird and Grant Allen became well known in the United States through their own writings and through the publicity given their ideas by the American press. Mona Caird was a feminist whose essays appeared for the most part in high-quality limited circulation periodicals. Her most controversial proposal was an attempt to substitute for divorce short-term marriage contracts whose expiration would leave both parties free to separate or to negotiate a new contract.[32]

Grant Allen's best-known statement on the question was a sensational novel boosting feminism and free love entitled The Woman Who Did.[33] Allen was really calling for an end to marriage altogether, but his polemics against the institution supported divorce as much as free love. Within a few years the radical attack on marriage enlisted such big guns as H. G. Wells, who in a characteristically exuberant preview of the future in 1901 announced that monogamy was dissolving and sexual standards relaxing to the point where in a hundred years the present moral code "would remain nominally operative in sentiment and practice, while being practically disregarded. . . ."[34] Marriage was also under fire from the new moralists like the mystical Edward Carpenter, Havelock Ellis and his wife Edith, and the South African feminist Olive Schreiner, among others.[35]

The effect of this stream of marriage propaganda was to invigorate and inspire those Americans who believed in the right to divorce. Few respectable Americans were prepared to go as far as new moralists like Wells and Carpenter, but a substantial number of liberals were beginning to feel that traditional marriage was needlessly tyrannical and repressive, that it discriminated against women, and that divorce was not only an escape hatch for abused women but offered real opportunities for a reform of the whole marriage system. At the bottom of most, if not all, of this sentiment was the feminist impulse, for most divorce liberals were acutely conscious of the usefulness of divorce as an instrument for the emancipation of women.

Unlike the new moralists whose feminism was concerned with freeing women for a fuller sex life, the American feminist was inclined to defend divorce because it freed women from sex. Benjamin O. Flower, who edited the populistic *Arena*, called for easier divorce laws as a way of protecting women from the excessive sexual appetites of their husbands. He argued that the common prostitute was "far freer than the wife who is nightly the victim of the unholy passion of her master. . . . "[36] By 1914 this argument had become so familiar that it was thought fit for the respectable readers of the cautious *Good Housekeeping* magazine. In that year Jesse Lynch Williams, feminist and playwright, asked rhetorically, "is allowing herself to be owned body and soul by a man she loathes doing right?" before going on to delicately suggest "that seems rather like a dishonorable institution more ancient than marriage."[37]

Many feminists contended that not only did traditional marriage make women the sexual victims of their husbands, but it also exaggerated the importance of sex by denying women the chance to develop their other traits of character through work and education, and by forcing them to compete in the marriage market largely on the basis of their sexual attractions. The most desirable women had the best marital opportunities and so, through a kind of natural selection, sexuality prospered at the expense of other attributes. Divorce, along with expanded opportunities for education and employment, was a way of combatting this pernicious tendency.[38]

If the impulse to defend divorce came first from feminists who agreed with Elizabeth Cady Stanton on the need for a "larger freedom in the marriage relation," social scientists performed a crucial service in coping with the public's fear of the social consequences of divorce.[39] The first man of stature to defend divorce was Carrol Wright, U.S. Commissioner of Labor Statistics and a self-trained social scientist, who at the national Unitarian convention in 1891 boldly declared himself for liberal divorce laws. A few years later he wrote:

> The pressure for divorce finds its impetus outside of laws, outside of our institutions, outside of our theology; it springs from the rebellion of the human heart against that slavery which binds in the cruelest bonds human beings who have by their haste, their want of wisdom, or the intervention of friends, missed the divine purpose as well as the civil purpose of marriage.[40]

But it was not until 1904 that a leading professionally trained social scientist joined the fight. In his massive *A History of Matrimonial Institutions* and subsequent writings George E. Howard, an eminent historian and sociologist, tried to show how the divorce rate was the product of forces which were dramatically improving American society.[41] He argued that industrialization, urbanization, and the other pressures which were breaking up the old patriarchal family produced not only more divorces but a new kind of marriage marked by higher spiritual standards and greater freedom. Closing with the problem of individualism which so alarmed the enemies of divorce, he declared that the growing power of the state was tending to make the individual and not the family the functional unit of society and that this process not only freed the individual from familial authoritarianism but elevated the family by abolishing its coercive power and transforming it into a "spiritual and psychic association of parent and child based on persuasion."[42]

Within a few years Wright and Howard were joined by a host of social scientists including most of the leading men in the field.[43] The weight of sociological opinion was solidly on the side of divorce by 1908 when the American Sociological Society devoted its third annual meeting to the family.[44] President William G. Sumner, the crusty, aging president of the society who had done so much to establish sociology as an academic discipline, opened the proceedings by observing gloomily that "the family has to a great extent lost its position as a conservative institution and has become a field for social change."[45] The program of the convention confirmed Sumner's fears for virtually every paper described the changes affecting the family, called for more changes, or did both. Charlotte P. Gilman read a paper summarizing her *Women and Economics,* and a group of papers dealt with the damage inflicted on the family by urban, industrial life.[46]

The high point of the meeting was George Howard's "Is the Freer Granting of Divorce an Evil?" Howard repeated his now familiar views and touched off a controversy which showed the drift of professional opinion.[47] He was attacked by Samuel Dike, who insisted that divorce was produced by a dangerous individualism and the decline of ideals, and by Walter George Smith. Smith was prominent Catholic lawyer who had advocated stricter divorce laws for many years and was a leader in the campaign for uniform divorce legislation. His criticisms stressed divorce's incompatibility with orthodox religion and he accused Howard of condoning a social revolution that destroyed the divinely constituted order of things. Nothing, he declared, could alter the fact of feminine inferiority. Howard replied that marriage was a purely social institution "to be freely dealt with by men according to human needs."[48]

Despite this unusually spirited clash, Smith and his friends were making an illusory show of strength. The moralistic flavor of their language, so different in tone from Howard's, revealed their professional isolation. Theirs was the faintly anachronistic rhetoric of a discredited tradition of social criticism. The opponents of Howard's position were, moreover, all laymen with the exception of President Sumner and Albion Small, while on his side were ranged most of the speakers, including E. A. Ross, James

Lichtenberger, and other leading scientists. As a profession then, sociology was committed to a positive view of divorce at a time when virtually every other organized group in the country was opposed to it. But although heavily outnumbered, the sociologists were the only people who could claim to speak on the problem with expert authority, and in the Progressive Era expertise was coming to be highly valued. As experts, the social scientists conferred respectability on the cause of free divorce at the same time as they did much to allay public anxiety over its effects.

A final problem that remained for the divorce liberals was finding some way to weaken the general conviction that divorce was forbidden by the Bible and to diminish the impact of the clergy's opposition to divorce. It was here that the handful of liberal ministers who supported divorce performed a signal, and indeed indispensable, service. Simply by saying that divorce was a morally acceptable device, the liberal ministers endowed it with a certain degree of legitimacy. If supporting divorce with their moral prestige was the more important function performed by the liberal ministers, some went beyond this and effectively disputed the traditional charge that the Bible specifically prohibited divorce.

One of the most impressive statements of the liberal position was delivered by William G. Ballentine, classicist, Bible scholar, onetime president of Oberlin College, and for twenty years editor of the *Bibliotheca Sacra.* Ballentine argued that "even if all thoughtful Christian men were today united in a resolute purpose of conformity to the letter of Scripture the path of duty would be far from plain."[49] He pointed out that a Biblical injunction against divorce cited by Bishop Doane in a recent magazine article appeared in the same passage as the admonition to resist evil. How, he asked, were Christians to know which commandment to obey and which to ignore? Ballentine described the life of Jesus as a struggle against Talmudic literalism:

> During His whole life, He fought against the tyranny of mere words, and for the lordship of the present living spiritual man. In his discourse He suggested great truths by parables, by questions, by metaphors, by paradoxes, by hyperboles, by every device that could elude the semblance of fixed judicial formulas. It is **the** irony of history that such language should be seized upon for statute law.[50]

Other scholars, theologians, and Higher Critics attacked the presumed Biblical sanctions against divorce in different ways, but the effect of their work was to undercut the general belief that the Bible clearly forbade divorce.[51]

On a more popular level the Rev. Minot J. Savage declared that as love was the essence of marriage, two people who no longer loved each other had every reason to get divorced.[52] This same conviction informed the writings of John H. Holmes, a great civil libertarian and advocate of liberal Christianity, who believed that the passing of love destroyed marriage in fact if not in name.[53]

Gradually the climate of opinion began to change. As noted earlier there was a substantial organized opposition to divorce during the Progressive period, but despite local victories, the movement to retard divorce by legal and political means was resoundingly unsuccessful. There were other signs which demonstrated that attitudes were being modified. Samuel Dike died in 1913 and his League expired shortly thereafter. It was essentially a one-man operation, but it was supported by the enemies of divorce, whose financial contributions had declined sharply even before his death, to the point where receipts after 1910 were about half of what they had been in the 1890s.[54] The Committee on the Family which was routinely formed by the Federal Council of Churches in 1911 was singularly inactive, and in 1919 it was dropped altogether.[55]

At the same time the solid wall of opposition to divorce maintained by the nation's press was repeatedly breached. Before 1900 no important American magazine defended the right to divorce except the radical *Arena*. Articles favorable to divorce were very rare in the general press. After about 1900, however, a few bold magazines like the *Independent* endorsed the right of divorce editorially, and many more began to print occasional articles defending divorce. The *North American Review*, which was more interested in the problem than any other major periodical, began the new century with a rousing attack on the opponents of divorce by the aging but still magnificent Elizabeth Cady Stanton.[56] Other magazines, too numerous to mention, also began to print articles favoring divorce. Even the uncompromisingly hostile *Outlook* unbent to this extent, and in 1910 it conceded editorially that there were times when divorce was permissible.[57] This shift influenced popular as well as serious magazines. In 1910 the slick monthly *World's Work* announced that "The True View of Increasing Divorce" was that the divorce rate was not alarming, and that divorces should not be subject to excessive restrictions.[58]

Obviously the changes in public opinion which these articles represented did not constitute a general recognition of the desirability of divorce. Although a few journals accepted the liberal argument that divorce was a therapeutic social mechanism, most did not. In many cases nothing more was involved than the admission that there were probably two sides to the question. This of itself, however, was a form of moral relativism on the issue which would have been unthinkable in the 1890s. This new tolerance of divorce coincided with the eruption of a number of curious phenomena like the dance craze and the white slave panic which marked the onset of the revolution in morals.[59]

Divorce was a part of the complex transformation of moral values and sexual customs which was to help give the 1920s their bizarre flavor. It was not only the most visible result of this vast social upheaval, but in many ways it was the most compatible with traditional modes of thought. It was, on the whole, an orderly, public, and institutionalized process which took due account of the formal difference between right and wrong, guilt and innocence. It had the blessings of the highest soiological authorities, and it was recommended by many feminists as a cure for the brutalizing sexual indignities known to occur in some marriages. Conservatives could, therefore, more easily resign themselves to divorce than to other, more extravagant, demonstrations of the changing moral order.

Although divorce has today assumed proportions undreamed of in the Progressive Era, the nature of the American response to mass divorce was determined at that time. Between 1905, when the magnitude of divorce as a social problem had become fully apparent, and 1917, when the movement to limit or direct the spread of divorce had clearly failed, something of importance for American social history had occurred. This was the recognition by moral conservatives that they could not prevent the revolution in morals represented by mass divorce. Their failure of morale in the immediate prewar period paved the way for spectacular changes which took place after the war.

# NOTES

1. The definitive statistical study is Paul H. Jacobson, *American Marriage and Divorce* (New York, 1959). Two great government reports contain the raw materials—they are U. S. Bureau of Labor, *Marriage and Divorce 1867-1887 (1889)* and the later more comprehensive U. S. Bureau of the Census, *Marriage and Divorce 1867-1906* (1909). Interesting contemporary analyses are contained in E. A. Ross, *Changing America* (New York, 1912) and William B. Bailey, *Modern Social Conditions* (New York, 1906).

2. Its origins are described in an untitled autobiographical manuscript by Samuel Warren Dike in the Dike Papers, Library of Congress.

3. The legal and political history of divorce is described very fully in Nelson Manfred Blake, *The Road to Reno* (New York, 1962).

4. See M. A. DeWolfe Howe, *The Life and Labors of Bishop Hare* (New York, 1912), *passim*, Blake, "Divorce in South Dakota," *Nation*, IX (January 26, 1893), 61.

5. National League for the Preservation of the Family, *Some Fundamentals of the Divorce Question* (Boston, 1909). A pamphlet written by Samuel Dike and published by his organization, which had undergone two changes of name since its founding, deals with these changes at some length. They involved extending the time required to obtain divorces and limiting the causes for which they could be granted.

6. U. S. Congressional Record, 52 Cong., 1st Sess. (February 3, 1892), p. 791.

7. See Senator Shortridge's candid remarks to this effect during hearings on a similar resolution years later. *Senate Judiciary Committee*. "Hearings on S. J. Res. 31" (November 1, 1921), *passim*.

8. "Secretary's Memorandum," *Proceedings of the 26th Annual Meeting of the NCCUSL* (1916).

9. See Blake, 140-145, and *Proceedings of the Adjourned Meeting of the National Congress on Uniform Divorce Laws* (Harrisburg, Pa., 1907).

10. "The Canon on Marriage and Divorce," *Public Opinion*. October 27, 1898.

11. "Remarriage After Divorce," *Outlook*, October 22, 1904.

12. The positions of the principal denominations on divorce and the efforts to change them are summarized in James P. Lichtenberger, *Divorce: A Study in Social Causation* (New York, 1909), chap. vii.

13. Daniel Bell, "The Myth of Crime Waves" (New York, 1961), pp. 151-174.

14. Roy Lubove, "The Progressives and the Prostitute," *The Historian*, XXIV (May 1962), 308-329.

15. Generalizations of this sort which depend upon a close acquaintance with the popular literature are notoriously hard to document. My own conclusions are derived from an examination of almost everything dealing with marriage and divorce published either in book form or in more than thirty leading periodicals from 1889 through 1919. For details see my unpublished "The Divorce Crisis of the Progressive Era" (Doctor's dissertation, Berkeley, Calif., 1963).

16. By dismissing the moral side of the opposition to divorce so casually I do not mean to imply that it was not important but only that it was unremarkable and required no detailed

analysis. Divorce was considered immoral because it was forbidden by the New Testament and because it encouraged lust. Naturally the clergymen who opposed divorce supported themselves with Scriptural citations. One of the most elaborate efforts to relate divorce to licentiousness was Samuel Dike's first major address on the subject, reprinted in *Christ and Modern Thought: The Boston Monday Lectures 1880-1881*. ed. Joseph Cook (Boston, 1882).

17. "The Right to Be Divorced," *Lutheran Church Review*, XXVIII (October 1909), 661.

18. W. E. Campbell, "Wells, the Family, and the Church," *Catholic World*, XCI (July 1910), 483.

19. "The Worst Anarchism," *Outlook*, August 11, 1906, p. 826.

20. Bureau of the Census, *Marriage and Divorce 1867-1906*, p. 4.

21. *Marriage and Divorce* (New York, 1915), p. 15.

22. Henry Neumann, *Spokesmen for Ethical Religion* (Boston, 1951), deals with Adler's career at some length.

23. Rebecca Harding Davis, Rose Terry Cooke, Marion Harland, Catherine Owen, Amelia E. Barr, *North American Review*, CXLVIII (May 1889).

24. Boston, 1909.

25. Among the frequent male efforts to sentimentalize over the role and nature of woman were Lyman Abbott, *Christianity and Social Problems* (Boston, 1896) and Robert Lawton, *The Making of a Home* (Boston, 1914).

26. "The Change in the Feminine Ideal," *Atlantic Monthly*, CV (March 1910), 295; see also her interesting autobiography: *Golden Yesterdays* (New York, 1940).

27. Ibid., p. 297.

28. *The Making of a Home*, p. 594.

29. "The Ethics of Divorce," *Ethical Record*. II (April 1890), 207.

30. *Sociology and Modern Social Problems* (New York, 1913).

31. *Jesus Christ and the Social Question* (New York, 1903), p. 145.

32. *The Morality of Marriage and Other Essays on the Status and Destiny of Women*, London, 1897. A collection of articles which had previously appeared in the *North American Review*, the *Fortnightly Review*, the *Westminster Review* and the *Nineteenth Century*. Typical of the American press's treatment of her ideas are "The Millenium of Marriage—Mona Caird's Views," *Current Literature*, XVI (July 1894), reprinted from the *Boston Herald*. "The Practice of Marriage," *Current Literature*, XVIII (October 1895), reprinted from the *Saturday Review*.

33. Boston, 1895.

34. "Anticipations; An Experiment in Prophecy—II," *North American Review*, CLXXIII (July 1901), 73-74.

35. Carpenter, *Love's Coming of Age* (New York, 1911). *Little Essays of Love and Virtue* (New York, 1921), summarized the ideas Havelock Ellis had been advocating for years and the *New Horizon in Love and Life* (London, 1921), contains the thoughts of his wife, who died in 1916. Schreiner, *Woman and Labor* (New York, 1911).

36. "Prostitution Within the Marriage Bond," *Arena*, XIII (June 1895), 68

37. "The New Marriage," *Good Housekeeping*, LII (February 1914), 184.

38. Charlotte Perkins Gilman, *Women and Economics* (Boston, 1898), was an especially influential exposition of this point of view. For other information on this remarkable woman's life and work see Carl N. Degler's appreciative article, "Charlotte Perkins Gilman on the Theory and Practice of Feminism," *American Quarterly*. VIII (Spring 1956). See also Rheta Childe Dorr, *What Eight Million Women Want* (Boston, 1910), and C. Gasquoine Hartley, *The Truth About Women* (London, 1914).

39. "Divorce vs. Domestic Warfare," *Arena*, I (April 1890), 568. Alone of the great feminist leaders, Mrs. Stanton was a lifelong supporter of divorce, and in her later years it became one of her major interests. In this respect she was hardly a typical feminist, for while most divorce liberals were also feminists, they remained very much a minority within the women's movement.

40. *Outline of Practical Sociology* (New York, 1900), p. 176.

41. Chicago, 1904.

42. "Social Control and the Function of the Family," Congress of Arts and Sciences, *Proceedings*, VII (St. Louis, 1904), 701. This abbreviated summary may not bring out the markedly utopian flavor which permeated discussions on the family by liberal sociologists and feminists during the Progressive period. Indeed, they entertained hopes for the future of the family which seem fantastically imaginative by the standards of our own more somberly clinical age. This visionary strain in Progressive social thought has been underestimated by historians in recent years, especially by Richard Hofstadter, whose influential *The Age of Reform* (New York, 1955), ignores the role played by feminism and the new morality in shaping the Progressive mood.

43. So many statements were made on marriage and divorce by sociologists during these years that I can list only a few of them here. Walter F. Willcox, *The Divorce Problem* (New York, 1891), was a seminal monograph that laid the statistical base for most later studies of divorce but which was not well known outside of the profession and did not have the impact of other works which were more widely publicized. Elsie Clews Parsons, *The Family* (New York, 1906), caused a minor sensation by calling for trial marriages. Mrs. Parsons was a student of Franz Boas and the most radical of the academicians who dealt with the problem. Arthur W. Calhoun, *A Social History of the American Family, From the Civil War* (Cleveland, 1919), Vol. III, was written from an avowedly socialist point of view and is still the only comprehensive work on the history of the American family.

44. *Papers and Proceedings of the American Sociological Society*, III (Chicago, 1909).

45. Ibid., p. 15.

46. "How Home Conditions React Upon the Family," *Papers . . . of American Sociological Society*, pp. 16–29. Margaret F. Byington, "The Family in a Typical Mill Town," pp. 73–84. Edward T. Devine, "Results of the Pittsburgh Survey," pp. 85–92; Charles R. Henderson, "Are Modern Industry and City Life Unfavorable to the Family?" pp. 93–105, among others.

47. *Papers . . . of American Sociological Society*. pp. 150–160.

48. Ibid., p. 180.

49. "The Hyperbolic Teachings of Jesus," *North American Review*, CLXXIX (September 1904), 403.

50. Ibid., p. 447.

51. E.g., Ernest D. Burton, "The Biblical Teachings Concerning Divorce," *Biblical World*, XXIX (February and March 1907). Norman Jones, "Marriage and Divorce: The Letter of the Law," *North American Review*, CLXXXI (October 1905). Thomas S. Potwin, "Should Marriage Be Indissoluble?" *New Englander and Yale Review*, LVI (January 1892).

52. *Men and Women* (Boston, 1902).

53. *Marriage and Divorce* (New York, 1913).

54. *Annual Reports* of the Executive Committee of the Federal Council of Churches of Christ in America.

56. "Are Homogenous Divorce Laws in all the States Desirable?" *North American Review*, CLXX (March 1900).

57. E. R. Stevens, "Divorce in America: The Problem," *Outlook*, June 1, 1907; "Just Grounds for Divorce," November 23, 1910.

58. *World's Work*, XIX (January 1910).

59. Henry F. May, *The End of American Innocence* (New York, 1959), II, Part IV, 333, 343–344.

# SELECTED READINGS FOR PART TWO

BARNETT, JAMES H. *Divorce and the American Divorce Novel.* 1937. Reprint. New York: Russell and Russell, 1968.

DAVIS, KINGSLEY. "The American Family in Relation to Demographic Change." In *Demographic and Social Aspects of Population Growth.* Vol. 1. United States Commission on Population Growth and the American Future. Washington, D.C.: Government Printing Office, 1972, pp. 235–266.

FASS, PAULA S. *The Damned and the Beautiful: American Youth in the 1920s.* New York: Oxford University Press, 1977.

GORDON, MICHAEL, AND CHARLES BERNSTEIN. "Mate Choice and Domestic Life in the Nineteenth-Century Marriage Manual." *Journal of Marriage and the Family,* 32 (1970), 665–674.

HERMAN, SONDRA R. "Loving Courtship or the Marriage Market? The Ideal and Its Critics, 1871–1911." *American Quarterly,* 25 (1973), 235–252.

JACOBSON, PAUL H. *American Marriage and Divorce.* New York: Rinehart, 1959.

MCGOVERN, JAMES R. "The American Women's Pre-World War I Freedom in Manners and Morals." *Journal of American History,* 55 (1968), 315–333.

MAY, ELAINE T. "The Pursuit of Domestic Perfection: Marriage and Divorce in Los Angeles, 1890–1920." Diss. University of California, Los Angeles, 1975.

MEEHAN, THOMAS R. "'Not Made Out of Levity': Evolution of Divorce in Early Pennsylvania." *Pennsylvania Magazine of History and Biography,* 92 (1968), 441–464.

NORTON, SUSAN. "Marital Migration in Essex County, Massachusetts, in the Colonial and Early Federal Periods." *Journal of Marriage and the Family,* 35 (1973), 406–418.

WALLER, WILLARD, "The Rating Dating Complex," *American Sociological Review,* 2 (1937), 727–734.

WEISBERG, D. KELLY. "Under Great Temptations Heer: Women and Divorce in Puritan Massachusetts." *Feminist Studies,* 2 (1975), 183–194.

WILLCOX, WALTER. "Divorce in the United States." *Columbia University Studies in History, Economics and Public Law,* 1, No. 67 (1891).

# PART THREE |

# STAGES OF LIFE

Perhaps the single most influential book published in the field of family history since World War II has been Philippe Ariès's *Centuries of Childhood* (1962)* in which he drew attention to the fact that childhood as a life stage is a modern phenomenon. More specifically, Ariès's point is that the medieval world readily integrated children into the work and play of adults just as soon as they were no longer dependent on their nurses or mothers. Between the twelfth and seventeenth centuries the modern notion of childhood emerged. The child came to be seen as having a distinct personality, an innocence which required preservaton and a life which had to be fitted into an age-graded system supervised by a school. Although the evidence Ariès garnered in support of his thesis was sketchy, the impact of his work was substantial.

In "Infancy and Childhood in the Plymouth Colony" John Demos seems to feel that the concept of childhood in the Plymouth Colony conformed with Ariès's medieval one, since from the age of six or seven the Puritan child appears to have been incorporated into the adult world. As was the case with Ariès, Demos's evidence is far from overwhelming and relies on such externals as change in dress. More recently other historians have questioned whether there was not, in fact, greater recognition among the Puritans of the distinctiveness of childhood than Demos realized (e.g., Beales, 1975). But what we are probably dealing with here are matters of degree and emphasis. If childhood as a unique stage of life was several centuries in developing, should we not expect the settlers of seventeenth-century New England to have a foot in both worlds?

What makes Demos's work of interest is not the Ariès controversy so much as the picture he provides of central themes involved in Puritan child rearing, especially the one of breaking the child's will. This theme has led to misunderstanding about seventeenth-century child rearing and to an undue emphasis on its harshness. It might be argued that the stress on breaking the child's will should be understood in the context of a belief in original sin, with the child's willfulness being a manifestation of it which had to be extirpated to improve chances of salvation. Certainly, some might argue that given the belief in predestination this should hardly be a parental concern; nevertheless, the Puritans saw education as something which, if nothing else, might provide the "main channels through which grace could flow (Morgan, 1966:95)."

*Complete citations for works referred to are in the selected readings on p. 257.

153

"The Stages of Life, 1790–1840" is a chapter from Joseph F. Kett's book and deals with the early years of the New Republic. His conceptualization of life stages relies heavily on the idea of dependence. Adulthood is defined in terms of the degree of economic independence a young person is able to maintain and whether this is a permanent or temporary situation. Kett's ideas differ from Demos's since they deal not with the extent to which a young person was "integrated" with adult society but the extent to which he was financially autonomous. Kett argues that the period from 1790–1840 continued the colonial practice of child placement, which, while putting the child under the control of surrogate parents, still gave the child's labor some tangible value. The teen years are characterized by Kett as a period of "semi-independence." He uses this term to convey how, in contrast to their counterparts in Greven's Andover, young men at the beginning of the nineteenth century ventured from their homes to seek their fortunes. Some returned once or twice to the parental fold, and even those who left permanently usually felt that they had financial obligations to their parents that had to be honored until their majority. This obligation reflected parental responsibilities to see that their children were equipped, by skill or capital, to make their way in the world. Adolescence, then, in the sense in which we have come to understand the word, was really not a stage of life or a concept that can be meaningfully applied to the period from 1790 to 1840. Young people, aged ten to twenty-one, were not segregated from direct participation in the adult world as they are today; rather, they moved in and out of that sphere as their fortunes and, in some instances, the seasons dictated.

"Social Change and Transitions to Adulthood in Historical Perspective," by John Modell, Frank F. Furstenberg, and Theodore Hershberg complements Kett's chapter in substance, although methodologically it is a rather different brand of history. Notably, it is the only work in this volume that is a collaborative effort of two historians and a sociologist (Furstenberg). Since it is a rather technical article students should expect to have to read it slowly and carefully. In it the authors compare 1880 to 1970 in terms of a number of aspects of the transition to adulthood. In contrast to the largely biographical approach adopted by Kett to establish the fluctuation between independence and dependence that characterized the ages between ten and twenty-one in the 1790 to 1840 period, Modell, Furstenberg, and Hershberg are concerned with "the *distribution* of ages at which members of a population make a given transition." The authors use a multidimensional approach to study the transition to adulthood; that is, they look at when young people leave school, start work, marry, and establish their own households in terms of their prevalence, timing, spread, age congruity, and integration. In this way the authors are trying to investigate how certain life-stage events cohered at two different time intervals separated by almost a century. Their results indicate that in the interval between 1880 and 1970 "the process of growing up has become more prevalent, less prolonged and more concentrated then it was a century ago."

By reading this article in conjunction with Kett's we see that the state he characterized as "semi-independence" persisted in some degree throughout most of the nineteenth century. Given the fact that we have only two points in time in the Modell, Furstenberg, and Hershberg study, we cannot say when and at what rate things changed nor, for that matter, how much change occurred in the middle of the nineteenth century. Nevertheless, these two selections convey the value of considering the way in which the sequencing of certain events, such as school-leaving or marriage, change over time.

John Demos's article "Old Age in Early New England" deals with a dramatically different life stage, though the question of sequence continues to be relevant. While sociologists have been studying old age for some time, historians have only recently begun to systematically consider what constituted old age. In the process historians have forced us to reconsider some former idealized versions of what it meant to be old.

The fact that the study of old age is a new area has not prevented it from stirring up controversies. David Hackett Fischer's *Growing Old in America* (1977) called forth a scathing review by Lawrence Stone (1977) and produced a subsequent exchange between Fischer and Stone. Fischer argues that during the Colonial era the situation of the elderly, at least in terms of authority, was strengthened, but that starting about 1780 youth appeared to gain new value as gerontophobia reared its head. The elderly suffered a loss of authority although simultaneously their interpersonal relations with younger people improved. Fischer's explanation of this lies more in the ideology of the American and French revolutions than in economic changes. In addition, Fischer maintains that at the turn of the present century, old age was seen as a social problem. Stone's disagreement with Fischer is based on both interpretation and fact, though some of the points are subtle. He takes as given that the period between 1770 and 1820 in the United States was one of social revolution and that the core of this revolution was a general democratization of relationships. Such a phenomenon was bound to undermine the position of the elderly, not the exaltation of youth and the gerontophobia that Fischer argues for. In Stone's words, "I believe that Professor Fischer has seen a small part of the picture but has mistaken it for the whole . . ."

In "Old Age in Early New England" Demos acknowledges what, in many respects, is at the heart of the Fischer-Stone dispute, namely, the problem of evidence. Most of what we know about old age comes from diaries and indirect evidence such as meeting-house seating arrangements, age heaping, and so on; and this problem of evidence is particularly aggravated for aged women. For Demos, the question of when old age began is tricky, involving as it does both chronology and capacity. Those who were seen as elderly were honored for their wisdom and their spiritual quality. Yet, at the same time, the infirmities and shortcomings of the elderly were also recognized, and this evoked a certain amount of scorn and ridicule. After exploring several aspects of the situation of the elderly in colonial New England, Demos comes to the conclusion that, in terms of their ability to "command honor and respect," the elderly were well placed—largely because of their control of land and other wealth. But the elderly's situation was "psychologically disadvantageous," that is, they were not successful in gaining the empathy and affection of their own children, much less of the younger generation as a whole. Demos ends at the point of transition that fueled the Fischer/Stone controversy, but he helps us to appreciate both how complex the situation of the elderly was in colonial New England and how much more research must be done before we can assert anything about this phenomenon with any certainty.

What emerges from this section is an awareness of the extent to which students of the family have become concerned with the stages of life and how they were arranged and experienced over the course of American history. This is an area of family history which will probably experience considerable growth over the next decade.

# 9 | INFANCY AND CHILDHOOD IN THE PLYMOUTH COLONY

## JOHN DEMOS

Surely no event in the life cycle displays a greater difference between the conditions prevalent then and now than the first one—the crisis of birth itself. The usual setting, in its most general outlines, is easily imagined. Delivery would take place at home. Tradition has it that the "inner room" . . . in the familiar house plan was also known as the "borning room," in reference to its special use in times of childbirth. There the mother was brought to bed, and there presumably she remained until she and her infant child were strong enough to venture forth into the household at large. Her attendants were older women experienced in such matters and acting in the role of midwives.

In our own culture childbirth normally presents few difficulties of any magnitude; but in the seventeenth century it was quite another story. We . . . note . . . the evidence that in one out of thirty deliveries the mother would lose her life,[1] or, stated another way, that every fifth woman in the Old Colony died from causes associated with childbirth. The mortality rate for newborn infants is more difficult to determine, but one in ten would seem a reasonable guess. These figures may seem surprisingly low when set alongside more traditional notions of life in the seventeenth century; but they nonetheless describe a very real danger. And this danger must have profoundly affected the perceptions of everyone directly involved in any given delivery.

When a baby was safely past the hazards of his first few days of life, he was doubtless incorporated quickly into the ongoing routine of his household. One major public event in which he took center stage was his baptism. Usually this occurred within six months of birth,[2] and on some occasions, particularly in wintertime, it must have been quite an ordeal. Otherwise, he enjoyed a continuing round of sleep and nourishment. The matter of how and where he slept is uncertain. Wooden and wicker cradles are among the most appealing artifacts of the seventeenth century to have come down to us today; but they are not found often in the inventory lists. Perhaps some of them were too crude and of too little value to bother with in adding up a man's estate. Perhaps, too, some other kind of makeshift bed was contrived for the newborn; or possibly he would for a short period sleep alongside his parents. It does seem that within a few months he was moved elsewhere—most likely to a trundle bed, which he might share with some of his older siblings. One rather gruesome notation in the Court Records serves to illustrate this type of arrangement. A small child of "about halfe a yeer old" had been "found dead in the morning . . . lying in bed with Waitstill Elmes and Sarah Hatch, the childs sister." An official board of inquest studied the matter and concluded that "either it was stiffled by lying on its face or accidentally over layed in the bed."[3]

The infant's clothing was probably quite simple. Previous studies of this subject have turned up no evidence of swaddling or otherwise binding the child so as to restrict his movement.[4] Some type of linen smock seems to have been standard dress for seventeenth-century babies; and doubtless, too, they were frequently under several layers of woolen blankets.

The baby's nourishment consisted, it appears, entirely of breast milk. The subject is not much discussed in any documents extant today, but there are occasional, incidental references to it.[5] There is also the indirect evidence which derives from the study of birth intervals. We touched on this matter briefly in an earlier section, but it deserves a more extended statement here. In the average family, we noted, children were spaced roughly two years apart (or a bit longer near the end of the wife's child-bearing span). This pattern is consistent with a practice of breast feeding a child for about twelve months, since lactation normally presents a biological impediment to a new conception.[6] The exceptions can nearly always be explained in the same terms. When one finds an interval of only twelve or fifteen months between two particular deliveries, one also finds that the older baby died at or soon after birth. (Here there would be no period of breast feeding, to speak of, and hence nothing to delay the start of another pregnancy.)[7]

We can try to pull together these various bits of evidence bearing on infancy as customarily experienced in the Old Colony. And in doing so, we are left with the impression—no stronger word could be justified—that for his first year or so a baby had a relatively comfortable and tranquil time. The ebb and flow of domestic life must have been constantly around him: large families in small houses created an inevitable sense of intimacy. Often he must have been set close to the fireside for warmth. His clothing was light and not especially restrictive, yet the covers laid over him heightened his sense of protection. And most important, he had regular access to his mother's breast[8]—with all that this implies in the way of emotional reassurance, quite apart from the matter of sound physical nourishment. Illness was, of course, a real danger; the death rate for infants under one year seems to have been substantially higher than for any later age. But this fact may well have encouraged an attitude of particular concern and tenderness towards infants.

All such statements are highly conjectural and so too is any impression we may try to form of the subsequent phases of a child's life. Still, with this strong word of warning, it seems worth proceeding somewhat further. Let us return once again to the writings of John Robinson for a most arresting pronouncement on the requirements of the child by way of discipline: "And surely there is in all children . . . a stubborness, and stoutness of mind arising from natural pride, which must, in the first place, be broken and beaten down; that so the foundation of their education being laid in humility and tractableness, other virtues may, in their time, be built thereon . . . For the beating, and keeping down of this stubborness parents must provide carefully . . . that the children's wills and wilfulness be restrained and repressed, and that, in time; lest sooner than they imagine, the tender sprigs grow to that stiffness, that they will rather break than bow. Children should not know, if it could be kept from them, that they have a will in their own, but in their parents' keeping; neither should these words be heard from them, save by way of consent, 'I will' or 'I will not.'"[9]

Translated into the language of modern psychology this statement amounts to a blanket indictment of the child's striving toward self-assertion and particularly of any impulses of direct aggression. The terms "break" and "beat down" ("destroy" is also used further on ) seem to admit of no qualification. Robinson urged, moreover, that this sort of discipline be started very early. It had to be accorded "the first place" in a whole sequence of socialization, because until the child's inherent "stubbornness" was thoroughly restrained training in the more positive virtues would not really take hold.

Precisely what age Robinson had in mind here is not clear, but we may suspect that it was somewhere between one and two years. This, at any rate, is the period when *every* child develops the ability to assert his own will far more directly and effectively than was possible earlier. His perceptions of himself as apart from other people grow progressively sharper; his world is for the first time explicitly organized in terms of "I" and "you," "mine" and "yours." He makes rapid progress with muscular control and coordination, and thus gains new power to express all his impulses. Even today, with our much more permissive style of child rearing, the second year is a time for establishing limits and often for the direct clash of wills between parent and child.[10] In all likelihood these first raw strivings of the infant self seemed to sincere Puritans a clear manifestation of original sin—the "fruit of natural corruption and root of actual rebellion against God and man," as Robinson himself put it. Such being the case, the only appropriate response from the parents was a repressive one.

And there was more still. The second year of life was for many children bounded at either end by experiences of profound loss. Somewhere near its beginning, we have surmised, the child was likely to be weaned; and near its end the arrival of a new baby might be expected. All this would serve to heighten the crisis imposed by the crushing of the child's assertive and aggressive drives.

The pattern is striking in itself; but it gains added significance when set alongside an important theme in the *adult* life of the colonists—namely the whole atmosphere of contention, of chronic and sometimes bitter enmity, to which we have already alluded.[11] This point merits the strongest possible emphasis, because it serves to call in question some extremely venerable and widespread notions about Puritanism. It has long been assumed that the people of this time and culture were peculiarly concerned— were effectively "neurotic," if you will—about all aspects of sex. But there is now a growing body of evidence to the contrary (some of which will be examined shortly); and it might even be argued that the Puritans took sex more nearly in their stride than most later generations of Americans.[12] Perhaps, though, there was a *different* bugbear in their lives—and psyches—namely, a tight cluster of anxieties about aggression. To read the records of Plymouth, and also those of the other New England settlements, is to sense a very special sort of preoccupation with any overt acts of this character. Here, it seems, was the one area of emotional and interpersonal life about which the Puritans were most concerned, confused, conflicted.

John Robinson's thoughts are pertinent once again, right at this point. His *Works* contain a number of short essays dealing successively with each of the most basic human instincts and emotions; and the one entitled "Of Anger" stands out in a very special way. Robinson could find nothing at all to say in favor of anger—no circumstance which could ever truly justify its expression, no perspective from which its appearance was less than totally repellent. The imagery which he summoned to describe it is intensely vivid. Anger, he wrote, "God so brands, as he scarce doth any created affection"; for it "hath always evil in it." The "wrathful man" is like a "hideous monster," with "his eyes burning, his lips fumbling, his face pale, his teeth gnashing, his mouth foaming, and other parts of his body trembling, and shaking."[13]

But anger, of course, is not easily avoided: efforts to suppress it can succeed only partially and at a very considerable cost. This leads us back to the opening stages in the life of a Puritan child. If his experience was, first, a year or so of general indulgence, and then a radical turn towards severe discipline—if, in particular, his earliest efforts at self-assertion were met with a crushing counterforce—it should not be surprising to find that aggression was a theme of special potency in the culture at large. Patterns of this kind are usually mediated, to a great extent, by fundamental practices and commitments in the area of child rearing.[14] The latter create what psychologists call a "fixation." Some essential part of the child's personality becomes charged with strong feelings of guilt, anxiety, fear—and fascination. And later experiences cannot completely erase these trends.

The developmental theory of Erik Erikson, more directly applied, helps to fill out this picture: it suggests quite powerfully certain additional lines of connection between infant experience and Puritan character structure. The time between one and two years forms the second stage in Erikson's larger developmental sequence, and he joins its characteristic behaviors under the general theme of "autonomy." "This stage," he writes, "becomes decisive for the ratio between love and hate, for that between freedom of self-expression and its suppression." Further: while the goal of this stage is autonomy, its negative side—its specific vulnerability—is the possibility of lasting "shame and doubt." It is absolutely vital that the child receive support in "his wish to 'stand on his own feet' lest he be overcome by that sense of having exposed himself prematurely and foolishly which we call shame, or that secondary mistrust, that 'double-take,' which we call doubt." If a child does not get this type of support—if, indeed, his efforts to assert himself are firmly "beaten down"—then a considerable preoccupation with shame can be expected in later life as well. At just this point the evidence on the Puritans makes a striking fit; for considerations of shame (and of "face-saving"—its other side) loom very large in a number of areas of their culture. Such considerations are manifest, for example, throughout the legion of Court cases that had to do with personal disputes and rivalries. Many of these cases involved suits for slander or defamation—where the issue of public exposure, the risk of shame, was absolutely central. Moreover, when a conviction was obtained, the defendant was normally required to withdraw his slanderous statements, and to apologize for them, *in public*. Note, too, that a common punishment, for many different types of offense, was a sentence to "sit in the stocks." Presumably the bite here was the threat of general ridicule.

A second point, more briefly: Erikson contends that each of man's early stages can be fundamentally related to a particular institutional principle. And for the stage we are now discussing he cites "the principle of *law and order*, which in daily life as well as in the high courts of law apportions to each his privileges and his limitations, his obligations and his rights." Surely few people have shown as much concern for "law and order" as the Puritans.[15]

Once established in the manner outlined above, the same style of parental discipline was probably maintained with little significant change for quite a number of years. The average child made his adjustments to it and became fully absorbed into the larger pattern of domestic life. With several older siblings on hand (or younger ones to come) he attracted no special attention. What concessions may have been made to his youth, what his playthings were, and what his games—if any—there is no way of knowing. All such details are hidden from us. As noted previously, however, the fact that children were dressed like adults does seem to imply a whole attitude of mind. The young boy appeared as a miniature of his father and the young girl as a miniature of her mother. There was no idea that each generation required separate spheres of work or recreation.[16] Children learned the behavior appropriate to their sex and station by sharing in the activities of their parents. Habits of worship provide a further case in point: the whole family went to the same church service, and the young no less than the old were expected to digest the learned words that flowed from the pulpit.

Yet this picture needs one significant amendment: it probably did *not* apply to the very earliest period of childhood. There is, for example, some evidence of a distinctive type of dress for children of less than six or seven years old.[17] Until this age boys and girls seem to have been clothed alike, in a kind of long robe which opened down the front. This garment, while generally similar to the customary dress of grown women, was set off by one curious feature: a pair of ribbons hanging from the back of the shoulders. The switch from this to the "adult" style of dress was quite a symbolic step, and must have been perceived as such by the children themselves.

One other kind of material bearing on the same aspect of development comes from the contracts of apprenticeship (or just plain "service"). Many of these applied to very young children—young, that is, by the standards which we might think appropriate. Six to eight seems to have been the most common age for such arrangements in Plymouth Colony. Here, then, we find a kind of convergence of the evidence, alerting us to the likelihood that the culture attached a very special importance to this particular time of life. Further "proof" is lacking,[18] but perhaps it was now that children began to assume the role of little adults. After all, if apprentices and servants were considered able to begin to work effectively at the age of six or seven, it seems reasonable to think that the same judgment might apply to children who remained at home.

In psychological terms there is nothing surprising about any of this. Indeed the culture was reacting in an intuitive way to inherent developmental changes that are widely recognized by behavioral scientists of our own time. A substantial body of recent research on "cognitive development" treats the period from six to eight years as a vital crux. The child leaves behind the disordered and "magical" impressions that characterize his earliest years and becomes for the first time capable of "logical thinking." He begins, for example, to understand cause and effect, and other such abstract relationships.[19] Emotionally, too, there are changes of great magnitude. According to psychoanalytic theory this is the period when the child effects a massive repression of his oedipal wishes for the parent of the opposite sex. He does so, in part, by identifying with the parent of the same sex—by trying, in short, to imitate various aspects of adult behavior and style.[20] More generally, he wishes to "learn to accomplish things which one would never have thought of by oneself, things which owe their attractiveness to the very fact that they are not the product of play and fantasy but the product of reality, practicality, and logic; things which thus provide a token sense of participation in the real world of adults."[21]

Virtually all cultures accord some special recognition to this stage of development. In complex (and literate) societies like our own it is the usual time for beginning school. Among "primitive" peoples the child starts now to master "the basic skills of technology"; he learns "to handle the utensils, the tools, and the weapons used by the big people: he enters the technology of his tribe very gradually but also very directly."[22] Naturally, this too is an important kind of "instruction," which capitalizes on the child's new mental and emotional capacities.

In this respect Plymouth probably was closest to the model of the primitive cultures. The training that began at the age of six or seven was, it seems, chiefly of a "technological" kind. The boy starting to work with his father at planting or fencemending, and the girl helping her mother with cooking or spinning or candlemaking, were both learning to master "the utensils, the tools, and the weapons used by the big people." But this society was at least partially literate, and it is possible that some training of a more academic sort was also begun about now. Perhaps there was a new intensity in the religious tutelage or "catechizing" provided for children; and perhaps they began to learn the "three R's." Unfortunately, however, such questions can be raised only in a speculative way since the historical record becomes at this point quite mute.[23]

But what of education in a more formal sense? Were there no bona fide schools for the children of Plymouth? A brief answer to this question would have to be negative, at least if one thinks in overall terms for the whole of the Old Colony period. For the first forty odd years of settlement there is only indirect evidence of the intent to found schools[24] and no evidence at all of schools in actual operation. Later on, admittedly, the picture did start to change. In December of 1670, for example, John Morton appeared before the Plymouth town meeting and "proffered to teach the children and youth of the towne to Reade and write and Cast accounts on Reasonable considerations."[25] The following year he renewed his proposal and the townsmen responded with a plan to raise money "for and toward the Maintenance of the free Scoole now begun and erected."[26] Meanwhile the General Court was taking similar steps on a Colony-wide basis. A fishing excise was to be allocated to any towns that could show a school actually underway.[27] In 1673 this money was awarded to Plymouth. In 1681 it went partly to Rehoboth and partly to "Mr Ichabod Wiswalls schoole at Duxburrow." In 1683 it was distributed among five different towns: Barnstable, Duxbury, Taunton, Rehoboth, and Bristol.[28]

Thus the trend in these later years was generally in the direction of increased facilities for formal schooling. Yet not until long afterward—well into the eighteenth century—would it produce a really firm and widespread system. The town of Plymouth itself can be cited to illustrate the point. Its achievement in starting a school during the 1670s was apparently not sustained, for two decades later its citizens repeatedly went on record with directives that the selectmen "should Indeavor to get A schoolmaster to teach Children to Reade and write."[29] Education under these conditions was definitely a sometime thing.

The whole subject of education in the American colonies was somewhat misconceived until a fascinating essay by Bernard Bailyn (published in 1960) supplied a new and much more meaningful focus.[30] Bailyn was the first to point out that formal schools constituted only a small part of the total educational process, at least with the first generations of settlers. Indeed, they formed a kind of appendage to other, far more important and more comprehensive agencies: the church, the community at large, and above all the family itself. This situation was to change radically before the end of the colonial period, owing to the corrosive effects of the New World environment on Old World habits and institutions. By the time of the Revolution the web of connections between family, church, and community was irrevocably broken, and schools were increasingly called upon to fill a part of the resultant social void.

But only the first part of Bailyn's story seems relevant to Plymouth Colony. To be sure, there were certain glimmerings of the cultural disruption to which he ascribes such importance; and near the end of the Colony's lifetime the process of institutionalizing education, the proliferation of schools, was clearly under way. But for most children of this period and place the major kinds of learning occurred at home. Here, in the context of the total household environment, values, manners, literacy, vocation were all transmitted from one generation to the next. The process was none the less real for being only partly conscious.

## NOTES

1. *A Little Commonwealth: Family Life in the Plymouth Colony*, by John Demos (New York: Oxford University Press, 1970), p. 66

2. Such at least is the impression one gains from examining the vital records of the Old Colony towns. In a considerable number of cases the records show both a date of birth and a date of baptism.

3. *Records of the Colony of New Plymouth, in New England,* ed. Nathaniel B. Shurtleff and David Pulsifer (Boston, 1855–1861), VI, 45.

4. My authority in this matter is Earle, *Child Life in Colonial Days,* 21 ff., 34 ff.

5. For example, Lidia Standish, testifying in connection with a trial for fornication, spoke of herself as "a mother of many children my selfe and have Nursed many." Ms. deposition, in the "Davis Scrapbooks," Ill, 12, at Pilgrim Hall, Plymouth, Mass.

6. On the question of the relationship between lactation and fertility, see Robert G. Potter et al., "Application of Field Studies to Research on the Physiology of Human Reproduction," in *Journal of Chronic Diseases,* XVIII (1965), 1125–1140.

7. There is one alternative explanation for these data which must at least be considered. It is just possible that the settlers maintained a taboo against sexual relations between husband and wife whenever the latter was nursing a child. A custom of this type has been noted among *many* preindustrial peoples in the world today. (For example: the Ojibwa and the Jivaro, among American Indian tribes; the Nuer, the Fang, and the Yoruba, all of Africa; the Trobriands and Samoans, in Oceania.) Specific documentation can be obtained by consulting the appropriate category (#853) in the Human Relations Area File. There is no evidence for such a practice in any European culture of the seventeenth century; but this is not the kind of thing that would likely show up either in written comment from the period or in secondary works by modern historians.

8. Admittedly, to put it this way skirts one very important question: what *sort* of feeding schedule the infant experiences. It makes considerable difference, of course, both for his immediate comfort and for his later development whether (1) he can obtain the breast simply by crying out for it, or (2) his mother adheres to a firm timetable of feedings at fixed intervals, regardless of his own demands. But there is simply no way of ascertaining what was the usual practice in Plymouth Colony.

9. *The Works of John Robinson,* ed. Robert Ashton (Boston, 1851), I, 246–247.

10. These few sentences represent the briefest summary of a huge psychological literature. For a useful introduction to this literature, see Paul H. Mussen, John J. Conger, and Jerome Kagan, *Child Development and Personality* (New York, 2nd ed., 1963), ch. 7. The same overall viewpoint is apparent in a number of popular books as well—most notably, perhaps, in Dr. Benjamin Spock's famous *Baby and Child Care* (New York, 1945). And finally I would like to acknowledge a special debt in this connection to Alison Demos, age twenty-one months, for a vivid *personal* demonstration of "autonomy" and related themes. Any parent of a child about this age will know what I mean.

11. Demos, *op. cit.,* p. 49.

12. The only useful study of this matter is Edmund Morgan, "The Puritans and Sex," *New England Quarterly,* XV (1942), 591–607.

13. *The Works of John Robinson* I, 226.

14. There is an enormous literature in anthropology, tending to bear out this point of view. And among anthropologists it is particularly associated with the work of the so-called "culture and personality" school. See, for example, Abram Kardiner, *The Psychological Frontiers of Society* (New York, 1945).

15. The material contained in these two paragraphs is drawn particularly from Erik Erikson, *Identity and the Life Cycle* (New York, 1959), 65–74. Re "shame" in Puritan child rearing, note the following attributed to John Ward in Cotton Mather, *Magnalia Christi Americana* (Hartford, 1853), I, 522: "Of young persons he would himself give this advice: 'Whatever you do, be sure to maintain shame in them; for if that be once gone, there is no hope that they'll ever come to good.'" I am indebted to Nancy Falik for bringing this passage to my attention.

16. A word of caution must be entered here. It is quite possible that certain tasks around the house or farm were normally left to children—that, in short, there was some notion of "children's work." No concrete evidence survives; but if this was the case, it would indicate at least a limited recognition of difference between the child and the adult. Still, the basic lines of contrast relative to the pattern prevalent in our own period remain firm.

17. Earle, *Child Life in Colonial Days,* 41, 44. And, for an extended discussion of the same practice in Europe at this time, see Philippe Aries, *Centuries of Childhood.* trans. Robert Baldick (New York, 1962), ch. 3.

18. Perhaps, though, there is a relevant datum in the Court's handling of bastardy cases. The usual practice was to oblige the father of an illegitimate child to pay a certain sum each week for maintenance, over a period of six or seven years. What would happen *after* this time is never indicated, but possibly it was felt that the child would then be able to earn his own keep, either in helping his mother and her family or in being "put out" to some foster family. See, for example, the case of Rebecca Littlefield vs. Israel Woodcock, *Plymouth Colony Records*, V, 161; and that of Elizabeth Woodward vs. Robert Stedson, *ibid.*, V, 181. Edmund Morgan, in *The Puritan Family* (New York, 1966), 66, calls attention to a statement by John Cotton that is also interesting in this connection. Cotton believed that it was perfectly normal for very young children to "spend much time in pastime and play, for their bodyes are too weak to labour, and their mind to study are too shallow . . . even the first seven years are spent in pastime, and God looks not much at it."

19. This is a central theme in many studies of cognitive psychology; but it is associated, above all, with the work of Jean Piaget. See, for example, Barbel Inhelder and Jean Piaget. *The Growth of Logical Thinking from Childhood to Adolescence*, trans. Anne Parsons and Stanley Milgram (New York, 1958).

20. Of course, the Oedipus complex has an absolutely central place in the whole psychoanalytic scheme, and the writings which deal with it are legion. But for a good short summary, see Otto Fenichel, *The Psychoanalytic Theory of Neurosis* (New York, 1945), chs. V, VI.

21. Erikson, *Identity and the Life Cycle*, 84.

22. Ibid., 83.

23. Or at least there is no evidence for Plymouth. The case seems otherwise for Massachusetts Bay. Morgan's *Puritan Family*. 96 ff., quotes some interesting statements by various Massachusetts clergymen on the subject of the religious instruction of the child. The statements imply a rather limited and fragmentary approach to the youngest children, followed later on by a switch to a more intense and systematic program. They do not indicate the precise age at which this switch was appropriate, but one is tempted to make a guess of six or seven. And what was true of the one Puritan colony was likely also to be true of its Puritan neighbor, Plymouth.

24. The Marshfield Town Records show that at a meeting in 1645 there was discussion of a proposal to raise money "for one to teach school." Ms. collections, Clerk's Office, Marshfield, Mass. See also John A. Goodwin, *The Pilgrim Republic* (Boston, 1888), 494–495. Goodwin cites some early indications of an intent to found schools which I have not been able to trace.

25. *Records of the Town of Plymouth* (Plymouth, 1889), I, 115.

26. Ibid., 124.

27. *Plymouth Colony Records*, V, 107–108.

28. Ibid., 108; VI, 81; VI, 102–103.

29. *Records of the Town of Plymouth*, I, 224, 245.

30. Bernard Bailyn, *Education in the Forming of American Society* (Chapel Hill, N.C., 1960).

# 10 | THE STAGES OF LIFE

## JOSEPH F. KETT

### THE LANGUAGE OF AGE

In preindustrial America the language of age had a nebulous quality. The term "infancy," for example, did not refer to suckling babes but the years of maternal control over the child. Infant schools, popular in the 1820s and 1830s, accepted those from eighteen months to six years of age. "Childhood" also had a broad connotation, often applying to anyone under eighteen or even twenty-one. A revivalist in the 1790s remarked that "young children" aged seven to sixteen had shown signs of religious change. An educator declared in 1819 that the Pestalozzian system of education was best suited to "young children" between the ages of six and sixteen. Isaac Ray, the psychologist, described the period between six and thirteen as "the first few years of childhood." Words like "youth," "young people" and "young men" had a similarly broad extension. Alvan Hyde still described himself as a youth at the age of twenty-four. William Gilmore Simms, in his biography of Nathanael Greene, extended his subject's wild and heady youth up to Greene's marriage at the age of thirty-two, although Green had been elected to the Rhode Island general assembly while still in his twenties. Cotton Mather distinguished only three age groups: children, young men, and old men.[1]

Expressions of age were not only broad but also interchangeable. In some of his sermons Cotton Mather equated "young people" with "children," in others with "young men." John Comly related that during the winter of 1780 he had often been carried to school "by a large boy, or young man, who lived with my father." Perhaps Comly's indifference to more precise terminology reflected his own education, for his approved reading prior to his eleventh birthday was a magazine called *The Young Man's Companion*. Confusion about age and levels of psychological development also applied to the content of children's literature. An issue of *Every Youth's Gazette* in 1842 contained a pedantic lecture on the role of the affections in learning followed by the story of Little Red Riding Hood.[2]

This nebulous language of age might suggest that contemporaries, while able to distinguish a seven year old and a seventeen year old, viewed such differences as unimportant and, as a corollary, were unfamiliar with any distinctive experiences that would mark youth as an intermediate stage of development between childhood and adulthood. In this view, "youth" was merely a word, interchangeable with other words, to describe the growing child. Yet such a conclusion would be misleading for several reasons.

Although contemporaries did not consistently assign a specific age range to youth, they often made distinctions between age groups. In seventeenth-century Massachusetts, for example, boys aged seven and over were separated from those younger by a variety of methods, including a prohibition against sleeping with their sisters and female servants, while special provisions existed for the military instruction of boys aged ten to sixteen. In these cases, consistent verbal distinctions between childhood and youth did not accompany practical distinctions between age groups. In other cases, those who made clear verbal and conceptual distinctions between childhood and youth did not specify the age range appropriate to each. Without mentioning chronological age, David Barnes devoted part of his 1796 address to the trustees of Derby Academy to the importance of adjusting subject matter and instructional methods to the different needs of children and youth.[3] In still other cases, verbal distinctions harmonized with distinctions between age groups. Describing the age and sex distribution of converts in the religious revivals of the 1790s and early 1800s, ministers consistently distinguished between children and "young people," usually equating the latter with the age group between twelve and twenty-two or twenty-three.[4] Moralists, in addition, often spoke of a "critical" period of youth between the ages of fourteen and twenty-one (or, at times, twenty-five).[5] Just as distinctions between children and youth were drawn, so too were they made between youth and adults. For penal purposes Roman law distinguished not only *infantia* (birth to six) and *pueritia* (seven to thirteen) but also *pubertas* (fourteen to twenty) and adulthood. In addition, the common law principle *malitia supplet aetatem* (in effect, malicious intent is more important than age) gave juries both in Britain and America an element of discretion in dealing with teenage offenders.[6]

Inasmuch as distinctions between children, youths, and adults were made, what did the often slack quality of the language of age signify? In part, it reflected the fact that many people in preindustrial society did not know their own exact age, much less those of acquaintances, friends, and relatives. In agricultural communities physical size, and hence capacity for work, was more important than chronological age, a fact which explains the popularity of terms like "large boy" or "great boy." During the Revolutionary War a committee declined to administer an oath of allegiance to William Akerly, "being a Lad of about fifteen years of age." Increase Mather, as well educated as any Puritan minister, precisely stated his brother's age at death, but his statement was off by three years.[7] In part, a loose vocabulary of age underscored the broad range of ages in most peer groups and institutions. Late eighteenth-century colleges, for example, often included young men of twenty-five as well as boys of fourteen, a fact which discouraged precision in the language of age without altering the status of the college as an institution for "youth." Finally, the vocabulary of age reflected an underlying indefiniteness in the timing of life experiences. In the absence of set ages for leaving home or going to school or starting out in a profession or vocation, terms designated different statuses which individuals passed into and out of at varying times. "Young people," for example, signified a village cohort. In the 1740s, Ebenezer Parkman, a Massachusetts minister, recorded in his diary that he "warmly inveighed against the Libertys allowed to Young People."[8] As late as the 1890s the same term appeared in the titles of various adult-sponsored institutions for youth, such as the Young People's Society for

Christian Endeavor. In the early nineteenth century "youth" increasingly connoted independent status away from home. A seventeen year old who still followed the plow was a "large boy" at work and a "young person" at play, but a fourteen year old who had gone off to an urban countinghouse was a "youth" or "young man" (terms often used interchangeably).

The overlap of terms is revealing and important in itself, but also frustrating for the historian who seeks to describe patterns of experience among young people in the past. Any attempt to get beyond an enumeration of curious happenings runs into the problem of radical divergence between and among individuals. What "patterns" were there in the life of a John Levy, born in the West Indies in 1797, who was bound out as a carpenter's apprentice, became a sailor, was robbed by pirates, was impressed into the British Navy, and then deserted, went into business for himself selling crockery on the Isle of Man, and finally made his way to Boston, all before the age of twenty? Where does one fit William Otter, born in Yorkshire in 1789, who by age sixteen had run away from home after a brutal beating by his father, signed onto a merchant ship going to Greenland, been shipwrecked, been impressed into the British Navy, deserted, returned home to find that his parents had gone to America, and smuggled himself to New York on an American merchant ship, finally becoming an apprentice?[9]

Perhaps such instances were exceptions, but exceptions to what? And why need they have been so exceptional? Shipwrecks were not unusual, and impressment was a time-honored practice of the British Navy. Boys often ran away from home after quarrels with their parents; those who did would have little way of knowing whether their parents would still be there on return. Early nineteenth-century society could exert about as much control over the comings and goings of young people as over epidemics or business cycles—which is to say, not much. Just as the age grading of the experiences of young people in our society makes it possible to apply horizontal concepts such as adolescence to, say, all fourteen year olds, radical differences among youth in the past render numerical age a poor guide to stages of development. Rather, it is preferable to begin with the types of status—dependency, semidependency, and independence—which different individuals passed through at varying ages. These terms did not correspond to our own stages of development, such as childhood, adolescence, and adulthood. Dependency in the early nineteenth century was briefer than our own period of childhood, while semidependency lasted longer than does present-day adolescence and possessed fundamentally different characteristics.

## FROM DEPENDENCE TO SEMIDEPENDENCE

Total dependence, or complete reliance on parents for financial support without the compensatory performance of serious labor, began at birth and usually ended before puberty. Until he or she was big enough, a child could scarcely perform useful labor on a farm. More hindrance than help, children were placed under the care of females, their mother or older sisters. Not only were families in the early 1800s larger than now, but the age range within families was greater. A child of five was likely to have older siblings, often much older siblings. Female influence extended to educational experiences as well, for in rural areas district schools had summer sessions, taught by women and attended by boys and girls under seven and by girls over seven during the busy months of planting, haying and harvesting.[10]

While female influence was the norm during the years of "infancy," exceptions occurred, especially in the case of orphans. To be orphaned by the death of either or both parents was a much more common experience then than now, not only because of primitive medical care but also because of the way in which births were spaced. Today, parents usually have their children within the span of a few years, but in 1800 a father who began to have children at twenty-five might not cease until he was forty-five or older. As a matter of statistical probability, the father would be dead before the youngest children reached maturity. The same applied to mothers. What the twentieth century has considered to be the "typical" life cycle of a woman—survival at least until her youngest children reach maturity—was untypical in the first half of the nineteenth century, occurring in only about 20 percent of the cases. Institutional care for orphans, although becoming more available after 1820, was still the exception. Orphaned children were more often sent to live with relatives, older siblings, or uncles and aunts. This was true even when one parent remained alive; a mother with three or four children could not always carry on by herself.[11]

Shocks caused by the sudden death of a parent differed in degree but not in kind from the other dislocations of families which were so common as to be almost normal in the early nineteenth century. Dependence on female influence did not mean that the experience of "infancy" was secure or stable. The need to find work or cheaper housing often propelled whole families into move after move. Alongside the well-documented westward migrations of the period, historians have more recently pointed to the constant swirling of population around settled areas in the East, with even large cities often little more than funnels for people heading in new and different directions.[12] Contemporaries were well aware of their peripatetic habits. As a biographer of the Universalist clergyman and author E. H. Chapin wrote: "The youthful days of Chapin were spent in various towns, wherever his father could gain employment in his profession [medicine]. He knew not the full worth of homestead, but only of the boarding and tenement house."[13] The childhood diary of Emily Chubbock is replete with instances of sudden and desperate moves by her family, as she and her parents sought to stave off pauperism in rural New York during the 1820s.[14] As a young diarist wrote in 1820:

> The time has come when I must leave this place where I have been residing, for a time to pursue my studies, under the tuition of Mr. M. Hallock. This is just according to the course of the world. We reside in one place a short time, and then leave it—*then* in another a while, and then leave *that*.[15]

For many children infancy was the last as well as the first stage of life. In Bedford, Massachusetts, between 1808 and 1822 more deaths occurred among those four and under than among those five through twenty-nine;

as many died four and under as from forty through sixty-nine. In Edgartown, Massachusetts, between 1780 and 1793 almost as many died aged four and under as from thirty through sixty-nine.[16]

If we define infancy as the period in which feminine control was paramount, its end would have come when a child began to perform serious farm labor during the summer months. Thereafter a child was likely to attend school, if at all, only in the winter months. Just as summer sessions were taught by women and attended by small boys and by girls of varying ages, winter sessions of district schools were taught by men and attended by girls and older boys. This transition usually took place between ages six and twelve, with the timing conditioned by a host of factors, including size of the farm, the presence or absence of older siblings to help with work, and the health of one's father. Verbal references suggest that the change often occurred between ten and twelve, at least among children of landowners. Elias Smith said that in late eighteenth-century Connecticut, boys were kept at home for farm work in the summer after age eleven or twelve; Samuel A. Foot began to work on his father's farm when he was ten years old, but added that this was earlier than most of the boys in his neighborhood and attributable to his father's failing health.[17] Maternal associations, organized in a number of eastern cities and towns in the 1820s and 1830s for the exchange of childrearing advice and mutual encouragement, explicitly defined their scope as the first ten years of life and assumed that older children would be principally under male control.[18] A few communities characterized by tight control over their members and by more or less rigid age groupings among dependents used twelve as a critical age in determining work assignments. In North Carolina the Moravians had separate categories for small and large boys, with those aged twelve to eighteen classed as large boys and expected to perform heavy labor.[19] At John Humphrey Noyes's Oneida Community, children between two and ten or eleven lived in a separate building, while boys aged twelve to seventeen and girls ten and over were "considered as having graduated from the Children's Department" and were organized separately for purposes of work and religious instruction.[20]

Drawn from various times and places, evidence of this sort is suggestive rather than conclusive and, in any event, says little about the amount of labor performed by a working child. In his influential study of French family life, Philippe Ariès claims that children in medieval France were incorporated fully into the work force at around the age of seven, an assertion that some historians have greeted skeptically. Our evidence indicates that in early nineteenth-century America, entrance into the labor force occurred as a rule after the age of seven but before puberty. "Full" incorporation, moreover, probably occurred around the time of puberty—that is, at fifteen or sixteen, when a boy was judged physically able to carry a man's work load. Prior to the middle of the nineteenth century, contemporaries associated puberty with rising power and energy rather than with the onset of an awkward and vulnerable stage of life which would later become known as adolescence. Census classifications also underscored the importance attached to the age of fifteen or sixteen, for after 1740 censuses generally distinguished those under sixteen, the "dependent" ages, from those between sixteen and sixty, the "productive" ages.[21]

Since children entered the work force in stages, it is not surprising that contemporaries customarily distinguished infancy, boyhood, and young manhood. A second measure of passage out of infancy, the commencement of departures from home, points toward a similar conclusion. Nineteenth-century lithographs depicted the act of leaving home as a single and irrevocable event, with the young man disappearing into the mist and out of range of the muffled cries of grieving parents. Yet sporadic home leaving, a pattern of departures for brief periods followed by returns to home, antedated the final departure by several years. As far back as the seventeenth century, colonial parents had placed children in the homes of neighbors, relatives, and even strangers.[22]

Various reasons lay behind the practice. Sometimes a child might be sent for tutorial purposes to live as a boarder in the house of a minister or lawyer. Ezra Stiles Gannett, a grandson of the Yale president, was sent to live and to study with a minister at age eight.[23] Educated people often took in a number of boys and conducted "family boarding schools."[24] But education was not always or even principally the motive, for educated people such as ministers placed their own children out in families. The diary of Ebenezer Parkman provides a running commentary on the difficulties an attentive father might encounter in trying to place out an incorrigible son. In April, 1747, Parkman sent his son Thomas to live with a Mr. Emms of Boston; but by June, Parkman was forced to relate that "my hopes [are] all blasted representing his living with Mr. Emms, who is discouraged and throws up."[25] Whatever the exact nature of Emms's discomfiture, this was not the end of Parkman's woes, for a year later he again confided in his diary that another master had sent Thomas back home in disgust.

Although placing a child out might have educational advantages, the motives often lay in another direction. The older and larger a child, the more space and food he took up, and the greater the economic incentive to send him to live elsewhere. This was especially true where there were younger children who, in effect, pushed the older ones out. James R. Newhall, whose father was a widower with six children, was sent at eleven to live with an uncle in Marblehead, Massachusetts, as a "boy of all work," a common expression which connoted running errands, chopping wood, drawing water, and, in the country, leading cows to pasturage. Children placed out in this way were servants rather than apprentices, for they were not yet learning a particular trade. Their work involved making themselves generally useful but not learning the intricacies of a craft. Of course, the time of apprentices was often taken up by the same sort of busywork, but the usual age of apprenticeship was fourteen, with variations as likely to be up as down the age ladder, while the boy of all work was likely to be between seven and fourteen.[26]

A second form of home leaving was for a young person to go out on a seasonal basis in search of work or perhaps advanced education. In the case of landowning farmers, winter was the preferred season to allow a boy to leave. "Farmers spared their boys in the winter," Octavius B. Frothingham wrote, "reckoning that their labor was about equivalent to their board; but in the summer, if they went away from home while under age, they must pay the labor of a substitute."[27] At times this arrangement endured even after the attainment of majority. When Theodore Parker left home for the final time at twenty-three, he hired a cousin to work for his father.[28] The winter occupations of young people who left home on a seasonal basis were varied, ranging from lumbering and construction to schoolteaching and school attendance. Edgar J. Sherman, in a pattern duplicated by countless New England and southern boys in the early nineteenth century, attended district school in his hometown in the winter, went to an academy in Vermont in the spring, and worked on his father's farm in the summer.

The fact that this seasonal pattern of home leaving and homecoming extended to education as well as work can be grasped more firmly by an examination of the academies, the distinctive educational innovation of late eighteenth-century America. Academies ranged from established, incorporated academies such as Andover, Exeter, Leicester, and Worcester to unincorporated and often ephemeral institutions whose "appointments" amounted to a room over a shoe store. One feature common to virtually all academies, however, was a broad range of ages. At Exeter in 1812, for example, the age range was ten to twenty-eight; at an academy in Hampton, New Hampshire, in 1811 it was eight to twenty-two. The spread at New Ipswich, in New Hampshire, was almost as broad, as Table 1 shows.[30]

**Table 1.** AGES OF STUDENTS AT NEW IPSWICH ACADEMY, 1831

| Age | 12 | 13 | 14 | 15 | 16 | 17 | 18 | 19 | 20 | 21 | 22 | 23 | 24 | 25 |
|---|---|---|---|---|---|---|---|---|---|---|---|---|---|---|
| Number | 1 | 1 | 1 | 1 | 2 | 3 | 1 | 1 | 2 | 2 | 3 | 1 | 0 | 1 |

The broad age span common to most academies was not the result of prolonged education but of a combination of late starts and random attendance stretched out over a number of years, with sizable gaps between sessions attended and with attendance in a given year rarely embracing more than a month or two. Although some academies published graded curriculum sequences covering three or four years, few students appear to have remained long enough in a given academy to have benefited from whatever advantages such sequences offered. The low level of persistence from term to term is indicated by the records of Pinkerton Academy for the academic year 1850–1851. Of thirty male students enrolled in the winter term, only ten were still in attendance in the spring term, while thirteen of the original thirty reenrolled in the fall of 1851. In 1862–1863 at Leicester Academy, seventeen of the thirty-five students enrolled originally in the fall term reenrolled in the winter.[31]

All other considerations aside, the ease with which seasonal labor patterns could be combined with academy attendance contributed to the latter's popularity. The academy provided, in other words, a form of seasonal education to complement seasonal labor patterns in preindustrial American society. Not surprisingly, academies were popular, although their evanescent and protean character prevents precise statements about enrollment. Bernard Bailyn has suggested that Henry Barnard's estimate—6,085 academies served by 12,260 teachers and enrolling over a quarter of a million students in 1850—was probably an understatement. Bailyn's suggestion is reinforced by the fact that Alexander Inglis counted

640 academies in Massachusetts in 1860, only a decade after Barnard had put the total at 400.[32]

The expenses connected with education at academies were modest. For an incorporated academy, tuition rarely ran to more than $4.50 for an eleven week term for the classical course and $3.50 for the English course. The same institution estimated board at $1.17 a week and room at $1 to $3 a week, depending on quality. Taking the higher of each optional figure, but excluding travel and entertainment, the cost per term was a little under $50. At unincorporated academies the costs were probably even lower. Furthermore, the seasonal quality of education at academies made it possible for students to earn money to defray expenses. Students could also easily find employment while in attendance. Academies were not boarding schools; rather, students lived in licensed dwellings in the town and could earn money in their free time. Young George Moore, for example, worked as a court clerk and took an active part in town affairs while studying at Concord Academy in the 1820s.[33]

Nevertheless, there were limits to the academies' appeal. The very looseness of structure which made academies accessible led many young men to despair of ever obtaining a thorough education at institutions that simultaneously embraced remedial, preparatory, and terminal education. Further, modest as they were, the costs of academy education were enough to deter unskilled laborers or poor farmers from sending their children. Academies were truly "colleges of the middling classes," but "middling" here means not the dead center of the income spectrum in antebellum America but the children of substantial farmers, professional men, and artisans.[34]

Analogies existed, however, between the seasonal quality of academy attendance and the educational experiences of boys and girls who for one reason or another, never went beyond primary school. Although attendance at academies fluctuated from term to term, in district schools it fluctuated from day to day and hour to hour. George Moore's diary indicates why schoolmasters in rural areas did not complain heatedly about truancy. The idea of truancy presupposes an anterior concept of normal attendance, and the latter could not exist as long as students drifted in and out of school at random, at virtually any hour of the morning or afternoon. Moore had only the haziest idea of which scholars "belonged" to his school until several weeks into the term. The age range of students in district schools was also broad. Contemporaries said that it ran from infancy to manhood. One day in 1828, Moore recorded the ages of all of his pupils at Acton, Massachusetts, so that "I may see what will become of them hereafter."[35] (See Table 2.)

In Moore's school, girls were as likely as boys to attend between ages seven and twelve; girls began younger but were less likely to be found in school in their late teens. Nearly half the boys were fifteen or over, but less than a quarter of the girls. Contemporary accounts of district school life suggest that Moore's snapshot of his school was representative of conditions elsewhere in the 1820s and 1830s. Complaints about the tendency of girls to conclude their schooling at fifteen or sixteen were as common as laments about the number of "large boys" of sixteen or seventeen and young

**Table 2.** AGE RANGE OF PUPILS AT ACTON DISTRICT SCHOOL, MARCH 28, 1828
*Boys*

| Age | 6 | 7 | 8 | 9 | 10 | 11 | 12 | 13 | 14 | 15 | 16 | 17 | 18 | 19 | 20 |
| --- | --- | --- | --- | --- | --- | --- | --- | --- | --- | --- | --- | --- | --- | --- | --- |
| Number | 2 | 2 | 1 | 4 | 3 | 3 | 0 | 2 | 2 | 5 | 1 | 4 | 5 | 1 | 1 |

*Girls*

| Age | 4 | 5 | 6 | 7 | 8 | 9 | 10 | 11 | 12 | 13 | 14 | 15 | 16 | 17 | 18 |
| --- | --- | --- | --- | --- | --- | --- | --- | --- | --- | --- | --- | --- | --- | --- | --- |
| Number | 1 | 1 | 1 | 8 | 2 | 3 | 2 | 4 | 1 | 1 | 2 | 4 | 0 | 3 | 1 |

men of eighteen or twenty in district schools.[36] But for either sex, education in district schools beyond age twelve was an extensive rather than intensive experience, with school taking up a few weeks or perhaps months each winter, for winter after winter. Further, students still attending district schools at eighteen or twenty were not the ones with advantages of birth or wealth. The duration of seasonal schooling varied from youth to youth, but was almost negatively correlated with social class. The son of a merchant was likely to have finished his "literary" education in an academy or family boarding school at fourteen or fifteen, but the plowboy with few prospects might stay around the district school till eighteen or nineteen.[37] In a general way, the same was true of college students, among whom the age range was likely to run from the middle teens to the middle twenties; those graduated from college at twenty-five rather than at eighteen were likely to be young men who did not begin any serious literary or classical education until the approach of majority because their teen years were taken up by farming. Broadly speaking, the higher a young man's social status, the faster he would move through his preparatory period and the sooner he would "get out into life" (see pp. 183–184).

To talk about getting out into life or starting in life made sense only for young men who were going somewhere, who had aspirations beyond farm service. But what about children of poor families? In the late nineteenth century it became fashionable to portray preindustrial American society as a time when wealth and luxury had not yet raised up classes. In industrial and urban America in the 1880s and 1890s, class distinctions were highly visible and were reinforced by residential segregation and strife between capital and labor. In preindustrial America class gradations were probably less visible, but they were no less sharp. Because mortality was higher among the poor, the disruption of families by the death of parents was more common. Because poor fathers owned no land or very little land, they were unable to utilize directly the labor of their children. Thus, while poor children remained dependent, parents had little incentive to keep them at home. As soon as these children were able to work, they had to leave home to find it.[38]

The autobiography of Asa Sheldon casts light on the nature of dependency in poor agricultural families in the early part of the nineteenth century. Born in 1788, Sheldon was a farmer who spent his life in the area of Wilmington, Massachusetts. At the age of seven he began to hire himself out for short periods:

When 7 years of age, I made a contract with Clark and Epps, of Lyndboro, N. H., and Col. Flint of North Reading, drovers, to drive their cattle and sheep from our house to Jerre Upton's tavern, two miles distant, that they might ride ahead and take breakfast while I drove them on, for four coppers each trip, which occurred weekly.[39]

The same pattern continued for the next few years. In the spring of 1796, Asa was employed by local farmers to drive oxen to plow at a shilling a day. A year later a Mr. David Parker came to Sheldon's house "to get a boy to live with him" and selected Asa. "because he is the youngest."[40] Sheldon called this his first home leaving, "an important event in the history of a youth." Sheldon also suggested by implication the reason for his parents' consent to Parker's request:

My father owning but a few acres of land, worked much of his time stoning wells and cellars, and consequently was with his family but little. Generally working in Salem, we saw but little of him, except on the Sabbath.[41]

If this laconic comment suggests that rural families might not have been such tightly knit units as some historians have claimed, it also underscores the earlier suggestion that departures from home at early ages, under twelve or thirteen, were often responses to economic necessity; by eight or nine years of age Asa would be of little use to his father but a burden on his mother.

After working from his ninth to thirteenth year as a servant to Parker, Sheldon was formally bound to Parker by his father. Sheldon's father was to receive $20 from Parker, and Asa was to receive $100 at age 21. As an apprentice, Asa had an element of freedom hitherto missing in his working arrangements. Following the common practice not only of farm servants but also of sons living at home, Asa often performed "stints" or extra work in return for cash rewards or free time. More complete freedom came at fifteen when Asa, increasingly at odds with the domineering Parker, walked out on his indenture, citing as his justification the recent death of his father. Now it was Parker's turn to bargain, for if Asa is to be believed, Parker soon missed the boy's strong back and willing spirit. Parker journeyed to Sheldon's home, now managed by Asa's mother, and persuaded Asa to return, but only after agreeing to sign a contract raising the latter's cash reward at attainment of majority to $200, while adding the promise of a new suit of clothes and a month's education each winter. Asa's troubles with Parker were not at an end, however, for the latter soon reverted to his despotic ways. In protest, Asa hired himself out part-time to another farmer. Technically still bound to Parker and, in fact, forced to return the agreed-on suit of clothes each Sunday night after meeting, Sheldon now had attained a further measure of freedom within the general context of semidependency. Shortly thereafter, now with Asa in his late teens, he walked out on all obligations to Parker and passed the remainder of his minority in a variety of service jobs.[42]

After his eighth birthday, Sheldon had little family life in the sense of warm and intimate bonds with parents. His father had been a remote and distant figure even before his death; his mother could not keep Asa at home, for that would have entailed feeding and lodging him without deriving any wages in return. So Asa left at an early age and became a "youth" in semidependent service. He described his parents with respect but not emotion, and in this respect followed the custom of his day. Where the simplest kinds of security were absent, affection lavished was likely to be affection frustrated. Parents and children were not unfeeling toward one another, but as long as children lived, affection had to be kept in check. The same emotional restraint governed relationships between siblings. Emily Chubbock's diary contains the following subdued description of a brother's homecoming: "March, 1830. Benjamin came home (he had been for five years in the employ of a farmer), and he and father commenced building fences and other spring work."[43]

Behind this emotional restraint lay family priorities and values very different from our own. Children provided parents in preindustrial society with a form of social security, unemployment insurance, and yearly support. As soon as children were able to work, in or out of the home, they were expected to contribute to the support of their parents; when parents were no longer able to work, children could look after them. A parent's first obligation was to have children sufficiently numerous to ensure that enough would survive. The second obligation was to supervise the placement of children between their seventh and twenty-first birthdays. Parents of means had a third obligation, to give children a "start in life," a stake in the form of capital or land that would enable the children to achieve economic independence. These three obligations are listed not only in chronological sequence but also in order of importance, for many parents, because of death or poverty, were in no position to discharge the third obligation.[44]

Social class conditioned childhood experiences in various ways, but certain common elements united the experiences of children of wealthy, comfortable, and poor parents. The ravages of mortality fell heaviest on the poor but struck all social classes. Leaving home was also an experience common to youth of different classes, although its nature differed from class to class. Landowning farmers sanctioned seasonal departures of sons from home but wanted their children back in the spring and summer. Wealthy merchants often sent their sons out as cabin boys at eight or nine or as supercargo at fifteen or sixteen as part of a process of grooming that was to lead to a junior partnership at twenty-one. Differences between rich and poor were often those of motive rather than deed; children of the wealthy left home because of parental preference rather than stark necessity.[45]

A source which throws light on the elements of similarity in the experiences of youth of different classes is a collection of biographies of New England manufacturers compiled in 1876 by J. D. Van Slyck, an enterprising journalist.[46] Van Slyck's collection was largely free of the fulsome ornamentation that often pervaded late nineteenth-century biographies, and it has the added merit of being based on autobiographical data submitted by the subjects, data which provides unusually precise information about the sequence of jobs during youth. Obviously, at the end of their careers Van Slyck's subjects had risen far above the average level of attainment, and even at birth they were not a cross section of the society from which they sprang. Although only about 1 percent attended college, all of them had some formal education, and many were able to benefit from parental assistance at key points in their careers. In view of this class bias, it is interesting to note the similarities between their occupations during their teens and those of Asa Sheldon.

A majority of Van Slyck's manufacturers were sons of farmers (86 out of 145 on whom data was available), but a sizable minority came from the artisan or petty manufacturing class (44 of 145). The proportion from other backgrounds was negligible; only seven were sons of professional men, while eight were sons of merchants. Those who came from farming families fell into two general classes. The larger proportion passed their early and middle teens as plowboys, going out first as farm servants but returning home frequently. Philip Corbin, born in Connecticut in 1824, worked seasonally at farm labor away from home between ages fifteen and nineteen, when, tiring of the agricultural routine, he went to New Britain and entered a factory as a "boy," doing menial jobs for a locksmith who paid him according to the value of his labor. This lasted for a year, at which point Corbin had learned enough of locksmithing to begin as an independent contractor.[47] Jared Beebe, born in Wilbraham, Massachusetts, in 1815, similarly worked on a farm and attended district school until he was twenty, when he entered a woolen mill as a spinner. Beebe's rise thereafter was slow, and it was not until 1852 that he had amassed enough capital to enter a partnership.[48] It is, indeed, a little ironic that late nineteenth-century business leaders romanticized rural boyhood, for the evidence indicates that a farm boyhood was essentially a drag on careers. Half the manufacturers who were sons of farmers did not follow any nonagricultural occupation until they were eighteen or over. Even then, many of them merely became store clerks and were several steps away from a small manufacturing partnership.

A smaller proportion of the manufacturers from agricultural backgrounds were sons of farmers who also had some other identifiable trade, often blacksmithing, which was carried on as a way to increase a family's earnings during slack seasons. Many of Van Slyck's subjects picked up their initial experience with tools in small shops attached to the farmhouse or located in an outlying shed. Such experiences might have prompted them to try their luck in manufacturing establishments, a conclusion which is supported by the fact that manufacturers whose fathers had some occupation ancillary to agriculture were more likely than the average to move into artisan or manufacturing jobs before age eighteen.

Although delays of various sorts marked the movement of sons of farmers into industry, they usually began to work at early ages at agricultural tasks, attending school only in the winter and only for a few weeks at a time. Even those of Van Slyck's subjects who had some advanced education usually spent no more than a term or two at an academy in their late teens. Similarly, artisans and petty manufacturers, including ones who could have provided advanced education for their sons, placed little premium on schooling beyond the rudiments. Of forty-four individuals from artisan or manufacturing families, fourteen had taken some form of steady employment before they reached age fourteen, while an additional thirteen began to work at fifteen and sixteen.

The difference lay, of course, in the kind of work performed, for the sons of artisans proceeeded directly into learning the routine of mills and shops. Compared to Philip Corbin, caught in the routine of farm labor until he was nineteen, Baxter D. Whitney moved down a well-greased track. Whitney was born in Winchendon, Massachusetts, in 1817; his father owned a small woolen mill. At the age of six, Whitney began to work at piecing rolls in his father's mill, a task which occupied him full- time until he was eleven, except for two weeks spent each summer and winter in school. At eleven he was sent to work at carding, at twelve on repairs. A year later his father sent him to Worcester to assist a firm of machinists in constructing looms for the senior Whitney's mill. Four years later Whitney, now seventeen, entered Fitchburg Academy for a term before returning to Winchendon as a repair foreman for a company which had bought his father's mill.[49]

The same shifting of situations every few years marked the youth of Moses Pierce, born in Pawtucket in 1808. After attending school until age eleven, Pierce was placed in the spinning room of a mill. A year later he entered the yarning room and stayed there until 1822, when he took employment in a succession of factory stores in Pawtucket and Valley Falls. After six years in various stores, Pierce was given charge of a small cotton factory in Willimantic, Connecticut, where he rewarded his employer's confidence by introducing a new system of bookkeeping at a time when any system of bookkeeping was a novelty. Finally, at twenty-one, he entered into a partnership to manufacture bleach.[50]

Pierce and Whitney were typical of the New England manufacturers in that both managed to pack an impressive number of experiences into their first twenty years and neither served a seven-year apprenticeship. Those who maintain that apprenticeship fixed the status of youth before the dramatic expansion of school enrollment at the end of the nineteenth century ignore the fluid quality of youthful experience in the early Republic. Indeed, long apprenticeships were never common, either in America or Britain, except for a few highly skilled crafts and for the binding out of pauper children.[51]

More interesting is the fact that, despite all their shifting around and apparent independence as teenagers, Pierce, Whitney, and the others continued to be caught up in a curious form of dependence. Perhaps they went into a variety of situations, but, more accurately, they were *sent* into various positions. The ties which held them were often stretched to the limit, but they were still there. In some cases, the bonds were plainly visible, for while seven-year apprenticeships were rare, three-year apprenticeships were common. Albert Curtis abandoned farm work at age seventeen to become an apprentice in a machine shop in Worcester. His contract ran for three years, stipulating that he was to receive board plus $40, $60, and $80 in each successive year. Then, at twenty-one he became a journeyman in the same shop at $1.25 a day.[52] At times, apprenticeship survived in an invisible form even after it had ceased to be visible. The father of Estus Lamb sent him at age thirteen to live with a cousin to learn the millwright trade (although the senior Lamb was also a millwright). There was no formal apprenticeship here, although Lamb was obviously an apprentice for all practical purposes. After learning the trade, Lamb left his cousin at age eighteen to work as a millwright at Oxford Plains, Massachusetts, agreeing to a contract of $200 in pay for two years' work. This was not a formal apprenticeship, but the level of remuneration suggests that Lamb was still in a semidependent and subordinate position, as does the fact that Lamb's father claimed the entire $200, "relinquishing, however, his claim for the remaining year of his son's minority."[53]

Dependency at times took horizontal rather than vertical forms, with younger brothers dependent on older brothers. Samuel Walker, an orphan, was "given away" to an older brother at seven. The brother kept him until age eleven and then placed him out on a neighboring farm. The older brother assumed many of the functions of a father, not the least being that he claimed Samuel's labor in return for board and oversight until Samuel reached majority. In practice, it did not work out quite that way. After returning to live with his brother for a short period, Samuel decided to strike out on his own. The brother agreed, but only on condition that Samuel pay him cash in lieu of time. Since Samuel did not have any money, the brother's condition presented obvious difficulties, which were resolved by an agreement that Samuel would leave, pick up whatever work he could, and then at nineteen pay off the stipulated sum. Strangely, Samuel's relations with his brother, if not exactly characterized by warmth, were not freighted with antagonism either. Samuel lived up to his part of the deal, and after he turned twenty-one, his brother helped him out in business by endorsing small notes.[54]

Whatever forms dependency took, it did not necessarily involve prolonged residence under the parental roof. The factory apprentice who lived at home was an exception, although those who spent their teens moving around from mill to mill were often placed with relatives, particularly with older brothers and uncles. The father of Phinehas Adams, for example, combined the occupations of farmer, mechanic, and petty mill owner, and was sufficiently well off to give Phinehas a private education up to age thirteen. Then, Phinehas was placed as a bobbin boy in a mill for which his father acted as agent. A short time later, Phinehas entered another mill for which his uncle was agent. Then, at nineteen, he linked up with his father in yet another mill.[55]

This kind of movement under the supervision of relatives or parents was not always possible and was much less likely to occur in the case of young plowboys like Philip Corbin, who stumbled into factory work without benefit of connections. Even the petty manufacturers often sent their children away from home for various reasons without requiring that they be placed with relatives and without granting them independence. Oliver Chace was not a poor man, but he seems to have thought nothing of placing his son Harvey in a mill as a bobbin boy at age nine, and then sending him around Rhode Island as a teenager to supervise the installation of machinery in whatever factories the elder Chace had acquired a financial interest. Dependency and residence at home were not interchangeable concepts before the middle of the nineteenth century.[56]

Relatives not only provided supervision for young men during their minority, but they also supplied capital to help the young people start on their own. Prior to the middle of the nineteenth century the partnership rather than the corporation was the preferred form of business enterprise, and relatives (especially brothers and cousins) were the preferred partners in many cases. An example of the manner in which close ties between brothers provided a crude form of family continuity and economic security is the case of John and Salmon Putnam, born in New Hampshire in 1812 and 1815, respectively. Their father was a scythe maker who, lacking capital, worked on contract for merchants and hence was forced to shift the family repeatedly around New Hampshire. The eldest of the two brothers, John, became an apprentice at fourteen to Loammi Chamberlain, a machinist in Mason Village. It is not clear whether anything was actually written down, but John was to receive board and clothing for five years, with permission to attend school one month a year. The apprenticeship ended when John turned nineteen, and he continued as a journeyman in Chamberlain's service for a dollar a day. Saving his money, John hired part of Chamberlain's shop in 1835 and began to make cotton machinery on contract. Meanwhile, the failure of a contractor for whom the senior Putnam was working had reduced the family to penury and forced it to dispose of Salmon, the younger brother, by sending him off at eight years of age to work in a New Ipswich mill where a relative was overseer. Later, Salmon went to Lowell, Massachusetts, and obtained employment with one of the larger cotton factories, rising by age seventeen to become overseer of the spinning room. Two or three years later, he linked up with John, who was just beginning business as a contractor. In 1836 the brothers went to Trenton, New Jersey, and started a machine shop. Caught short by the Panic of 1837, they left Trenton, stored their tools in Mason Village, and took separate jobs in different parts of New Hampshire until better times permitted them to establish a machine shop in Fitchburg, Massachusetts. There they continued in partnership until 1858, when they converted the business to a stock company ultimately capitalized at over a quarter of a million dollars.[57] The careers of the Putnam brothers primarily illustrate the importance of sibling relationships in early nineteenth-century business enterprise, but they also underscore the importance of work in machine shops, which required a high degree of technical skill but a relatively small amount of capital, in facilitating the movement of artisans' sons into manufacturing enterprises.

The early career of Milton Morse offers an apt summary of the oscillation between independence and dependence, between home leaving and homecoming, in the early nineteenth century. Morse was the son of a sometime carpenter and farmer, Oliver Morse, and Waitstill Stratton, a woman whose Puritan surname was scarcely descriptive of her later mobility. Milton was born in 1799 in Foxboro, his mother's hometown, but soon moved with his family to Wrentham, Massachusetts, where Milton was put to work in a small cotton factory, picking cotton by hand and putting it on the cards. After doing this for two years, Milton was apprenticed to a blacksmith, with the stipulated term to run until his twenty-first birthday. Milton was still under thirteen at the binding; we know this because at thirteen he walked out on his apprenticeship and returned to his parents. The family then moved to Attleboro, where the senior Morse engaged as a woodworker in nearby Pawtucket, while Milton continued to work at his single skill of picking cotton. Still in his teens, Milton took a job as a handyman in a mill at Seekonk, learning various phases of the routine until age twenty-one. On coming of age, Milton left Seekonk to join his father, who had rented a farm at East Providence, and worked for him a year before hiring himself out as a farmhand to his uncle at Foxboro. For the next six or seven years Milton returned periodically to farm labor, probably for no more than a few months at a time, certainly not often enough to keep him from working as a journeyman mechanic and overseer on a seasonal basis. All the while he amassed capital without the risks of ownership, and when a business slump in the late 1820s forced a number of failures, Morse and an acquaintance formed a partnership to manufacture cotton goods.[58] He went on to become a celebrated manufacturer and a pillar of New England industrial society, until he died in 1877 from injuries caused by a falling derrick.

"Semidependence" has been used at a number of points to describe the status of youth aged ten to twenty-one in the early part of the nineteenth century. The word is intended to signify two aspects of the economic experience of young people. First, as young people grew older, they customarily experienced greater freedom and acquired new responsibilities. They left home, took different jobs, and moved again in search of still more jobs. But "semidependence" also signifies a different view of growth, not as a gradual removal of restraints but as a jarring mixture of complete freedom and total subordination. Autobiographers who lapsed routinely into the passive voice when describing the events of their youth were unconsciously conveying an important aspect of nineteenth-century family life, for in the quasi-contractual relationship between fathers and sons, the obligation to work lay heavily on the son.[59]

As noted earlier, the conditions of semidependence were affected by social class. Poor farm children were forced out of the home early; children of prosperous, landowning farmers left home at a somewhat later age and returned home more frequently; children of wealthy manufacturers and merchants left early but because of parental preference rather than necessity. The degree of freedom also depended on social class. To the extent that poor households were more frequently disrupted than wealthy ones, poor children often had more de facto freedom (unless bound as paupers), although, it must be added, there was little that they could do with their freedom.

Social class is one variable; another is historical periodization. To what extent have we described timeless components of preindustrial society and to what extent have we identified patterns unique to the period from 1790 to 1840?

The tendency to send children away from home before puberty was well established in early nineteenth-century America for the same reason it had been well established in England during the sixteenth and seventeenth centuries. High birthrates in both cases made the labor of children redundant

in the home and forced their removal. Moreover, the element of patriarchalism so evident in labor contracts between sons and fathers was a characteristic feature of American society in the period between 1650 and 1790,
just as it was after 1790.[60] Some of the basic features of semidependence in
1800 or 1820 were rooted in the preindustrial nature of society.

Yet the period 1790–1840 departed in important ways from earlier
times. By the late eighteenth century, American social structure had become notably more complex and differentiated than in the seventeenth
and early eighteenth centuries. Whether the social structure was also becoming more stratified remains an open question, but by 1800 one could
identify in most regions large numbers of commercial as well as subsistence farmers, several gradations of wealth among commercial farmers, a
growing class of artisans and shopkeepers in towns and cities, and a fluid
body of nondependent, propertyless urban workers. Asa Sheldon's occupational career, the early parts of which have already been sketched, illustrates the direction of change. Late in life Sheldon described himself as a
farmer, and, indeed, he did engage in farming, but he was primarily an enterprising Yankee jobber who supported himself in his mature years by
working on contract to provide farmers and tradesmen with lumber and to
develop real estate.[61]

The growth of urbanization during the first half of the nineteenth century did not have a revolutionary effect on young people, mainly because
class differences around 1800 were not reflected as sharply in the teen
years as in mature life. On farms and in shops and stores young people of
different classes mingled in an atmosphere of informality, although their
ultimate destinations would be different. Moreover, urban tradesmen and
industrialists often operated farms on which their sons supplied the
labor.[62] Nor was the nature of the early factories such as to transform the
time and work rhythms of agricultural society; an alternation of seasonal
labor and seasonal education marked the lives of factory youth as well as
farm youth. Eleven-year-old Emily Chubbock recorded this laconic comment in her diary: "December, 1828. The ice stopped the water wheel and
the factory was closed for a few months. January, 1829. Entered district
school."[63]

Yet economic change altered the experiences of young people in important ways. The transportation revolution between 1815 and 1840 stimulated large numbers of young men to abandon agriculture for commercial
and industrial occupations in towns and cities and for construction jobs
both in rural and in urban areas. In the seventeenth and early eighteenth
centuries young men had usually remained dependent until marriage or
their father's death; by 1820, however, increasing numbers of young men
were pushing out on their own in their late teens and early twenties.[64]
Large towns and cities could sustain a range of political, educational, and
social institutions which small towns and rural areas could not, so that the
corporate life of youth shifted from involuntary associations (family and
village) to voluntary associations such as academies, young men's societies, and political clubs. In the curious balance between dependence and
independence which together made up semidependence, the weight was increasingly on the side of independence.

## FROM SEMIDEPENDENCE TO INDEPENDENCE

No clear and distinct barrier divided semidependence from independence; no consensus existed as to the moment when a boy became a man. Few institutions marked the passage from one stage of life to the next, and in any event, young people passed less time in 1800 than now in institutional settings. Various criteria for the attainment of full manhood can be advanced, each with some justification; the age of marriage, the age at which a young man left home for the final time, perhaps even the age at which one joined a church.

For the moment, without dismissing any of these, we will examine a different criterion, the age at which an upwardly mobile youth entered one of the learned professions. The unimposing quality of professional and pre-professional requirements in the early nineteenth century lends plausibility to the idea that early entry into the professions was normal. With the exception of the ministry of a few orthodox denominations, a college degree was not a prerequisite for professional practice, while professional education itself was normally shortened for college graduates. Since legal and medical apprenticeships could be entered at sixteen (and sometimes earlier), a nongraduate could have been ready to practice at twenty-one, the legal minimum. Some individuals did begin to practice law or medicine at twenty-one; indeed, some began at seventeen or eighteen, either ignoring the law or benefiting from legislative dispensations. But the more pronounced tendency was toward late entrance, "late" in this context meaning from twenty-five to the early thirties. In 1894 a New Hampshire lawyer and antiquarian, Charles Bell, published a collection of biographies of nearly every lawyer known to have practiced in the state.[65] The great majority of Bell's lawyers were born between 1780 and 1830. Fully two-thirds were twenty-five or over at the start of legal practice; a quarter were twenty-eight or over. A few individuals were not admitted to the bar until their forties or fifties; in their case, law was less a career than an avocation, taken up in middle life and ancillary to their main occupation. But for most of the New Hampshire lawyers, entrance to legal practice was the result of a more or less permanent vocational choice made in young manhood but toward the end rather than the beginning of young manhood. (See Table 3.)

What took them so long? Considering the relatively low barriers guarding access to professions in antebellum America, why all the foot dragging? A high proportion of Bell's 780 lawyers (63 percent) were college

**Table 3.** NEW HAMPSHIRE LAWYERS: AGES AT ENTRY TO PRACTICE

| Age Range | 18–24 | 25–27 | 28 and Over |
|---|---|---|---|
| Total: N = 500 | 37.0% | 34.2% | 28.8% |
| Sons of lawyers | 68.8 | 25.0 | 6.2 |
| Had relatives other than father in legal profession | 45.5 | 39.4 | 15.1 |
| Sons of farmers | 14.9 | 25.9 | 59.2 |

graduates. But this fact does not explain the frequency of delays into the late twenties, and in any event, the nongraduates among his lawyers were actually slightly older on average than the graduates at entry to practice. The fact that fully 75 percent of the college graduates among Bell's lawyers began to practice within four years of graduation provides a valuable clue. Many of those who began to practice late left college late, not at eighteen or nineteen but at twenty-three or twenty-four. Such late graduations were very common at colleges outside the South in the first half of the nineteenth century; twenty-three- and twenty-four-year- old graduates formed a procession of which Bell's lawyers were merely the tail end.[66] The likeliest explanation for late graduations, in turn, lies in late decisions to prepare for college for preparation itself was not time consuming. Logically, such late decisions would be more frequent where the young men's families lacked ties to professions or to merchant houses where advanced education was valuable. In other words, these young men were originally destined for some other line. In fact, only a tiny fraction of Bell's lawyers (40 of 780) were themselves sons of lawyers. An equally small fraction (36 of 780) had close relatives in the law. But if most did not come from legal backgrounds, what kind of families did they come from? Here the limitations of evidence are severe, but we might take a clue from Bell, who said that New Hampshire lawyers were very often raised on farms. If so—and prior to 1830 alternatives to agriculture were meager in New Hampshire— it is likely that many of Bell's lawyers experienced the drag force of a farm boyhood in their early years. Mired in obligations to their parents, they must have also suffered from their lack of personal connections to the state's professional life and from their inability to find patrons to smooth their path. The difference between the age at entrance to practice of those of Bell's subjects who were sons of lawyers and those known to have been raised on farms is striking, all the more so because the sons of lawyers were almost without exception college graduates.

Bell's collection happens to be unparalleled for completeness, but collections of biographies do exist for other states and other professions. Data on Massachusetts and New Hampshire Congregationalist and Presbyterian clergymen born before 1830 point to a similar pattern of late access, with ordination usually delayed until the late twenties or early thirties.[67] Perhaps date of ordination is misleading as an indicator, since ordination coincided with installation rather than with the completion of preparation for the ministry. But even if we take the other possible indicator, date of licensing to preach, or "approbation," the picture does not change significantly. More than three-quarters of the candidates of the Essex North Massachusetts ministerial association, for example, were twenty-five or over at licensing; a third were twenty-eight or over.

That orthodox clergymen experienced delays before licensing is not surprising in view of the value placed in New England on an educated clergy. But allowing three years for professional education and assuming college graduation at twenty-one, approbation should not have been postponed much beyond age twenty-four. In fact, the traditional assumption was that only five years should elapse between the commencement of Latin grammar and the first sermon.[68] But much longer delays were clearly common, delays caused less by time spent in professional education than by late graduation from college. Nearly a third of the Essex North ministers were twenty-five or over at college graduation; more than two-thirds were twenty-three or over. Two points can be made about this tendency toward late graduation and late approbation. First, only 13 percent of the Essex North ministers were themselves sons of ministers. Predictably, sons of ministers were younger at graduation than the average. Secondly, in early nineteenth-century New England, periodic waves of religious enthusiasm, supplemented by the benevolent work of various educational societies, were pulling numbers of young men from the plow and workbench and propelling them in the direction of college and ministerial education.[69] It is likely that in the ministry as in law, track switching, with all its concomitant effects, was inducing marked delays in the ages at which young men entered professions in the early nineteenth century.[70]

The life of one Alfred Poore, born in 1818 in West Haverhill, Massachusetts, provides an illustration of these forces and, incidentally, suggests how an individual with meager preprofessional and professional training might not reach the level of formal qualification for a profession before age twenty-eight. Poore was the son of a farmer and cordwainer; in his youth he learned the latter trade, practicing it except for interim periods of farm labor and district schooling. Like many farm boys, he was nearly twenty when he stopped attending district school. In the winter of 1837–1838 he spent one term at Atkinson Academy, deriving in the words of a laconic memorialist "an increased desire for knowledge."[71] He then entered the Bradford Teachers' Seminary but never actually taught school. Instead, he conceived the desire to study medicine and, after a brief apprenticeship, he spent one term in the medical department of Dartmouth College, receiving a preceptor's certificate in 1846. One could end the story there, with Poore finally entering a profession, but for the fact that he never did practice medicine. Rather, he spent the next ten years clerking in a country store and farming before finally turning to antiquarianism, a field in which he won sufficient notice to merit a brief obituary in 1908 in the *New England Historical and Genealogical Register*.

To what extent did these particular groups or individuals represent the nation? Was delayed entry into professions normal or aberrant? Part of the answer lies in the fact that, even in New England, the tendency toward late access concealed a less conspicuous but equally important trend, the wide distribution of ages at entry, since there were individual cases of lawyers practicing at eighteen or ministers preaching at twenty-one. We are really confronted, then, by two distinct tendencies, late entry as a probability and early entry as a possibility. Significant deviations from the model of late access, moreover, did exist in other professions and other sections of the country. Physicians, for example, usually began to practice at earlier ages than either Bell's lawyers or the New England clergymen. Analysis of a sample of 500 doctors drawn from William B. Atkinson's directory *Physicians and Surgeons of the United States* provides some illuminating comparisons.[72] Only about half of Atkinson's physicians, most of whom were born between 1810 and 1850, were twenty-five or over at entrance to practice; the proportion of very late entries, twenty-eight or over, was much lower than among Bell's lawyers. (See Table 4.)

Several explanations help to account for the lower age of entry into

**Table 4.**  AGES AT ENTRY: DOCTORS BY REGION OF ORIGIN

| Age Range | 18–24 | 25–27 | 28 and Over |
|---|---|---|---|
| Total: N=500 | 59.0% | 29.2% | 11.8% |
| New England | 36.0 | 43.7 | 20.3 |
| Middle Atlantic | 69.9 | 18.8 | 11.3 |
| Midwest | 52.5 | 31.5 | 16.0 |
| South (incl. Md. and Ky.) | 72.0 | 19.2 | 8.8 |

medicine. Prior to 1870 the medical profession was probably the least prestigious of the professions and certainly the most accessible. A medical degree was not a prerequisite to practice, and by 1845 most states had abandoned licensing efforts, in effect throwing medical practice open to all comers.[73] But there were important regional differences in the ages at which Atkinson's doctors began to practice. Physicians born in New England were older at entrance to practice than those born in the Middle Atlantic states, and much older than those born in the South. New England doctors, in fact, were almost as old at the start of practice as Bell's lawyers. Southerners, in contrast, often began to prescribe drugs and to treat patients when scarcely out of adolescence.

The pattern of early access in the South was not confined to medicine. In sharp contrast to the New Hampshire pattern, Southern lawyers generally started to practice in their early twenties. Variations were as often downward into the late teens as upward, despite the fact that professional standards in many parts of the South where early entry predominated were comparable to those of New England.[74] Why, then, did southerners move so much more rapidly than northerners? Part of the answer probably lies in the survival of so many elements of prescriptive status and hierarchy in the antebellum South at a time of their erosion in the North. Among southern aristocrats, family name acted as a guarantor of maturity and responsibility almost without regard to chronological age. This helps to explain why in South Carolina some of the leading judges in the state were only in their mid-twenties. The antebellum South, especially states like Virginia and South Carolina, carried over the tradition which decreed that status rather than age determined a man's position. This tradition accounted for many of those astonishing instances of precocity which, like that of William Pitt, the twenty-four-year-old prime minister of Great Britain, can so easily be ripped out of context to "prove" that youth in the past routinely achieved eminence at much earlier ages than now.

Just as the accelerated development of privileged southern youth reflected the continued vitality of such traditions in the South, delays among northern youth in entering professions reflected the withering of traditions of status and hierarchy in the North. Pointing to a variety of youth movements spawned by modernization, a recent student has described European youth between 1770 and 1870 as "troubled." There are good reasons to apply the same adjective to American youth between 1790 and 1840, but a more comprehensive description of northern youth in the latter period would be "restless." To a greater extent than in the South, urbanization in the North was bringing into existence a kind of town life that had few antecedents before the Revolution. After 1820 the growth of metropolises had a dramatic effect on all age groups, but for a young man around 1800 the town was the key development. The presence of an increasing number of towns of about 5,000 people, combined with pressure on available land, tempted young men to abandon agriculture without, at the same time, providing new beacons to guide them.[75]

## CONCLUSION

A model which divided early nineteenth-century life experiences into childhood, adolescence, and adulthood, corresponding to age groups of one to thirteen, fourteen to twenty, and twenty-one and upward, would fail to convey the real complexity of the situation. Few apprenticeships began at fourteen and ended at twenty-one; some began at twelve, some at sixteen or eighteen. Moreover, young people often had more than one apprenticeship, whether formal or informal. Apprenticeship did not necessarily mark the first leaving of home; many left at eight or nine as servants. Those who left home in boyhood often returned for longer or shorter periods, a fact which prompted the distinction between sporadic (in, out, and in again) home leaving and the final departure, or "start in life," which might come at fourteen but usually came later.

If childhood is defined as a period of protected dependency within the home, then its extent was much shorter then than now. If adolescence is defined as the period after puberty during which a young person is institutionally segregated from casual contacts with a broad range of adults, then it can scarcely be said to have existed at all, even for those young people who attended school beyond age fourteen. Nevertheless, it is possible to speak of youth in the early nineteenth century, either as an often lengthy period of semidependence between ages ten and twenty-one or as a time of indecision between ages fifteen and twenty-five. Of course, there were still young men who plunged into the business of life like comets. A few months after his arrival in America, the German-born scholar Francis Lieber, recorded the following in his diary:

> Story from real life. I arrived here in October, 1835. In January, 1836, W_____ and another student were expelled [from college] on account of a duel. Since that time W_____ has:
> First. Shot at his antagonist in the streets of Charleston.
> Second. Studied (?) law with Mr. De Saussure in Charleston
> Third. Married.
> Fourth. Been admitted to the Bar.
> Fifth. Imprisoned for two months in the above shooting.
> Sixth. Become father of a fine girl.
> Seventh. Practised law for some time.
> Eighth. Been elected a member of the legislature.
> Now he is only twenty-two years old. What a state of society this requires and must produce![76]

But such prodigies, always rare, were becoming even rarer. In the ensuing decades, the idea of youth as a period of prolonged indecision would rise to prominence.

# NOTES

1. Dean May and Maris A. Vinovskis, "A Ray of Millennial Light: Early Education and Social Reform in the Infant School Movement in Massachusetts, 1826–1840," in Tamara K. Hareven, ed., *Family and Kin in American Urban Communities, 1800–1940* (New York, forthcoming); "Plymouth Church Records, 1620–1859," in *Publications of the Colonial Society of Massachusetts* 22 (1920): 378; quoted in Henry Barnard, *Pestalozzi and His Educational System* (Syracuse, 1881), p. 397; "The Proper Time for Sending Children to School," *Common School Journal* 13 (August 15, 1851):248; on Alvan Hyde, see Heman Humphrey, *Revival Sketches and Manual, in Two Parts* (New York, 1859), p. 132; William Gilmore Simms, ed., *The Life of Nathanael Greene, Major-General in the Army of the Revolution* (New York, 1861), pp. 21, 28–29; Cotton Mather, *Youth in Its Brightest Glory* (Boston, 1709), pp. 3–6.

2. Cotton Mather, *The Best Ornaments of Youth* (Boston, 1707), pp. 22–23, 25; Mather, *Repeated Warnings: Another Essay to Warn Young People Against Rebellions That Must Be Repented Of* (Boston, 1712), p. 4; *Journal of the Life and Religious Labors of John Comly, Late of Byberry, Pennsylvania* (Philadelphia, 1853), pp. 8, 11; *Every Youth's Gazette* 1 (January 22, 1842.

3. David Barnes, *Sermons* (Boston, 1815), pp. 44–70.

4. "The Visit," *Western New York Baptist Magazine* 2 (February 1817):154; "Revival of Religion in Rupert," *Connecticut Evangelical Magazine* 5 (September 1804):113.

5. J. William Frost, *The Quaker Family in Colonial America: A Portrait of the Society of Friends* (New York, 1973), chap. 7.

6. Wiley B. Sanders, ed., *Juvenile Offenders for a Thousand Years: Selected Readings from Anglo-Saxon Times to 1900* (Chapel Hill, 1970), pp. 60–62.

7. "Minutes of the Committee and of the First Commission for Detecting Conspiracies in the State of New York, 1776–1778," *Collections of the New-York Historical Society* 58 (1924):169; on Increase Mather, see "Biographical Sketch and Diary of Rev. Joseph Green, of Salem Village," *Historical Collections of the Essex Institute* 8 (June 1866):166n.

8. Francis Walett, ed., "The Diary of Ebenezer Parkman," *Proceedings of the American Antiquarian Society* 74, pt. 1 (April 16, 1964):46.

9. *The Life and Adventures of John Levy* (Lawrence, Mass., 1871); William Otter, *History of My Own Times, or the Life and Adventures of William Otter* (Emmitsburg, Md., 1835).

10. The greatest change in family size since 1790 has been the decline by nearly 100 percent in families of seven or more members; see U.S. Bureau of the Census, *A Century of Population Growth: From the First Census to the Twelfth* (Baltimore, 1970), p. 12. While family size has changed over time, historians have modified the older view of very large, extended families giving way to small, nuclear ones; see Philip J. Greven, Jr. *Four Generations: Population, Land, and Family in Colonial Andover, Massachusetts* (Ithaca, 1970), pp. 15–16, 121, 220, and John Demos, *A Little Commonwealth: Family Life in Plymouth Colony* (New York, 1970), pp. 64, 68, 192, 194. Greven found a range of family types from nuclearity to extension in Andover. He observed that kinship was a major factor in determining social relations and in regulating social conduct but added that the basic household was most often nuclear, with kin living nearby in the community (p. 16). See also Peter Laslett, "Size and Structure of the Household in England Over Three Centuries," *Population Studies* 23 (July 1969):199–223.

11. For an illustration of the kinds of arrangements made for orphans, see *Autobiography of Benjamin Hallowell*, 2nd ed. (Philadelphia, 1884), p. 15; for the radical changes in female cohort mortality between 1830 and 1920, see P. R. Uhlenburg, "A Study of Cohort Life Cycles: Cohorts of Native-Born Massachusetts Women, 1830–1920," *Population Studies* 23 (November 1969):407–420.

12. Peter R. Knights, *The Plain People of Boston, 1830–1860; A Study in City Growth* (New York, 1971), chaps. 2, 4, 7.

13. Anson Tufts, "Rev. Edwin H. Chapin, D.D., LL.D.," *New England Historical and Genealogical Register* (Hereinafter *NEHGR*) 38 (April 1884):122.

14. Asahel C. Kendrick, *The Life and Letters of Mrs. Emily C. Judson* (New York, 1861), pp. 1–20; George T. Day, *The Life of Martin Cheney* (Providence, 1853), pp. 6–31.

15. "Memoirs of Isaac T. Packard," *The Guardian* 3 (February 1821):45.

16. "Some Records of Deaths in Bedford, Mass.," *NEHGR* 62 (January 1908):69–73; "Deaths at Edgartown, Mass.," *NEHGR* 53 (January 1889):102; Bernard Farber, *Guardians of Virtue: Salem Families in 1800* (New York, 1970), p. 177.

17. Elias Smith, *The Life, Conversion, Preachings, Travels and Sufferings of Elias Smith* (Portsmouth, N.H., 1816), p. 22; Samuel A. Foot, *Autobiography* 2 vols. (New York, 1873), vol. 1, p. 10; "Send Your Children to the Summer School," *School Journal and Vermont Agriculturalist* 3 (May 1849):4–5.

18. *The Mother's Magazine* 1 (January 1833):3.

19. Adelaide L. Fries, ed., *Records of the Moravians of North Carolina*, 8 vols. (Raleigh, 1922–1954), vol. 1, pp. 420–421.

20. Constance N. Robertson, *Oneida Community: An Autobiography 1851–1876* (Syracuse, 1970), pp. 311, 315–316.

21. Philippe Ariès, *Centuries of Childhood: A Social History of Family Life*, trans. Robert Baldick (New York, 1962), p. 368 and passim; David Hunt, *Parents and Children in History: The Psychology of Family Life in Early Modern France* (New York, 1970); Evarts B. Greene and Virginia D. Harrington, *American Population Before the Federal Census of 1790* (New York, 1932), pp. 98–99.

22. Edmund Morgan, *The Puritan Family: Religious and Domestic Relations in Seventeenth-Century New England*, rev. ed. (New York, 1966), p. 77; see also Roger Smith, "Early Victorian Household Structure: A Case Study of Nottinghamshire," *International Review of Social History* 15 (1970):68–84; John R. Gillis, *Youth and History: Tradition and Change in European Age Relations, 1770–Present* (New York, 1974), pp. 16–18.

23. William C. Gannett, *Ezra Stiles Gannett, Unitarian Minister in Boston, 1824–1871: A Memoir* (Boston, 1875), p. 17; Otis P. Lord, "Memoir of Asahel Huntington," *Historical Collections of the Essex Institute* 11 (July–October 1871):833.

24. "Rev. Henry Griswold Jessup, A.M.," *NEHGR* 59 (1904, suppl.):xcvi.

25. Walett, ed., "The Diary of Ebenezer Parkman, 1745–1746," *Proceedings of the American Antiquarian Society* 72, pt. 2 (October 16, 1962):189.

26. Gillis, *Youth and History*, pp. 16–17; James R. Newhall, *The Legacy of an Octogenarian* (Lynn, Mass., 1897), p. 114; Elias H. Johnson, ed., *Ezekial Gilman Robinson: An Autobiography, With a Supplement by H. C. Wayland and Critical Estimates* (New York, 1896), pp. 10–13; John E. Todd, ed., *John Todd: The Story of His Life, Told Mainly by Himself* (New York, 1876), pp. 53–54; William Stickney, ed., *Autobiography of Amos Kendall* (Boston, 1872), p. 11.

27. Octavius B. Frothingham, *Theodore Parker: A Biography* (Boston, 1874), p. 25.

28. Ibid., pp. 26–27; see also Smith *Life, Conversion, Preaching*, p. 119, and Jason Whitman, *A Memoir of the Rev. Bernard Whitman* (Boston, 1837), p. 34.

29. Edgar J. Sherman, *Some Recollections of a Long Life* (Boston, 1908), p. 13; Solon J. Buck, *William Watts Folwell: The Autobiography of a Pioneer of Culture* (Minneapolis, 1933), pp. 40–43; *Memoirs of the Life and Religious Experience of Ray Potter, . . . Written by Himself* (Providence, 1829), chaps. 1–2.

30. *General Catalogue of the Officers and Students of the Phillips Exeter Academy, 1783–1903* (Exeter, 1903); *Catalogue of the Trustees, Instructors, and Students of New Ipswich Academy, 1831* (Keene, N.H., 1831); Joseph Dow, *History of the Town of Hampton, New Hampshire*, 2 vols. (Salem, Mass., 1893), vol. 1, p. 493. The Exeter catalogue lists ages. For the other academies, I have deduced ages from family registers in town histories.

31. *Catalogue of the Trustees, Instructors and Students of Pinkerton Academy, Derry, N.H., 1850–1851* (Boston, 1851); *Catalogue of the Trustees, Instructors and Students of Leicester Academy, Massachusetts, 1862–1863* (Worcester, 1863).

32. Bernard Bailyn, "Education as a Discipline: Some Historical Notes," in John Walton and James L. Keuthe, eds., *The Discipline of Education* (Madison, 1963), p. 135; Theodore R. Sizer, ed., *The Age of the Academies* (New York, 1964).

33. *Catalogue of the Trustees, Instructors and Students of Leicester Academy, Massachusetts, 1838* (Worcester, 1838), passim; George Moore, "Diaries," 4 vols. (Harvard College Library), vol. 1, October 31, 1829–January 24, 1830.

34. *A Catalogue of the Officers and Students of Haverhill Academy, 1837* (Concord, N.H., 1837). Using various sources, I have traced the occupation of fathers of thirty students

at Haverhill. Nine were merchants or involved in "general trade"; five were lawyers; two were innkeepers and two were cabinetmakers; one was a banker and one was a furniture dealer; three were listed merely as "Capt." and one was a "Capt." and a farmer; two were in tanning; four were farmers. All of the farmers held town office.

35. Moore, "Diaries," vol. 1, March 28, 1828.

36. Warren Burton, *The District School As It Was* (Boston, 1833).

37. On merchants see Kenneth W. Porter, *The Jacksons and the Lees: Two Generations of Massachusetts Merchants, 1765-1844,* 2 vols. (Cambridge, 1937), vol. 1, pp. 7-11.

38. Gillis, *Youth and History,* pp. 16-18 and passim; Farber, *Guardians of Virtue,* pp. 199-200.

39. *The Life of Asa G. Sheldon, Wilmington Farmer* (Woburn, Mass., 1862), p. 16.

40. Ibid., p. 23.

41. Ibid., pp. 20-21.

42. Ibid., pp. 24-38.

43. Kendrick, *Life and Letters of Mrs. Emily C. Judson,* p. 21.

44. For a comparable pattern in Europe, see Gillis, *Youth and History,* pp. 9-14.

45. Porter, *The Jacksons and the Lees,* vol. 1, pp. 7-11; "Mr. Boyden's Reminiscences," *Proceedings of the Worcester Society of Antiquity. 1889* 9 (1890):65-66.

46. J. D. Van Slyck, ed., *New England Manufacturers and Manufactories,* 2 vols. (Boston, 1876).

47. Ibid., vol. 1, pp. 186-187.

48. Ibid., pp. 77-79; see also ibid., pp. 63-65, 238-239.

49. Ibid., vol. 2, pp. 700-701.

50. Ibid., pp. 468-471; ibid., vol. 1, pp. 182-184.

51. Lawrence W. Towner, "The Indentures of Boston's Poor Apprentices: 1734-1805," *Publications of the Colonial Society of Massachusetts* 43 (1956-1963):417-418; Margaret G. Davies, *The Enforcement of English Apprenticeship: A Study in Applied Mercantilism, 1563- 1642* (Cambridge, Mass., 1956), p. 263.

52. Van Slyck, *Manufacturers,* vol. 1. pp. 210-212.

53. Ibid., pp. 391-393.

54. Ibid., vol. 2, pp. 633-634.

55. Ibid., pp. 597-598.

56. Ibid., vol. 1, pp. 172-173.

57. Ibid., vol. 2, pp. 495-499; ibid., vol. 1, pp. 213-214.

58. Ibid., vol. 2, pp. 450-451.

59. William Paret, *Reminiscences* (Philadelphia, 1911), pp. 15-20; W. J. Stillman, *The Autobiography of a Journalist* 2 vols. (London, 1901), vol. 1, pp. 14-15.

60. Gillis, *Youth and History,* pp. 16-18; Greven, *Four Generations,* chap. 4.

61. *Life of Asa G. Sheldon,* pp. 108-235; Jackson T. Main, *The Social Structure of Revolutionary America* (Princeton, 1965), pp. 17, 23, 27; James A. Henretta, "Economic Development and Social Structure in Colonial Boston," *William and Mary Quarterly* 22 (January 1965):75-92; Aubrey C. Land, "Economic Base and Social Structure: The Northern Chesapeake in the Eighteenth Century," *Journal of Economic History* 25 (December 1965): 639-654; James T. Lemon and Gary B. Nash, "The Distribution of Wealth in Eighteenth-Century America: A Century of Change in Chester County, Pennsylvania, 1693- 1802," *Journal of Social History* 2 (Fall 1968):1-24; Kenneth A. Lockridge, "Social Change and the Meaning of the American Revolution," *Journal of Social History* 6 (Summer 1973):403-439.

62. Richard D. Brown, "The Emergence of Urban Society in Rural Massachusetts, 1760-1820," *Journal of American History* 61 (June 1974):31-32.

63. Kendrick, *Life and Letters of Mrs. Emily C. Judson,* p. 17.

64. Daniel Scott Smith has indicated that parental control over marriage patterns weakened after the middle of the eighteenth century; see his "Parental Power and Marriage Patterns: An Analysis of Historical Trends in Hingham, Massachusetts," *Journal of Marriage*

*and the Family* 35 (August 1973):419–428. See also Brown, "The Emergence of Urban Society," 49–50.

65. Charles Bell, *The Bench and Bar of New Hampshire* (Boston, 1894). Bell sought "to include the name of every member of the bar who has ever lived or practiced in New Hampshire, but not those practitioners who were never admitted to the bar; nor members of the bar who practiced here, but whose homes were out of New Hampshire; nor those admitted to the bar who never practiced, or who practiced elsewhere" (p. 5). I have based my conclusions concerning age of entry to practice on a sample of 500 (out of 780) of Bell's lawyers.

66. W. Scott Thomas, "Changes in the Age of College Graduation," *Report of the Commissioner of Education, 1902,* 2 vols. (Washington, D.C., 1903), vol. 2, pp. 2199–2206.

67. Daniel H. Calhoun, *Professional Lives in America: Structure and Aspiration, 1750–1850* (Cambridge, 1965), chap. 4. Calhoun relied on Henry A. Hazen, *Congregational and Presbyterian Ministry and Churches of New Hampshire* (Boston, 1875), and concluded that the typical New Hampshire minister was about thirty at ordination. For Massachusetts ministers of the same denominations, I have used *Contributions to the Ecclesiastical History of Essex County, Massachusetts* (Boston, 1865), pp. 57–219.

68. Calhoun, *Professional Lives,* p. 214, note 56.

69. Ibid., p. 111; David F. Allmendinger, Jr. *Paupers and Scholars: The Transformation of Student Life in Nineteenth-Century New England* (New York, 1975), chap. 1.

70. Calhoun notes that between the eighteenth and nineteenth centuries there was a rise of about three years in the age of ordination, and he doubts that the change was the result of the appearance of formal professional training for ministers; see Calhoun, *Professional Lives,* pp. 147–151.

71. Sidney Perley, "Alfred Poore," *NEHGR* 62 (January 1908):53.

72. William B. Atkinson, *Physicians and Surgeons of the United States* (Philadelphia, 1878). Atkinson included "all professors, hospital physicians and surgeons, officers of the more important medical societies, [and] authors, together with those who by length of service or success in the profession had become of eminence" (p. 3). My conclusions are based on a sample of 500 of the 2,700 physicians and surgeons in the directory.

73. Joseph F. Kett, *The Formation of the American Medical Profession: The Role of Institutions, 1780–1860* (New Haven, 1968), chaps. 1–3.

74. A work which bears comparison to Bell's collection of New Hampshire biographies is John B. O'Neall's *Sketches of the Bench and Bar of South Carolina,* 2 vols. (Charleston, 1859). More than two-thirds of the sixty-four lawyers in O'Neall's collection began to practice before the age of twenty-five, with more than a quarter beginning between eighteen and twenty-one. Many of the late starters in South Carolina actually were raised in New England. Similarly, a sample of 400 antebellum lawyers drawn from the *Biographical Directory of the American Congress, 1774–1961* (Washington, D.C., 1961) reveals that congressmen who were born and admitted to the bar in the North were about twice as likely as their southern counterparts to have entered legal practice at late ages. Of the northerners, 52.7 percent were admitted to the bar between the ages of eighteen and twenty-four, 30.7 percent between twenty-five and twenty-seven, and 16.6 percent at twenty-eight or over. Of the southerners (including natives of Maryland and Kentucky), 74.7 percent were admitted between eighteen and twenty-four, 17.3 percent between twenty-five and twenty-seven, and 8 percent at twenty-eight or over.

75. Gillis, *Youth and History,*, chap. 2.

76. Quoted in Thomas S. Perry, ed., *The Life and Letters of Francis Lieber* (Boston, 1882), p. 126.

# 11 | SOCIAL CHANGE AND TRANSITIONS TO ADULTHOOD IN HISTORICAL PERSPECTIVE[1]

JOHN MODELL, FRANK F. FURSTENBERG, JR.
AND THEODORE HERSHBERG

Rules can be found in every society governing the passage to adulthood. In some social systems this transition is sharply demarcated, highly routinized, and carefully coordinated, while in others it is far less easy to chart the course through which social members come of age. Sociologists and historians have shown little taste for studying patterns of transition, relegating these problems to anthropologists or social psychologists instead. Remarkably little work has been done on the scheduling of critical life events in our society, and on the existence of and changes in social timetables (Neugarten, 1968). How such scheduling is articulated with the requirements of other social institutions, though a subject of some speculation, has been generally neglected as a topic for empirical investigation (Elder, 1975).

Although this paper explicitly addresses only the problem of youth, we regard the transition to adulthood as an illustrative case of a more general set of problems concerning how institutional constraints bear on the construction of the life course. The present paper may be seen as an exploratory study of some gross contrasts between youth "then"—in the late nineteenth century—and "now" in 1970. At the same time, it proposes a series of analytic distinctions and a methodology, the implications of which will be discussed more fully further on.

## I. YOUTH AND UNCERTAINTY

Discomfort, even turmoil, commonly characterize the period we have come to call youth, a stage of life during which major transitions of status are accomplished. These transitions, no doubt, are stressful in themselves,

John Modell is Associate Professor of History, University of Minnesota, and Research Associate, Philadelphia Social History Project. Frank F. Furstenberg, Jr. is Associate Professor of Sociology, University of Pennsylvania. Theodore Hershberg is Associate Professor of History, University of Pennsylvania, and Director, Philadelphia Social History Project. An earlier version of this paper was presented at the annual meetings of the American Sociological Association in San Francisco, August, 1975.

but our appreciation of the turmoil of youth typically rests on assumptions about the fit between the transition period and the society within which it occurs. It is widely held that this fit has changed substantially since industrialization. Most commentators have argued that the period of youth has been moved later in the life course (Musgrave, 1965; Keniston, 1972), extended (Flacks, 1971; Panel on Youth, 1974), removed for better or for worse from meaningful contact with the adult world (Coleman, 1961; Berger, 1971), and experienced as meandering and arbitrary. They contrast this to a vision of the past in which youth was a relatively brief period (lacking even a name) of substantial and near adult responsibility (Demos and Demos, 1969).

As is often the case, our historical image is the product of no research in particular but is instead based on nostalgia and the need for a contrasting image to our concept of youth today. Happily, in recent years a genuine historiography has developed. Joseph Kett's (1971; 1973; 1974) description indicates that the experience of rural youth in the nineteenth century was surely different from what we see today. But it was anything but brief and consistently filled with adult-like responsibility.

Michael Katz' intensive study (1975) of family behavior in a mid-nineteenth-century Canadian city also finds growing up then to have been a qualitatively different process from what it has become. His lucid exposition is the fullest treatment now available. "Most young people," Katz maintains, passed through "a semiautonomous state," having entered some adult statuses but not having completed the entire set of transitions. Katz finds, moreover, that the length of this period of life—or even its occurrence at all—was quite responsive to local economic conditions, becoming rarer among youths during time of economic stringency.

Kett's account indicates that even within narrower segments of the population, fixed and regular patterns of transition were not much in evidence, and points out several ways in which the life course of the preadult was far less predictable. Early life in nineteenth-century America might be said to be "disorderly," to borrow Harold Wilensky's (1968) characterization of some types of work careers. Youth was not a clearly progressive and irreversible status sequence but was variable and seemingly capricious.

Many commentators on contemporary youth would dispute the claim that the transition to adulthood has become more orderly and predictable during the twentieth century. Some writers contend that it has now become more difficult to grow up because passage to adulthood has become *less* and not *more* clearly charted. Protracted schooling, economic dependency upon the family, and the complex nature of career decisions are taken as signs that the timing in the transition to adulthood has become more prolonged and the sequence of movement less clearly prescribed. Alienation follows from the lack of clarity; weak institutionalization rather than its excess is seen as a defect of American society today.

Needless to say, these varying interpretations are possible because we possess relatively little systematic information that bears directly upon the question of what kinds of changes have occurred in the organization of the life course. Indeed, we lack even a clear conceptual basis on which to conduct empirical inquiry, despite widespread agreement that the "latitude," "predictability," or "clarity" of the transition to adulthood may have varied over time.

Students of youth typically have stressed learning in their models of growing older. Gerontologists, by contrast, studying a population deemed progressively incompetent to perform their former tasks, have often seen growing older in terms of a reallocation of roles. Growing older, of course, empirically involves both learning and role allocation, at all ages. The gerontological perspective, however, should be appealing to those studying social change, since it suggests the inexorable but variable process of replacement, which the social demographer, Norman Ryder (1965; 1974) has identified as a main feature of "social metabolism." This bio-social process, Ryder argues, gives rise to a set of conventions for moving individuals in and out of social patterns.

The most enlightening statement of the nature of this problem, by Matilda Riley and her collaborators (1969; 1972), divides the social-metabolic process into two conceptually distinct though empirically overlapped processes: "allocation"—the role-assignment and exchange process as seen from the structural point of view, and "socialization"—the motivation and instruction of role occupants. The timing of any particular transition in our complex society is rarely a simple reflection of an age norm but is rather the cumulative outcome of the allocational needs of the society (the whole set of roles available and their age-related definitions), the time required for adequate socialization for the performance of these roles, and individual volition. Social schedules, Riley and her collaborators argue, reduce dangerous conflicts and minimize incompetence. Age norms limit the field of contestants for desired positions to a manageable number of relatively well-prepared persons. Yet even if one accepts the premises, one need not necessarily endorse the assumption that this is desirable.[2]

The present paper has three purposes: (1) We wish to turn this geronto-logical-demographic perspective to the question of youth. (2) We will do so especially by examining the distribution, timing, and sequencing of a series of transitions, thereby suggesting the juncture between the societal perspective of allocation and the individual perspective of the career. And (3) we intend to do these things while developing the points historically, indicating thereby some long-term shifts in the meaning of "youth" in American society.

When we speak of the transition to adulthood, we are already dealing with a somewhat artificial construct. It is an open question whether individuals in any given society hold a common notion of adulthood. We can be reasonably certain that at the present time there would be imperfect agreement among Americans about when and how someone attains adult status in our society. One can, however, safely assume that both in the past and now, becoming an adult involves a *series* of changes in status which moves an individual from economic dependence upon parents or their surrogates to economic independence (or dependence upon a spouse), and from participation in the family of orientation to establishment of a family of procreation (or, far less commonly, to move out of the family of orientation into lifetime roles as spinster or bachelor). These events may not universally announce adulthood, but they certainly bear an overwhelming and apparent association with participation in the adult world. In our construction of the complex transition to adulthood, we shall center our attention on five particular transitions for which data are available: exit from school; entrance to the work force; departure from the family of origin; marriage; and the establishment of a household.

## II. METHODS AND DATA

The purposes of this paper are exploratory, aiming to look at a large subject with a new perspective and fresh information. The data we press into service are admittedly crude, though, we think, not inadequate to the purposes to which they are put. The same might be said about the methods. Taken together, these cautions argue that only where findings are strong and mutually supporting can we speak with certainty. Though our arguments are ineradicably quantitative, they do not pretend to be precise or refined.

What little systematic information we possess on tempo and organization of the transition to adulthood has relied heavily on the methods devised by Paul Glick for depicting changes in the life cycle of Americans. Glick's life-cycle approach presented a pioneering effort to describe the shifts which have taken place during the twentieth century in the spacing of critical family events such as marriage, childbirth, and family dissolution. Thus, for example, Glick was able to show that the domestic careers of women have become increasingly concentrated in the early portions of their lives, leaving a lengthy period of time within marriage after the last child has departed from the home (Glick and Parke, 1965; and see Wells, 1973, for a still longer historical sweep).

The application of the Glick method has brought some interesting findings to light, but it is a rough tool at best for characterizing the timing and arrangement of events over the life span. What Glick and his followers have done is to estimate mean ages at which certain events occur. These means, taken in sequence, are a convenient way of expressing years "of experience" in particular life-cycle stages for the population taken as a whole. But if we wished to arrive at a typical life course by arranging these averages in chronological order, we would need to assume that all transitions take place at the mean age and that everyone undergoes all transitions.[3] Moreover, if variance is high (or changing) the notion of average intervals is highly suspect. Based on aggregate averages, the interval between entering marriage and setting up a household may be far smaller than when computed on the basis of individual experiences.[4] Or, a significant minority may delay household formation substantially, while for the majority it occurs simultaneously with marriage.

Throughout our analysis, we employ a rather simple quantitative device, the intent and assumptions of which should be discussed here. Our treatment of transitions differs from the usual "age-at" basis (seen most typically in examinations of marriage), for our concern is not so much with central tendencies as with dispersion in timing. Accordingly, our technique calls for the analysis of the *distribution* of ages at which members of a population make a given transition. But our data are not from a

registration of life-course events for individuals (such as a marriage register). What we have, instead, is an enumeration of statuses occupied by individuals, classified by their age and sex (from a census). Our problem is
to infer from this count what set of age-specific events might have produced it. We can do this by assigning equal sizes to all equally-bounded
age groups, and by assuming that only transitional events (which are irreversible) account for changes in distribution of statuses within succeeding age groups, not death or migration.[5]

A source of uncertainty in inferring timing from a momentary distribution of statuses by age is the fact that entry into many statuses does not
preclude subsequent exit; many transitions are, to a degree, reversible.
Our nomenclature prevents us from thinking a widowed or divorced person "unmarried," but one could never know from age-specific labor-force
participation rates that for males the process of youthful attachment and
senescent detachment from work often involves a shuttling in and out of
the work force. Were we to examine this feature of status transitions,
longitudinal data would be required to measure reversibility. In a real
sense, however, reversibility is not relevant, for our concern is with binding transitions—what Howard Becker calls "commitment" (Becker, 1960).
To marry is to incur obligations and relationships that are generally
lasting. While a casual job may not impose permanent obligation, commitment to regular work (even if at casual labor) does, and such commitment undoubtedly occurs close to the time of entry to the labor force.

If we had uniform, smooth data on these statuses for single years of age
for men and women separately for 1880 and 1970, we would have no com-
putational problems with the data (given the above operational assumptions). But we do not. Whereas we have all-United States data for 1970
from the published census, only sometimes available with single-year-of-
age detail, our data for 1880 are fresh tabulations from a large, every Nth
sample of Philadelphia whites from the Federal Population Manuscript
Schedules.[6] Wherever possible, we also present calculations based on age-
by-status data available for other nineteenth-century American populations, for the sake of comparison. In the broad terms in which we cast our
argument, these data validate the general applicability of our Philadelphia
materials, though of course there are differences of detail.[7] Where inter-
polation is necessary, we have interpolated linearly, unless the result is absurd. Where we have had to smooth, we have used the simplest arithmetic
methods that seemed to give reasonable figures. For the most part, we
have been able to make our categories for 1880 line up pretty well with
those for 1970, although we do not know precisely how often a person in
the nineteenth-century census lacking an "occupation" was really out of
the work force. There is no reason to believe, however, that the distribution by age is seriously biased.

As much as possible, we have tried to use techniques of data analysis
which remain intuitively comprehensible, and to remain close enough to
the data so that the approximateness of our procedures will not be forgotten. Thus, we rely heavily in Section III upon calculating the approximate
ages at which increasing cumulative deciles of the population had completed certain transitions—when the first 10 percent were married, the

next 10 percent, and so on—and deriving measures from this. These will be described in detail below. Only one measure could not be accomplished with this intuitive simplicity: the measure of the interrelatedness of a pair of statuses. Here we required a measure which would be applicable across age groups in which marginal distributions for each of the statuses varied widely; a measure of association in which the effects of *both* sets of marginal frequencies are eliminated. Accordingly, we have computed Goodman's λ for the interaction of the two variables.[8]

The concepts we are developing are, perhaps, more complicated than our measurements. This is especially the case because the thrust of our argument is moving toward seeing experience as *longitudinal* and understood in *cohort* form. The ideal ending point of this inquiry would be a distribution of careers, which might be categorized by starting age, sequence of transitions, and intervals among transitions. To know this distribution of careers would permit us substantial insight into how they were constructed. But our data permit us only to compare cross sections, in order to draw implications for patterns of events within individual life courses.[9]

The concepts we will introduce here are designed to begin to bridge our present capabilities and our ambitions. We shall discuss five dimensions of status transitions. A sixth, reversibility, has not been introduced for methodological reasons. Within certain logical limits, these several dimensions of status passage are independent of one another. In reality, however, they form a coherent configuration linked to other features of a social system. Of these five dimensions, the first three are simple, referring to a property of a single status transition. The last two are complex, referring to the interrelationship of two or more status transitions. All five measures are meaningful at the aggregate level of analysis only.

(1) The **prevalence** of a transition is the measure of the proportion of a population (ignoring mortality) which experiences a given transition. Some transitions are quite rare, others almost universal.

(2) **Timing**, when considered in the aggregate, refers to typical points in the life course at which transitions occur. We shall employ three measures of timing: the age at which half the population has experienced the transition under question, and the ages at which the first and fifth deciles make the transition (the latter two based only on those who ever make the transition). Timing may be early or late.

(3) **Spread** is the period of time required for a fixed proportion in a population to undergo a particular transition. As our measure of spread, we use the central 80 percent of those who make the transition, but some other figure would be equally appropriate. A transition can have a brief or protracted spread.[10]

(4) The **age congruity** of a pair of transitions refers to the degree of overlap of their spreads. A population will undergo a pair of congruous transitions over the same period. If the transitions are incongruous, the population first accomplishes one transition, then the next. This dimension is a joint property of a pair of aggregate distributions and does not refer to the closeness in time of transitions of the individual level.

(5) **Integration**, on the other hand, is a summary measure of individual-

level relationships. The dimension refers to the degree to which status transitions are contigent upon one another at the individual level, apart from their degree of age-congruity. (Without longitudinal data, we cannot measure directly the contingency of transitions, but we can measure the contingency of statuses. Goodman's , mentioned above, measures this interaction for narrow age groups.) A pair of transitions may be consistently integrated or unintegrated, or its integration may vary with age.[11]

### III. THE PACE OF TRANSITION TO ADULTHOOD

In the analysis which follows we take up several different ways of assessing whether the timetable for coming of age has changed. For each method we shall consider the five events which we identified earlier as important transitions in the early life course.

**Prevalence**   We can assume even in the absence of data that a fraction of the population will not make certain transitions at any point in their lives. Some individuals (even ignoring mortality in youth or before) never enter and thus never leave school, never go to work, marry, or depart from the households of their families of origin. To the extent that these transitions have become more prevalent, we may conclude the social timetable of becoming an adult may have become more rigidly prescribed.[12]

Table 1 presents prevalence estimates for the five events at different points in time for males and females separately. Considering the fact that the census data from the nineteenth century are more likely to omit information, and hence fail to record occupancy of a status, the figures do not reveal striking differences. In both centuries most individuals attended school, entered the work force, marrried, and ultimately left their household of origin to establish one of their own. The drift of the figures, however, is toward generally greater prevalence.

Not surprisingly, the greatest difference occurs in the proportion showing up as school attenders. In the twentieth century, we discover that virtually all youth attend school at some age. The figure (99.7 per cent) is identical for both males and females. The rates of the two sexes are similar, too, in the nineteenth century, but the figure is lower— between 80 and 90 percent. Again, we should caution the reader that the nineteenth-century data undoubtedly understate the proportion of individuals who *ever* attended school, but even so, few would dispute the claim that what is today virtually universal was in the nineteenth century merely commonplace. In that sense, we now see greater uniformity in the process of growing up.

Entrance to the work force reveals a similar pattern for females though it is questionable whether gainful employment for women has been a relevant part of the transition to adulthood. In both centuries nearly all males—over 95 percent—enter the work force at some point while, by contrast, the figures for females are dramatically lower. Given the temporary nature of female participation in the work force, at least up until the present era, we must regard these prevalence estimates with some suspicion. Nevertheless, it does seem likely that a higher proportion of women in the nineteenth century never had another occupation than housewife.

**TABLE 1.** PREVALENCE, SPREAD, TIMING OF FIRST AND FIFTH DECILES, AND POPULATION MEDIAN TIMING OF TRANSITIONS, BY SEX, 1880 AND 1970

| | Leaving School | | | Entering Work Force | | | Leaving Household of Origin | | | Marriage | | | Establishing Own Household | | |
|---|---|---|---|---|---|---|---|---|---|---|---|---|---|---|---|
| | 1880 PHILA. | OTHER 19th C. | 1970 US | 1880 PHILA. | OTHER 19th C. | 1970 US | 1880 PHILA. | OTHER 19th C. | 1970 US | 1880 PHILA. | OTHER 19th C. | 1970 US | 1880 PHILA. | OTHER 19th C. | 1970 US |
| **MALES** | | | | | | | | | | | | | | | |
| Prevalence | 86.6% | 82.0%[a] | 99.7% | b | 97.9%[c] | 95.4% | d | d,f | d | 88.7% | 93.7%[c] | 93.7% | 86.5% | 85.9%[f] | 86.4% |
| Spread | 5.0 | 7.5 | 7.5 | 6.9 | 9.6 | 8.1 | 16.0 | | 12.4 | 17.1 | 19.7 | 7.1 | 18.1 | | 13.6 |
| Timing: 1st decile | 11.9 | 11.4 | 16.4 | 12.4 | 12.4 | 14.5 | 17.7 | | 15.8 | 21.2 | 19.9 | 19.6 | 21.6 | | 17.0 |
| Timing: 5th decile | 14.4 | 14.9 | 19.1 | 15.3 | 16.5 | 17.3 | 23.2 | | 20.1 | 26.0 | 26.4 | 21.8 | 25.8 | | 23.9 |
| Timing: Median | g | g | g | 15.7 | 16.6 | 17.5 | g | | g | 26.8 | 26.9 | 22.3 | 27.7 | | 25.7 |
| **FEMALES** | | | | | | | | | | | | | | | |
| Prevalence | 88.0% | 82.0%[a] | 99.7% | b | 42.3%[c] | 58.3% | d | d,f | d | 80.3% | 92.9%[c] | 93.0% | 83.8% | 81.3%[f] | 90.1% |
| Spread | 5.8 | 6.2 | 7.6 | 6.7 | 7.3 | 4.8 | 19.0 | | 12.7 | 11.7 | 15.0 | 7.9 | 17.0 | | 12.4 |
| Timing: 1st decile | 11.3 | 10.8 | 16.3 | 11.3 | 11.0 | 14.3 | 17.0 | | 16.1 | 18.5 | 17.4 | 17.1 | 19.1 | | 16.8 |
| Timing: 5th decile | 14.3 | 14.1 | 18.6 | 14.6 | 14.7 | 17.0 | 20.1 | | 20.5 | 22.7 | 22.3 | 20.2 | 24.0 | | 22.0 |
| Timing: Median | g | g | g | never | never | 19.8 | g | | g | 25.0 | 23.0 | 20.5 | 25.7 | | 23.8 |

a. Selected areas of Dutchess County, New York. From Calhoun (1973:348).

b. The prevalence figure for Philadelphia is probably somewhat low because a small number of rare occupations had not yet received a code at the time we made our calculations. Persons thus occupied were temporarily recorded as though not in the work force. Occurrence of these miscoded people was essentially random by age (though not by sex).

c. All United States, 1890. U.S. Department of the Interior (1896:21).

d. "Child" prevalence is a function of orphanhood, not of abandonment of child status in the process of becoming adult. In a trivial sense, everyone surviving his parents ceases being a "child." No figures are presented.

e. All United States, 1890. U.S. Census Bureau (1906:832).

f. Massachusetts, 1885. (Massachusetts, Bureau of Statistics of Labor, 1887, I, part 1:482–483.) The unfortunately broad age groups available in this publication for household status by age and sex did not permit the calculation of sufficiently precise spread and timing figures to justify the enterprise. As nearly as can be seen, however, the figures conform to the Philadelphia nineteenth-century pattern, and diverge markedly from the twentieth-century pattern.

g. The notion of half a population leaving a status which not all of them have ever occupied is self-contradictory. No figures are presented.

Looking at the departure from home, again we find greater uniformity in the twentieth century. According to the 1970 census, there are ages when virtually everyone lives as a child in a family. The pattern in the nineteenth century suggests that even at very early ages (under eight), nearly a tenth of the sample were not living in the households of their parents, presumably the result of orphanhood, separation from both parents, or residence in more complex households which their parents did not head.

For the other two statuses which we examined, marriage and household headship, we discovered little or no variation in prevalence between the pattern of a century ago and the contemporary mode. Roughly the same proportion—over 90 percent—married at some point in the life course.[13] Males and females differed little in this respect. Headship rates were also almost identical over time. Again, our estimate certainly understates the actual prevalence, yet indicates that in both centuries at least 86 percent of surviving individuals in the population set up their own household at some point.

With the exception of female participation in the work force, the prevalence data presented in Table 1 indicate that both males and females today more uniformly experience the five transitions. While this fact in itself does not necessarily imply a greater degree of determinacy in the process of entering adulthood, it is at least consistent with this interpretation.

**Spread** Many commentators on the problem of youth in contemporary society have remarked on the extended nature of the transition to adulthood. It seems to take longer to grow up today than it did in times past. We have examined this supposition by looking at the typical ages at which most individuals have entered adulthood, but we must also measure the length of the transition process as it occurred in both centuries. Here we are not referring to the time it takes any one individual to pass from childhood but the period of years it requires for an entire cohort to make the transition. In short, we want to know how many years it takes a cohort to leave school, enter the work force, and so on.

The spread of the five transitions we are discussing—exit from school, entrance to the work force, departure from home, marriage, and establishing a household—changes a bit in the nineteenth century, but it is minor in comparison to the historical trends we shall discuss below. In other words, cohort behavior in the previous century was probably relatively stable.[14] A good deal of variation always occurs at the extremes—the points at which the transition begins and concludes—and, in order not to give undue weight to these two tails we shall define the spread as the period it takes for 80 percent of a given population to achieve a particular transition. Since the prevalence figures are generally quite high at both periods, this causes no problem in comparing the transition spreads within or between periods.

As the figures in Table 1 reveal, the trend toward extended schooling is evident in the larger spread in the period during which the 1970 youth exit from school. It took 6.5 years for the central 80 percent of the population to complete the process of transition in 1970 whereas the comparable figure in the nineteenth-century Philadelphia was only 4.3 years. Though the estimates of spread square with our intuitions about the prolongation of this transition, they are not quite as dramatic as we might have expected. Even in the nineteenth century, the transition from schooling was not sudden or abrupt in the sense that most individuals left school at just the same age. We have reason to believe that in certain localities, the transition was quite gradual; indeed, the spread was hardly different from what we find today. For example, in Dutchess County, New York in 1850, it took 7.5 years for the central 80 percent of the males to make the transition from schooling. Although schooling is more prevalent today and extends over a far greater proportion of the life span, the length of time required by individuals to depart from schooling was not very much more concentrated during the last century. Despite the greater institutional pressures to attend school today, the spread in the transition out of school has only been extended by about two years.

Turning to entrance to the work force, the historical trend in spread is less obvious, though Table 1 shows a slight increase for males. During the nineteenth century, the entrance to work revealed a great deal of variation. Some individuals had occupations listed while quite young, while others acquired them only in their late teens or early twenties. Nevertheless, it seems unlikely that the time required to enter the work force was more extended in the past than now. In fact, there is some indication that the spread for males decreased in the mid-twentieth century, as entrance was delayed by child labor legislation but not deferred to the extent that it is today by prolonged schooling and the inability of young people to find work. In other words, the transition may have been more concentrated in the near past than the more distant past, when economic conditions both prescribed and favored the entrance of young people into the work force.

In the three familial transitions, there is a clear trend in the evidence we have assembled. Unquestionably, it now takes *less* time for young people to move out of their parents' household, marry, and set up their own home. Among both males and females there is a decidedly shorter pattern of departure from the family of origin. This corresponds to a strikingly different spread in the period over which marriage occurred. For both sexes the period in which 80 percent of the population marry is about half as long as was once the case.[15] Finally, setting up a separate household also occurs with more alacrity. Young people complete this transition in about two-thirds the time it took a century ago.

The narrowing of the spread in the years that it takes youth to make the transition from the family of orientation to the family of procreation is unmistakable. Like the figures presented earlier on prevalence, these findings reenforce the notion that the passage to adulthood has become more determinate, at least in respect to the familial transitions. In contrast to a century ago, young people today are more likely to be similar to one another in the age at which they leave home, enter marriage, and set up their own households. The greater rapidity of this transition is somewhat inconsistent with our notion that the stage of youth has become more protracted, though it is consonant with the view that this period of life has become more routinized.

**Timing** The question of whether or not the period of youth has become more prolonged during the twentieth century cannot be completely settled by our measure of spread. Transitions may be concentrated into fewer years, as we have found, but that period in which the transition occurs may come later in the life course. In other words, most individuals may not arrive as early even if the passage takes less time because, in effect, they begin the movement later. Thus, the timing of the entrance to adulthood may be independent of the length of the period in which the transition takes place.

Certainly, what we know about the extension of schooling supports the supposition that entrance to adulthood has been delayed. Formal education has become more protracted for most young people today as compared to their forbears. Table 1 presents two sets of figures on the timing of the departure from school. The first is the age at which the first decile of the school population has left, broken down by historical period and sex. The second is the median point for leaving school, correcting for the fact that not all individuals in the population attend school. The figures in the table are all ages in years.

Regardless of which figure we examine, there is little doubt that the age of departure from school has risen dramatically during the past century. The median age of school departure for both males and females is roughly four-and-a-half years later today—19.1 in 1970 as compared to 14.4 in the nineteenth century. The same degree of variation is evident at the first decile.

It is easy to understand why so many observers have been persuaded that the extension of schooling has delayed the entrance to adulthood. Yet if we look at the other transitions, the picture is different. Not surprisingly, as schooling has lengthened, entrance to the work force has occurred later. The differences over time, however, are less than impressive. The census data reveal that entrance to the work force occurs only one to two years later today than it did in the latter part of the nineteenth century.

Clearly, there are certain problems in making these inferences. The concept and measurement of occupational status have changed, and, more importantly, the significance of entrance to the work force has altered. Part-time work may well have proliferated among youths. While we need to take note of these differences, we should not exaggerate them. Like their counterparts today, most working youth in the nineteenth century were not economically independent but were contributing to the family economy. To be sure, their contribution may have been more substantial and more necessary than is now the case. Not only economic independence but also the establishment of a family were portrayed in literary sources as essential components of adulthood in the late nineteenth century.[16]

As Table 1 reveals, the age pattern of family formation in the nineteenth century was markedly different from current practice. As implied by our figures on the spread, many individuals delayed departure from the home a century ago. Although the pattern of boarding and lodging was quite common, most young people did not leave home until their early twenties, several years later than is the custom today. Even more disparity is apparent at the extremes. A fifth of the young people in the nineteenth century remained in the household of their family of origin until their late twenties; this pattern is extremely unusual today.

Age of marriage changed even more over the time period we are studying. Whereas at the present time, most of those who eventually marry do so by their early twenties, a century ago a substantial proportion of the females and most of the males did not wed until their late twenties or early thirties. There are, of course, certain variations according to the time and region, but the figures presented in Table 1 point to distinctly different configurations from those today.

Underscoring these patterns of family formation are the data on household establishment. Again, we discover sharp contrasts in the age at which most individuals formed separate residential units. At the median point, this even occurred several years later in the previous century, and at the extremes the differences were far more pronounced. Frequently, household formation did not occur until the early thirties for nineteenth-century males, and a delay between marriage and the establishment of a separate household was frequent. During this period, the newlyweds resided in the home of parents or boarded with another family. From the source material we have examined, there is good reason to suspect that many young people did not feel prepared to marry until after they had discharged obligations to their family as well as accumulated some resources to support a family of their own. In that particular sense, the period of preparation for adult responsibility was extensive and often was characterized by a good deal of uncertainty.

We can summarize some of these differences by creating an overall measure of the period of youth, examining the time elapsed between the point when the first quintile passed through the first status transition (leaving school, or entering the work force) and the last quintile arrived at the final status transition—headship of a household. This measure reveals the degree to which the transition to adulthood has become more concentrated. For males, the period was reduced by a third, taking 21.7 years in 1880 but only 14.4 years in 1970. While most of this concentration resulted from a truncation of the *end* of the period of "youth" some is attributable to a slightly later point of entrance to "youth" today. For nineteenth-century Philadelphia males, the period of youth extended from 12.6 years to 34.3 years. Their counterparts in 1970 entered youth at 14.2 and completed the series of transitions at 28.6. For females the duration was and is shorter (because it ends earlier) though the increase in concentration is nearly as great.

When looked at from this vantage point, it would be difficult to substantiate the position that growing up in contemporary America has become more problematic because it takes a longer period of time or because the expectations for becoming an adult are more blurred than was once the case. If anything, the information of the pacing of the transition to adulthood suggests that the process of growing up has become more prevalent, less prolonged, and more concentrated than it was a century ago.

## IV. COMPLEX MEASURES:
## AGE CONGRUITY AND INTEGRATION

There are two additional measures—age congruity and integration—which can be used to discover whether the transition to adulthood has become increasingly determinate over the last century. Unlike the "simple" measures, which dealt with the different dimensions of each status transition separately, these complex measures deal with two status transitions considered in conjunction.

Age congruity indicates the degree of overlap between the spreads of two transitions. To provide a summary measure, we have constructed an index of age congruity (Table 2). A value of 0.00 indicates complete incongruity or no overlap between spreads. In such an instance, almost all members of a cohort have completed one transition before beginning the other. A value of 1.00 indicates the opposite, complete congruity or overlap of spreads, or the simultaneous occurrence of the two transitions.

**Table 2.** AGE CONGRUITY OF TRANSITION PAIRS, BY SEX, 1880, AND 1970

|  | Males | | Females | |
|---|---|---|---|---|
|  | 1880 | 1970 | 1880 | 1970 |
| Nonfamily transition: | | | | |
| School/work force | .76 | .79 | .93 | .45 |
| Family transitions: | | | | |
| "Child"/marriage | .72 | .73 | .80 | .77 |
| Marriage/head-spouse | .66 | .69 | .77 | .78 |
| Mixed transitions: | | | | |
| School/"child" | .00 | .75 | .01 | .75 |
| School/marriage | .00 | .59 | .00 | .91 |
| School/head-spouse | .00 | .64 | .00 | .71 |
| Work force/"child" | .14 | .60 | .08 | .34 |
| Work force/marriage | .00 | .39 | .00 | .31 |
| Work force/head-spouse | .00 | .51 | .00 | .27 |

*Computing formula:* Congruity = $\dfrac{2 \times \text{years overlapped (central 80\%) between two transitions}}{\text{transition}_a + \text{transition}_b}$

*Sources:* See Table 1. All 1880 figures based on Philadelphia data.

In our discussion of the five statuses considered separately, we noted that although the proportion of persons experiencing the statuses (prevalence) remained roughly the same in both centuries, there were significant changes in the spread and timing of the transitions. Two major findings emerged: the two nonfamilial status transitions (school leaving and work-force entry) started earlier in the nineteenth century (timing) and required slightly less time to reach completion (spread); second, the three familial transitions started later and required considerably more years for completion.

Prior to these changes, significant age congruity for males and females was found in 1880 only in the three wholly familial or wholly nonfamilial-type transitions. All six mixed pairs of transitions (involving statuses from both the nonfamilial and familial categories) were quite age incongruous, with the slight exception of work-force entry and leaving home (0.14 for males and 0.08 for females). Logic suggests that shorter spreads in 1970 should have resulted in reduced age overlap, yet we find the opposite: shorter spreads in the twentieth century were accompanied by increased overlap in spreads. What explains this apparent paradox is that the changes in spread did not occur in a vacuum. The reduction in spreads was more than offset by changes in timing which moved the spreads toward each other.

The movement toward each other of spreads in the mixed-pair category was brought about by legislation affecting the spread and timing of school leaving and work-force entry, and economic forces, which affected the spread and timing of leaving home, marriage, and headship. Yet it is important to note that these same forces did not produce a significant increase by 1970 in the degree of overlap of wholly nonfamilial or of wholly familial pairs of transitions. These remained age-congruous to roughly the same extent as they had been in the last century. In summary, family transitions are now, (as they were not a century ago), mixed with nonfamilial aspects of the complex transition to adulthood. No longer do youth segregate into distinct phases the entrance into the world of work climaxed by the entrance into the family world of adults. Graphs 1A and 1B show how the development of rather massive overlap between marriage and labor-force entrance has at least formally *complicated* the sequencing decisions faced by contemporary youths.

The changes in spread and timing, then, had the effect by 1970 of collapsing or concentrating the transition to adulthood into a smaller number of years situated earlier in life. These changes raise questions about the nature of the organization of the life course today. Life-course organization in the nineteenth century was substantially the product of age congruity. Most members of a cohort left one status before any entered another. Individuals today are forced to make more complex

**GRAPH 1A**   Age at Completion of First Through Ninth Deciles: Transition Spread, Work Force, and Marriage, Males, 1880 and 1970.

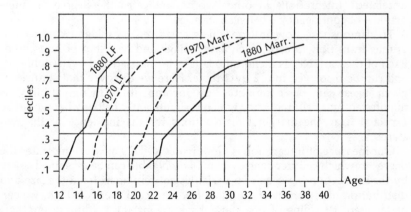

**GRAPH 1B** AGE AT COMPLETION OF FIRST THROUGH NINTH DECILES: TRANSITION SPREAD, WORK FORCE, AND MARRIAGE, FEMALES, 1880 AND 1970.

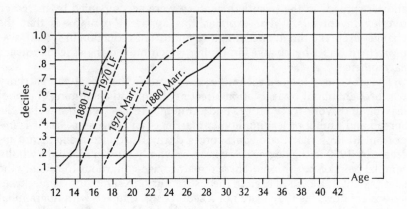

career decisions in a briefer period of time because increased age congruity, in theory, makes possible the holding of several statuses simultaneously. Considered in the abstract, increased age congruity is not necessarily accompanied by greater determinacy in the life course. Age congruity only makes possible simultaneous occupancy of statuses; it does not by itself tell if or how status transitions will be coordinated with each other. We wish to learn, therefore, whether the process of decision making has become more helter-skelter or more orderly. Is the high degree of age congruity today associated with a reduction in the determinacy of the path to adulthood; that is, with large numbers of individuals holding once incompatible statuses simultaneously?

This question bears directly on our understanding of the turmoil of youth today. To answer it we use a measure which we call integration. Here we are concerned with the degree to which *pairs* of statuses affect each other. Do they complement each other as do marriage and headship? Conflict with each other as do school and marriage? Or are they unrelated? Integration, in other words, indicates the degree of interaction—of contingency—between statuses.

To demonstrate how integration is measured, consider two age-congruous transition spreads, such as marriage and headship of household. Each of the variables is dichotomous (single/married and head/nonhead) and can be displayed in a 2 by 2 table. Here we discover that statuses at given ages can be compatible or incompatible. Incompatibility is manifested by a cell frequency which is significantly below what would be expected from the marginal distributions for the incidence of the two statuses.

Our measure of integration is Goodman's $\lambda$. This measure indicates the degree to which cell frequencies in an N by N table can be explained solely by the interaction between two variables entirely apart from the size and distribution of either set of marginal frequencies. When $\lambda$ is high, we can better predict holding of one status by knowing the holding of another.

Since we have calculated λ values for specific ages, we are also able to see whether the interaction between statuses varied with age for each sex, and how this interaction changed between 1880 and 1970.

Let us now consider the interaction between status pairs in the three categories: nonfamilial, familial, and mixed. In the one nonfamilial pair (school leaving and work-force entry), being in school, as one would expect, consistently and strongly precluded labor-force participation (Graphs 2A and 2B portray this visually.)[17] While this was true in both centuries, the interaction was considerably stronger in 1880 than in 1970. This relationship weakened decidedly with age for both sexes in 1880 and for females in 1970.

**GRAPH 2A**  INTEGRATION BETWEEN SCHOOL ATTENDANCE AND WORK-FORCE. PARTICIPATION, MALES, 1880 AND 1970. (NEGATIVE LAMBDA INDICATES SCHOOL ATTENDANCE MAKES WORK-FORCE PARTICIPATION LESS LIKELY.)

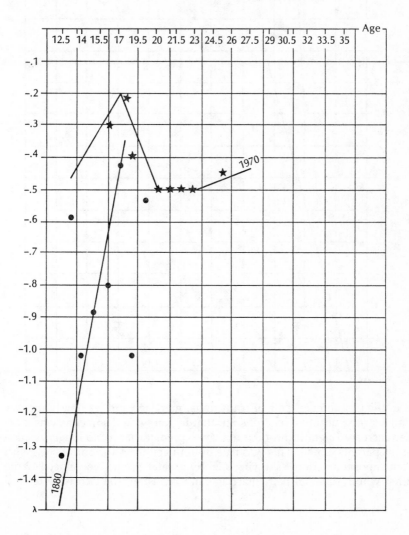

**GRAPH 2B**  INTEGRATION BETWEEN SCHOOL ATTENDANCE AND WORK-FORCE PARTICIPATION, FEMALES, 1880 AND 1970. (NEGATIVE LAMBDA INDICATES ATTENDANCE MAKES WORK-FORCE PARTICIPATION LESS LIKELY.)

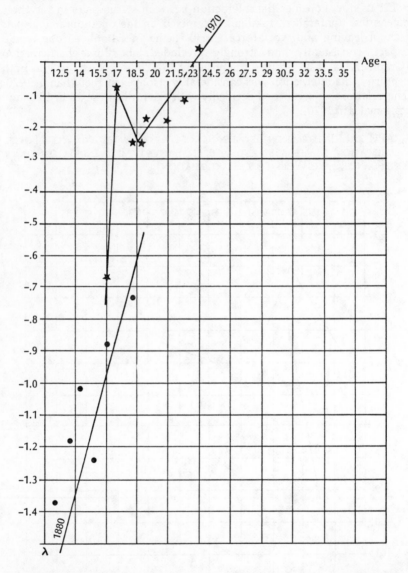

In the first familial pair of transitions, marriage and leaving home, we find a strong negative relationship; that is, knowing if someone was married increased significantly our ability to predict that he no longer resided in his parents' home. This was true in both centuries for both sexes, with contemporary patterns showing slightly greater predictive value. For the other wholly familial pair, marriage and headship, the two were related positively and strongly. Holding one status much increased the likelihood of holding the other; slightly more so in 1970 than in 1880. In addition, the interaction for males was sharply age-graded in both centuries, that is, predictive value declined with age, while for females the strength of the interaction increased until roughly 28–29, falling thereafter. In the instances noted above, both age congruity and integration were found in both centuries, but while the degree of congruity remained constant over time, the degree of integration increased to an even greater peak in the twentieth century. We conclude that family decisions are highly orchestrated, especially through a very tight pattern of status integration.

Let us now consider the degree of integration found in the mixed category, among the six pairs each of which includes a nonfamilial and a familial status. The high congruity between school departure and marriage is one of the most dramatic instances of the increased complexity of transition to adulthood today.

Since this pair of transitions was age-incongruous in the nineteenth century, thus obviating the need for, or possibility of, integration, it is especially interesting to discover whether the transitions have by now become integrated. The two transitions might not now interact, even though they are simultaneous. What we, in fact, find to a significant degree is conflict between school and marriage in 1970 (though by no means so much as in some other pairs, like marriage and "child" family status). There is a striking difference between the sexes in integration: the degree of integration for women is generally twice as high as it is for men, though for both sexes $\lambda$ declines steadily with age. For contemporary women (especially those at younger ages) school must be tightly meshed into the schedule of family transitions. For contemporary men, while school and marriage are still integrated, the greater instrumental worth of continued education to men means that more is to be gained by staying in school even when married. A common expression of this pattern is for a newly-married wife to leave school and go to work in order to permit her husband to remain in school.

The nature of integration between headship and school, and its change over the century, is sufficiently like that between marriage and school departure that we need not discuss it at length. School attendance and departure from the family of origin is another question. Indeed, the patterns shown for this pair of transitions are as perplexing as any revealed by our data. What is especially striking is that lambda is generally low and unstable over the relevant age ranges. In 1880 there is something of a predominance of positive $\lambda$ values, indicating that those youth not yet departed from their parents' households (most often into statuses like "boarder" or "servant" rather than to headship) were more likely to be in school. But these positive figures were low. In 1970 the strongest generalization possible is that at the central transition ages, departure from family origin was almost unrelated to school attendance, although extreme ages show signs of a relationship. Residence at school may explain this in part.

Turning to the relationship between entrance into the work force and family transitions, it is important to remember that for women, work-force entry is by no means irreversible. Predictably, the patterns of integration break down quite differently by sex. For males, "child" status in 1880 had a rather unstable integration with work-force participation. In 1880 at all ages but the youngest (where sons were *less* prone to work) the relationship is small and essentially insignificant. For females the pattern is consistent both by age and over time: daughters were more likely to work than women who had left their families of origin. The degree of integration between the two statuses is roughly similar over time.

Among males integration between marriage and work-force entrance was almost absent in 1880 (Graphs 3A and 3B). By 1970 a strong and significant positive relationship between marriage and work-force participation existed. The responsibilities of marriage typically include employment for men; a greater proportion of young men's work-force participation can now be attributed to marriage than was formerly the case. Our supposition is that work-force participation in 1880 was so general by the age when people began to marry that nonworkers were usually disabled or disinclined men, conditions rarely affected by a change in marital status.

Similar patterns can be seen in the other family and work-force transitions for males. Headship and work-force participation were to a great extent age-incongruous in 1880, but unlike the marriage/work-force relationship just examined, even at that early date there are some signs that the statuses were contingent upon each other. By 1970 this relationship between the two appears to have become even stronger and is consistently more impressive than the marriage/work-force relationship. It would appear that the 1970 pattern was foreshadowed in 1880. Integration between work and family formation has been facilitated by institutional innovations. Thus, for example, for those in the work force, housing (rented as well as owned) is now easier to come by, making family headship more feasible.

Headship of household is the last of our transitions in sequence and in that sense for males usually the culmination of a series of earlier moves. For women in 1880, by contrast, *departure* from the work force was often seen as the culmination of the transition to adulthood following marriage and household formation. Accordingly, in 1880, females displayed a strong integration between marriage and work-force participation, and between headship (most often "wife" status) and work-force participation, but in the *opposite* direction from that for males. The relationship, moreover, was remarkably stable across a wide band of ages. In 1970 major fragments of this convention remained, but it was not intact. The negative relationship is markedly weaker than in 1880 and is presently primarily at the younger ages. As women in 1970 entered their thirties, a new configuration took shape and a positive trend emerged between the married state and work-force participation.[18]

Leaving aside specific considerations, overall there is no doubt that the concentration of transition decisions in a briefer period of time has not resulted in a random or helter-skelter response. In contrast to the age incongruity of the nineteenth century, an integrated mode has emerged in the twentieth century.

**GRAPH 3A**  INTEGRATION BETWEEN MARRIAGE AND WORK-FORCE PARTICIPA-
TION, MALES, 1880 AND 1970. (POSITIVE LAMBDA INDICATES MARRIAGE MAKES
WORK-FORCE PARTICIPATION MORE LIKELY.)

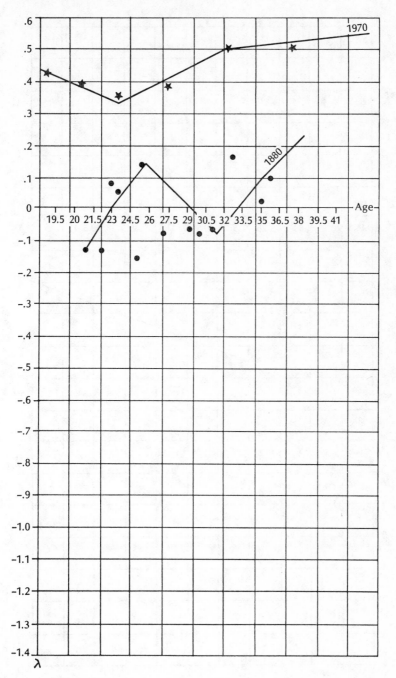

**GRAPH 3B** INTEGRATION BETWEEN MARRIAGE AND WORK-FORCE PARTICIPA-
TION, FEMALES, 1880 AND 1970. (POSITIVE LAMBDA INDICATES MARRIAGE MAKES
WORK-FORCE PARTICIPATION MORE LIKELY.)

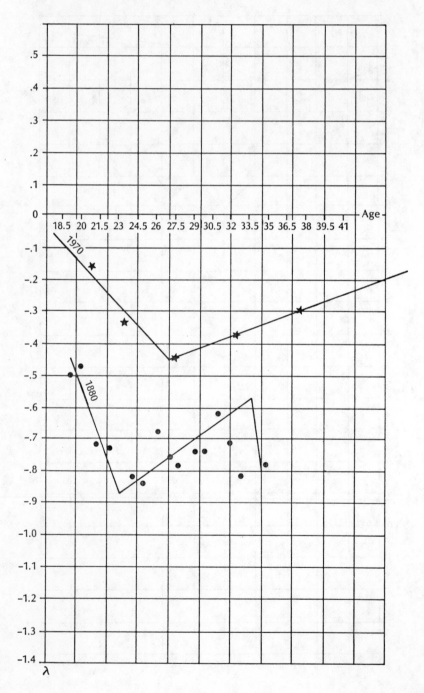

## V. CONCLUSIONS

The burden of this paper has been to present evidence suggesting that over the last century there has been change in the pattern of the transition to adulthood. As a result, the early life course today is to an important degree organized differently, with different consequences for youth. Our quantitative evidence expands and refines Kett's argument that the broad latitude of choice that characterized growing up in the nineteenth century has been replaced today by a more prescribed and tightly defined schedule of life-course organization. The prevalence of the usual transitions has increased somewhat, and for most of the transitions the spread has narrowed, sometimes markedly. The relative timing of the several statuses—notably the moving together of the familial and the nonfamilial transitions—has created a situation of far greater age congruity. A far larger proportion of a cohort growing up today is faced with choices about sequencing and combining statuses.

We can perhaps understand the slight increase of prevalence and the narrowing of spread as an aspect of the homogenizing over time of the regional, urban/rural, and ethnic differences in this country, each subgroup in the nineteenth century putatively living within its own age-graded system. Only further research into the sources of variation of age norming can determine to what degree this was actually the case. Surely, however, young people today face more complex sequencing decisions, rendered stressful by their very individuation and preferential basis. Our use of the individual level Philadelphia data (regionally and ecologically homogeneous), demonstrates that the change in the mechanisms of life-course organization from the age incongruity of the nineteenth century to the integration of the twentieth century represents a real historical development.

The distinction between familial and nonfamilial transitions has appeared in all our discussions to this point. Our understanding of how growing up has changed is bound up with this dichotomy. Characteristics of familial and nonfamilial transitions, distinct from each other in the nineteenth century, today have become increasingly alike. They resemble each other in spread and timing, and they are more age-congruous and integrated with one another. No longer are the family transitions the predominately consequential ones: today school departure and work-force entry are far more important in shaping the subsequent work career than a century ago. And today the familial transitions are not so enduring as was once the case. In the nineteenth century the family was a unique institution, standing alone; in the twentieth, it is one of many; or rather, one of the many in and out of which individuals have to thread their way.

The past century witnessed a radical alteration in the nature and functioning of the household economy as the family passed through its developmental cycle. Notable in regard to the transition to adulthood we are discussing has been a major change in the function of the labor of "dependents." In the nineteenth century most urban American families were able to operate with a margin of comfort to the degree that they could count on a steady contribution from their laboring children of both sexes. A young man or woman in 1880 Philadelphia typically would enter the work force and contribute to a family income for about seven years (barring mortality). By contrast, the 1970 family economy depends upon husband and wife alone. Children, while they are briefly (2.5 years) of working age but still living with their parents, either spend the money they earn on consumption goods, or accumulate for their own subsequent families (usually by investing in their own education), rather than contributing their earnings to the families of origin.

Michael Anderson (1971) describes well the predictably unpredictable quality of nineteenth-century urban family life which made the family such a special institution. His focus, rightly we feel, is on the exigencies brought on by premodern urban morbidity and mortality, and by the narrow economic marginality which characterized family life as early industrialization transformed society. Sudden death, maiming accidents, frequent and extended layoffs, sickness, and other such devastating events made it essential for families to have a reserve of obligations to aid at times of such calamities. If the family, with its small knowledge and limited risk pool, were to perform as actuary, it needed the ability to call upon able members over many years. This period extended beyond what "youth" subsumes today and would be incompatible with current standards of adult independence.[19]

A major historical development of the past century has been the creation of nonfamilial responses to meet the material exigencies of life. Public health clinics, workmen's compensation, unemployment insurance, pensions, and the like have rendered life far more predictable and the risk-balancing role of the family far less important. At the same time, the affluence of industrial society has created a surplus that frees families from dependence on the labor of their "dependents." Individuals now find that their course to adulthood is far more involved than before with nonfamilial institutions, especially those concerned with training and occupation, and relatively free from familial obligations. In short, affluence has made participation in the family economy unnecessary and children have the luxury of leaving home earlier and hence can afford to set up their own family at a much earlier point in the life course. Here we are not arguing the desirability of an earlier schedule for family formation but stating that what was once uncommon in the nineteenth century has today become more nearly normative.

It is important to bear in mind that the legislation which raised the ages of leaving school and entering the work force was *not* accompanied by other legislation governing the age-graded sequence of status decisions which constitute a social career. Indeed, if anything, to a larger extent than before, the career is for the individual to determine. Career decisions have in many cases become criteria for social evaluation, placing greater pressure on the individual to choose correctly.

Transitions are today more contingent, more integrated, because they are constrained by a set of formal institutions. The institutions with which individuals must increasingly deal call for and reward precise behavior. By contrast, the nineteenth-century family allowed for far greater latitude, providing individuals were prepared to satisfy their familial obligations. "Timely" action to nineteenth-century families consisted of helpful response in times of trouble; in the twentieth century, timeliness connotes adherence to a schedule.

Whatever the sources for the change in the mode of the transitions, it should be obvious enough that the shift to the contemporary pattern of allocation, the "integrated mode," has not been without stress. While we can make a case that in certain respects the current pattern of transition both allows more individual discretion and seems to display more articulation between statuses, the integrated mode does not, in our way of thinking, imply the reduction of strain. Growing up, as a process, has become briefer, more normful, bounded and consequential[20]—and thereby more demanding on the individual participants.

Scholars who see today's period of youth as extended, normless, lacking bounds, and without consequential decisions are responding—we believe—not to its essential characteristics but to the expressions of those experiencing the phase of life. They reflect rather than analyze turmoil.

## NOTES

1. The authors wish to thank the Center for Studies of Metropolitan Problems, NIMH, whose financial support (MH16621) has made possible the research of the Philadelphia Social History Project, of which this is a part.

2. That rigid schedules may be at the source of social-psychological problems is apparent from several of Bernice Neugarten's studies, which point to such consequences when individuals are forced to adhere to schedules they do not accept, or prove unable to conform to schedules they hold legitimate.

3. Peter Uhlenberg's alternative approach (1969, 1974) creates from demographic parameters a set of typical careers reflecting different experience, and estimates their prevalence in the population. Like the Glick approach, however, Uhlenberg's method makes nothing of the fact of *variance* in the timing of events.

4. This paradox depends on the possibility that for many persons establishing households precedes marriage.

5. For analogous inferences, well-established procedures are available, notably John Hajnal's (1953) method of estimating age at marriage directly from a single set of census data. Like Hajnal, we will make two assumptions: first, that the distribution of statuses by age has not been effected by rapid change; and, second, that in- and out-migration and mortality are not differential by the statuses we are considering. For purposes of simplicity (and since we are concerned with comparing distributions rather than determining absolute ages) we use a pair of techniques related to but distinct from Hajnal's "singulate mean age at marriage." To determine timing, we use a variant of Hajnal's "singulate median" age at marriage; and to get measures of the age-spread of the marriage transition, we use a crude "process of differencing" to estimate the number of marriages during each successive year of experience. Thus if 40 percent of 21-year olds are still single but only 30 percent of the 22-year olds, we can estimate that 10 percent of the population in question marries between 21 and 22 years of age.

6. The data are drawn from a far larger base collected by the Philadelphia Social History Project. Directed by Theodore Hershberg, The PSHP focuses on the impact which urbanization, industrialization, and immigration had upon: social and family structure; the formation and transformation of neighborhoods; the organization, mechanization, and journey-to-work; the development of an intra-urban transportation network; the spatial differentiation

of residence, commerce, and industry; and patterns of migration and social mobility. Blacks (about 4 percent of the population) and members of households headed by persons born outside of the United States, Ireland, and Germany (about 5 percent of the population) are omitted from our tabulations. The blacks introduced thorny problems of household definition we preferred to sidestep; the others omitted were for substantive reasons never a part of the Project sample.

7. We have been able to make the most thorough comparisons for marriage and workforce participation. In the former, Philadelphia's pattern of age by marital status essentially resembles that for Boston in 1845, Rhode Island in 1875, United States cities in 1890, and all United States in 1890. Philadelphia's age-pattern of work-force participation is similar to that for Massachusetts in 1885 and the United States in 1890. Finer analysis of the Massachusetts materials reveals that age at entrance to the work force did not vary widely there by urban/rural distinctions; while data from the United States census of 1910 shows minor differences in this regard. We feel entirely justified distinguishing "nineteenth-century" patterns (which Philadelphia shared) from "contemporary" ones. We include supplementary "nineteenth-century material in Table 1, but for subsequent presentation of data, we rely on Philadelphia in 1880, since only for Philadelphia are our data uniform and useful for examining individual-level relationships.

8. The statistic is a by-product of the ECTA program for iteratively fitting different "models" to a given set of cell frequencies and, for our purposes, are derived from the "fully-saturated" model in which all the marginal frequencies are determined by the given data.

9. Were the distribution of such careers known, we would, of course, know also the distribution of the component transition ages; but, equally obviously, the reverse is not the case. The connectedness of information about careers is considerably greater than that of information about a set of transitions examined singly.

10. Saveland and Glick (1969) anticipate our measure of "spread" in their discussion of marriage patterns, noting that by comparison with the American experience for the 1920–40 period, "the 'spread' of age at first marriage tended to become narrower by 1958–60." The authors draw no conclusions about trends, however, explaining the observed narrowing by the Depression.

11. These dimensions do not exhaust all aspects of the scheduling of transitions. For the moment, we should list two more dimensions: (1) *reversibility*, already discussed, and (2) *order*, referring to the time sequence of two or more transitions, summed over a population. The order of a pair of transitions, summed over a population. The order of a pair of transitions may be relatively fixed or relatively variable.

12. Unfortunately, census data from the nineteenth century, lacking retrospective items, do not indicate the proportion of individuals within a given cohort who ever went to school, worked, married, left home, or set up a separate household. Since some of these statuses are "reversible" it is difficult to ascertain exact prevalence estimates from cross-sectional data. As a rough approximation, we shall measure the prevalence by the maximum proportion achieving the transition in any age group. Needless to say, this is a conservative measure of prevalence because it does not take into account individuals who had achieved the transition by the age at which most other members of the population had "retired." Yet, it is most unlikely that these limitations do great violence to the comparisons we are drawing since in both instances we are relying on similar types of census material.

13. In reporting these differences, we are choosing to ignore the fact that at certain points the prevalence of marriage in the past was slightly lower. We prefer to disregard minor variations, concentrating instead on gross differentials.

14. While our "modern" picture could undoubtedly be improved by working out cohort-based figures really representing the experience of a given birth cohort, once again the differences would not be so substantial as to vitiate our major point: that the age-based organization of the process of transition to adulthood changed markedly over the century.

15. Carter and Glick (1970:78–80) note that "first marriages have (in the past few decades) been increasingly concentrated within a narrower range of years," and use an interquatile range of age at marriage as their measure. They concentrate, however, on the quantitatively less significant shift upward in the younger portion of marriages, explaining this hypotheti-

cally by "widespread expressions of disapproval of very young marriages." They ignore the more substantial foreshortening of the marriage transitions at the older end and fail to consider the implications of the narrowing of the spread.

16. Six students under the direction of Frank Furstenberg examined a variety of forms of literature from the late nineteenth century—including marriage manuals, popular fiction, journalism, and sermons—seeking information about the timing of transitional events. The literatures (which shared a middle-class bias) included almost nothing about leaving school or entering the work force. The decision to leave the family of origin was discussed occasionally, as was also headship. Marriage was a favorite topic, a fact suggesting the importance of the event for the entrance to adulthood.

17. The trend lines are simply drawn in freehand between single-year-of-age observations to suggest a sense of orderliness. Economies of space preclude printing graphs for all relationships, and a simple summary measure has eluded our imaginations.

18. Whether or not the obscuring of a once-strong pattern of integration pointed to a general lack of integration of work-force departure and family formation, or whether instead it pointed to the presence of a pair (or more) of mutually effacing patterns in the population (a "liberated pattern" opposed to a "traditional feminine" pattern) cannot be discovered with the data at hand.

19. The other side of the coin, however, was a necessarily tolerant outlook upon individual and situational variation in behavior, unusually high by our current standards. The nineteenth-century family could ill-afford to exact precise behavior, since what it needed most was emergency backing. The study of transitions, seen in this light, fits neatly into our understanding of larger themes of family behavior.

20. The data below are excerpted from a remarkably rich table presented in Carter and Glick (1970:107), based on 1960 census compilations. By controlling for age (men 45 to 54 years old only are included), educational background, occupational type, and race, we are enabled to document the assertion that timing has substantial consequences, though we cannot with single-observation data specify the routes. The table, at any rate, shows that age at first marriage, within a single occupational stratum, has an effect on subsequent income twenty or more years later. Very crudely put, to marry early was about as consequential for income prospects as to marry late; and for this occupational stratum, the scheduling of marriage rightly was worth about as much as continuing on into high school, or entering college.

MEAN EARNINGS IN 1959 FOR WHITE MEN 45–54 YEARS OLD WHO ARE OPERATIVES AND KINDRED WORKERS, BY EDUCATIONAL LEVEL AND AGE AT FIRST MARRIAGE.

|  | Married 14–20 | Married 21–26 | Married 27–33 | Married 34+ |
| --- | --- | --- | --- | --- |
| 0–8 years' education | $4384 | $4658 | $4600 | $4339 |
| Some high school | $5131 | $5302 | $5283 | $4814 |
| Finish high school | $5407 | $5686 | $5513 | $5072 |
| Some college | $5394 | $6151 | $5733 | $5340 |

# BIBLIOGRAPHY

ANDERSON, MICHAEL. 1971. Family Structure in Nineteenth Century Lancashire. Cambridge, England: The University Press.

BECKER, HOWARD S. 1960. "Notes on the Concept of Commitment." American Journal of Sociology 66:32–40.

BERGER, BENNETT M. 1971. Looking for America: Essays on Youth, and Suburbia, and Other American Obsessions. Englewood Cliffs, N.J.: Prentice-Hall.

BOSTON. 1845. Census of the City of Boston, 1845.

CALHOUN, DANIEL HOVEY. 1973. The Intelligence of a People. Princeton: Princeton University Press.

CARTER, HUGH AND PAUL C. GLICK. 1970. Marriage and Divorce: a Social and Economic Study. "Vital and Health Statistics Monographs," American Public Health Association. Cambridge: Harvard University Press.

COALE, ANSLEY J. 1971. "Age Patterns at Marriage." Population Studies 25:193–214.

COLEMAN, JAMES S. 1961. The Adolescent Society. New York: Free Press of Glencoe.

DAVIS, JAMES A. 1972a. "The Goodman System for Significance Tests in Multivariate Contingency Tables." Unpublished paper, April 1972. National Opinion Research Center, University of Chicago.

_____. 1927b. "The Goodman Log Linear System for Assessing Effects in Multivariate Contingency Tables." Unpublished paper, June, 1972. National Opinion Research Center, University of Chicago.

DEMOS, JOHN AND VIRGINIA DEMOS. 1969. "Adolescence in Historical Perspective." Journal of Marriage and the Family 31: 632–638.

ELDER, GLEN. 1975. "Age Differentiation and the Life Course." In Annual Review of Sociology. Palo Alto, California: Annual Reviews.

FLACKS, RICHARD. 1971. Youth and Social Change. Chicago: Markham.

GLICK, PAUL C. 1957. American Families. New York: Wiley.

GLICK, PAUL C. AND ROBERT PARKE. 1965. "New Approaches in Studying the Life Cycle of the Family." Demography 2:187–202.

HAJNAL, JOHN. 1953. "Age at Marriage and Proportions Marrying." Population Studies 7:111–136.

KATZ, MICHAEL. 1975. The People of Hamilton, Canada West. Cambridge: Harvard University Press.

KENISTON, KENNETH. 1972. "Youth: a 'New' Stage of Life." In Thomas J. Cottle, ed., The Prospect of Youth. Boston: Little, Brown.

KETT, JOSEPH. 1971. "Growing up in Rural New England, 1800–1840." In Tamara K. Hareven, ed., Anonymous Americans: Explorations in Nineteenth-Century Social History. Englewood Cliffs, New Jersey: Prentice-Hall, Inc.

_____. 1973. "Adolescence and Youth in Nineteenth-Century America." In Theodore K. Rabb and Robert I. Rotberg, eds., The Family in History: Interdisciplinary Essays. New York: Harper & Row.

_____. 1974. "Part I." In Panel on Youth of the President's Science Advisory Committee. Transition to Adulthood. Chicago: University of Chicago Press.

MASSACHUSETTS, BUREAU OF THE STATISTICS OF LABOR. 1887. Census of Massachusetts: 1885. Volume I, parts 1 and 2.

MUSGROVE, F. 1965. Youth and the Social Order. Bloomington: Indiana University Press.

NEUGARTEN, BERNICE L., (ed.). 1968. Middle Age and Aging: A Reader in Social Psychology. Chicago: University of Chicago Press.

PANEL ON YOUTH OF THE PRESIDENT'S SCIENCE ADVISORY COMMITTEE. 1974. Transition to Adulthood. Chicago: University of Chicago Press.

RILEY, MATILDA WHITE, MARILYN JOHNSON, AND ANNE FONER. 1972. Aging and Society. Volume Three: A Sociology of Age Stratification. New York: Russell Sage Foundation.

RILEY, MATILDA WHITE, et al. 1969. "Socialization for the Middle and Later Years." In David A. Goslin, ed., Handbook of Socialization Theory and Research. Chicago: Rand-McNally.

RYDER, NORMAN B. 1965. "The Cohort as a Concept in the Study of Social Change." American Sociological Review 30:843–861.

_____. 1974. "The Demography of Youth." In James S. Coleman, ed., Youth: Transition to Adulthood. Chicago: University of Chicago Press.

SAVELAND, WALT AND PAUL C. GLICK. 1969. "First-Marriage Decrement Tables by Color and Sex for the United States in 1958–60." Demography 6:243–255.

UHLENBERG, PETER R. 1969. "A Study of Cohort Life Cycles: Cohorts of Native Born Massachusetts Women, 1830–1920." Population Studies 23:407–420.

_____. 1974. "Cohort Variations in Family Life Cycle Experience of United States Females." Journal of Marriage and the Family 36:284–289.

UNITED STATES, BUREAU OF THE CENSUS. 1906. Fifteenth Census of the United States: 1900. Special Reports. Supplementary Analysis and Derivative Tables.

_____. 1972. Census of Population: 1970, Subject Report 4C, Marital Status.

_____. 1973a. Census of Population: 1970, Subject Report 4A, Family Composition.

_____. 1973b. Census of Population: 1970, Subject Report 4B, Persons by Family Characteristics.

_____. 1973c. Census of Population: 1970, Subject Report 5A, School Enrollment.

_____. 1973d. Census of Population: 1970, Subject Report 6A, Employment Status and Work Experience.

UNITED STATES, DEPARTMENT OF THE INTERIOR, DIVISION OF THE ELEVENTH CENSUS. 1896. Special Report on the Statistics of Occupations.

WELLS, ROBERT V. 1973. "Demographic Change and the Life Cycle in American Families." In Theodore K. Rabb and Robert I. Rotberg, eds. The Family in History: Interdisciplinary Essays. New York: Harper & Row.

WILENSKY, HAROLD. 1968. "Orderly Careers and Social Participation: the Impact of Work History on Social Integration in the Middle Mass." In Bernice L. Neugarten, ed., Middle Age and Aging: A Reader in Social Psychology. Chicago: University of Chicago Press.

# 12 | OLD AGE IN EARLY NEW ENGLAND

JOHN DEMOS

## I

Within the past decade or so scholars have come to appreciate the significance of *age* as a determinant of historical experience. At first their interest
was directed largely to childhood, then to adolescence, and now—in appropriate sequence—to the later parts of the life course. For historians,
among others, old age is a time whose idea has come.

The overall topography of the field has recently been charted in a bold
and brilliant book by David Hackett Fischer: *Growing Old in America.*[1] In
the span of little more than two hundred pages Fischer has ranged through
the entire history of old age in the United States and added some brief but
vivid forays across the oceans to Europe and to Asia, back down the centuries to ancient and medieval times, and even (in a closing chapter)
through the looking glass into the future. At the heart of his study Fischer
has fashioned an interpretive scheme—a "model" of the history of age relations—which seems likely to influence research in this field for years to
come. Other scholars will now wish to cover particular sections of the
larger territory more slowly and with a somewhat sharper focus.

Some such justification is needed for the present essay. For the concern
here is with a small and rather remote corner of the American past. Little
attention is given to issues of chronological development and change. Instead, the main goal is to present a rounded view of old age in one particular setting; the materials are explored and, where possible, connected
on a "horizontal" rather than a "vertical" basis.

Even within this modest framework of intentions, problems arise and
limits must be accepted. There are, for one thing, severe problems of evidence. The historical record of early New England includes a substantial
corpus of prescriptive statements on old age—chiefly sermons and essays
by leading clergymen. There is, however, a dearth of evidence directly reflecting behavior by and toward the elderly. Thus the scholar is obliged to
pursue *in*direct methods: for example, demographic reconstruction, the
analysis of legal materials, and assorted forms of collective biography.
Some important questions inevitably slip by unanswered. The most glar-
ing *lacunae* in the present case involve the experience of New England
women. Quite possibly male and female aging were significantly different;

For valuable comment and criticism on an earlier draft of this essay I am
grateful to: Rudolph Binion, David Hackett Fischer, David Gutmann, Nancy
Roelker, and David Rothman.

but the data seem too meager to permit even an opinion about this, let alone any solid conclusions.

It may be unfair to hold the evidence entirely to blame for such deficiencies. After all, historical evidence responds to—and, in a sense, is created by—the asking of particular questions. And in any "new field" the questions themselves are problematic. It thus seems prudent to specify in advance the questions to be asked here. First, we shall consider how old age was conceived—was thought about—in early New England. Second, we shall assess the elderly as a demographic presence: how many they were, and how they were situated in the larger population. Third, we will consider the social experience of old people: their work, their leisure, the nature of their power and prestige. The essay will close with some interpretative suggestions—and a residual agenda of questions for the future.

## II

Rev. Cotton Mather of Boston, in publishing a treatise entitled "The Old Man's Honour," included a fulsome dedication to his elderly friend and mentor, Major John Richards. He wrote in part:

> Were there nothing else to commend my regards for you, besides the Old Age, which your out-living of threescore winters has brought you to the border of, that were enough to give you a room in my esteem, and reverence, and veneration.[2]

This passage helps to illumine two central questions pertaining to old age in early New England: its chronological definition and its claims for attention in the culture at large. Each point merits detailed consideration.

The view of age sixty as a "border" appears in various written statements, and is implied in a different way by certain forms of legislative enactment. A clergyman noted "the considerable number of aged persons" in his congregation: "For there are many who have attained to three score, and such are everywhere accounted old men."[3] A town voted to exempt older persons from particular civic obligations and established "60 years of age" as the official cutoff point.[4] A provincial assembly set requirements of regular service in paramilitary units—for all male inhabitants "between the ages of 16 and 60 years."[5]

Here, then, one finds an apparent consensus as to the beginning of old age. And yet its application in specific instances was far from precise. The requirement of military service called forth some especially revealing evidence. When a man wished to be "freed from training" (i.e., with his local militia unit), he was obliged to petition the courts for a personal waiver. Thus: (1) "John Leigh, being about seventy years of age, [is] discharged from ordinary training." (2) "Robert Kinsman, being above three score years of age and having the 'seattyca,' was freed from training." (3) "John Cooly, being aged, and having fits whereby he falls, is freed from training." (4) "William Lord of Salem, aged seventy-seven, [is] discharged from training, on account of age and many bodily infirmities."[6] The list of such actions could be lengthened indefinitely, but the larger point is immediately clear. The actual age invoked was often more (and occasionally less) than sixty, was sometimes omitted altogether, and was usually linked to the physical condition of the man in question. This implies a certain looseness or flexibility in the application of age norms and, more, a functional attitude toward the process of growing old. Aging was measured, in part, by numbers but also by the survival (or decline) of inherent capacity. The tendency of our own time is much more exclusively formal: chronology is usually the decisive consideration (e.g., in retirement); biology counts for relatively little.

Cotton Mather's dedication to Major Richards spoke of "esteem, and reverence, and veneration" as appropriate attitudes toward the aged. Here, too, he expressed a widespread cultural convention. "Honour old age": so it was written in the Scriptures and endlessly repeated in the sermon literature of early New England. There were various ways to justify this prescription. In the first place, the elderly are wiser than other persons; their "counsel" should therefore carry disproportionate weight in civil and religious affairs. Their wisdom derived, in turn, from the sheer element of accumulated experience. When the "Pilgrim pastor," John Robinson, described the preferment due to older people, he noted in particular "their manifold advantages . . . for the getting of wisdom."[7] When the poetess Anne Bradstreet composed her verses on "The Four Ages of Life," she chose a special way of portraying the last one. She listed the numerous "private changes" and "various times of state" to which an old man of her era might bear witness, virtually defining him as a repository of experience.[8] It is not easy for us today to recapture the strength of these associations; they seem insubstantial or simply trite. Our culture has many ways of storing experience—most obviously, in written documents. But in communities where literacy was less extensive, it was often other *people*—elderly ones—that provided a sense of contact with the past. And to the extent that the past was honored, they were honored too.

For so-called Puritans there was a special, religious dimension to the accumulated experience of old age. The elderly were thought to have "a peculiar acquaintance with the Lord Jesus Christ."[9] In fact, this acquaintance verged on likeness: "there is something of the image of God in age," an almost physical resemblance.[10] God, after all, "is the Ancient of Days," and when his "majesty and eternity are set forth in Scripture, it is with white hair."[11] Hence "the fear of God and honoring the old man is commanded with the same breath and linked together in the same sentence."[12] These brief quotations, stitched together from various New England sermons, reflect an idea widely noted in studies of premodern society. Elderly persons are literally and figuratively closer than others to God. They stand, as it were, near the boundary between the natural and supernatural worlds. Indeed, they are in a special position to mediate between these worlds—which explains, in part, the preferments they customarily enjoy.[13]

To restate these prescriptive standards for dealings with the aged is to consider only one side of a highly complicated picture. Did old people, in their actual behavior, justify the confidence associated with age? Did their particular traits and tendencies inspire feelings of "esteem and reverence and veneration"? What was the typical predisposition of the elderly, in terms of what we now call character or personality? Such questions are also treated in the literature of early New England—and in ways that jar uncomfortably with the ritual exhortation to "honour old age."

Consider, for example, the opinion of William Bridge, sometime fellow of Harvard College and author of the earliest treatise on this subject published anywhere in the colonies. "Old age is a dry and barren ground," he begins. "The state of old age is a state of weakness and of much infirmity." Bridge proceeds to spell this out in great detail, separating the natural from the moral infirmities. The moral ones make an especially long list. Older people are likely to be "too drowsy and remiss in the things of God . . . too covetous and tenacious for the things of this world . . . too timorous and fearful . . . too touchy, peevish, angry, and forward . . . very unteachable . . . [since] they think they know more than others . . . hard to be pleased, and as hard to please others . . . full of complaints of the present times . . . [and] full of suspicions, and very apt to surmise, suspect, and fear the worst."[14] Parts of this portrait show up in other writings from the period; the overall effect is certainly unflattering.[15]

The matter of "natural infirmities" in old age also received much attention. Cotton Mather, for one, and the aforementioned William Bridge, for another, catalogued the physical aspects of aging in somewhat gruesome detail. Here is a short sample:

The sun, the light, the moon, and the stars
begin to be darkened with you; that is,
your parts are under a decay; your fancy,
your judgement are failing you . . .
Your hands now shake and shrink, and must
lean upon a staff . . . Your thighs and
legs now buckle under you . . . Your teeth
grow weak and few, and are almost all
rotted out . . . Your eyes become dim, and
clouds disturb the visive powers in them . . .
You become deaf and thick of hearing . . .
You can't without some difficulty go up
a pair of stairs, and are in danger of
stumbling at every stone in the street . . .
Your backs are so feeble that instead of
carrying anything else they can scarce bear
themselves . . . [16]

Loss, decline, decay: these were the central images. There is a note of distaste here, almost of repulsion, which betrays an important preconscious attitude.

And there is more. One feels, in the sermon literature, a sharp, even scornful quality insofar as such literature is directed to the elderly themselves. Thus we find Cotton Mather, at the ripe age of twenty-nine, hectoring his older parishioners to repent their sins and threatening them with dreadful figures of hell. At one point Mather enumerates six particular "virtues . . . which all old men should be studious of": sobriety, gravity, temperance, orthodoxy, charity, and patience. Yet in discussing these, one by one, he emphasizes not the beauty of the virtue itself but rather the ugliness of its associated vice. Sobriety, for example, is contrasted with drunkenness, and the terms which Mather chooses to frame the comparison express a certain relish. "For them that stagger with age, at the same time to stagger with drink; to see an old man reeling, spewing, stinking with the excesses of the tavern, 'tis too loathsome a thing to be mentioned without a very zealous detestation."[17]

Indeed, all the vices of the elderly seemed especially detestable, and *visible*. One more striking image, from the essay by William Bridge, will help to make the point: "When the leaves are off the trees, we see the birds' nests in the trees and bushes. Now in our old age our leaves are off, then therefore we may see these nests of sin, and lusts in our hearts and lives, which we saw not before, and so be sensible and repent of them."[18] Among other things, in short, old age brought exposure; personal character was stripped of its protective covering and made to seem ridiculous, even contemptible.

## III

We cannot proceed much further in this investigation without bringing forward demographic considerations. We need to assess the actual presence of the elderly in the total population of colonial New England. How numerous was the "old" cohort in comparison to other age groups? What were the chances that individuals might survive to old age? To what degree was personal contact with elderly people a regular feature of life? Answers to these questions should permit us to decide whether there was something intrinsically "special" and exotic about old age, within the larger frame of social experience.

Among modern-day Americans the age group of persons sixty years old and more comprises some 15 percent of the total. We have no precisely comparable figures for early America—no figures for large populations—but assorted findings from local communities are helpful in establishing approximate trends and tendencies. There follows a brief summary of such findings, based on the study of five different New England towns.

(1) In 1678 all male inhabitants (over the age of sixteen) of Newbury, Massachusetts, were required to take an oath of allegiance to the Crown; in the process their names and ages were recorded on a list which is still extant in the files of the Essex County Courts.[19] The total number of these oath takers was 206. Twenty-eight of them were at least sixty years old; eleven were at least seventy. The entire male population of Newbury in this year (i.e., including those younger than sixteen as well) can be estimated at 420. Thus the over-sixty cohort represented about 6.7 percent of the whole. For the over-seventy category the figure is 2.6 percent.

(2) The age structure of the population of Windsor, Connecticut, has been analyzed for the years 1640 and 1686. In the former case 1.3 percent of the settled inhabitants were found to be sixty or older; in the latter, 4.1 percent.[20]

(3) Hampton, New Hampshire, has been studied by equivalent methods and also for two different points in time. Careful reconstitution of Hamp-

ton families in the year 1656 yields a roster of some 356 local inhabitants. At least 14 of these people were more than sixty years old—or 4 percent of the entire list. More than two decades later (1680) the male adults resident in Hampton were "rated" for tax purposes. Their number was 126 overall; 120 of them can be assigned at least approximate ages. In addition, 90 women can be definitely associated with these men (i.e., as wives or widows), and the entire population of the town (including children) can be estimated at about 525. At least 33 of the adults (22 men, 11 women) were older than sixty at this time—which translates to 6.3 percent of the total.[21]

(4) Still another investigation of this type has been made with the townspeople of Wethersfield, Connecticut, as of the year 1668.[22] The results are: a total population of 413, an over-sixty cohort of 9 (or 2.2 percent). If the latter figures seem very small, they need to be considered in the light of a temporary demographic anomaly. The Wethersfield citizenry of 1668 included a disproportionately *large* group of persons in their fifties (26 altogether). Thus the officially "old" cohort must, within a few years, have grown considerably.

(5) There exists for the town of Bristol, Rhode Island, in 1689 an actual (and quite unique) census of local inhabitants.[23] An absence of reliable vital records precludes any full analysis of age groups in this case; however, approximate ages can be assigned to the 68 adult women on the list. Within the latter group only two may possibly have been as old as sixty, and even there the evidence is ambiguous. Another local census was made in Bristol nearly a century later (1774). By then, it can be shown, the over-sixty cohort had risen to 5.6 percent of the total citizenry. (See Table 1.)

These somewhat scattered findings must now be sorted so as to yield a more general conclusion. In five of eight instances (Newbury, 1678; Windsor, 1686; Hampton, 1656; Hampton, 1680; Bristol, 1774) the "old" cohort

**Table 1.** AGE STRUCTURES: NEW ENGLAND TOWNS, SEVENTEENTH AND EIGHTEENTH CENTURIES

| Town | Year | Persons Over Sixty | Total Population | Percent Over Sixty | Total Adults (over twenty) | Percent Over Sixty |
|---|---|---|---|---|---|---|
| Newbury, Mass. | 1678 | 28 | 420* | 6.7%* | 206** | 13.5% |
| Windsor, Conn. | 1640 | — | — | 1.3% | — | 4.1% |
| Windsor, Conn. | 1686 | — | — | 4.1% | — | 8.5% |
| Hampton, N. H. | 1656 | 14 | 356 | 4.0% | 136 | 10.3% |
| Hampton, N. H. | 1680 | 33 | 525* | 6.3%* | 240 | 13.8% |
| Wethersfield, Conn. | 1668 | 9 | 413 | 2.2% | 174 | 5.3% |
| Bristol, R. I. | 1689 | 2 (?) | — | — | 68 | 2.9%(?) |
| Bristol, R. I. | 1774 | — | — | 5.6% | — | 10.6% |

Sources: *Records and Files of the Quarterly Courts of Essex County, Massachusetts* (Salem, Mass.: The Essex Institute, 1911-1921), VII, pp. 156-157. Linda Auwers Bissell, "Family, Friends, and Neighbors: Social Interaction in Seventeenth Century Windsor, Connecticut" (Ph.D. diss., Brandeis University, 1973), p. 41.

Local records, Hampton, N.H., and Wethersfield, Conn. Family reconstitution by the author.

John Demos "Families in Colonial Bristol, R.I.: An Exercise in Historical Demography," *William and Mary Quarterly,* third series, XXV pp. 40-57.

Note: Newbury, Mass. (1678) includes males only. Bristol, R.I. (1689) includes females only.
*estimate.
**over sixteen yrs. old; elsewhere adults means over twenty.

falls within a range of 4 to 7 percent of the total population. The remaining three cases (Wethersfield, 1668; Windsor, 1640; Bristol, 1689) all produce significantly lower results. We have seen, however, that the first was subject to a quirk in the numbers themselves. And there were special circumstances affecting the other two as well. Windsor in 1640 and Bristol in 1689 were new communities, barely removed from a wilderness state. Evidently the settlement process was an affair of young people, or at least of those not old. For some years, in such places, the age structure of inhabitants was foreshortened. Later, as the communities themselves aged, so, too, did their populations, with an "old" cohort gradually filling out at the farther end of the demographic spectrum. These changes belonged to a regular morphology of town growth and development.

We may therefore regard 4–7 percent as the likely portion of elderly people in established New England communities. Yet these findings need to be refined in one additional connection. With fertility limited only by natural constraints (e.g., menopause and the contraceptive effects of lactation) the birthrate was consistently high; hence colonial populations were everywhere skewed toward youth. Persons under twenty normally made up a majority of the whole, and the relative size of all older cohorts was diminished accordingly. Perhaps, then, we should measure the elderly in relation to *other adults*. In modern America the over-sixty age group is some 23 percent of the larger adult population (defined, for the moment, as all those who are at least twenty). In our five leading cases from the colonial era the comparable figures are: 8.5 percent (Windsor, 1686); 10.3 percent (Hampton, 1656); 10.6 percent (Bristol, 1774); 13.5 percent (Newbury, 1678); 13.8 percent (Hampton, 1680). This is to say that the numerical presence of old people, among adults generally, was about half as large in colonial New England as it is now. The difference is certainly substantial, but it does not seem overwhelming.

We shall now alter our line of approach, translating our interest in age structures and "cohorts" into questions about personal expectation of life. To what extent, as individuals, did New Englanders actually survive to old age? Was this a prospect only for a very few, or was it something that many younger people might reasonably anticipate? The evidence is less full and less reliable than scholars might ideally wish, and the currently available results show some points of difference and disagreement. Still, most signs point strongly in one general direction, with implications for the study of aging that are truly profound.

The first substantial research on "survivorship" in early New England appeared about a decade ago. Its geographical focuses were the Massachusetts towns of Andover and Ipswich and the colony at Plymouth.[24] In each case local populations were scanned for information on age at death; and the results, taken together, showed a very considerable pattern of longevity. In all three settings the majority of recorded deaths occurred among persons distinctly "old." (Indeed, at both Plymouth and Andover the most common age-decade for mortality was the seventies.) Given what is known of other premodern populations, these figures seemed quite incredible, and some scholars found them literally so.

Indeed, the Plymouth, Andover, and Ipswich studies displayed a number of methodological shortcomings. Particularly troublesome was the question of bias in the various sample populations. (Were short-lived persons less likely than others to find their way into the records?) New studies were called for which would deal with this possibility more effectively; the returns are just now coming in. One very recent investigation has canvassed all deponents in the quarterly courts of Middlesex County, Massachusetts during the period 1661–1675.[25] By comparing age at the time of witnessing (usually recorded in the deposition itself) with age at death (where known), it was possible to construct a "life table" for this particular group. At birth 44.5 percent of the population might expect to live to age sixty or more, and 20.8 percent to at least seventy. Among those who survived to age twenty, the percentages rose to 54.9 and 34.6 respectively. Mean life expectation among the twenty year olds was an additional 40.5 years. (See Table 2.)

An alternative strategy is to analyze the entire populations of particular town-communities at given points in time. These populations can, with only marginal error, be reconstructed from local censuses, tax lists, meetinghouse plans, and other town records. Once again, a process of linkage to individual death dates yields an approximate life table. Unfortunately, however, the deaths of some persons were not recorded; in their cases, the method substitutes the latest date when they are known to have been living. (This amounts to an assumption that all such persons died in the same year when they last appeared in the records—clearly an overestimate of mortality.) The result is a two-part construction, establishing an upper bound of survivorship (based only on known ages at death) and a lower one (based on the entire population at risk). Presumably the actual rate of survivorship lay somewhere in between.

This method has been applied, for the present study, to two different local communities: Hampton, New Hampshire, in the year 1656 and Wethersfield, Connecticut, in 1668. In the case of Hampton, the chances of survival from age twenty to at least sixty were between 61 percent and 77 percent. Mean expectation of life for young people of about twenty was between forty-two and forty-seven years; for children of ten the comparable figures were forty-seven and fifty-two. (Life expectation at birth is harder to calculate, owing to irregular recording of infant deaths; however, a reasonable guess would be forty-four to fifty-two years.) The

Table 2. SURVIVORSHIP: SEVENTEENTH-CENTURY NEW ENGLAND

| Town/Colony | % of Twenty-Year-Olds Surviving to at Least Age Sixty |
|---|---|
| Plymouth Colony | 68.0% |
| Andover, Mass.: | |
| first generation (born 1640–1669) | 60.4 |
| second generation (born 1670–1699) | 65.7 |
| Ipswich, Mass. | 71.7 |
| Middlesex County, Mass. | 54.9 |

Sources: John Demos, *A Little Commonwealth: Family Life in Plymouth Colony* (New York: Oxford University Press, 1970), p. 193.

Philip J. Greven, Jr., *Four Generations: Population, Land, and Family in Colonial Andover, Massachusetts* (Ithaca, N.Y.: Cornell University Press, 1970), pp. 27, 110.

Susan L. Norton, "Population Growth in Colonial America: A Study of Ipswich, Mass.", *Population Studies,* XXV, p. 40.

Carol Shuchman, "Examining Life Expectancies in Seventeenth-Century Massachusetts" (Unpublished paper, Brandeis University, 1976).

Wethersfield figures are not quite so high. Survivorship from age twenty to age sixty was between 60 and 62 percent. Life expectation at the same age averaged thirty-nine years; at age ten it was forty-four years. (See Table 3 for a fuller summary of these findings.)

Taken altogether, these results do not markedly alter the picture of longevity drawn in the earlier studies. Additional research is surely needed—especially for larger, more commercial communities, such as Boston and Newport—but the evidence at hand is already fairly substantial. And *all* of it suggests that survival to old age was a better-than-even prospect for young people in colonial New England.

Some questions remain, finally, about actual contacts between the generations in these various communities. Granted that the "old" cohort was a definite part of the larger age structure; granted, too, that survival to old age was a reasonable expectation for many of the New Englanders; we may yet wish to know how much, and in what ways, the elderly were *known* by others in the course of daily experience.

A partial answer to this question can be obtained by reconverting the age-structure percentages to numbers of individual people. If an average New England community contained some 500 inhabitants, and if the over-sixty cohort was normally in a range of 4–7 percent, the total of the elderly

**Table 3.** LIFE EXPECTATION AND SURVIVORSHIP: HAMPTON, N.H. (1656) AND WETHERSFIELD, CONN. (1668)

| Life Expectation | Hampton (males and females) | | | Wethersfield (males only) | | |
|---|---|---|---|---|---|---|
| at Ages: | HIGH | LOW | MEDIUM | HIGH | LOW | MEDIUM |
| 0–5 yrs. | 51.6 yrs. | 44.0 yrs. | 47.8 yrs. | 60.3 yrs. | 54.0 yrs. | 57.2 yrs. |
| 6–15 yrs. | 52.5 | 47.1 | 49.8 | 45.9 | 41.2 | 43.6 |
| 16–25 yrs. | 47.0 | 41.9 | 44.5 | 39.3 | 38.3 | 38.8 |
| *Surviving to* | | | | | | |
| *Age 60 from Ages:* | | | | | | |
| 0–5 yrs. | 57.5% | 41.0% | 49.3% | 63.6% | 57.1% | 60.4% |
| 6–15 yrs. | 62.9 | 48.6 | 55.8 | 42.9 | 38.0 | 40.5 |
| 16–25 yrs. | 77.4 | 60.9 | 69.2 | 61.8 | 60.0 | 60.9 |
| *Surviving to* | | | | | | |
| *Age 70 from Ages:* | | | | | | |
| 0–5 yrs. | 40.0% | 25.3% | 32.7% | 50.0% | 39.3% | 44.7% |
| 6–15 yrs. | 51.4 | 36.7 | 44.1 | 26.2 | 22.0 | 24.1 |
| 16–25 yrs. | 58.1 | 43.5 | 50.8 | 26.4 | 22.5 | 24.5 |

Sources: Local records and genealogies from Hampton, N.H., and Wethersfield, Conn. Family reconstitution by the author.

"High" estimates are based exclusively on persons for whom the age at death is known. "Low" estimates add to this group all other known residents of the town; in their cases death is assumed to have occurred immediately following the date when they are last noted as being alive in any of the extant records. The latter procedure clearly overstates actual mortality. The "medium" estimate simply averages "high" and "low" in each instance.

The age groups for which the material is organized (see left-hand column) are meant to produce rough averages for ages 3, 10, and 20. The findings are summarized accordingly in the text.

The Wethersfield data is flawed, for the earliest ages, by incomplete recording of infant deaths. The findings for the age group 0–5 years cannot, therefore, be given much credence.

in such places must have fallen between a low of about 20 and a high of about 35. The figures for smaller and larger communities are easily computed according to the same principle. This, in short, is a simple way of gauging the numerical possibilities for intergenerational contact.

However, the question should ideally be redefined so as to express specific *forms* of contact. Here one rather direct line of approach suggests itself. New Englanders of the colonial era were deeply responsive to family ties; and perhaps the family offered, at least to some of them, early and powerful experience of older people. The reference, of course, is to grandparents. It was suggested in a scholarly review of some years ago that grandparents may well have been a "New England . . . invention, at least in terms of scale";[26] but we have as yet virtually no published research on the subject. The following paragraphs are intended as a very modest beginning.

What can be learned about the *qualitative* aspects of the grandparent-grandchild relationship? There is, for a start, important evidence scattered through probate records: direct bequests by elderly testators to their children's children. Examples abound: "I give and bequeathe unto my granddaughter Hubbard . . . one cow [named] Primrose." And: "As concerning my grandchild Abiel Sadler . . . I do give and bequeathe unto the said Abiel Sadler my lasts and tools belonging to my trade." And again: "I give and bequeathe unto my five grandchildren, the children of my son John Neal by Mary his now wife: viz. Jeremiah, John, Jonathan, Joseph, and Lydia Neale, fifty pounds sterling between them." Considered overall, grandchildren formed the second most important category of beneficiaries in New England wills (surpassed only by the testators' own children). The records also offer passing glimpses of the same impulse at work while the old yet lived—for example, this note in an estate inventory from 1678: "My mother in her lifetime disposed of her wearing apparel by her particular desire to her granddaughter Hannah Blaney."[27]

Moreover, it is clear that grandparents and grandchildren were sometimes involved in the exchange of personal help and services. When young children were orphaned, grandparents might be called to serve *in loco parentis*: for example: (a court order) "John Cheney, sr., of Newbury, was chosen guardian to his grandchild, Abiel Chandler, aged about two years"; and also (a clause from a will) "my mind is to bequeathe my two daughters unto my dear mother-in-law Mrs. Elvin in Great Yarmouth, entreating her and my loving father Mr. Elvin, her husband, to take care of them." Sometimes a testator would make these arrangements in advance, contingent on a subsequent remarriage by his spouse: "in case [my wife] . . . shall marry, again, then my will is that if my father William White pleases he shall have full power to take my son John home to himself, and have the sole and whole care of his education and power to dispose and order him." Occasionally such transfers occurred even when both parents were living: "Philip Fowler the elder, of Ipswich, in the presence of Joseph his son and Martha his wife, and with their full consent, adopted as his own son Philip, the son of the said Joseph and Martha."[28]

But if grandparents often cared for young children, the reverse was also true. Again the probates are a useful source. One Massachusetts resident made a special bequest to his granddaughter "because of her diligent attendence on me." Another noted a prior "covenant, or agreement, betwixt myself and my grandchild," according to which the latter was promised valuable properties in exchange "for his managing my affairs." Occasionally such arrangements drew special attention from the courts. Thus "Capt. Thomas Topping of Brandford requested the Governor and this county court to grant an exemption from public service to his grandson, sent by the youth's father from Long Island to help him in his old age in his domestic affairs and occasions." (The court responded affirmatively, citing "defects" in the old man's "sight and hearing . . . so far that he needs constant attendance upon his person and occasions.")[29]

One final piece of evidence bearing on these cross-generational ties is a striking admonition in an essay on childrearing by Rev. John Robinson. "Grandfathers are more affectionate towards their children's children than to their immediates," wrote Robinson, "as seeing themselves further propagated in them, and by their means proceeding on to a further degree of eternity, which all desire naturally, if not in themselves, yet in their posterity. And hence it is that children brought up with their grandfathers or grandmothers seldom do well, but are usually corrupted by their too great indulgence."[30]

Unfortunately, the extant records do not support any firm calculations as to the number of children actually "brought up with their grandfathers or grandmothers"—though it cannot have been very large. What can be calculated, at least on a limited scale, is the numerical presence of grandparents and grandchildren within a single community. Once again, the demographic reconstruction of Hampton, New Hampshire, provides a test case. In 1680 the population of Hampton included approximately 290 children and "youth" under the age of nineteen. For some 200 of these there is complete information about the survival (and death) of grandparents. Over 90 percent had at least one grandparent currently alive (and, with only a few possible exceptions, resident in Hampton). For obvious reasons the pattern was strongest with respect to very young children. Thus no child under five years old was altogether without grandparents; indeed, a clear majority of this age group had three or four grandparents still living. But older children were affected too: in the age group ten through nineteen nearly half had at least two grandparents living. These findings refer only to blood relationships; they must be revised upwards when stepgrandparents are taken into account. For example, over 80 percent of the entire sample population had at least two living grandparents of either the natural or the step variety. (See Table 4.)

The same data can be used to depict sequences of developmental experience with grandparents. Of course, such experience varied markedly, depending on a child's position in the birth order. A first- or second-born child was likely to know all his grandparents in his earliest years and to have two or three still surviving as he entered his teens. A middle child (third-, fourth-, or fifth-born) would have, perhaps, one grandparent less at each equivalent stage along the way. And a child born near the lower end of the birth order (below fifth) was lucky to have two living grandparents at the outset and one as he grew up. The median age, for each of these groups, at the death of the *last* surviving grandparent was approx-

**Table 4.** CHILDREN AND GRANDPARENTS: HAMPTON, N.H., 1680

| Children's Ages | Percent of Children with Living Grandparents, as Follows | | | | | |
|---|---|---|---|---|---|---|
| | 0 | 1 | 2 | 3 | 4 | (N) |
| 0–4 yrs. | 0% | 18% | 23% | 46% | 9% | (79) |
| 5–9 yrs. | 2 | 30 | 38 | 23 | 8 | (53) |
| 10–14 yrs. | 6 | 31 | 31 | 25 | 8 | (36) |
| 15–19 yrs. | 44 | 34 | 6 | 16 | 0 | (32) |
| | Percent of Children with Living Grandparents and Stepgrandparents, as Follows | | | | | |
| | 0 | 1 | 2 | 3 | 4 | (N) |
| 0–4 yrs. | 0% | 5% | 22% | 20% | 53% | (79) |
| 5–9 yrs. | 2 | 11 | 32 | 17 | 38 | (53) |
| 10–14 yrs. | 6 | 6 | 36 | 17 | 36 | (36) |
| 15–19 yrs. | 44 | 13 | 22 | 13 | 9 | (32) |

Source: *Documents and Records Relating to the Province of New Hampshire,* edited by Nathaniel Benton (Concord, N.H., 1867). I. p. 424.

Town Book of Hampton. 2 volumes (manuscript volumes in Town Offices, Hampton, N.H.).

Joseph Dow, *History of the Town of Hampton, New Hampshire* (Salem, Mass.: Salem Press, 1893).

Sybil Noyes, Charles Thornton Libby, and Walter Goodwin Davis, *Genealogical Dictionary of Maine and New Hampshire* (Baltimore: Genealogical Publishing Company, 1972).

Note: Sample includes 200 children, from 61 different families. Another 86 children, from 21 families, were *not* included because of incomplete information as to the pertinent relationships.

imately twenty-five (first- or second-born), twenty (third through fifth), and twelve (fifth or below).

These materials suggest, in conclusion, that grandparent-grandchild ties were (potentially) close and (relatively) widespread. Many children received exposure, in the context of family experience, to the ways and wisdom of the elderly. There was much interest and affection in this relationship, at least on the side of the grandparents; occasionally, there was coresidence and mutual dependence. Whether or not grandparenthood was "invented" in early New England, it certainly seems to have flourished there.

Our detour into demography has, at length, yielded valuable results. It is evident now that old age was (1) an attribute of a small but not insignificant portion of local populations in colonial New England; (2) a life stage at which many individual persons would eventually arrive; and (3) a human condition which almost everyone, as children, observed from close-up. There was, in short, nothing intrinsically unusual about growing—or being—old.

## IV

Just as the culture at large recognized old age as a distinct time of life, so, too, were elderly people conscious of their own aging. They thought about it and talked about it, and in various ways they acted from a particular sense of age-appropriate needs and requirements. "Old age is come upon me," wrote one man in beginning a letter to his brother. "This is a matter of great grief to us now in our old age," stated an elderly couple when obliged to testify in court about a quarrel with their daughter and son-in-law. And there were set phrases included in various New England wills as a kind of explanatory preface: "being ancient and weak of body," or "considering my great age and the many infirmities accompanying the same," or (more grandly) "having through God's goodness lived in this world unto old age, and now finding my strength to decay [and] not knowing how near my glass is run." A rare seventeenth-century diary throws indirect light on the same point: Thomas Minor of Stonington, Connecticut began to note his *birthdays* only when he had reached a fairly advanced age. Minor kept his diary on a fairly regular basis from 1653 until 1684, covering the age span in his own life from forty-five to seventy-six. The first of the birthday entries was made on April 23, 1670: "I was 62 years old." The next one came in 1675; similar notations appeared thereafter on April 23rd of each year.[31]

But if Thomas Minor counted the passing of his final years, numbers were not ordinarily the chief criterion of old age. As noted earlier, chronological age was imprecisely specified on various official documents (e.g., those that certified release from military training); indeed, there is reason to think that many New Englanders did not know, or did not care, precisely how old they were. More important, surely, to the subjective experience of aging was the whole dimension of physical change and decline. Again we should note the relevant phrases from the wills, which invariably coupled "age" and "infirmity." (In some cases the former is *subsumed* under the latter: e.g., "by reason of my great age and other infirmities.")[32]

We touch here on the physiology of aging, a particularly difficult and elusive subject for historical study. Lacking any equivalent of modern geriatric data, we can reach only a few relatively simple conclusions. Demographic materials suggest that the elderly in colonial New England were not a great deal more liable to mortal illness and injury than their twentieth-century counterparts. Life expectation at age sixty appears to have been at least 15 years; at seventy, about 10; at eighty, about 5. These figures are only a little lower than the comparable ones for today.[33]

Yet there is no doubting the depth of the association between age and physical depletion in the minds of the New Englanders. "Infirmity," "deformity," "weakness," "natural decays," "ill savors," "the scent of rottenness": such terms recur throughout their writings on old age. Anne Bradstreet's poem, "The Four Ages of Man," puts some especially pungent description into the mouth of a fictive representative of the elderly:

> My almond-tree (gray hairs) doth flourish now,
> And back, once straight, begins apace to bow,
> My grinders now are few, my sight doth fail,
> My skin is wrinkled, and my cheeks are pale.
> No more rejoice at music's pleasant noise,
> But do awake at the cock's clanging voice.
> I cannot scent savors of pleasant meat,
> Nor sapors find in what I drink or eat.
> My hands and arms, once strong, have lost their might.
> I cannot labor, nor can I fight.
> My comely legs, as nimble as the roe,
> Now stiff and numb, can hardly creep or go.[34]

Language such as this implies some particular element of stress and shock in physical aging, as typically experienced by the New Englanders. Was morbidity, their presumed vulnerability to illness, the critical factor here? Perhaps—but the evidence is ambiguous at best. Old people in this setting certainly suffered from frequent and protracted bouts of illness; but so, too, did many others still young and vigorous. Compared to our own time, morbidity was not particularly age-specific; hence this factor alone would not well distinguish old age from the earlier phases of life.

In fact, the literary materials on old age make little reference to illness; they stress instead the loss of capacities and skills. Just here lies an important clue. We can scarcely overestimate the importance of *physical exertion* in premodern times: the "strong arms" and "nimble legs" of which Bradstreet wrote were directly engaged by the work of the farm, the routines of the household, travel, transport, and a host of other quite mundane activities. In this context "infirmity" was bound to have a very intense and focused meaning. It seems likely, moreover, that physical decline was often postponed until quite late in life. Even today the pace of such changes varies markedly from one individual and one setting to another. Strength, coordination, and a relatively trim physique can be preserved long after youth has passed, by regular exertion and exercise. Conversely, physical decline can be hastened, given a more inactive and sedentary style of life. We may suppose that the former pattern best approximates the experience of the early New Englanders. If so, their subjective sense of the life course was shaped accordingly. Nowadays physical aging is typically, and often powerfully, associated with the passage from youth to middle age; here, indeed, lies an important part of what we call the "midlife crisis." But centuries ago an equivalent crisis may well have marked the entrance to *old* age.

These considerations should help to explain some distinctly negative undertones in the attitudes of the elderly toward their own aging. For despite the "honor" that was prescribed as their due, few of them seem to have enjoyed being old. Increase Mather advised "aged servants of the Lord" to "comfort themselves with this consideration: God will never forsake them. They may live to be a burden to themselves and others; their nearest relations may grow weary of them; but then the Everlasting Arm will not grow weary in supporting them." Another minister, himself past sixty, urged his peers to avoid any semblance of "foolish" or "ridiculous" behavior. He particularly warned against "everything in our old age which may look as if we were loath to be thought old" (for example: "vain boasts of the faculties yet potent with us"). The same man three decades earlier had rebuked all "trifling and childish and frolicsome sort of carriage" in the elderly. "We cannot reverence you unless your grave looks, as well as your gray hairs, demand it of us."[35]

It is impossible to know how well and widely the elderly maintained their "grave looks"; there are, however, some grounds for speculation about their "gray hairs." Near the end of the seventeenth century there arose in Massachusetts a sharp controversy about what one man called "the evil fashions and practices of this age, both in apparel and [in] that general disguisement of long, ruffianlike hair."[36] Centrally at issue here was the widespread and increasing use of wigs. Rev. Nicholas Noyes of

Salem sounded the tune of those who opposed the trend in a lengthy "Essay Against Periwigs." "The beauty of old men is the gray head," wrote Noyes, citing Scripture. And he continued:

> The frequent sight of gray hairs is a lecture
> to men against levity, vanity, and youthful
> vagaries and lusts . . . Others are obliged to
> rise up before and honor the old man, the
> demonstrative token of which is his gray
> hairs. But strangers to old men cannot so well
> distinguish of the age they converse with,
> when youthful hairs are grafted on a gray head,
> as is oftentimes [true] in the case of periwigs . . .
> and when periwigged men are known to be old,
> though they do the utmost to conceal their age,
> yet such levity and vanity appears in their
> affecting youthful shows as renders them contemptible
> and is in itself ridiculous.[37]

Unless the concerns of Rev. Noyes were totally removed from social reality, some elderly men preferred to appear younger than they actually were. In fact, although the symbolic importance of gray hair was everywhere recognized in New England society, the context of such recognition was at least occasionally pejorative. Here is a small but revealing instance. Two older, and locally eminent, men—Mr. Edward Woodman and Capt. William Gerrish—were arguing opposite positions before the town meeting at Newbury, Massachusetts. In the heat of the debate Gerrish made a slighting reference to the "gray hairs" of his adversary. The rejoinder was reported as follows. "Mr. Woodman said . . . that his gray hairs would stand where Capt. Gerrish, his bald pate, would."[38] It appears, then, that the "demonstrative token" of old age did not always elicit "honor," even from the elderly themselves.

But, most of all, old people dreaded what the young might think or say about them. "Our patience will be tried," declared Cotton Mather in his mid-sixties, "by the contempt which the base may cast upon us, and our beholding or fancying ourselves to be *lamps despised* among those who see we are going out." A generation earlier Increase Mather had composed a tract of *Solemn Advice to Young Men*, in which the following idea was central: "It is from pride that young men do not show that respect to their superiors, or unto aged ones, which God commandeth them to do . . . Such especially whose parts and abilities are through age decayed: proud youth despiseth them." And elsewhere the same author wrote:

> To deride aged persons because of those
> natural infirmities which age has brought
> upon them is a great sin. It may be they
> are become weak and childish: they that laugh
> at them on that account, perhaps if they should
> live to their age will be as childish as they.
> And would they be willing to be made a laughing-
> stock by those that are younger than they?

This preoccupation with ridicule—whatever its relation to actual experience—implies a considerable insecurity in the aged themselves.[39]

There is one additional device—an ingenious creation of Professor Fischer—for measuring attitudes toward aging. For all sorts of reasons and in many different settings, individual persons misreport their age. This tendency is evident even in our own day, but it was much stronger in pre-modern times. Its chief manifestation in colonial New England was in rounding off the exact figures to one or another multiple of ten: twenty-nine sometimes became thirty, sixty-two might be reduced to sixty, and so forth. When these reports were grouped (e.g., in a large population list-ing), they showed an effect now called "age heaping"—a disproportionate clustering around the aforementioned ten-year levels. Thus five times as many people were likely to report themselves as being fifty than forty-nine or fifty-one—and likewise at the comparable points across the entire age spectrum. An interesting question in the present context is the direction of this effect: did more people round off *up* or *down*? Did they prefer to make themselves a little older, or a little younger, than they actually were? If the former was true, we may infer an "age bias"; if the latter, a "youth bias"—in the population at large.[40]

The only large sample of age reports currently available for seven-teenth-century New England involves some 4,000 Massachusetts residents called as witnesses in trial proceedings before the Essex County Court. (Witnesses were normally required to give their age before testifying.) The critical data are the ages within two years on either side of the "rounded" levels (e.g., 38, 39, 41, and 42, around the figure 40). Careful tabulation shows a preponderance of *down*ward revision—in short, a "youth bias." (See Table 5.) Curiously, the pattern weakens somewhat near the end of

**Table 5.** AGE–HEAPING RATIOS: ESSEX COUNTY, MASS.

| Age levels | Ratios |
|------------|--------|
| 28–29 | 0.920 |
| 30 | 2.349 |
| 31–32 | 0.667 |
| 38–39 | 0.754 |
| 40 | 3.109 |
| 41–42 | 0.621 |
| 48–49 | 0.976 |
| 50 | 3.232 |
| 51–52 | 0.460 |
| 58–59 | 0.627 |
| 60 | 3.222 |
| 61–62 | 0.535 |
| 68–69 | 0.511 |
| 70 | 2.764 |
| 71–72 | 0.748 |

Source: *Records and Files of the Quarterly Courts of Essex County, Massachusetts* (Salem, Mass.: The Essex Institute, 1911–1921).

Note: Ratio is computed by dividing actual number of persons of given age by number of those reporting the age. ("Actual" numbers are determined by averaging reports for age levels within five years on either side of the given age.)

Under-reporting can be expected within two years on either side of the ten-year inter-vals, and the material has been organized accordingly.

All data has been taken from age reports given by deponents in the Quarterly Courts of Essex County, Massachusetts, 1636–1682.

the life cycle and disappears altogether for people of seventy and more. (However, the sample numbers are probably too small at the most advanced age levels to yield results of much significance.) Taken as a whole, the material shows a personal orientation toward aging that is markedly *un*favorable.

V

We turn now from subjective considerations—the "self" view of aging—to questions of social experience. Here, fortunately, the evidence becomes more ample and varied, and conclusions can be more directly reached.

There is the important matter of domestic location—how the elderly were positioned in relation to home and family. In our own time a considerable number of people lose their homes, or find themselves living alone, as they pass into old age; the "nest" is empty or abandoned altogether. In colonial New England such conditions were rare.

For one thing most New Englanders continued to live in their own homes even after their children had grown up and moved out to begin separate families. There was no general pattern of relocation for the elderly in response to altered needs for space and/or altered resources. In fact, the issue of resources was crucial: the majority of older people were well-off when compared to those in other age groups. The evidence for this conclusion derives from tax and probate records. When age is correlated with wealth—both for decedents whose estates were inventoried and for household-heads "rated" by local tax committees—a consistent pattern emerges. Average wealth was lowest for the age group of men in their twenties, rose strongly through the thirties and forties, reached a peak in the fifties, and declined gradually thereafter. (See Table 6.) The reason for the eventual downward turn is obvious: men past sixty were deeding away property to their grown children. But if the elderly had somewhat less wealth overall than their "middle-aged" neighbors, they also had greatly lessened needs.

**Table 6.** CORRELATIONS OF AGE AND WEALTH IN COLONIAL NEW ENGLAND

| Age groups | Hampton (N.H.) tax list (1653) | Hampton (N.H.) tax list (1680) | Easthampton L.I. tax list (1675) | Inventories, 5 towns:** 17th century | Inventories: Lyme, Conn. 1676–1776 |
|---|---|---|---|---|---|
| 20–29 | 43.7* | 86.7* | 41.3* | £112 | £72 |
| 30–39 | 41.2 | 61.3 | 37.0 | 134 | 224 |
| 40–49 | 36.1 | 45.8 | 17.6 | 431 | 442 |
| 50–59 | 13.9 | 28.1 | 9.0 | 555 | 517 |
| 60–69 | 22.0 | 39.0 | 16.4 | 434 | 335 |
| 70–79 | 55.0 | 42.3 | — | 308 | 262 |
| 80–89 | — | 94.5 | — | 286 | — |
| (N) | (73) | (123) | (34) | (196) | |

Sources: Local records and genealogies from the towns involved. Family reconstitution by the author.
   Jackson Turner Main, "The Economic and Social Structure of Early Lyme," in *A Lyme Miscellany,* ed. George Willauer, Jr. (Middletown, Conn.: Wesleyan University Press, 1977), p. 33.
   *average rank, relative to all other taxpayers on complete list.
   **sample includes estate inventories for men whose age at death can be determined, from the following towns: Hampton (N.H.), Springfield (Mass.), Northampton (Mass.), Wethersfield (Conn.), Easthampton, L.I. (Conn.).

A household in which the head was forty or fifty would normally include a number of young children, including some too young to earn their keep by contributing meaningful labor. The same household twenty years later was much reduced in size. The (by then) old man might well have no one to support beyond himself and his spouse. He might perhaps be labor-poor, but much of his property would remain intact—and this with many fewer mouths to feed.

Let us try to visualize other aspects of the same man's situation. His children, grown by now and established in their own households, were still a part of his social environment. The lure of new lands and fresh opportunities might possibly have drawn one or two to distant locations, but most of them would be living nearby.[41] The details of these intrafamilial relationships remain obscure, and there are no grounds for assuming any special elements of closeness or harmony. Still, the simple fact of the children's presence within the same community was important in its own right.

To the children, moreover, were added the grandchildren. We have already considered this matter from the standpoint of the young, but we should look at it again from the farther end of the life course. Most elderly New Englanders were grandparents many times over. Two cases, drawn from the Hampton data, will serve to illustrate the common pattern. Isaac Perkins and his wife Susannah were born in about 1610 and 1615 respectively and were married in 1636. Together they produced twelve children, three of whom died before reaching adulthood. Of the nine children who married, eight produced children of their own. The eldest of the latter was born in the year 1660, when Isaac and Susannah were approximately fifty and forty-five. (Susannah bore her last child the year *after* the birth of her first grandchild, thus did the generations overlap.) By 1670, when Isaac had reached sixty and Susannah fifty-five, there were twelve grandchildren; a decade later there were thirty-one. When Isaac died in his mid-seventies there were thirty-nine grandchildren; when Susannah died at eighty-four the total had risen to fifty-six. By this time, too, great-grandchildren were starting to arrive. The experience of the Perkins' neighbors, Morris and Sarah Hobbs, can be more quickly summarized. The first of their grandchildren was born when they were about fifty and forty-five years old; thirteen more had arrived by the time Sarah died at sixty-one. Morris lived on another twenty years. At seventy he had twenty-three grandchildren; at seventy-five, thirty-six grandchildren and two great-grandchildren; and at eighty-six (the year of his death), forty-four grandchildren and seventeen great-grandchildren.

These figures seem extraordinary by the standards of our own day; but, given the arithmetic of high fertility and surprisingly long life expectation, they are plausible—indeed, virtually inevitable. Again, they establish only the statistical presence of grandchildren; but stray notations gleaned from court records hint at the qualitative dimension as well. Thus one old man remembered dispatching his grandson "to the cowhouse . . . to scare the fowls from my hogs' meat"; another, needing spectacles to read a neighbor's will, "sent his grandchild Mary . . . to Henry Brown's and she brought a pair."[42]

While presumably enjoying their proximity to kin, elderly couples preferred to look after themselves. Thus Gov. George Willys of Connecticut wrote, in concluding a long letter to his son about various matters of inheritance: "I will say no more; for you know, as it is a way of prudence, so it also my judgement and shall be my practice, not so to dispose to any child but that (God preserving my estate in an ordinary course of Providence) I may have to maintain myself and not to be expecting from any of them." An Essex County farmer invoked the same principle when asked whether he might not increase the "portion" of his married son: "He answered that he had been advised to keep his estate in his own hands as long as he lived, and as they were young and lusty, they could work to get themselves necessaries."[43]

It appears that most elderly couples succeeded in remaining self-sufficient; as noted previously, they retained on average a relatively high level of wealth. Inevitably, however, there were some circumstances in which they required assistance. The most obvious and certainly the most common of these was widowhood. When a man died, his wife was placed in a position of some doubt or even of jeopardy. If she was still young, she might look forward to remarriage, which would automatically supply her deficiencies. But if she was elderly, her prospects that way were greatly reduced.[44] In any case, her rights to her late husband's property must be secured through appropriate action in the courts. The principle of the widow's "thirds" was long established in custom and in common law: she would have the use of one-third of the family lands during her lifetime, plus full title to a third of all moveable properties.[45] Often the wills of the decedents added explicit provisions for her daily maintenance. "My will is," wrote Jonathan Platt of Rowley, Massachusetts shortly before his death, "that my two sons John and Jonathan do provide well for my beloved wife, and that they let her want nothing that is needful for herself so long as she remaineth my widow." Similarly, John Cheney of Newbury "enjoined" his son Daniel to supply his widow with "whatever necessaries . . . her age shall require during the time of her normal life."[46]

In many instances these arrangements were spelled out with extraordinary precision. Typically, the widow was guaranteed appropriate space for her lodging ("the parlor end of the house . . . with the cellar that hath lock and key to it"); access to other parts of the household ("free liberty to bake, brew, and wash, etc. in the kitchen"); a fuel supply ("firewood, ready cut for the fire, at her door"); furnishings ("the bedstead we lie on, and the bedding . . . thereunto belonging . . . and the best green rug . . . the best low chair . . . and a good cushion"); and household implements ("pots, kettles, and other vessels commonly made use of").[47] She might also be given domestic animals ("two cows, by name Reddy and Cherry, and one yearling heifer") and regular assistance in caring for them ("kept for her use by my heir, wintered and summered at his charge, and brought into the yard daily, as his own is, to be milked"); a share in the fruits of the garden ("apples, pears, and plums for her use"); and a means of travel ("a gentle horse or mare to ride to meeting or any other occasion she may have").[48] Less often—and chiefly where there was considerable wealth in the family—she would receive regular payments in money or produce ("eight pounds per year, either in wheat, barley, or indian corn"); personal service ("Maria, the little Negro girl, to be with her so long as my wife lives"); and special sustenance for mind ("the book called *The Soul's Preparation for Christ*, and that of Perkins upon the creed") or body ("her beer, as she hath now").[49]

These provisions, reflecting a broad range of probate settlements, directly involved the testator's children (and heirs) in his widow's care. Frequently, the widow herself was empowered to see to their fulfillment. Thus one man directed that "if Nathaniel [his son] fail of anything he is to do for my wife, my will is that he shall forfeit ten pounds every year he fails"; and another left all his moveable property for his wife to bequeath "to my children accordingly as she shall see cause and they deserve, in their carriage and care of her in her widow's estate."[50]

Sometimes elderly men made formal arrangements for their own care following the death of their wives. One old farmer promised a bequest to his son-in-law on condition that the latter "be helpful towards the maintenance of him while he lived." And a second, noting his "weak body . . . and solitary condition," conveyed his entire estate to a relative who would "find and provide for me wholesome and sufficient food and raiment, lodging, attendance, washing, and other necessaries, as well in sickness and weakness of old age as in health." Similar arrangements could be made even while both spouses survived: "I bequeathe to my cousin Daniel Gott all my neat cattle and sheep and horse-carts, chains, plow, and tools . . . in consideration that he is to remove his family and come to live with me and my wife Lynn during our lives and carry on our husbandry affairs."[51]

The care of old and infirm persons did not, of course, always require a legal document; sometimes it was managed informally—or simply developed out of familial closeness and affection. Here and there the wills afford a retrospective glimpse. "Forasmuch as my eldest son and his family hath in my extreme old age and weakness been tender and careful of me," wrote one testator, in identifying the chief beneficiary of his estate. Another—a woman making "her last will . . . upon her death bed"—particularly remembered "my daughter Ann, in consideration of her staying with me in my old age and being helpful to me."[52]

When such "considerations" were not specifically acknowledged in probate documents, they might give rise to legal proceedings. The relatives, even the children, of the deceased were quite ready to put a price on their "tendance and care." When the courts settled the estate of Jeffrey Massey of Salem, Massachusetts, a son filed bills for his "charges . . . with my father and mother in the time of their age and weakness . . . both food, physick, and tendance for the space of four years." Occasionally such claims were disputed by other family members, and witnesses were called to establish particulars. Thus one dutiful son was described as having taken such "great trouble and care . . . with his mother that he could hardly spare time to go abroad about his business." Another had helped his aging father to frame a house, and—a witness remembered—"did almost all the work"; the father had subsequently remarked "that his son was the best friend he had."[53]

At least a few elderly New Englanders, finding themselves in need of help but without relatives living nearby, were obliged to appeal to public authority. Usually the local meeting would supervise their care. Particular tasks and services were assigned to individual townspeople, who were subsequently reimbursed out of town funds. The financial accounts of Watertown, Massachusetts, for the year 1670 reveal the process at work in a specific case:

|  | £ s d |
|---|---|
| To widow Bartlett, for dieting old Bright | 10-00-00 |
| To John Bisko, for a bushel of meal to old Bright, and 7 loads of wood | 01-11-06 |
| To William Perry, for work for old Bright | 00-03-03 |
| To Michael Bairstow . . . for cloth for a coat for old Bright | 01-18-06 |

The recipient of these charities, Goodman Henry Bright, was "old" indeed—95 years old by the best available estimate. The local records of New Haven, Connecticut, show a similar involvement with a man identified only as "old Bunnill." The town voted him "maintainance" of two shillings per week (among other benefits). Eventually "the town was informed that old Bunnill is desirous to go to old England . . . where he saith he hath some friends to take care of him," and public funds were authorized to pay for his passage.[54]

## VI

The problems created by infirmity were only one part of the experience of old age. Many elderly New Englanders retained a substantial capacity for work, for public service, for ordinary forms of social intercourse. The same thing is true, even more so, of our own society; however, the context is now vastly changed.

To make such comparisons with modern conditions is to spotlight at once the issue of "retirement." Did the New Englanders retire from active pursuits as they crossed the "borders" of old age? A quick answer is likely to be negative. Almost any set of local records can be used to observe old people in the postures of their workaday world. Here are several examples, culled from the files of the Essex County Courts: Edward Guppy, age sixty, "employed by Edmund Batter to mow salt water grass in the marsh"; William Nichols, age seventy, hauling grist to the local mill; Evan Morris, age sixty-six, working "as a retainer" at the Rowley ironworks; William Boynton, age sixty-eight, hired by a merchant to transport "rugs and blanketing" to Boston; George Kesar, age sixty-seven, tanning leather for his neighbors; James Brown, age seventy-four, still active as a glazier; Edmund Pickard, age sixty, "master of the [ship] Hopewell"; Wayborough Gatchell, age seventy, continuing "her services as midwife"; and—most remarkably of all—Henry Stich, age 102, working as a "collier" at Saugus.[55]

As in everyday labor, so, too, in public service did older people play substantial parts. The various governors and assistants of Plymouth Colony seem, for the most part, to have retained their offices until the end of their lives. The careers of New England clergymen were also extremely prolonged; in a sample of thirty-five only three were terminated by causes other than death.[56] Individual cases are no less impressive. In 1700 the Hampton vital records gave special notice to the death of "Henry Green, Esq., aged about 80 years, for several years a member of the Council of New Hampshire until by age he laid down that place, but a Justice till he died which was the 5th of August." In 1669 Thomas Minor of Connecticut made the following entry in his diary: "I am by my own accounts sixty-one years old. I was by the town this year chosen to be a selectman, the town's treasurer, the town's recorder, the brander of horses, [and] by the General Court recorded the head officer of the train-band . . . one of the four that have the charge of the militia of the whole county, and chosen and sworn commissioner and one to assist in keeping the county court."[57]

Yet the total picture is complicated, and the evidence does not run entirely in a single direction. Henry Green, after all, had "laid down" one of his offices on account of age. And there are similar indications in the careers of other public officials—such as the notorious Samuel Sewall of Massachusetts. When Sewall was sixty-five years old and long established as a magistrate, he put his name forward for the position of chief justice. The governor was evasive in his reply: he recognized Sewall's qualifications but "did not know but that by reason of my age I had rather stay at home." Sewall "humbly thanked His Excellency" for this mark of personal consideration—and continued his quest for the position. Ten years later, though, it was Sewall himself who cited the exigencies of age: "I went to the Lieut. Governor and desired to lay down my place in the Superior Court. I was not capable to do the work, and therefore was not willing to hold the place." Thomas Munson of New Haven made a similar plea while seeking, at the age of sixty-three, to retire from his post as Lieutenant in the local militia: "He said he had been an officer to the company long, and had willingly served to the best of his ability, but he finds such decays in himself, and thereby [feels himself] unfit to serve in that place and office any longer."[58]

Lieut. Munson seems, in fact, a better case for our purposes than either Green or Sewall; as a *local* (not provincial) official he more closely approximated average experience. But the study of local leadership is most usefully pursued by way of collective biography. Were selectmen, for example, often men of advanced years? Might they continue to serve until the time of their death? A modest sample of Hampton selectmen has been investigated with these questions in mind, and the results establish distinct trends in relation to age. The largest portion of the sample comprised men between the ages of fifty and fifty-nine years (32 percent); the next largest group were in their forties (27 percent). A smaller, though still considerable, number were in their sixties (18 percent); however, very few (3 percent) were seventy or more. (See Table 7.)

A subsample drawn from the same material yields an even clearer picture of withdrawal from office holding in relation to old age. The nineteen selectmen in this group all served at least three terms, and all died at ages of at least seventy. Their mean age at the time of final service was 65.8.

**Table 7.**  SELECTMEN'S AGES: HAMPTON, N.H. (1645–1720)

| Age group | Number of Selectmen | Percentage of Sample |
|---|---|---|
| 20–29 | 2 | 1% |
| 30–39 | 31 | 19 |
| 40–49 | 45 | 27 |
| 50–59 | 52 | 32 |
| 60–69 | 30 | 18 |
| 70+ | 5 | 3 |

Sources: Town Book of Hampton. 2 volumes (ms. volumes in Town Offices, Hampton, N.H.).
  Joseph Dow, *History of the Town of Hampton, New Hampshire* (Salem, Mass.: Salem Press, 1893).
  Sybil Noyes, Charles Thornton Libby, and Walter Goodwin Davis, *Genealogical Dictionary of Maine and New Hampshire* (Baltimore: Genealogical Publishing Company, 1972).

Only one of them actually died in office, and fully 90 percent lived at least five years longer. Indeed, the average interval between final term and time of death was more than eleven years. (See Table 8.)

Thomas Minor qualifies as a "local leader" in another settlement (Stonington, Connecticut), and his diary offers a unique opportunity to study the career of an older man in detail. Minor's varied responsibilities as an

**Table 8.**  SELECTMEN'S AGES AT RETIREMENT AND DEATH: HAMPTON, N.H. (1645–1720)

| Age in last term as selectman | | Interval between last term and death | |
|---|---|---|---|
| AGE | N | YEARS | N |
| 59 or less | 2 | 0 | 1 |
| 60 | 1 | 1 | — |
| 61 | 1 | 2 | 1 |
| 62 | — | 3 | — |
| 63 | 2 | 4 | — |
| 64 | 2 | 5 | 1 |
| 65 | — | 6 | — |
| 66 | 1 | 7 | 3 |
| 67 | — | 8 | 1 |
| 68 | 4 | 9 | 1 |
| 69 | 1 | 10 | 2 |
| 70 | — | 11 | 1 |
| 71 | 1 | 12 | 1 |
| 72 | 3 | 13 | 1 |
| 73 | — | 14 | 1 |
| 74 | 1 | 15 | 2 |
| 75 and over | — | 16 | — |
| | | 17 | 3 |
| | | 18 and over | — |
| Average = 65.8 yrs. | | Average = 10.3 yrs. | |

Sources: Town Book of Hampton. 2 volumes (Ms. volumes, Town Offices, Hampton, N.H.).
  Joseph Dow, *History of the Town of Hampton, New Hampshire* (Salem, Mass.: Salem Press, 1893).
  Sybil Noyes, Charles Thornton Libby, and Walter Goodwin Davis, *Genealogical Dictionary of Maine and New Hampshire* (Baltimore: Genealogical Publishing Company, 1972).
Note: The sample includes nineteen men, all of whom died at ages of at least seventy, having served at least three terms as town selectman.

officeholder in his sixty-first year have already been noted. He continued to serve, in similar ways, for some while longer and was even "employed in the country's service about the Indian War" at the age of sixty-seven. After seventy, however, the pattern seems to have changed. The diary makes no further reference to office holding or, indeed, to any other form of public responsibility.[59]

Minor's life as a private citizen is also fully chronicled; again there is evidence of vigorous activity well into his seventh decade. Here is the record of a typical month in his sixty-sixth year:

> The third month is May and hath 31 days. Friday the first: this week I made my cart. Friday the 8: a town meeting. Monday the 11: I and my wife was at New London. Friday the 15: we pulled down the chimneys. Monday the 18 day: Thomas Park began to build. Friday 22: we shore the sheep and had home one of the mantel-trees. 25: we had a town meeting. 27 Wednesday: we laid out Bay grants on the east side [of the] Poquatuck . . .[60]

Beyond the age of seventy Minor continued to work on his farm, to visit friends, and the like—but at a somewhat reduced pace. By this time he was receiving considerable help from others. In the spring of his seventy-third year, for example, one of his sons "took all the corn to sow and to plant, to halves for this year."[61]

One final test has been made of the effects of aging on Thomas Minor, by coding the events noted in his diary on a simple "self/other" basis. Minor's reports of his own activity (any event in which he is himself a chief agent) can then be compared with his references to the doings of others. The results, briefly summarized, show a modest lowering of the ratio (self/other) as Minor passed into his sixties, and a very marked decline in his early seventies. (See Table 9.) Though this measure is admittedly crude, it allows us to glimpse the deeper rhythms of aging in one particular case.

The retirement question evokes, in sum, a complex and divided answer

**Table 9.**  Thomas Minor (Stonington, Conn.): Activities Pattern

| Years | Minor's Age | Self | Other | Ratio |
|---|---|---|---|---|
| 1654–1657 | (45–48) | 98 | 25 | 3.92 |
| 1658–1661 | (49–52) | 149 | 44 | 3.39 |
| 1662–1665 | (53–56) | 129 | 50 | 2.58 |
| 1666–1669 | (57–60) | 151 | 52 | 2.90 |
| 1670–1673 | (61–64) | 156 | 88 | 1.77 |
| 1674–1677 | (65–68) | 144 | 68 | 2.12 |
| 1678–1680 | (69–71) | 88 | 41 | 2.15 |
| 1681–1684 | (72–75) | 88 | 93 | 0.95 |

Source: Thomas Minor, *The Diary of Thomas Minor, Stonington, Connecticut, 1653 to 1684,* edited by Sidney Miner and George D. Stanton (New London, Conn.: Day Publishing Company).

Note: The first six calendar months of each year (January–June) were coded for references to personal activity. The numbers in the "self" column include all activities in which Minor describes himself as a major participant. The "other" column includes activities which Minor attributes to other people in his local environment. (The following kinds of activity are *not* included: marriages, births, deaths, sicknesses, injuries, holidays, and religious observances.)

from the New England source materials. It appears that most men past sixty voluntarily reduced their activities in work and/or public service. Yet nearly always this was a gradual process—a quantitative rather than a qualitative change—and rarely did it lead to complete withdrawal. There were two main categories of exceptions: those ministers and magistrates whose exalted rank exempted them from even a partial retirement, and those among the ordinary folk whose "infirmities" were simply incapacitating.

We should understand, too, that the idea of retirement was not entirely unknown to the New Englanders. The Mathers, father and son, both remarked on its sometimes painful aspect. "It is a very undesirable thing for a man to outlive his work," wrote Increase, "although if God will have it so, His Holy Will must be humbly and patiently submitted unto."[62] Cotton pursued the same thought at greater length:

> Old folks often can't endure to be judged less able than ever they were for public appearances, or to be put out of offices. But good sir, be so wise as to disappear of your own accord, as soon and as far as you lawfully may. Be glad of a dismission from any post, that would have called for your activities. . . . Let your quietus gratify you. Be pleased with the retirement which you are dismissed unto.[63]

Comments like these seem to reach forward to our own time; yet the similarities, no less than the differences, are liable to overstatement. The germ of modern retirement was present three centuries ago—but only the germ. What was then gradual, partial, and indefinite at many points has now become abrupt, total, and rigid in its specific applications. A process with intrinsic biological connections has become a moment plucked from the calendar.

## VII

There is one more aspect of social experience to which our study should make some approach. We established at the outset that the normative code of colonial New England was decidedly favorable to old age. "Honor," "respect," even "veneration" were the terms most frequently used in prescribing attitudes toward the elderly. Younger people were urged to "rise up . . . before the old man," and conduct themselves with "a bashful and modest reverence." The elderly, for their part, would "use a kind of authority and confidence in their words and carriage." But were these precepts actually followed in practice?[64]

Occasionally—very occasionally—some fragment of the documentary record allows us to glimpse people of different generations dealing with one another face to face. A few of these have been noted already; one more will be added now. Two residents of Scituate, Massachusetts, were arguing one summer day in 1685 about a debt for several bolts of cloth. One was Nathaniel Parker, age twenty-three, the other Edward Jenkins, age approximately sixty-five. (The site was Jenkins' own house.) Tempers flared—and then: "Nathaniel Parker ran to Edward Jenkins and took Edward Jenkins by the collar or neckcloth that was about Edward Jenkins' neck; and Nathaniel Parker said, 'God damn me, if thou were not an old man, I would bat thy teeth down thy throat.'" Shall we count this as an expression of deference to age? Literally, yes—but, in context, no. Certainly it was not the kind of deference prescribed in the published literature on old age. Parker's comment seems, in fact, to imply *contempt* for his adversary's weakness as an "old man."[65]

The connotations, in the New England setting, of the word "old" deserve our further consideration. Again and again in local records we find elderly people mentioned in a special way: "old Bright," "old Bunnill," "old Woodward," "old Hammond." Their given names are, in effect, discounted, and age itself becomes an identifying mark. (For younger persons the pattern of reference was consistently otherwise; in their case, given name and surname appeared together.) This usage was not, moreover, a matter of indifference to the elderly themselves. Increase Mather made the point very clearly: "To treat aged persons with disrespectful or disdainful language only because of their age is a very criminal offense in the sight of God; yet how common is it to call this or the other person 'old such an one,' in a way of contempt on the account of their age."[66] A list of householders, in the records of Watertown, Massachusetts, includes five men designated in precisely this way. Their age, as determined from independent evidence, ranged between sixty-seven and eighty-two. Interestingly, there are other men of equivalent age on the same list who are not called "old." The distinction was one of social rank, pure and simple. Thus the man listed as "Simon Stone" (age seventy-two) was wealthy, a deacon of the Watertown church, and frequently a town officer; whereas "old Knapp" (age seventy-four) was a sometime carpenter of little means and no public responsibilities whatsoever. The implicitly pejorative prefix could only be applied in the latter instance.[67] Probate documents afford parallel evidence on the same matter. Testators called themselves "ancient" or "aged" (when they referred to such things at all), but never "old." It was fine to describe property that way—"old housing," "old lumber," "old cows," or whatever—but not the *person* writing the will.[68]

So much for individual terms of reference; were there no formal—perhaps even institutional—expressions of deference to the elderly? One possibility comes immediately to mind. The inhabitants of New England towns, like people in traditional communities everywhere, came together at regular intervals to honor in a ceremonial way their deepest values and spiritual commitments. Weekly (sometimes twice-weekly) they gathered for worship in the village meetinghouse. On these occasions they reaffirmed not only the shared basis of their corporate life but also the hierarchical arrangement of its constituent parts. Every meetinghouse was carefully "seated"—that is, all adult members of the community occupied places assigned to them in accordance with their individual status. The basic principle was: the higher the rank of the person involved, the closer his seat to the front.[69] The official criteria for making these status evaluations invariably included "age"—along with "estate" (i.e., wealth), "office" (public service), "dignity of descent" (pedigree), and "pious disposition."[70] Here, then, was an unmistakable mark of the preferment deemed appropriate for older citizens.

However, we may well ask to what extent, and in what ways, this criterion of status was actually applied in conjunction with all the others. Fortunately, detailed seating plans have survived in various town archives; *un*fortunately, they have not as yet received much systematic attention from scholars.[71] That they deserve such attention seems indisputable, for they are virtual "sociograms" that would tell us much about seventeenth-century life. But for the moment we have only one set of results on which to base some very tentative conclusions.

**Table 10.** HAMPTON (N.H.) MEETINGHOUSE PLAN, 1650 STATUS-DISCREPANT CASES

| NAME | (3–4 Quintiles) AGE (IN QUINTILES) | WEALTH | SEAT ROW | (SECTION) |
|---|---|---|---|---|
| Brown, John | 4 | 1* | 1 | (s) |
| Cole, Eunice | 1 | 5* | 5 | (e) |
| Cole, William | 1 | 5* | 3 | (w) |
| Elkins, Gershom | 2 | 5* | 3 | (w) |
| Elkins, Mary | 2 | 5* | 4 | (e) |
| Fuller, Frances | 4 | 1* | 1 | (s) |
| Huggins, John | 2 | 5* | 5 | (w) |
| Moulton, Margaret | 5 | 2 | 2 | (s) |
| Sanborn, John | 5 | 2 | 2 | (s) |
| Ward, Margaret | 5 | 1* | 2 | (s) |
| Ward, Thomas | 4 | 1* | 1 | (w) |

| NAME | (2 Quintiles) AGE (IN QUINTILES) | WEALTH | SEAT ROW | (SECTION) |
|---|---|---|---|---|
| Brown, Sarah | 3 | 1* | 1 | (e) |
| Estow, Mary | 1 | 3* | 2 | (s) |
| Estow, William | 1* | 3 | Table | |
| Green, Henry | 5 | 3* | 2 | (w) |
| Leavitt, Thomas | 4 | 2 | 2 | (w) |
| Marston, Mary | 5* | 3 | 3 | (s) |
| Moulton, William | 4 | 2 | 2 | (s) |
| Philbrick, Thomas | 1* | 3 | 1 | (s) |
| Sanborn, Mary | 4 | 2 | 2 | (e) |
| Sanborn, Mary | 5 | 3 | 2 | (e) |
| Sanborn, William | 5 | 3* | 2 | (s) |
| Sleeper, Thomas | 3 | 5* | 3 | (w) |
| Smith, Deborah | 3 | 5* | 4 | (e) |
| Smith, John | 3 | 5* | 4 | (w) |
| Swain, William | 1* | 3 | 1 | (s) |
| Taylor, Anthony | 2 | 4* | 3 | (s) |

Sources: *Town Book of Hamnpto,* 2 volumes (Ms. volumes in Town Offices, Hampton, N.H.).

Sybil Noyes, Charles Thornton Libby, and Walter Goodwin Davis, *Genealogical Dictionary of Maine and New Hampshire* (Baltimore: Genealogical Publishing Company, 1772).

Joseph Dow, *History of the Town of Hampton, New Hampshire* (Salem, Mass.: Salem Press, 1893).

Note: Ages have been computed (in some cases estimated) from vital records, genealogies, etc. Wealth was determined by averaging positions (relative to all other taxpayers) on tax lists of 1647 and 1653. Asterisk indicates factor apparently given greatest weight in seating assignment.

The Hampton (New Hampshire) meetinghouse was seated in the early months of the year 1650.[72] The design of the building was relatively simple. The pulpit was on the north side; just below, and roughly in the middle of the floor space, was a "table" where men of the highest rank were privileged to sit. The other male members of the congregation were assigned to one of eight benches in the west and southwest parts of the building; the women occupied comparable places directly opposite. We do not know precisely what instructions were given to the committee that took the measure of every single individual named on the plan; nor could we, in any case, deal with such intangibles as "pious disposition." We can, however, investigate the importance of age and wealth relative to one another.

Predictably, age and wealth were substantially intercorrelated overall, and in many individual cases they simply cannot be distinguished. Older men (or women) who were also wealthy had a double claim on front-row seats, while those who were both young and poor invariably occupied places near the rear. In other instances, however, there were sharp status discrepancies—for example, a young and rich man, an old and poor one. What places were thought appropriate for *them*? Most such people were seated on the basis of wealth. For example, William Cole, at seventy-nine the oldest resident of the town, had one of the lowest tax assessments; he sat on a back bench in the meetinghouse. By contrast, Thomas Ward, only thirty-one but already near the top in terms of wealth, was assigned to the front row. Cole and Ward belonged to a group of eleven particularly discrepant cases (i.e., where rankings for age and wealth are at least three quintiles apart). In nine of these, wealth was the decisive factor for seating position; in the remaining two there was something of a compromise. An additional group of sixteen cases, in which the age/wealth discrepancy was less (two quintiles), includes eight which favored wealth, four which favored age, and four in the compromise category. (See Table 10.) In truth, the Hampton materials from 1650 are not the best imaginable for this inquiry. The town had been settled barely a decade earlier, and few of its people were truly old. The data strongly suggests that age *in general* was not an important criterion of social rank, but it might yet be shown, on other evidence, that *old* age was treated specially.

## VIII

This long excursion through an extremely varied and tortuous body of source materials is now at an end; there remains, however, the question of central themes and tendencies. Here we may allow ourselves to be quite openly speculative. Moreover, we may look for help to the social sciences, where the study of aging has been more extensively pursued.

We are told by sociologists that the status of old people, in any culture, turns on a cluster of institutional factors. Among these the following seem especially important: (1) property ownership; (2) the possession of strategic knowledge; (3) the predominant modes and styles of economic productivity; (4) an ethos of mutual dependence (or, conversely, of "individualism"); (5) the importance of received traditions (especially religious ones); (6) the strength of family and kinship ties; (7) the range and character of community life.[73]

Measured against this checklist, the position of the elderly in colonial New England looks strong. We know, for example, that some of them (merchants, artisans, or particularly successful yeomen) controlled large amounts of property and that old people in general were well-off in comparison to most other age groups. "Strategic knowledge" was also an acquirement of the elderly. Farming, marketing, domestic craftsmanship: these things they knew at least as well as their younger neighbors. In addition—and more important—they controlled a variety of significant information about the community's past. Much that pertained to the settlement of legal questions—boundaries, contracts, the details of ownership—was never written down and had to be recalled in some appropriate forum by those who could bear personal witness from long ago.[74] ("John Emery, Sr., aged about eighty-one years, testified that about forty years ago he saw laid out to William Estow, then of Newbury, a four acre lot . . . ")[75] In a society only partially literate and without comprehensive record keeping the *memories* of old people gave them a certain advantage.

Other institutional factors can be followed in the same way—and to roughly parallel conclusions. Thus the fact that early New England was land-rich and labor-poor enhanced the productive value even of marginal workers (such as the "aged and infirm"). The principle of reciprocity was established at the very core of the value structure: "we must be knit together in this work as one man," John Winthrop had said in a famous speech prepared enroute to the New World.[76] The force of tradition was appreciated, even venerated, throughout New England society. Most people were well supplied with kinfolk, and there was a vigorous network of neighborly relationships. In sum, the position of the elderly was supported, even enhanced, by prevailing social arrangements. Certainly their power and influence compare very favorably with what obtains for their counterparts in our own time.

We may now feel that we have finally uncovered the basis in social reality for the *dictum* "honor old age." And yet, too, we have seen how that *dictum* was subject to varying interpretations—and was often directly controverted by actual behavior. To understand these somewhat paradoxical findings, it is necessary to look beyond social structure to considerations of psychological functioning. Just here there are valuable suggestions to be taken from anthropological research on the aging process in a variety of premodern cultures.[77] This research can be summarized only at the risk of gross oversimplification, but the effort is worth making nonetheless. In most, if not all, premodern settings, the elderly occupy a position of far greater social importance than is true in our culture; in part, this is based on their control of valuable resources and, in part, on their presumed status as being "closer to God." But however powerful, they are not invariably *secure*. In some societies the elderly elicit great respect and affection; in others they are the object of deep resentment and mistrust, and live in a chronic state of fear. The difference is not based on their institutional position, which may be strong in both cases, but rather on the predominant style of affective and interpersonal life in the culture—in technical language, on a culture-specific capacity for "object relations."

In fact, older people everywhere are liable to be considered alien, different, strange; given certain preconditions, they arouse in their younger culture-mates mixed feelings of awe and apprehension. In a society where interpersonal relations are more or less relaxed, where there is little subjective tension between the claims of self and others, where psychosocial conditions favor the formation of "internalized objects"—in such a society the elderly remain secure. As one scholar has written, "by keeping his 'object' status the older person avoids becoming the *stranger* . . . [who arouses] fear and revulsion."[78] Or—to put it in still another way—the older person is experienced fully as an individual being in whom the past (what he formerly *was*) and the present (what he now *is*) are implicitly joined. But things are not always so. In other societies—where object relations are narrower, less differentiated, more narcissistic in tone—the aged (and sometimes also the very young) are distinctly at risk. Their strangeness is highlighted and often deeply feared. No matter what their socioeconomic power and official prestige, they are vulnerable to various forms of covert, even overt, attack.

These two situations are, in fact, the opposite ends of a single spectrum. And we must now ask where on that spectrum to locate the New Englanders. The question seems impossibly large, yet the materials discussed in the preceding pages suggest at least some parts of an answer. The people of early New England had many strong and admirable qualities, but there was, indeed, something problematic about their "object relations." In the doings of many of them one feels a thin edge of psychic vulnerability—a sense of self somewhat insecurely held, a view of others not fully three-dimensional. Committed always to goals of "peaceableness," they often disappointed themselves: inner and outer conflict was the actual condition of their lives. The doubt, the distress, the occasional rages which fueled such conflict are manifest all through the documentary record they have left to us.[79] Inevitably, under such conditions, there was some narrowing of their perception and understanding of others. The very qualities of "otherness" were hard for them to appreciate. Their view of the American Indians, for example, was notoriously constricted: Indians must behave in all things like Englishmen, else they are "savages" and "beasts."[80] Even their attitudes toward their own children expressed a certain lack of empathy. They were determined, insofar as possible, to "beat down" infantile expressions of willfulness, and they insisted on confronting their young with painful reminders of sin and death.[81] This does not imply an absence of parental love but simply an inability to credit fully the inherent childishness of childhood.

And what about the bearing of such considerations on old age? First, the elderly themselves were burdened with an especially difficult experience of their own aging. Growing old always creates some narcissistic imbalance, but for persons who are already sensitive on that count the problems are greatly compounded. Here, then, is one way to account for the "peevish," "suspicious," and "complaining" character usually attributed to the aged in colonial New England. But we must also look at the matter in terms of what the others, the not-old, contributed. For reasons related to their own character structure, they were frequently unable to "see" the elderly in a way that embraced the full richness of human individuality.[82] To them the old person was, indeed, something of a stranger. Thus they tended to stereotype him (calling him "old such an one"), to fear him (especially for his alleged "covetousness"), and indirectly to ridicule him (witness the figure of the "staggering, spewing, old drunkard," and the metaphor of the tree with its leaves off).

To summarize these rather diverse and cross-cutting materials, we may say that the position of the elderly in early New England was sociologically advantageous but psychologically *dis*advantageous. Their control of important resources seemed to command honor and respect but not affection or sympathetic understanding. Simone de Beauvoir has written that the only sure protection for old people is "that which their children's love provides."[83] And precisely here the situation of old New Englanders was doubtful.

## IX

We have pressed about as far as our evidence will carry us—perhaps, indeed, a bit farther. And yet there are important questions which we have scarcely touched. As noted at the start, most of the available data concerns aging in *men*, but sooner or later we will need to find some parallel way of investigating the experience of women. Another major *lacuna* in the present treatment is the matter of attitudes toward death. In all cultures and epochs the elderly must anticipate death by one means or another, and such anticipation was expressed with great emphasis in early New England. But death makes a huge subject in itself; fortunately, there are other studies which approach it more directly and at considerable length.[84]

One further issue should be confronted, if only in a speculative way, before we conclude. Can we say anything about our material in relation to historical *change*? Were the central tendencies in aging gradually altered as time and circumstance moved them along? And what was their eventual direction, seen in retrospect?

There is reason to think that the position of elderly people was improved between the middle of the seventeenth and the middle of the eighteenth centuries. Some of our own measures, when applied to later materials, strongly suggest as much. "Age heaping," for example, begins to show an age bias after 1700. A meetinghouse plan from the year 1774 seems to give strong priority to age (as compared with wealth). Wigs were increasingly designed to make their owners look older, not younger, than was the case—likewise the sartorial fashions of the eighteenth century. The unfriendly undertones, so persistent in seventeenth-century literature on old age, appear to have faded thereafter.[85] It seems possible, then, that the decades immediately preceding the American Revolution were a time of maximum advantage for old people.

If so, we may well wonder *why*—and it is worth recording certain points of plausible relevance from out of the present research. We have learned that life expectation for the early New Englanders was surprisingly long. Evidently, they survived to old age in numbers unequalled elsewhere in the colonies or in old England across the seas.[86] Perhaps, under these conditions, the aura of strangeness around elderly people was gradually dissipated.

Perhaps, too, there were complementary changes of inner life. This possibility is hard to explore on an empirical basis, but it does link up with reigning themes in New England historiography. Thus the harsh lines of Calvinist belief are thought to have softened somewhat after the middle of the seventeenth century. The balance of social concern tipped away from religion toward secular experience; in terms of cultural types, the shift went "from Puritan to Yankee."[87] There was, moreover, an ecological shift spanning roughly the same time period. The "wilderness," in which personal security and cultural integrity both seemed at risk, gave way to a settled society with its various protections and amenities. New England character was modified accordingly. The claims of self were now more freely acknowledged, and this, in turn, broadened the psychic space available for experiencing others—indeed, "otherness" in general.[88] The inherited social core remained intact (Anglo-Saxon, Christian, adult, and effectively male), but people on the margins were less vulnerable to implicit or explicit stereotyping. And old people were particular beneficiaries.

A further consideration—no easier to specify, but probably no less important—was the meaning of age in a society still relatively new. The example of the "planters" seems to have gained a deeper and deeper significance as the decades passed. These redoubtable men and women were the roots of the growing community. History had opened to them a uniquely creative path, and they had followed it unswervingly. Their success in "settlement" would remain, for all their descendants, an achievement of stunning proportions. To be sure, the effect on their *immediate* descendants was problematic: the sons of the planters found it hard to measure up. Tension built to a peak in roughly the third quarter of the seventeenth century: the religious controversies of that era represented, in part, a crisis in age relations.[89] The members of the settler generation were leaving "the earthly stage" *enroute* to their reward beyond. Their deaths occasioned special comment in local diaries and some notably elaborate funerals; perhaps, too, there was a connection with the dominant religious motif of "declension."[90] There were signs of sharpened age consciousness overall: increasingly, for example, individual people identified themselves as being old.[91]

In time, of course, the "crisis" eased. Gone as a living presence, the planters survived as the heroic figures of legend. The ambivalence they had aroused in their own children yielded to the unqualified admiration of succeeding generations. The residue of this process was a growing regard for age: old people were closest to the hallowed beginnings of New England, and that alone gave them a certain *cachet*. Here is Samuel Sewall, writing in his diary in the spring of 1726: "The honored, ancient, elder Faunce . . . kindly visited me. *Laus Deo*." Thomas Faunce was then about eighty and had served for many years as deacon of the first church at Plymouth. He is said to have "kept in cherished remembrance the first settlers, many of whom he well knew. He used to identify the rock on which they landed."[92] Another venerable link to the same era, Goodwife Ann Pollard, was memorialized in a famous portrait of 1721. She was then past 100, old enough to have come to Boston with the very earliest settlers. Indeed, she was known as a *raconteur* of that experience and claimed to have been the first person ashore—a spry girl of ten, leading Governor Winthrop and his colleagues onto the site of what would later become New England's greatest city.[93]

When Ann Pollard was young, Charles I was king of England, and Sir Walter Raleigh had only just died: by her last years Benjamin Franklin was already a young man. The life of the "honored, ancient, elder Faunce" ran from the old age of William Bradford to the childhood of John Adams and Thomas Jefferson. Franklin, Adams, and Jefferson would, in time, lead a political revolution and launch a new nation on its collective life course. Franklin was the most famous old man of the Revolutionary era, and, indeed, he capitalized on that fact. Adams and Jefferson, too, would be admired, even "venerated," in their old age. And yet a new "revolution in age relations"—as Professor Fischer has called it—was coming: "young America" of the nineteenth century was less and less inclined to acknowledge the claims of age. From the ambivalent circumstances of the settlement period—the main concern of the present essay—old people's experience had moved through a long cycle of change. More cycles, more changes would follow. It was, and is, a fascinating story, which historians are only beginning to tell.

## NOTES

1. (New York: Oxford University Press, 1977).

2. Cotton Mather, *Addresses to Old Men and Young Men and Little Children* (Boston: R. Pierce, 1690), dedication page.

3. Increase Mather, *Two Discourses* (Boston: B. Green, 1716), p. 120.

4. *Records of the Colony and Plantation of New Haven, from 1638 to 1649*, Charles J. Hoadly, ed. (Hartford, Conn.: Case, Tiffany, and Company, 1857), p. 375.

5. *Records of the Colony or Jurisdiction of New Haven, from May, 1653 to the Union*, Charles J. Hoadly, ed. (Hartford, Conn.: Case, Lockwood, and Company, 1858), p. 602.

6. *Records and Files of the Quarterly Courts of Essex County, Massachusetts* (Salem, Mass.: The Essex Institute, 1911-1921), I, 336, 179, 187, 380.

7. *The Works of John Robinson*, Robert Ashton, ed. (Boston: Doctrinal Tract and Book Society, 1851), I, 253.

8. *The Works of Anne Bradstreet*, Jeannine Hensley, ed. (Cambridge, Mass.: Harvard University Press, 1967), pp. 61-62.

9. Cotton Mather, *Addresses to Old Men*, p. 6.

10. Increase Mather, *Two Discourses*, p. 65.

11. Nicholas Noyes, "An Essay Against Periwigs," in *Remarkable Providences*, ed. John Demos, (New York: George Braziller, 1972), p. 215.

12. William Bridge, *A Word to the Aged* (Boston: John Foster, 1679), p. 5.

13. See, for example, David Gutmann, "The Cross-Cultural Perspective: Notes Toward a

Comparative Psychology of Aging," in *Handbook of the Psychology of Aging*, ed. James E. Birren and K. Warner Schaie (New York: Van Nostrand Reinhold Company, 1977), pp. 302–326.

14. Bridge, *Word to the Aged*, pp. 3–4.

15. Cotton Mather, *Addresses to Old Men*, pp. 37ff.

16. Ibid., p. 40.

17. Ibid., p. 37.

18. Bridge, *Word to the Aged*, p. 11.

19. *Records and Files of the Quarterly Courts*, VII, 156–157.

20. Linda Auwers Bissell, "Family, Friends and Neighbors: Social Interaction in Seventeenth-Century Windsor, Connecticut" (Ph.D. diss., Brandeis University, 1973), p. 40.

21. The reconstitution of Hampton families in 1656 has been done by the author of this essay. The 1680 tax list is published in *Documents and Records Relating to the Province of New Hampshire*, ed. Nathaniel Benton (Concord, N. H., 1867), I, 424.

22. Also by the author of this essay.

23. "Census of Bristol in Plymouth Colony, Now in Rhode Island, 1689," *New England Historical and Genealogical Register*, XXXIV (1880), 404–405.

24. Philip J. Greven, Jr., *Four Generations: Population, Land, and Family in Colonial Andover, Massachusetts* (Ithaca, N. Y.: Cornell University Press, 1970); Susan L. Norton, "Population Growth in Colonial America: A Study of Ipswich, Mass.," *Population Studies* XXV (1971), 433–452; John Demos, *A Little Commonwealth: Family Life in Plymouth Colony* (New York: Oxford University Press, 1970).

25. Carol Shuchman, "Examining Life Expectancies in Seventeenth-Century Massachusetts" (unpublished paper, Brandeis University, 1976).

26. John M. Murrin, "Review Essay," *History and Theory* XI (1972), 238.

27. *The Probate Records of Essex County, Massachusetts* (Salem, Mass.: The Essex Institute, 1916–1920), II, 61; II, 54; II, 50.

28. *Probate Records*, I, 150; I, 76; II, 108; I, 132.

29. *Probate Records*, III, 266; III, 11. *County Court Records, New Haven County*, I, folio 153 (ms. volume at the Connecticut State Library, Hartford, Conn.).

30. *Works of John Robinson*, I, 246.

31. Correspondence of Thomas Leeds and William Leeds, in *Remarkable Providences*, p. 151. *Records and Files of the Quarterly Courts*, IV, 81. *Probate Records*, III, 13; III, 278; III, 141. *The Diary of Thomas Minor, Stonington, Connecticut, 1653 to 1684*, ed. Sidney Miner and George D. Stanton (New London, Conn.: Day Publishing Company, 1899), pp. 95, 128, 135, 141, 148 154, 160, 166, 172, 183.

32. *Probate Records*, II, 441.

33. Demos, *Little Commonwealth*, p. 192; Shuchman, "Examining Life Expectancies," p. 15.

34. *Works of Anne Bradstreet*, pp. 62–63.

35. Increase Mather, *Two Discourses*, p. 105. Cotton Mather, *A Brief Essay on the Glory of Aged Piety* (Boston: S. Kneeland and T. Green, 1726), p. 27. Cotton Mather, *Addresses to Old Men*, p. 37.

36. *Probate Records*, I, 332.

37. Noyes, *"Essay Against Periwigs,"* p. 215.

38. *Records and Files of the Quarterly Courts*, IV, 123.

39. Cotton Mather, *Glory of Aged Piety* pp. 29–30; Increase Mather, *Solemn Advice to Young Men* (Boston: B. Green, 1695), p. 20; Increase Mather, *Two Discourses*, p. 99.

40. On the analysis of age heaping, see Ansley J. Coale and Melvin Zelnick, *New Estimates of Fertility and Population in the United States* (Princeton, N. J.: Princeton University Press, 1963).

41. On geographic mobility in seventeenth-century New England, see Greven, *Four Generations*, ch. 2; Kenneth A. Lockridge, "The Population of Dedham, Massachusetts,

1636–1736," *Economic History Review*, XIX (1966), 318–344; Bissell, "Family, Friends, and Neighbors," pp. 59–71.

42. *Records and Files of the Quarterly Courts*, VII, 356; IV, 347.

43. *Collections of the Connecticut Historical Society*, Volume XXI: *The Willys Papers* (Hartford, Conn.: The Connecticut Historical Society, 1924), p. 71; *Records and Files of the Quarterly Courts*, VII, 269.

44. Rates of remarriage have been calculated for seventeenth-century Windsor, Connecticut. Among younger widows (those whose first marriage lasted less than ten years) the portion remarrying was 67 percent; among older ones (with a first marriage lasting at least twenty years) the comparable figure was slightly under 25 percent. See Bissell, "Family, Friends, and Neighbors," p. 56. The actual numbers of widows in local populations at given points in time can be calculated from census, land, and tax records. In 1670 the Connecticut towns of Hartford, Wethersfield, and Windsor were found to contain a total of 335 heads of household; 18 of these (slightly more than 5 percent) were widows. A land-allotment list from New Haven in 1680 contained the names of 220 proprietors—25 of whom were widows (11 percent). See *Collections of the Connecticut Historical Society* Volume XXI: *The Willys Papers* pp. 191–199; *New Haven Town Records, 1662–1684*, Franklin Bowditch Dexter, ed., (New Haven Conn.: The New Haven Colony Historical Society, 1919), pp. 405–410. For an excellent discussion of widowhood in a slightly later period, see Alexander Keyssar, "Widowhood in Eighteenth-Century Massachusetts: A Problem in the History of the Family," *Perspectives in American History*, VIII (1974), 83–119.

45. Richard B. Morris, *Studies in the History of American Law* (New York: Columbia University Press, 1930), ch. 3; Demos, *Little Commonwealth*, p. 85.

46. *Probate Records*, III, 390; II, 52.

47. Ibid., III, 223; *The Mayflower Descendant*, XXX, 101; *Probate Records*, II, 221; II, 63; *Mayflower Descendant*, II, (1900), 184–185.

48. *Probate Records*, I, 96; II, 346; II, 263; *Mayflower Descendant*, II, (1900), 184–185.

49. *Probate Records*, III, 48; *Mayflower Descendant*, II, (1900), 184–185; *Probate Records*, II, 64; III, 175.

50. *Probate Records*, II, 239; *Mayflower Descendant*, XVII, (1915), 34–36.

51. *Mayflower Descendant*, XI, (1909), 92–93; *Probate Records*, III, 351; II, 251.

52. *Mayflower Descendant*, VI, (1904), 81; *Probate Records*, II, 171.

53. *Probate Records*, III, 150–151; III, 377; II, 144.

54. *Watertown Records*, I (Watertown, Mass., 1894), part one, 101; *New Haven Town Records, 1649–1662*, Franklin Bowditch Dexter, ed. (New Haven, Conn.: The New Haven Colony Historical Society, 1917), pp. 116, 208.

55. *Records and Files of the Quarterly Courts*, III, 276; V, 29; V, 396; V, 188; VI, 77; VI, 44; VII, 326; VIII, 345; II, 97.

56. See Demos, *Little Commonwealth*, pp. 174–175; David Hackett Fischer, *Growing Old in America* (New York: Oxford University Press, 1977), p. 45.

57. Quoted in Joseph Dow, *History of the Town of Hampton, New Hampshire* (Salem, Mass.: Salem Press Publishing and Printing Company, 1893), II, 740; *Diary of Thomas Minor*, pp. 207–208.

58. Diary of Samuel Sewall, *Collections of the Massachusetts Historical Society*, fifth series, VII (Boston, Mass.: The Massachusetts Historical Society, 1882), pp. 168, 382; *New Haven Town Records, 1662–1684*, p. 331.

59. *Diary of Thomas Minor*, p. 133, *passim*.

60. Ibid., pp. 122–123.

61. Ibid., p. 165.

62. Increase Mather, *Two Discourses* p. 134.

63. Cotton Mather, *Glory of Aged Piety*, p. 28.

64. Noyes, "Essay Against Periwigs," p. 215; *Works of John Robinson*, p. 251.

65. *Davis Scrapbooks*, III, 8 (ms. volumes, Pilgrim Hall, Plymouth, Mass.).

66. Increase Mather, *Two Discourses* pp. 98–99.

67. *Watertown Records*, I, part one, 53.

68. See, for example, *Probate Records*, II, 4, 229, 315, 345, 352, 426, 441; III, 13, 183, 187, 278, 329, 345, 375.

69. On the practice of seating the meetinghouse, see Robert J. Dinkin, "Provincial Massachusetts: A Deferential or a Democratic Society" (Ph.D. diss. Columbia University, 1968).

70. See, for example, *Watertown Records*, I, part one, 47; *Town Votes, Wethersfield, Conn.*, I, folios 115–116 (ms. volumes, Connecticut State Library, Hartford, Conn.).

71. See John Coolidge, "Hingham Builds a Meetinghouse," *New England Quarterly*, XXXIV (1961), 435–461. Coolidge makes some approach to the issue of seating and social rank in Hingham and clearly believes that older persons received favored positions. However, he does not seem to have attempted systematic comparison of the age factor with other variables like wealth.

72. *Town Book of Hampton*, I, folios 28–29 (ms. volume, Town Offices, Hampton, N. H.).

73. See Irving Rosow, *Socialization to Old Age* (Berkeley, Calif.: University of California Press, 1974), ch. 1.

74. The effect of this pattern can be measured quantitatively from legal records. Persons over sixty, we know, comprised 10 percent or so of the total adult population of early New England; yet they account for some 15 percent of all witnesses in court cases in mid-seventeenth-century Massachusetts. Data compiled by the author from *Records and Files of the Quarterly Courts, passim.*

75. Ibid., VII, 194.

76. John Winthrop, "A Model of Christian Charity," in *Puritan Political Ideas*, ed. Edmund Morgan (New York: The Bobbs-Merrill Company, Inc., 1965), p. 92.

77. The best summary of this viewpoint is found in Gutmann, "Notes Toward a Comparative Psychology of Aging," pp. 302–326.

78. Ibid., pp. 315–316.

79. See Demos, *Little Commonwealth*, pp. 136ff; Richard L. Bushman, *From Puritan to Yankee: Character and the Social Order in Connecticut, 1690–1765* (Cambridge, Mass.: Harvard University Press, 1967), pp. 20–21; Darrett B. Rutman, "The Mirror of Puritan Authority," in *Puritanism and the American Experience*, ed. Michael McGiffert (Reading, Mass.: Addison-Wesley Publishing Company, 1969), pp. 65–79; Emory Elliott, *Power and the Pulpit in Puritan New England* (Princeton, N. J.: Princeton University Press, 1975), pp. 76ff.

80. See Neal Salisbury, "Conquest of the 'Savage': Puritans, Puritan Missionaries, and Indians, 1620–1680," (Ph.D. diss. University of California at Los Angeles, 1972).

81. See Demos, *Little Commonwealth*, pp. 134ff; Edmund Morgan, *The Puritan Family* (New York: Harper & Row, 1966), ch. 3; David E. Stannard, in "Death and the Puritan Child," *Death in America*, ed. David E. Stannard (Philadelphia: University of Pennsylvania Press, 1975), pp. 9–29.

82. This line of argument draws heavily on recent work in the clinical theory of psychoanalysis, especially the so-called "psychology of the self." See the writings of Heinz Kohut: *The Analysis of the Self* (New York: International Universities Press, 1971) and *The Restoration of the Self* (New York: International Universities Press, 1977).

83. Quoted in Gutmann, "Notes Toward a Comparative Psychology of Aging," p. 314.

84. David E. Stannard, "Death and Dying in Puritan New England," *American Historical Review*, LXXVIII (1973), 1305–1330, and *The Puritan Way of Death: A Study in Religion, Culture, and Social Change* (New York: Oxford University Press, 1977).

85. This evidence, and much more from eighteenth-century sources, is presented in Fischer, *Growing Old in America*, pp. 39, 85–90, and *passim.*

86. For a summary of the comparative material, see Ibid., pp. 225–227.

87. See, for example, Bushman, *From Puritan to Yankee*; Kenneth A. Lockridge, *A New England Town: The First Hundred Years* (New York: W. W. Norton and Company, 1970).

88. See Richard Brown, *Modernization: The Transformation of American Life* (New York: Hill and Wang, 1976), ch. 5; John Demos, "Introduction," *Remarkable Providences*, pp. 19–22.

89. This idea is fruitfully explored in John M. Murrin, "Review Essay," *History and Theory*, XI (1972), 235–240.

90. See Perry Miller, "Declension in a Bible Commonwealth," *Nature's Nation* (Cambridge, Mass.: Harvard University Press, 1967), pp. 14–49.

91. Elderly people writing wills did not, before about 1660, make reference to their age; after that time they did so with growing regularity. See, for example, the wills included in *Probate Records*, I–III, *passim*.

92. "Diary of Samuel Sewall," *Collections of the Massachusetts Historical Society*, fifth series, VII (Boston: The Massachusetts Historical Society, 1882), p. 376. The comment on elder Faunce's personal connections with the Pilgrim fathers is by Sewall's editor.

93. On the portrait of Ann Pollard, and her stories of arriving in Boston with the Winthrop group, see James Thomas Flexner, *First Flowers of Our Wilderness* (Boston: Houghton Mifflin Company, 1947), pp. 46–49.

# SELECTED READINGS FOR PART THREE

ACHENBAUM, ANDREW. "The Obsolescence of Old Age in America." *Journal of Social History*, 8 (1974), 48–62.

ARIÈS, PHILLIPPE. *Centuries of Childhood: A Social History of Family Life.* New York: Vintage, 1962.

BEALES, ROSS W., JR. "In Search of the Historical Child: Miniature Adulthood and Youth in Colonial New England." *American Quarterly*, 27 (1975), 379–398.

DE MAUSE, LLOYDE, ed. *The History of Childhood.* New York: Harper & Row, 1975.

DEMOS, JOHN, AND VIRGINIA DEMOS. "Adolescence in Historical Perspective." *Journal of Marriage and the Family*, 31 (1969), 632–638.

ELDER, GLEN H., JR. *Children of the Great Depression.* Chicago: University of Chicago Press, 1974.

———. "Family History and the Life Course." *Journal of Family History*, 2 (1977), 276–304.

FISCHER, DAVID HACKETT. *Growing Old in America.* New York: Oxford University Press, 1977.

HINER, N. RAY. "Adolescence in Eighteenth-Century America." *History of Childhood Quarterly*, 3 (1975), 253–280.

KATZ, MICHAEL. *The People of Hamilton, Canada West.* Cambridge: Harvard University Press, 1975.

KENISTON, KENNETH. "Youth as a Stage of Life." *The American Scholar*, 39 (1970), 631–654.

KETT, JOSEPH. *Rites of Passage: Adolescence in America; 1790 to the Present.* New York: Basic Books, 1977.

MECHLING, JAY. "Advice to Historians on Advice to Mothers." *Journal of Social History*, 9 (1975), 45–63.

MORGAN, EDMUND S. *The Puritan Family.* 1944. Reprint. New York: Harper & Row, 1966.

RAPSON, RICHARD L. "The American Child as Seen by British Travelers, 1845–1935." *American Quarterly*, 17 (1965), 520–534.

SHORTER, EDWARD. *The Making of the Modern Family.* New York: Basic Books, 1975.

STEARNS, PETER N. *Old Age in European Society.* New York: Holmes and Meier, 1977.

STONE, LAWRENCE. Review of David H. Fischer's *Growing Old in America* in *New York Review of Books*, 24 (May 12, 1977), 10–16.

ZUCKERMAN, MICHAEL. "Dr. Spock: The Confidence of Man." In *The Family in History.* Ed. Charles Rosenberg. Philadelphia: University of Pennsylvania Press, 1975.

# PART FOUR |

# WOMEN: ROLES AND RELATIONSHIPS

The presence of a section on women might cause some eyebrows to be raised. Why, some might ask, not just have a section on people or sex roles? The justification is this: if we consider all the changes in the family over the last few centuries, the roles that have been most altered are those of wife and mother. In a certain sense, then, one might argue that the history of family change in the West has really been a history of the changing place of women in that institution.

Lois Green Carr and Lorena S. Walsh's article "The Planter's Wife: The Experience of White Women in Seventeenth-Century Maryland" illustrates one way in which the field has grown since the first edition of this book; namely, researchers are now expanding their interest to include sections of colonial America other than New England. Like Greven, whose article on Andover, Massachusetts, is in part one of this book, Carr and Walsh study seventeenth-century familial patterns. However, they focus on Maryland rather than on Massachusetts and on women rather than men; in addition, they are far more interested in comparisons between Maryland and England than between Maryland and Massachusetts. Nevertheless, readers will do well to keep Greven's article in mind as they read Carr and Walsh's article and to make comparisons where appropriate. A central theme of Carr and Walsh's selection is the extent to which certain aspects of the position of women in the Chesapeake are attributable to the demographic situation there. In their words: "These facts— immigrant predominance, early death, late marriage, and sexual imbalance—created circumstances of social and demographic disruption that deeply affected family and community life."

The settlers of New England came largely in family groups and engaged in subsistence agriculture of several crops. In Maryland, however, tobacco, a cash crop, dominated the region, and the planters who came there to make their fortune usually arrived without families. As a result, indentured servants and those working to pay out their passage were the main sources of plantation labor. Relatively few of these servants were women, and what women there were were avidly and competitively sought as wives after they had served out their time. That was despite the fact that these women had a large number of illegitimate births. Contributing to the high rate of illegitimacy was the fact that even if the father of the child were willing to marry the mother, he could not do so unless he could afford to purchase her from her master. Yet, given the shortage of women, the stigma of having borne a child out of wedlock did not seem to significantly reduce the chances of a woman marrying. As further evidence of a rather easy-going morality, the figures for one Maryland county show that a third of the brides were already pregnant as they went to the altar.

Once married, women in this southern colony appeared to have had both the respect and the trust of their husbands. Evidence for this is found in wills that give widows considerable control over their spouses' estates. As Carr and Walsh scrupulously point out, it has not been firmly established that husbands in seventeenth-century England did not often grant their widows such financial discretion; however, the available evidence suggests that they did not.

Carr and Walsh offer much interesting material, including, for example, a discussion of the differences between English-born and Maryland-born women in mortality and age at marriage. While the authors express a creditable scholarly diffidence in not wanting to make too great claims for their findings and interpretations, they nevertheless have produced an important piece of research.

Louise Tilly, John W. Scott, and Miriam Cohen's article "Women's Work and European Fertility Patterns" is one of the few selections in this edition which deals with European rather than American data. It has been included for several reasons. For one thing, it is a response to a series of articles by Edward Shorter (e.g., 1973)* whose arguments the authors summarize while offering a critique and an alternative. Briefly, Shorter has argued that the increase in both marital and nonmarital fertility in the second half of the eighteenth century was an outgrowth of the "emancipation" being experienced by the women of the new urban working class. These women had left their country homes to find work in the city; in the process they attained freedom from parental and communal supervision and developed a new sense of selfhood that expressed itself in a more hedonistic sexual attitude. These developments supposedly lead to more births in and out of marriage. Tilly, Scott, and Cohen contend that Shorter provides more argument than data, and they attempt to set things right. The reader would be wrong, however, to conclude that their article represents a demolition of Shorter's thesis. Certainly, some of their data seriously weaken the foundation of his argument, but ultimately they, too, offer only a speculative explanation of why the change occurred.

At this point the reader may wonder how this material is related to the American scene. The relationship is simple: the United States manifests similar patterns, at least with regard to illegitimacy (see Smith's article in part five of this book), over the same period. Moreover, the issue being raised is a universal one. How did the coming of industrialization affect the position of women both in terms of the market place, and, perhaps inseparably, their relationships with men? Tilly, Scott, and Cohen do not interpret the rise in marital and nonmarital fertility as an indicator of a new, expressive sexuality flowing from economic emancipation. Rather, they believe that the increase was caused by the traditional desire to marry being stymied by economic problems at the same time that traditional con-

---

*Complete citations for works referred to are in the selected readings on p. 359.

trols were being weakened. It might be argued that this conclusion tells us more about illegitimacy than it does about marital fertility, but the authors do attempt to fit the latter into their interpretive scheme as well. The issue they are dealing with is a key one, the data they bring to bear on it are illuminating, and their interpretation is a provocative one.

Whereas Tilly, Scott, and Cohen give some insight into the way in which working-class women experienced the early stages of industrialization, Barbara Welter considers their middle-class counterparts in "The Cult of True Womanhood: 1820–1860." These women did not seek work outside the home either before or after marriage. Instead, they were elevated to a pedestal as symbols of the sanctity and purity of the home, a sanctity and purity that were seen as being threatened by the relentless onslaughts of urban industrialism. This idealization of women went hand in hand with the appearance of the role of the housewife and the development of a companionate form of marriage. While the housewife performs tasks that are economically important and contribute to the participation of the male breadwinner in the labor force, she has lost the direct participation which characterized her role in the preindustrial economy. This is the case especially among the middle class, where the activities of married women in the home often were more managerial than menial.

Each of the feminine ideals of "piety, purity, submissiveness, and domesticity" reflect a different aspect of the "cult of true womanhood," but together they can be viewed as the price middle-class women paid for their beatified status. It was a price which effectively excluded them from a direct participation in the economy. Nonetheless, it gave them a certain leverage and a degree of power, though one might argue that the sphere in which it could be exercised was limited.

A question might be raised regarding the extent to which what Welter describes represents a literary ideal rather than social reality. The sources on which she constructs her argument are, indeed, literary, and there is an absence of other types of data. Yet, even if this were only an ideal presented to women—and it probably was much more than that—it still helped mold their self-concepts and provided them with criteria with which to judge themselves and be judged by others, especially male "others."

Carroll Smith-Rosenberg's "The Female World of Love and Ritual: Relationships Between Women in Nineteenth Century America" is a true pioneering effort. Not only does it cover historical ground that previously has been neglected, but it also forces us to confront current assumptions about human relationships. Drawing upon an analysis of letters and diaries, Smith-Rosenberg argues that relationships between American women from 1760 to 1880 were characterized by patterns of support and an intensity of affect that are difficult to interpret within the psychosocial framework employed by most current commentators on human relationships. The extent to which these relationships involved sexual intimacy—especially when they occurred between age peers or near age peers—is difficult to assess, but great emotional involvement was often evident. Many of these relationships lasted throughout the women's lives, even when they were separated by long distances.

The reader must approach the interpretative section of this article critically because Smith-Rosenberg offers some rather revolutionary conclusions. She questions the extent to which Victorian society was as repressive and prudish as is commonly believed and at the same time challenges reigning notions about homosexuality and heterosexuality. It is her thesis that women in nineteenth-century America had more freedom to explore relationships with other women than may be true today; further, they did not run the risk of being branded as "perverts." Moreover, their participation in such relationships did not seem to preclude their participation in conventional heterosexual relationships. Thus she asks us to reconsider the dichotomy between homosexuality and heterosexuality and the pathological label that is often attached to the former. In dealing with this theme there is, perhaps, one question that Smith-Rosenberg never adequately confronts; namely, the extent to which these relationships confirm the validity of the repressive picture of Victorian sexuality. More specifically, in what way, if any, can these relationships between women be seen as compensatory for the failure of relationships between men and women during this same period? To raise this question is not to argue that people will only turn to members of their own sex for support, affection, and sex when these things are lacking in their heterosexual relationships but, rather, to ask the reader if he or she is ready to accept without qualification the last sentence of Smith-Rosenberg's article: " . . . the supposedly repressive and destructive Victorian sexual ethos, may have been more flexible and responsive to the needs of particular individuals than those of mid-twentieth century." Irrespective of one's answer, the significance of this article remains unquestioned.

# 13 | THE PLANTER'S WIFE: THE EXPERIENCE OF WHITE WOMEN IN SEVENTEENTH-CENTURY MARYLAND

## LOIS GREEN CARR and LORENA S. WALSH

Four facts were basic to all human experience in seventeenth-century Maryland. First, for most of the period the great majority of inhabitants had been born in what we now call Britain. Population increase in Maryland did not result primarily from births in the colony before the late 1680s and did not produce a predominantly native population of adults before the first decade of the eighteenth century. Second, immigrant men could not expect to live beyond age forty-three, and 70 percent would die before age fifty. Women may have had even shorter lives. Third, perhaps 85 percent of the immigrants, and practically all the unmarried immigrant women, arrived as indentured servants and consequently married late. Family groups were never predominant in the immigration to Maryland and were a significant part for only a brief time at mid-century. Fourth, many more men than women immigrated during the whole period.[1] These facts—immigrant predominance, early death, late marriage, and sexual imbalance—created circumstances of social and demographic disruption that deeply affected family and community life.

We need to assess the effects of this disruption on the experience of women in seventeenth-century Maryland. Were women degraded by the hazards of servitude in a society in which everyone had left community and kin behind and in which women were in short supply? Were traditional restraints on social conduct weakened? If so, were women more exploited or more independent and powerful than women who remained in England? Did any differences from English experience which we can observe in the experience of Maryland women survive the transformation from an immigrant to a predominantly native-born society with its own kinship networks and community traditions? The tentative argument put forward here is that the answer to all these questions is Yes. There were degrading aspects of servitude, although these probably did not characterize the lot of most women; there were fewer restraints on social conduct, especially in courtship, than in England; women were less protected but also more powerful than those who remained at home; and at least some

Ms. Carr is the historian and Ms. Walsh a research associate at the St. Mary's City Commission. The authors wish to thank Russell R. Menard for sharing his data and insights into family history in the Chesapeake.

of these changes survived the appearance in Maryland of New World creole communities. However, these issues are far from settled, and we shall offer some suggestions as to how they might be further pursued.

Maryland was settled in 1634, but in 1650 there were probably no more than six hundred persons and fewer than two hundred adult women in the province. After that time population growth was steady; in 1704 a census listed 30,437 white persons, of whom 7,163 were adult women.[2] Thus in discussing the experience of white women in seventeenth-century Maryland we are dealing basically with the second half of the century.

Marylanders of that period did not leave letters and diaries to record their New World experience or their relationships to one another. Nevertheless, they left trails in the public records that give us clues. Immigrant lists kept in England and documents of the Maryland courts offer quantifiable evidence about the kinds of people who came and some of the problems they faced in making a new life. Especially valuable are the probate court records. Estate inventories reveal the kinds of activities carried on in the house and on the farm, and wills, which are usually the only personal statements that remain for any man or woman, show something of personal attitudes. This essay relies on the most useful of the immigrant lists and all surviving Maryland court records, but concentrates especially on the surviving records of the lower Western Shore, an early-settled area highly suitable for tobacco. Most of this region comprised four counties: St. Mary's, Calvert, Charles, and Prince George's (formed in 1696 from Calvert and Charles). Inventories from all four counties, wills from St. Mary's and Charles, and court proceedings from Charles and Prince George's provide the major data.[3]

Because immigrants predominated, who they were determined much about the character of Maryland society. The best information so far available comes from lists of indentured servants who left the ports of London, Bristol, and Liverpool. These lists vary in quality, but at the very least they distinguish immigrants by sex and general destination. A place of residence in England is usually given, although it may not represent the emigrant's place of origin; and age and occupation are often noted. These lists reveal several characteristics of immigrants to the Chesapeake and, by inference, to Maryland.[4]

Servants who arrived under indenture included yeomen, husbandmen, farm laborers, artisans, and small tradesmen, as well as many untrained to any special skill. They were young: over half of the men on the London lists of 1683–1684 were aged eighteen to twenty-two. They were seldom under seventeen or over twenty-eight. The women were a little older; the great majority were between eighteen and twenty-five, and half were aged twenty to twenty-two. Most servants contracted for four or five years service, although those under fifteen were to serve at least seven years.[5] These youthful immigrants represented a wide range of English society. All were seeking opportunities they had not found at home.

However, many immigrants—perhaps about half[6]—did not leave England with indentures but paid for their passage by serving according to the custom of the country. Less is known about their social characteristics, but some inferences are possible. From 1661, customary service was set by Maryland laws that required four-year (later five-year) terms for men and women who were twenty-two years or over at arrival and longer terms for those who were younger. A requirement of these laws enables us to determine something about age at arrival of servants who came without indentures. A planter who wished to obtain more than four or five years of service had to take his servant before the county court to have his or her age judged and a written record made. Servants aged over twenty-one were not often registered, there being no incentive for a master to pay court fees for those who would serve the minimum term. Nevertheless, a comparison of the ages of servants under twenty-two recorded in Charles County, 1658–1689, with those under twenty-two on the London list is revealing. Of Charles County male servants (N=363), 77.1 percent were aged seventeen or under, whereas on the London list (N=196), 77.6 percent were eighteen or over. Women registered in Charles County court were somewhat older than the men, but among those under twenty-two (N=107), 5.5 percent were aged twenty-one, whereas on the London list (N=69), 46.4 percent had reached this age. Evidently, some immigrants who served by custom were younger than those who came indentured, and this age difference probably characterized the two groups as a whole. Servants who were not only very young but had arrived without the protection of a written contract were possibly of lower social origins than were servants who came under indenture. The absence of skills among Charles County servants who served by custom supports this supposition.[7]

Whatever their status, one fact about immigrant women is certain: many fewer came than men. Immigrant lists, headright lists, and itemizations of servants in inventories show severe imbalance. On a London immigrant list of 1634–1635 men outnumbered women six to one. From the 1650s at least until the 1680s most sources show a ratio of three to one. From then on, all sources show some, but not great, improvement. Among immigrants from Liverpool over the years 1697–1707 the ratio was just under two and one half to one.[8]

Why did not more women come? Presumably, fewer wished to leave family and community to venture into a wilderness. But perhaps more important, women were not as desirable as men to merchants and planters who were making fortunes raising and marketing tobacco, a crop that requires large amounts of labor. The gradual improvement in the sex ratio among servants toward the end of the century may have been the result of a change in recruiting the needed labor. In the late 1660s the supply of young men willing to emigrate stopped increasing sufficiently to meet the labor demands of a growing Chesapeake population. Merchants who recruited servants for planters turned to other sources, and among these sources were women. They did not crowd the ships arriving in the Chesapeake, but their numbers did increase.[9]

To ask the question another way, why did women come? Doubtless, most came to get a husband, an objective virtually certain of success in a land where women were so far outnumbered. The promotional literature, furthermore, painted bright pictures of the life that awaited men and women once out of their time; and various studies suggest that for a while, at least, the promoters were not being entirely fanciful. Until the 1660s, and to a less degree the 1680s, the expanding economy of Maryland and Virginia offered opportunities well beyond those available in England to men without capital and to the women who became their wives.[10]

Nevertheless, the hazards were also great, and the greatest was untimely death. Newcomers promptly became ill, probably with malaria, and many died. What proportion survived is unclear; so far no one has devised a way of measuring it. Recurrent malaria made the woman who survived seasoning less able to withstand other diseases, especially dysentery and influenza. She was especially vulnerable when pregnant. Expectation of life for everyone was low in the Chesapeake, but especially so for women.[11] A woman who had immigrated to Maryland took an extra risk, though perhaps a risk not greater than she might have suffered by moving from her village to London instead.[12]

The majority of women who survived seasoning paid their transportation costs by working for a four- or five-year term of service. The kind of work depended on the status of the family they served. A female servant of a small planter—who through about the 1670s might have had a servant[13]—probably worked at the hoe. Such a man could not afford to buy labor that would not help with the cash crop. In wealthy families women probably were household servants, although some are occasionally listed in inventories of well-to-do planters as living on the quarters—that is, on plantations other than the dwelling plantation. Such women saved men the jobs of preparing food and washing linen but doubtless also worked in the fields.[14] In middling households experience must have varied. Where the number of people to feed and wash for was large, female servants would have had little time to tend the crops.

Tracts that promoted immigration to the Chesapeake region asserted that female servants did not labor in the fields, except "nasty" wenches not fit for other tasks. This implies that most immigrant women expected, or at least hoped, to avoid heavy field work, which English women—at least those above the cottager's status—did not do.[15] What proportion of female servants in Maryland found themselves demeaned by this unaccustomed labor is impossible to say, but this must have been the fate of some. A study of the distribution of female servants among wealth groups in Maryland might shed some light on this question. Nevertheless, we still would not know whether those purchased by the poor or sent to work on a quarter were women whose previous experience suited them for field labor.

An additional risk for the woman who came as a servant was the possibility of bearing a bastard. At least 20 percent of the female servants who came to Charles County between 1658 and 1705 were presented to the county court for this cause.[16] A servant woman could not marry unless someone was willing to pay her master for the term she had left to serve.[17] If a man made her pregnant, she could not marry him unless he could buy her time. Once a woman became free, however, marriage was clearly the usual solution. Only a handful of free women were presented in Charles County for bastardy between 1658 and 1705. Since few free women remained either single or widowed for long, not many were subject to the risk. The hazard of bearing a bastard was a hazard of being a servant.[18]

This high rate of illegitimate pregnancies among servants raises lurid questions. Did men import women for sexual exploitation? Does John Barth's Whore of Dorset have a basis outside his fertile imagination?[19] In our opinion, the answers are clearly No. Servants were economic investments on the part of planters who needed labor. A female servant in a household where there were unmarried men must have both provided and faced temptation, for the pressures were great in a society in which men outnumbered women by three to one. Nevertheless, the servant woman was in the household to work—to help feed and clothe the family and make tobacco. She was not primarily a concubine.

This point could be established more firmly if we knew more about the fathers of the bastards. Often the culprits were fellow servants or men recently freed but too poor to purchase the woman's remaining time. Sometimes the master was clearly at fault. But often the father is not identified. Some masters surely did exploit their female servants sexually. Nevertheless, masters were infrequently accused of fathering their servants' bastards, and those found guilty were punished as severely as were other men. Community mores did not sanction their misconduct.[20]

A female servant paid dearly for the fault of unmarried pregnancy. She was heavily fined, and if no one would pay her fine, she was whipped. Furthermore, she served an extra twelve to twenty-four months to repay her master for the "trouble of his house" and labor lost, and the fathers often did not share in this payment of damages. On top of all, she might lose the child after weaning unless by then she had become free, for the courts bound out bastard children at very early ages.[21]

English life probably did not offer a comparable hazard to young unmarried female servants. No figures are available to show rates of illegitimacy among those who were subject to the risk,[22] but the female servant was less restricted in England than in the Chesapeake. She did not owe anyone for passage across the Atlantic; hence it was easier for her to marry, supposing she happened to become pregnant while in service. Perhaps, furthermore, her temptations were fewer. She was not 3,000 miles from home and friends, and she lived in a society in which there was no shortage of women. Bastards were born in England in the seventeenth century, but surely not to as many as a fifth of the female servants.

Some women escaped all or part of their servitude because prospective husbands purchased the remainder of their time. At least one promotional pamphlet published in the 1660s described such purchases as likely, but how often they actually occurred is difficult to determine.[23] Suggestive is a 20 percent difference between the sex ratios found in a Maryland headright sample, 1658-1681, and among servants listed in lower Western Shore inventories for 1658-1679.[24] Some of the discrepancy must reflect the fact that male servants were younger than female servants and therefore served longer terms; hence they had a greater chance of appearing in an inventory. But part of the discrepancy doubtless follows from the purchase of women for wives. Before 1660, when sex ratios were even more unbalanced and the expanding economy enabled men to establish themselves more quickly, even more women may have married before their terms were finished.[25]

Were women sold for wives against their wills? No record says so, but nothing restricted a man from selling his servant to whomever he wished. Perhaps some women were forced into such marriages or accepted them as the least evil. But the man who could afford to purchase a wife—especially a new arrival—was usually already an established landowner.[26] Probably most servant women saw an opportunity in such a marriage. In addition, the shortage of labor gave women some bargaining power. Many masters must have been ready to refuse to sell a woman who was unwilling to marry a would-be purchaser.

If a woman's time was not purchased by a prospective husband, she was virtually certain to find a husband once she was free. Those famous spinsters, Margaret and Mary Brent, were probably almost unique in seventeenth-century Maryland. In the four counties of the lower Western Shore only two of the women who left a probate inventory before the eighteenth century are known to have died single.[27] Comely or homely, strong or weak, any young woman was too valuable to be overlooked, and most could find a man with prospects.

The woman who immigrated to Maryland, survived seasoning and service, and gained her freedom became a planter's wife. She had considerable liberty in making her choice. There were men aplenty, and no fathers or brothers were hovering to monitor her behavior or disapprove her preference. This is the modern way of looking at her situation, of course. Perhaps she missed the protection of a father, a guardian, or kinfolk, and the participation in her decision of a community to which she felt ties. There is some evidence that the absence of kin and the pressures of the sex ratio created conditions of sexual freedom in courtship that were not customary in England. A register of marriages and births for seventeenth-century Somerset County shows that about one-third of the immigrant women whose marriages are recorded were pregnant at the time of the ceremony—nearly twice the rate in English parishes.[28] There is no indication of community objection to this freedom so long as marriage took place. No presentments for bridal pregnancy were made in any of the Maryland courts.[29]

The planter's wife was likely to be in her mid-twenties at marriage. An estimate of minimum age at marriage for servant women can be made from lists of indentured servants who left London over the years 1683–1684 and from age judgments in Maryland county court records. If we assume that the 112 female indentured servants going to Maryland and Virginia whose ages are given in the London lists served full four-year terms, then only 1.8 percent married before age twenty, but 68 percent after age twenty-four.[30] Similarly, if the 141 women whose ages were judged in Charles County between 1666 and 1705 served out their terms according to the custom of the country, none married before age twenty-two, and half were twenty-five or over.[31] When adjustments are made for the ages at which wives may have been purchased, the figures drop, but even so the majority of women waited until at least age twenty-four to marry.[32] Actual age at marriage in Maryland can be found for few seven-teenth-century female immigrants, but observations for Charles and Somerset counties place the mean age at about twenty-five.[33]

Because of the age at which an immigrant woman married, the number of children she would bear her husband was small. She had lost up to ten years of her childbearing life[34]—the possibility of perhaps four or five children, given the usual rhythm of childbearing.[35] At the same time, high mortality would reduce both the number of children she would bear over the rest of her life and the number who would live. One partner to a marriage was likely to die within seven years, and the chances were only one in three that a marriage would last ten years.[36] In these circumstances, most women would not bear more than three or four children—not counting those stillborn—to any one husband, plus a posthumous child were she the survivor. The best estimates suggest that nearly a quarter, perhaps more, of the children born alive died during their first year and that 40 to 55 percent would not live to see age twenty.[37] Consequently, one of her children would probably die in infancy, and another one or two would fail to reach adulthood. Wills left in St. Mary's County during the seventeenth century show the results. In 105 families over the years 1660 to 1680 only twelve parents left more than three children behind them, including those conceived but not yet born. The average number was 2.3, nearly always minors, some of whom might die before reaching adulthood.[38]

For the immigrant woman, then, one of the major facts of life was that although she might bear a child about every two years, nearly half would not reach maturity. The social implications of this fact are far-reaching. Because she married late in her child-bearing years and because so many of her children would die young, the number who would reach marriageable age might not replace, or might only barely replace, her and her husband or husbands as child-producing members of the society. Consequently, so long as immigrants were heavily predominant in the adult female population, Maryland could not grow much by natural increase.[39] It remained a land of newcomers.

This fact was fundamental to the character of seventeenth-century Maryland society, although its implications have yet to be fully explored. Settlers came from all parts of England and hence from differing traditions—in types of agriculture, forms of landholding and estate management, kinds of building construction, customary contributions to community needs, and family arrangements, including the role of women. The necessities of life in the Chesapeake required all immigrants to make adaptations. But until the native-born became predominant, a securely established Maryland tradition would not guide or restrict the newcomers.

If the immigrant woman had remained in England, she would probably have married at about the same age or perhaps a little later.[40] But the social consequences of marriage at these ages in most parts of England were probably different. More children may have lived to maturity, and even where mortality was as high newcomers are not likely to have been the main source of population growth.[41] The locally born would still dominate the community, its social organization, and its traditions. However, where there were exceptions, as perhaps in London, late age at marriage, combined with high mortality and heavy immigration, may have had consequences in some ways similar to those we have found in Maryland.

A hazard of marriage for seventeenth-century women everywhere was death in childbirth, but this hazard may have been greater than usual in the Chesapeake. Whereas in most societies women tend to outlive men, in this malaria-ridden area it is probable that men outlived women. Hazards of childbirth provide the likely reason that Chesapeake women died so young. Once a woman in the Chesapeake reached forty-five, she tended to outlive men who reached the same age. Darrett and Anita Rutman have found malaria a probable cause of an exceptionally high death rate among pregnant women, who are, it appears, peculiarly vulnerable to that disease.[42]

This argument, however, suggests that immigrant women may have lived longer than their native-born daughters, although among men the opposite was true. Life tables created for men in Maryland show that those native-born who survived to age twenty could expect a life span three to ten years longer than that of immigrants, depending upon the region where they lived. The reason for the improvement was doubtless immunities to local diseases developed in childhood.[43] A native woman developed these immunities, but as we shall see, she also married earlier than immigrant women usually could and hence had more children.[44] Thus she was more exposed to the hazards of childbirth and may have died a little sooner. Unfortunately, the life tables for immigrant women that would settle this question have so far proved impossible to construct.

However long they lived, immigrant women in Maryland tended to outlive their husbands—in Charles County, for example, by a ratio of two to one. This was possible, despite the fact that women were younger than men at death, because women were also younger than men at marriage. Some women were widowed with no living children, but most were left responsible for two or three. These were often tiny, and nearly always not yet sixteen.[45]

This fact had drastic consequences, given the physical circumstances of life. People lived at a distance from one another, not even in villages, much less towns. The widow had left her kin 3,000 miles across an ocean, and her husband's family was also there. She would have to feed her children and make her own tobacco crop. Though neighbors might help, heavy labor would be required of her if she had no servants, until—what admittedly was usually not difficult—she acquired a new husband.

In this situation dying husbands were understandably anxious about the welfare of their families. Their wills reflected their feelings and tell something of how they regarded their wives. In St. Mary's and Charles counties during the seventeenth century, little more than one-quarter of the men left their widows with no more than the dower the law required—one-third of his land for her life, plus outright ownership of one-third of his personal property. (See Table 1.) If there were no children, a man almost always left his widow his whole estate. Otherwise there were a variety of arrangements. (See Table 2.)

During the 1660s, when testators begin to appear in quantity, nearly a

**Table 1.** Bequests of Husbands to Wives, St. Mary's and Charles Counties, Maryland, 1640 to 1710

|  |  | Dower or Less | |
| --- | --- | --- | --- |
|  | N | N | % |
| 1640s | 6 | 2 | 34 |
| 1650s | 24 | 7 | 29 |
| 1660s | 65 | 18 | 28 |
| 1670s | 86 | 21 | 24 |
| 1680s | 64 | 17 | 27 |
| 1690s | 83 | 23 | 28 |
| 1700s | 74 | 25 | 34 |
| Totals | 402 | 113 | 28 |

Source: Wills, I–XIV, Hall of Records, Annapolis, Md.

fifth of the men who had children left all to their wives, trusting them to see that the children received fair portions. Thus in 1663 John Shircliffe willed his whole estate to his wife "towards the maintenance of herself and my children into whose tender care I do Commend them Desireing to see them brought up in the fear of God and the Catholick Religion and Chargeing them to be Dutiful and obedient to her."[46] As the century progressed, husbands tended instead to give the wife all or a major part of the estate for her life, and to designate how it should be distributed after her death. Either way, the husband put great trust in his widow, considering that he knew she was bound to remarry. Only a handful of men left estates to their wives only for their term of widowhood or until the children came of age. When a man did not leave his wife a life estate, he often gave her land outright or more than her dower third of his movable property. Such bequests were at the expense of his children and showed his concern that his widow should have a maintenance which young children could not supply.

**Table 2.** Bequests of Husbands to Wives With Children, St. Mary's and Charles Counties, Maryland, 1640 to 1710

|  |  | All Estate | | All or Dwelling Plantation for Life | | All or Dwelling Plantation for Widowhood | | All or Dwelling Plantation for Minority of Child | | More than Dower in Other Form | | Dower or Less or Unknown | |
| --- | --- | --- | --- | --- | --- | --- | --- | --- | --- | --- | --- | --- | --- |
|  | N | N | % | N | % | N | % | N | % | N | % | N | % |
| 1640s | 3 | 20 | 37 | 33 | | | | | | | | 2 | 67 |
| 1650s | 16 | 1 | 6 | 2 | 13 | 1 | 6 | 1 | 6 | 4 | 25 | 7 | 44 |
| 1660s | 45 | 8 | 18 | 8 | 18 | 2 | 4 | 3 | 7 | 9 | 20 | 15 | 33 |
| 1670s | 61 | 4 | 7 | 21 | 34 | 2 | 3 | 3 | 5 | 13 | 21 | 18 | 30 |
| 1680s | 52 | 5 | 10 | 19 | 37 | 2 | 4 | 2 | 4 | 11 | 21 | 13 | 25 |
| 1690s | 69 | 1 | 1 | 31 | 45 | 7 | 10 | 2 | 3 | 10 | 14 | 18 | 26 |
| 1700s | 62 | | | 20 | 32 | 6 | 10 | 2 | 3 | 14 | 23 | 20 | 32 |
| Totals | 308 | 20 | 6 | 101 | 33 | 20 | 6 | 13 | 4 | 61 | 20 | 93 | 30 |

Source: Wills, I–XIV.

A husband usually made his wife his executor and thus responsible for paying his debts and preserving the estate. Only 11 percent deprived their wives of such power.[47] In many instances, however, men also appointed overseers to assist their wives and to see that their children were not abused or their property embezzled. Danger lay in the fact that a second husband acquired control of all his wife's property, including her life estate in the property of his predecessor. Over half of the husbands who died in the 1650s and 1660s appointed overseers to ensure that their wills were followed. Some trusted to the overseers' "Care and good Conscience for the good of my widow and fatherless children." Others more explicitly made overseers responsible for seeing that "my said child . . . and the other [expected child] (when pleases God to send it) may have their right Proportion of my Said Estate and that the said Children may be bred up Chiefly in the fear of God."[48] A few men—but remarkably few—authorized overseers to remove children from households of stepfathers who abused them or wasted their property.[49] On the whole, the absence of such provisions for the protection of the children points to the husband's overriding concern for the welfare of his widow and to his confidence in her management, regardless of the certainty of her remarriage. Evidently, in the politics of family life women enjoyed great respect.[50]

We have implied that this respect was a product of the experience of immigrants in the Chesapeake. Might it have been instead a reflection of English culture? Little work is yet in print that allows comparison of the provisions for Maryland widows with those made for the widows of English farmers. Possibly, Maryland husbands were making traditional wills which could have been written in the communities they left behind. However, Margaret Spufford's recent study of three Cambridgeshire villages in the late sixteenth century and early seventeenth century suggests a different pattern. In one of these villages, Chippenham, women usually did receive a life interest in the property, but in the other two they did not. If the children were all minors, the widow controlled the property until the oldest son came of age, and then only if she did not remarry. In the majority of cases adult sons were given control of the property with instructions for the support of their mothers. Spufford suggests that the pattern found in Chippenham must have been very exceptional. On the basis of village censuses in six other counties, dating from 1624 to 1724, which show only 3 percent of widowed people heading households that included a married child, she argues that if widows commonly controlled the farm, a higher proportion should have headed such households. However, she also argues that widows with an interest in land would not long remain unmarried.[51] If so, the low percentage may be deceptive. More direct work with wills needs to be done before we can be sure that Maryland husbands and fathers gave their widows greater control of property and family than did their English counterparts.

Maryland men trusted their widows, but this is not to say that many did not express great anxiety about the future of their children. They asked both wives and overseers to see that the children received "some learning." Robert Sly made his wife sole guardian of his children but admonished her "to take due Care that they be brought up in the true fear of God and instructed in such Literature as may tend to their improvement." Widowers, whose children would be left without any parent, were often the most explicit in prescribing their upbringing. Robert Cole, a middling planter, directed that his children "have such Education in Learning as [to] write and read and Cast accompt I mean my three Sonnes my two daughters to learn to read and sew with their needle and all of them to be keept from Idleness but not to be keept as Comon Servants." John Lawson required his executors to see that his two daughters be reared together, receive learning and sewing instruction, and be "brought up to huswifery."[52] Often present was the fear that orphaned children would be treated as servants and trained only to work in the fields.[53] With stepfathers in mind, many fathers provided that their sons should be independent before the usual age of majority, which for girls was sixteen but for men twenty-one. Sometimes fathers willed that their sons should inherit when they were as young as sixteen, though more often eighteen. The sons could then escape an incompatible stepfather, who could no longer exploit their labor or property. If a son was already close to age sixteen, the father might bind him to his mother until he reached majority or his mother died, whichever came first. If she lived, she could watch out for his welfare, and his labor could contribute to her support. If she died, he and his property would be free from a stepfather's control.[54]

What happened to widows and children if a man died without leaving a will? There was great need for some community institution that could protect children left fatherless or parentless in a society where they usually had no other kin. By the 1660s the probate court and county orphans' courts were supplying this need.[55] If a man left a widow, the probate court—in Maryland a central government agency—usually appointed her or her new husband administrator of the estate with power to pay its creditors under court supervision. Probate procedures provided a large measure of protection. These required an inventory of the movable property and careful accounting of all disbursements, whether or not a man had left a will. William Hollis of Baltimore County, for example, had three stepfathers in seven years, and only the care of the judge of probate prevented the third stepfather from paying the debts of the second with goods that had belonged to William's father. As the judge remarked, William had "an uncareful mother."[56]

Once the property of an intestate had been fully accounted and creditors paid, the county courts appointed a guardian who took charge of the property and gave bond to the children with sureties that he or she would not waste it. If the mother were living, she could be the guardian, or if she had remarried, her new husband would act. Through most of the century bond was waived in these circumstances, but from the 1690s security was required of all guardians, even of mothers. Thereafter the courts might actually take away an orphan's property from a widow or stepfather if she or he could not find sureties—that is, neighbors who judged the parent responsible and hence were willing to risk their own property as security. Children without any parents were assigned new families, who at all times found surety if there were property to manage. If the orphans inherited land, English common law allowed them to choose guardians for themselves at age fourteen—another escape hatch for children in conflict with stepparents. Orphans who had no property, or whose property was insufficient to provide an income that could maintain them, were expected to work for their guardians in return for their maintenance. Every year the county courts were expected to check on the welfare of orphans of intestate parents and remove them or their property from guardians who abused them or misused their estates. From 1681, Maryland law required that a special jury be impaneled once a year to report neighborhood knowledge of mistreatment of orphans and hear complaints.

This form of community surveillance of widows and orphans proved quite effective. In 1696 the assembly declared that orphans of intestates were often better cared for than orphans of testators. From that time forward, orphans' courts were charged with supervision of all orphans and were soon given powers to remove any guardians who were shown false to their trusts, regardless of the arrangements laid down in a will. The assumption was that the deceased parent's main concern was the welfare of the child, and that the orphans' court, as "father to us poor orphans," should implement the parent's intent. In actual fact, the courts never removed children—as opposed to their property—from a household in which the mother was living, except to apprentice them at the mother's request. These powers were mainly exercised over guardians of orphans both of whose parents were dead. The community as well as the husband believed the mother most capable of nurturing his children.

Remarriage was the usual and often the immediate solution for a woman who had lost her husband.[57] The shortage of women made any woman eligible to marry again, and the difficulties of raising a family while running a plantation must have made remarriage necessary for widows who had no son old enough to make tobacco. One indication of the high incidence of remarriage is the fact that there were only sixty women, almost all of them widows, among the 1,735 people who left probate inventories in four southern Maryland counties over the second half of the century.[58] Most other women must have died while married and therefore legally without property to put through probate.

One result of remarriage was the development of complex family structures. Men found themselves responsible for stepchildren as well as their own offspring, and children acquired half-sisters and half-brothers. Sometimes a woman married a second husband who himself had been previously married, and both brought children of former spouses to the new marriage. They then produced children of their own. The possibilities for conflict over the upbringing of children are evident, and crowded living conditions, found even in the households of the wealthy, must have added to family tensions. Luckily, the children of the family very often had the same mother. In Charles County, at least, widows took new husbands three times more often than widowers took new wives.[59] The role of the mother in managing the relationships of half-brothers and half-sisters or stepfathers and stepchildren must have been critical to family harmony.

Early death in this immigrant population thus had broad effects on Maryland society in the seventeenth century. It produced what we might call a pattern of serial polyandry, which enabled more men to marry and to father families than the sex ratios otherwise would have permitted. It produced thousands of orphaned children who had no kin to maintain them or preserve their property, and thus gave rise to an institution almost unknown in England, the orphans' court, which was charged with their protection. And early death, by creating families in which the mother was the unifying element, may have increased her authority within the household.

When the immigrant woman married her first husband, there was usually no property settlement involved, since she was unlikely to have any dowry. But her remarriage was another matter. At the very least, she owned or had a life interest in a third of her former husband's estate. She needed also to think of her children's interests. If she remarried, she would lose control of the property. Consequently, property settlements occasionally appear in the seventeenth-century court records between widows and their future husbands. Sometimes she and her intended signed an agreement whereby he relinquished his rights to the use of her children's portions. Sometimes he deeded to her property which she could dispose of at her pleasure.[60] Whether any of these agreements or gifts would have survived a test in court is unknown. We have not yet found any challenged. Generally speaking, the formal marriage settlements of English law, which bypassed the legal difficulties of the married woman's inability to make a contract with her husband, were not adopted by immigrants, most of whom probably came from levels of English society that did not use these legal formalities.

The wife's dower rights in her husband's estate were a recognition of her role in contributing to his prosperity, whether by the property she had brought to the marriage or by the labor she performed in his household. A woman newly freed from servitude would not bring property, but the benefits of her labor would be great. A man not yet prosperous enough to own a servant might need his wife's help in the fields as well as in the house, especially if he were paying rent or still paying for land. Moreover, food preparation was so time-consuming that even if she worked only at household duties, she saved him time he needed for making tobacco and corn. The corn, for example, had to be pounded in the mortar or ground in a handmill before it could be used to make bread, for there were very few water mills in seventeenth-century Maryland. The wife probably raised vegetables in a kitchen garden; she also milked the cows and made butter and cheese, which might produce a salable surplus. She washed the clothes, and made them if she had the skill. When there were servants to do field work, the wife undoubtedly spent her time entirely in such household tasks. A contract of 1681 expressed such a division of labor. Nicholas Maniere agreed to live on a plantation with his wife and child and a servant. Nicholas and the servant were to work the land; his wife was to "Dresse the Victualls milk the Cowes wash for the servants and Doe allthings necessary for a woman to doe upon the s[ai]d plantation."[61]

We have suggested that wives did field work; the suggestion is supported by occasional direct references in the court records. Mary Castleton, for example, told the judge of probate that "her husband late Deceased in his Life time had Little to sustaine himselfe and Children but what was produced out of ye ground by ye hard Labour of her the said Mary."[62] Household inventories provide indirect evidence. Before about 1680 those of poor men and even middling planters on Maryland's lower Western Shore—the bottom two-thirds of the married decedents[63]—show few signs of household industry, such as appear in equivalent English estates.[64] Sheep and woolcards, flax and hackles, and spinning wheels all were a rarity, and such things as candle molds were nonexistent. Women in these households must have been busy at other work. In households with bound labor the wife doubtless was fully occupied preparing food and washing clothes for family and hands. But the wife in a household too poor to afford bound labor—the bottom fifth of the married decedent group—might well tend tobacco when she could.[65] Eventually, the profits of her labor might enable the family to buy a servant, making greater profits possible. From such beginnings many families climbed the economic ladder in seventeenth-century Maryland.[66]

The proportion of servantless households must have been larger than is suggested by the inventories of the dead, since young men were less likely to die than old men and had had less time to accumulate property. Well over a fifth of the households of married men on the lower Western Shore may have had no bound labor. Not every wife in such households would necessarily work at the hoe—saved from it by upbringing, ill-health, or the presence of small children who needed her care—but many women performed such work. A lease of 1691, for example, specified that the lessee could farm the amount of land which "he his wife and children can tend."[67]

Stagnation of the tobacco economy, beginning about 1680, produced changes that had some effect on women's economic role.[68] As shown by inventories of the lower Western Shore, home industry increased, especially at the upper range of the economic spectrum. In these households women were spinning yarn and knitting it into clothing.[69] The increase in such activity was far less in the households of the bottom fifth, where changes of a different kind may have increased the pressures to grow tobacco. Fewer men at this level could now purchase land, and a portion of their crop went for rent.[70] At this level, more wives than before may have been helping to produce tobacco when they could. And by this time they were often helping as a matter of survival, not as a means of improving the family position.

So far we have considered primarily the experience of immigrant women. What of their daughters? How were their lives affected by the demographic stresses of Chesapeake society?

One of the most important points in which the experience of daughters differed from that of their mothers was the age at which they married. In this woman-short world, the mothers had married as soon as they were eligible, but they had not usually become eligible until they were mature women in their middle twenties. Their daughters were much younger at marriage. A vital register kept in Somerset County shows that some girls married at age twelve and that the mean age at marriage for those born before 1670 was sixteen and a half years.

Were some of these girls actually child brides? It seems unlikely that girls were married before they had become capable of bearing children. Culturally, such a practice would fly in the face of English, indeed Western European, precedent, nobility excepted. Nevertheless, the number of girls who married before age sixteen, the legal age of inheritance for girls, is astonishing. Their English counterparts ordinarily did not marry until their mid- to late twenties or early thirties. In other parts of the Chesapeake, historians have found somewhat higher ages at marriage than appear in Somerset, but everywhere in seventeenth-century Maryland and Virginia most native-born women married before they reached age twenty-one.[71] Were such early marriages a result of the absence of fathers? Evidently not. In Somerset County, the fathers of very young brides—those under sixteen—were usually living.[72] Evidently, guardians were unlikely to allow such marriages, and this fact suggests that they were not entirely approved. But the shortage of women imposed strong pressures to marry as early as possible.

Not only did native girls marry early, but many of them were pregnant before the ceremony. Bridal pregnancy among native-born women was not as common as among immigrants. Nevertheless, in seventeenth-century Somerset County 20 percent of native brides bore children within eight and one half months of marriage. This was a somewhat higher percentage than has been reported from seventeenth-century English parishes.[73]

These facts suggest considerable freedom for girls in selecting a husband. Almost any girl must have had more than one suitor, and evidently many had freedom to spend time with a suitor in a fashion that allowed her to become pregnant. We might suppose that such pregnancies were not incurred until after the couple had become betrothed, and that they were consequently an allowable part of courtship, were it not that girls whose fathers were living were usually not the culprits. In Somerset, at least, only 10 percent of the brides with fathers living were pregnant, in contrast to 30 percent of those who were orphans.[74] Since there was only about one year's difference between the mean ages at which orphan and nonorphan girls married, parental supervision rather than age seems to have been the main factor in the differing bridal pregnancy rates.[75]

Native girls married young and bore children young; hence they had more children than immigrant women. This fact ultimately changed the composition of the Maryland population. Native-born females began to have enough children to enable couples to replace themselves. These children, furthermore, were divided about evenly between males and females. By the mid-1680s, in all probability, the population thus began to grow through reproductive increase, and sexual imbalance began to decline. In 1704 the native-born preponderated in the Maryland assembly for the first time and by then were becoming predominant in the adult population as a whole.[76]

This appearance of a native population was bringing alterations in family life, especially for widows and orphaned minors. They were acquiring kin. St. Mary's and Charles counties wills demonstrate the change.[77] (See Table 3.) Before 1680, when nearly all those who died and left families had been immigrants, three-quarters of the men and women who left widows

**Table 3.** RESIDENT KIN OF TESTATE MEN AND WOMEN WHO LEFT MINOR CHILDREN, ST. MARY'S AND CHARLES COUNTIES 1640 TO 1710

| | FAMILIES N | NO KIN % FAMILIES | ONLY WIFE % FAMILIES | GROWN CHILD % FAMILIES | OTHER KIN % FAMILIES |
|---|---|---|---|---|---|
| | | | A. | | |
| 1640–1669 | 95 | 23 | 43 | 11 | 23 |
| 1670–1679 | 76 | 17 | 50 | 7 | 26 |
| 1700–1710 | 71 | 6 | 35[a] | 25 | 34[b] |
| | | | B. | | |
| 1700–1710 | | | | | |
| Immigrant | 41 | 10 | 37 | 37 | 17 |
| Native | 30 | | 33[c] | 10 | 57[d] |

Source: Wills, I–XIV.

Notes:

a. If information found in other records is included, the percentage is 30.
b. If information found in other records is included, the percentage is 39.
c. If information found in other records is included, the percentage is 20.
d. If information found in other records is included, the percentage is 70.

For a discussion of wills as a reliable source for discovery of kin see n. 78. Only 8 testators were natives of Maryland before 1680s; hence no effort has been made to distinguish them from immigrants.

and/or minor children made no mention in their wills of any other kin in Maryland. In the first decade of the eighteenth century, among native-born testators, nearly three-fifths mention other kin, and if we add information from sources other than wills—other probate records, land records, vital registers, and so on—at least 70 percent are found to have had such local connections. This development of local family ties must have been one of the most important events of early Maryland history.[78]

Historians have only recently begun to explore the consequences of the shift from an immigrant to a predominantly native population.[79] We would like to suggest some changes in the position of women that may have resulted from this transition. It is already known that as sexual imbalance disappeared, age at first marriage rose, but it remained lower than it had been for immigrants over the second half of the seventeenth century. At the same time, life expectancy improved, at least for men. The results were longer marriages and more children who reached maturity.[80] In St. Mary's County after 1700, dying men far more often than earlier left children of age to maintain their widows, and widows may have felt less inclination and had less opportunity to remarry.[81]

We may speculate on the social consequences of such changes. More fathers were still alive when their daughters married, and hence would have been able to exercise control over the selection of their sons-in-law. What in the seventeenth century may have been a period of comparative independence for women, both immigrant and native, may have given way to a return to more traditional European social sontrols over the creation of new families. If so, we might see the results in a decline in bridal pregnancy and perhaps a decline in bastardy.[82]

We may also find the wife losing ground in the household polity, although her economic importance probably remained unimpaired. Indeed, she must have been far more likely than a seventeenth-century immigrant woman to bring property to her marriage. But several changes may have caused women to play a smaller role than before in household decision-making.[83] Women became proportionately more numerous and may have lost bargaining power.[84] Furthermore, as marriages lasted longer, the proportion of households full of stepchildren and half-brothers and half-sisters united primarily by the mother must have diminished. Finally, when husbands died, more widows would have had children old enough to maintain them and any minor brothers and sisters. There would be less need for women to play a controlling role, as well as less incentive for their husbands to grant it. The provincial marriage of the eighteenth century may have more closely resembled that of England than did the immigrant marriage of the seventeenth century.

If this change occurred, we should find symptoms to measure. There should be fewer gifts from husbands to wives of property put at the wife's disposal. Husbands should less frequently make bequests to wives that provided them with property beyond their dower. A wife might even be restricted to less than her dower, although the law allowed her to choose her dower instead of a bequest.[85] At the same time, children should be commanded to maintain their mothers.

However, St. Mary's County wills do not show these symptoms. (See Table 4.) True, wives occasionally were willed less than their dower, an arrangement that was rare in the wills examined for the period before 1710. But there was no overall decrease in bequests to wives of property beyond their dower, nor was there a tendency to confine the wife's interest to the term of her widowhood or the minority of the oldest son. Children were not exhorted to help their mothers or give them living space. Widows evidently received at least enough property to maintain themselves, and husbands saw no need to ensure the help of children in managing it. Possibly, then, women did not lose ground, or at least not all ground, within the family polity. The demographic disruption of New World settlement may have given women power which they were able to keep even after sex ratios became balanced and traditional family networks appeared. Immigrant mothers may have bequeathed their daughters a legacy of independence which they in turn handed down, despite pressures toward more traditional behavior.

It is time to issue a warning. Whether or not Maryland women in a creole society lost ground, the argument hinges on an interpretation of English behavior that also requires testing. Either position supposes that women in seventeenth-century Maryland obtained power in the household which wives of English farmers did not enjoy. Much of the evidence for Maryland is drawn from the disposition of property in wills. If English wills show a similar pattern, similar inferences might be drawn about English women. We have already discussed evidence from English wills that supports the view that women in Maryland were favored; but the position of seventeenth-century English women—especially those not of gentle status—has been little explored.[86] A finding of little difference between bequests to women in England and in Maryland would greatly weaken the

**Table 4.** BEQUESTS OF HUSBANDS TO WIVES WITH CHILDREN, ST. MARY'S COUNTY, MARYLAND, 1710 TO 1776

| | N | All Estate | All or Dwelling Plantation for Life | All or Dwelling Plantation for Widowhood | All or Dwelling Plantation for Minority of Child | More than Dower in Other Form | Dower or Less or Unknown | Maintenance or House Room |
|---|---|---|---|---|---|---|---|---|
| | | % | % | % | % | % | % | % |
| 1710–1714 | 13 | 0 | 46 | 0 | 0 | 23 | 31 | 0 |
| 1715–1719 | 25 | 4 | 24 | 4 | 0 | 28 | 36 | 4 |
| 1720–1724 | 31 | 10 | 42 | 0 | 0 | 28 | 23 | 3 |
| 1725–1729 | 34 | 3 | 29 | 0 | 0 | 24 | 41 | 3 |
| 1730–1734 | 31 | 6 | 16 | 13 | 0 | 29 | 35 | 0 |
| 1735–1739 | 27 | 0 | 37 | 4 | 4 | 19 | 37 | 0 |
| 1740–1744 | 35 | 0 | 40 | 0 | 3 | 23 | 34 | 0 |
| 1745–1749 | 39 | 3 | 31 | 8 | 0 | 31 | 28 | 0 |
| 1750–1754 | 43 | 2 | 35 | 7 | 0 | 16 | 40 | 0 |
| 1755–1759 | 34 | 3 | 41 | 3 | 0 | 41 | 12 | 0 |
| 1760–1764 | 48 | 2 | 46 | 10 | 2 | 13 | 27 | 0 |
| 1765–1769 | 45 | 4 | 27 | 11 | 2 | 18 | 33 | 4 |
| 1770–1774 | 46 | 4 | 26 | 7 | 2 | 37 | 26 | 0 |
| 1775–1776 | 19 | 5 | 32 | 26 | 0 | 5 | 32 | 0 |
| Totals | 470 | 3 | 33 | 7 | 1 | 24 | 31 | 1 |

Source: Wills, XIV–XLI.

argument that demographic stress created peculiar conditions especially favorable to Maryland women.

If the demography of Maryland produced the effects here described, such effects should also be evident elsewhere in the Chesapeake. The four characteristics of the seventeenth-century Maryland population— immigrant predominance, early death, late marriage, and sexual imbalance—are to be found everywhere in the region, at least at first. The timing of the disappearance of these peculiarities may have varied from place to place, depending on date of settlement or rapidity of development, but the effect of their existence upon the experience of women should be clear. Should research in other areas of the Chesapeake fail to find women enjoying the status they achieved on the lower Western Shore of Maryland, then our arguments would have to be revised.[87]

Work is also needed that will enable historians to compare conditions in Maryland with those in other colonies. Richard S. Dunn's study of the British West Indies also shows demographic disruption.[88] When the status of wives is studied, it should prove similar to that of Maryland women. In contrast were demographic conditions in New England, where immigrants came in family groups, major immigration had ceased by the mid-seventeenth century, sex ratios balanced early, and mortality was low.[89] Under these conditions, demographic disruption must have been both less severe and less prolonged. If New England women achieved status similar to that suggested for women in the Chesapeake, that fact will have to be explained. The dynamics might prove to have been different;[90] or a dynamic we have not identified, common to both areas, might turn out to have been the primary engine of change. And, if women in England shared the status— which we doubt—conditions in the New World may have had secondary importance. The Maryland data establish persuasive grounds for a hypothesis, but the evidence is not all in.

## NOTES

1. Russell R. Menard, "Economy and Society in Early Colonial Maryland" (Ph.D. diss., University of Iowa, 1975), 153–212, and "Immigrants and Their Increase: The Process of Population Growth in Early Colonial Maryland," in Aubrey C. Land, Lois Green Carr, and Edward C. Papenfuse, eds., *Law, Society, and Politics in Early Maryland* (Baltimore, 1977), 88–110, hereafter cited as Menard, "Immigrants and Their Increase"; Lorena S. Walsh and Russell R. Menard, "Death in the Chesapeake: Two Life Tables for Men in Early Colonial Maryland," *Maryland Historical Magazine*, LXIX (1974), 211–227. In a sample of 806 headrights Menard found only two unmarried women who paid their own passage ("Economy and Society," 187).

2. Menard, "Immigrants and Their Increase," Fig. I; William Hand Browne et al., eds., *Archives of Maryland* (Baltimore, 1883–    ), XXV, 256, hereafter cited as *Maryland Archives.*

3. Court proceedings for St. Mary's and Calvert counties have not survived.

4. The lists of immigrants are found in John Camden Hotten, ed., *The Original Lists of Persons of Quality; Emigrants; Religious Exiles; Political Rebels; . . . and Others Who Went from Great Britain to the American Plantations, 1600–1700* (London, 1874); William

Dodgson Bowman, ed., *Bristol and America: A Record of the First Settlers in the Colonies of North America, 1654-1685* (Baltimore, 1967 [orig. publ. London, 1929]); C. D. P. Nicholson, comp., *Some Early Emigrants to America* (Baltimore, 1965); Michael Ghirelli, ed., *A List of Emigrants to America, 1682-1692* (Baltimore, 1968); and Elizabeth French, ed., *List of Emigrants to America from Liverpool, 1697-1707* (Baltimore, 1962 [orig. publ. Boston, 1913]). Folger Shakespeare Library, MS. V.B. 16 (Washington, D.C.), consists of 66 additional indentures that were originally part of the London records. For studies of these lists see Mildred Campbell, "Social Origins of Some Early Americans," in James Morton Smith, ed., *Seventeenth-Century America: Essays in Colonial History* (Chapel Hill, N.C., 1959), 63–89; David W. Galenson, "'Middling People' or 'Common Sort'?: The Social Origins of Some Early Americans Reexamined," *William and Mary Quarterly* (forthcoming). See also Menard, "Immigrants and Their Increase," Table 4.1, and "Economy and Society," Table VIII-6; and Lorena S. Walsh, "Servitude and Opportunity in Charles County," in Land, Carr, and Papenfuse, eds., *Law, Society, and Politics in Early Maryland*, 112–114, hereafter cited as Walsh, "Servitude and Opportunity."

5. Campbell, "Social Origins of Some Early Americans," in Smith, ed., *Seventeenth-Century America*, 74–77; Galenson, "'Middling People' or 'Common Sort'?" *WMQ* (forthcoming). When the ages recorded in the London list (Nicholson, comp., *Some Early Emigrants*) and on the Folger Library indentures for servants bound for Maryland and Virginia are combined, 84.5 percent of the men (N = 354) are found to have been aged 17 to 30, and 54.9 percent were 18 through 22. Of the women (N = 119), 81.4 percent were 18 through 25; 10 percent were older, 8.3 percent younger, and half (51.2 percent) immigrated between ages 20 and 22. Russell Menard has generously lent us his abstracts of the London list.

6. This assumption is defended in Walsh, "Servitude and Opportunity," 129.

7. Ibid., 112–114, describes the legislation and the Charles County data base. There is some reason to believe that by 1700, young servants had contracts more often than earlier. Figures from the London list include the Folger Library indentures.

8. Menard, "Immigrants and Their Increase," Table 1.

9. Menard, "Economy and Society," 336–356; Lois Green Carr and Russell R. Menard, "Servants and Freedmen in Early Colonial Maryland," in Thad W. Tate and David A. Ammerman, eds., *Essays on the Chesapeake in the Seventeenth Century* (Chapel Hill, N.C., forthcoming); E. A. Wrigley, "Family Limitation in Pre-Industrial England," *Economic History Review*, 2d Ser., XIX (1966), 82–109; Michael Drake, "An Elementary Exercise in Parish Register Demography," ibid., XIV (1962), 427–445; J. D. Chambers, *Population, Economy, and Society in Pre-Industrial England* (London, 1972).

10. John Hammond, *Leah and Rachel, or, the Two Fruitfull Sisters Virginia and Maryland . . .*, and George Alsop, *A Character of the Province of Mary-land . . .*, in Clayton Colman Hall, ed., *Narratives of Early Maryland, 1633-1684*, Original Narratives of Early American History (New York, 1910), 281–308, 340–387; Russell R. Menard, P. M. G. Harris, and Lois Green Carr, "Opportunity and Inequality: The Distribution of Wealth on the Lower Western Shore of Maryland, 1638-1705," *Md. Hist. Mag.*, LXIX (1974), 169–184; Russell R. Menard, "From Servant to Freeholder: Status Mobility and Property Accumulation in Seventeenth-Century Maryland," *WMQ*, 3d Ser., XXX (1973), 37–64; Carr and Menard, "Servants and Freedmen," in Tate and Ammerman, eds., *Essays on the Chesapeake*; Walsh, "Servitude and Opportunity," 111–133.

11. Walsh and Menard, "Death in the Chesapeake," *Md. Hist. Mag.*, LXIX (1974), 211–227; Darrett B. and Anita H. Rutman, "Of Agues and Fevers: Malaria in the Early Chesapeake," *WMQ*, 3d Ser., XXXIII (1976), 31–60.

12. E. A. Wrigley, *Population and History* (New York, 1969), 96–100.

13. Menard, "Economy and Society," Table VII-5.

14. Lorena S. Walsh, "Charles County, Maryland, 1658-1705: A Study in Chesapeake Political and Social Structure" (Ph.D. diss., Michigan State University, 1977), chap. 4.

15. Hammond, *Leah and Rachel*, and Alsop, *Character of the Province*, in Hall, ed., *Narratives of Maryland*, 281–308, 340–387; Mildred Campbell, *The English Yeoman Under Elizabeth and the Early Stuarts*, Yale Historical Publications (New Haven, Conn., 1942), 255–261; Alan Everitt, "Farm Labourers," in Joan Thirsk, ed., *The Agrarian History of England and Wales, 1540-1640* (Cambridge, 1967), 432.

16. Lorena S. Walsh and Russell R. Menard are preparing an article on the history of illegitimacy in Charles and Somerset counties, 1658–1776.

17. Abbot Emerson Smith, *Colonists in Bondage: White Servitude and Convict Labor in America, 1607–1776* (Chapel Hill, N.C., 1947), 271–273. Marriage was in effect a breach of contract.

18. Lois Green Carr, "County Government in Maryland, 1689–1709" (Ph.D. diss., Harvard University, 1968), text, 267–269, 363. The courts pursued bastardy offenses regardless of the social status of the culprits in order to ensure that the children would not become public charges. Free single women were not being overlooked.

19. John Barth, *The Sot-Weed Factor* (New York, 1960), 429.

20. This impression is based on Walsh's close reading of Charles County records, Carr's close reading of Prince George's County records, and less detailed examination by both of all other seventeenth-century Maryland court records.

21. Walsh, "Charles County, Maryland," chap. 4; Carr, "County Government in Maryland," chap. 4, n. 269. Carr summarizes the evidence from Charles, Prince George's, Baltimore, Talbot, and Somerset counties, 1689–1709, for comparing punishment of fathers and mothers of bastards. Leniency toward fathers varied from county to county and time to time. The length of time served for restitution also varied over place and time, increasing as the century progressed. See Charles County Court and Land Records, MS, L #1, ff. 276–277, Hall of Records, Annapolis, Md. Unless otherwise indicated, all manuscripts cited are at the Hall of Records.

22. Peter Laslett and Karla Osterveen have calculated illegitimacy ratios—the percentage of bastard births among all births registered—in 24 English parishes, 1581–1810. The highest ratio over the period 1630–1710 was 2.4. Laslett and Osterveen, "Long Term Trends in Bastardy in England: A Study of the Illegitimacy Figures in the Parish Registers and in the Reports of the Registrar General, 1561–1960," *Population Studies*, XXVII (1973), 267. In Somerset County, Maryland, 1666–1694, the illegitimacy ratio ranged from 6.3 to 11.8. Russell R. Menard, "The Demography of Somerset County, Maryland: A Preliminary Report" (paper presented to the Stony Brook Conference on Social History, State University of New York at Stony Brook, June 1975), Table XVI. The absence of figures for the number of women in these places of childbearing age but with no living husband prevents construction of illegitimacy rates.

23. Alsop, *Character of the Province*, in Hall, ed., *Narratives of Maryland*, 358.

24. Maryland Headright Sample, 1658–1681 (N = 625); 257.1 men per 100 women; Maryland Inventories, 1658–1679 (N = 584); 320.1 men per 100 women. Menard, "Immigrants and Their Increase," Table 1.

25. A comparison of a Virginia Headright Sample, 1648–1666 (N = 4,272) with inventories from York and Lower Norfolk counties, 1637–1675 (N = 168) shows less, rather than more, imbalance in inventories as compared to headrights. This indicates fewer purchases of wives than we have suggested for the period after 1660. However, the inventory sample is small.

26. Only 8 percent of tenant farmers who left inventories in four Maryland counties of the lower Western Shore owned labor, 1658–1705. St. Mary's City Commission Inventory Project, "Social Stratification in Maryland, 1658–1705" (National Science Foundation Grant GS-32272), hereafter cited as "Social Stratification." This is an analysis of 1,735 inventories recorded from 1658 to 1705 in St. Mary's, Calvert, Charles, and Prince George's counties, which together constitute most of the lower Western Shore of Maryland.

27. Sixty women left inventories. The status of five is unknown. The two who died single died in 1698. Menard, "Immigrants and Their Increase," Table 1.

28. Menard, "Demography of Somerset County," Table XVII; Daniel Scott Smith and Michael S. Hindus, "Premarital Pregnancy in America, 1640–1971: An Overview," *Journal of Interdisciplinary History*, V (1975), 541. It was also two to three times the rate found in New England in the late seventeenth century.

29. In Maryland any proceedings against pregnant brides could have been brought only in the civil courts. No vestries were established until 1693, and their jurisdiction was confined to the admonishment of men and women suspected of fornication unproved by the conception

of a child. Churchwardens were to inform the county court of bastardies. Carr, "County Government in Maryland," text, 148–149, 221–223.

30. The data are from Nicholson, comp., *Some Early Emigrants.*

31. Charles County Court and Land Records, MSS, C #1 through B #2.

32. Available ages at arrival are as follows:

| Age | under 12 | 13 | 14 | 15 | 16 | 17 | 18 | 19 | 20 | 21 | 22 | 23 | 24 | 25 | 26 | 27 | 28 | 29 | 30 |
|---|---|---|---|---|---|---|---|---|---|---|---|---|---|---|---|---|---|---|---|
| Indentured (1682–1687) | | | | 1 | 1 | 6 | 2 | 9 | 9 | 82 | 19 | 6 | 5 | 6 | 2 | 3 | 1 | 2 | 3 |
| Unindentured (1666–1705) | 8 | 5 | 12 | 4 | 7 | 18 | 16 | 13 | 34 | 9 | 11 | 2 | 1 | 1 | | | | | |

Terms of service for women without indentures from 1666 on were 5 years if they were aged 22 at arrival; 6 years if 18–21; 7 years if 15–17; and until 22 if under 15. From 1661 to 1665 these terms were shorter by a year, and women under 15 served until age 21. If we assume that (1) indentured women served 4 years; (2) they constituted half the servant women; (3) women under age 12 were not purchased as wives; (4) 20 percent of women aged 12 or older were purchased; and (5) purchases were spread evenly over the possible years of service, then from 1666, 73.9 percent were 23 or older at marriage, and 66.0 percent were 24 or older; 70.8 percent were 23 or older from 1661 to 1665, and 55.5 percent were 24 or older. Mean ages at eligibility for marriage, as calculated by dividing person-years by the number of women, were 24.37 from 1666 on and 23.42 from 1661 to 1665. All assumptions except (3) and (5) are discussed above. The third is made on the basis that native girls married as young as age 12.

33. Walsh, "Charles County, Maryland," chap. 2; Menard, "Demography of Somerset County," Tables XI, XII.

34. The impact of later marriages is best demonstrated with age-specific marital fertility statistics. Susan L. Norton reports that women in colonial Ipswich, Massachusetts, bore an average of 7.5 children if they married between ages 15 and 19; 7.1 if they married between 20 and 24; and 4.5 if they married after 24. Norton, "Population Growth in Colonial America: A Study of Ipswich, Massachusetts," *Pop. Studies,* XXV (1971), 444. Cf. Wrigley, "Family Limitation in Pre-Industrial England," *Econ. Hist. Rev.,* 2d Ser., XIX (1966), 82–109.

35. In Charles County the mean interval between first and second and subsequent births was 30.8, and the median was 27.3 months. Walsh, "Charles County, Maryland," chap. 2. Menard has found that in Somerset County, Maryland, the median birth intervals for immigrant women between child 1 and child 2, child 2 and child 3, child 3 and child 4, and child 4 and child 5 were 26, 26, 30, 27 months, respectively ("Demography of Somerset County," Table XX).

36. Walsh, "Charles County, Maryland," chap. 2.

37. Walsh and Menard, "Death in the Chesapeake," *Md. Hist. Mag.,* LXIX (1974), 222.

38. Menard, using all Maryland wills, found a considerably lower number of children per family in a similar period: 1.83 in wills probated 1660–1665; 2.20 in wills probated 1680–1684 ("Economy and Society," 198). Family reconstitution not surprisingly produces slightly higher figures, since daughters are often underrecorded in wills but are recorded as frequently as sons in birth registers. In seventeenth-century Charles County the mean size of all reconstituted families was 2.75. For marriages contracted in the years 1658–1669 (N = 118), 1670–1679 (N = 79), and 1680–1689 (N = 95), family size was 3.15, 2.58, and 2.86, respectively. In Somerset County, family size for immigrant marriages formed between 1665 and 1695 (N = 41) was 3.9. Walsh, "Charles County, Maryland," chap. 2; Menard, "Demography of Somerset County," Table XXI.

39. For fuller exposition of the process see Menard, "Immigrants and Their Increase."

40. P. E. Razell, "Population Change in Eighteenth-Century England. A Reinterpretation," *Econ. Hist. Rev.,* 2d Ser., XVIII (1965), 315, cites mean age at marriage as 23.76 years for 7,242 women in Yorkshire, 1662–1714, and 24.6 years for 280 women of Wiltshire, Berkshire, Hampshire, and Dorset, 1615–1621. Peter Laslett, *The World We Have Lost: England before the Industrial Age,* 2d ed. (London, 1971), 86, shows a mean age of 23.58 for 1,007 women in the Diocese of Canterbury, 1619–1690. Wrigley, "Family Limitation in Pre-Industrial England," *Econ. Hist. Rev.,* 2d Ser., XIX (1966), 87, shows mean ages at marriage for 259 women in Colyton, Devon, ranging from 26.15 to 30.0 years, 1600–1699.

41. For a brief discussion of Chesapeake and English mortality see Walsh and Menard, "Death in the Chesapeake," *Md. Hist. Mag.,* LXIX (1974), 224–225.

42. George W. Barclay, *Techniques of Population Analysis* (New York, 1958), 136n; Darrett B. and Anita H. Rutman, "'Now-Wives and Sons-in-Law': Parental Death in a Seventeenth-Century Virginia County," in Tate and Ammerman, eds., *Essays on the Chesapeake*; Rutman and Rutman, "Of Agues and Fevers," *WMQ*, 3d Ser., XXXIII (1976), 31–60. Cf. Peter H. Wood, *Black Majority: Negroes in Colonial South Carolina from 1670 through the Stono Rebellion* (New York, 1974), chap. 3.

43. Walsh and Menard, "Death in the Chesapeake," *Md. Hist. Mag.*, LXIX (1974) 211–227; Menard, "Demography of Somerset County."

44. In Charles County immigrant women who ended childbearing years or died before 1705 bore a mean of 3.5 children (N = 59); the mean for natives was 5.1 (N = 42). Mean completed family size in Somerset County for marriages contracted between 1665 and 1695 was higher, but the immigrant–native differential remains. Immigrant women (N = 17) bore 6.1 children, while native women (N = 16) bore 9.4 Walsh, "Charles County, Maryland," chap. 2; Menard, "Demography of Somerset County," Table XXI.

45. Among 1735 decedents who left inventories on Maryland's lower Western Shore, 1658–1705, 72 percent died without children or with children not yet of age. Only 16 percent could be proved to have a child of age. "Social Stratification."

46. Wills, I, 172.

47. From 1640 to 1710, 17 percent of the married men named no executor. In such cases, the probate court automatically gave executorship to the wife unless she requested someone else to act.

48. Wills, I, 96, 69.

49. Ibid., 193–194, 167, V, 82. The practice of appointing overseers ceased around the end of the century. From 1690 to 1710, only 13 percent of testators who made their wives executors appointed overseers.

50. We divided wills according to whether decedents were immigrant, native born, or of unknown origins, and found no differences in patterns of bequests, choice of executors, or tendency to appoint overseers. No change occurred in seventeenth-century Maryland in these respects as a native-born population began to appear.

51. Margaret Spufford, *Contrasting Communities: English Villagers in the Sixteenth and Seventeenth Centuries* (Cambridge, 1974), 85–90, 111–118, 161–164.

52. Wills, I, 422, 182, 321.

53. For example, ibid., 172, 182.

54. Lorena S. Walsh, "'Till Death Do Us Part': Marriage and Family in Charles County, Maryland, 1658–1705," in Tate and Ammerman, eds., *Essays on the Chesapeake*.

55. The following discussion of the orphans' court is based on Lois Green Carr, "The Development of the Maryland Orphans' Court, 1654–1715," in Land, Carr, and Papenfuse, eds., *Law, Society, and Politics in Early Maryland*, 41–61.

56. Baltimore County Court Proceedings, D. ff. 385–386.

57. In seventeenth-century Charles County two-thirds of surviving partners remarried within a year of their spouse's death. Walsh, "Charles County, Maryland," chap. 2.

58. See n. 26.

59. Walsh, "'Till Death Do Us Part,'" in Tate and Ammerman, eds., *Essays on the Chesapeake*.

60. Ibid.

61. *Maryland Archives*, LXX, 87. See also ibid., XLI, 210, 474, 598, for examples of allusions to washing clothes and dairying activities. Water mills were so scarce that in 1669 the Maryland assembly passed an act permitting land to be condemned for the use of anyone willing to build and operate a water mill. Ibid., II, 211–214. In the whole colony only four condemnations were carried out over the next 10 years. Ibid., LI, 25, 57, 86, 381. Probate inventories show that most households had a mortar and pestle or a hand mill.

62. Testamentary Proceedings, X, 184–185. Cf. Charles County Court and Land Records, MS, I #1, ff. 9–10, 259.

63. Among married decedents before 1680 (N = 308), the bottom two-thirds (N = 212) were those worth less than £150. Among all decedents worth less than £150 (N = 451), only 12 (about 3 percent) had sheep or yarn-making equipment, "Social Stratification."

64. See Everitt, "Farm Labourers," in Thirsk, ed., *Agrarian History of England and Wales*, 422–426, and W. G. Hoskins, *Essays in Leicestershire History* (Liverpool, 1950), 134.

65. Among married decedents, the bottom fifth were approximately those worth less than £30. Before 1680 these were 17 percent of the married decedents. By the end of the period, from 1700 to 1705, they were 22 percent. Before 1680, 92 percent had no bound labor. From 1700 to 1705, 95 percent had none. Less than 1 percent of all estates in this wealth group had sheep or yarn-making equipment before 1681. "Social Stratification."

66. On opportunity to raise from the bottom to the middle see Menard, "From Servant to Freeholder," *WMQ*, 3d Ser., XXX (1973), 37–64; Walsh, "Servitude and Opportunity," 111–133, and Menard, Harris, and Carr, "Opportunity and Inequality," *Md. Hist. Mag.*, LXIX (1974), 169–184.

67. Charles County Court and Land Records, MS, R #1, f. 193.

68. For seventeenth-century economic development see Menard, Harris, and Carr, "Opportunity and Inequality," *Md. Hist. Mag.*, LXIX (1974), 169–184.

69. Among estates worth £150 or more, signs of diversification in this form appeared in 22 percent before 1681 and in 67 percent after 1680. Over the years 1700–1705, the figure was 62 percent. Only 6 percent of estates worth less than £40 had such signs of diversification after 1680 or over the period 1700–1705. Knitting rather than weaving is assumed because looms were very rare. These figures are for all estates. "Social Stratification."

70. After the mid-1670s information about landholdings of decedents becomes decreasingly available, making firm estimates of the increase in tenancy difficult. However, for householders in life-cycle 2 (married or widowed decedents who died without children of age) the following table is suggestive. Householding decedents in life-cycle 2 worth less than £40 (N = 255) were 21 percent of all decedents in this category (N = 1,218).

| | £, 0–19 | | | | £, 20–39 | | |
|---|---|---|---|---|---|---|---|
| | DECEDENTS | LAND UNKN. | WITH LAND | WITH LAND | DECEDENTS | LAND UNKN. | WITH LAND | WITH LAND |
| | N | N | N | % | N | N | N | % |
| To 1675 | 10 | 0 | 7 | 70 | 34 | 2 | 29 | 91 |
| 1675 on | 98 | 22 | 40- | 53 | 113 | 16 | 64 | 66 |

In computing percentages, unknowns have been distributed according to knowns.

A man who died with a child of age was almost always a landowner, but these were a small proportion of all decedents (see n. 45).

Several studies provide indisputable evidence of an increase in tenancy on the lower Western Shore over the period 1660–1706. These compare heads of households with lists of landowners compiled from rent rolls made in 1659 and 1704–1706. Tenancy in St. Mary's and Charles counties in 1660 was about 10 percent. In St. Mary's, Charles, and Prince George's counties, 1704–1706, 30–35 percent of householders were tenants. Russell R. Menard, "Population Growth and Land Distribution in St. Mary's County, 1634–1710" (ms report, St. Mary's City Commission, 1971, copy on file at the Hall of Records); Menard, "Economy and Society," 423; Carr, "County Government in Maryland," text, 605.

71. Menard, "Immigrants and Their Increase," Table III: n. 40 above.

72. Menard, "Demography of Somerset County," Table XIII.

73. Ibid., Table XVII; P. E. H. Hair, "Bridal Pregnancy in Rural England in Earlier Centuries," *Pop. Studies*, XX (1966), 237; Chambers, *Population, Economy, and Society in England*, 75; Smith and Hindus, "Premarital Pregnancy in America," *Jour. Interdisciplinary Hist.*, V (1975), 537–570.

74. Menard, "Demography of Somerset County," Table XVIII.

75. Adolescent subfecundity might also partly explain lower bridal pregnancy rates among very young brides.

76. Menard develops this argument in detail in "Immigrants and Their Increase." For the assembly see David W. Jordan, "Political Stability and the Emergence of a Native Elite in Maryland, 1660–1715," in Tate and Ammerman, eds., *Essays on the Chesapeake*. In Charles County, Maryland, by 1705 at least half of all resident landowners were native born. Walsh, "Charles County, Maryland," chaps. 1 7.

77. The proportion of wills mentioning nonnuclear kin can, of course, prove only a proxy of the actual existence of these kin in Maryland. The reliability of such a measure may vary greatly from area to area and over time, depending on the character of the population and on local inheritance customs. To test the reliability of the will data, we compared them with data from reconstituted families in seventeenth-century Charles County. These reconstitution data draw on a much broader variety of sources and include many men who did not leave wills. Because of insufficient information for female lines, we could trace only the male lines. The procedure compared the names of all married men against a file of all known county residents, asking how many kin in the male line might have been present in the county at the time of the married man's death. The proportions for immigrants were in most cases not markedly different from those found in wills. For native men, however, wills were somewhat less reliable indicators of the presence of such kin; when nonnuclear kin mentioned by testate natives were compared with kin found by reconstitution, 29 percent of the native testators had nonnuclear kin present in the county who were not mentioned in their wills.

78. Not surprisingly, wills of immigrants show no increase in family ties, but these wills mention adult children far more often than earlier. Before 1680, only 11 percent of immigrant testators in St. Mary's and Charles counties mention adult children in their wills; from 1700 to 1710, 37 percent left adult children to help the family. Two facts help account for this change. First, survivors of early immigration were dying in old age. Second, proportionately fewer young immigrants with families were dying, not because life expectancy had improved, but because there were proportionately fewer of them than earlier. A long stagnation in the tobacco economy that began about 1680 had diminished opportunities for freed servants to form households and families. Hence, among immigrants the proportion of young fathers at risk to die was smaller than in earlier years.

In the larger population of men who left inventories, 18.2 percent had adult children before 1681, but in the years 1700–1709, 50 percent had adult children. "Social Stratification."

79. Examples of some recent studies are Carole Shammas, "English-Born and Creole Elites in Turn-of-the-Century Virginia," in Tate and Ammerman, eds., *Essays on the Chesapeake*; Jordan, "Political Stability and the Emergence of a Native Elite in Maryland," ibid.; Lois Green Carr, "The Foundations of Social Order: Local Government in Colonial Maryland," in Bruce C. Daniels, ed., *Town and Country: Essays on the Structure of Local Government in the American Colonies* (Middletown, Conn., forthcoming); Menard, "Economy and Society." 396–440.

80. Allan Kulikoff has found that in Prince George's County the white adult sex ratio dropped significantly before the age of marriage rose. Women born in the 1720s were the first to marry at a mean age above 20, while those born in the 1740s and marrying in the 1760s, after the sex ratio neared equality, married at a mean age of 22. Marriages lasted longer because the rise in the mean age at which men married—from 23 to 27 between 1700 and 1740—was more than offset by gains in life expectancy. Kulikoff, "Tobacco and Slaves: Population, Economy, and Society in Eighteenth-Century Prince George's County, Maryland" (Ph.D. diss., Brandeis University, 1976), chap. 3; Menard, "Immigrants and Their Increase."

81. Inventories and related biographical data have been analyzed by the St. Mary's City Commission under a grant from the National Endowment for the Humanities, "The Making of a Plantation Society in Maryland" (R 010585-74-267). From 1700 through 1776 the percentage of men known to have had children, and who had an adult child at death, ranged from a low of 32.8 percent in the years 1736–1738 to a high of 61.3 percent in the years 1707–1709. The figure was over 50 percent for 13 out of 23 year-groups of three to four years each. For the high in 1707–1709 see comments in n. 78.

82. On the other hand, these rates may show little change. The restraining effect of an increased parental control may have been offset by a trend toward increased sexual activity that appears to have become general throughout Western Europe and the United States by the mid-nineteenth century. Smith and Hindus, "Premarital Pregnancy in America," *Jour. Interdisciplinary Hist.*, V (1975), 537–570; Edward Shorter, "Female Emancipation, Birth Control, and Fertility in European History," *American Historical Review*, LXXVIII (1973), 605–640.

83. Page Smith has suggested that such a decline in the wife's household authority had occurred in the American family by—at the latest—the beginning of the nineteenth century (*Daughters of the Promised Land: Women in American History* [Boston, 1970], chaps. 3, 4).

84. There is little doubt that extreme scarcity in the early years of Chesapeake history enhanced the worth of women in the eyes of men. However, as Smith has observed, "the functioning of the law of supply and demand could not in itself have guaranteed status for colonial women. Without an ideological basis, their privileges could not have been initially established or subsequently maintained" (ibid., 38–39). In a culture where women were seriously undervalued, a shortage of women would not necessarily improve their status.

85. Acts 1699, chap. 41, *Maryland Archives*, XXII, 542.

86. Essays by Cicely Howell and Barbara Todd, printed or made available to the authors since this article was written, point out that customary as opposed to freehold tenures in England usually gave the widow the use of the land for life, but that remarriage often cost the widow this right. The degree to which this was true requires investigation. Howell, "Peasant Inheritance in the Midlands, 1280–1700," in Jack Goody, Joan Thirsk, and E. P. Thompson, eds., *Family and Inheritance: Rural Society in Western Europe, 1200–1800* (Cambridge, 1976), 112–155; Todd, " 'In Her Free Widowhood': Succession to Property and Remarriage in Rural England, 1540–1800" (paper delivered to the Third Berkshire Conference of Women Historians, June 1976).

87. James W. Deen, Jr., "Patterns of Testation: Four Tidewater Counties in Colonial Virginia," *American Journal of Legal History*, XVI (1972), 154–176, finds a life interest in property for the wife the predominant pattern before 1720. However, he includes an interest for widowhood in life interest and does not distinguish a dower interest from more than dower.

88. Richard S. Dunn, *Sugar and Slaves: The Rise of the Planter Class in the English West Indies, 1624–1713* (Chapel Hill, N.C., 1972), 326–334. Dunn finds sex ratios surprisingly balanced, but he also finds very high mortality, short marriages, and many orphans.

89. For a short discussion of this comparison see Menard, "Immigrants and Their Increase."

90. James K. Somerville has used Salem, Massachusetts, wills from 1660 to 1770 to examine women's status and importance within the home ("The Salem [Mass.] Woman in the Home, 1660–1770," *Eighteenth-Century Life*, I [1974], 11–14). See also Alexander Keyssar, "Widowhood in Eighteenth-Century Massachusetts: A Problem in the History of the Family," *Perspectives in American History*, VIII (1974), 83–119, which discusses provisions for 22 widows in eighteenth-century Woburn, Massachusetts. Both men find provisions for houseroom and care of the widow's property enjoined upon children proportionately far more often than we have found in St. Mary's County, Maryland, where we found only five instances over 136 years. However, part of this difference may be a function of the differences in age at widowhood in the two regions. Neither Somerville nor Keyssar gives the percentage of widows who received a life interest in property, but their discussions imply a much higher proportion than we have found of women whose interest ended at remarriage or the majority of the oldest son.

# 14 | WOMEN'S WORK AND EUROPEAN FERTILITY PATTERNS

## LOUISE A. TILLY, JOAN W. SCOTT, AND MIRIAM COHEN

During the nineteenth century most commentators on the "condition of the working classes" attributed large families and frequent illegitimacy among the poor to social, economic, or moral pathology. For Engels over-populated working-class families were the offspring of industrial capital-ism. For Malthus they were evidence of imprudence, of an inability to make rational calculations. For both, as for many government investiga-tors and social reformers, high rates of fertility among married and single workers were both indicators and causes of misery and deprivation. Since the nineteenth century, of course, there have been many debates about the effects of industrialization on the standard of living of workers and on their demographic behavior. There have been some studies of family size among occupational groups, and there have been attempts to describe and explain changes in working-class fertility patterns. Most of these studies lack the explicit moralizing of the nineteenth-century commentators, al-though some implicitly retain those biases. Few, however, maintain that large families and numerous bastards were positive developments.[1]

Now Edward Shorter has advanced such an argument. In an intriguing and provocative piece, Shorter speculates that "female emancipation" led to increased rates of legitimate and illegitimate fertility in Western Europe at the end of the eighteenth century.[2] His subject is not economic depriva-tion; indeed, that is an irrelevant consideration for him. Instead, he main-tains that industrialization early led to the sexual emancipation of work-ing-class women by offering employment opportunities outside the home. Work led to sexual liberation, according to Shorter, by revolutionizing women's attitudes about themselves: they became individualistic and self-seeking; they rebelled against traditional constraints and sought pleasure

Louise A. Tilly is Assistant Professor of History and Director of Women's Studies Program at the University of Michigan. She is the author of numerous ar-ticles on social history. Joan W. Scott is Associate Professor of History at the Uni-versity of North Carolina, Chapel Hill and the author of *The Glassworkers of Carmaux: French Crafstmen and Political Action in a 19th-Century City* (Cam-bridge, Mass., 1974). Miriam Cohen is a Ph.D. candidate at the University of Michigan.

The authors would like to thank for their help Charles Tilly, Michael Hanagan, Lawrence Stone, Peter Laslett, Peter Stearns, Robert Lerner, Daniel Scott Smith, Ellen Sewell, Michael Marrus, Anne Bobroff and Kathryn Kish Sklar.

and fulfillment in uninhibited sexual activity. In the absence of birth control, heightened sexual activity inevitably meant more children. Indeed, toward the end of the nineteenth century, as information about contraception became available, fertility rates sharply declined.

Shorter's is a novel interpretation with some important contributions to women's history as well as to demographic history. Above all, he must be commended for bringing together hitherto scattered evidence about European fertility patterns. He has established that from about 1750–1790 there were widespread increases in illegitimate fertility rates in both urban and rural areas. He has collected evidence to suggest that there were also increases in legitimate fertility, especially among young married women in some areas of Western Europe and the United States. The question of marital fertility, however, is still unresolved, in spite of Shorter's definitive statements about it.[3] In addition, Shorter insists that the social and economic experiences of women are central to fertility changes. In so doing, he implicitly challenges the conventional view of women's history, which sees political emancipation as the source of all other changes in women's lives in the modern world. This view, which echoes some of the more simplistic literature on political development, suggests that a change in political consciousness during the nineteenth century led to political enfranchisement for women in the twentieth century, and, only then, to their expanded social and economic activity. Shorter, on the contrary, points out the social, economic, and demographic changes in women's lives that predated political emancipation by more than 100 years.

Despite these contributions, however, Shorter's article is misleading. It confuses the connections between fertility patterns and women's experience instead of clarifying them. If Shorter accurately describes changes in illegitimate fertility, he nonetheless explains them incorrectly. Although he is justified in insisting that women's history must be considered by historical demographers, he fails seriously to examine that history. The clarity and simplicity of Shorter's logic may be persuasive, yet the historical evidence that he offers is scant. In fact, his only evidence that attitudes changed is the *consequence* of that presumed change. In other words, increased illegitimacy rates are the only real proof which he has that women's attitudes and sexual behavior did change.

There is, despite Shorter's neglect of it, a growing body of evidence about women's role in preindustrial and industrial society. This evidence was available to Shorter. We do not claim new and dramatic findings, yet we seriously question both Shorter's premise about the position of preindustrial women and his central assertion that a change in popular attitudes led to increased illegitimate and, possibly, legitimate fertility.

In this article we first examine Shorter's hypothesis. Then we present the historical evidence about women's work experiences before and during industrialization. Finally, we offer an alternative model to explain fertility changes, which is based on that evidence.

## SHORTER'S HYPOTHESIS

When Shorter began writing about illegitimacy, he attributed its increase between 1790 and 1860 to a sexual revolution, but he carefully related sexual behavior to social situations. Social instability, he suggested, would tend to decrease the likelihood that marriage would follow a sexual encounter; in stable social situations, however, marriage more regularly legitimized sexual relationships. The model which he constructed was more complicated than we have described, and we have serious disagreements with it; but it is unnecesssary here to review it at length. The important point is that in his earlier work Shorter indicated that sexual relationships and marriage patterns (hence, fertility rates) were extremely sensitive to social and economic realities and to changes in them.[4]

In his article in the *American Historical Review*, Shorter has sharpened and simplified this argument. He builds his case by correlating a number of events: industrialization, migration, changes in women's work, changes in fertility rates, etc. He then argues that since they all involve fertility, they can be reduced to a single causal sequence, constructed on a premise about a change in women's attitudes. Structural considerations are pushed aside, and so are alternative explanations. According to Shorter, a change in fertility rates can only mean a change in sexual practices, which has to mean a change in attitudes, particularly of women. The sequence must be linear and direct. As Shorter argues:

> It seems a plausible proposition that people assimilate in the market place an integrated, coherent set of values about social behavior and personal independence and that these values quickly inform the noneconomic realm of individual mentalities. If this logic holds true, we may identify exposure to the market place as a prime source of female emancipation.[5]

This statement, as its language clearly reveals, is based on a chain of reasoning, not on evidence. Shorter offers nothing to prove that more women worked in the capitalist marketplace in this period. He merely assumes that they did. Similarly, he assumes that women at the end of the eighteenth century had different family roles and attitudes from their predecessors. And he assumes as well that changes in work opportunities immediately changed values.[6] Ideas, in his opinion, instantly reflect one's current economic experience. Shorter employs a mechanistic notion of "value transfer" to explain the influence of changes in occupational structure on changes in collective mentalities: "In the eighteenth and early nineteenth centuries the market economy encroached steadily at the cost of the moral economy, and the values of individual self-interest and competitiveness that people learned in the market were soon transferred to other areas of life."[7]

For Shorter, sexual behavior echoes market behavior at every point. "Emancipated" women gained a sense of autonomy at work that the subordinate and powerless women of preindustrial society had lacked. That work, created by capitalist economic development, necessarily fostered values of individualism in those who participated in it, and individualism was expressed in part by a new desire for sexual gratification. Young women working outside the home, Shorter insists, were by definition rebelling against parental authority. Indeed, they sought work in order to gain the independence and individual fulfillment that could not be attained at home. It follows, in Shorter's logic, that sexual behavior, too, must have been defiant of parental restraint. As the market economy spread there arose a new, libertine, proletarian subculture "indulgent of eroticism." Once married, the independent young working women engaged in frequent intercourse because they and their husbands took greater pleasure in sex. Female "emancipation" thus began among the young and poor. In the absence of birth control, the sexual gratification of single working girls increased the illegitimate birthrate; that of married women (who worked or had worked) inflated the legitimate birthrate. In this fashion Shorter answers a central question of European historical demography. The fertility increase in the late eighteenth century was simply the result of the "emancipation," occupational and sexual, of working-class women.

Shorter then attributes the fall in fertility at the end of the nineteenth century to the diffusion of birth control knowledge and techniques. Middle-class women were the first to use birth control. Later, it was adopted as well by lower-class women "mentally prepared for small families" by their experiences with motherhood and work. Presumably single, lower-class women were even more willing to curb fertility once they knew how. Meanwhile, middle-class women became personally emancipated. The chronological coincidence of the search for individual autonomy, which originated among the lower classes, and of techniques of birth control, known first to the middle classes, caused the late nineteenth-century fertility decline. Shorter concludes by suggesting that the movement for women's political rights was the final outcome of the growth of capitalism, industrialization, and changes in women's work which had started more than a century earlier.

It is now time to examine the historical evidence that Shorter neglected on women's role in preindustrial society; on the effects of industrialization on women's work and on their attitudes; and on the motives which sent young girls out into the "marketplace" at the end of the eighteenth and beginning of the nineteenth century. None of the evidence that we have found supports Shorter's argument in any way. Women were not powerless in "traditional" families; they played important economic roles which gave them a good deal of power within the family. Industrialization did not significantly modernize women's work in the period when fertility rates rose; in fact, the vast majority of working women did not work in factories, but at customary women's jobs. Women usually became wage earners during the early phases of industrialization not to rebel against their parents or declare independence from their husbands, but to augment family finances. Indeed, women in this period must be studied in their family settings, for the constraints of family membership greatly affected their opportunities for individual autonomy. No change in attitude, then, increased the numbers of children whom working women bore. Rather, old attitudes and customary behavior interacted with greatly changed circumstances—particularly in the composition of populations—and led to increased illegitimate fertility.

Women eventually shed many outdated priorities, and by the end of the nineteenth century some working women had clearly adopted "modern" life styles. But these changes involved a more gradual and complex adaptation than Shorter implies. The important point, however, is that the years around 1790 were not a watershed in the history of women's economic emancipation—despite the fact that the locus of women's work began to move outside the home. These *were* crucial years for the increases in fertility in Europe. All of the evidence is not in, by any means; what we offer, however, indicates that in this period, women of the popular classes simply were not searching for freedom or experiencing emancipation. The explanation for changed fertility patterns lies elsewhere.

## WOMEN'S PLACE IN "TRADITIONAL" FAMILIES

In the preindustrial family, the household was organized as a family or domestic economy. Men, women, and children worked at tasks which were differentiated by age and sex, but the work of all was necessary for survival. Artisans' wives assisted their husbands in their work as weavers, bakers, shoemakers, or tailors. Certain work, like weaving, whether carried on in the city or the country, needed the cooperation of all family members. Children and women did the spinning and carding; men ran the looms. Wives also managed many aspects of the household, including family finances. In less prosperous urban families, women did paid work which was often an extension of their household chores: they sewed and made lace; they also took odd jobs as carters, laundresses, and street cleaners. Unmarried women also became servants. Resourcefulness was characteristic of poor women: when they could not find work which would enable them to contribute to the family income, they begged, stole, or became prostitutes. Hufton's work on the Parisian poor in the eighteenth century and Forrest's work on Bordeaux both describe the crucial economic contribution of urban working-class women and the consequent central role which these women played in their families.[8]

In the country, the landowning peasant's family was also the unit of productive activity. The members of the family worked together, again at sex-differentiated tasks. Children—boys and girls—were sent to other farms as servants when their help was not needed at home. Their activity, nonetheless, contributed to the well-being of the family. They sent their earnings home, or, if they were not paid wages, their absence at least relieved the family of the burden of feeding and boarding them. Women's responsibilities included care of the house, barnyard, and dairy. They managed to bring in small net profits from marketing of poultry and dairy products and from work in rural domestic industry. Management of the household and, particularly, of finances led to a central role for women in these families. An observer in rural Brittany during the nineteenth century reported that the wife and mother of the family made "the important decisions, buying a field, selling a cow, a lawsuit against a neighbor, choice of a future son-in-law." For rural families who did not own land, women's work was even more vital: from agricultural work, spinning, or petty trading, they contributed their share to the family wage—the only economic resource of the landless family.[9]

In city and country, among propertied and propertyless, women of the popular classes had a vital economic role which gave them a recognized and powerful position within the household. It is impossible to guess what sort of sexual relations were practiced under these circumstances. We *can* say, however, that women in these families were neither dependent nor powerless. Hence, it is impossible to accept Shorter's attempt to derive women's supposed sexual subordination from their place in the preindustrial household.

## WHY WOMEN WORKED

Shorter attributes the work of women outside the home after 1750, particularly that of young, single women, to a change in outlook: a new desire for independence from parental restraints. He argues that since seeking work was an individualistic rebellion against traditionalism, sexual behavior, too, reflected a defiance of parental authority. The facts are that daughters of the popular classes were most often sent into service or to work in the city by their families. Their work represented a continuation of practices customary in the family economy. When resources were scarce or mouths at home too numerous, children customarily sought work outside, generally with family approval.

Industrialization and urbanization created new problems for rural families but generated new opportunities as well. In most cases, families strategically adapted their established practices to the new context. Thus, daughters sent out to work went farther away from home than had been customary. Most still defined their work in the family interest. Sometimes arrangements for direct payment in money or foodstuffs were made between a girl's parents and her employer. In other cases, the girls themselves regularly sent money home. Commentators observed that the girls considered this a normal arrangement—part of their obligation to the family.[10]

In some cases the conditions of migration for young working girls emphasized their ties to family and in many ways limited their independence. In Italy and France, factory dormitories housed female workers, and nuns regulated their behavior and social lives. In the needle trades in British cities, enterprising women with a little capital turned their homes into lodging houses for pieceworkers in their employ.[11] Of course, these institutions permitted employers to control their employees by limiting their mobility and regulating their behavior. The point is not that they were beneficent practices, but that young girls lived in households which permitted them limited autonomy. Domestic service, the largest single occupation for women, was also the most traditional and most protective of young girls. They would be sent from one household to another and thus be given security. Châtelain argues that domestic service was a safe form of migration in France for young girls from the country. They had places to live, families, food, and lodgings and had no need to fend for themselves in the unknown big city as soon as they arrived.[12] It is true that servants often longed to leave their places, and that they resented the exploitation of their mistresses (and the advances of their masters). But that does not change the fact that, initially, their migration was sponsored by a set of traditional institutions which limited their individual freedom.

In fact, individual freedom did not seem to be at issue for the daughters of either the landed or the landless, although clearly their experiences differed. It seems likely that peasant families maintained closer ties with their daughters, even when the girls worked in distant cities. The family interest in the farm (the property that was the birthright of the lineage and not of any individual) was a powerful influence on individual behavior. Thus, farm girls working as domestics continued to send money home. Married daughters working as domestics in Norwegian cities sent their children home to be raised on the farm by grandparents. But even when ties of this sort were not maintained, it was seldom from rebellious motives. Braun describes the late eighteenth-century situation of peasants in the hinterland of Zurich. These peasants were willing to divide their holdings for their children because of new work opportunities in cottage industry. These young people married earlier than they would have if the farm had been held undivided, and they quickly established their own families. Braun suggests that the young workers soon lost touch with their parents. The process, as he describes it, however, was not rebellion; rather, the young people went into cottage industry to lessen the burden that they represented for the family. These motives were welcomed and encouraged by the parents. Family bonds were stretched and broken, but that was a consequence, not a cause, of the new opportunities for work.[13]

Similarly, among urban artisans, older values informed the adaptation to a new organization of work and to technological change. Initially, artisans as well as their political spokesmen insisted that the old values of association and cooperation could continue to characterize their work relationships in the new industrial society. Artisan subculture in cities during the early stages of industrialization was not characterized by an individualistic, self-seeking ideology, as Thompson, Hufton, Forrest, Soboul, Gossez, and others have clearly shown.[14] With no evidence that urban artisans adopted the values of the marketplace at work, Shorter's deduction about a "libertine proletarian subculture" has neither factual nor logical validity. It seems more likely that artisan families, like peasant families, sent their wives and daughters to work to help bolster their shaky economic situation. These women undoubtedly joined the ranks of the unskilled who had always constituted the urban female work force. Wives and daughters of the unskilled and propertyless had worked for centuries at service and manufacturing jobs in cities. In the nineteenth century there were more of them because the proportions of unskilled propertyless workers increased.

Eighteenth- and early nineteenth-century cities grew primarily by migration. The urban working class was thus constantly renewed and enlarged by a stream of rural migrants. Agricultural change drove rural laborers and peasants cityward at the end of the eighteenth century, and technological change drove many artisans and their families into the ranks of the unskilled. Women worked outside the home because they had to. Changed attitudes did not propel them into the labor force. Family interest and not self-interest was the underlying motive for their work.

## WOMEN'S WORK

What happened in the mid-eighteenth century with the spread of capitalism, the growth of markets, and industrialization? Did these economic changes bring new work experiences for women, with the consequences which Shorter describes? Did women, earning money in the capitalist marketplace, find a new sense of self that expressed itself in increased sexual activity? In examining the historical evidence for the effects on women's work of industrialization and urbanization, we find that the location of women's work did change—more young women worked outside the home and in large cities than ever before. But they were recruited from the same groups which had always sent women to work.

The female labor force of nineteenth-century Europe, like that of seventeenth- and eighteenth-century Europe, consisted primarily of the daughters of the popular classes and, secondarily of their wives. The present state of our knowledge makes it difficult to specify precisely the groups within the working classes from which nineteenth-century women wage earners came. It is clear, however, that changes in the organization of work must have driven the daughters and wives of craftsmen out of the family shop. Similarly, population growth (a result of declining mortality and younger age at marriage due to opportunities for work in cottage industry) created a surplus of hands within the urban household and on the family farm. Women in these families always had been expected to work. Increasingly, they were sent away from home to earn their portion of the family wage.[15]

Shorter's notion that the development of modern capitalism brought new kinds of opportunities to working-class women as early as the middle of the eighteenth century is wrong. There was a very important change in the location of work from rural homes to cities, but this did not revolutionize the nature of the work that most women did. Throughout the nineteenth century, most women worked at traditional occupations. By the end of the century, factory employment was still minimal.

Domestic service, garment making, and textiles had long been the chief nonagricultural employers of women. This continued to be the case during the nineteenth century. In France, in 1866, 69 percent of women working outside agriculture were employed in these three fields; in 1896, the figure was 59 percent. In England, the occupational opportunities for women were similarly stable. In the 1840s, Pinchbeck notes, women served in traditional female occupations—the largest percentage were in domestic service, the next largest in textiles, the next in clothing manufacture. In her study of women in the labor force in 1915, Hutchins noted that as late as 1911, two-thirds of working women were in the same three fields: domestic service (including laundry) 35 percent; textiles 19.5 percent; and garment making 15.6 percent.[16]

It is worthwhile to examine the case of England more closely. England was the first country to industrialize, and its fertility rates probably rose with industrialization.[17] Yet, contrary to Shorter's assumption that new work experiences for women led to increased illegitimacy, nothing indicates that women's work there changed significantly. During the early phases of British industrialization the proportion of women entering the work force did not increase; nor did women work in factories in significant numbers in the crucial late eighteenth-century period when fertility rates began to rise. (And it is this factory experience, particularly, that Shorter emphasizes as "liberating.")

Aggregate statistics on the number of women workers before 1841 do not exist, but several studies have shown that opportunities for women to participate in the economy actually shrank with early industrialization. The reorganization of agriculture displaced women who had worked on the family plot. (A portion of these women became wage laborers toward the end of the eighteenth century, but only temporarily. Their numbers declined toward the middle of the nineteenth century as did all employment in agriculture.) In the manufacturing sector, the mechanization of cotton spinning at the end of the eighteenth century first deprived women of that age-old occupation. Until the second decade of the next century, women had to compete with children for jobs assisting men who operated the large new machines. It was not until after the power loom was introduced into the factory (after 1820) that opportunities were created for large numbers of women to participate in the factory work force. The experience of wool workers was similar. As the industry was concentrated into workshops, long before power-driven machinery was introduced, women were excluded from the preparation process. Although some women competed with men as handloom weavers in the early nineteenth century, it was not until the 1860s that the power loom brought many women into the wool factories. Because the mill-based woolen industry was concentrated in Yorkshire and Nottinghamshire, many female domestic wool workers elsewhere were left permanently unemployed.[18] Finally, as a consequence of changes in the organization of craft work, many artisans' wives who had heretofore taken an active part in their husbands' work were deprived of their occupations.

Not all women employed in manufacturing were engaged in textile spinning and weaving. Women's occupations also included millinery, corset, boot and shoe making, dress and artificial flower making, bookbinding, food production and canning, and matchmaking. Such were the industries which employed women, primarily in London and other cities. In Birmingham, an unusual number of women engaged in small metal trades. In the course of the nineteenth century, many of these activities were moved into small workshops and larger factories, but this happened long after the factory organization of textile production.[19] Thus, it was primarily in the textile industry, and then only after the 1820s, that the number of women factory workers increased.

In England women moved very slowly into "modern occupations." Let us compare the number of women in the British population from 1841 to 1911, the number of women in the labor force outside agriculture as a whole, and the number of women who were occupied in work other than domestic service. Our category for modern occupations, it should be noted, is a rough one, including all nonservant, nonagricultural occupations. This includes not only factory jobs, but all manufacturing jobs, in whatever kind of setting, and nonmanufacturing jobs, such as those in commerce and the professions. The following facts are evident. First, the number of women in the labor force outside agriculture at the middle of the nineteenth century was relatively small (24.4 percent); the nonagricultural female work force did not increase apace with the female population after mid-century. In 1841 as in 1891, the largest proportion of women was engaged in domestic and other personal service occupations such as laundering. There was an increase in nonservant occupations between 1841 and 1851, but between 1861 and 1891 servants increased at approximately the same rate as all other occupations. Until 1891, the growth in modern occupations absorbed neither the natural increase in the female population nor the increase of unemployed females which, as noted above, resulted from structural changes in industry and agriculture. In mid-nineteenth-century England, a century after Shorter's supposed revolution in women's work experience, a large proportion of working women were still in domestic service, and most others were still engaged in traditionally organized industries. Throughout the greater part of the nineteenth century, women's factory work was almost exclusively in textiles, and the number of women employed in factories was a small proportion of the entire female work force. The major early effect of industrialization and urbanization on the fields of work open to women was to increase the numbers of women in domestic service and in the artisan industries which were being transformed by the new division of labor.

In cities, matters were no different. Urban women remained in traditional occupations. Domestic service persisted as the most important, claiming in 1891, one-third of all working women. In 1910, the London County Council reported a similar proportion. The next largest occupation was dressmaking, then laundering and tailoring. Of the manufacturing enterprises, many were still domestic endeavors. A report on women's employment in Birmingham based on the 1901 census showed a relatively high proportion of women in the labor force: 37 percent. Of these, almost half were engaged in domestic service, charring, the professions, or commerce. This meant that even in this manufacturing city, about 20 percent of women were employed in industry, with about half that number still in domestic outwork.[20]

Shorter is also incorrect in his assumption that the working woman was able to live independently of her family because she had the economic means to do so. Evidence for British working women indicates that this was not the case. Throughout the nineteenth century, British working women's wages were considered supplementary incomes—supplementary, that is, to the wages of other family members. It was assumed by employers that women, unlike men, were not responsible for earning their own living. Female wages were always far lower than male. In the Lancashire cotton mills in 1833, where female wages were the highest in the country, females aged 16–21 earned 7/3.5 weekly, while males earned 10/3. Even larger differentials obtained among older workers. In London in the 1880s, there was a similar differential between the average earnings of the sexes: 72 percent of the males in the bookbinding industry earned over 30/- weekly; 42.5 percent of women made less than 12/-. In precious metals, clocks, and watch manufacturing, 83.5 percent of the males earned 30/- or more weekly; females earned 9–12/-. Women in small clothing workshops earned 10–12/- weekly, while women engaged in outwork in the clothing trades made only 4/- a week. In Birmingham, in 1900, the average weekly wage for working women less than age 21 was 10/-, for men 18/-. Women's work throughout this period, as in the eighteenth century, was for the most part unskilled. Occupations were often seasonal or ir-

**Figure 1** PERCENTAGE PARTICIPATION OF WOMEN IN THE BRITISH LABOR FORCE

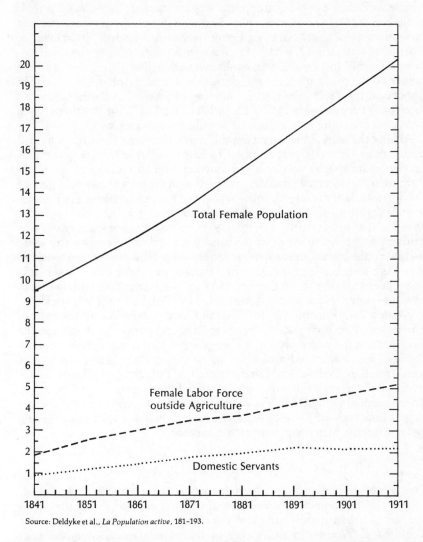

Source: Deldyke et al., *La Population active*, 181–193.

regular, leaving women without work for many months during the year.[21] Is it possible that there were many single women who could enjoy a life of independence when the majority could not even afford to live adequately on their personal wages?

Finally, throughout the period, British women tended to give up work outside the home when they married, although many worked at home or moved in and out of the labor force when necessary. This demonstrates that women, married or single, were motivated to work by economic necessity and not by a drive for "liberation" in Shorter's sense. We can cite only a few examples here, based mostly on age evidence. In 1833, the bulk of women in the Lancashire cotton mills were between the ages of 16 and

21. In 1841, in six out of seven districts in Lancashire 75 percent of the female work force in the cotton mills was unmarried. In the woolen mills of the north and in Gloucestershire, 50 percent of working women left the mills after age 21; of those remaining, few were married. Retirement of married women from the labor force was most noticeable in the textile industry. In mill towns, children could be employed at young ages and the family could count on their wages to take the place of the mother's. In London in the 1880s, the greatest number of women in the female work force were between ages 15 and 25. In 1911, in all of Great Britain only 9.6 percent of the entire married female population was employed.[22]

Among the married women who did work, domestic industry provided occupations for the largest number. In East London in the 1880s, Booth's survey found that most employed married women worked at home. In Birmingham, twenty years later, married women were the largest part of the domestic labor force, as, indeed, married women had been for decades in most countries of Western Europe.[23] In contrast to middle-class women, who could afford servants, the work experience for lower-class wives was neither psychologically nor economically rewarding, except in the sense that it supplemented an inadequate family wage. If these women worked, they were torn between the cares of a mother and those of a worker. It is no wonder that they much preferred to stay home and supervise their own families—a preference amply documented by the labor force statistics.

Women's work from 1750 to 1850 (and much later) did not provide an experience of emancipation. Work was hard and poorly paid and, for the most part, it did not represent a change from traditional female occupations. Those women who traveled to cities did find themselves free of some traditional village and family restraints. But, as we shall see, the absence of these restraints was more often burdensome than liberating. Young women with inadequate wages and unstable jobs found themselves caught in a cycle of poverty which increased their vulnerability. Having lost one family, many sought to create another.

## THE ORIGINS OF INCREASED ILLEGITIMACY

The compositional change which increased the numbers of unskilled, propertyless workers in both rural and urban areas and raised their proportion in urban populations also contributed to an increase in rates of illegitimacy. Women in this group of the population always had contributed the most illegitimate births. An increase in the number of women in this group, therefore, meant a greater incidence of illegitimacy.

A recent article by Laslett and Oosterveen speaks directly to Shorter's speculations: "The assumption that illegitimacy figures directly reflect the prevalence of sexual intercourse outside marriage, which seems to be made whenever such figures are used to show that beliefs, attitudes and interests have changed in some particular way, can be shown to be very shaky in its foundations." Using data from Colyton, collected and analyzed by E. A. Wrigley, they argue that one important component in the incidence of illegitimacy is the existence of illegitimacy-prone families, which bring forth bastards generation after generation. Nevertheless, they warn, "this projected sub-society never produced all the bastards, all the bastard-bearers."[24]

The women who bore illegitimate children were not pursuing sexual pleasure, as Shorter would have us believe. Most expected to get married, but the circumstances of their lives—propertylessness, poverty, large-scale geographic mobility, occupational instability, and the absences of traditional social protection—prevented the fulfillment of this expectation. A number of pressures impelled young working girls to find mates. One was the loneliness and isolation of work in the city. Another was economic need: wages were low and employment for women, unstable. The logical move for a single girl far from her family would be to find a husband with whom she might reestablish a family economy. Yet another pressure was the desire to escape the confines of domestic service, an occupation which more and more young women were entering.

Could not this desire to establish a family be what the domestic servants, described by the Munich police chief in 1815, sought? No quest for pleasure is inherent in the fact that "so many young girls leave service. . . . But they do little real work and let themselves be supported by boyfriends; they become pregnant and then are abandoned."[25] It seems a sad and distorted version of an older family form, but an attempt at it, nevertheless. Recent work has shown, in fact, that for many French servants in the nineteenth century, this kind of transfer to urban life and an urban husband was often successful.[26]

Was it a search for sexual fulfillment that prompted young women to become "engaged" to young men and then sleep with them in the expectation that marriage would follow? Not at all. In rural and urban areas premarital sexual relationships were common.[27] What Shorter interprets as sexual libertinism, as evidence of an individualistic desire for sexual pleasure, is more likely an expression of the traditional wish to marry. The attempt to reconstitute the family economy in the context of economic deprivation and geographic mobility produced unstable and stable "free unions."

Free or consensual unions had two different kinds of consequences for those who entered into them, but both resulted in illegitimate children. One consequence, the more stable, was common-law marriage, a more or less permanent relationship. The other was less stable and involved desertion of the woman, or a series of short-lived encounters, or prostitution. Middle-class observers were most disturbed by the unstable side of consensual union, and especially by the increase in the numbers of abandoned pregnant women and prostitutes.

When asked how she let herself get into difficult and immoral situations, the woman most frequently answered that the man had promised to marry her. In Nantes, in the eighteenth century, information drawn from declarations to midwives at childbirth shows that mothers of illegitimate children were, for the most part, servants and working women. These women testified that promises of work and of marriage usually preceded intercourse with the fathers of their bastards. In Aix in 1787–1788, according to Fairchilds, the *declarations de grossesse* show that the vast majority of all illegitimate pregnancies were preceded by promises of marriage. A needleworker explained her plight to Henry Mayhew in 1851: "He told me if I came to live with him he'd care I should not want, and both mother and me had been very bad off before. He said he'd make me his lawful wife. . . ."[28]

The absence of traditional constraints—family, local community, and church—led to the disappointments of many marital expectations. What Shorter deems "freedom" here, in all of its normative implications, is in fact the opposite, for the absence of traditional constraints increased women's vulnerability. Lack of money or a lost job, the opportunity for work in a distant city, all kept men from fulfilling their promises, and the women's families were nowhere at hand to enforce them. Eighteenth-century evidence from Lille, also based on women's declarations during childbirth, shows that most unmarried mothers had come to the city as textile workers or as servants, all poorly paid occupations. Fully 70 percent of these women came from families broken by the death of at least one parent. The men involved were in professions marked by unstable tenure, such as servants, traveling workers, or soldiers. Lottin concludes that work outside the family weakened traditional family authority and "facilitated the emancipation of the girls." But like Shorter, his evidence for this statement is illegitimate birth statistics only. Lottin's other point seems more likely in light of the evidence about the occupations and backgrounds of the women whom he studied: "All the same, seducers could pursue their ends more easily, because they did not fear an avenging father, often violent, ready to make them pay for the dishonor."[29]

Cobb's sympathetic evocation of lower-class life during Year III of the French Revolution notes that "women and girls born in the provinces were easier to recruit to prostitution and were less protected. (They were also much more exposed to seduction and to unemployment . . . ) . . . prostitution witnesses for the feminine population as a whole, emphasizes its fluidity, its insecurity, the enormous risks encountered by the provincial girl. . . ." In 1836, in Paris, Parent-Duchâtelet reported that the majority of the prostitutes whom he studied were recent migrants. Almost one-third were household servants and many had been initially seduced by promises of marriage and then abandoned, pregnant or with an infant. He also remarked on the instability of women's employment which drove them to prostitution when they could not find work. Some years later, and across the Channel, abandoned women told Mayhew some of the reasons that their hoped-for marriages never took place: sometimes there was no money for a proper wedding; sometimes the men moved on to search for work; sometimes poverty created unbearable emotional stress.[30] Overall, the traditional contexts which identified and demanded "proper" behavior were absent. There is obviously much still to be learned about young working girls and about the behavior and motives of their suitors. The central point here is that no major change in values or mentality was necessary to create these cases of illegitimacy. Rather, older expectations operating in a changed context yielded unanticipated (and often unhappy) results.

If they were left far from their families with illegitimate children, young women were forced to become independent. But theirs was an independence or self-reliance based on desperation and disillusionment, and not on the carefree, self-seeking individualism of Shorter's description. Evidence for this can be found in the reasons for their prostitution given by women in the Year III: "to get bread"; "to be able to live"; "to feed my child"; "to pay for a wet nurse." "What are we?" exclaimed a Paris prostitute; "Most of us are unfortunate women, without origins, without education, servants, maids for the most part. . . ." These bitter tones are echoed by the London working girls who told Mayhew that they "went wrong" in order to support their children.[31]

Prostitution, in turn, produced more illegitimate children. Many prostitutes were domestic servants or girls from the garment industry out of work—women whose need sent them into the streets. In an ironic way, even this kind of activity had its historical roots. Hufton's catalog of the resources developed by lower-class women in pre-Revolutionary France in their roles as providers of food includes begging, the renting out of their children to other beggars, flirtation, and sexual favors. Many of the girls testifying to Mayhew of their "shame" explained it as the only way to provide food for their children and keep them out of the workhouse. This attitude would have been recognizable to peasant women, although they would have found the life style associated with it unfamiliar and abhorrent: a woman's body was her last resource in a desperate effort to support her family.

The sheer increase in the numbers of prostitutes and deserted pregnant women was not alone responsible for the increase in illegitimacy rates. Charitable institutions, developed at this time for the care of illegitimate children, lengthened their lives or, at least, registered their births. From the mid-seventeenth century on, reformers who established new foundling hospitals or improved old ones explicitly defined their goal as the elimination of infanticide. St. Vincent de Paul's work in Paris, for example, culminated in the dedication of the Bicêtre for this purpose in 1690. A Foundling Hospital was opened in Dublin in 1704. And, in 1739, the London Hospital was incorporated, "to prevent the frequent murders of poor miserable children at their birth, and to suppress the inhuman custom of exposing new-born infants to perish in the streets." Similarly such hospitals were opened in Strasbourg (in 1748) and in Moscow and St. Petersburg during the reign of Catherine. Malthus, in fact, criticized the Russian institutions for discouraging marriage by making it too easy for illegitimate children to be cared for by others.[32] The incidence of infanticide in the sixteenth and seventeenth centuries has never been quantified, as far as we know, but qualitative evidence suggests that death was the common fate of children of illicit unions, whether the mother was deserted or the parents simply too poor to support another child. The hospitals, of course, often simply institutionalized infanticide, but they guaranteed registration of the birth in their baptismal records. The eighteenth-century foundling hospital "civilized" the care of illegitimate children by baptizing them, but it failed in the majority of cases to nurture these children to adulthood.

Domestic servants, prostitutes, and deserted women were not the only mothers of illegitimate children in the eighteenth and nineteenth centuries.

Often bastards were the products of stable consensual unions which sometimes even ended in legal marriage. Although we do not yet have hard evidence, it seems likely that the number of these unions increased as the population of unskilled, propertyless workers grew in cities. These unions were not a new phenomenon; instead, they represented the continuation of a practice long common with the urban working class. From mid-seventeenth-century Aix comes this comment on the urban poor: "They almost never know the sanctity of marriage and live together in shameful fashion."[33] Ford characterizes mid-eighteenth-century Strasbourg as "a society where cohabitations frequently began with the formal announcement of intended marriage. This practice did not enjoy full social or religious approval to be sure, but neither did it create any particular scandal." Children born out of wedlock were frequently legitimated by marriage, Ford says, but even when this did not happen, the mother's family recognized its responsibility for her child. Similar practices were noted by Frederic Le Play in his biographies of urban workers in the middle of the nineteenth century and by novelists of working-class life such as Emile Zola. Agulhon also describes the existence of free unions among the working class of Toulon before 1849.[34]

Free unions seem to have increased as more and more young men and women left their native towns and villages and moved to larger towns or cities. For some, there was no point in legalizing a union because there was no property to protect. For others, consensual union was the prelude to marriage—the period during which women worked and accumulated the dowry required for a "proper" marriage. Children born in this period were legitimated at the wedding ceremony. Often young people did not marry because they did not know priests or ministers to perform the ceremony. Many, too, scorned the rituals of the church. Others simply were too busy working, and, if they were migrants, they may well have been ignorant of the place where one went to secure a civil act. In some German states, marriage was forbidden to those without sufficient economic resources. Couples simply lived together without the blessing of the state.[35]

Illegitimacy was the product of free unions, and free unions seem to have increased during the late eighteenth and early nineteenth centuries, most probably because industrialization and urbanization moved many people out of their traditional occupational, social, and geographic contexts. Mobility, in fact, was the recurring experience for those people responsible for increased illegitimacy from about 1750 to 1850. Geographic mobility meant that men and women left familiar and family settings and therefore lost the protection and constraint they provided. Shorter himself describes this kind of situation, in discussing the factors which led to illegitimacy in rural areas. Itinerant workers seduced young girls and then moved on. "The hapless young girls were still giving the traditional response to what they thought was the customary signal." Shorter here acknowledges the traditionalism of the rural women's responses, but he insists that the *men* had changed their attitudes. Again the evidence for this alleged mentality change is the consequence of it—abandoned pregnant women. But it is equally plausible, and more congruent with the evidence, that the economic pressures on young men prevented them from fulfilling their obligations.[36]

Rising rates of illegitimacy, then, did not signify a "sexual revolution." They followed, instead, from structural and compositional changes associated with urbanization and industrialization. There is no evidence, moreover, that these changes immediately gave rise to changes in attitude. On the contrary, men and women engaged in intercourse with established expectations but in changed or changing contexts. As a result, illegitimacy increased.

## A MODEL FOR THE RISE AND FALL OF EUROPEAN FERTILITY RATES

We have dealt so far with the rise in illegitimate fertility which occurred in most of Europe toward the end of the eighteenth century. Shorter also sees this as the central issue to be explained, but he places it in a much larger context: the rise of all illegitimate fertility, and possibly legitimate fertility, in the eighteenth century and the decline of both kinds of fertility at the end of the nineteenth century. His model is wrong. We offer an alternative to it.

We start with declining mortality. Early in the eighteenth century, in much of Western Europe, mortality began to drop, presumably as a result of increased food supply. Subsistence crises ended, and the rate of population growth increased. The growth in population was almost surely distributed differentially by class. In the wealthy and upper levels of the popular classes (propertied peasants and prosperous artisans), adult and child mortality decreased earlier in time than it did in poor and unpropertied classes. As more of these children survived to adulthood, the problems of "placing" them and of avoiding fragmentation of property became acute. Thus, the ranks of the propertyless were swelled with the surplus children of more prosperous families, who were forced to seek a living with no expectation of inheritance.

Fortunately, new occupational opportunities were another by-product of population growth. Increasing population meant increased demand. This, together with a complex of technological and agricultural changes, launched in England the process which became industrialization. But even in England, and *a fortiori* throughout the rest of Western Europe, the early effect of increased demand was the expansion of cottage industry, of market agriculture, and of consumer and service industries in administrative and commercial cities. Despite their abundance, however, these jobs often turned out to be quite unstable, as British stocking frame knitters and handloom weavers or French cotton textile workers learned after 1780. In consumer services and domestic service, as in cottage industry, employment fluctuated enormously according to seasons and business cycles.

Far from home, cut off from possible property ownership, no longer required by craft organizations to postpone marriage until the completion of long apprenticeships, and in difficult economic straits, the men and women in cottage, consumer, and service industries acted in what contemporaries called "improvident" ways: they married younger and did not control their fertility as compulsively as peasant and artisan families had tended to.[37] Why? A number of related factors were involved. The abandonment of late marriage itself represented the relinquishing of the chief means that families had used to control fertility. Associated with this was a decline in the numbers of those who never married. Stearns has reminded us that in preindustrial society fertility was controlled through the celibacy of a large minority of men and women. The likelihood that such celibacy could be enforced decreased with propertylessness and with migration; hence, the rates of partnerships of all sorts, including marriage, were likely to increase, and with them, the number of children born. The economic necessity which required both partners to work for the survival of the family led young mothers to relinquish the practice of nursing their own young. This, and high levels of infant mortality which also reduced the nursing period shortened the interval between successive births.[38] The possibility of employment for young children encouraged families to continue high fertility strategies even as child mortality fell. Above all, however, high rates of infant mortality determined family strategies of high fertility. In order to guarantee the survival of one or two children, families experiencing high rates of infant mortality had traditionally produced many children. This continued to be the case.

Le Play's example of the Parisian carpenter's family well illustrates the pressures which led to high fertility. The carpenter's wife worked in the early years of her marriage. She sold fruits and vegetables at Les Halles and polished metal at home. In a period of eight years she bore six children. Four of them were bottle-fed, and all died before the age of 18 months. Bottle feeding (a necessity for a mother working away from home who could not afford or did not want to send her baby to a wet nurse) was undoubtedly a factor in the short interval between the births as well as in the deaths. This high rate of infant mortality made a strategy of high fertility appropriate, especially if a son were to live to inherit his father's membership in the carpentering trade, but also if two or three children were to survive to an age when they could earn wages and thus free their mother of the need to work.[39]

Illegitimate fertility increased, too, because of a growth in the population of propertyless working men and women. In rural areas, geographically mobile men established relationships with women, became betrothed, engaged in intercourse, and then moved on. In cities, engagement often led to abandonment, or to a free union. In all cases, illegitimacy was a by-product. The migration of these "surplus" children, then, resulted in an even larger population of mobile men and of sexually vulnerable women, far from the protection of their families. The consequences of the increase in this population were increased incidence of abandoned pregnant women; increased prostitution of abandoned or unemployed women; increased incidence and duration of consensual or free union. All three of these alternatives produced illegitimate children.

Illegitimate and legitimate fertility rose simultaneously, then, because of a complex of changes stemming from declining mortality during the eighteenth century. These changes increased the numbers of young people physically and materially removed from their families and from work within the traditional household. They were also removed from the constraints on personal and marital behavior of property; for many of them, the link between legal marriage and property had been broken. There is little evidence to indicate, however, that changes in sexual attitudes, particularly those of women, preceded these developments. Instead, the various attempts at union whether successful or not, represented the pursuit of older goals, an endorsement of established male-female relationships. In every kind of situation, the woman's goal, at least, seems to have been to reestablish the family economy, the partnership of economic enterprise and of social and, perhaps, emotional sustenance. These women sought not sexual fulfillment but economic cooperation and all of the other things which traditional marriage implied. That they often failed to find them, and that their attempts to establish a family took a variety of forms does not prove anything about their motivation. The form of male-female relationships was created not by the revolutionized sexual attitudes of the partners, but by a complex interaction of values and expectations and changing social and economic circumstances. And it is those circumstances that must be examined if rising rates of fertility are to be explained.

. Why did fertility decline toward the end of the nineteenth century? Above all, because infant mortality declined among the working classes as economic prosperity increased. The explanation offered by Banks for the decline of middle-class fertility applies at a later date to working-class marital fertility. He argues that middle-class family size shrank because of the parents' expectations about their own standard of living and because of their rising ambitions for their children.[40] Among the working classes, child mortality declined in the nineteenth century. For the first time, the children of working-class families, once they survived infancy, were not subject to continuing high mortality risk. As long as children could work, though, fertility does not appear to have fallen. As factory legislation reduced possibilities of child labor and educational opportunity became available to the working classes after 1870, family outlooks changed. Finally, the standard of living of workers improved during this period with two important results: many mothers of young children could withdraw from outside work because the family could live on the husband's wages; children were no longer needed as additional wage earners. With fewer children, a man's wages went farther and there would be more money for the education of children. (An investment in education was a contribution to a child's future and might function as apprenticeship and property had earlier.) At this point, the working-class family acted on what was clearly its own interest by adopting family limitation, and its marital fertility fell.[41]

What about illegitimate fertility? In an article written with Knodel and van de Walle, Shorter preemptorily discounts any kind of prosperity model.

> It is unlikely that higher incomes moved unwed mothers to curb their illegitimate fertility so as to plan better the educational future of their bastards on hand. Possibly improvements in the standard of living during the last quarter of the nineteenth century restricted illegitimate fertility through some other mechanism. But *ad hoc* rummaging about for alternate linkages in an "economic prosperity" model is unlikely to result in any generalizable kind of explanation.[42]

Shorter and his associates assume here that individual decisions—of un-wed mothers—lay behind falling illegitimacy rates. Yet, it can be shown that *fin-de-siècle* prosperity did bring about some compositional changes in European populations that tended to reduce the size of the population which produced illegitimate births. First, the number of women in sexually vulnerable situations, particularly servants and other female migrants to cities, began to wane. From about the last decade of the nineteenth century the rate of increase of women in domestic service began to drop; eventual-ly the number of domestic servants absolutely declined.[43] Both the in-crease in factory jobs for women and the increase in working-class pros-perity reduced the number of women working on their own, far from their families. Second, increased prosperity led to a decrease in the number of extremely mobile, propertyless men restlessly moving about in search of work. Third, increased prosperity led to a new emphasis on marriage, as the urban working classes began to acquire goods and even landed prop-erty in working-class suburbs. Formal and legalized marriage which spell-ed out the disposition and use of this property led to a decline in consen-sual unions. In addition, children's work was limited by law, and there was greater educational opportunity for them. Unwed mothers whose il-legitimate children were the results of seduction and abandonment or of prostitution might not be able to decide to marry, but it behooved couples whose children were equally illegitimate to reach the altar when conven-tional marriage meant improved opportunity for themselves and their children. Regular employment and better wages clearly opened up new vistas for workers, and the custom of free union became less widespread.

The movement to the cities, of course, did not end with the nineteenth century. Why did later urbanization and geographic mobility not result in compositional changes like those of the late eighteenth and early nine-teenth centuries? They probably did, but migrants were a smaller propor-tion of the population. Furthermore, cities were no longer the same types of administrative and commercial centers with greatest employment op-portunity in unstable areas. Industrial growth broadened and changed oc-cupational opportunities in twentieth-century cities. Also, most rural migrants to these cities were not as economically vulnerable as their nineteenth-century predecessors. They now came from rural areas where fertility was also controlled. Their families thus had greater resources with which to sponsor their migration and maintain contacts with them.

Women's work in the late eighteenth and early nineteenth centuries was not "liberating" in any sense. Most women stayed in established occupa-tions. They were so poorly paid that economic independence was pre-cluded. Furthermore, whether married or single, most women often entered the labor force in the service of the family interest. The evidence available points to several causes for illegitimacy, none related to the "emancipation" of women: economic need, causing women to seek work far from the protection of their families; occupational instability of men which led to *mariages manqués* (sexual intercourse following a promise of marriage which was never fulfilled). Finally, analysis of the effects of population growth on propertied peasants and artisans seems to show that the bifurcation of marriage and property arrangements began to change the nature of marriage arrangements for propertyless people.

Our alternative model has the advantage of being built on evidence. Much more of this evidence is needed before the model can be confirmed. Nevertheless, the negative evidence which we have offered for Shorter's model and his own lack of evidence lead us to believe that less sensational but no less dramatic, more complex but less speculative explanations are in order for the fertility changes in Europe from 1750 to 1900. This examination of the history of working-class women and their families in the eighteenth and nineteenth centuries has shown that *continuities* in mentality mark the fertility rise. The fertility fall, a consequence of economic prosperity and family limitation, opened the way for a changed consciousness among women.

## NOTES

1. Friedrich Engels, *The Condition of the Working Class in England in 1844* (London, 1892); Thomas Malthus, *First Essay on Population 1798* (reprinted, Ann Arbor, 1959).

2. "Female Emancipation, Birth Control and Fertility in European History," *American Historical Review*, LXXVIII (1973), 605–640.

3. On illegitimacy see Edward Shorter, "Illegitimacy, Sexual Revolution and Social Change in Modern Europe," *Journal of Interdisciplinary History*, II (1971), 261–269. Shorter's general statement about the rise in illegitimacy is borne out most strongly in large cities and in German rural and urban areas. There is, however, a great deal more variety in French rural areas. On marital fertility see Shorter, "Female Emancipation," 633–640. As noted in the text, the marital fertility figures are incomplete. Some are ambiguous; others contradict his claims.

4. Other articles by Shorter which treat the same question are "Sexual Change and Illegitimacy: The European Experience," in Robert J. Bezucha (ed.), *Modern European Social History* (Lexington, Mass., 1972), 231–269; "Capitalism, Culture and Sexuality: Some Competing Models," *Social Science Quarterly*, LIII (1972), 338–356. See also Shorter, John Knodel, and Etienne van de Walle, "The Decline of Non-Marital Fertility in Europe, 1880–1940," *Population Studies*, XXV (1971), 375–393.

5. "Female Emancipation," 622.

6. The weakness of Shorter's evidence on these points is striking. For example, the source of his description of peasant and working-class women's roles in traditional society is Helmut Möller's study of the eighteenth-century petty bourgeois family in Germany (*Die kleinburgerliche Familie im 18. Jahrhundert: Verhalten und Gruppenkultur* [Berlin, 1966], 69). For his proposition about the free and easy sexuality of the early nineteenth-century European working class, Shorter draws his evidence from post–World War II West Germany.

7. "Female Emancipation," 621.

8. Olwen Hufton, "Women in Revolution, 1789–1796," *Past & Present*, LIII (1971), 93; Alan Forrest, "The Condition of the Poor in Revolutionary Bordeaux," ibid., LIX (1973), 151–152. See also Natalie Z. Davis, "City Women and Religious Change in Sixteenth-Century France," in Dorothy Gies McGuigan (ed.), *A Sampler of Women's Studies* (Ann Arbor, 1973), 21–22; Michael Anderson, *Family Structure in Nineteenth Century Lancashire* (Cambridge, 1971), 96.

9. Y. Brekelien, *La vie quotidienne des paysans en Bretagne au XIX$^c$ siècle* (Paris, 1966), 69. On the family basis of the peasant economy see Daniel Thorner, Basile Kerblay, and R. E. F. Smith (eds.), *A. V. Chayanov on the Theory of Peasant Economy* (Homewood, Ill., 1966), 21, 60; Teodor Shanin, "The Peasantry as a Political Factor," in Shahin (ed.), *Peasants*

*and Peasant Societies: Selected Readings* (Harmondsworth, 1971), 241–244; Basile Kerblay, "Chayanov and the Theory of Peasantry as a Specific Type of Economy," in ibid., 151. For Western Europe see "Giunta per la Inchiesta Agraria e sulle condizioni della classe agricola," *Atti* (Rome, 1882), *passim*; Henri Mendras, *The Vanishing Peasant: Innovation and Change in French Agriculture* (Cambridge, Mass., 1970), 74–76; Jean-Marie Gouesse, "Parenté, famille et marriage en Normandie aux XVII$^c$ et XVIII$^c$ siècles," *Annales E.S.C.*, XXVII (1972), 1146–1147 and Annexe V, 1153–1154; Martin Nadaud, *Memoires de Leonard, ancien garçon maçon* (Paris, 1895; reissued, 1948), 130; Michael Drake, *Population and Society in Norway, 1735–1865* (Cambridge, 1969), 137–144.

10. Rudolf Braun, "The Impact of Cottage Industry on an Agricultural Population," in David Landes (ed.), *The Rise Of Capitalism* (New York, 1966), 61–63; R.-H. Hubscher, "Une contribution a la connaissance des milieux populaires ruraux au XIX$^c$ siècle: Le livre de compte de la famille Flauhaut, 1881–1887," *Revue d'histoire économique et sociale*, XLVII (1969), 395–396; Evelyne Sullerot, *Histoire et sociologie du travail féminin* (Paris, 1968), 91–94; Anderson, *Lancashire* 22; Peter Stearns, "Working Class Women in Britain, 1890–1914," in Martha Vicinus (ed.), *Suffer and Be Still* (Bloomington, Ind., 1972), 110; Marie Hall Ets, *Rosa, The Life of an Italian Immigrant* (Minneapolis, 1970), 138–140; Frédéric Le Play, *Les Ouvriers européens* (Paris, 1855–1878), V, 122.

11. Ets, *Rosa*, 87–115; Italy, Ufficio del Lavoro, *Rapporti sulla ispezione del Lavoro (1 dicembre 1906–30 giugno 1908)* (Milan, 1909), 93–94; Sullerot, *Histoire*, 91–94, 100; Jules Simon, *L'Ouvrière* (Paris, 1871, 53–54. Eileen Yeo and E. P. Thompson, *The Unknown Mayhew* (New York, 1972), 116–180.

12. Abel Châtelain, "Migrations et domesticité feminine urbaine en France, XVIII$^c$ siècle–XX$^c$ siècle," *Revue d'histoire économique et sociale*, XLVII (1969), 508.

13. Drake, *Population*, 138; Braun, "Impact of Cottage Industry," 63–64.

14. Hufton, "Women in Revolution"; Forrest, "Condition of the Poor"; Albert Soboul, *Les Sans-Culottes parisiens en l'an II* (Paris, 1958); Rémi Gossez, *Les Ouvriers de Paris* (Paris, 1967), I; E. P. Thompson, *The Making of The English Working Class* (London, 1963).

15. For an elaboration of this see Joan W. Scott and Louise A. Tilly, "Women's Work and the Family in Nineteenth-Century Europe," *Comparative Studies in Society and History*, XVII (1975), 36–64.

16. T. Deldycke, H. Gelders, and J.-M. Limbor, *La Population active et sa structure* (Brussels, 1969), 169. Ivy Pinchbeck, *Women Workers and the Industrial Revolution, 1750–1850* (New York, 1930), 84. Similar distributions can be found in Germany and Italy; see Adna Ferrin Weber, *The Growth of Cities in the Nineteenth Century* (New York, 1967), 375; Louise A. Tilly, "Women at Work in Milan, Italy, 1880–World War I," unpub. paper, read to the American Historical Association (1972). B. L. Hutchins, *Women in Modern Industry* (London, 1915), 84.

17. Shorter, "Female Emancipation," 633. See also Peter Laslett and Karla Oosterveen, "Long-term Trends in Bastardy in England: A Study of the Illegitimacy Figures in the Parish Registers and in the Reports of the Registrar General, 1461–1960," *Population Studies*, XXVII (1973), 225–286.

18. Pinchbeck, *Women Workers*, 117–121, 152–153, 155–156; Neil Smelser, *Social Change in the Industrial Revolution: An Application of Theory to the British Cotton Industry* (Chicago, 1959), 184, ff.

19. Edward Cadbury, M. Cecile Matheson, and George Shann, *Women's Work and Wages: A Phase of Life in An Industrial City* (Chicago, 1907), 44–46; Gareth Stedman Jones, *Outcast London* (Oxford, 1971), 83–87. Pinchbeck, *Women Workers*, 315.

20. Cadbury, Matheson, and Shann, *Women's Work*, 44–45.

21. Pinchbeck, *Women Workers*, 193; Charles Booth, *Life and Labour of the People of London* (London, 1895) IV, *passim*; Cadbury, Matheson, and Shann, *Women's Work*, 121; Stedman Jones, *Outcast London*, 83–87.

22. Pinchbeck, *Women Workers*, 219; Booth, *Life and Labour*, IX, 52; Deldycke, et al., *La Population*, 185.

23. Booth, *Life and Labour*, I, *passim*; Cadbury, Matheson, and Shann, *Women's Work*, 14.

24. Laslett and Oosterveen, "Long-term Trends," 257–258, 284.

25. Quoted in Shorter, "Female Emancipation," 618. Sex ratios discussed in Weber, *Growth of Cities*, 285–300, 320, 325–327.

26. Theresa McBride, "Rural Tradition and the Process of Modernization: Domestic Servants in Nineteenth Century France" (Ph.D. diss., Rutgers University, 1973).

27. Shorter, Knodel, and van de Walle, "Decline of Non-Marital Fertility," 384; Le Play, *Les Ouvriers*, V, 150–154. Pierre Caspard attacks Shorter's notion of a sexual revolution as the cause of increased prenuptial conceptions in "Conceptions prénuptiales et développement du capitalisme dans la Principauté de Neuchâtel (1678–1820)," *Annales E.S.C.*, XXIX (1974), 989–1008.

28. Shorter, "Sexual Revolution and Social Change," 258; Jacques De Pauw, "Amour illégitime et société a Nantes au XVIIIᶜ siècle," *Annales E.S.C.*, XXVII (1972), 1163–1166; M. Cl. Murtin, "Les abandons d'enfants a Bourg et dans le département de l'Ain à la fin du XVIIIᶜ siècle et dans la première moitée du XIXᶜ," *Cahiers d'histoire*, II (1965), 135–166. Cissie Catherine Fairchilds, "Poverty and Charity in Aix-en-Provence 1640–1789" (Ph.D. diss., Johns Hopkins University, 1972). Yeo and Thompson, *Mayhew*, 148.

29. Alain Lottin, "Naissances Illégitimies et filles-mères à Lille au XVIIIᶜ siècle," *Revue d'histoire moderne et contemporaine*, XVII (1970), 309 (authors' translation).

30. Richard Cobb, *The Police and the People: French Popular Protest 1789–1820* (Oxford, 1970), 235, 238; Alexandre Parent-Duchâtelet, *De la Prostitution dans la Ville De Paris* (Paris, 1836), 73–75, 93–94. Yeo and Thompson, *Mayhew*, 116–180. See also Massimo Livi Bacci, *A Century of Portuguese Fertility* (Princeton, 1971), 71–73.

31. Cobb, *Police and the People*, 234, 237, 238. See also Henry Mayhew, *London Labour and the London Poor* (London, 1851; reprinted, 1967), IV, 220, 255, 256.

32. *Encyclopedia Britannica* (New York, 1911), X, 746–747, "Foundling hospitals"; Franklin Ford, *Strasbourg in Transition* (New York, 1966) 177–179. The graph of illegitimacy in Paris supplied by Shorter, "Sexual Revolution and Social Change," 265, is based on figures in E. Charlot and J. Dupaquier, "Mouvement annuel de la population de la Ville de Paris de 1670 à 1821," *Annales du Demographie historique*, I (1967), 512–513. See also William Langer, "Checks on Population Growth: 1750–1850," *Scientific American*, CCXXVI (1972), 92–99; J. F. Terme et J.-B. Monfalcon, *Histoire des enfants trouvés* (Paris, 1840).

33. Fairchilds, "Poverty and Charity," citing *La mendicité abolie dans la ville d'Aix par l'Hôpital général ou Maison de charité*, an undated pamphlet which she dates from the late seventeenth century.

34. Ford, *Strasbourg*, 178; Maurice Agulhon, *Une Ville ouvrière au temps du socialisme utopique. Toulon de 1815 à 1851* (Paris, 1970), 99. See also Pierre Pierrard, *La Vie ouvrière a Lille sous le Second Empire* (Paris, 1965), 118–120; Edith Thomas, *Les Petroleuses* (Paris, 1963), 20–23; Richard Cobb, "The Women of the Commune," in his *Second Identity: Essays on France and French History* (London, 1969), 231.

35. The whole question of the place and meaning of legal sanctification of marriage needs further exploration. There may have existed among the poor a moral concept of the family, similar to the "moral economy" described by E. P. Thompson. Indeed, common-law marriage in England and consensual union in France were both recognized in law. It may well be, despite the laws imposed by centralizing states and churches, that a popular tradition of nonlegal, nonsanctified marriage continued. See John Knodel, "Law, Marriage and Illegitimacy in Nineteenth-Century Germany," *Population Studies*, XX (1966–1967), 279–294; U. R. Q. Henriques, "Bastardy and the New Poor Law," *Past & Present*, XXXVII (1967), 103–129; Régine Pernoud, "La vie de famille du Moyen Age à l'ancien Régime," in Robert Prigent (ed.), *Renouveau des idées sur la famille* (Paris, 1954), 29; E. P. Thompson, "The Moral Economy of the English Crowd in the Eighteenth Century," *Past & Present*, L (1971), 76–136.

36. Shorter, "Capitalism, Culture and Sexuality," 342; Shorter accepts the initial importance of population growth in "Sexual Change and Illegitimacy," 249, as well as the connection of migration and increased illegitimacy and the end of the linkage of marriage and property settlement.

37. On improvident marriages, see Henriques, "Bastardy," 111–112; Braun, "Impact of Cottage Industry," 59; Matti Sarmela, *Reciprocity Systems of the Rural Society in the Finnish-Karelian Culture Area with Special Reference to Social Intercourse of the Youth* (Helsinki, 1969), 57.

38. Peter Stearns, private communication, 30 Nov. 1973. *Annales de l'Assemblee Na-*

*tionale,* T. XXXII, 5 juin–7 juillet 1874, Annexe No. 2446 (Paris, 1874), annexe, 48–133; see esp. 54, 59, 74, 84–85. See also, Margaret Hewitt, *Wives and Mothers in Victorian Industry* (London, 1958). John Knodel, "Two and a Half Centuries of Demographic History in a Bavarian Village," *Population Studies,* XXIV (1970), 353–376.

39. Le Play, *Les Ouvriers,* V, 427.

40. James A Banks, *Prosperity and Parenthood: A Study of Family Planning among the Victorian Middle Classes* (London, 1954). See also Charles Tilly, "Population and Pedagogy in France," *History of Education Quarterly,* XIII (1973), 113–128. See also H. J. Habakkuk, *Population Growth and Economic Development since 1750* (New York, 1971), 63; Michael Young and Peter Wilmott, *The Symmetrical Family: A study of Work and Leisure in the London Region* (London, 1973), 39.

41. It appears that decisions about family strategy were more important than the technology of birth control. Most evidence indicates that workers used age-old methods, particularly *coitus interruptus.* The technological revolution appears to have reached the lower class at a much later date than Shorter implies. See, for example, R. P. Newman, "Industrialization and Sexual Behavior: Some Aspects of Working Class Life in Imperial Germany," in Bezucha (ed.), *Modern European Social History,* 270–298. Infant mortality did not fall decisively in the nineteenth century until fertility began to decline. Public health measures and increased parental awareness improved the life chances of infants. See E. A. Wrigley, *Industrial Growth and Population Change: A Regional Study of the Coalfield Areas of North-West Europe in the Later Nineteenth Century* (Cambridge, 1961), 102–103; Great Britain, National Health Insurance Medical Research Committee, *The Mortalities of Birth, Infancy and Childhood* (London, 1917), xiii–xiv.

42. Shorter, Knodel, and van de Walle, "Decline of Non-Marital Fertility," 393.

43. See the historical tables on labor force composition for France, England, Germany, and Italy in Deldycke, et al, *La Population active,* 165–177, 181–193, 129–139, 106–107, for the proportionate decline in domestic service as a woman's occupation.

# 15 | THE CULT OF TRUE WOMANHOOD: 1820–1860

## BARBARA WELTER

The nineteenth-century American man was a busy builder of bridges and railroads, at work long hours in a materialistic society. The religious values of his forebears were neglected in practice if not in intent, and he occasionally felt some guilt that he had turned this new land, this temple of the chosen people, into one vast countinghouse. But he could salve his conscience by reflecting that he had left behind a hostage, not only to fortune, but to all the values which he held so dear and treated so lightly. Woman, in the cult of True Womanhood[1] presented by the women's magazines, gift annuals, and religious literature of the nineteenth century, was the hostage in the home.[2] In a society where values changed frequently, where fortunes rose and fell with frightening rapidity, where social and economic mobility provided instability as well as hope, one thing at least remained the same—a true woman was a true woman, wherever she was found. If anyone, male or female, dared to tamper with the complex of virtues which made up True Womanhood, he was damned immediately as an enemy of God, of civilization, and of the Republic. It was a fearful obligation, a solemn responsibility, which the nineteenth-century American woman had—to uphold the pillars of the temple with her frail white hand.

The attributes of True Womenhood, by which a woman judged herself and was judged by her husband, her neighbors, and society could be divided into four cardinal virtues—piety, purity, submissiveness, and domesticity. Put them all together and they spelled mother, daughter, sister, wife—woman. Without them, no matter whether there was fame, achievement, or wealth, all was ashes. With them she was promised happiness and power.

Religion or piety was the core of woman's virtue, the source of her strength. Young men looking for a mate were cautioned to search first for piety, for if that were there, all else would follow.[3] Religion belonged to woman by divine right, a gift of God and nature. This "peculiar susceptibility" to religion was given her for a reason: "the vestal flame of piety, lighted up by Heaven in the breast of woman" would throw its beams into the naughty world of men.[4] So far would its candle power reach that the "Universe might be Enlightened, Improved, and Harmonized by WOMAN!!"[5] She would be another, better Eve, working in cooperation with the Redeemer, bringing the world back "from its revolt and sin."[6] The world would be reclaimed for God through her suffering, for "God increased the

313

cares and sorrows of woman, that she might be sooner constrained to accept the terms of salvation."[7] A popular poem by Mrs. Frances Osgood, "The Triumph of the Spiritual Over the Sensual" expressed just this sentiment, woman's purifying passionless love bringing an erring man back to Christ.[8]

Dr. Charles Meigs, explaining to a graduating class of medical students why women were naturally religious, said that "hers is a pious mind. Her confiding nature leads her more readily than men to accept the proffered grace of the Gospel."[9] Caleb Atwater, Esq., writing in *The Ladies' Repository*, saw the hand of the Lord in female piety: "Religion is exactly what a woman needs, for it gives her that dignity that best suits her dependence."[10] And Mrs. John Sandford, who had no very high opinion of her sex, agreed thoroughly: "Religion is just what woman needs. Without it she is ever restless or unhappy. . . . "[11] Mrs. Sandford and the others did not speak only of that restlessness of the human heart, which St. Augustine notes, that can only find its peace in God. They spoke rather of religion as a kind of tranquilizer for the many undefined longings which swept even the most pious young girl and about which it was better to pray than to think.

One reason religion was valued was that it did not take a woman away from her "proper sphere," her home. Unlike participation in other societies or movements, church work would not make her less domestic or submissive, less a True Woman. In religious vineyards, said the *Young Ladies' Literary and Missionary Report*, "you may labor without the apprehension of detracting from the charms of feminine delicacy." Mrs. S. L. Dagg, writing from her chapter of the Society in Tuscaloosa, Alabama, was equally reassuring: "As no sensible woman will suffer her intellectual pursuits to clash with her domestic duties" she should concentrate on religious work "which promotes these very duties."[12]

The women's seminaries aimed at aiding women to be religious, as well as accomplished. Mt. Holyoke's catalogue promised to make female education "a handmaid to the Gospel and an efficient auxiliary in the great task of renovating the world."[13] The Young Ladies' Seminary at Bordentown, New Jersey, declared its most important function to be "the forming of a sound and virtuous character."[14] In Keene, New Hampshire, the Seminary tried to instill a consistent and useful character" in its students, to enable them in this life to be "a good friend, wife and mother" but more important, to qualify them for "the enjoyment of Celestial Happiness in the life to come."[15] And Joseph M. D. Mathews, Principal of Oakland Female Seminary in Hillsborough, Ohio, believed that "female education should be preeminently religious."[16]

If religion was so vital to a woman, irreligion was almost too awful to contemplate. Women were warned not to let their literary or intellectual pursuits take them away from God. Sarah Josepha Hale spoke darkly of those who, like Margaret Fuller, threw away the "One True Book" for others, open to error. Mrs. Hale used the unfortunate Miss Fuller as fateful proof that "the greater the intellectual force, the greater and more fatal the errors into which women fall who wander from the Rock of Salvation, Christ the Savior. . . . "[17]

One gentleman, writing on "Female Irreligion" reminded his readers that "Man may make himself a brute, and does so very often, but can woman brutify herself to his level—the lowest level of human nature— without exerting special wonder?" Fanny Wright, because she was godless, "was no woman, mother though she be." A few years ago, he recalls, such women would have been whipped. In any case, "woman never looks lovelier than in her reverence for religion" and, conversely, "female irreligion is the most revolting feature in human character."[18]

Purity was as essential as piety to a young woman, its absence as unnatural and unfeminine. Without it she was, in fact, no woman at all, but a member of some lower order. A "fallen woman" was a "fallen angel," unworthy of the celestial company of her sex. To contemplate the loss of purity brought tears; to be guilty of such a crime, in the woman's magazines at least, brought madness or death. Even the language of the flowers had bitter words for it: a dried white rose symbolized "Death Preferable to Loss of Innocence."[19] The marriage night was the single great event of a woman's life, when she bestowed her greatest treasure upon her husband, and from that time on was completely dependent upon him, an empty vessel,[20] without legal or emotional existence of her own.[21]

Therefore all True Women were urged, in the strongest possible terms, to maintain their virtue, although men, being by nature more sensual than they, would try to assault it. Thomas Branagan admitted in *The Excellency of the Female Character Vindicated* that his sex would sin and sin again—they could not help it—but woman, stronger and purer, must not give in and let man "take liberties incompatible with her delicacy." "If you do," Branagan addressed his gentle reader, "You will be left in silent sadness to bewail your credulity, imbecility, duplicity, and premature prostitution."[22]

Mrs. Eliza Farrar, in *The Young Lady's Friend*, gave practical logistics to avoid trouble: "Sit not with another in a place that is too narrow; read not out of the same book; let not your eagerness to see anything induce you to place your head close to another person's."[23]

If such good advice was ignored, the consequences were terrible and inexorable. In *Girlhood and Womanhood: Or Sketches of My Schoolmates*, by Mrs. A. J. Graves (a kind of mid-nineteenth-century *The Group*), the bad ends of a boarding-school class of girls are scrupulously recorded. The worst end of all is reserved for "Amelia Dorrington: The Lost One," Amelia died in the almshouse "the wretched victim of depravity and intemperance" and all because her mother had let her be high-spirited not prudent." These girlish high spirits had been misinterpreted by a young man, with disastrous results. Amelia's "thoughtless levity" was "followed by a total loss of virtuous principle" and Mrs. Graves editorializes that "the coldest reserve is more admirable in a woman a man wishes to make his wife, than the least approach to undue familiarity."[24]

A popular and often-reprinted story by Fanny Forester told the sad tale of "Lucy Dutton." Lucy "with the seal of innocence upon her heart, and a rose-leaf on her cheek" came out of her vine-covered cottage and ran into a city slicker. "And Lucy was beautiful and trusting, and thoughtless: and he was gay, selfish and profligate. Needs the story be told? . . . Nay, censor, Lucy was a child—consider how young, how very untaught—oh! her innocence was no match for the sophistry of a gay, city youth! Spring came and shame was stamped upon the cottage at the foot of the hill." The baby died; Lucy went mad at the funeral and finally died herself. "Poor, poor Lucy Dutton! The grave is a blessed couch and pillow to the wretched. Rest thee there, poor Lucy!"[25] The frequency with which derangement follows loss of virtue suggests the exquisite sensibility of woman and the possibility that, in the women's magazines at least, her intellect was geared to her hymen, not her brain.

If, however, a woman managed to withstand man's assaults on her virtue, she demonstrated her superiority and her power over him. Eliza Farnham, trying to prove this female superiority, concluded smugly that "the purity of women is the everlasting barrier against which the tides of man's sensual nature surge."[26]

A story in *The Lady's Amaranth* illustrates this dominance. It is set, improbably, in Sicily, where two lovers, Bianca and Tebaldo, have been separated because her family insisted she marry a rich old man. By some strange circumstance the two are in a shipwreck and cast on a desert island, the only survivors. Even here, however, the rigid standards of True Womanhood prevail. Tebaldo unfortunately forgets himself slightly so that Bianca must warn him: "We may not indeed gratify our fondness by caresses, but it is still something to bestow our kindest language, and looks and prayers, and all lawful and honest attentions on each other." Something, perhaps, but not enough, and Bianca must further remonstrate: "It is true that another man is my husband, but you are my guardian angel." When even that does not work she says in a voice of sweet reason, passive, and proper to the end, that she wishes he wouldn't but "still, if you insist, I will become what you wish; but I beseech you to consider, ere that decision, that debasement which I must suffer in your esteem." This appeal to his own double standards holds the beast in him at bay. They are rescued, discover that the old husband is dead, and after "mourning a decent season" Bianca finally gives in, legally.[27]

Men could be counted on to be grateful when women thus saved them from themselves. William Alcott, guiding young men in their relations with the opposite sex, told them that "Nothing is better calculated to preserve a young man from contamination of low pleasures and pursuits than frequent intercourse with the more refined and virtuous of the other sex." And he added, one assumes in equal innocence, that youths should "observe and learn to admire, that purity and ignorance of evil which is the characteristic of well-educated young ladies, and which, when we are near them, raises us above those sordid and sensual considerations which hold such sway over men in their intercourse with each other."[28]

The Rev. Jonathan F. Stearns was also impressed by female chastity in the face of male passion and warned woman never to compromise the source of her power: "Let her lay aside delicacy, and her influence over our sex is gone."[29]

Women themselves accepted, with pride but suitable modesty, this priceless virtue. *The Ladies' Wreath,* in "Woman the Creature of God and the Manufacturer of Society" saw purity as her greatest gift and chief means of discharging her duty to save the world: "Purity is the highest beauty—the true pole-star which is to guide humanity aright in its long, varied, and periious voyage."[30]

Sometimes, however, a woman did not see the dangers to her treasure. In that case they must be pointed out to her, usually by a male. In the nineteenth century any form of social change was tantamount to an attack on woman's virtue, if only it was correctly understood. For example, dress reform seemed innocuous enough and the bloomers worn by the lady of that name and her followers were certainly modest attire. Such was the reasoning only of the ignorant. In another issue of *The Ladies' Wreath* a young lady is represented in dialogue with her "Professor." The girl expresses admiration for the bloomer costume—it gives freedom of motion, is healthful, and attractive. The "Professor" sets her straight. Trousers, he explains, are "only one of the many manifestations of that wild spirit of socialism and agrarian radicalism which is at present so rife in our land." The young lady recants immediately: "If this dress has any connexion with Fourierism or Socialism, or fanaticism in any shape whatever, I have no disposition to wear it at all . . . no true woman would so far compromise her delicacy as to espouse, however unwittingly, such a cause."[31]

America could boast that her daughters were particularly innocent. In a poem on "The American Girl" the author wrote proudly:

> Her eye of light is the diamond bright,
> Her innocence the pearl,
> And these are ever the bridal gems
> That are worn by the American girl.[32]

Lydia Maria Child, giving advice to mothers, aimed at preserving that spirit of innocence. She regretted that "want of confidence between mothers and daughters on delicate subjects" and suggested a woman tell her daughter a few facts when she reached the age of twelve to "set her mind at rest." Then Mrs. Child confidently hoped that a young lady's "instinctive modesty" would "prevent her from dwelling on the information until she was called upon to use it."[33] In the same vein, a book of advice to the newly married was titled *Whisper to a Bride*.[34] As far as intimate information was concerned, there was no need to whisper, since the book contained none at all.

A masculine summary of this virtue was expressed in a poem "Female Charms":

> I would have her as pure as the snow on the mount—
> As true as the smile that to infamy's given—
> As pure as the wave of the crystalline fount,
> Yet as warm in the heart as the sunlight of heaven.
> With a mind cultivated, not boastingly wise,
> I could gaze on such beauty, with exquisite bliss;
> With her heart on her lips and her soul in her eyes—
> What more could I wish in dear woman than this.[35]

Man might, in fact, ask no more than this in woman, but she was beginning to ask more of herself, and in the asking was threatening the third powerful and necessary virtue, submission. Purity, considered as a moral imperative, set up a dilemma which was hard to resolve. Woman must preserve her virtue until marriage and marriage was necessary for her happiness. Yet marriage was, literally, an end to innocence. She was told not to question this dilemma but simply to accept it.

Submission was perhaps the most feminine virtue expected of women. Men were supposed to be religious, although they rarely had time for it, and supposed to be pure, although it came awfully hard to them, but men were the movers, the doers, the actors. Women were the passive, submissive responders. The order of dialogue was, of course, fixed in Heaven. Man was "woman's superior by God's appointment, if not in intellectual dowry, at least by official decree." Therefore, as Charles Elliot argued in *The Ladies' Repository*, she should submit to him "for the sake of good order at least."[36] In *The Ladies Companion* a young wife was quoted approvingly as saying that she did not think woman should "feel and act for herself" because "When, next to God, her husband is not the tribunal to which her heart and intellect appeals—the golden bowl of affection is broken."[37] Women were warned that if they tampered with this quality they tampered with the order of the Universe.

*The Young Lady's Book* summarized the necessity of the passive virtues in its readers' lives: "It is, however, certain, that in whatever situation of life a woman is placed from her cradle to her grave, a spirit of obedience and submission, pliability of temper, and humility of mind, are required from her."[38]

Woman understood her position if she was the right kind of woman, a true woman. "She feels herself weak and timid. She needs a protector," declared George Burnap, in his lectures on *The Sphere and Duties of Woman*. "She is in a measure dependent. She asks for wisdom, constancy, firmness, perseverance, and she is willing to repay it all by the surrender of the full treasure of her affections. Woman despises in man every thing like herself except a tender heart. It is enough that she is effeminate and weak; she does not want another like herself."[39] Or put even more strongly by Mrs. Sandford: "A really sensible woman feels her dependence. She does what she can, but she is conscious of inferiority, and therefore grateful for support."[40]

Mrs. Sigourney, however, assured young ladies that although they were separate, they were equal. This difference of the sexes did not imply inferiority, for it was part of that same order of Nature established by Him "who bids the oak brave the fury of the tempest, and the alpine flower lean its cheek on the bosom of eternal snows."[41] Dr. Meigs had a different analogy to make the same point, contrasting the anatomy of the Apollo of the Belvedere (illustrating the male principle) with the Venus de Medici (illustrating the female principle). "Woman," said the physician, with a kind of clinical gallantry, "has a head almost too small for intellect but just big enough for love."[42]

This love itself was to be passive and responsive. "Love, in the heart of a woman," wrote Mrs. Farrar, "should partake largely of the nature of gratitude. She should love, because she is already loved by one deserving her regard."[43]

Woman was to work in silence, unseen, like Wordsworth's Lucy. Yet, "working like nature, in secret" her love goes forth to the world "to regulate its pulsation, and send forth from its heart, in pure and temperate flow, the life-giving current."[44] She was to work only for pure affection, without thought of money or ambition. A poem, "Woman and Fame," by Felicia Hemans, widely quoted in many of the gift books, concludes with a spirited renunciation of the gift of fame:

> Away! to me, a woman, bring
> Sweet flowers from affection's spring.[45]

"True feminine genius," said Grace Greenwood (Sara Jane Clarke) "is ever timid, doubtful, and clingingly dependent; a perpetual childhood." And she advised literary ladies in an essay on "The Intellectual Woman"—"Don't trample on the flowers while longing for the stars."[46] A wife who submerged her own talents to work for her husband was extolled as an example of a true woman. In *Women of Worth: A Book for Girls*, Mrs. Ann Flaxman, an artist of promise herself, was praised because she "devoted herself to sustain her husband's genius and aid him in his arduous career."[47]

Caroline Gilman's advice to the bride aimed at establishing this proper order from the beginning of a marriage: "Oh, young and lovely bride, watch well the first moments when your will conflicts with his to whom God and society have given the control. Reverence his *wishes* even when you do not his *opinions*."[48]

Mrs. Gilman's perfect wife in *Recollections of a Southern Matron* realizes that "the three golden threads with which domestic happiness is woven" are "to repress a harsh answer, to confess a fault, and to stop (right or wrong) in the midst of self-defense, in gentle submission." Woman could do this, hard though it was because in her heart she knew she was right and so could afford to be forgiving, even a trifle condescending. "Men are not unreasonable," averred Mrs. Gilman. "Their difficulties lie in not understanding the moral and physical nature of our sex. They often wound through ignorance, and are surprised at having offended." Wives were advised to do their best to reform men, but if they couldn't, to give up gracefully. "If any habit of his annoyed me, I spoke of it once or twice, calmly, then bore it quietly."[49]

A wife should occupy herself "only with domestic affairs—wait till your husband confides to you those of high importance—and do not give your advice until he asks for it," advised the *Lady's Token*. At all times she should behave in a manner becoming a woman, who had "no arms other than gentleness." Thus "if he is abusive, never retort."[50] A *Young Lady's Guide to the Harmonious Development of a Christian Character* suggested that females should "become as little children" and "avoid a controversial spirit."[51] *The Mother's Assistant and Young Lady's Friend* listed "Always Conciliate" as its first commandment in "Rules for Conjugal and Domestic Happiness." Small wonder that these same rules ended with the succinct maxim: "Do not expect too much."[52]

As mother, as well as wife, woman was required to submit to fortune. In *Letters to Mothers* Mrs. Sigourney sighed: "To bear the evils and sorrows which may be appointed us, with a patient mind, should be the continual effort of our sex. . . . It seems, indeed, to be expected of us; since the passive and enduring virtues are more immediately within our province." Of these trials "the hardest was to bear the loss of children with submission" but the indomitable Mrs. Sigourney found strength to murmur to the bereaved mother: "The Lord loveth a cheerful giver."[53] *The Ladies' Parlor Companion* agreed thoroughly in "A Submissive Mother," in which a mother who had already buried two children and was nursing a dying baby saw her sole remaining child "probably scalded to death. Handing over the infant to die in the arms of a friend, she bowed in sweet submission to the double stroke." But the child "through the goodness of God survived, and the mother learned to say 'Thy will be done.'"[54]

Woman then, in all her roles, accepted submission as her lot. It was a lot she had not chosen or deserved. As *Godey's* said, "the lesson of submission is forced upon woman." Without comment or criticism the writer affirms that "To suffer and to be silent under suffering seems the great command she has to obey."[55] George Burnap referred to a woman's life as "a series of suppressed emotions."[56] She was, as Emerson said, "more vulnerable, more infirm, more mortal than man."[57] The death of a beautiful woman, cherished in fiction, represented woman as the innocent victim, suffering without sin, too pure and good for this world but too weak and passive to resist its evil forces.[58] The best refuge for such a delicate creature was the warmth and safety of her home.

The true woman's place was unquestionably by her own fireside—as daughter, sister, but most of all as wife and mother. Therefore domesticity was among the virtues most prized by the women's magazines. "As society is constituted," wrote Mrs. S. E. Farley, on the "Domestic and Social Claims on Woman," "the true dignity and beauty of the female character seem to consist in a right understanding and faithful and cheerful performance of social and family duties."[59] Sacred Scripture reenforced social pressure: "St. Paul knew what was best for women when he advised them to be domestic," said Mrs. Sandford. "There is composure at home; there is something sedative in the duties which home involves. It affords security not only from the world, but from delusions and errors of every kind."[60]

From her home woman performed her great task of bringing men back to God. *The Young Ladies' Class Book* was sure that "the domestic fireside is the great guardian of society against the excess of human passions."[61] *The Lady at Home* expressed its convictions in its very title and concluded that "even if we cannot reform the world in a moment, we can begin the work by reforming ourselves and our households—It is woman's mission. Let her not look away from her own little family circle for the means of producing moral and social reforms, but begin at home."[62]

Home was supposed to be a cheerful place, so that brothers, husbands, and sons would not go elsewhere in search of a good time. Woman was expected to dispense comfort and cheer. In writing the biography of Margaret Mercer (every inch a true woman) her biographer (male) notes: "She never forgot that it is the peculiar province of woman to minister to the comfort, and promote the happiness, first, of those most nearly allied to her, and then of those, who by the Providence of God are placed in a state of dependence upon her."[63] Many other essays in the women's journals showed woman as comforter: "Woman, Man's Best friend," "Woman, the Greatest Social Benefit," "Woman, A Being to Come Home To," "The Wife: Source of Comfort and the Spring of Joy."[64]

One of the most important functions of woman as comforter was her role as nurse. Her own health was probably, although regrettably, delicate.[65] Many homes had "little sufferers," those pale children who wasted away to saintly deaths. And there were enough other illnesses of youth and age, major and minor, to give the nineteenth-century American woman nursing experience. The sickroom called for the exercise of her higher qualities of patience, mercy, and gentleness as well as for her housewifely arts. She could thus fulfill her dual feminine function—beauty and usefulness.

The cookbooks of the period offer formulas for gout cordials, ointment for sore nipples, hiccough and cough remedies, opening pills and refreshing drinks for fever, along with recipes for pound cake, jumbles, stewed calf's head, and currant wine.[66] *The Ladies' New Book of Cookery* believed that "food prepared by the kind hand of a wife, mother, sister, friend" tasted better and had a "restorative power which money cannot purchase."[67]

A chapter of *The Young Lady's Friend* was devoted to woman's privilege as "ministering spirit at the couch of the sick." Mrs. Farrar advised a soft voice, gentle and clean hands, and a cheerful smile. She also cautioned against an excess of female delicacy. That was all right for a young lady in the parlor but not for bedside manners. Leeches, for example, were to be regarded as "a curious piece of mechanism . . . their ornamental stripes should recommend them even to the eye, and their valuable services to our feelings." And she went on calmly to discuss their use. Nor were women to shrink from medical terminology, since "If you cultivate right views of the wonderful structure of the body, you will be as willing to speak to a physician of the bowels as the brains of your patient."[68]

Nursing the sick, particularly sick males, not only made a woman feel useful and accomplished but increased her influence. In a piece of heavy-handed humor in *Godey's*, a man confessed that some women were only happy when their husbands were ailing that they might have the joy of nursing him to recovery "thus gratifying their medical vanity and their love of power by making him more dependent upon them."[69] In a similar vein a husband sometimes suspected his wife "almost wishes me dead—for the pleasure of being utterly inconsolable."[70]

In the home women were not only the highest adornment of civilization, but they were supposed to keep busy at morally uplifting tasks. Fortunately most of housework, if looked at in true womanly fashion, could be regarded as uplifting. Mrs. Sigourney extolled its virtues: "The science of housekeeping affords exercise for the judgment and energy, ready recollection, and patient self-possession, that are the characteristics of a superior mind."[71] According to Mrs. Farrar, making beds was good exercise, the repetitiveness of routine tasks inculcated patience and perseverance, and proper management of the home was a surprisingly complex art: "There is more to be learned about pouring out tea and coffee, than most young ladies are willing to believe."[72] *Godey's* went so far as to suggest coyly, in "Learning vs. Housewifery" that the two were complementary, not opposed: chemistry could be utilized in cooking, geometry in dividing cloth, and phrenology in discovering talent in children."[73]

Women were to master every variety of needlework, for, as Mrs. Sigourney pointed out, "Needle-work, in all its forms of use, elegance, and ornament, has ever been the appropriate occupation of woman."[74] Embroidery improved taste; knitting promoted serenity and economy.[75] Other forms of artsy-craftsy activity for her leisure moments included painting on glass or velvet. Poonah work, tussy-mussy frames for her own needlepoint or water colors, stands for hyacinths, hair bracelets, or baskets of feathers.[76]

She was expected to have a special affinity for flowers. To the editors of *The Lady's Token* "A Woman never appears more truly in her sphere, than when she divides her time between her domestic avocations and the culture of flowers."[77] She could write letters, an activity particularly feminine since it had to do with the outpourings of the heart,[78] or practice her drawingroom skills of singing and playing an instrument. She might even read.

Here she faced a bewildering array of advice. The female was dangerously addicted to novels, according to the literature of the period. She should avoid them, since they interfered with "serious piety." If she simply couldn't help herself and read them anyway, she should choose edifying ones from lists of morally acceptable authors. She should study history since it "showed the depravity of the human heart and the evil nature of sin." On the whole, "religious biography was best."[79]

The women's magazines themselves could be read without any loss of concern for the home. *Godey's* promised the husband that he would find his wife "no less assiduous for his reception, or less sincere in welcoming his return" as a result of reading their magazine.[80] *The Lily of the Valley* won its right to be admitted to the boudoir by confessing that it was "like its namesake humble and unostentatious, but it is yet pure, and, and we trust, free from moral imperfections."[81]

No matter what later authorities claimed, the nineteenth century knew that girls *could* be ruined by a book. The seduction stories regard "exciting and dangerous books" as contributory causes of disaster. The man without honorable intentions always provides the innocent maiden with such books as a prelude to his assault on her virtue.[82] Books which attacked or seemed to attack woman's accepted place in society were regarded as equally dangerous. A reviewer of Harriet Martineau's *Society in America* wanted it kept out of the hands of American women. They were so susceptible to persuasion, with their "gentle yielding natures" that they might listen to "the bold ravings of the hard-featured of their own sex." The frightening result: "such reading will unsettle them for their true station and pursuits, and they will throw the world back again into confusion."[83]

The debate over women's education posed the question of whether a "finished" education detracted from the practice of housewifely arts. Again it proved to be a case of semantics, for a true woman's education was never "finished" until she was instructed in the gentle science of home-making.[84] Helen Irving, writing on "Literary Women," made it very clear that if women invoked the muse, it was as a genie of the household lamp. "If the necessities of her position require these duties at her hands, she will perform them nonetheless cheerfully, that she knows herself capable of higher things." The literary woman must conform to the same standards as any other woman: "That her home shall be made a loving place of rest and joy and comfort for those who are dear to her, will be the first wish of every true woman's heart."[85] Mrs. Ann Stephens told women who wrote to make sure they did not sacrifice one domestic duty. "As for genius, make it a domestic plant. Let its roots strike deep in your house. . . ."[86]

The fear of "blue stockings" (the eighteenth-century male's term of derision for educated or literary women) need not persist for nineteenth-century American men. The magazines presented spurious dialogues in which bachelors were convinced of their fallacy in fearing educated wives. One such dialogue took place between a young man and his female cousin. Ernest deprecates learned ladies ("A *Woman* is far more lovable than a *philosopher*"), but Alice refutes him with the beautiful example of their Aunt Barbara who "although she *has* perpetrated the heinous crime of writing some half dozen folios" is still a model of "the spirit of feminine gentleness." His memory prodded, Ernest concedes that, by George, there was a woman: "When I last had a cold she not only made me a bottle of cough syrup, but when I complained of nothing new to read, set to work and wrote some twenty stanzas on consumption."[87]

The magazines were filled with domestic tragedies in which spoiled young girls learned that when there was a hungry man to feed French and china painting were not helpful. According to these stories many a marriage is jeopardized because the wife has not learned to keep house. Harriet Beecher Stowe wrote a sprightly piece of personal experience for *Godey's*, ridiculing her own bad housekeeping as a bride. She used the same theme in a story "The Only Daughter," in which the pampered beauty learns the facts of domestic life from a rather difficult source, her mother-in-law. Mrs. Hamilton tells Caroline in the sweetest way possible to shape up in the kitchen, reserving her rebuke for her son: "You are her husband—her guide—her protector—now see what you can do," she admonishes him. "Give her credit for every effort: treat her faults with tenderness; encourage and praise whenever you can, and depend upon it, you will see another woman in her." He is properly masterful, she properly domestic, and in a few months Caroline is making lumpless gravy and keeping up with the darning. Domestic tranquillity has been restored and the young wife moralizes: "Bring up a girl to feel that she has a responsible part to bear in promoting the happiness of the family, and you make a reflecting being of her at once, and remove that lightness and frivolity of character which makes her shrink from graver studies."[88] These stories end with the heroine drying her hands on her apron and vowing that *her* daughter will be properly educated, in piecrust as well as Poonah work.

The female seminaries were quick to defend themselves against any suspicion of interfering with the role which nature's God had assigned to women. They hoped to enlarge and deepen that role but not to change its setting. At the Young Ladies' Seminary and Collegiate Institute in Monroe

City, Michigan, the catalogue admitted few of its graduates would be likely "to fill the learned professions." Still, they were called to "other scenes of usefulness and honor." The average woman is to be "the presiding genius of love" in the home, where she is to "give a correct and elevated literary taste to her children, and to assume that influential station that she ought to possess as the companion of an educated man."[89]

At Miss Pierce's famous school in Litchfield, the students were taught that they had "attained the perfection of their characters when they could combine their elegant accomplishments with a turn for solid domestic virtues."[90] Mt. Holyoke paid pious tribute to domestic skills: "Let a young lady despise this branch of the duties of woman, and she despises the appointments of her existence." God, nature, and the Bible "enjoin these duties on the sex, and she cannot violate them with impunity." Thus warned, the young lady would have to seek knowledge of these duties elsewhere, since it was not in the curriculum at Mt. Holyoke. "We would not take this privilege from the mother."[91]

One reason for knowing her way around a kitchen was that America was "a land of precarious fortunes," as Lydia Maria Child pointed out in her book *The Frugal Housewife: Dedicated to Those Who Are Not Ashamed of Economy.* Mrs. Child's chapter "How To Endure Poverty" prescribed a combination of piety and knowledge—the kind of knowledge found in a true woman's education, "a thorough religious *useful* education."[92] The woman who had servants today, might tomorrow, because of a depression or panic, be forced to do her own work. If that happened she knew how to act, for she was to be the same cheerful consoler of her husband in their cottage as in their mansion.

An essay by Washington Irving, much quoted in the gift annuals, discussed the value of a wife in case of business reverses: "I have observed that a married man falling into misfortune is more apt to achieve his situation in the world than a single one . . . it is beautifully ordained by Providence that woman, who is the ornament of man in his happier hours, should be his stay and solace when smitten with sudden calamity."[93]

A story titled simply but eloquently "The Wife" dealt with the quiet heroism of Ellen Graham during her husband's plunge from fortune to poverty. Ned Graham said of her: "Words are too poor to tell you what I owe to that noble woman. In our darkest seasons of adversity, she has been an angel of consolation—utterly forgetful of self and anxious only to comfort and sustain me." Of course she had a little help from "faithful Dinah who absolutely refused to leave her beloved mistress," but even so Ellen did no more than would be expected of any true woman.[94]

Most of this advice was directed to woman as wife. Marriage was the proper state for the exercise of the domestic virtues. "True Love and a Happy Home," an essay in *The Young Ladies' Oasis,* might have been carved on every girl's hope chest.[95] But although marriage was best, it was not absolutely necessary. The women's magazines tried to remove the stigma from being an "Old Maid." They advised no marriage at all rather than an unhappy one contracted out of selfish motives.[96] Their stories showed maiden ladies as unselfish ministers to the sick, teachers of the young, or moral preceptors with their pens, beloved to the entire village. Usually the life of single blessedness resulted from the premature death of a fiancé, or was chosen through fidelity to some high mission. For example, in "Two Sisters," Mary devotes herself to Ellen and her abandoned children, giving up her own chance for marriage. "Her devotion to her sister's happiness has met its reward in the consciousness of having fulfilled a sacred duty."[97] Very rarely, a "woman of genius" was absolved from the necessity of marriage, being so extraordinary that she did not need the security or status of being a wife.[98] Most often, however, if girls proved "difficult," marriage and a family were regarded as a cure.[99] The "sedative quality" of a home could be counted on to subdue even the most restless spirits.

George Burnap saw marriage as "that sphere for which woman was originally intended, and to which she is so exactly fitted to adorn and bless, as the wife, the mistress of a home, the solace, the aid, and the counsellor of that ONE, for whose sake alone the world is of any consequence to her."[100] Samuel Miller preached a sermon on women: "How interesting and important are the duties devolved on females as WIVES . . . the counsellor and friend of the husband; who makes it her daily study to lighten his cares, to soothe his sorrows, and to augment his joys; who, like a guardian angel, watches over his interests, warns him against dangers, comforts him under trials; and by her pious, assiduous, and attractive deportment, constantly endeavors to render him more virtuous, more useful, more honourable, and more happy."[101] A woman's whole interest should be focused on her husband, paying him "those numberless attentions to which the French give the title of *petits soins* and which the woman who loves knows so well how to pay . . . she should consider nothing as trivial which could win a smile of approbation from him."[102]

Marriage was seen not only in terms of service but as an increase in authority for woman. Burnap concluded that marriage improves the female character "not only because it puts her under the best possible tuition, that of the affections, and affords scope to her active energies, but because it gives her higher aims, and a more dignified position."[103] *The Lady's Amaranth* saw it as a balance of power: "The man bears rule over his wife's person and conduct. She bears rule over his inclinations: he governs by law; she by persuasion. . . . The empire of the woman is an empire of softness . . . her commands are caresses, her menaces are tears."[104]

Woman should marry but not for money. She should choose only the high road of true love and not truckle to the values of a materialistic society. A story "Marrying for Money" (subtlety was not the strong point of the ladies' magazines) depicts Gertrude, the heroine, rueing the day she made her crass choice: "It is a terrible thing to live without love. . . . A woman who dares marry for aught but the purest affection, calls down the just judgments of heaven upon her head."[105]

The corollary to marriage, with or without true love, was motherhood, which added another dimension to her usefulness and her prestige. It also anchored her even more firmly to the home. "My Friend," wrote Mrs. Sigourney, "If in becoming a mother, you have reached the climax of your happiness, you have also taken a higher place in the scale of being . . . you have gained an increase of power."[106] The Rev. J. N. Danforth pleaded in *The Ladies' Casket*, "Oh, mother, acquit thyself well in thy humble sphere, for thou mayest affect the world."[107] A true woman naturally loved her children; to suggest otherwise was monstrous.[108]

America depended upon her mothers to raise up a whole generation of Christian statesmen who could say "all that I am I owe to my angel mother."[109] The mothers must do the inculcating of virtue since the fathers, alas, were too busy chasing the dollar. Or as *The Ladies' Companion* put it more effusively, the father "weary with the heat and burden of life's summer day, or trampling with unwilling foot the decaying leaves of life's autumn, has forgotten the sympathies of life's joyous springtime. . . . The acquisition of wealth, the advancement of his children in worldly honor—these are his self-imposed tasks." It was his wife who formed "the infant mind as yet untainted by contact with evil . . . like wax beneath the plastic hand of the mother."[110]

*The Ladies' Wreath* offered a fifty-dollar prize to the woman who submitted the most convincing essay on "How May An American Woman Best Show Her Patriotism." The winner was Miss Elizabeth Wetherell who provided herself with a husband in her answer. The wife in the essay, of course, asked her husband's opinion. He tried a few jokes first—"Call her eldest son George Washington," "Don't speak French, speak American"— but then got down to telling her in sober prize-winning truth what women could do for their country. Voting was no asset, since that would result only in "a vast increase of confusion and expense without in the smallest degree affecting the result." Besides, continued this oracle, "looking down at their child," if "we were to go a step further and let the children vote, their first act would be to vote their mothers at home." There is no comment on this devastating male logic, and he continues: "Most women would follow the lead of their fathers and husbands," and the few who would "fly off on a tangent from the circle of home influence would cancel each other out."

The wife responds dutifully: "I see all that. I never understood so well before." Encouraged by her quick womanly perception, the master of the house resolves the question—an American woman best shows her patriotism by staying at home, where she brings her influence to bear "upon the right side for the country's weal." That woman will instinctively choose the side of right he has no doubt. Besides her "natural refinement and closeness to God"; she has the "blessed advantage of a quiet life" while man is exposed to conflict and evil. She stays home with "her Bible and a well-balanced mind" and raises her sons to be good Americans. The judges rejoiced in this conclusion and paid the prize money cheerfully, remarking "they deemed it cheap at the price."[111]

If any woman asked for greater scope for her gifts, the magazines were sharply critical. Such women were tampering with society, undermining civilization. Mary Wollstonecraft, Frances Wright, and Harriet Martineau were condemned in the strongest possible language—they were read out of the sex. "They are only semi-women, mental hermaphrodites." The Rev. Harrington knew the women of America could not possibly approve of such perversions and went to some wives and mothers to ask if they did want a "wider sphere of interest" as these nonwomen claimed. The answer was reassuring. " 'NO!' they cried simultaneously, 'Let the men take care of politics, *we will take care of the children!*'" Again female discontent resulted only from a lack of understanding: women were not subservient, they were rather "chosen vessels." Looked at in this light the conclusion was inescapable: "Noble, sublime is the task of the American mother."[112]

"Women's Rights" meant one thing to reformers but quite another to the True Woman. She knew her rights,

> The right to love whom others scorn,
> The right to comfort and to mourn,
> The right to shed new joy on earth,
> The right to feel the soul's high worth . . .
> Such women's rights, and God will bless
> And crown their champions with success.[113]

The American woman had her choice—she could define her rights in the way of the women's magazines and insure them by the practice of the requisite virtues, or she could go outside the home, seeking other rewards than love. It was a decision on which, she was told, everything in her world depended. "Yours it is to determine," the Rev. Mr. Stearns solemnly warned from the pulpit, "whether the beautiful order of society . . . shall continue as it has been" or whether "society shall break up and become a chaos of disjointed and unsightly elements."[114] If she chose to listen to other voices than those of her proper mentors, sought other rooms than those of her home, she lost both her happiness and her power—"that almost magic power, which, in her proper sphere, she now wields over the destinies of the world."[115]

But even while the women's magazines and related literature encouraged this ideal of the perfect woman, forces were at work in the nineteenth century which impelled woman herself to change, to play a more creative role in society. The movements of social reform, westward migration, missionary activity, utopian communities, industrialism, the Civil War—all called forth responses from woman which differed from those she was trained to believe were hers by nature and divine decree. The very perfection of True Womanhood, moreover, carried within itself the seeds of its own destruction. For if woman was so very little less than the angels, she should surely take a more active part in running the world, especially since men were making such a hash of things.

Real women often felt they did not live up to the ideal of True Womanhood: some of them blamed themselves, some challenged the standard, some tried to keep the virtues and enlarge the scope of womanhood.[116] Somehow through this mixture of challenge and acceptance, of change and continuity, the True Woman evolved into the New Woman—a transformation as startling in its way as the abolition of slavery or the coming of the machine age. And yet the stereotype, the "mystique" if you will, of what woman was and ought to be persisted, bringing guilt and confusion in the midst of opportunity.[117]

The women's magazines and related literature had feared this very dislocation of values and blurring of roles. By careful manipulation and interpretation they sought to convince woman that she had the best of both worlds—power and virtue—and that a stable order of society depended upon her maintaining her traditional place in it. To that end she was identified with everything that was beautiful and holy.

"Who Can Find a Valiant Woman?" was asked frequently from the pulpit and the editorial pages. There was only one place to look for her—at home. Clearly and confidently these authorities proclaimed the True Woman of the nineteenth century to be the Valiant Woman of the Bible, in whom the heart of her husband rejoiced and whose price was above rubies.

## NOTES

1. Authors who addressed themselves to the subject of women in the mid-nineteenth century used this phrase as frequently as writers on religion mentioned God. Neither group felt it necessary to define their favorite terms; they simply assumed—with some justification—that readers would intuitively understand exactly what they meant. Frequently what people of one era take for granted is most striking and revealing to the student from another. In a sense this analysis of the ideal woman of the mid-nineteenth century is an examination of what writers of that period actually meant when they used so confidently the vague phrase True Womanhood.

2. The conclusions reached in this article are based on a survey of almost all of the women's magazines published for less than three years; all the gift books cited in Ralph Thompson, *American Literary Annuals and Gift Books, 1825-1865* (New York, 1936) deposited in the Library of Congress, the New York Public Library, the New York Historical Society, Columbia University Special Collections, Library of the City College of the University of New York, Pennsylvania Historical Society, Massachusetts Historical Society, Boston Public Library, Fruitlands Museum Library, the Smithsonian Institution and the Wisconsin Historical Society; hundreds of religious tracts and sermons in the American Unitarian Society and the Galatea Collection of the Boston Public Library; and the large collection of nineteenth-century cookbooks in the New York Public Library and the Academy of Medicine of New York. Corroborative evidence not cited in this article was found in women's diaries, memoirs, autobiographies, and personal papers, as well as in all the novels by women which sold over 75,000 copies during this period, as cited in Frank Luthor Mott, *Golden Multitudes: The Story of Best Sellers in the United States* (New York, 1947) and H. R. Brown, *The Sentimental Novel in America, 1789-1860* (Durham, N. C., 1940). This latter information also indicated the effect of the cult of True Womanhood on those most directly concerned.

3. As in "The Bachelor's Dream," in *The Lady's Gift: Souvenir for All Seasons* (Nashua, N. H., 1849), p. 37.

4. *The Young Ladies' Class Book: A Selection of Lessons for Reading in Prose and Verse*, ed. Ebenezer Bailey, Principal of Young Ladies' High School, Boston (Boston, 1831), p. 168.

5. A Lady of Philadelphia, *The World Enlightened, Improved, and Harmonized by WOMAN!!!* A lecture, delivered in the City of New York, before the Young Ladies' Society for Mutual Improvement, on the following question, proposed by the society, with the offer of $100 for the best lecture that should be read before them on the subject proposed;—What is the power and influence of woman in moulding the manners, morals, and habits of civil society? (Philadelphia, 1840), p. 1.

6. *The Young Lady's Book: A Manual of Elegant Recreations, Exercises, and Pursuits* (Boston, 1830), p. 29.

7. *Woman As She Was, Is, and Should Be* (New York, 1849), p. 206.

8. "The Triumph of the Spiritual Over the Sensual: An Allegory," in *Ladies' Companion: A Monthly Magazine Embracing Every Department of Literature, Embellished With Original Engravings and Music*, XVII (New York) (1842), 67.

9. *Lecture on Some of the Distinctive Characteristics of the Female,* delivered before the class of the Jefferson Medical College, Jan. 1847 (Philadelphia, 1847), p. 13.

10. "Female Education," *Ladies' Repository and Gatherings of the West: A Monthly Periodical Devoted to Literature and Religion,* I (Cincinnati), 12.

11. *Woman, in Her Social and Domestic Character* (Boston, 1842), pp. 41–42.

12. *Second Annual Report of the Young Ladies' Literary and Missionary Association of the Philadelphia Collegiate Institution* (Philadelphia, 1840), pp. 20, 26.

13. *Mt. Holyoke Female Seminary: Female Education. Tendencies of the Principles Embraced, and the System Adopted in the Mt. Holyoke Female Seminary* (Boston, 1839), p.3.

14. *Prospectus of the Young Ladies' Seminary at Bordentown, New Jersey* (Bordentown, 1836), p. 7.

15. *Catalogue of the Young Ladies' Seminary in Keene, New Hampshire* (n.p., 1832), p. 20.

16. "Report to the College of Teachers, Cincinnati, October, 1840" in *Ladies' Repository,* I (1841), 50.

17. *Woman's Record: or Sketches of All Distinguished Women from 'The Beginning' Till A. D. 1850* (New York, 1853), pp. 665, 669.

18. "Female Irreligion," *Ladies' Companion,* XIII (May-Oct. 1840), 111.

19. *The Lady's Book of Flowers and Poetry,* ed. Lucy Hooper (New York, 1842), has a "Floral Dictionary" giving the symbolic meaning of floral tributes.

20. See, for example, Nathaniel Hawthorne, *The Blithedale Romance* (Boston, 1852), p. 71, in which Zenobia says: "How can she be happy, after discovering that fate has assigned her but one single event, which she must contrive to make the substance of her whole life? A man has his choice of innumerable events."

21. Mary R. Beard, *Woman As Force in History* (New York, 1946) makes this point at some length. According to common law, a woman had no legal existence once she was married and therefore could not manage property, sue in court, etc. In the 1840s and 1850s laws were passed in several states to remedy this condition.

22. *Excellency of the Female Character Vindicated: Being an Investigation Relative to the Cause and Effects on the Enroachments of Men Upon the Rights of Women and the Too Frequent Degradation and Consequent Misfortunes of The Fair Sex* (New York, 1807), pp. 277, 278.

23. By a Lady (Eliza Ware Rotch Farrar,), *The Young Lady's Friend* (Boston, 1837), p. 293.

24. *Girlhood and Womanhood; or, Sketches of My Schoolmates* (Boston, 1844), p. 140.

25. Emily Chubbuck, *Alderbrook* (Boston, 1847), 2nd. ed., II, 121, 127.

26. *Woman and Her Era* (New York, 1864), p. 95.

27. "The Two Lovers of Sicily," *The Lady's Amaranth: A Journal of Tales, Essays, Excerpts—Historical and Biographical Sketches, Poetry and Literature in General* (Philadelphia), II (Jan. 1839), 17.

28. *The Young Man's Guide* (Boston, 1833), pp. 229, 231.

29. *Female Influence: and the True Christian Mode of Its Exercise; a Discourse Delivered in the First Presbyterian Church in Newburyport, July 30, 1837* (Newburyport, 1837), p. 18.

30. W. Tolles, "Woman The Creature of God and the Manufacturer of Society," *Ladies' Wreath* (New York), III (1852), 205.

31. Prof. William M. Heim, "The Bloomer Dress," *Ladies' Wreath,* III (1852), 247.

32. *The Young Lady's Offering: or Gems of Prose and Poetry* (Boston, 1853), p. 283. The American girl, whose innocence was often connected with ignorance, was the spiritual ancestress of the Henry James heroine. Daisy Miller, like Lucy Dutton, saw innocence lead to tragedy.

33. *The Mother's Book* (Boston, 1831), pp. 151, 152.

34. Mrs. L. H. Sigourney, *Whisper to a Bride* (Hartford, 1851), in which Mrs. Sigourney's approach is summed up in this quotation: "Home! Blessed bride, thou art about to enter this sanctuary, and to become a priestess at its altar!," p. 44.

35. S. R. R., "Female Charms," *Godey's Magazine and Lady's Book* (Philadelphia), XXXIII (1846), 52.

36. Charles Elliot, "Arguing With Females," *Ladies' Repository*, I (1841), 25.

37. *Ladies' Companion*, VIII (Jan. 1838), 147.

38. *The Young Lady's Book* (New York, 1830), American edition, p. 28. (This is a different book than the one of the same title and date of publication cited in note 6.)

39. *Sphere and Duties of Woman* (5th ed., Baltimore, 1854), p. 47.

40. *Woman*, p. 15.

41. *Letters to Young Ladies* (Hartford, 1835), p. 179.

42. *Lecture*, p. 17.

43. *The Young Lady's Friend*, p. 313.

44. Maria J. McIntosh, *Woman in America: Her Work and Her Reward* (New York, 1850), p. 25.

45. *Poems and a Memoir of the Life of Mrs. Felicia Hemans* (London, 1860), p. 16.

46. Letter "To an Unrecognized Poetess, June, 1846" (Sara Jane Clarke), *Greenwood Leaves* (2nd ed.; Boston, 1850), p. 311.

47. "The Sculptor's Assistant: Ann Flaxman," in *Women of Worth: A Book for Girls* (New York, 1860), p. 263.

48. Mrs. Clarissa Packard (Mrs. Caroline Howard Gilman), *Recollections of a House-keeper* (New York, 1834), p. 122.

49. *Recollections of a Southern Matron* (New York, 1838), pp. 256, 257.

50. *The Lady's Token: or Gift of Friendship*, ed. Colesworth Pinckney (Nashua, N. H., 1848), p. 119.

51. Harvey Newcomb, *Young Lady's Guide to the Harmonious Development of Christian Character* (Boston, 1846), p. 10.

52. "Rules for Conjugal and Domestic Happiness," *Mother's Assistant and Young Lady's Friend*, III (Boston), (April 1843), 115.

53. *Letters to Mothers* (Hartford, 1838), p. 199. In the diaries and letters of women who lived during this period, the death of a child seemed consistently to be the hardest thing for them to bear and to occasion more anguish and rebellion, as well as eventual submission, than any other event in their lives.

54. "A Submissive Mother," *The Ladies' Parlor Companion: A Collection of Scattered Fragments and Literary Gems* (New York, 1852), p. 358.

55. "Woman," *Godey's Lady's Book*, II (Aug. 1831), 110.

56. *Sphere and Duties of Woman*, p. 172.

57. Ralph Waldo Emerson, "Woman," *Complete Writings of Ralph Waldo Emerson* (New York, 1875), p. 1180.

58. As in Donald Fraser, *The Mental Flower Garden* (New York, 1857). Perhaps the most famous exponent of this theory is Edgar Allan Poe who affirms in "The Philosophy of Composition" that "the death of a beautiful woman is unquestionably the most poetical topic in the world. . . ."

59. "Domestic and Social Claims on Woman," *Mother's Magazine*, VI (1846), 21.

60. *Woman*, p. 173.

61. *The Young Ladies' Class Book*, p. 166.

62. T. S. Arthur, *The Lady at Home: or, Leaves from the Every-Day Book of an American Woman* (Philadelphia, 1847), pp. 177, 178.

63. Caspar Morris, *Margaret Mercer* (Boston, 1840), quoted in *Woman's Record*, p. 425.

64. These particular titles come from: *The Young Ladies' Oasis: or Gems of Prose and Poetry*, ed. N. L. Ferguson (Lowell, 1851), pp. 14, 16; *The Genteel School Reader* (Philadelphia, 1849), p. 271; and *Magnolia*, I (1842), 4. A popular poem in book form, published in England, expressed very fully this concept of woman as comforter: Coventry Patmore, *The*

*Angel in the Home* (Boston, 1856 and 1857). Patmore expressed his devotion to True Womanhood in such lines as:

> The gentle wife, who decks his board
> And makes his day to have no night,
> Whose wishes wait upon her Lord,
> Who finds her own in his delight. (p. 94)

65. The women's magazines carried on a crusade against tight lacing and regretted, rather than encouraged, the prevalent ill health of the American woman. See, for example, *An American Mother, Hints and Sketches* (New York, 1839), pp. 28 ff. for an essay on the need for a healthy mind in a healthy body in order to better be a good example for children.

66. The best single collection of nineteenth-century cookbooks is in the Academy of Medicine of New York Library, although some of the most interesting cures were in hand-written cookbooks found among the papers of women who lived during the period.

67. Sarah Josepha Hale, *The Ladies' New Book of Cookery: A Practical System for Private Families in Town and Country* (5th ed.; New York, 1852), p. 409. Similar evidence on the importance of nursing skills to every female is found in such books of advice as William A. Alcott, *The Young Housekeeper* (Boston, 1838), in which, along with a plea for apples and cold baths, Alcott says "Every female should be trained to the angelic art of managing properly the sick," p. 47.

68. *The Young Lady's Friend*, pp. 75–77, 79.

69. "A Tender Wife," *Godey's*, II (July 1831), 28.

70. "MY WIFE! A Whisper," *Godey's*, II (Oct. 1831), 231.

71. *Letters to Young Ladies*, p. 27. The greatest exponent of the mental and moral joys of housekeeping was the *Lady's Annual Register and Housewife's Memorandum Book* (Boston, 1838), which gave practical advice on ironing, hair curling, budgeting, and marketing, and turning cuffs—all activities which contributed to the "beauty of usefulness" and "joy of accomplishment" which a woman desired (I, 23).

72. *The Young Lady's Friend*, p. 230.

73. "Learning vs. Housewifery," *Godey's*. X (Aug. 1839), 95.

74. *Letters to Young Ladies*, p. 25. W. Thayer, *Life at the Fireside* (Boston, 1857), has an idyllic picture of the woman of the house mending her children's garments, the grandmother knitting and the little girl taking her first stitches, all in the light of the domestic hearth.

75. "The Mirror's Advice," *Young Maiden's Mirror* (Boston, 1858), p. 263.

76. Mrs. L. Maria Child, *The Girl's Own Book* (New York, 1833).

77. P. 44.

78. T. S. Arthur, *Advice to Young Ladies* (Boston, 1850), p. 45.

79. R. C. Waterston, *Thoughts on Moral and Spiritual Culture* (Boston, 1842), p. 101. Newcomb's *Young Lady's Guide* also advised religious biography as the best reading for women (p. 111).

80. *Godey's*, I (1828), 1. (Repeated often in *Godey's* editorials.)

81. *The Lily of the Valley*, n. v. (1851), p. 2.

82. For example, "The Fatalist," *Godey's*, IV (Jan. 1834), 10, in which Somers Dudley has Catherine reading these dangerous books until life becomes "a bewildered dream. . . . O Passion, what a shocking perverter of reason thou art!"

83. Review of *Society in America* (New York, 1837) in *American Quarterly Review* (Philadelphia), XXII (Sept. 1837), 38.

84. "A Finished Education," *Ladies' Museum* (Providence), I (1825), 42.

85. Helen Irving, "Literary Women," *Ladies' Wreath*, III (1850), 93.

86. "Women of Genius," *Ladies' Companion*, XI (1839), 89.

87. "Intellect vs. Affection in Woman," *Godey's* XVI (1846), 86.

88. "The Only Daughter," *Godey's*, X (Mar. 1839), 122.

89. *The Annual Catalogue of the Officers and Pupils of the Young Ladies' Seminary and Collegiate Institute* (Monroe City, 1855), pp. 18, 19.

90. *Chronicles of a Pioneer School* from 1792 to 1833: Being the History of Miss Sarah Pierce and Her Litchfield School, Compiled by Emily Noyes Vanderpoel; ed. Elizabeth C. Barney Buel (Cambridge, 1903), p. 74.

91. *Mt. Holyoke Female Seminary*, p. 13.

92. *The American Frugal Housewife* (New York, 1838), p. 111.

93. "Female Influence," in *The Ladies' Pearl and Literary Gleaner: A Collection of Tales, Sketches, Essays, Anecdotes, and Historical Incidents* (Lowell), I (1841), 10.

94. Mrs. S. T. Martyn, "The Wife," *Ladies' Wreath*, II (1848-1849), 171.

95. *The Young Ladies' Oasis*, p. 26.

96. "On Marriage," *Ladies' Repository*, I (1841), 133; "Old Maids," *Ladies' Literary Cabinet* (Newburyport), II (1822) (Microfilm), 141; "Matrimony," *Godney's* II (Sept. 1831), 174; and "Married or Single," *Peterson's Magazine* (Philadelphia) IX (1859), 36, all express the belief that while marriage is desirable for a woman it is not essential. This attempt to reclaim the status of the unmarried woman is an example of the kind of mild crusade which the women's magazines sometimes carried on. Other examples were their strictures against an overly genteel education and against the affectation and aggravation of ill health. In this sense the magazines were truly conservative, for they did not oppose all change but only that which did violence to some cherished tradition. The reforms they advocated would, if put into effect, make woman even more the perfect female, and enhance the ideal of True Womanhood.

97. *Girlhood and Womanhood*, p. 100. Mrs. Graves tells the stories in the book in the person of an "Old Maid," and her conclusions are that "single life has its happiness too" for the single woman "can enjoy all the pleasures of maternity without its pains and trials" (p. 140). In another one of her books, *"Woman in America* (New York, 1843), Mrs. Graves speaks out even more strongly in favor of "single blessedness" rather than "a loveless or unhappy marriage" (p. 130).

98. A very unusual story is Lela Linwood, "A Chapter in the History of a Free Heart," *Ladies' Wreath*, III (1853), 349. The heroine, Grace Arland, is "sublime" and dwells "in perfect light while we others struggle yet with the shadows." She refuses marriage and her friends regret this but are told her heart "is rejoicing in its *freedom.*" The story ends with the plaintive refrain:

> But is it not a happy thing,
> All fetterless and free,
> Like any wild bird, on the wing,
> To carol merrily?

But even in this tale the unusual, almost unearthly rarity of Grace's genius is stressed; she is not offered as an example to more mortal beings.

99. Horace Greeley even went so far as to apply this remedy to the "dissatisfactions" of Margaret Fuller. In his autobiography, *Recollections of a Busy Life* (New York, 1868) he says that "noble and great as she was, a good husband and two or three bouncing babies would have emancipated her from a deal of cant and nonsense" (p. 178).

100. *Sphere and Duties of Woman*, p. 64.

101. *A Sermon: Preached March 13, 1808, for the Benefit of the Society Instituted in the City of New York, For the Relief of Poor Widows with Small Children* (New York, 1808), pp. 13, 14.

102. *Lady's Magazine and Museum: A Family Journal* (London) IV (Jan. 1831), 6. This magazine is included partly because its editorials proclaimed it "of interest to the English speaking lady at home and abroad" and partly because it shows that the preoccupation with True Womanhood was by no means confined to the United States.

103. *Sphere and Duties of Woman*, p. 102.

104. "Matrimony," *Lady's Amaranth*, II (Dec. 1839), 271.

105. Elizabeth Doten, "Marrying for Money," *The Lily of the Valley*, n. v. (1857), p. 112.

106. *Letters to Mothers*, p. 9.

107. "Maternal Relation," *Ladies' Casket* (New York, 1850?), p. 85. The importance of the mother's role was emphasized abroad as well as in America. *Godey's* recommended the book by the French author Aimée-Martin on the education of mothers to "be read five times," in the original if possible (XIII, Dec. 1842, 201). In this book the highest ideals of True Womanhood are upheld. For example: "Jeunes filles, jeunes épouses, tendres mères, c'est dans votre âme bien plus que dans les lois du législateur que reposent aujourd'hui l'avenir de l'Europe et les destinées du genre humain," L. Aimée-Martin, *De l'Education des Mères de famille ou De la civilisation du genre humain par les femmes* (Bruxelles, 1857), II, 527.

108. *Maternal Association of the Amity Baptist Church:* Annual Report (New York, 1847), p. 2: "Suffer the little children to come unto me and forbid them not, is and must ever be a sacred commandment to the Christian woman."

109. For example, Daniel Webster, "The Influence of Woman," in *The Young Ladies' Reader* (Philadelphia, 1851), p. 310.

110. Mrs. Emma C. Embury, "Female Education," *Ladies' Companion.* VIII (Jan. 1838), 18. Mrs. Embury stressed the fact that the American woman was not the "mere plaything of passion" but was in strict training to be "the mother of statesmen."

111. "How May An American Woman Best Show Her Patriotism?" *Ladies' Wreath,* III (1851), 313. Elizabeth Wetherell was the pen name of Susan Warner, author of *The Wide Wide World* and *Queechy.*

112. Henry F. Harrington, "Female Education," *Ladies' Companion,* IX (1838), 293, and "Influence of Woman—Past and Present," *Ladies Companion,* XIII (1840), 245.

113. Mrs. E. Little, "What Are the Rights of Women?" *Ladies' Wreath,* II (1848–1849), 133.

114. *Female Influence,* p. 18.

115. Ibid., p. 23.

116. Even the women reformers were prone to use domestic images, i.e., "sweep Uncle Sam's kitchen clean," and "tidy up our country's house."

117. The "Animus and Anima" of Jung amounts almost to a catalogue of the nineteenth-century masculine and female traits, and the female hysterics whom Freud saw had much of the same training as the nineteenth-century American woman. Betty Friedan, *The Feminine Mystique* (New York, 1963), challenges the whole concept of True Womanhood as it hampers the "fulfillment" of the twentieth-century woman.

# 16 | THE FEMALE WORLD OF LOVE AND RITUAL: RELATIONS BETWEEN WOMEN IN NINE- TEENTH-CENTURY AMERICA

## CARROLL SMITH-ROSENBERG

The female friendship of the nineteenth century, the long-lived, intimate, loving friendship between two women, is an excellent example of the type of historical phenomena which most historians know something about, which few have thought much about, and which virtually no one has writ- ten about.[1] It is one aspect of the female experience which consciously or unconsciously we have chosen to ignore. Yet an abundance of manuscript evidence suggests that eighteenth- and nineteenth-century women routine- ly formed emotional ties with other women. Such deeply felt, same-sex friendships were casually accepted in American society. Indeed, from at least the late eighteenth through the mid-nineteenth century, a female world of varied and yet highly structured relationships appears to have been an essential aspect of American society. These relationships ranged from the supportive love of sisters, through the enthusiasms of adolescent girls, to sensual avowals of love by mature women. It was a world in which men made but a shadowy appearance.[2]

Defining and analyzing same-sex relationships involves the historian in deeply problematical questions of method and interpretation. This is especially true since historians, influenced by Freud's libidinal theory, have discussed these relationships almost exclusively within the context of individual psychosexual developments or, to be more explicit psycho- pathology.[3] Seeing same-sex relationships in terms of a dichotomy be- tween normal and abnormal, they have sought the origins of such ap- parent deviance in childhood or adolescent trauma and detected the symp- toms of "latent" homosexuality in the lives of both those who later became "overtly" homosexual and those who did not. Yet theories concerning the nature and origins of same-sex relationships are frequently contradictory or based on questionable or arbitrary data. In recent years such hypoth- eses have been subjected to criticism both from within and without the

Research for this paper was supported in part by a grant from the Grant Foundation, New York, and by National Institutes of Health trainee grant 5 FO3 HD-18800-03. I would like to thank several scholars for their assistance and criticism in preparing this paper: Erving Goff- man, Roy Schafer, Charles E. Rosenberg, Cynthia Secor, Anthony Wallace. Judy Breault, who has just completed a biography of an important and introspective nineteenth-century feminist, Emily Howland, served as a research assistant for this paper and her knowledge of nineteenth-century family structure and religious history proved invaluable.

psychological professions. Historians who seek to work within a psychological framework, therefore, are faced with two hard questions: do sound psychodynamic theories concerning the nature and origins of same-sex relationships exist? If so, does the historical datum exist which would permit the use of such dynamic models?

I would like to suggest an alternative approach to female friendships—one which would view them within a cultural and social setting rather than from an exclusively individual psychosexual perspective. Only by thus altering our approach will we be in the position to evaluate the appropriateness of particular dynamic interpretations. Intimate friendships between men and men and women and women existed in a larger world of social relations and social values. To interpret such friendships more fully they must be related to the structure of the American family and to the nature of sex-role divisions and of male-female relations both within the family and in society generally. The female friendship must not be seen in isolation; it must be analyzed as one aspect of women's overall relations with one another. The ties between mothers and daughters, sisters, female cousins and friends, at all stages of the female life cycle constitute the most suggestive framework for the historian to begin an analysis of intimacy and affection between women. Such an analysis would not only emphasize general cultural patterns rather than the internal dynamics of a particular family or childhood; it would shift the focus of the study from a concern with deviance to that of defining configurations of legitimate behavioral norms and options.[4]

This analysis will be based upon the correspondence and diaries of women and men in thirty-five families between the 1760s and the 1880s. These families, though limited in number, represented a broad range of the American middle class, from hard-pressed pioneer families and orphaned girls to daughters of the intellectual and social elite. It includes families from most geographic regions, rural and urban, and a spectrum of Protestant denominations ranging from Mormon to orthodox Quaker. Although scarcely a comprehensive sample of America's increasingly heterogeneous population, it does, I believe, reflect accurately the literate middle class to which the historian working with letters and diaries is necessarily bound. It has involved an analysis of many thousands of letters written to women's friends, kin, husbands, brothers and children at every period of life from adolescence to old age. Some collections encompass virtually entire life spans; one contains over 100,000 letters as well as diaries and account books. It is my contention that an analysis of women's private letters and diaries which were never intended to be published permits the historian to explore a very private world of emotional realities central both to women's lives and the middle-class family in nineteenth-century America.[5]

The question of female friendships is peculiarly elusive; we know so little or perhaps have forgotten so much. An intriguing and almost alien form of human relationship, they flourished in a different social structure and amidst different sexual norms. Before attempting to reconstruct their social setting, therefore, it might be best first to describe two not atypical friendships. These two friendships, intense, loving, and openly avowed, began during the women's adolescence and, despite subsequent marriages and geographic separation, continued throughout their lives. For nearly half a century these women played a central emotional role in each other's lives, writing time and again of their love and of the pain of separation. Paradoxically to twentieth-century minds, their love appears to have been both sensual and platonic.

Sarah Butler Wister first met Jeannie Field Musgrove while vacationing with her family at Stockbridge, Massachusetts, in the summer of 1849.[6] Jeannie was then sixteen, Sarah fourteen. During two subsequent years spent together in boarding school, they formed a deep and intimate friendship. Sarah began to keep a bouquet of flowers before Jeannie's portrait and wrote complaining of the intensity and anguish of her affection.[7] Both young women assumed nom de plumes, Jeannie a female name, Sarah a male one; they would use these secret names into old age.[8] They frequently commented on the nature of their affection: "If the day should come," Sarah wrote Jeannie in the spring of 1861, "when you failed me either through your fault or my own, I would forswear all human friendship thenceforth." A few months later Jeannie commented: "Gratitude is a word I should never use toward you. It is perhaps a misfortune of such intimacy and love that it makes one regard all kindness as a matter of course, as one has always found it, as natural as the embrace in meeting."[9]

Sarah's marriage altered neither the frequency of their correspondence nor their desire to be together. In 1864, when twenty-nine, married, and a mother, Sarah wrote to Jeannie: "I shall be entirely alone [this coming week]. I can give you no idea how desperately I shall want you. . . ." After one such visit Jeannie, then a spinster in New York, echoed Sarah's longing: "Dear darling Sarah! How I love you & how happy I have been! You are the joy of my life. . . . I cannot tell you how much happiness you gave me, nor how constantly it is all in my thoughts. . . . My darling how I long for the time when I shall see you. . . ." After another visit Jeannie wrote: "I want you to tell me in your next letter, to assure me, that I am your dearest. . . . I do not doubt you, & I am not jealous but I long to hear you say it once more & it seems already a long time since your voice fell on my ear. So just fill a quarter page with caresses & expressions of endearment. Your silly Angelina." Jeannie ended one letter: "Goodbye my dearest, dearest lover—ever your own Angelina." And another, "I will go to bed . . . [though] I could write all night—A thousand kisses—I love you with my whole soul—your Angelina."

When Jeannie finally married in 1870 at the age of thirty-seven, Sarah underwent a period of extreme anxiety. Two days before Jeannie's marriage Sarah, then in London, wrote desperately: "Dearest darling—How incessantly have I thought of you these eight days—all today—the entire uncertainty, the distance, the long silence—are all new features in my separation from you, grevious to be borne. . . . Oh Jeannie. I have thought & thought & yearned over you these two days. Are you married I wonder? My dearest love to you wherever and *who*ever you are."[10] Like many other women in this collection of thirty-five families, marriage brought Sarah and Jeannie physical separation; it did not cause emotional distance. Although at first they may have wondered how marriage would affect their relationship, their affection remained unabated throughout their lives, underscored by their loneliness and their desire to be together.[11]

During the same years that Jeannie and Sarah wrote of their love and need for each other, two slightly younger women began a similar odyssey of love, dependence, and—ultimately—physical, though not emotional, separation. Molly and Helena met in 1868 while both attended the Cooper Institute School of Design for Women in New York City. For several years these young women studied and explored the city together, visited each other's families, and formed part of a social network of other artistic young women. Gradually, over the years, their initial friendship deepened into a close intimate bond which continued throughout their lives. The tone in the letters which Molly wrote to Helena changed over these years from "My dear Helena," and signed "your attached friend," to "My dearest Helena," "My Dearest," "My Beloved," and signed "Thine always" or "thine Molly."[12]

The letters they wrote to each other during these first five years permit us to reconstruct something of their relationship together. As Molly wrote in one early letter:

> I have not said to you in so many or so few words that I was happy with you during those few so incredibly short weeks but surely you do not need words to tell you what you must know. Those two or three days so dark without, so bright with firelight and contentment within I shall always remember as proof that, for a time, at least—I fancy for quite a long time—we might be sufficient for each other. We know that we can amuse each other for many idle hours together and now we know that we can also work together. And that means much, don't you think so?

She ended: "I shall return in a few days. Imagine yourself kissed many times by one who loved you so dearly."

The intensity and even physical nature of Molly's love was echoed in many of the letters she wrote during the next few years, as, for instance in this short thank-you note for a small present: "Imagine yourself kissed a dozen times my darling. Perhaps it is well for you that we are far apart. You might find my thanks so expressed rather overpowering. I have that delightful feeling that it doesn't matter much what I say or how I say it, since we shall meet so soon and forget in that moment that we were ever separated. . . . I shall see you soon and be content."[13]

At the end of the fifth year, however, several crises occurred. The relationship, at least in its intense form, ended, though Molly and Helena continued an intimate and complex relationship for the next half-century. The exact nature of these crises is not completely clear, but it seems to have involved Molly's decision not to live with Helena, as they had originally planned, but to remain at home because of parental insistence. Molly was now in her late twenties. Helena responded with anger and Molly became frantic at the thought that Helena would break off their relationship. Though she wrote distraught letters and made despairing attempts to see Helena, the relationship never regained its former ardor—possibly because Molly had a male suitor.[14] Within six months Helena had decided to marry a man who was, coincidentally, Molly's friend and publisher. Two years later Molly herself finally married. The letters toward the end of this

period discuss the transition both women made to having male lovers—
Molly spending much time reassuring Helena, who seemed depressed
about the end of their relationship and with her forthcoming marriage.[15]

It is clearly difficult from a distance of 100 years and from a post- Freudian cultural perspective to decipher the complexities of Molly and
Helena's relationship. Certainly Molly and Helena were lovers—emotionally if not physically. The emotional intensity and pathos of their love becomes apparent in several letters Molly wrote Helena during their crisis: "I
wanted so to put my arms round my girl of all the girls in the world and
tell her . . . I love her as wives do love their husbands, as *friends* who
have taken each other for life—and believe in her as I believe in my God.
. . . If I didn't love you do you suppose I'd care about anything or have ridiculous notions and panics and behave like an old fool who ought to
know better. I'm going to hang on to your skirts. . . . You can't get away
from [my] love." Or as she wrote after Helena's decision to marry: "You
know dear Helena, I really was in love with you. It was a passion such as I
had never known until I saw you. I don't think it was the noblest way to
love you." The theme of intense female love was one Molly again expressed in a letter she wrote to the man Helena was to marry: "Do you
know sir, that until you came along I believe that she loved me almost as
girls love their lovers. *I know I loved her so.* Don't you wonder that I can
stand the sight of you." This was in a letter congratulating them on their
forthcoming marriage.[16]

The essential question is not whether these women had genital contact
and can therefore be defined as heterosexual or homosexual. The twentieth-century tendency to view human love and sexuality within a dicho-
tomized universe of deviance and normality, genitality and platonic love,
is alien to the emotions and attitudes of the nineteenth century and fundamentally distorts the nature of these women's emotional interaction. These
letters are significant because they force us to place such female love in a
particular historical context. There is every indication that these four
women, their husbands and families—all eminently respectable and socially conservative—considered such love both socially acceptable and fully
compatible with heterosexual marriage. Emotionally and cognitively,
their heterosocial and their homosocial worlds were complementary.

One could argue, on the other hand, that these letters were but an example of the romantic rhetoric with which the nineteenth century surrounded
the concept of friendship. Yet they possess an emotional intensity and a
sensual and physical explicitness that is difficult to dismiss. Jeannie longed
to hold Sarah in her arms; Molly mourned her physical isolation from
Helena. Molly's love and devotion to Helena, the emotions that bound
Jeannie and Sarah together, while perhaps a phenomenon of nineteenth-
century society were not the less real for their Victorian origins. A survey
of the correspondence and diaries of eighteenth- and nineteenth-century
women indicates that Molly, Jeannie, and Sarah represented one very real
behavioral and emotional option socially available to nineteenth-century
women.

This is not to argue that individual needs, personalities, and family dynamics did not have a significant role in determining the nature of particular relationships. But the scholar must ask if it is historically possible and, if possible, important, to study the intensely individual aspects of psychosexual dynamics. Is it not the historian's first task to explore the social structure and the world view which made intense and sometimes sensual female love both a possible and an acceptable emotional option? From such a social perspective a new and quite different series of questions suggests itself. What emotional function did such female love serve? What was its place within the hetero- and homosocial worlds which women jointly inhabited? Did a spectrum of love-object choices exist in the nineteenth century across which some individuals, at least, were capable of moving? Without attempting to answer these questions it will be difficult to understand either nineteenth-century sexuality or the nineteenth-century family.

Several factors in American society between the mid-eighteenth and the mid-nineteenth centuries may well have permitted women to form a variety of close emotional relationships with other women. American society was characterized in large part by rigid gender-role differentiation within the family and within society as a whole, leading to the emotional segregation of women and men. The roles of daughter and mother shaded imperceptibly and ineluctably into each other, while the biological realities of frequent pregnancies, childbirth, nursing, and menopause bound women together in physical and emotional intimacy. It was within just such a social framework, I would argue, that a specifically female world did indeed develop, a world built around a generic and unself-conscious pattern of single-sex or homosocial networks. These supportive networks were institutionalized in social conventions or rituals which accompanied virtually every important event in a woman's life, from birth to death. Such female relationships were frequently supported and paralleled by severe social  restrictions on intimacy between young men and women. Within such a world of emotional richness and complexity, devotion to and love of other women became a plausible and socially accepted form of human interaction.

An abundance of printed and manuscript sources exists to support such a hypothesis. Etiquette books, advice books on child rearing, religious sermons, guides to young men and young women, medical texts, and school curricula all suggest that late eighteenth- and most nineteenth-century Americans assumed the existence of a world composed of distinctly male and female spheres, spheres determined by the immutable laws of God and nature.[17] The unpublished letters and diaries of Americans during this same period concur, detailing the existence of sexually segregated worlds inhabited by human beings with different values, expectations, and personalities. Contacts between men and women frequently partook of a formality and stiffness quite alien to twentieth-century America and which today we tend to define as "Victorian." Women, however, did not form an isolated and oppressed subcategory in male society. Their letters and diaries indicate that women's sphere had an essential integrity and dignity that grew out of women's shared experiences and mutual affection and

that, despite the profound changes which affected American social structure and institutions between the 1760s and the 1870s, retained a constancy and predictability. The ways in which women thought of and interacted with each other remained unchanged. Continuity, not discontinuity, characterized this female world. Molly Hallock's and Jeannie
Fields's words, emotions, and experiences have direct parallels in the 1760s
and the 1790s.[18] There are indications in contemporary sociological and
psychological literature that female closeness and support networks have
continued into the twentieth century—not only among ethnic and working-class groups but even among the middle class.[19]

Most eighteenth- and nineteenth-century women lived within a world
bounded by home, church, and the institution of visiting—that endless
trooping of women to each others' homes for social purposes. It was a
world inhabited by children and by other women.[20] Women helped each
other with domestic chores and in times of sickness, sorrow, or trouble.
Entire days, even weeks, might be spent almost exclusively with other
women.[21] Urban and town women could devote virtually every day to visits, teas, or shopping trips with other women. Rural women developed a
pattern of more extended visits that lasted weeks and sometimes months,
at times even dislodging husbands from their beds and bedrooms so that
dear friends might spend every hour of every day together.[22] When husbands traveled, wives routinely moved in with other women, invited
women friends to teas and suppers, sat together sharing and comparing
the letters they had received from other close women friends. Secrets were
exchanged and cherished, and the husband's return at times viewed with
some ambivalence.[23]

Summer vacations were frequently organized to permit old friends to
meet at water spas or share a country home. In 1848, for example, a young
matron wrote cheerfully to her husband about the delightful time she was
having with five close women friends whom she had invited to spend the
summer with her; he remained at home alone to face the heat of Philadelphia and a cholera epidemic.[24] Some ninety years earlier, two young
Quaker girls commented upon the vacation their aunt had taken alone
with another woman; their remarks were openly envious and tell us something of the emotional quality of these friendships: "I hear Aunt is gone
with the Friend and wont be back for two weeks, fine times indeed I think
the old friends had, taking their pleasure about the country . . . and have
the advantage of that fine woman's conversation and instruction, while we
poor young girls must spend all spring at home. . . . What a disappointment that we are not together. . . ."[25]

Friends did not form isolated dyads but were normally part of highly integrated networks. Knowing each other, perhaps related to each other,
they played a central role in holding communities and kin systems
together. Especially when families became geographically mobile women's
long visits to each other and their frequent letters filled with discussions of
marriages and births, illness and deaths, descriptions of growing children,
and reminiscences of times and people past provided an important sense of
continuity in a rapidly changing society.[26] Central to this female world
was an inner core of kin. The ties between sisters, first cousins, aunts, and

nieces provided the underlying structure upon which groups of friends and their network of female relatives clustered. Although most of the women within this sample would appear to be living within isolated nuclear families, the emotional ties between nonresidential kin were deep and binding and provided one of the fundamental existential realities of women's lives.[27] Twenty years after Parke Lewis Butler moved with her husband to Louisiana, she sent her two daughters back to Virginia to attend school, live with their grandmother and aunt, and be integrated back into Virginia society.[28] The constant letters between Maria Inskeep and Fanny Hampton, sisters separated in their early twenties when Maria moved with her husband from New Jersey to Louisiana, held their families together, making it possible for their daughters to feel a part of their cousins' network of friends and interests.[29] The Ripley daughters, growing up in western Massachusetts in the early 1800s, spent months each year with their mother's sister and her family in distant Boston; these female cousins and their network of friends exchanged gossip-filled letters and gradually formed deeply loving and dependent ties.[30]

Women frequently spent their days within the social confines of such extended families. Sisters-in-law visited each other and, in some families, seemed to spend more time with each other than with their husbands. First cousins cared for each other's babies—for weeks or even months in times of sickness or childbirth. Sisters helped each other with housework, shopped and sewed for each other. Geographic separation was borne with difficulty. A sister's absence for even a week or two could cause loneliness and depression and would be bridged by frequent letters. Sibling rivalry was hardly unknown, but with separation or illness the theme of deep affection and dependency reemerged.[31]

Sisterly bonds continued across a lifetime. In her old age a rural Quaker matron, Martha Jefferis, wrote to her daughter Anne concerning her own half-sister, Phoebe: "In sister Phoebe I have a real friend—she studies my comfort and waits on me like a child. . . . She is exceedingly kind and this to all other homes (set aside yours) I would prefer—it is next to being with a daughter." Phoebe's own letters confirmed Martha's evaluation of her feelings. "Thou knowest my dear sister," Phoebe wrote, "there is no one . . . that exactly feels [for] thee as I do, for I think without boasting I can truly say that my desire is for thee."[32]

Such women, whether friends or relatives, assumed an emotional centrality in each others' lives. In their diaries and letters they wrote of the joy and contentment they felt in each others' company, their sense of isolation and despair when apart. The regularity of their correspondence underlines the sincerity of their words. Women named their daughters after one another and sought to integrate dear friends into their lives after marriage.[33] As one young bride wrote to an old friend shortly after her marriage: "I want to see you and talk with you and feel that we are united by the same bonds of sympathy and congeniality as ever."[34] After years of friendship one aging woman wrote of another: "Time cannot destroy the fascination of her manner . . . her voice is music to the ear. . . ."[35] Women made elaborate presents for each other, ranging from the Quakers' frugal pies and breads to painted velvet bags and phantom bouquets.[36] When a friend died, their grief was deeply felt. Martha Jefferis was unable to write to her daughter for three weeks because of the sorrow she felt at the death of a dear friend. Such distress was not unusual. A generation earlier a young Massachusetts farm woman filled pages of her diary with her grief at the death of her "dearest friend" and transcribed the letters of condolence other women sent her. She marked the anniversary of Rachel's death each year in her diary, contrasting her faithfulness with that of Rachel's husband who had soon remarried.[37]

These female friendships served a number of emotional functions. Within this secure and empathetic world women could share sorrows, anxieties, and joys, confident that other women had experienced similar emotions. One mid-nineteenth-century rural matron in a letter to her daughter discussed this particular aspect of women's friendships: "To have such a friend as thyself to look to and sympathize with her—and enter into all her little needs and in whose bosom she could with freedom pour forth her joys and sorrows—such a friend would very much relieve the tedium of many a wearisome hour. . . . " A generation later Molly more informally underscored the importance of this same function in a letter to Helena: "Suppose I come down . . . [and] spend Sunday with you quietly," she wrote Helena ". . . that means talking all the time until you are relieved of all your latest troubles, and I of mine. . . . "[38] These were frequently troubles that apparently no man could understand. When Anne Jefferis Sheppard was first married, she and her older sister Edith (who then lived with Anne) wrote in detail to their mother of the severe depression and anxiety which they experienced. Moses Sheppard, Anne's husband, added cheerful postscripts to the sisters' letters—which he had clearly not read—remarking on Anne's and Edith's contentment. Theirs was an emotional world to which he had little access.[39]

This was, as well, a female world in which hostility and criticism of other women were discouraged, and thus a milieu in which women could develop a sense of inner security and self-esteem. As one young woman wrote to her mother's longtime friend: "I cannot sufficiently thank you for the kind unvaried affection & indulgence you have ever shown and expressed both by words and actions for me. . . . Happy would it be did all the world view me as you do, through the medium of kindness and forbearance."[40] They valued each other. Women, who had little status or power in the larger world of male concerns, possessed status and power in the lives and worlds of other women.[41]

An intimate mother-daughter relationship lay at the heart of this female world. The diaries and letters of both mothers and daughters attest to their closeness and mutual emotional dependency. Daughters routinely discussed their mother's health and activities with their own friends, expressed anxiety in cases of their mother's ill health and concern for her cares.[42] Expressions of hostility which we would today consider routine on the part of both mothers and daughters seem to have been uncommon indeed. On the contrary, this sample of families indicates that the normal relationship between mother and daughter was one of sympathy and understanding.[43] Only sickness or great geographic distance was allowed to cause extended separation. When marriage did result in such separation, both viewed the distance between them with distress.[44] Something of this sympathy and love between mothers and daughters is evident in a letter Sarah Alden Ripley, at age sixty-nine, wrote her youngest and recently married daughter: "You do not know how much I miss you, not only when I struggle in and out of my mortal envelop and pump my nightly potation and no longer pour into your sympathizing ear my senile gossip, but all the day I muse away, since the sound of your voice no longer rouses me to sympathy with your joys or sorrows. . . . You cannot know how much I miss your affectionate demonstrations."[45] A dozen aging mothers in this sample of over thirty families echoed her sentiments.

Central to these mother-daughter relations is what might be described as an apprenticeship system. In those families where the daughter followed the mother into a life of traditional domesticity, mothers and other older women carefully trained daughters in the arts of housewifery and motherhood. Such training undoubtedly occurred throughout a girl's childhood but became more systematized, almost ritualistic, in the years following the end of her formal education and before her marriage. At this time a girl either returned home from boarding school or no longer divided her time between home and school. Rather, she devoted her energies on two tasks: mastering new domestic skills and participating in the visiting and social activities necessary to finding a husband. Under the careful supervision of their mothers and of older female relatives, such late-adolescent girls temporarily took over the household management from their mothers, tended their young nieces and nephews, and helped in childbirth, nursing, and weaning. Such experiences tied the generations together in shared skills and emotional interaction.[46]

Daughters were born into a female world. Their mother's life expectations and sympathetic network of friends and relations were among the first realities in the life of the developing child. As long as the mother's domestic role remained relatively stable and few viable alternatives competed with it, daughters tended to accept their mother's world and to turn automatically to other women for support and intimacy. It was within this closed and intimate female world that the young girl grew toward womanhood.

One could speculate at length concerning the absence of that mother-daughter hostility today considered almost inevitable to an adolescent's struggle for autonomy and self-identity. It is possible that taboos against female aggression and hostility were sufficiently strong to repress even that between mothers and their adolescent daughters. Yet these letters seem so alive and the interest of daughters in their mothers' affairs so vital and genuine that it is difficult to interpret their closeness exclusively in terms of repression and denial. The functional bonds that held mothers and daughters together in a world that permitted few alternatives to domesticity might well have created a source of mutuality and trust absent in societies where greater options were available for daughters than for mothers. Furthermore, the extended female network—a daughter's close ties with her own older sisters, cousins, and aunts—may well have permitted a diffusion and a relaxation of mother-daughter identification and so have aided a daughter in her struggle for identity and autonomy. None of these explanations are mutually exclusive; all may well have interacted to produce the degree of empathy evident in those letters and diaries.

At some point in adolescence, the young girl began to move outside the matrix of her mother's support group to develop a network of her own. Among the middle class, at least, this transition toward what was at the same time both a limited autonomy and a repetition of her mother's life seemed to have most frequently coincided with a girl's going to school. Indeed, education appears to have played a crucial role in the lives of most of the families in this study. Attending school for a few months, for a year, or longer, was common even among daughters of relatively poor families, while middle-class girls routinely spent at least a year in boarding school.[47] These school years ordinarily marked a girl's first separation from home. They served to wean the daughter from her home, to train her in the essential social graces, and, ultimately, to help introduce her into the marriage market. It was not infrequently a trying emotional experience for both mother and daughter.[48]

In this process of leaving one home and adjusting to another, the mother's friends and relatives played a key transitional role. Such older women routinely accepted the role of foster mother; they supervised the young girl's deportment, monitored her health and introduced her to their own network of female friends and kin.[49] Not infrequently women, friends from their own school years, arranged to send their daughters to the same school so that the girls might form bonds paralleling those their mothers had made. For years Molly and Helena wrote of their daughters' meeting and worried over each others' children. When Molly finally brought her daughter east to school, their first act on reaching New York was to meet Helena and her daughters. Elizabeth Bordley Gibson virtually adopted the daughters of her school chum, Eleanor Custis Lewis. The Lewis daughters soon began to write Elizabeth Gibson letters with the salutation "Dearest Mama." Eleuthera DuPont, attending boarding school in Philadelphia at roughly the same time as the Lewis girls, developed a parallel relationship with her mother's friend. Elizabeth McKie Smith. Eleuthera went to the same school and became a close friend of the Smith girls and eventually married their first cousin. During this period she routinely called Mrs. Smith "Mother." Indeed, Eleuthera so internalized the sense of having two mothers that she casually wrote her sisters of her "Mamma's" visits at her "mother's" house—that is at Mrs. Smith's.[50]

Even more important to this process of maturation than their mother's friends were the female friends young women made at school. Young girls helped each other overcome homesickness and endure the crises of adolescence. They gossiped about beaux, incorporated each other into their own kinship systems, and attended and gave teas and balls together. Older girls in boarding school "adopted" younger ones, who called them "Mother."[51] Dear friends might indeed continue this pattern of adoption and mothering throughout their lives; one woman might routinely assume the nurturing role of pseudomother, the other the dependency role of daughter. The pseudomother performed for the other woman all the services which we normally associate with mothers; she went to absurd lengths to purchase items her "daughter" could have obtained from other sources, gave advice, and functioned as an idealized figure in her "daughter's" imagination. Helena played such a role for Molly, as did Sarah for Jeannie. Elizabeth Bordley Gibson bought almost all Eleanor Parke Custis Lewis's necessities—from shoes and corset covers to bedding and harp strings—and sent them from Philadelphia to Virginia, a procedure that sometimes took months. Eleanor frequently asked Elizabeth to take back her purchases, have them redone, and argue with shopkeepers about prices. These were favors automatically asked and complied with. Anne Jefferis Sheppard made the analogy very explicitly in a letter to her own mother written shortly after Anne's marriage, when she was feeling depressed about their separation: "Mary Paulen is truly kind, almost acts the part of a mother and trys to aid and *comfort me*, and also to *lighten my new cares.*"[52]

A comparison of the references to men and women in these young women's letters is striking. Boys were obviously indispensable to the elaborate courtship ritual girls engaged in. In these teenage letters and diaries, however, boys appear distant and warded off—an effect produced both by the girl's sense of bonding and by a highly developed and deprecatory whimsy. Girls joked among themselves about the conceit, poor looks, or affectations of suitors. Rarely, especially in the eighteenth and early nineteenth centuries, were favorable remarks exchanged. Indeed, while hostility and criticism of other women were so rare as to seem almost tabooed, young women permitted themselves to express a great deal of hostility toward peer-group men.[53] When unacceptable suitors appeared, girls might even band together to harass them. When one such unfortunate came to court Sophie DuPont she hid in her room, first sending her sister Eleuthera to entertain him and then dispatching a number of urgent notes to her neighboring sister-in-law, cousins, and a visiting friend who all came to Sophie's support. A wild female romp ensued, ending only when Sophie banged into a door, lacerated her nose, and retired, with her female cohorts, to bed. Her brother and the presumably disconcerted suitor were left alone. These were not the antics of teenagers but of women in their early and mid-twenties.[54]

Even if young men were acceptable suitors, girls referred to them formally and obliquely: "The last week I received the unexpected intelligence of the arrival of a friend in Boston," Sarah Ripley wrote in her diary of the young man to whom she had been engaged for years and whom she would shortly marry. Harriet Manigault assiduously kept a lively and gossipy diary during the three years preceding her marriage, yet did not once comment upon her own engagement nor, indeed, make any personal references to her fiance—who was never identified as such but always referred to as Mr. Wilcox.[55] The point is not that these young women were hostile to young men. Far from it; they sought marriage and domesticity. Yet in these letters and diaries men appear as an other or out group, segregated into different schools, supported by their own male network of friends and kin, socialized to different behavior, and coached to a proper formality in courtship behavior. As a consequence, relations between young women and men frequently lacked the spontaneity and emotional intimacy that characterized the young girls' ties to each other.

Indeed, in sharp contrast to their distant relations with boys, young women's relations with each other were close, often frolicsome, and surprisingly long lasting and devoted. They wrote secret missives to each other, spent long solitary days with each other, curled up together in bed at night to whisper fantasies and secrets.[56] In 1862 one young woman in her early twenties described one such scene to an absent friend: "I have sat up to midnight listening to the confidences of Constance Kinney, whose heart was opened by that most charming of all situations, a seat on a bedside late at night, when all the household are asleep only oneself & one's confidante survive in wakefulness. So she has told me all her loves and tried to get some confidences in return but being five or six years older than she, I know better. . . . "[57] Elizabeth Bordley and Nelly Parke Custis, teenagers in Philadelphia in the 1790s, routinely secreted themselves until late each night in Nelly's attic, where they each wrote a novel about the other.[58] Quite a few young women kept diaries, and it was a sign of special friendship to show their diaries to each other. The emotional quality of such exchanges emerges from the comments of one young girl who grew up along the Ohio frontier:

> Sisters CW and RT keep diaries & allow me the inestimable pleasure of reading them and in turn they see mine—but O shame covers my face when I think of it; theirs is so much better than mine, that every time. Then I think well now I *will* burn mine but upon second thought it would deprive me the pleasure of reading theirs, for I esteem it a very great privilege indeed, as well as very improving, as we lay our hearts open to each other, it heightens our love & helps to cherish & keep alive that sweet soothing friendship and endears us to each other by that soft attraction.[59]

Girls routinely slept together, kissed and hugged each other. Indeed, while waltzing with young men scandalized the otherwise flighty and highly fashionable Harriet Manigault, she considered waltzing with other young women not only acceptable but pleasant.[60]

Marriage followed adolescence. With increasing frequency in the nineteenth century, marriage involved a girl's traumatic removal from her mother and her mother's network. It involved, as well, adjustment to a husband, who, because he was male came to marriage with both a different world view and vastly different experiences. Not surprisingly, marriage was an event surrounded with supportive, almost ritualistic, practices. (Weddings are one of the last female rituals remaining in twentieth-century America.) Young women routinely spent the months preceding their marriage almost exclusively with other women—at neighborhood sewing bees and quilting parties or in a round of visits to geographically distant friends and relatives. Ostensibly they went to receive assistance in the practical preparations for their new home—sewing and quilting a trousseau and linen—but of equal importance, they appear to have gained emotional support and reassurance. Sarah Ripley spent over a month with friends and relatives in Boston and Hingham before her wedding; Parke Custis Lewis exchanged visits with her aunts and first cousins throughout Virginia.[61] Anne Jefferis, who married with some hesitation, spent virtually half a year in endless visiting with cousins, aunts, and friends. Despite their reassurance and support, however, she would not marry Moses Sheppard until her sister Edith and her cousin Rebecca moved into the groom's home, met his friends, and explored his personality.[62] The wedding did not take place until Edith wrote to Anne: "I can say in truth I am entirely willing thou shouldst follow him even away in the Jersey sands believing if thou are not happy in thy future home it will not be any fault on his part. . . . "[63]

Sisters, cousins, and friends frequently accompanied newlyweds on their wedding night and wedding trip, which often involved additional family visiting. Such extensive visits presumably served to wean the daughter from her family of origin. As such they often contained a note of ambivalence. Nelly Custis, for example, reported homesickness and loneliness on her wedding trip. "I left my Beloved and revered Grandmamma with sincere regret," she wrote Elizabeth Bordley. "It was sometime before I could feel reconciled to traveling without her." Perhaps they also functioned to reassure the young woman herself, and her friends and kin, that though marriage might alter it would not destroy old bonds of intimacy and familiarity.[64]

Married life, too, was structured about a host of female rituals. Childbirth, especially the birth of the first child, became virtually a *rite de passage*, with a lengthy seclusion of the woman before and after delivery, severe restrictions on her activities, and finally a dramatic reemergence.[65] This seclusion was supervised by mothers, sisters, and loving friends. Nursing and weaning involved the advice and assistance of female friends and relatives. So did miscarriage.[66] Death, like birth, was structured around elaborate unisexed rituals. When Nelly Parke Custis Lewis rushed to nurse her daughter who was critically ill while away at school, Nelly received support, not from her husband, who remained on their plantation, but from her old school friend, Elizabeth Bordley. Elizabeth aided Nelly in caring for her dying daughter, cared for Nelly's other children, played a major role in the elaborate funeral arrangements (which the father did not attend), and frequently visited the girl's grave at the mother's request. For years Elizabeth continued to be the confidante of Nelly's anguished recollections of her lost daughter. These memories, Nelly's letters make clear, were for Elizabeth alone. "Mr. L. knows nothing of this," was a frequent comment.[67] Virtually every collection of letters and diaries in my sample contained evidence of women turning to each other for comfort when facing the frequent and unavoidable deaths of the eighteenth and nineteenth centuries.[68] While mourning for her father's death, Sophie DuPont received elaborate letters and visits of condolence—all from women. No man wrote or visited Sophie to offer sympathy at her father's death.[69] Among rural Pennsylvania Quakers, death and mourning rituals assumed an even more extreme same-sex form, with men or women largely barred from the deathbeds of the other sex. Women relatives and friends slept with the dying woman, nursed her, and prepared her body for burial.

Eighteenth- and nineteenth-century women thus lived in emotional proximity to each other. Friendships and intimacies followed the biological ebb and flow of women's lives. Marriage and pregnancy, childbirth and weaning, sickness and death involved physical and psychic trauma which comfort and sympathy made easier to bear. Intense bonds of love and intimacy bound together those women who, offering each other aid and sympathy, shared such stressful moments.

These bonds were often physical as well as emotional. An undeniably romantic and even sensual note frequently marked female relationships. This theme, significant throughout the stages of a woman's life, surfaced first during adolescence. As one teenager from a struggling pioneer family in the Ohio Valley wrote in her diary in 1808: "I laid with my dear R[ebecca] and a glorious good talk we had until about 4[A.M.]—O how hard I do *love* her. . . . "[71] Only a few years later Bostonian Eunice Callender carved her initials and Sarah Ripley's into a favorite tree, along with a pledge of eternal love, and then waited breathlessly for Sarah to discover and respond to her declaration of affection. The response appears to have been affirmative.[72] A half-century later urbane and sophisticated Katherine Wharton commented upon meeting an old school chum: "She was a great pet of mine at school & I thought as I watched her light figure how often I had held her in my arms—how dear she had once been to me." Katie maintained a long intimate friendship with another girl. When a young man began to court this friend seriously, Katie commented in her diary that she had never realized "how deeply I loved Eng and how fully." She wrote over and over again in that entry: "Indeed I love her!" and only with great reluctance left the city that summer since it meant also leaving Eng with Eng's new suitor.[73]

Peggy Emlen, a Quaker adolescent in Philadelphia in the 1760s, expressed similar feelings about her first cousin, Sally Logan. The girls sent love poems to each other (not unlike the ones Elizabeth Bordley wrote to Nellie Custis a generation later), took long solitary walks together, and even haunted the empty house of the other when one was out of town. Indeed Sally's absences from Philadelphia caused Peggy acute unhappiness. So strong were Peggy's feelings that her brothers began to tease her about her affection for Sally and threatened to steal Sally's letters, much to both girls' alarm. In one letter that Peggy wrote the absent Sally she elaborately described the depth and nature of her feelings: "I have not words to express my impatience to see My Dear Cousin, what would I not give just now for an hours sweet conversation with her, it seems as if I had a thousand things to say to thee, yet when I see thee, everything will be forgot thro' joy. . . . I have a very great friendship for several Girls yet it dont give me so much uneasiness at being absent from them as from thee. . . . [Let us] go and spend a day down at our place together and there unmolested enjoy each others company."[74]

Sarah Alden Ripley, a young, highly educated woman, formed a similar intense relationship, in this instance with a woman somewhat older than herself. The immediate bond of friendship rested on their atypically intense scholarly interests, but it soon involved strong emotions, at least on Sarah's part. "Friendship," she wrote Mary Emerson, "is fast twining about her willing captive the silken hands of dependence, a dependence so sweet who would renounce it for the apathy of self-sufficiency?" Subsequent letters became far more emotional, almost conspiratorial. Mary visited Sarah secretly in her room, or the two women crept away from family and friends to meet in a nearby woods. Sarah became jealous of

Mary's other young woman friends. Mary's trips away from Boston also thrust Sarah into periods of anguished depression. Interestingly, the letters detailing their love were not destroyed but were preserved and even reprinted in a eulogistic biography of Sarah Alden Ripley.

Tender letters between adolescent women, confessions of loneliness and emotional dependency, were not peculiar to Sarah Alden, Peggy Emlen, or Katie Wharton. They are found throughout the letters of the thirty-five families studied. They have, of course, their parallel today in the musings of many female adolescents. Yet these eighteenth- and nineteenth-century friendships lasted with undiminished, indeed often increased, intensity throughout the women's lives. Sarah Alden Ripley's first child was named after Mary Emerson. Nelly Custis Lewis's love for and dependence on Elizabeth Bordley Gibson only increased after her marriage. Eunice Callender remained enamored of her cousin Sarah Ripley for years and rejected as impossible the suggestion by another woman that their love might some day fade away.[76] Sophie DuPont and her childhood friend, Clementina Smith, exchanged letters filled with love and dependency for forty years while another dear friend, Mary Black Couper, wrote of dreaming that she, Sophie, and her husband were all united in one marriage. Mary's letters to Sophie are filled with avowals of love and indications of ambivalence toward her own husband. Eliza Schlatter, another of Sophie's intimate friends, wrote to her at a time of crisis: "I wish I could be with you present in the body as well as the mind & heart—I would turn your *good husband out of bed*—and snuggle into you and we would have a long talk like old times in Pine St.—I want to tell you so many things that are not *writable*. . . . "[77]

Such mutual dependency and deep affection is a central existential reality coloring the world of supportive networks and rituals. In the case of Katie, Sophie, or Eunice—as with Molly, Jeannie, and Sarah—their need for closeness and support merged with more intense demands for a love which was at the same time both emotional and sensual. Perhaps the most explicit statement concerning women's lifelong friendships appeared in the letter abolitionist and reformer Mary Grew wrote about the same time, referring to her own love for her dear friend and lifelong companion, Margaret Burleigh. Grew wrote, in response to a letter of condolence from another woman on Burleigh's death: "Your words respecting my beloved friend touch me deeply. Evidently . . . you comprehend and appreciate, as few persons do . . . the nature of the relation which existed, which exists, between her and myself. Her only surviving niece . . . also does. To me it seems to have been a closer union than that of most marriages. We know there have been other such between two men and also between two women. And why should there not be. Love is spiritual, only passion is sexual."[78]

How then can we ultimately interpret these long-lived intimate female relationships and integrate them into our understanding of Victorian sexuality? Their ambivalent and romantic rhetoric presents us with an ultimate puzzle: the relationship along the spectrum of human emotions between love, sensuality, and sexuality.

One is tempted, as I have remarked, to compare Molly, Peggy, or

Sophie's relationships with the friendships adolescent girls in the twentieth century routinely form—close friendships of great emotional intensity. Helena Deutsch and Clara Thompson have both described these friendships as emotionally necessary to a girl's psychosexual development. But, they warn, such friendships might shade into adolescent and postadolescent homosexuality.[79]

It is possible to speculate that in the twentieth century a number of cultural taboos evolved to cut short the homosocial ties of girlhood and to impel the emerging women of thirteen or fourteen toward heterosexual relationships. In contrast, nineteenth-century American society did not taboo close female relationships but rather recognized them as a socially viable form of human contact—and, as such, acceptable throughout a woman's life. Indeed, it was not these homosocial ties that were inhibited but rather heterosexual leanings. While closeness, freedom of emotional expression, and uninhibited physical contact characterized women's relationships with each other, the opposite was frequently true of male-female relationships. One could thus argue that within such a world of female support, intimacy, and ritual it was only to be expected that adult women would turn trustingly and lovingly to each other. It was a behavior they had observed and learned since childhood. A different type of emotional landscape existed in the nineteenth century, one in which Molly and Helena's love became a natural development.

Of perhaps equal significance are the implications we can garner from this framework for the understanding of heterosexual marriages in the nineteenth century. If men and women grew up as they did in relatively homogeneous and segregated sexual groups, then marriage represented a major problem in adjustment. From this perspective we could interpret much of the emotional stiffness and distance that we associate with Victorian marriage as a structural consequence of contemporary sex-role differentiation and gender-role socialization. With marriage both women and men had to adjust to life with a person who was, in essence, a member of an alien group.

I have thus far substituted a cultural or psychosocial for psychosexual interpretation of women's emotional bonding. But there are psychosexual implications in this model which I think it only fair to make more explicit. Despite Sigmund Freud's insistence on the bisexuality of us all or the recent American Psychiatric Association decision on homosexuality, many psychiatrists today tend explicitly or implicitly to view homosexuality as a totally alien or pathological behavior—as totally unlike heterosexuality. I suspect that in essence they may have adopted an explanatory model similar to the one used in discussing schizophrenia. As a psychiatrist can speak of schizophrenia and of a borderline schizophrenic personality as both ultimately and fundamentally different from a normal or neurotic personality, so they also think of both homosexuality and latent homosexuality as states totally different from heterosexuality. With this rapidly dichotomous model of assumption, "latent homosexuality" becomes the indication of a disease in progress— seeds of a pathology which belie the reality of an individual's heterosexuality.

Yet at the same time we are well aware that cultural values can affect choices in the gender of a person's sexual partner. We, for instance, do not necessarily consider homosexual-object choice among men in prison, on shipboard or in boarding schools a necessary indication of pathology. I would urge that we expand this relativistic model and hypothesize that a number of cultures might well tolerate or even encourage diversity in sexual and nonsexual relations. Based on my research into this nineteenth-century world of female intimacy, I would further suggest that rather than seeing a gulf between the normal and the abnormal, we view sexual and emotional impulses as part of a continuum or spectrum of affect gradations strongly affected by cultural norms and arrangements, a continuum influenced in part by observed and thus learned behavior. At one end of the continuum lies committed heterosexuality, at the other uncompromising homosexuality; between, a wide latitude of emotions and sexual feelings. Certain cultures and environments permit individuals a great deal of freedom in moving across this spectrum. I would like to suggest that the nineteenth century was such a cultural environment. That is, the supposedly repressive and destructive Victorian sexual ethos, may have been more flexible and responsive to the needs of particular individuals than those of mid-twentieth century.

## NOTES

1. The most notable exception to this rule is now eleven years old: William R. Taylor and Christopher Lasch, "Two 'Kindred Spirits': Sorority and Family in New England, 1839–1846," *New England Quarterly* 36 (1963): 25–41. Taylor has made a valuable contribution to the history of women and the history of the family with his concept of "sororial" relations. I do not, however, accept the Taylor-Lasch thesis that female friendships developed in the mid-nineteenth century because of geographic mobility and the breakup of the colonial family. I have found these friendships as frequently in the eighteenth century as in the nineteenth and would hypothesize that the geographic mobility of the mid-nineteenth century eroded them as it did so many other traditional social institutions. Helen Vendler (*Review of Notable American Women, 1607–1950,* ed. Edward James and Janet James, *New York Times*) [November 5, 1972]: sec. 7) points out the significance of these friendships.

2. I do not wish to deny the importance of women's relations with particular men. Obviously, women were close to brothers, husbands, fathers, and sons. However, there is evidence that despite such closeness, relationships between men and women differed in both emotional texture and frequency from those between women. Women's relations with each other, although they played a central role in the American family and American society, have been so seldom examined either by general social historians or by historians of the family that I wish in this article simply to examine their nature and analyze their implications for our understanding of social relations and social structure. I have discussed some aspects of male-female relationships in two articles: "Puberty to Menopause: The Cycle of Femininity in Nineteenth-Century America," *Feminist Studies* 1 (1973): 58–72, and, with Charles Rosenberg, "The Female Animal: Medical and Biological Views of Women in 19th Century America," *Journal of American History* 59 (1973): 331–356.

3. See Freud's classic paper on homosexuality, "Three Essays on the Theory of Sexuality," in *The Standard Edition of the Complete Psychological Works of Sigmund Freud,* trans. James Strachey (London: Hogarth Press, 1953), 7:135–172. The essays originally appeared in 1905. Prof. Roy Shafer, Department of Psychiatry, Yale University, has pointed out that Freud's view of sexual behavior was strongly influenced by nineteenth-century evolutionary thought. Within Freud's schema, genital heterosexuality marked the height of human

development (Schafer, "Problems in Freud's Psychology of Women," *Journal of the American Psychoanalytic Association* 22 [1974]: 459–485.

4. For a novel and most important exposition of one theory of behavioral norms and options and its application to the study of human sexuality, see Charles Rosenberg, "Sexuality, Class and Role," *American Quarterly* 25 (1973): 131–153.

5. See, e.g., the letters of Peggy Emlen to Sally Logan, 1768–1772, Wells Morris Collection, Box 1 Historical Society of Pennsylvania; and the Eleanor Parke Custis Lewis Letters, Historical Society of Pennsylvania, Philadelphia.

6. Sarah Butler Wister was the daughter of Fanny Kemble and Pierce Butler. In 1859 she married a Philadelphia physician, Owen Wister. The novelist Owen Wister is her son. Jeannie Field Musgrove was the half-orphaned daughter of constitutional lawyer and New York Republican politician David Dudley Field. Their correspondence (1859–1898) is in the Sarah Butler Wister Papers, Wister Family Papers, Historical Society of Pennsylvania.

7. Sarah Butler, Butler Place, S.C., to Jeannie Field, New York, September 14, 1855.

8. See, e.g., Sarah Butler Wister, Germantown, Pa., to Jeannie Field, New York, September 25, 1862, October 21, 1863; or Jeannie Field, New York, to Sarah Butler Wister, Germantown, July 3, 1861, January 23 and July 12, 1863.

9. Sarah Butler Wister, Germantown, to Jeannie Field, New York, June 5, 1861, February 29, 1864; Jeannie Field to Sarah Butler Wister November 22, 1861, January 4 and June 14, 1863.

10. Sarah Butler Wister, London, to Jeannie Field Musgrove, New York, June 18 and August 3, 1870.

11. See, e.g., two of Sarah's letters to Jeannie: December 21, 1873, July 16, 1878.

12. This is the 1868–1920 correspondence between Mary Hallock Foote and Helena, a New York friend (the Mary Hallock Foote Papers are in the Manuscript Division, Stanford University). Wallace E. Stegner has written a fictionalized biography of Mary Hallock Foote (*Angle of Repose* [Garden City, N.Y.: Doubleday & Co., 1971]). See, as well, her autobiography: Mary Hallock Foote, *A Victorian Gentlewoman in the Far West: The Reminiscences of Mary Hallock Foote*, ed. Rodman W. Paul (San Marino, Calif.: Huntington Library, 1972). In many ways these letters are typical of those women wrote to other women. Women frequently began letters to each other with salutations such as "Dearest," "My Most Beloved," "You Darling Girl," and signed them "tenderly" or "to my dear dear sweet friend, good-bye." Without the least self-consciousness, one woman in her frequent letters to a female friend referred to her husband as "my other love." She was by no means unique. See, e.g., Annie to Charlene Van Vleck Anderson, Appleton, Wis., June 10, 1871, Anderson Family Papers, Manuscript Division, Stanford University; Maggie to Emily Howland, Philadelphia, July 12, 1851, Howland Family Papers, Phoebe King Collection, Friends Historical Library, Swarthmore College; Mary Jane Burleigh to Emily Howland, Sherwood, N. Y., March 27, 1872, Howland Family Papers, Sophia Smith Collection, Smith College; Mary Black Couper to Sophia Madeleine DuPont; Wilmington, Del.: n.d. [1834] (two letters), Samuel Francis DuPont Papers, Eleutherian Mills Foundation, Wilmington, Del.; Phoebe Middleton, Concordville, Pa., to Martha Jefferis, Chester County , Pa., February 22, 1848; and see in general the correspondence (1838–1849) between Rebecca Biddle of Philadelphia and Martha Jefferis, Chester County, Pa., Jefferis Family Correspondence, Chester County Historical Society, West Chester, Pa.; Phoebe Bradford Diary, June 7 and July 13, 1832, Historical Society of Pennsylvania; Sarah Alden Ripley, to Abba Allyn, Boston, n.d. [1818–1820], and Sarah Alden Ripley to Sophia Bradford, November 30, 1854, in the Sarah Alden Ripley Correspondence, Schlesinger Library, Radcliffe College; Fanny Canby Ferris to Anne Biddle, Philadelphia, October 11 and November 19, 1811, December 26, 1813, Fanny Canby to Mary Canby. May 27, 1801, Mary R. Garrigues to Mary Canby, five letters n.d., [1802–1808], Anne Biddle to Mary Canby, two letters n.d., May 16, July 13, and November 24, 1806, June 14, 1807, June 5, 1808, Anne Sterling Biddle Family Papers, Friends Historical Society, Swarthmore College; Harriet Manigault Wilcox Diary, August 7, 1814, Historical Society of Pennsylvania. See as well the correspondence between Harriet Manigault Wilcox's mother, Mrs. Gabriel Manigault, Philadelphia, and Mrs. Henry Middleton, Charleston, S.C., between 1810 and 1830, Cadwalader Collection, J. Francis Fisher Section, Historical Society of Pennsylvania. The basis and nature of such friendships can be seen in the comments of Sarah Alden Ripley to her sister-in-law and long-time friend, Sophia Bradford: "Hearing that you are not well reminds me of what it would be

to lose your loving society. We have kept step together through a long piece of road in the weary journey of life. We have loved the same beings and wept together over their graves" (Mrs. O. J. Wister and Miss Agnes Irwin, eds., *Worthy Women of Our First Century* [Philadelphia: J. B. Lippincott & Co., 1877] p. 195).

13. Mary Hallock [Foote] to Helena, n.d. [1869–1870], n.d. [1871–1872], Folder 1, Mary Hallock Foote Letters, Manuscript Division, Stanford University.

14. Mary Hallock [Foote] to Helena, September 15 and 23, 1873, n.d. [October 1873], October 12, 1873.

15. Mary Hallock [Foote] to Helena, n.d. [January 1874], n.d. [Spring 1874].

16. Mary Hallock [Foote] to Helena, September 23, 1873; Mary Hallock [Foote] to Richard, December 13, 1873. Molly's and Helena's relationship continued for the rest of their lives. Molly's letters are filled with tender and intimate references, as when she wrote, twenty years later and from 2,000 miles away: "It isn't because you are good that I love you—but for the essence of you which is like perfume" (n.d. [1890s?]).

17. I am in the midst of a larger study of adult gender-roles and gender-role socialization in America, 1785–1895. For a discussion of social attitudes toward appropriate male and female roles, see Barbara Welter, "The Cult of True Womanhood: 1820–1860," *American Quarterly* 18 (Summer 1966): 151–174; Ann Firor Scott, *The Southern Lady: From Pedestal to Politics 1830–1930* (Chicago: University of Chicago Press, 1970), chaps. 1–2; Smith-Rosenberg and Rosenberg.

18. See, e.g., the letters of Peggy Emlen to Sally Logan, 1768–1772, Wells Morris Collection, Box 1, Historical Society of Pennsylvania; and the Eleanor Parke Custis Lewis Letters, Historical Society of Pennsylvania.

19. See esp. Elizabeth Botts, *Family and Social Network* (London: Tavistock Publications, 1957); Michael Young and Peter Willmott, *Family and Kinship in East London*, rev. ed. (Baltimore: Penguin Books, 1964).

20. This pattern seemed to cross class barriers. A letter that an Irish domestic wrote in the 1830s contains seventeen separate references to women and but only seven to men, most of whom were relatives and two of whom were infant brothers living with her mother and mentioned in relation to her mother (Ann McGrann, Philadelphia, to Sophie M. DuPont, Philadelphia, July 3, 1834, Sophie Madeleine DuPont Letters, Eleutherian Mills Foundation).

21. Harriett Manigault Diary, June 28, 1814, and passim; Jeannie Field, New York, to Sarah Butler Wister, Germantown, April 19, 1863; Phoebe Bradford Diary, January 30, February 19, March 4, August 11, and October 14, 1832, Historical Society of Pennsylvania; Sophie M. DuPont, Brandywine, to Henry DuPont, Germantown, July 9, 1827, Eleutherian Mills Foundation.

22. Martha Jefferis to Anne Jefferis Sheppard, July 9, 1843; Anne Jefferis Sheppard to Martha Jefferis, June 28, 1846; Anne Sterling Biddle Papers, passim, Biddle Family Papers, Friends Historical Society, Swarthmore College; Eleanor Parke Custis Lewis, Virginia, to Elizabeth Bordley Gibson, Philadelphia, November 24 and December 4, 1820, November 6, 1821.

23. Phoebe Bradford Diary, January 13, November 16–19, 1832, April 26 and May 7, 1833; Abigail Brackett Lyman to Mrs. Catling, Litchfield, Conn., May 3, 1801, collection in private hands; Martha Jefferis to Anne Jefferis Sheppard, August 28, 1845.

24. Lisa Mitchell Diary, 1860s, passim, Manuscript Division, Tulane University; Eleanor Parke Custis Lewis to Elizabeth Bordley [Gibson] February 5, 1822; Jeannie McCall, Cedar Park, to Peter McCall, Philadelphia, June 30, 1849, McCall Section, Cadwalader Collection, Historical Society of Pennsylvania.

25. Peggy Emlen to Sally Logan, May 3, 1769.

26. For a prime example of this type of letter, see Eleanor Parke Custis Lewis to Elizabeth Bordley Gibson, passim, or Fanny Canby to Mary Canby, Philadelphia, May 27, 1801, or Sophie M. DuPont, Brandywine, to Henry DuPont, Germantown, February 4, 1832.

27. Place of residence is not the only variable significant in characterizing family structure. Strong emotional ties and frequent visiting and correspondence can unite families that do not live under one roof. Demographic studies based on household structure alone fail to reflect such emotional and even economic ties between families.

28. Eleanor Parke Custis Lewis to Elizabeth Bordley Gibson, April 20 and September 25, 1848.

29. Maria Inskeep to Fanny Hampton Correspondence, 1823–1860, Inskeep Collection, Tulane University Library.

30. Eunice Callender, Boston, to Sarah Ripley [Stearns], September 24 and October 29, 1803, February 16, 1805, April 29 and October 9, 1806, May 26, 1810.

31. Sophie DuPont filled her letters to her younger brother Henry (with whom she had been assigned to correspond while he was at boarding school) with accounts of family visiting (see, e.g., December 13, 1827, January 10 and March 9, 1828, February 4 and March 10, 1832; also Sophie M. DuPont to Victorine DuPont Bauday, September 26 and December 4, 1827, February 22, 1828; Sophie M. DuPont, Brandywine, to Clementina B. Smith, Philadelphia, January 15, 1830; Eleuthera DuPont, Brandywine, to Victorine DuPont Bauday, Philadelphia, April 17, 1821, October 20, 1826; Evelina DuPont [Biderman] to Victorine DuPont Bauday, October 18, 1816). Other examples, from the Historical Society of Pennsylvania, are Harriet Manigault [Wilcox] Diary, August 17, September 8, October 19 and 22, December 22, 1814; Jane Zook, Westtown School, Chester County, Pa., to Mary Zook, November 13, December 7 and 11, 1870, February 26, 1871; Eleanor Parke Custis [Lewis] to Elizabeth Bordley [Gibson], March 30, 1796, February 7 and March 20, 1798; Jeannie McCall to Peter McCall, Philadelphia, November 12, 1847; Mary B. Ashew Diary, July 11 and 13, August 17, Summer and October 1858, and, from a private collection, Edith Jefferis to Anne Jefferis Sheppard, November 1841, April 5, 1842; Abigail Brackett Lyman, Northampton, Mass., to Mrs. Catling, Litchfield, Conn., May 13, 1801; Abigail Brackett Lyman, Northampton, to Mary Lord, August 11, 1800. Mary Hallock Foote vacationed with her sister, her sister's children, her aunt, and a female cousin in the summer of 1874; cousins frequently visited the Hallock farm in Milton, N.Y. In later years Molly and her sister Bessie set up a joint household in Boise, Idaho (Mary Hallock Foote to Helena, July [1874?] and passim). Jeannie Field, after initially disliking her sister-in-law, Laura, became very close to her, calling her "my little sister" and at times spending virtually every day with her (Jeannie Field [Musgrove] New York, to Sarah Butler Wister, Germantown, March 1, 8, and 15, and May 9, 1863).

32. Martha Jefferis to Anne Jefferis Sheppard, January 12, 1845; Phoebe Middleton to Martha Jefferis, February 22, 1848. A number of other women remained close to sisters and sisters-in-law across a long lifetime (Phoebe Bradford Diary, June 7, 1832, and Sarah Alden Ripley to Sophia Bradford, cited in Wister and Irwin, p. 195).

33. Rebecca Biddle to Martha Jefferis, 1838–1849, passim; Martha Jefferis to Anne Jefferis Sheppard, July 6, 1846; Anne Jefferis Sheppard to Rachael Jefferis, January 16, 1865; Sarah Foulke Farquhar [Emlen] Diary, September 22, 1813, Friends Historical Library, Swarthmore College; Mary Garrigues to Mary Canby [Biddle], 1802–1808, passim; Anne Biddle to Mary Canby [Biddle], May 16, July 13, and November 24, 1806, June 14, 1807, June 5, 1808.

34. Sarah Alden Ripley to Abba Allyn, n.d., Schlesinger Library.

35. Phoebe Bradford Diary, July 13, 1832.

36. Mary Hallock [Foote] to Helena, December 23 [1868 or 1869]; Phoebe Bradford Diary, December 8, 1832; Martha Jefferis and Anne Jefferis Sheppard letters, passim.

37. Martha Jefferis to Anne Jefferis Sheppard, August 3, 1849; Sarah Ripley [Stearns] Diary, November 12, 1808, January 8, 1811. An interesting note of hostility or rivalry is present in Sarah Ripley's diary entry. Sarah evidently deeply resented the husband's rapid remarriage.

38. Martha Jefferis to Edith Jefferis, March 15, 1841; Mary Hallock Foote to Helena, n.d. [1874–1875?]; see also Jeannie Field, New York, to Sarah Butler Wister, Germantown, May 5, 1863, Emily Howland Diary, December 1879, Howland Family Papers.

39. Anne Jefferis Sheppard to Martha Jefferis, September 29, 1841.

40. Frances Parke Lewis to Elizabeth Bordley Gibson, April 29, 1821.

41. Mary Jane Burleigh, Mount Pleasant, S.C., to Emily Howland, Sherwood, N.Y., March 27, 1872, Howland Family Papers; Emily Howland Diary, September 16, 1879, January 21 and 23, 1880; Mary Black Couper, New Castle, Del., to Sophie M. DuPont, Brandywine, April 7, 1834.

42. Harriet Manigault Diary, August 15, 21 and 23, 1814 Historical Society of Pennsylvania; Polly [Simmons] to Sophie Madeleine DuPont, February 1822; Sophie Madeleine DuPont to Victorine Bauday, December 4, 1827; Sophie Madeleine DuPont to Clementina

Beach Smith, July 24, 1828, August 19, 1829; Clementina Beach Smith to Sophie Madeleine DuPont, April 29, 1831; Mary Black Couper to Sophie Madeleine DuPont, December 24, 1828, July 21, 1834. This pattern appears to have crossed class lines. When a former Sunday school student of Sophie DuPont's (and the daughter of a worker in her father's factory) wrote to Sophie she discussed her mother's health and activities quite naturally (Ann McGrann to Sophie Madeleine DuPont, August 25, 1832; see also Elizabeth Bordley to Martha, n.d. [1797], Eleanor Parke Custis [Lewis] to Elizabeth Bordley [Gibson], May 13, 1796, July 1, 1798; Peggy Emlen to Sally Logan, January 8, 1786. All but the Emlen/Logan letters are in the Eleanor Parke Custis Lewis Correspondence, Historical Society of Pennsylvania).

43. Mrs. S. S. Dalton, "Autobiography," (Circle Valley, Utah, 1876), pp. 21–22, Bancroft Library, University of California, Berkeley; Sarah Foulke Emlen Diary, April 1809; Louisa G. Van Vleck, Appleton, Wis., to Charlena Van Vleck Anderson, Göttingen, n.d. [1875], Harriet Manigault Diary, August 16, 1814, July 14, 1815; Sarah Alden Ripley to Sophy Fisher [early 1860s], quoted in Wister and Irwin (n. 12 above), p. 212. The Jefferis family papers are filled with empathetic letters between Martha and her daughters, Anne and Edith. See, e.g., Martha Jefferis to Edith Jefferis, December 26, 1836, March 11, 1837, March 15, 1841; Anne Jefferis Sheppard to Martha Jefferis, March 17, 1841, January 17, 1847; Martha Jefferis to Anne Jefferis Sheppard, April 17, 1848, April 30, 1849. A representative letter is this of March 9, 1837 from Edith to Martha: "My heart can fully respond to the language of my own precious Mother, that absence has not diminished our affection for each other, but has, if possible, strengthened the bonds that have united us together & I have had to remark how we had been permitted to mingle in sweet fellowship and have been strengthened to bear one another's burdens. . . ."

44. Abigail Brackett Lyman, Boston, to Mrs. Abigail Brackett (daughter to mother), n.d. [1797], June 3, 1800; Sarah Alden Ripley wrote weekly to her daughter, Sophy Ripley Fisher, after the latter's marriage (Sarah Alden Ripley Correspondence, passim): Phoebe Bradford Diary, February 25, 1833, passim, 1832–1833; Louisa G. Van Vleck to Charlena Van Vleck Anderson, December 15, 1873, July 4, August 15 and 29, September 19, and November 9, 1875. Eleanor Parke Custis Lewis's long correspondence with Elizabeth Bordley Gibson contains evidence of her anxiety at leaving her foster mother's home at various times during her adolescence and at her marriage, and her own longing for her daughters, both of whom had married and moved to Louisiana (Eleanor Parke Custis [Lewis] to Elizabeth Bordley [Gibson], October 13, 1795, November 4, 1799, passim, 1820s and 1830s). Anne Jefferis Sheppard experienced a great deal of anxiety on moving two days' journey from her mother at the time of her marriage. This loneliness and sense of isolation persisted through her marriage until, finally a widow, she returned to live with her mother (Anne Jefferis Sheppard to Martha Jefferis, April 1841, October 16, 1842, April 2, May 22, and October 12, 1844, September 3, 1845, January 17, 1847, May 16, June 3, and October 31, 1849; Anne Jefferis Sheppard to Susanna Lightfoot, March 23, 1845, and to Joshua Jefferis, May 14, 1854). Daughters evidently frequently slept with their mothers—into adulthood (Harriet Manigault [Wilcox] Diary, February 19, 1815; Eleanor Parke Custis Lewis to Elizabeth Bordley Gibson, October 10, 1832). Daughters also frequently asked mothers to live with them and professed delight when they did so. See, e.g., Sarah Alden Ripley's comments to George Simmons, October 6, 1844, in Wister and Irwin, p. 185: "It is no longer 'Mother and Charles came out one day and returned the next,' for mother is one of us: she has entered the penetratice, been initiated into the mystery of the household gods, . . . Her divertissement is to mend the stockings . . . whiten sheets and napkins, . . . and take a stroll at evening with me to talk of our children, to compare our experiences, what we have learned and what we have suffered, and, last of all, to complete with pears and melons the cheerful circle about the solar lamp. . . ." We did find a few exceptions to this mother-daughter felicity (M.B. Ashew Diary, November 19, 1857, April 10 and May 17, 1858). Sarah Foulke Emlen was at first very hostile to her stepmother (Sarah Foulke Emlen Diary, August 9, 1807), but they later developed a warm supportive relationship.

45. Sarah Alden Ripley to Sophy Thayer, n.d. [1861].

46. Mary Hallock Foote to Helena [winter 1873] (no. 52); Jossie, Stevens Point, Wis., to Charlena Van Vleck [Anderson], Appleton, Wis., October 24, 1870; Pollie Chandler, Green Bay, Wis., to Charlena Van Vleck [Anderson], Appleton, n.d. [1870]; Eleuthera DuPont to Sophie DuPont, September 5, 1829; Sophie DuPont to Eleuthera DuPont, December 1827; Sophie DuPont to Victorine Bauday, December 4, 1827; Mary Gilpin to Sophie DuPont,

September 26, 1827; Sarah Ripley Stearns Diary, April 2, 1809; Jeannie McCall to Peter Mc-Call, October 27 [late 1840s]. Eleanor Parke Custis Lewis's correspondence with Elizabeth Bordley Gibson describes such an apprenticeship system over two generations—that of her childhood and that of her daughters. Indeed, Eleanor Lewis's own apprenticeship was quite formal. She was deliberately separated from her foster mother in order to spend a winter of domesticity with her married sisters and her remarried mother. It was clearly felt that her foster mother's (Martha Washington) home at the nation's capital was not an appropriate place to develop domestic talents (October 13, 1795, March 30, May 13, and [summer] 1796, March 18 and April 27, 1797, October 1827).

47. Education was not limited to the daughters of the well-to-do. Sarah Foulke Emlen, the daughter of an Ohio Valley frontier farmer, for instance, attended day school for several years during the early 1800s. Sarah Ripley Stearns, the daughter of a shopkeeper in Green-field, Mass., attended a boarding school for but three months, yet the experience seemed very important to her. Mrs. S. S. Dalton, a Mormon woman from Utah, attended a series of poor country schools and greatly valued her opportunity, though she also expressed a great deal of guilt for the sacrifices her mother made to make her education possible (Sarah Foulke Emlen Journal, Sarah Ripley Stearns Diary, Mrs. S. S. Dalton, "Autobiography").

48. Maria Revere to her mother [Mrs. Paul Revere], June 13, 1801, Paul Revere Papers, Massachusetts Historical Society. In a letter to Elizabeth Bordley Gibson, March 28, 1847, Eleanor Parke Custis Lewis from Virginia discussed the anxiety her daughter felt when her granddaughters left home to go to boarding school. Eleuthera DuPont was very homesick when away at school in Philadelphia in the early 1820s (Eleuthera DuPont to Sophie Madeleine DuPont, Wilmington Del., February and April 3, 1821).

49. Elizabeth Bordley Gibson, a Philadelphia matron, played such a role for the daughters and nieces of her lifelong friend, Eleanor Parke Custis Lewis, a Virginia planter's wife (Eleanor Parke Custis Lewis to Elizabeth Bordley Gibson, January 29, 1833, March 19, 1826, and passim through the collection). The wife of Thomas Gurney Smith played a similar role for Sophie and Eleuthera DuPont (see, e.g., Eleuthera DuPont to Sophie Madeleine DuPont, May 22, 1825; Rest Cope to Philema P. Swayne [niece] West Town School, Chester County, Pa., April 8, 1829, Friends Historical Library, Swarthmore College). For a view of such a social pattern over three generations, see the letters and diaries of three generations of Manigault women in Philadelphia: Mrs. Gabrielle Manigault, her daughter, Harriet Manigault Wilcox, and granddaughter, Charlotte Wilcox McCall. Unfortunately the papers of the three women are not in one family collection (Mrs. Henry Middleton, Charleston, S.C., to Mrs. Gabrielle Manigault, n.d. [mid 1800s]; Harriet Manigault Diary, vol. 1; December 1, 1813, June 28, 1814; Charlotte Wilcox McCall Diary, vol. 1, 1842, passim. All in Historical Society of Philadelphia).

50. Frances Parke Lewis, Woodlawn, Va., to Elizabeth Bordley Gibson, Philadelphia, April 11, 1821, Lewis Correspondence; Eleuthera DuPont, Philadelphia, to Victorine DuPont Bauday, Brandywine, December 8, 1821, January 31, 1822; Eleuthera DuPont, Brandywine, to Margaretta Lammont [DuPont], Philadelphia, May 1823.

51. Sarah Ripley Stearns Diary, March 9 and 25, 1810; Peggy Emlen to Sally Logan, March and July 4, 1769; Harriet Manigault [Wilcox] Diary, vol. 1, December 1, 1813, June 28 and September 18, 1814, August 10, 1815; Charlotte Wilcox McCall Diary, 1842, passim; Fanny Canby to Mary Canby, May 27, 1801, March 17, 1804; Deborah Cope, West Town School, to Rest Cope, Philadelphia, July 9, 1828, Chester County Historical Society, West Chester, Pa.; Anne Zook, West Town School, to Mary Zook, Philadelphia, January 30, 1866, Chester County Historical Society, West Chester, Pa.; Mary Gilpin to Sophie Madeleine DuPont, February 25, 1829; Eleanor Parke Custis [Lewis] to Elizabeth Bordley [Gibson], April 27, July 2, and September 8, 1797, June 30, 1799, December 29, 1820; Frances Parke Lewis to Elizabeth Bordley Gibson, December 20, 1820.

52. Anne Jefferis Sheppard to Martha Jefferis, March 17, 1841.

53. Peggy Emlen to Sally Logan, March 1769, Mount Vernon, Va.; Eleanor Parke Custis [Lewis] to Elizabeth Bordley [Gibson], Philadelphia, April 27, 1797, June 30, 1799; Jeannie Field, New York, to Sarah Butler Wister, Germantown, July 3, 1861, January 16, 1863, Harriet Manigault Diary, August 3 and 11–13, 1814; Eunice Callender, Boston, to Sarah Ripley [Stearns], Greenfield, May 4, 1809. I found one exception to this inhibition of female hostili-

ty. This was the diary of Charlotte Wilcox McCall, Philadelphia (see, e.g., her March 23, 1842 entry).

54. Sophie M. DuPont and Eleuthera DuPont, Brandywine, to Victorine DuPont Bauday, Philadelphia, January 25, 1832.

55. Sarah Ripley [Stearns] Diary and Harriet Manigault Diary, passim.

56. Sophie Madeleine DuPont to Eleuthera DuPont, December 1827; Clementina Beach Smith to Sophie Madeleine DuPont, December 26, 1828; Sarah Faulke Emlen Diary, July 21, 1808, March 30, 1809; Annie Hethroe, Ellington, Wis., to Charlena Van Vleck [Anderson], Appleton, Wis., April 23, 1865; Frances Parke Lewis, Woodlawn, Va., to Elizabeth Bordley [Gibson], Philadelphia, December 20, 1820; Fanny Ferris to Debby Ferris, West Town School, Chester County, Pa., May 29, 1826. An excellent example of the warmth of women's comments about each other and the reserved nature of their references to men are seen in two entries in Sarah Ripley Stearns's diary. On January 8, 1811 she commented about a young woman friend: "The amiable Mrs. White of Princeton . . . one of the loveliest most interesting creatures I ever knew, young fair and blooming . . . beloved by everyone . . . formed to please & to charm. . . ." She referred to the man she ultimately married always as "my friend" or "a friend" (February 2 or April 23, 1810).

57. Jeannie Field, New York, to Sarah Butler Wister, Germantown, April 6, 1862.

58. Elizabeth Bordley Gibson, introductory statement to the Eleanor Parke Custis Lewis Letters [1850s], Historical Society of Pennsylvania.

59. Sarah Foulke [Emlen] Diary, March 30, 1809.

60. Harriet Manigault Diary, May 26, 1815.

61. Sarah Ripley [Stearns] Diary, May 17 and October 2, 1812; Eleanor Parke Custis Lewis to Elizabeth Bordley Gibson, April 23, 1826; Rebecca Ralston, Philadelphia, to Victorine Du-Pont [Bauday], Brandywine, September 27, 1813.

62. Anne Jefferis to Martha Jefferis, November 22 and 27, 1840, January 13 and March 17, 1841; Edith Jefferis, Greenwich, N.J., to Anne Jefferis, Philadelphia, January 31, February 6 and February 1841.

63. Edith Jefferis to Anne Jefferis, January 31, 1841.

64. Eleanor Parke Custis Lewis to Elizabeth Bordley, November 4, 1799. Eleanor and her daughter Parke experienced similar sorrow and anxiety when Parke married and moved to Cincinnati (Eleanor Parke Custis Lewis to Elizabeth Bordley Gibson, April 23, 1826). Helena DeKay visited Mary Hallock the month before her marriage; Mary Hallock was an attendant at the wedding; Helena again visited Molly about three weeks after her marriage; and then Molly went with Helena and spent a week with Helena and Richard in their new apartment Mary Hallock [Foote] to Helena DeKay Gilder [Spring 1874] (no. 61), May 10, 1874 [May 1874], June 14, 1874 [Summer 1874]. See also Anne Biddle, Philadelphia, to Clement Biddle (brother), Wilmington, March 12 and May 27, 1827; Eunice Callender, Boston, to Sarah Ripley [Stearns], Greenfield, Mass., August 3, 1807, January 26, 1808; Victorine DuPont Bauday, Philadelphia, to Evelina DuPont [Biderman], Brandywine, November 25 and 26, December 1, 1813; Peggy Emlen to Sally Logan, n.d. (1769–1770?); Jeannie Field, New York, to Sarah Butler Wister, Germantown, July 3, 1861).

65. Mary Hallock to Helena DeKay Gilder [1876] (no. 81); n.d. (no. 83), March 3, 1884; Mary Ashew Diary, vol. 2, September–January, 1860, Louisa Van Vleck to Charlena Van Vleck Anderson, n.d. [1875]; Sophie DuPont to Henry DuPont, July 24, 1827; Benjamin Ferris to William Canby, February 13, 1805; Benjamin Ferris to Mary Canby Biddle, December 20, 1825; Anne Jefferis Sheppard to Martha Jefferis, September 15, 1884; Martha Jefferis to Anne Jefferis Sheppard, July 4, 1843, May 5, 1844, May 3, 1847, July 17, 1849; Jeannie McCall to Peter McCall, November 26, 1847, n.d. [late 1840s]. A graphic description of the ritual surrounding a first birth is found in Abigail Lyman's letter to her husband Erastus Lyman, October 18, 1810.

66. Fanny Ferris to Anne Biddle, November 19, 1811; Eleanor Parke Custis Lewis to Elizabeth Bordley Gibson, November 4, 1799, April 27, 1827; Martha Jefferis to Anne Jefferis Sheppard, January 31, 1843, April 4, 1844; Martha Jefferis to Phoebe Sharpless Middleton, June 4, 1846; Anne Jefferis Sheppard to Martha Jefferis, August 20, 1843, February 12, 1844;

Maria Inskeep, New Orleans, to Mrs. Fanny G. Hampton, Bridgeton, N.J., September 22, 1848; Benjamin Ferris to Mary Canby, February 14, 1805; Fanny Ferris to Mary Canby [Biddle], December 2, 1816.

67. Eleanor Parke Custis Lewis to Elizabeth Bordley Gibson, October –November 1820, passim.

68. Emily Howland to Hannah, September 30, 1866; Emily Howland Diary, February 8, 11, and 27, 1880; Phoebe Brandford Diary, April 12 and 13, and August 4, 1833; Eunice Callender, Boston, to Sarah Ripley [Stearns], Greenwich, Mass., September 11, 1802, August 26, 1810; Mrs. H. Middleton, Charleston, to Mrs. Gabrielle Manigault, Philadelphia, n.d. [mid 1800s]; Mrs. H. C. Paul to Mrs. Jeannie McCall, Philadelphia, n.d. [1840s]; Sarah Butler Wister, Germantown, to Jeannie Field [Musgrove], New York, April 22, 1864; Jeannie Field [Musgrove] to Sarah Butler Wister, August 25, 1861, July 6, 1862; S. B. Randolph to Elizabeth Bordley [Gibson], n.d. [1790s]. For an example of similar letters between men, see Henry Wright to Peter McCall, December 10, 1852; Charles McCall to Peter McCall, January 4, 1860, March 22, 1864; R. Mercer to Peter McCall, November 29, 1872.

69. Mary Black [Couper] to Sophie Madeleine DuPont, February 1827, [November 1, 1834], November 12, 1834, two letters [late November 1834]; Eliza Schlatter to Sophie Madeleine DuPont, November 2, 1834.

70. For a few of the references to death rituals in the Jefferis papers see: Martha Jefferis to Anne Jefferis Sheppard, September 28, 1843, August 21 and September 25, 1844, January 11, 1846, summer 1848, passim; Anne Jefferis Sheppard to Martha Jefferis, August 20, 1843; Anne Jefferis Sheppard to Rachel Jefferis, March 17, 1863, February 9, 1868. For other Quaker families, see Rachel Biddle to Anne Biddle, July 23, 1854; Sarah Foulke Farquhar [Emlen] Diary, April 30, 1811, February 14, 1812; Fanny Ferris to Mary Canby, August 31, 1810. This is not to argue that men and women did not mourn together. Yet in many families women aided and comforted women and men, men. The same-sex death ritual was one emotional option available to nineteenth-century Americans.

71. Sarah Foulke [Emlen] Diary, December 29, 1808.

72,. Eunice Callender, Boston, to Sarah Ripley [Stearns] Greenfield, Mass., May 24, 1803.

73. Katherine Johnstone Brinley [Wharton] Journal, April 26, May 30, and May 29, 1856, Historical Society of Pennsylvania.

74. A series of roughly fourteen letters written by Peggy Emlen to Sally Logan (1768–1771) has been preserved in the Wells Morris Collection, Box 1, Historical Society of Pennsylvania (see esp. May 3 and July 4, 1769, January 8, 1768).

75. The Sarah Alden Ripley Collection, the Arthur M. Schlesinger, Sr., Library, Radcliffe College, contains a number of Sarah Alden Ripley's letters to Mary Emerson. Most of these are undated, but they extend over a number of years and contain letters written both before and after Sarah's marriage. The eulogistic biographical sketch appeared in Wister and Irwin (n. 12 above). It should be noted that Sarah Butler Wister was one of the editors who sensitively selected Sarah's letters.

76. See Sarah Alden Ripley to Mary Emerson, November 19, 1823. Sarah Alden Ripley routinely, and one must assume ritualistically, read Mary Emerson's letters to her infant daughter, Mary. Eleanor Parke Custis Lewis reported doing the same with Elizabeth Bordley Gibson's letters, passim. Eunice Callender, Boston, to Sarah Ripley [Stearns], October 18, 1808.

77. Mary Black Couper to Sophie M. DuPont, March 5, 1832. The Clementina Smith–Sophie DuPont correspondence of 1,678 letters is in the Sophie DuPont Correspondence. The quotation is from Eliza Schlatter, Mount Holly, N.J., to Sophie DuPont, Brandywine, August 24, 1834. I am indebted to Anthony Wallace for informing me about this collection.

78. Mary Grew, Providence, R.I., to Isabel Howland, Sherwood, N.Y., April 27, 1892, Howland Correspondence, Sophia Smith Collection, Smith College.

79. Helena Deutsch, *Psychology of Women* (New York: Grune & Stratton, 1944), vol. 1, chaps. 1–3; Clara Thompson, *On Women*, ed. Maurice Green (New York: New American Library, 1971).

# SELECTED READINGS FOR PART FOUR

BRANCA, PATRICIA. "A New Perspective on Women's Work: A Comparative Typology." *Journal of Social History*, 9 (1975), 129–153.

CHAFE, WILLIAM H. *The American Women*. New York: Oxford University Press, 1972.

CLARK, ALICE. *Working Life of Women in the Seventeenth Century*. 1919. Reprint. New York: Augustus Kelley, 1968.

COTT, NANCY. *The Bonds of Womanhood*. New Haven: Yale University Press, 1977.

DAVIDOFF, LEONORE. "Mastered for Life: Servant and Wife in Victorian and Edwardian England." *Journal of Social History*, 7 (1974), 406–428.

DUBLIN, THOMAS. "Women, Work and the Family: Female Operatives in the Lowell Mills, 1830–1860." *Feminist Studies*, 3 (1975), 30–39.

FILENE, PETER G. *Him, Her, Self: Sex Roles in Modern America*. New York: Mentor, 1974.

KLEINBERG, SUSAN J. "Technology and Women's Work: The Lives of Working-Class Women in Pittsburgh, 1870–1900." *Labor History*, 17 (1976), 58–72.

LERNER, GERDA. "The Lady and the Mill Girl: Changes in the Status of Women in the Age of Jackson." *Midcontinent American Studies*, 10 (1969), 5–14.

OAKLEY, ANN. *Woman's Work*. New York: Pantheon, 1975.

PINCHBECK, IVY. *Women Workers and the Industrial Revolution, 1750–1850*. 1930. Reprint. London: Frank Cass, 1969.

PLECK, ELIZABETH H. "Two Worlds in One: Work and Family." *Journal of Social History*, 10 (1976), 178–195.

SHORTER, EDWARD. "Female Emancipation, Birth Control, and Fertility in European History." *American Historical Review*, 78 (1973), 605–636.

SMITH, DANIEL S. "Family Limitation, Sexual Control, and Domestic Feminism in Victorian America." *Feminist Studies*, 1 (1973), 40–57

SMITH-ROSENBERG, CARROLL, AND CHARLES ROSENBERG. "The Female Animal: Medical and Biological Views of Women and Her Role in Nineteenth-Century America." *Journal of American History*, 60 (1973), 332–356.

STRICKER, FRANK. "Cookbooks and Law Books: The Hidden History of Career Women in Twentieth-Century America." *Journal of Social History*, 10 (1976), 1–19.

UHLENBERG, PETER R. "A Study of Cohort Life Cycles: Cohorts of Native-Born Massachusetts Women, 1830–1920." *Population Studies*, 23 (1969), 404–420.

# PART FIVE | SEX: BEHAVIOR AND IDEOLOGY

Of the four articles included in this section, three appeared in the first edition; this is testimony to both their quality and the fact that sex continues to be a somewhat neglected area. Part of the problem is the relative inaccessibility, historically, of this aspect of life. While demographic records can establish whether or not a couple walked to the altar with the bride already pregnant, and literary sources inform us of what people were told they should and should not do (in the case of legal infraction, e.g., adultery, we can sometimes find out what happened to people who did what they shouldn't have), the more private aspects of sex still elude us. This is why the Mosher interviews used by Carl N. Degler in "What Ought to Be and What Was: Women's Sexuality in the Nineteenth Century" were seen as such a windfall. Yet, one suspects that social historians in years to come will find some way of getting more answers on this topic from our ancestors since they have done so well in other areas.

Edmund Morgan's classic article "The Puritans and Sex" is the only selection in this volume that was published prior to the 1960s; to that extent it might be thought of as an example of the "old" social history of the family. Old or new, it is a fine piece of scholarship and raises serious questions about stereotypes of Puritan sexual attitudes and behavior. Obviously, an important distinction has to be made between the realistic, though by no means permissive, stance taken on these matters by the Puritans and the prudery and downright repressiveness we encounter during the mid-nineteenth century, if only in public statements and law. It is unfortunate that these two distinct periods in the history of America's sexual customs are often lumped together and spoken of as if they were of the same cloth when, in fact, they are very different.

G. J. Barker-Benfield's essay "The Spermatic Economy: A Nineteenth Century View of Sexuality," later elaborated on in his book *The Horrors of the Half-Known Life* (1976), offers a most provocative thesis. Simply put, he maintains that the growth of gynecological surgery, especially the removal of ovaries, was a masculine response to anxieties about male and female sexuality. Similarly, masturbation phobia and the general concern about the "wastage" of semen (hence the title "The Spermatic Economy") also reflect the ambiguity and ambivalence about sexuality during this era. Barker-Benfield traces these phenomena to the conditions of nineteenth-century America, when rapid expansion and great opportunity for individual accomplishment resulted in the home being viewed as a sanctuary from the dangerous outside world in which the struggle to succeed raged (see Welter's article in part four). He takes us from the frontier and factory to the bedroom and the surgery but, perhaps, some of the connections are

361

not as evident as they should be. Were these surgeons reflecting the ideology that Barker-Benfield claims, or were they simply misled by reigning medical misconceptions? A question like this is extraordinarily difficult to answer. Still, the author has confronted an issue few historians or sociologists have the audacity to face. He tries not merely to describe practices but to explain how they are linked to a key motif confronting the society as a whole. Thus this essay offers an interpretation of the sources of nineteenth-century prudery and sexual schizophrenia. Barker-Benfield's work will probably continue to be one of the more controversial papers in this anthology, and this is one of its virtues.

Carl Degler's paper deals with what he sees as a contradiction between what female sexuality was *supposed* to have been like in nineteenth-century America and what his research—drawn largely from a previously undiscovered set of interviews carried out by a female physician—suggest it actually was. We have long been accustomed to an image of Victorian women desiring sex only for procreative purposes and otherwise only tolerating it to mollify their husband's more imperious sexuality. The problem with Degler's paper is that the evidence he brings to bear in challenging this image is drawn almost exclusively from the last quarter of the century, a period which other researchers see as a transitional one during which female sexuality and nonprocreative marital sex gained legitimacy. Nevertheless, by carefully exploring the more general literature of the period, Degler challenges whether, during the earlier part of the century, there was as much behavioral prudery as there was written prudery. This is one of the key questions for scholars interested in American sexuality during the nineteenth century.

For a decade now sociologists have been speaking about a revolution in American sexual behavior that supposedly occurred in the 1920s. This misconception stems largely from the findings of the Kinsey group, though notions of the disruptive effects of World War I on American life are also contributing factors. Daniel Scott Smith's analysis of the facts in "The Dating of the American Sexual Revolution: Evidence and Interpretation" stands in marked contrast to this point of view. He seems to feel that the take-off point for the changes we have been seeing in this area throughout the twentieth century probably occurred in the second half of the nineteenth century. In addition, Smith shows that American sexual behavior has followed a cyclical pattern, with the eighteenth and twentieth centuries being periods which manifest elevated rates of premarital sex—in the case of the eighteenth century, as indicated by bridal pregnancy— though the meaning and context of premarital sex in the eighteenth century was different from today. The author draws upon a variety of sources to fill out his picture of American sexual attitudes and behavior, and he presents us with an excellent discussion of some of the methodological problems encountered in trying to work with historical data.

# 17 | THE PURITANS AND SEX

## EDMUND S. MORGAN

Henry Adams once observed that Americans have "ostentatiously ignored" sex. He could think of only two American writers who touched
upon the subject with any degree of boldness—Walt Whitman and Bret
Harte. Since the time when Adams made this penetrating observation,
American writers have been making up for lost time in a way that would
make Bret Harte, if not Whitman, blush. And yet there is still more truth
than falsehood in Adams's statement. Americans, by comparison with
Europeans or Asiatics, are squeamish when confronted with the facts of
life. My purpose is not to account for this squeamishness, but simply to
point out that the Puritans, those bogeymen of the modern intellectual,
are not responsible for it.

At the outset, consider the Puritans' attitude toward marriage and the
role of sex in marriage. The popular assumption might be that the Puritans
frowned on marriage and tried to hush up the physical aspect of it as much
as possible, but listen to what they themselves had to say. Samuel Willard,
minister of the Old South Church in the latter part of the seventeenth century and author of the most complete textbook of Puritan divinity, more
than once expressed his horror at "that Popish conceit of the Excellency of
Virginity."[1] Another minister, John Cotton, wrote that

> Women are Creatures without which there is no comfortable Living for man: it
> is true of them what is wont to be said of Governments, *That bad ones are bet-
> ter than none:* They are a sort of Blasphemers then who dispise and decry them,
> and call them *a necessary Evil,* for they are *a necessary Good.*[2]

These sentiments did not arise from an interpretation of marriage as a
spiritual partnership, in which sexual intercourse was a minor or incidental matter. Cotton gave his opinion of "Platonic love" when he recalled the
case of

> one who immediately upon marriage, without ever approaching the *Nuptial
> Bed,* indented with the *Bride,* that by mutual consent they might both live such
> a life, and according did sequestring themselves according to the custom of
> those times, from the rest of mankind, and afterwards from one another too, in
> their retired Cells, giving themselves up to a Contemplative life; and this is re-
> corded as an instance of no little or ordinary Vertue; but I must be pardoned in
> it, if I can account it no other than an effort of blind zeal, for they are the dic-
> tates of a blind mind they follow therein, and not of the Holy Spirit, which saith
> *It is not good that man should be alone.*[3]

Here is as healthy an attitude as one could hope to find anywhere. Cotton certainly cannot be accused of ignoring human nature. Nor was he an
isolated example among the Puritans. Another minister stated plainly that

"the Use of the Marriage Bed" is "founded in mans Nature," and that consequently any withdrawal from sexual intercourse upon the part of husband or wife "Denies all reliefe in Wedlock unto Human necessity: and sends it for supply vnto Beastiality when God gives not the gift of Continency."[4] In other words, sexual intercourse was a human necessity and marriage the only proper supply for it. These were the views of the New England clergy, the acknowledged leaders of the community, the most Puritanical of the Puritans. As proof that their congregations concurred with them, one may cite the case in which the members of the First Church of Boston expelled James Mattock because, among other offenses, "he denyed Coniugall fellowship vnto his wife for the space of 2 years together vpon pretense of taking Revenge upon himself for his abusing of her before marryage."[5] So strongly did the Puritans insist upon the sexual character of marriage that one New Englander considered himself slandered when it was reported, "that he Brock his deceased wife's hart with Greife, that he wold be absent from her 3 weeks together when he was at home, and wold never come nere her, and such Like."[6]

There was just one limitation which the Puritans placed upon sexual relations in marriage: sex must not interfere with religion. Man's chief end was to glorify God, and all earthly delights must promote that end, not hinder it. Love for a wife was carried too far when it led a man to neglect his God:

> . . . sometimes a man hath a good affection to Religion, but the love of his wife carries him away, a man may bee so transported to his wife, that hee dare not bee forward in Religion, lest hee displease his wife, and so the wife, lest shee displease her husband, and this is an inordinate love, when it exceeds measure.[7]

Sexual pleasures, in this respect, were treated like other kinds of pleasure. On a day of fast, when all comforts were supposed to be foregone in behalf of religious contemplation, not only were tasty food and drink to be abandoned but sexual intercourse, too. On other occasions, when food, drink and recreation were allowable, sexual intercourse was allowable too, though of course only between persons who were married to each other. The Puritans were not ascetics; they never wished to prevent the enjoyment of earthly delights. They merely demanded that the pleasures of the flesh be subordinated to the greater glory of God: husband and wife must not become "so transported with affection, that they look at no higher end than marriage it self." "Let such as have wives," said the ministers, "look at them not for their own ends, but to be fitted for Gods service, and bring them nearer to God."[8]

Toward sexual intercourse outside marriage the Puritans were as frankly hostile as they were favorable to it in marriage. They passed laws to punish adultery with death, and fornication with whipping. Yet they had no misconceptions as to the capacity of human beings to obey such laws. Although the laws were commands of God, it was only natural—since the fall of Adam—for human beings to break them. Breaches must be punished lest the community suffer the wrath of God, but no offense, sexual or otherwise, could be occasion for surprise or for hushed tones of voice.

How calmly the inhabitants of seventeenth-century New England could contemplate rape or attempted rape is evident in the following testimony offered before the Middlesex County Court of Massachusetts:

> The examination of Edward Wire taken the 7th of october and alsoe Zachery Johnson. who sayeth that Edward Wires mayd being sent into the towne about busenes meeting with a man that dogd hir from about Joseph Kettles house to goody marches. She came into William Johnsones and desired Zachery Johnson to goe home with her for that the man dogd hir. accordingly he went with her and being then as far as Samuell Phips his house the man over tooke them. which man caled himselfe by the name of peter grant would have led the mayd but she oposed itt three times: and coming to Edward Wires house the said grant would have kist hir but she refused itt: wire being at prayer grant dragd the mayd between the said wiers and Nathanill frothinghams house. hee then flung the mayd downe in the streete and got atop hir; Johnson seeing it hee caled vppon the fellow to be sivill and not abuse the mayd then Edward wire came forth and ran to the said grant and took hold of him asking him what he did to his mayd, the said grant asked whether she was his wife for he did nothing to his wife: the said grant swearing he would be the death of the said wire. when he came of the mayd; he swore he would bring ten men to pul down his house and soe ran away and they followed him as far as good[y] phipses house where they mett with John Terry and George Chin with clubs in there hands and soe they went away together. Zachy Johnson going to Constable Heamans, and wire going home. there came John Terry to his house to ask for beer and grant was in the streete but afterward departed into the towne, both Johnson and Wire both aferme that when grant was vppon the mayd she cryed out severall times.
>
> Deborah hadlocke being examined sayth that she mett with the man that cals himselfe peeter grant about good prichards that he dogd hir and followed hir to hir masters and there threw hir downe and lay vppon hir but had not the use of hir body but swore several othes that he would ly with hir and gett hir with child before she got home.
>
> Grant being present denys all saying he was drunk and did not know what he did.[9]

The Puritans became inured to sexual offenses, because there were so many. The impression which one gets from reading the records of seventeenth-century New England courts is that illicit sexual intercourse was fairly common. The testimony given in cases of fornication and adultery—by far the most numerous class of criminal cases in the records—suggests that many of the early New Englanders possessed a high degree of virility and very few inhibitions. Besides the case of Peter Grant, take the testimony of Elizabeth Knight about the manner of Richard Nevars's advances toward her:

> The last publique day of Thanksgiving (in the year 1674) in the evening as I was milking Richard Nevars came to me, and offered me abuse in putting his hand, under my coates, but i turning aside with much adoe, saved my self, and when i was settled to milking he agen took me by the shoulder and pulled me backward almost, but i clapped one hand on the ground and held fast the cows teatt with the other hand, and cryed out, and then came to mee Jonathan Abbot one of my Masters Servants, whome the said Never asked wherefore he came, the said abbot said to look after you, what you doe unto the Maid, but the said Never bid Abbot goe about his businesse but I bade the lad to stay.[10]

One reason for the abundance of sexual offenses was the number of men in the colonies who were unable to gratify their sexual desires in marriage.[11] Many of the first settlers had wives in England. They had come to the new world to make a fortune, expecting either to bring their families after them or to return to England with some of the riches of America. Although these men left their wives behind, they brought their sexual appetites with them; and in spite of laws which required them to return to their families, they continued to stay, and more continued to arrive, as indictments against them throughout the seventeenth century clearly indicate.

Servants formed another group of men, and of women too, who could not ordinarily find supply for human necessity within the bounds of marriage. Most servants lived in the homes of their masters and could not marry without their consent, a consent which was not likely to be given unless the prospective husband or wife also belonged to the master's household. This situation will be better understood if it is recalled that most servants at this time were engaged by contract for a stated period. They were, in the language of the time, "covenant servants," who had agreed to stay with their masters for a number of years in return for a specified recompense, such as transportation to New England or education in some trade (the latter, of course, were known more specifically as apprentices). Even hired servants who worked for wages were usually single, for as soon as a man had enough money to buy or build a house of his own and to get married, he would set up in farming or trade for himself. It must be emphasized, however, that anyone who was not in business for himself was necessarily a servant. The economic organization of seventeenth-century New England had no place for the independent proletarian workman with a family of his own. All production was carried on in the household by the master of the family and his servants, so that most men were either servants or masters of servants; and the former, of course, were more numerous than the latter. Probably most of the inhabitants of Puritan New England could remember a time when they had been servants.

Theoretically no servant had a right to a private life. His time, day or night, belonged to his master, and both religion and law required that he obey his master scrupulously.[12] But neither religion nor law could restrain the sexual impulses of youth, and if those impulses could not be expressed in marriage, they had to be given vent outside marriage. Servants had little difficulty in finding the occasions. Though they might be kept at work all day, it was easy enough to slip away at night. Once out of the house, there were several ways of meeting with a maid. The simplest way was to go to her bedchamber, if she was so fortunate as to have a private one of her own. Thus Jock, Mr. Solomon Phipps's Negro man confessed in court

that on the sixteenth day of May 1682, in the morning, betweene 2 and one of the clock, he did force open the back doores of the House of Laurence Hammond in Charlestowne, and came in to the House, and went up into the garret to Marie the Negro.

He doth likewise acknowledge that one night the last week he forced into the House the same way, and went up to the Negro Woman Marie and that the like he hath done at severall other times before.[13]

Joshua Fletcher took a more romantic way of visiting his lady;

> Joshua Fletcher . . . doth confesse and acknowledge that three severall nights, after bedtime, he went into Mr Fiskes Dwelling house at Chelmsford, at an open window by a ladder that he brought with him. the said windo opening into a chamber, whose was the lodging place of Gresill Juell servant to mr. Fiske. and there he kept company with the said mayd. she sometimes having her cloathes on, and one time he found her in her bed.[14]

Sometimes a maidservant might entertain callers in the parlor while the family were sleeping upstairs. John Knight described what was perhaps a common experience for masters. The crying of his child awakened him in the middle of the night, and he called to his maid, one Sarah Crouch, who was supposed to be sleeping with the child. Receiving no answer, he arose and

> went downe the stayres, and at the stair foot, the latch of doore was pulled in. I called severall times and at the last said if shee would not open the dore, I would breake it open, and when she opened the doore shee was all undressed and Sarah Largin with her undressed, also the said Sarah went out of doores and Dropped some of her clothes as shee went out. I enquired of Sarah Crouch what men they were, which was with them. Shee made mee no answer for some space of time, but at last shee told me Peeter Brigs was with them, I asked her whether Thomas Jones was not there, but shee would give mee no answer.[15]

In the temperate climate of New England it was not always necessary to seek out a maid at her home. Rachel Smith was seduced in an open field "about nine of the clock at night, being darke, neither moone nor starrs shineing." She was walking through the field when she met a man who

> asked her where shee lived, and what her name was and shee told him. and then shee asked his name, and he told her Saijing that he was old Good-man Shepards man. Also shee saith he gave her strong liquors, and told her that it was not the first time he had been with maydes after his master was in bed.[16]

Sometimes, of course, it was not necessary for a servant to go outside his master's house in order to satisfy his sexual urges. Many cases of fornication are on record between servants living in the same house. Even where servants had no private bedroom, even where the whole family slept in a single room, it was not impossible to make love. In fact, many love affairs must have had their consummation upon a bed in which other people were sleeping. Take, for example, the case of Sarah Lepingwell. When Sarah was brought into court for having an illegitimate child, she related that one night when her master's brother, Thomas Hawes, was visiting the family, she went to bed early. Later, after Hawes had gone to bed, he called to her to get him a pipe of tobacco. After refusing for some time,

> at the last I arose and did lite his pipe and cam and lay doune one my one bead and smoaked about half the pip and siting vp in my bead to giue him his pip my bead being a trundell bead at the sid of his bead he reached beyond the pip and Cauth me by the wrist and pulled me on the side of his bead but I biding him let me goe he bid me hold my peas the folks wold here me and if it be replyed come why did you not call out I Ansar I was posesed with fear of my mastar least my

master shold think I did it only to bring a scandall on his brothar and thinking thay wold all beare witnes agaynst me but the thing is true that he did then begete me with child at that tim and the Child is Thomas Hauses and noe mans but his.

In his defense Hawes offered the testimony of another man who was sleeping "on the same side of the bed," but the jury nevertheless accepted Sarah's story.[17]

The fact that Sarah was intimidated by her master's brother suggests that maidservants may have been subject to sexual abuse by their masters. The records show that sometimes masters did take advantage of their position to force unwanted attentions upon their female servants. The case of Elizabeth Dickerman is a good example. She complained to the Middlesex County Court.

against her master John Harris senior for profiring abus to her by way of forsing her to be naught with him: . . . he has tould her that if she tould her dame: what cariag he did show to her shee had as good be hanged and shee replyed then shee would run away and he sayd run the way is before you: . . . she says if she should liwe ther shee shall be in fear of her lif.[18]

The court accepted Elizabeth's complaint and ordered her master to be whipped twenty stripes.

So numerous did cases of fornication and adultery become in seventeenth-century New England that the problem of caring for the children of extramarital unions was a serious one. The Puritans solved it, but in such a way as to increase rather than decrease the temptation to sin. In 1668 the General Court of Massachusetts ordered:

that where any man is legally convicted to be the Father of a Bastard childe, he shall be at the care and charge to maintain and bring up the same, by such assistance of the Mother as nature requireth, and as the Court from time to time (according to circumstances) shall see meet to Order: and in case the Father of a Bastard, by confession or other manifest proof, upon trial of the case, do not appear to the Courts satisfaction, then the Man charged by the Woman to be the Father, shee holding constant in it, (especially being put upon the real discovery of the truth of it in the time of her Travail) shall be the reputed Father, and accordingly be liable to the charge of maintenance as aforesaid (though not to other punishment) notwithstanding his denial, unless the circumstances of the case and pleas be such, on the behalf of the man charged, as that the Court that have the cognizance thereon shall see reason to acquit him, and otherwise dispose of the Childe and education therof.[19]

As a result of this law a girl could give way to temptation without the fear of having to care for an illegitimate child by herself. Furthermore, she could, by a little simple lying, spare her lover the expense of supporting the child. When Elizabeth Wells bore a child, less than a year after this statute was passed, she laid it to James Tufts, her master's son. Goodman Tufts affirmed that Andrew Robinson, servant to Goodman Dexter, was the real father, and he brought the following testimony as evidence:

Wee Elizabeth Jefts aged 15 ears and Mary tufts aged 14 ears doe testyfie that their being one at our hous sumtime the last winter who sayed that thear was a new law made concerning bastards that If aney man wear aqused with a bastard and the woman which had aqused him did stand vnto it in her labor that he should bee the reputed father of it and should mayntaine it Elizabeth Wells hearing of the sayd law she sayed vnto vs that if shee should bee with Child shee would bee sure to lay it vn to won who was rich enough abell to mayntayne it wheather it wear his or no and shee farder sayed Elizabeth Jefts would not you doe so likewise If it weare your case and I sayed no by no means for right must tacke place: and the sayd Elizabeth wells sayed If it wear my caus I think I should doe so.[20]

A tragic unsigned letter that somehow found its way into the files of the Middlesex County Court gives more direct evidence of the practice which Elizabeth Wells professed:

der loue i remember my loue to you hoping your welfar and i hop to imbras the but now i rit to you to let you nowe that i am a child by you and i wil ether kil it or lay it to an other and you shal have no blame at al for I haue had many children and none have none of them. . . . [i.e., none of their fathers is supporting any of them.][21]

In face of the wholesale violation of the sexual codes to which all these cases give testimony, the Puritans could not maintain the severe penalties which their laws provided. Although cases of adultery occurred every year, the death penalty is not known to have been applied more than three times. The usual punishment was a whipping or a fine, or both, and perhaps a branding, combined with a symbolical execution in the form of standing on the gallows for an hour with a rope about the neck. Fornication met with a lighter whipping or a lighter fine, while rape was treated in the same way as adultery. Though the Puritans established a code of laws which demanded perfection—which demanded, in other words, strict obedience to the will of God, they nevertheless knew that frail human beings could never live up to the code. When fornication, adultery, rape, or even buggery and sodomy appeared, they were not surprised, nor were they so severe with the offenders as their codes of law would lead one to believe. Sodomy, to be sure, they usually punished with death; but rape, adultery, and fornication they regarded as pardonable human weaknesses, all the more likely to appear in a religious community, where the normal course of sin was stopped by wholesome laws. Governor Bradford, in recounting the details of an epidemic of sexual misdemeanors in Plymouth, wrote resignedly:

it may be in this case as it is with waters when their streames are stopped or damned up, when they gett passage they flow with more violence, and make more noys and disturbance, then when they are suffered to rune quietly in their owne chanels. So wickednes being here more stopped by strict laws, and the same more nerly looked unto, so as it cannot rune in a comone road of liberty as it would, and is inclined, it searches every wher, and at last breaks out wher it getts vente.[22]

The estimate of human capacities here expressed led the Puritans not only to deal leniently with sexual offenses but also to take every precaution to prevent such offenses, rather than wait for the necessity of punishment. One precaution was to see that children got married as soon as possible. The wrong way to promote virtue, the Puritans thought, was to "ensnare" children in vows of virginity, as the Catholics did. As a result of such vows, children, "not being able to contain," would be guilty of "unnatural pollutions, and other filthy practices in secret: and too oft of horrid Murthers of the fruit of their bodies," said Thomas Cobbett.[23] The way to avoid fornication and perversion was for parents to provide suitable husbands and wives for their children:

> Lot was to blame that looked not out seasonally for some fit matches for his two daughters, which had formerly minded marriage (witness the contract be ween them and two men in *Sodom*, called therfore for his Sons in Law, which had married his daughters, Gen. 19. 14.) for they seeing no man like to come into them in a conjugall way . . . then they plotted that incestuous course, whereby their Father was so highly dishonoured. . . .[24]

As marriage was the way to prevent fornication, successful marriage was the way to prevent adultery. The Puritans did not wait for adultery to appear; instead, they took every means possible to make husbands and wives live together and respect each other. If a husband deserted his wife and remained within the jursidiction of a Puritan government, he was promptly sent back to her. Where the wife had been left in England, the offense did not always come to light until the wayward husband had committed fornication or bigamy, and of course there must have been many offenses which never came to light. But where both husband and wife lived in New England, neither had much chance of leaving the other without being returned by order of the county court at its next sitting. When John Smith of Medfield left his wife and went to live with Patience Rawlins, he was sent home poorer by ten pounds and richer by thirty stripes. Similarly Mary Drury, who deserted her husband on the pretense that he was impotent, failed to convince the court that he actually was so, and had to return to him as well as to pay a fine of five pounds. The wife of Phillip Pointing received lighter treatment: when the court thought that she had overstayed her leave in Boston, they simply ordered her "to depart the Towne and goe to Tanton to her husband." The courts, moreover, were not satisfied with mere cohabitation; they insisted that it be peaceful cohabitation. Husbands and wives were forbidden by law to strike one another, and the law was enforced on numerous occasions. But the courts did not stop there. Henry Flood was required to give bond for good behavior because he had abused his wife simply by "ill words calling her whore and cursing of her." The wife of Christopher Collins was presented for railing at her husband and calling him "Gurley gutted divill." Apparently in this case the court thought that Mistress Collins was right, for although the fact was proved by two witnesses, she was discharged. On another occasion the court favored the husband: Jacob Pudeator, fined for striking and kicking his wife, had the sentence moderated when th court was informed that she was a woman "of great provocation."[25]

Wherever there was strong suspicion that an illicit relation might arise between two persons, the authorities removed the temptation by forbidding the two to come together. As early as November, 1630, the Court of Assistants of Massachusetts prohibited a Mr. Clark from "cohabitacion and frequent keepeing company with Mrs. Freeman, vnder paine of such punishment as the Court shall thinke meete to inflict." Mr. Clark and Mrs. Freeman were both bound "in XX£ apeece that Mr. Clearke shall make his personall appearance att the nexte Court to be holden in March nexte, and in the meane tyme to carry himselfe in good behaviour towards all people and espetially towards Mrs. Freeman, concerneing whome there is stronge suspicion of incontinency." Forty-five years later the Suffolk County Court took the same kind of measure to protect the husbands of Dorchester from the temptations offered by the daughter of Robert Spurr. Spurr was presented by the grand jury

> for entertaining persons at his house at unseasonable times both by day and night to the greife of theire wives and Relations &c The Court having heard what was alleaged and testified against him do Sentence him to bee admonish't and to pay Fees of Court and charge him upon his perill not to entertain any married men to keepe company with his daughter especially James Minott and Joseph Belcher.

In like manner, Walter Hickson was forbidden to keep company with Mary Bedwell, "And if at any time hereafter hee bee taken in company of the saide Mary Bedwell without other company to bee forthwith apprehended by the Constable and to be whip't with ten stripes." Elizabeth Wheeler and Joanna Peirce were admonished "for theire disorderly carriage in the house of Thomas Watts being married women and founde sitting in other mens Laps with theire Armes about theire Necks." How little confidence the Puritans had in human nature is even more clearly displayed by another case, in which Edmond Maddock and his wife were brought to court "to answere to all such matters as shalbe objected against them concerning Haarkwoody and Ezekiell Euerells being at their house at unseasonable tyme of the night and her being up with them after her husband was gone to bed." Haarkwoody and Everell had been found "by the Constable Henry Bridghame about tenn of the Clock at night sitting by the fyre at the house of Edmond Maddocks with his wyfe a suspicious weoman her husband being on sleepe [sic] on the bedd." A similar distrust of human ability to resist temptation is evident in the following order of the Connecticut Particular Court:

> James Hallett is to returne from the Correction house to his master Barclyt, who is to keepe him to hard labor, and course dyet during the pleasure of the Court provided that Barclet is first to remove his daughter from his family, before the sayd James enter therein.

These precautions, as we have already seen, did not eliminate fornication, adultery, or other sexual offenses, but they doubtless reduced the number from what it would otherwise have been.[26]

In sum, the Puritan attitude toward sex, though directed by a belief in absolute, God-given moral values, never neglected human natures. The rules of conduct which the Puritans regarded as divinely ordained had been formulated for men, not for angels and not for beasts. God had created mankind in two sexes; He had ordained marriage as desirable for all, and sexual intercourse as essential to marriage. On the other hand, He had forbidden sexual intercourse outside of marriage. These were the moral principles which the Puritans sought to enforce in New England. But in their enforcement they took cognizance of human nature. They knew well enough that human beings since the fall of Adam were incapable of obeying perfectly the laws of God. Consequently, in the endeavor to enforce those laws they treated offenders with patience and understanding, and concentrated their efforts on prevention more than on punishment. The result was not a society in which most of us would care to live, for the methods of prevention of often caused serious interference with personal liberty. It must nevertheless be admitted that in matters of sex the Puritans showed none of the blind zeal or narrow-minded bigotry which is too often supposed to have been characteristic of them. The more one learns about these people, the less do they appear to have resembled the sad and sour portraits which their modern critics have drawn of them.

## NOTES

1. Samuel Willard, *A Compleat Body of Divinity* (Boston, 1726), 125 and 608–613.

2. John Cotton, *A Meet Help* (Boston, 1699), 14–15.

3. *A Meet Help*, 16.

4. Edward Taylor, Commonplace Book (manuscript in the library of the Massachusetts Historical Society).

5. Records of the First Church in Boston (manuscript copy in the library of the Massachusetts Historical Society), 12.

6. Middlesex County Court Files, folder 42.

7. John Cotton, *A Practical Commentary . . . upon the First Epistle Generall of John* (London, 1656), 126.

8. *A Practical Commentary*, 126.

9. Middlesex Files, folder 48.

10. Middlesex Files, folder 71.

11. Another reason was suggested by Charles Francis Adams in his scholarly article, "Some Phases of Sexual Morality and Church Discipline in Colonial New England," *Proceedings* of the Massachusetts Historical Society, XXVI, 477–516.

12. On the position of servants in early New England see *More Books*, XVII (September, 1942), 311–328.

13. Middlesex Files, folder 99.

14. Middlesex Files, folder 47.

15. Middlesex Files, folder 52.

16. Middlesex Files, folder 44.

17. Middlesex Files, folder 47.

18. Middlesex Files, folder 94.

19. William H. Whitmore, editor, *The Colonial Laws of Massachusetts. Reprinted from the Edition of 1660* (Boston, 1889), 257.

20. Middlesex Files, folder 52.

21. Middlesex Files, folder 30.

22. William Bradford, *History of Plymouth Plantation* (Boston, 1912), n, 309.

23. Thomas Cobbett, *A Fruitfull and Usefull Discourse touching the Honour due from Children to Parents and the Duty of Parents towards their Children* (London, 1656), 174.

24. Cobbett. 177.

25. Samuel E. Morison and Zechariah Chafee, editors, *Records of the Suffolk County Court, 1671–1680, Publications* of the Colonial Society of Massachusetts, XXIX and XXX,

121, 410, 524, 837–841, and 1158; George F. Dow, editor, *Records and File s of the Quarterly Courts of Essex County, Massachusetts* (Salem, 1911–1921), I, 274; and V, 377.

26. *Records of the Suffolk County Court*, 442–443 and 676; John Noble, editor, *Records of the Court of Assistants of the Colony of Massachusetts Bay* (Boston, 1901–1928), II, 8; *Records of the Particular Court of Connecticut, Collections* of the Connecticut Historical Society, XXII, 20; and a photostat in the library of the Massachusetts Historical Society, dated March 29, 1653.

# 18 | THE SPERMATIC ECONOMY: A NINETEENTH-CENTURY VIEW OF SEXUALITY

## G.J. BARKER-BENFIELD

In nineteenth-century America, the world outside the home was regarded by men as "a vast wilderness."[1] They were "naked and alone surrounded by savages";[2] their lives were consumed in "a rage of competitive battle."[3] Democratic leveling in the New World, the disintegration of class stability and of transgenerational family craftsmanship exposed all men to a perplexing choice of identities that they experienced as relentless pressure. Freedom of this kind proved a mortal burden. Potentially everyone could make it; but in effect almost no one could distinguish himself from the ruck of atoms all pressing in the same direction.[4] A man was forced to face this hostile world of relentless competition because he was born with a penis: "the whirl and contact with the world . . . is the inheritance of our sex."[5]

Woman's role as wife and mother was geared to this necessary strife among men. In addition to showing her menfolk a perpetually cheerful smile, a wife was deemed to impart morality to her husband and sons. But morality derived from woman-in-her-world was irrelevant to the life-style to which men were addicted.[6] In fact, women themselves were felt to be a persistently explosive threat to the survival and prosperity of men.

Hence the well-known and otherwise perplexing coexistence of an ideology[7] of male self-sufficiency with that of woman's moral power over men's lives.[8] Placing her on a pedestal symbolized the circumscription in such rhetoric. And from the early 1830s, a son could turn to a stream of self-help expertise from clergymen and assorted medical practitioners, the sheer numbers of whom, together with the numbers of books they sold, bear out the assumption Alexis de Tocqueville made of the irrelevance to men of the mother's educational function.[9] These advice manuals competed with the mother for the allegiance of the son old enough to read: they competed both in authority and in their assumption of the ideal of self-sufficiency. In addition, such experts as Amariah Brigham (1798–1849) and Isaac Ray (1807–1881) carried their challenge to the mother's putative authority in early childbearing. They urged the development of a "bodily constitution possessing extraordinary powers of endurance" to prepare the sons for confrontation with the withering blast of competitive, vicissitudinous democracy.[10] They were also concerned to check the dangerous development of the intellect of girls. Female education was, in the last resort, dispensable since girls should be designed only for robust motherhood.[11]

The Reverend John Todd (1800–1873), author of *The Student's Manual*, was among those offering a young man a program for success. His views of male psychology were typical of all kinds of nineteenth-century American writers from Emerson and Thoreau to John C. Calhoun and Ik Marvell as well as Brigham, Ray, and a host of other doctors including J. Marion Sims and Augustus Kinsley Gardner.

After brief and divisive ministries in Groton, Massachusetts, Northampton, and Philadelphia, Todd settled in Pittsfield in 1842 until his death and held powerful and ecclesiastical sway over his part of Massachusetts. Todd was the subject of Melville's short satire "The Lightning-Rod Man."[12] Melville's attack was based on Todd's role as behavioral stylist for hundreds of thousands, if not millions, of young men. A prolific writer, Todd came to see *The Student's Manual* as his most important work, although he did not see the irony of the book's title; it focused, in the final analysis, on masturbation. Within two years after its publication in 1835 the *Manual* had gone into seven editions; in the twenty-fourth edition of 1854 Todd pointed out that there had "never been less than one edition yearly published in this country." It remained as popular throughout the nineteenth century. Young men came to Todd to acknowledge, "I owe most or all of what I am to your pen."[13]

Paradoxically, Todd told young men how to become self-made. Self-making was the product of will and energy. Energy was one of the most frequent and most characteristic terms associated with male activity in this period (along with its synonyms: vigor, vitality, vital powers, and vital forces). Todd's books constantly break down into rules for the generation, hoarding, and miserly expenditure of "that moving active spirit."[14] Men "are naturally and practically indolent and . . . need powerful stimulants and heavy pressure to awaken their powers and call forth exertions."[15] Dr. Ray said that "most men go through life with a large amount of latent power undeveloped, and utterly unable to concentrate their energies on any particular point." Men needed a "course of suitable discipline,"[16] in addition to the useful "rivalry" and the "pressure" of frightening competition, which Todd asserted "we cannot get at home."[17] Men needed competition in developing a psychic system to defend themselves against the competition which made the system necessary, and so on.

The courses of discipline advocated by Amariah Brigham, Isaac Ray, and John Todd reflected two conventional assumptions about man's being. First was the somatic basis of the mind: the intellect depended on the material body for "vigor and power."[18] Properly developed, the mind itself could stimulate the body's resources: "mental excitement increases the flow of blood to the brain," the organ that "manifested" mind.[19] But too much exercise, too large a flow, could "enfeeble or derange the mind."[20] The second assumption was that the underlying model for the operation of the whole man, psychological and physiological, was economic.[21] Americans shared this convention with Europeans, some of whom Brigham cited. It was, he said, a "fundamental law of the distribution of vital powers . . . that when they are increased in one part, they are diminished in all the rest of the living economy . . . to increase the powers of one organ it is absolutely necessary that they should be diminished in all the others."[22] This law underlay Todd's and Ray's recommendations for the arousing and channeling of energies from latency and waste into self-education, railroading, business—in short, into the "majesty and destiny of Manhood. . . ."[23]

So men were committed to goals that they believed necessarily drove some of them insane. American doctors accepted the dicta of the French psychiatrist, Jean-Dominique Esquirol, that insanity was a disease of civilization, and that the number of the insane was in proportion to civilization's progress. Since America was regarded as the most advanced country, doctors found there the highest incidence of insanity: conditions thought to derange the mind were the unchecked nature of democratic ambitions; a lifetime's enervation by perplexing choice; and the chronic uncertainty of the modern economy. All were pressures experienced most directly by males.[24] Concentration of energies was the inevitable characteristic of the Faustian figures of nineteenth-century literature, from Melville's Ahab to Bradley Headstone in Dickens' *Our Mutual Friend.* In each case, fixity of purpose was described in the specific terms of the contemporary psychological definition of "monomania," the too successful concentration of energies on one "mad mark."[25]

Todd's young man had to be constantly on the watch for opportunities to incorporate energy and at the same time to prevent loss of his energy to others. A chapter in *The Student's Manual* is arranged according to the metaphor of thieves who steal time: for example, the thieves of sloth and sleep. All of one's experiences were reified and quantified into a drum-tight economic system in which every gain was someone's loss, every loss someone else's gain. This seems to have been a projection of the intrapersonal "law of animal economy" on to interpersonal relations.

Todd represented the assimilation of resources to oneself as a specific physical process: the incorporation of material that could be converted into "mental powers." "We want to have the mind continually expanding and creating new thoughts or at least feeding itself on manly thoughts. The food is to the blood, which circulates through your veins, what reading is to the mind."[26] Todd's image for the working of the male body under the stimulus of a properly resolute will was that of a "fountain"[27] of "unequaled . . . inconquerable energy" that showed itself best in the "pure" achievements of railroad building and related extractive industries out West—logging and mining.[28] Hanging on the walls of Todd's study in Pittsfield, where he turned his energy into successful tracts about turning energy, was a phallic arsenal of guns, spears, fishing rods, tools, canes and clubs. In the midst of all stood a covered, five-foot-three-inch high, indoor fountain, self-contained and ever replenished, furnishing the "waters of life." Todd proudly explained "I have only to touch a little brass cock" for the waters to "leap up" and generate "pearls dropping into a well, "golden balls falling into cups of silver."[29] A young man, he said, should regard books as "fountains'" from which he should draw "gold dust," converting his reading into an inner and permanent "fountain." "What you read today, will so be gone—expended or forgotten, and the mind must be continually filled up with new streams of knowledge. . . . It is the hand of the diligent which maketh rich."[30]

That reference to "hand" (where "eye" or "mind" would have seemed more appropriate) brings to mind the constant temptation faced by the young male reader to masturbate. Part of man's difficulty in self-government was his sexual eruptibility. Experts like Dr. Edward Jarvis emphasized that men were naturally appetitive beings who could break out from the social control that, they said, democracy had placed in individual and putatively autonomous hands. One manifestation of this lack of sexual control in men, uniquely recorded in American asylums, was masturbation.[31] The facility with which Todd attacked masturbation was analogous to the facility with which a young male reader found himself masturbating. Todd's work is pervaded with masturbation phobia, explicit and implicit. In the course of willing his energies into the proper channels to replenish or increase his "fountain," a young man was inevitably beset with the temptation to masturbate. The hoarding and concentration of energy—ultimately, of sexual energy—in an obsessively self-sufficient system that was preoccupied with masturbation (i.e., with avoiding it) was very much like the contemporary definition of the autonomous, secretive, addictive habit such a system was designed to avoid.[32] And, in fact, the treatment of masturbation, the absorption of a young man's energies in constructive male tasks, was the same as the course a normal non- (or undiscovered) masturbator would take. An article in the *New Orleans Medical and Surgical Journal* of 1855 described a "young man of fine physical development who wrote good verses and practiced masturbation to excess. [He] asked for medical advice . . . [and] was persuaded to try severe manual labor, he cleared six acres of heavily timbered beech and sugar tree bottoms—was cured and rose to distinction in civil life."[33] Todd's masturbator exactly reversed this productive relation with his surroundings. Instead of feeding one's blood with resources, the masturbator found "vipers" feeding on his own "life's blood."[34] The masturbator's "fountain" became "corrupted," the "ship" of his self-sufficient being having a "worm hole" in it. Clearly there was a proportionate relationship between positive and negative male behaviors. Masturbation was the most thoroughly appropriate sin for a society preoccupied with the autonomous accumulation of male energies (and monomania perhaps the most appropriate and extreme form of its "lunacy").[35]

The discharge of sperm, it was generally believed, "obliterated," "prostrated," and "blotted out" all of "the energies of the system." Instead of "concentrating" those energies onto the nonsexual end of success, the masturbator concentrated what was left of them onto his penis and testicles. "All the remaining energies of animal life seem to be concentrated in these organs, and all the remaining power to gratification left is in the exercise of this . . . loathsome and beastly habit." That the ejaculation of sperm then diminished and exhausted all of the rest of the body's energy suggests that, somehow, in its focusing on the genital organs the previously undefined energy was transformed into sperm.[36]

The significance attached to the ejaculation of sperm reflected an amalgam of popular ideas. Widespread in the eighteenth and nineteenth centuries was the belief in pangenesis—each part of the body contributed a fraction of itself to the sperm by way of the blood. The belief that sperm represented its bearer was probably intensified by Lamarck's elaboration in 1802 of the theory of the hereditability of acquired characteristics, a notion held both popularly and by such luminaries as Charles Lyell, Herbert Spencer, and Charles Darwin.[37] The American sex expert, Dr. Gardner, said in 1872, that sperm was "the concentrated powers of man's perfected being . . . " "Sperm is the purest extract of the blood and according to the expression of Feruel, *totus homo semen est.*"[38]

After mid-century, beliefs about sperm and the body's economy were influenced by the increasingly mechanistic, materialistic views associated with Hermann von Helmholtz's "conservation of force." But views of the body as an economic system, or a system of energies held in equilibrium by reason, "the balance wheel of the mind," were already traditional in the early part of the century. In fact, the application of "conservation of force" to human physiology looked back to Benjamin Rush, for example, with his vascular theory, and forward to Freud via his teachers Brucke, Meynert, and Breuer. American acceptance of Freudian theory, particularly the economy of the libido and sublimation, was governed to a large extent by the way in which they coincided with widespread indigenous views of a very similar kind.[39]

While the system was economic ("the spermatic economy" of the title of this essay), and "spermatic plethora" was, therefore, of some slight concern, that could be dealt with easily by pursuing a normal path of nonsexual activity.[40] The deeper anxiety was spermatic *loss*, with its concomitant losses of will and order. Such a belief made *any* uncontrolled expenditure of sperm potentially dangerous. To its remarks on masturbation, an article signed "W" (Samuel Woodward?) in the *Boston Medical and Surgical Journal* of 1835 added the warning that nature "designs that this drain upon the system [i.e. ejaculation of sperm in copulation] should be reserved to mature age and even then that it should be made but sparingly. . . . Sturdy manhood . . . loses its energy and bends under the too frequent expenditure of this important secretion: and so age or condition will protect a man from the dangers of unlimited indulgence, [even] legally and naturally exercised."[41] Expenditure was the term for which "spend" (i.e., reach orgasm) was the nickname (used, for example, in *Moby Dick* and the anonymous *My Secret Life*). Pangenesis and Lamarckism were expressed in the belief that "runts," feeble infants, and girls would be produced by debilitated sperm, old man's prostrated sperm, businessman's tired sperm, masturbator's exhausted, debaucher's exceeded, contraceptor's impeded, coward's unpatriotic, and newlywed's green, sperm.[42]

In his book, *Conjugal Sins* (1870), Dr. A. K. Gardner (1822–1876) laid out elaborate conditions and precautions for productive nondamaging procreation which reflected the specific stresses and strains of the nineteenth-century American male world and the law of animal economy. *Conjugal Sins* sold 30,000 copies in its first six years[43] and the preface to the ninth edition of 1923 claimed an increasing demand. If one followed its rules to the letter, in the normal run of things one could only copulate at high noon on Sundays. Failure to follow these rules would result in "nervous exhaustion."[44] One only survived if very lucky.

Physicians intervened in the marriage relationship to tell husband and wife that their joint concern was to keep the male's sperm souped up to a particular level of richness. The idea was to use neither more nor less sperm than was necessary for the production of a baby and for the preservation of the richness of sperm at the next copulation. At the same time, very significant concern was given to the appeasing of woman's coital appetite, which demanded the infusion of sperm.[45]

Perhaps the most famous American gynecologist of the nineteenth century, J. Marion Sims (1813–1883), was led to quantify sperm. "I do not know that anyone has thought of measuring the quantity of semen, ejected in the act of copulation. . . . I was induced on several occasions to remove semen with a syringe and to measure it subsequently, and I found that ordinarily there was about a drachm and ten minims."[46] Someone else had followed the logic of the translation of the body's economy into measure, this time of fiscal currency. He was the anonymous English author of *My Secret Life*, who said that on several occasions he stuffed money into a woman's vagina, to have her excrete it into a chamber pot for quantification.[47] Dr. Gardner called sperm "Danaean shower," that is, a shower of procreative gold.[48] The interpenetrative confusion of sexual and economic terms represented the two overriding preoccupations of nineteenth-century Western man, sex and money, which were rapidly becoming the only measures of his identity.[49] They also seemed to promise certain kinds of immortality. The ambiguity of the value of sperm in the author of *My Secret Life's* account also was true of American ideology. Masturbation was "pollution," a "stain," its vehicle a "curse . . . hang[ing] upon a man." Gardner's Danaean shower, a "life-giving emanation" under some conditions, was "unclean excretion" under others.[50]

The notion of concentrating the body's energies, whether on the genitals or on success, suggests how energies were something a man deployed from a preexisting form. In 1870, Dr. J. H. Walters used the word "organization" for such deployment. "In 1850, while yet an under-graduate student of medicine, I could not accept the doctrines of life, at that time generally received and taught. Those doctrines uniformly started with the assumption of some peculiar vital force or forces, either as existing independently of the matter of the organism, or as properties originally 'stamped' upon matters capable of assimilation, and which become phenomenal by the act of organization. How different soever might be the fancies as to the nature and origin of this peculiar force, it was assumed to account for those phenomena which are peculiar to living organisms, such as the development of special forms, nutrition, reproduction, etc.; and also to account for phenomena, it was assumed allowable to endow it with any imaginable property to meet every emergency, such as the capacity of being dormant or depressed on the one hand, or of being excited or stimulated on the other." Among the medical students vulnerable to such generally taught doctrine were Brigham (whose book appeared in Boston just three years before Todd's *Student Manual* in Northampton), Eli Todd and Samuel Woodward (both acknowledged by Todd to have influenced his views on masturbation), and Isaac Ray.[51]

According to Ray, everyone had a "given amount of original endowment," but he needed a course of suitable discipline to bring it to focus.

Such discipline was the willing of Walter's "organization." Todd's work was meant to supply the pattern for such organization. The two concentrations to which Todd addressed himself most insistently, reading and masturbation, occurred as alternatives to one another. The advance of one was at the expense of the other. If the young man followed Todd's advice, he would be able to "call forth the highest efforts of the whole man, body and soul, in enterprise that will do good to men" and over-ridingly, in attaining his own worldly success. One slip of imagination while reading would lead him to the perversion of his energies in masturbation. In short, sublimation, or something very like it, was a general belief long before Freud formulated and refined it. One of the most concise expressions of the pre-Freudian form (which I shall call "proto-sublimation") was Thoreau's in 1854: "the generative which when we are loose, dissipates and makes us unclean, when we are continent invigorates and inspires us." This was Dr. Gardner's version in 1872: the sexual "passion may be restrained within proper limitations. He who indulges in lascivious thoughts may stimulate himself to frenzy; but if his mind were under proper control he would find other employment for it, and his body, obedient to its potent sway, would not become master of the man."[52]

Man's command of the unrefined, passionate part of himself formed the model for his conquest of nature. The Faustian idea of assimilating nature's resources to male powers was again a familiar theme in nineteenth-century history, in Europe as well as in America. It was essentially Marx's and Freud's depiction of bourgeois activity, and it was John C. Calhoun's Kantian vision of the progress of Western man. Almost exactly a century before Freud's formulation of the creation of civilization as the work of male psychical energy, economically withdrawn from women for that purpose. Tocqueville pointed out that American democracy had been first in developing the postindustrial revolution's alignments of work and sex.[53] The barrier between the sexes inside the home extended to a barrier between the homosexual world of work and the (divided) heterosexual life in the family. American men uniquely took "constant care" in maintaining "two clear and distinct lines of action for the sexes." Men were the "head" of the body politic, women its "heart."[54]

Todd said the prayers at the union of the first transcontinental railroad at Promontory Point in 1869. For him this union was "a marriage, consummated under the bright sun."[55] It was sublimation, or "sanctification," according to Todd's own sexual psychology; an all-male equivalent of sexual intercourse, the energies invested in a "work so great it made all other works of this kind seem small and insignificant." Male heroes in the creation of American civilization were, in Todd's view, "taking the materialism of earth, and sanctifying it and making it not merely harmonize with but be a carrier of spiritual things."[56] Todd received one of the rings commemorating the union, made from the gold of the final spike. Its inscription, "The Mountain Wedding, May 10th, 1869,"[57] is evidence of the general assumption of the sexual meaning of ostensibly nonsexual events.

Mining was a second epitome of this proto-sublimation of natural resources, turning them into uncontaminated treasures. Todd's idea of "perfect democracy" was the California mining camps, "perfect" because they were free of women.[58] Melville similarly presented a microcosm of America without women, the *Pequod*, but with a different evaluation of it—its mission was self-destructive. The only man who survived had chosen to withdraw his allegiance from Ahab, and place his "conceit of attainable felicity" in "the wife, the hearth, the bed."[59] But even the men who stayed within settlement could relegate women to the edges of the day, and identify their all-male work world with the Western ideals they created and bought.[60]

At the same time, men like Todd characterized the earth that they worked and exploited as female: "man can turn the coarse of the pit into the hair-spring of the watch, or be able to take Nature in her wild state and turn her wastes into gardens of beauty."[61] This was a view of nature described, for example, by Henry Nash Smith in *Virgin Land*, and apostrophized as sexual in Smith's account of Thomas Hart Benton, one of Todd's idols.[62] Precious metals "laid away in the dark" of the continent's womb had awaited their transfiguration at the hands of man as an expression of his "power . . . to multiply the anthems of heaven to all eternity."[63] Woman's corresponding activity, confined to her own body, was gestation and birth. "If she must go down almost to the grave in a pilgrimage [i.e., gestation] she brings up priceless jewels in which the heart may rejoice to all eternity."[64] Man's infinitely greater work somehow duplicated woman's reproductive power. The meaning becomes clearest in Todd's image for wresting value from reading, the mind's life's blood. It occurs in his discussion of the temptation to masturbate: one had to find the valuable bits in Byron, Todd said, without being seduced into masturbation. "There are beautiful pearls in the slimy bottom of the ocean, but they are found only here and there, and would you dive after them if there were many probabilities that you would stick and die in the mud in which they were imbedded, or if not, that you certainly shorten and embitter life in the process of diving and obtaining them?"[65] Being lured into masturbation was like being trapped and drowned in the slimy, dirty, and dangerous bottom. Yet such a plunge into the depths was a necessary part of proto-sublimation, that is, the discovery, awakening and conversion of latent power. And, again, masturbation was in a contemporary sense simulative of addictive, excessive intercourse which functioned as a drain on the economic system.

Diving for pearls was equivalent to mining for gold and precious stones, Todd's metaphor for all male progress. Dying or sticking in mud doubly evoked the dangers of sexual intercourse: in the first place by way of Todd's deliberate image for masturbation, simulative of copulation; and in the second by way of Todd's often-expressed account of diving for value (or male consummation under the sun) as man's sexless substitute for sexual relations. Both elements were expressions of anxiety over the self-sufficient, "non-sticking" utilization of sexual energy, of which an underlying meaning was the fear of finding oneself held under, being absorbed by a vagina. The image of not getting out of the depths into which one plunged also conjured up the fear of not passing through the dangers of being born, of not being distinguished from woman, from the mass. Woman, Todd said elsewhere, could "lay the foundation of many suns" (for example, George Washington or Napoleon), or she could decide that a "new star" be "quenched shortly and lost in darkness and forgetfulness."[66] Todd eventually came to cope with woman's obliterative power by demanding that she be confined and controlled in the only kind of production he could not duplicate. The common images for the issue of woman's and the continent's body—in this case, precious minerals—linked them together as areas viewed by men as exploitable in the same way, and as expressions of man's mastery over his own resources. Todd also gave vent to the fantasy of doing without muddy woman altogether, in his construction of a fountain self-sufficiently, inexhaustibly "dropping pearls," and in his social ideal, the mining camp.

These assumptions about male activity and its relation to nature were interpenetrative with assumptions about woman and men's relations with her. (I should note that the women with whom this paper is concerned were those whose lives first reflected the effects of the industrial revolution in America through the historically unique role of the nonworking wife, the new trendsetting "women of the future" whom both Tocqueville and the experts took for "all women.")[67] Throughout the century men held some notion of woman as being of both body and mind, although the significance they attached to each greatly varied. In 1832 Brigham articulated anxiety about the social effects of the education of women, on their health, on their offspring, and on the future of society, but, like Todd in the same period, he concentrated on programs for the support and development of the *male* physique and intellect.[68] It was a typical belief that even if women could not govern feeling and affection by their weaker intellects, they did have an innate appetitivelessness that allowed them greater "self control" than men. At the same time "all the various and manifold derangements of the reproductive system, peculiar to females, add to the causes of insanity." It would seem difficult to separate the idea of woman's sexual self-control from this domination of her mind by her sexual organs. The division between woman's relative immunity to "sensuality," and her essential liability to her sexual organs was a version of the well-known two views of woman as sexless and entirely sensual, which represented perhaps men's wish for woman's sexlessness, and the fear out of which that wish originated.[69]

The circumstances that drove *men* to insanity were assumed to be givens of their society and of their sexual role within it. The characteristic disorder of boom and slump was, as Tocqueville put it, an "endemic disease" of the democratic "temperament."[70] The corollary of accepting such conclusions about men was to direct social/medical/psychological expertise at that area of society that was not held by men to be so inalienable as the nature of their own existences, and, consequently was controllable; that is, to direct it at women. And a step beyond that was to concentrate it on that part of woman that made her specially liable to insanity, her sexual organs.

The growing number of workless women and alarm over the possibility that their life-style might become a widespread trend,[71] together with the growing strength of the woman's rights movement intensified male anxieties. As the century wore on it was a function of those anxieties that the medically materialistic therapy of gynecological surgery got under way. The significance men attached to the body part of women increased in proportion to their devaluation of her mind. Dr. Charles Meigs advised his gynecological pupils in 1848 (the year of the first Woman's Rights Convention at Seneca Falls) that their studies necessarily should include woman's psychology, since her generative organs exercised a "strange" influence over her heart, mind, and soul. By 1871, Dr. Horatio Storer represented the general belief quite bluntly. "Woman was what she is [sic] in health, in character, in her charms, alike of body, mind and soul because of her womb alone."[72]

For gynecological purposes women became creatures entirely of body, a conviction expressed by a multitude of euphemisms. Woman's only function was to bear children. After menopause a woman was, in Gardner's words, "degraded to the level of a being who has no further duty to perform in this world."[73] Among the elements in this exclusion of women from the male world of work, rationalized by her psychological unfitness for it, was the fear of doubling the already severe competition that men faced. At the same time, both Todd and Gardner occasionally expressed simple jealousy at the escape of women from that harsh world, even though men demanded it.[74]

Gynecologists' labeling of sexual organs revealed the significance of that familiar synecdoche "the sex." Throughout J. Marion Sims' *Clinical Notes on Uterine Surgery* (1866) the vagina has a "mouth," the womb a "neck" and a "throat," and he compared the cervix to "the tonsils."[75] A woman's reproductive tract stood for her total identity as a man's face stood for his. The only criterion a reasonable man needed to have in selecting a wife was her capacity to bear children. Woman was simply a "natal mechanism," her menses "mechanical action."[76] Sims also advocated a "mechanical view" of sexual intercourse.[77] According to Gardner, frigidity "may or not accompany the act [of coitus]; the result is as independent of sensation"[78] in either case. Mechanically, of course, men had to put up with orgasm; not so women. Sims described the enjoyment of sex as "mere animal sensuality."[79] Doctors' adherence to the notion of the irrelevance of woman's pleasure in copulation and to the idea of her natural frigidity reflected and reinforced the general social belief that "sensuality is unusual in the sex."[80] The phenomenon of vaginismus (a condition where a woman's genitals frigidified or became so painful on being touched that they were impenetrable) was simply a more thoroughgoing version of James Fenimore Cooper's "shrinking delicacy."[81] Defining the absence of sexual desire in woman as normal, doctors came to see its presence as disease, for which some of them tested by manipulating clitoris or breasts.[82] Sexual appetite was a male quality (to be properly channeled of course). If a woman showed it, she resembled a man.

The paradox of confining a woman's identity to the distinction of her sexual organs while at the same time claiming she was sexless should be apparent. Sexless woman was a sexual definition. Men's fantastic and unappeasable demands that women not be what they were rested on what they could not avoid perceiving women to be. So Gardner's assertion that "woman when she has her period takes the greatest care to conceal it from all eyes," above all those of her husband, was a wish that she conform more nearly to the healthy norm of sexlessness. Gardner said woman considered menstruation "a blot or infirmity."[83] That is, an intrinsic part of her being was a temporary, even curable, anomaly. Menstruation, like woman's sexual desire, was a powerful reminder of woman's "animal" nature, a manifestation of "notorious appetite." Woman's menstrual blood was corrupt and virulent, imperiling an unwitting penis with "disease," "excoriations," and "blenorrhagias."[84] Not only was sex dangerous for men, it was dirty, "bestial," and "brutish." Sims, an internationally known gynecologist, hated to examine a woman's pelvic organs; Gardner found no "scenes . . . more appalling that [those] in the obstetric chamber. . . . "[85]

Above all, woman's latent boundlessness posed a threat to male energies, and through them, to civilization. A woman was a sperm absorber, "a drag on the energy, spirits and resolution of her partner."[86] Moreover, the repression of woman's sexual feelings represented sexual and social order generally. It demonstrated to man his subordination of his own dangerous but necessary sexual eruptibility. Desirous woman represented man's loss of control over himself. All women were potentially antagonistic to the fundamental value scheme of society. Female masturbation was universally attacked on the grounds that it raised woman to a state of sexual craving, that is, it made her a threat to men.[87] Even critics of gynecological-surgical excesses reserved the right to castrate "nymphomaniacs."[88] During the earlier phase of masturbation phobia (before the decade preceding the Civil War), the emphasis had been on how masturbation affected *male* health and energy, with no suggestion that masturbation addicted men to heterosexual craving. After mid-century, men became increasingly anxious about female masturbation and developed several drastic techniques to deal with it. Assertion of woman's natural sexlessness was the wishful thinking of men scared spermless, as it were, by woman's potential appetite. "To the man there is a limitation of physical capability which no stimulants from without or within can goad to excess. The erethism [i.e., sexual appetite] of woman has no boundary."[89] Stirred by an unwary bridegroom, allowed to masturbate, or placed in contact with a dance partner at the time of her menstruation, a woman became a vast impending menace: all body, when aroused she became all appetite.[90]

Consistent with the increasing projection of masturbation phobia on to women was the increasing projection on to her of both sexual explosiveness and of the spermatic economy.[91] J. A. Jackson's 1896 article describing the "torture" to a man of the thought of the loss of semen, and the identical anxiety by the anonymous quantifier of nocturnal emissions in 1904 were evidence of the continuation of the spermatic economy tradition (on which projection depended).[92] A.J. Himel's unacknowledged quotation in 1907 of Oliver Wendell Holmes' characterization of hysterical woman was a reminder that the fear of sperm absorbent woman also continued: "A woman of flesh and blood and with infinite variety will, like a vampire drain a man, *nolens volens*, of his life's blood." Himel generalized Holmes' characterization to all women.[93] The inference was that only a woman without flesh and without the blood that corresponds to the blood of the man she was draining would not so debilitate a man. It would seem that part of the fear men had of copulating with a woman at the time of menstruation was that she would be more likely at that time to regain from man's blood what she was losing. (And on the projective side, her loss of blood would remind him of his.) Man's absence of will in this fantasy of Himel's and the inevitability of woman's absorption of man (since all women were of flesh and blood) suggests, too, another aspect of nineteenth-century male psychology generally—a yearning to escape the necessity of facing manhood's relentless destiny, and making woman responsible for the escape.[94]

The connection between contemporary beliefs about the position and function of women and disease and treatment is suggested by the ambiguous term "disorder," used to denote both physical/psychical malfunctions, and social trespasses of a sexual and political kind. Gardner associated his patients, the new, workless women, with the whole range of subversive feminism—Bloomer wearers to women's righters, women doctors and midwives.[95] Todd linked his 1867 attack against contraception and abortion (for which he made women almost entirely responsible) with his attack on women's rights published in the same year. He detected among "the other sex [woman] . . . a widespread uneasiness, a discontentment with woman's lot, impatient of its burdens, rebellious against its sufferings,[with] an undefined hope of emancipation . . . by some great revolution . . . propagating theories, weak, foolish and criminal." The logic of describing woman's independence as "revolutionary" and "criminal" is obvious. Woman was "the sex," her highest and single function, reproduction: therefore contraception and abortion were rebellion against social order. Conversely any demand for social or political rights on the part of a being construed as entirely body was a sexual rebellion. Abortion, according to Todd, was "a direct war against human society, . . . [and] against the family order. . . . "[96] Gardner wrote Conjugal Sins to "Arrest the Rapid Extinction of the American People." Rebellious women threatened the United States with disintegration on the scale of the fall of the Roman Empire.[97]

Todd put such feelings into another historical context. The French Revolution had unleashed, he said, an infidel, fiendish, "voluptuous" and depraved experiment that threatened to dissolve ordered, God-fearing, American society. Revolutionaries had sunk so far as to ordain "the worship of a vile woman." Such "political vandals" still threatened to dismantle the family, the basic unit of order, and "substitute the vagrancy of desire, the rage of lust, and the solicitude [sic; solitude?], and disease and desolution which follow the footsteps of unregulated nature exhausted by excess."[98] Within the obvious fear of a leveled, disordered society were anxieties about isolation and the waste of undisciplined sexual energy, to both of which Todd's behavioral manuals contributed. Gardner's conceptions of the breaking down of the barriers of reason and morality and the abandonment of sexuality to "the hazards of free will," his personification of the will as a ruler with "potent sway" over the body so that it would "not become master of the man"[99] reflected a similar apprehension of a social struggle between hierarchy and anarchy, which, as I have suggested, was a projection of the individual's attempt to discipline and utilize his own bodily powers.

The metaphor of the body-politic linked man's view of the state to his most personal and indestructible source of identity, his body. The rational achievement of civilization seemed to rest on the subordination of the dark passions. Western man's apprehensions of a conflict between order and enthusiasm, reason and passion, head and heart, had been increasing in the period between the Reformation and the eighteenth-century Enlightenment. The Revolutions cut off the head, or at least seemed to bring it closer to the passions, to the genitals. And revolutionary rhetoric promised further leveling. Freud neatly represented what I would regard as a characteristically post-Revolutionary apprehension of the association between head and heart, and order and anarchy: "Civilization behaves towards sexuality as a people or a stratum of its population does which has subjected another one to its exploitation. Fear of a revolt by the suppressed elements drives it to stricter precautionary measures."[100] Freud's previous definition of civilization as male activity clearly put women into the subordinated stratum, just as Marx did. Marx's consideration of the bourgeois' exploitation of "his" wife makes that quite clear. The bourgeoisie was male.[101]

The absence in America of counter traditions of class and other established psychic benchmarks posed more immediate problems for social and individual identity than was the case in the more slowly leveled Europe.[102] (Americans were also denied the modern form of that ethnic identity, nationalism, on which the evolving mass societies in Europe could rely after the French Revolution.) Tocqueville's account of intrafamilial democracy in the relations between fathers and sons was interlocked with the effacement of what he called "class identity."[103] He observed that "hardly anything but money" remained to leveled society as a source of distinction, of identity.[104] He defined that "hardly anything" by suggesting that men fell back on body: as they "relinquish more and more the peculiar opinions and feelings of a caste, a profession, or a family, they simultaneously arrive at something nearer to the constitution of man, which is everywhere the same."[105] America was the freest field for the fulfillment of this tendency. White men constituted themselves the headship of American society on the basis of physiology (namely skin color and genital organs), and charted their superiority according to the differences in beings regarded as naturally lower on the great chain of being—closer to the animal, to dark passions, appetite. That, I think, is the explanation for Todd's reiterated use of the term "emancipation" in 1867 to label the goals of turbulent, revolutionary women. It followed by four years Lincoln's "Emancipation Proclamation."

Sexual identity was the persistent and explicit concern of all kinds of nineteenth-century literature, delineating "a gospel of real manhood and real womanhood."[106] Men's insistence on inexorable difference and separation seems to have indicated an anxiety that such distinctions would not be sustained. Men asseverated the exclusion of women from the arena of individuation-by-success within which men felt themselves so threatened already. A concern for identity based on body provided the authority for the claims by doctors to be social engineers. The reiterated fantasy that independent women could only become men similarly reflected the precarious, solipsistic vulnerability of sexual identity—that any challenge from a different group could only mean that they wanted to become you; that is, they wanted to remove your mark of distinction, your difference from them.

The need to control women in America intensified according to the stresses and strains of the social breakdown described, for example, by the modern historian Robert Wiebe in his account of the "search for order," 1877–1920.[107] In 1867 Todd turned his attention to the sexual transgressions of Anglo-Saxon women, who were aborting and contracepting, denying existence to governors, generals, lawyers, and judges of "our race," to the advantage of alien and "sexually potent" immigrants.[108] Todd's "watchful eye," and that of the native physician, observed that "while our foreign population have large families our own native American families are running out, and at this rate must entirely run out."[109] Todd repeated this fear again and again, as he watched the back-door threat to the long-term and representatively racist, Messianic vision of Anglo-Saxon energies reaching to China.[110] Like Todd, Gardner associated the "flood" of dirty, sexually vicious immigrants with the threat from rebellious women who were, he said, "a tide of error, sin and misery with which the community is being overwhelmed by unholy practices[sic]," flooding up from the lower depths to convert good, holy, and productive sexuality into "bestiality."[111]

The coterminous rise of eugenics and of drastic gynecology[112] were aspects of a renewed and more desperate attempt to control and shape procreative powers as if the American body politic were literally a body. Gardner declared that the "well-being of society demands that means shall be adopted to separate its good elements from the bad." In the future, he said, medical science would enable American men "to separate the pure from the impure."[113] He advocated the execution of all criminals and would have Anglo-Saxon parents reproduce on stock-breeding and stock-raising principles.[114] Restored to the pedestal, women would preserve "the blood of strong races in our veins," produce sons of a new "national physique," and thus "repulse the invaders" (whom Gardner called "dirty" and "effete") all of which would lead in his view to an advance in human rights.[115] One of the most frequent and putatively irrefutable rationales for the castration of women defined as somehow disorderly was that they would cease to contribute to the degeneracy of the American body politic.[116]

Gardner's assertion that it was a "crime" for women to be sick[117] in light of his world-view and of his commitment to the control of women, suggests the historical significance of the phenomenal preeminence of American gynecological surgery in nineteenth-century medical history.[118] It was an expression of the hypostasis of sexual identity. The gynecologists' underlying aims cannot be separated from the society in which they moved: these aims were retaliation against and control of women, and the assumption of as much of their reproductive power as possible,[119] all part and parcel of the projective meaning of the subordination of "the sex."

Late in the 1860s gynecologists began to practice surgical treatment of the psychological disorders of woman, identifying her sexual organs with her whole being. While hideous, Abraham Jacobi's recommendation in 1875 for the creation of a sore on the penis for the discouragement of masturbation in boy children[120] fell far short of the drastic surgery performed on girls' and women's genitals.[121] Clitoridectomy was performed for indications of masturbation and the duplicity associated with it, always with the idea of reestablishing order, regaining control. The British gynecologist who reinvented[122] clitoridectomy in 1858 was expelled from the London Obstetrical Society almost immediately after the published results of his clitoridectomies in 1866, and the operation was not performed in England thereafter.[123] But clitoridectomy was performed in the United States from 1867 (or earlier) until at least 1904, and perhaps until 1925.[124] Circumcision of females coexisted with clitoridectomy in the 1890s, and was widely advocated in response to what was gauged to be a growing incidence of masturbation and other dangerously unappeasable irritations of the clitoris. The operation removed a piece of skin, the "hood" above the clitoris.[125] Circumcision of both girls and adult women continued to be performed in the United States at least until 1937, its fundamental rationale the curbing of woman's masturbation and the unappeasable erethism induced by unsatisfactory intercourse.[126]

The difference in the recognition accorded clitoridectomy in England and America, and the length of time between the acceptance of contraception in each country,[127] were perhaps measures of the difference in attitudes toward women, and in the difference in pressures felt by men; so, too, the respective acceptance and elimination of the midwife. She was given governmental recognition and institutional status early in the twentieth century in England, where obstetrics is today the domain of women. American gynecologists reached the climax of their hundred years' war against midwives in the first two decades of the twentieth century, implementing a legislative and propaganda campaign, the latter to persuade women that "normal" pregnancy and parturition were the exception, and childbirth a "wound" that only the expertise of males could master. Midwives were finally driven out before World War II, and in 1968, 99 percent of all preganant women were delivered by men.[128]

A third surgical treatment of women's psychology was female castration, invented by Robert Battey of Rome, Georgia, in 1872.[129] Battey called it "normal ovariotomy" because this excision of the ovaries was indicated by nonovarian conditions—neurosis, insanity, abnormal menstruation, and practically anything untoward in female behavior. Among the indications were troublesomeness, eating like a ploughman, masturbation, attempted suicide, erotic tendencies, persecution mania, simple "cussedness," and dysmenorrhoea (painful menstruation, long held to be one consequence of masturbation). Most apparent in the enormous variety of symptoms doctors took to indicate castration was a strong current of sexual appetitiveness on the part of women. That is, castratable women evinced a quality held to be characteristic of men.[130]

Female castration was a very much more widespread and frequently performed operation in America than clitoridectomy. Women were castrated from New York to New Orleans, Youngs Crossroads in South Carolina to Ottumwa and Keokuk in Iowa, from Philadelphia to Portland, Oregon, from Boston to Los Angeles and San Francisco. Battey performed the first female castration in 1872 and the record continued until at least 1921. Infinitely more operations were performed than were written up and published. By the early 1890s female castration had reached the proportions of an "epidemic," a "rage," a "thriving industry,"[131] and continued to be performed in spite of the opposition that had begun in the early 1890s. A major part of the opposition was based on the rise of "conservative ovarian surgery," which itself came under fire for puncturing, burning, resecting and otherwise tampering with ovaries, and therefore can be placed in the same context with the operation it was largely introduced to replace.[132] Indeed, female castration gave way to further drastic gynecological surgery including salpingectomy (extirpation of the Fallopian tubes), hysterectomy, and the transplanting of ovaries. (The latter operation depended on the availability of "normal ovaries," that is, on Battey's operation and was initially performed, to a considerable extent, to solve the problems created by Battey's operation.[133] So gynecological transplanters were part of a cycle perpetuated by gynecologists who created and cured "their" own symptoms.) Doctors competed with each other in the number of ovaries they extirpated, and handed them around at medical society meetings on plates like trophies.[134] It was estimated in 1906 that for every one of the one hundred and fifty thousand doctors in the U.S. there was one sterilized woman; and "some of this large number [of doctors] have openly boasted . . . that they have removed from fifteen hundred to two thousand ovaries."[135]

In addition to the sheer volume, duration, and geographical spread of female castration, and the meanings of physicians' rhetoric explaining, advocating and justifying it, a salient feature of the operation was the early recognition of its failure to cure (indeed, of its tendency to exaggerate previous symptoms and to drive women insane). Battey quite soon tried to modify his initial assertion that the removal of normal, healthy ovaries for insanity was justified by arguing that *after* the operations had been performed the ovaries were always found to be diseased or abnormal.[136] That ground also crumbled as other gynecologists slowly came to realize that a *normal* ovary could be encysted, inflamed, enlarged, prolapsed and anteflexed, all of which had been regarded as indications of abnormalcy and disease.[137] In any case, Battey and other proponents of wholesale female castration continued to extirpate healthy ovaries for nonovarian indications.

Gynecologists treated their patients as if they were rebels or criminals. Defending the continued performance of demonstratedly useless castration, and suggesting that the operation would be effective if it included extirpation of the womb thus made useless, Dr. Arnold Praeger stated in 1895 that the "principles of surgery . . . resemble justice."[138] Dr. David Gilliam making a plea in 1896 for the "More General Adoption of Oophorectomy" applied the lesson of the beneficial effects of the castration of animals to the castration of women. "Why do we alter our colts and calves? Not that we expect to abate strength or endurance, nor yet to render them less intelligent; but that we may make them tractable and trustworthy, that we may convert them into faithful, well disposed servants." Bulls, and men, he said, were naturally and should remain belligerent. Like the other gynecologists, he integrated his surgical vision with the spermatic economy, of which his statement was even more concise than Thoreau's. "It is the equity of nature; procreative power and mental energy are inverse." But an emasculated creature's remaining sexual passion was "tempered with prudence and tame besides the fierce energy of untethered masculinity." Castrated women became "tractable, orderly, industrious and cleanly." A wife should be a faithful servant, as tractable and undemanding as a castrated animal.[139] In short, Gilliam justified female castration as a way of returning women to that ideally repressed and circumscribed self of Tocqueville's account and Todd's and Gardner's dreams. Many of the patients for whom doctor and husband claimed a cure had exhibited symptoms of unmanageableness at home, and were deemed "cured" when they were restored to their husband's management after castration.

Gynecologists' authority in matters pertaining to control of woman's disorders was much harder to dispute than husbands'. So it may well be that disorderly women were handed over to the gynecologist for castration by husbands unable to enforce their minimum identity guarantee. Women by and large shared men's beliefs about roles and social order; if such beliefs drove them inevitably to disorder, they went to the proper authorities. Many of the case reports describe husband and friends pressuring the woman to obtain freedom from "disorder," much as Tocqueville described the young woman pressured toward the yoke of marriage.[140]

Castrated patients were rich enough to afford a gynecologist, and all seem to have been nonworkers, homebodies; a high proportion was addicted to morphine or brandy, and quite a few were bedridden.[141] They seem to have been those women left workless by the change in work patterns accelerated by the industrial revolution, and reenslaved as possessions.[142] Moreover, the ascription by these women of their disorder (that is, of social displacement, and a lack of a sense of personal value and identity) to their sex organs reflected the male assumption that their identity must somehow reside in "the sex." One critic of wholesale castration, Dr. Ely Van de Warker, realized that the doctor's clamor about the ovaries had a "sociological reflex." "So constantly," he pointed out in 1906, "have they been held up before her as the one evil spot in her anatomy that she has grown to look with suspicion on her own organs."[143] Women pleaded with the gynecologist for castration, "fully convinced that all their grief emanates from their pelvis . . . this idea fostered and augmented by their friends."[144] Some gynecologists eventually realized that some patients came to them for the same reasons that others went to faith cures and Christian Science.[145] In short, this enormous phenomenon was symbiotic between patient and doctor, reflecting and refracting the largest contours of social beliefs and expectations.[146]

The meaning that both patients and doctors attached to sickness and cure, disorder and order, suggest that the variety of symptoms focused on woman's sex organs can be explained as a language of anxiety shaped by a language of conformity. In W. P. Manton's phrase, castratable women were mentally alienated.[147] But all women were supposed to be "alien" from the democratic norm. It was male. The doctors' own sexual values condemned them to sustain the disease of being female. Just as men confined women to the "butterfly" existence that made them sick,[148] and more demanding, more in need of more confinement (to bed, or to asylum or to both), so doctors created specific symptoms they attempted to cure, their therapy expressing the same social assumptions of a male identity that made it necessary to exclude and subordinate women, make them sick, and so on. Castration itself destroyed woman's one remaining thread of identity, her hope for children. Her symptoms intensified and men became still more desperate. But by the same standard of social beliefs generating disease, castration could and did work, although much less frequently than it proved iatrogenic.[149]

Impregnation could be as much a way of controlling woman as castration. Hence the paradox of the coexistence of castration and the inducing of fertility as areas of gynecological experiment, and the paradox of the general anxiety about the increasing sterility of Anglo-Saxon women, even as the Jeremiahs castrated some of them.[150] Gynecologists were in a better position than Todd to attempt procreation without diving into dangerous woman: for years Sims experimented in the impregnation of supposedly sterile women with a mechanical penis, and claimed some success.[151] Driving out midwives was an assertion of control at the end of gestation; and like Todd, Gardner compared the delivery of children to the mining of California gold.[152] The work of Gardner and Sims reveals the persistent desire to master the process of copulation, gestation, and delivery, while other male experts tried to preempt mother's power in childbearing. "From the foundation of the world man has been born of woman; and notwithstanding that his inventive genius has discovered steam . . . and harnessed him to his chariot, and sent lightning to do his bidding over the almost boundless extent of the world; yet we cannot hope that any change may be effected in this particular."[153] The complaint betrays the wish. To sever dependence on women for reproduction would be a feat surpassing the harnessing of steam and electricity, and would enable man to escape the deadly danger with which, like Todd, Gardner associated woman's reproductive power.[154]

Furthermore, Gardner and Sims (and the castrators generally) identified the mastery of woman's body both with man's encroachment on and utilization of nature's body. Sims' invention of his speculum for the examination of woman's reproductive tract enabled him to see "everything as no man had ever seen before. . . . I felt like an explorer in medicine who first views a new and important territory."[155] Battey, too, was depicted as a "pioneer" traveling "in paths hitherto untrod."[156] Gardner associated his sexual energies with the mechanized steam power of the new "iron horse," and represented the male sexual organ as a "railroad train" that could easily be thrown from its track by woman's rebellious contraception.[157] Just as a woman's body was a source of babes of gold who were to constitute the pure spermatic power of the new nation, so too "the mountains and forests" of the West were "vast reservoirs of health and strength" from which "we may annually recruit our exhausted energies at every fresh contact with our worthy mother earth." This assimilation of natural resources had a corresponding excretive dimension: the West was waiting to "draw off, through the mighty sluices of our continental railway lines" a "super-abundance of poverty," which otherwise "stagnates into cesspools of abomination . . . which breed plagues and pestilence."[158] Gardner, then, shared Todd's alimentary view of the use of resources, ingesting and excreting apt metaphors for the ambiguous evaluation of sperm, and for the fantasy of self-sufficiency.[159] Gynecologists saw themselves as being in a special position to mediate man's interaction with nature, of which woman was at once part and representative. Male energy was the icon to which man's vision of his relations with women, his appropriation of her power and that of nature, was captive. This accumulation of power, representing the three conquests of self, woman, and nature, betrayed in its own terms the fantasy of self-reproduction, the climax of male claims to self-making.

It would be misleading to end a sketch of nineteenth-century male anxieties about themselves and women on a note of assertion, that is, to suggest that men were unambiguous even in their fantasies. So I will conclude with some suggestions about the psychic ambiguities in men, warning the reader that the following remarks are the tip of an iceberg to be more fully uncovered with the publication of *The Horrors of the Half-Known Life.* The assertion of mastery over reproduction, and over the disorders of women had a self-destructive side. In the first place, such efforts were the displacement of anxieties over the inescapable anarchy of American malehood, intensified by the subversiveness of indolent women, which itself was the function of the displacement of the responsibility of male order on to women. The need for control could not be satisfied. Gynecological disciplines manifested the same "mad impatience" Tocqueville had perceived in democratic men generally, and their methods drove women to more sickness, demanding further gynecological disciplines, and so on.

Secondly, the gynecologists' "performances" of operations, their piling up of records, and their repeated attempts to innovate and prove priority in innovations (which they termed "conceptions," "bantlings," and "babies")[160] were held up to other *men's* eyes for judgment. So surgeons claimed to be self-made successes in virtue of the invention of an original operation (or operative technique); they then presented themselves for judgment at the hands of other surgeons. Accounts of this process (of which the cutting of a woman's body was a phase) were shot through with exactly the same legal metaphors the surgeons applied in their judgment of women.

The second installment of Battey's account of his first female castration illustrates this ambiguous process, that is, one both assertive and submissive toward other men. First Battey repeated his claim to be a Daniel Boone of the human dimension of virgin land—i.e., the female body— "carving out for myself a new pathway through consecrated ground [that phrase evoking the burial of dead bodies], upon which the foot of man has not dared willingly to tread." He then gave a more complicated picture of his psychic state at the time of his conception. "However pure may have been the motives actuating me, however cogent may have appeared, to my own mind, the reasons which have impelled me—I must of necessity stand before the bar of the medical world, and submit myself to its just judgment. It becomes me, too, to appear before you, my brothers and my peers, to answer for myself."[161] Robert Morris, a circumcisor and a castrator of females, and a transplanter of ovaries, warned that patients "must be classified carefully if physicians are not to be subjected to the humiliation of doing unnecessary and harmful surgery."[162] An overriding concern in his assertively autonomous performances was what other experts thought of the individual gynecologist. The process expressed the same circular world-view to which Todd's work testifies in behalf of men generally. Men defended themselves against a general, democratic hostility which was intensified by each individual's defense against it.

In 1901, A. Palmer Dudley (Professor of Gynecology, Harlem Post-Graduate Medical School and Hospital, and Dartmouth Medical College, New York City) expressed a similar apprehension to that of Robert Morris. Analysis of his words suggests how he confused his judgment of woman's genitals with his fear of being judged himself, and how that confusion reflected his uncertainty about his own sexual identity. He told his colleagues that "a man is put to the test at the operating table."[163] The gynecologist was reduced to his manhood; his physiological identity seemed to be at issue as well as his professional identity. If he was successful, he might be handing "his" ovaries around on a plate as part of his success, his affirmation of his professional identity and his manhood. What was important was not her, but himself. Her body furnished the material for his identity: in fact, he proved his manhood to other men by appropriating that part of her body that characterized her as a female. Her body stood for his. I have mentioned men's fear of becoming not-men, of becoming women. Yet here Dudley used woman's body for his manhood. Such a process of assimilation was the counterpart of the other sexually confused fantasy, that of "mannish" woman's righters (characterized as such by doctors like Gardner), of the "phallic" heroines of the popular literature cited by Henry Nash Smith.[164] Dudley's patient's complaint was sexual disorder; given the limited number of slots in the sexual order, the sexually disordered woman was construed to be a man. If a woman deviated from the contemporary standard of womanhood, she became a man. If a man deviated from the contemporary standard of manhood, he became a woman. So it may be that what was being put to the test was the ambiguity of Dudley's sexual identity. Robert Edes suggested in 1896 that gynecological surgery was performed to relieve the surgeon of the anxieties women occasioned him, rather than relieve her of her own sickness. "I have heard an eminent surgeon offer a vivid description of his sufferings from the importunities of a patient whom he had skillfully relieved of her ovaries but not of her sufferings say: 'I told her at last that she had better try Christian Science.'"[165] But relief was hard to come by, when, in the final analysis, it depended on other men, all of whom suffered from the same unresolvable tensions Dudley did, and all of whom were burdened by the pressure to depend for judgment on no one at all, to be self-sufficient. Neither success nor failure could protect a man from such pressure.

So on the one side, there was a powerful undercurrent of desire of gynecologists to reproduce themselves to the extent of designating female castration as reproduction. According to his and his contemporaries' metaphor, Battey's normal ovariotomy was his own baby. One irony in this psychic circle was that the removal of woman's ovaries made a castrated woman more like a man insofar as she did not menstruate or give birth; conversely it made men like the "sexless" kind of woman the pedestal rhetoric idealized. This latter irony represents the other side of castration's meaning, in its projective dimension—that men desired to be beyond the anxiety and responsibility to which they were committed by the existence of their penes and testicles, a desire in the work of both Gardner and Todd, as well as the castrating gynecologists. The following quotation is from an article in which Arnold Praeger was defending a gynecology he assumed to be synonymous with female castration. He said that opponents of castration implied that "gynecology is a sort of illegitimate appendage of medicine, which should be choked and strangled out of existence as a monster which has suddenly arisen to unsex and destroy lovely woman."[166] Most immediately, the image compared gynecological surgery to the diseased ovary it demanded to destroy. Both sides of the self-reproductive fantasy invoked a projective and introjective hall of mirrors which stood for the profound ambiguities of only negatively knowing who one was. Praeger's mixed metaphor conveys both the ambition of giving legitimate birth, and the ambition to experience the existence represented by the castrated, ornamental woman, free even of childbearing. The "natural" source of generation, the ovary, was monstrous.

Dudley's and Praeger's confusions reflected the ambiguities in being male that I have indicated in the earlier parts of this paper. Men maintained a rigid sex line yet felt it could dissolve at the drop of a hat; men wanted the competition they simultaneously dreaded; they were told by experts how not to rely on experts, in other words, to be self-sufficient; they accepted a model for behavior—obsessive energization—that they believed ran them into the danger of having their sanity destroyed (and, in fact, it was this particular psychic circularity men dealt with by projecting their incipient insanity on to women). Further circularities were these: the terms of antimasturbation tracts would themselves cause men to masturbate; men depended on the control and use of energy they also felt to be uncontrollable; they depended on copulation to implement their social vision, yet believed they ran dreadful risks (of debilitation, disease and death) in sexual intercourse. Men claimed to control reproduction when they were dependent on women for it; they saw women as entirely sex organs even as they claimed she was sexless. Furthermore, those views of women must have been as susceptible to her human reality as the definitions of blacks as property or animals were susceptible to their human reality (in spite of attempts of both women and blacks to fulfill white men's expectations of them). Gynecologists reflected such circularities: they attempted artificial insemination of woman, and they castrated her—both actions were intended to assume power over reproduction. By the late 1890s, they were transplanting ovaries to cure woman of castration, thereby relieving themselves of their own sufferings.

# NOTES

1. John Todd, *The Student's Manual* (Northampton: Hopkins, Bridgman, 1835), pp. 326–327.

2. Ibid., p. 372

3. George Rogers Taylor, *The Transportation Revolution* (New York: Harper and Row, 1968), pp. 22, 153.

4. Alexis de Tocqueville, *Democracy in America*, 2 vols. (New York: Vintage Books, 1945 [1st ed., Paris, 1835, 1840]) 2: bks. 2 and 3; see, too, Alexander Mitscherlich, *Society Without the Father*, trans. E. Mosbacher (New York: Harcourt, Brace and World, 1969); Dr. Edward Jarvis, "On the Supposed Increase of Insanity," *American Journal of Insanity*. 8 (April, 1852): 360–364.

5. John Todd, *The Young Man, Hints Addressed to the Young Men of the United States* (Northamptom: Hopkins, Bridgman, 1856 [1st ed., 1844]), p. 113.

6. Donald B. Meyer, *The Positive Thinkers* (Garden City: Doubleday, 1965), pp. 55–56.

7. I use the word in one of the ways in which Erik Erikson defines it: "The tendency at a given time to make facts amenable to ideas, and ideas to facts, in order to create a world image convincing enough to support the collective and individual sense of identity" (*Young Man Luther* [New York: W. W. Norton and Co., 1962], p. 22). It should be obvious that there was more to the ideology of nineteenth-century American males than "self-making."

8. For examples of the rhetoric see James Fenimore Cooper, *Notions of the Americans*, 2 vols. (London: Henry Colburn, 1828), 1: 140–142.

9. For Tocqueville's logic here, see pt. 1 of my book *The Horrors of the Half-Known Life* (New York: Harper and Row, 1976).

10. Isaac Ray, *Mental Hygiene* (reprint edition, New York: Hafner Publishing Co., 1968 [1st ed., 1863]), p. 58; Amariah Brigham, *Remarks on the Influence of Mental Cultivation and Mental Excitement upon Mental Health* (Boston: Marsh Capen and Lyon, 1833 [1st ed., 1832]), p. 16.

11. Brigham, *Remarks*, preface, pp. 81–82, 84; Ray, *Mental Hygiene*, p. 54.

12. See Egbert S. Oliver, "Explanatory Notes" to Melville, *Piazza Tales* (New York: Hendricks House, 1962), pp. 238–241; and see too Benfield, *The Horrors*.

13. John Todd, *The Story of His Life, Told Mainly by Himself*, comp. and ed. Jonathan Edwards Todd (New York: Harper and Brothers, 1876), p. 461, Dr. Augustus Kinsley Gardner said he and "thousands" were decisively influenced by *The Student's Manual*, particularly by the chapter on masturbation, "so potent to rob man of the high prerogatives of manhood. . . . " (*Conjugal Sins* [New York: J. S. Redfield, 1870], pp. 69–70).

14. Todd, *Life*, p. 280.

15. Todd, *Student's Manual*, p. 125. "We consist of two parts; the one inert, passive, utterly incapable of directing itself, barely ministerial to the other, moved, animated by it" (p. 176).

16. Ray, *Mental Hygiene*, p. 205. Ray saw this power being wasted on a national scale: "The amount of mental power which has . . . been destroyed is infinitely greater . . . than that which has been suffered to work out its destined purpose" (p. 53). This view may be compared to Freud's apprehension of one of civilization's sources of discontent, that "a piece of unconquerable nature may lay behind—this time a piece of our own psychical constitution" (*Civilization and Its Discontents*, trans. James Strachey [New York: W. W. Norton and Co., 1962], p. 33).

17. Todd, *Student's Manual*, p. 284.

18. Brigham, *Remarks*, pp. ix–x, 15, 36.

19. Ibid., p. 15.

20. Ibid., p. 36

21. This medical/psychological idea pervaded nineteenth-century literature with powerful undertones of "the spermatic economy." One example was the best seller in 1850: Ik Marvell

[pseud.], *Reveries of a Bachelor* (New York: Charles Scribner, 1859 [1st ed., 1850]), pp. 31, 96, 133.

22. Brigham, *Remarks*, pp. 45–46.

23. Todd, *The Young Man*, p. 43.

24. Edward Jarvis, "On the Supposed Increase of Insanity," *American Journal of Insanity*, 8 (1852): 349, 354–55; Ray, *Mental Hygiene*, pp. 228–229, 284; Norman Dain, *Concepts of Insanity* (New Brunswick: Rutgers University Press, 1964), pp. 89, 212, n. 9. Ray was explicit about this necessity for men to run the danger of going mad. "I do not suppose that insanity inducing excitement can be banished from every sphere of human activity, or that such a result would be desirable, if it could. It has its uses, and within certain limits it furnishes indispensable aid in realizing the purposes and aspirations of men" (*Mental Hygiene*, p. 191).

25. Herman Melville, *Moby Dick* (New York: Harper and Brothers, 1851), ch. XLI; Charles Dickens, *Our Mutual Friend* (London: Chapman and Hall), chs. XXXII, XLIV.

26. Todd, *Student's Manual*, pp. 375–376.

27. Todd, *Life*, p. 451.

28. John Todd, *The Sunset Land* (Boston: Lee and Shepard, 1871), pp. 226–233, 84–85.

29. Todd, *Life*, pp. 438, 429–431.

30. John Todd, *The Daughter at School* (Northamptom: Bridgman and Childs, 1868 [1st ed., 1853]), p. 110; idem, *Student's Manual*, p. 165.

31. Edward Jarvis, "Of the Comparative Liability of Males and Females to Insanity, and Their Comparative Curability and Mortality When Insane," *American Journal of Insanity*, 7 (1850): 158.

32. This is an argument I spell out in *The Horrors* (and one that Melville suggests in "The Lightning-Rod Man"). The characteristics of the masturbatory habit can be picked up from almost any case history, with which medical journals are replete, especially in the period c. 1830–1910. Three articles, published in the same year as *The Student's Manual*, give the idea. All are by 'W' and in the *Boston Medical and Surgical Journal*: "Remarks on Masturbation," 12, no. 6 (March, 1835): 94–97; "Insanity, Produced by Masturbation," 12, no 7 (March 1835): pp. 109–111 and "Effects of Masturbation, with Cases," 12, no. 9 (April, 1835): 138–141. It should be noted that the cases discussed at that early stage of the modern history of American masturbation phobia were all male. See, too, Ray, *Mental Hygiene*, 274–277.

33. Anon., "Legislative Control of Prostitution," *New Orleans Medical and Surgical Journal*, 11 (March 1855): 704.

34. Todd, *Student's Manual*, p. 209.

35. Todd, *The Young Man*, pp. 139–140. Compare Kai Erikson's account of the relations between deviant and normal behavior in *Wayward Puritans* (New York: John Wiley, 1966), pp. 19–21.

36. "W," "Insanity," p. 109.

37. Conway Zirkle, "The Early History of the Inheritance of Acquired Characters and of Pangenesis," *Transactions of the American Philosophical Society*, 35, pt. 2, (1946): pp. 141, 146. The history of ideas about sperm is complicated, and can be approached by way of Elizabeth Gasking, *Investigations of Generation*, 1651–1828 (London: Hutchinson, 1967). See too, B. Seeman, *The River of Life* (New York: Norton, 1961), pp. 26, 27, 31. Another tradition informing attitudes toward "healthy" human reproduction in nineteenth-century America was eighteenth-century English stockbreeding, transmitted by way of the French physiocrats by Thomas Jefferson, and applied by him to human beings. Jefferson, *Notes on Virginia* (New York: Harper Torchbooks, 1964). p. 133. The physiocrat to whom Jefferson was particularly indebted was D'Aubenton, as his frequent references attest (*Notes*, pp. 39, 44, 47, 48, 49, 53, 54).

38. Augustus Kinsley Gardner, *Our Children* (Hartford: Belknap and Bliss, 1872), pp. 51, 162–163.

39. John Bowlby, *Attachment* (New York: Basic Books, 1969), pp. 14–15; "W," "Insanity," p. 110; idem, "Remarks," p. 95; R. H. Shryock, *Medicine in America*, (Baltimore: Johns

Hopkins U. Press, 1966), p. 239; John Burnham, "Psychoanalysis and American Medicine: 1894–1918," *Psychological Issues* 5, no. 4 (1967): *passim*.

40. Gardner, *Conjugal Sins*, ch. IV.

41. "W," "Remarks," p. 96; see, too, Gardner, *Conjugal Sins*, pp. 174–175, 190, 193.

42. Augustus Kinsley Gardner, *Our Children* (Hartford: Belknap and Bliss, 1872), pp. 39–40, 323; idem, *Conjugal Sins*, pp. 174–175, 190–193, 83–84, 88, 78, 81. Spermatic waste, the associated disease of "spermatorrhoea," the idea of the economic use of sperm/energy, and its relation to a wider social context, are discussed in chapter 20 of Wayland Young's insightful *Eros Denied* (New York: Grove Press, 1964). Gardner quotes extensively from what he cites as "M. Lallemand. A practical treatise on the causes, symptoms and treatment of Spermatorrhoea, Philadelphia, 1853" (*Conjugal Sins*, pp. 81–82). Young's book describes the essential elements of a "spermatic economy" for nineteenth-century England; Michael Bliss has recorded the identical phenomenon in Canadian history in "Pure Books on Avoided Subjects; Pre-Freudian Sexual Ideas in Canada, " Read to the Canadian Historical Association, June 4, 1970.

43. *Ladies Home Journal*, February 27, 1876.

44. Gardner, *Conjugal Sins*, pp. 141–142.

45. J. Marion Sims, *Clinical Notes on Uterine Surgery* (New York: William Wood, 1866), p. 373; Gardner, *Conjugal Sins, passim*, esp. pp. 101–102.

46. Sims, *Clinical Notes*, p. 373.

47. Anon., *My Secret Life*, abr. ed. (New York: Grove Press, 1966 [1st private printing, c 1890]), pp. 525–557; the book describes a lifetime of sexual activity or fantasy stretching over decades prior to its first printing. Another figure, this time an anonymous American, was also driven to quantify sperm. From 1895 to 1903 he calculated that he averaged 3.43 nocturnal emissions each month. Since he was a bachelor and did not masturbate, he felt this was an accurate measure of permissible expenditures, and while 3.43 would vary for different men, it did represent the physiological limit that should be a warning to both "unmarried masturbator and married incontinent." His article is complete with statistics and a graph. "Nocturnal Emissions," *American Journal of Psychology*, 15 (January, 1904): 104–107.

48. Augustus Kinsley Gardner, *The Causes and Curative Treatment of Sterility* (New York: De Witt and Davenport, 1856), p. 9.

49. The evidence is overwhelming. I shall discuss sex in this context later; for money as one remaining source of identity, see Tocqueville, *Democracy*, 2, bk. 2, ch. 17: "When the reverence that belonged to what is old has vanished, birth, condition, and profession no longer distinguish men, or scarcely distinguish them; hardly anything but money remains to create strongly marked differences between them and to raise some of them above the common level. The distinction originating in wealth is increased by the disappearance or diminution of all other distinctions. Among aristocratic nations money reaches only to a few points in the vast circle of man's desires; in democracies it seems to lead to all."

50. Todd, *Student's Manual*, p. 147; Gardner, *Sterility*, p. 28; idem, *Conjugal Sins*, p. 50.

51. J. H. Walters, "Report on the Doctrine of Force, Physical and Vital," *Transactions of the American Medical Association*, 21 (1870): 273; Todd's acknowledgment of Eli Todd—a distant relative—and Samuel Woodward, is included in a footnote to his discussion of masturbation in *Student's Manual*, p. 148: this discussion was in Latin, and a translation is appended to G. J. Barker-Benfield, "The Horrors of the Half-Known Life: Aspects of the Exploitation of Women by Men," (Unpublished doctoral dissertation, University of California, Los Angeles, 1968).

52. Ray, *Mental Hygiene*, p. 205; Todd, *Student's Manual*, pp. 375–376 (for a full account of the meaning of reading in the ideology of self-making and masturbation-phobia, see chapters 14 and 15 of Benfield, *The Horrors*); Henry David Thoreau, *Walden* (New York: New American Library edition, 1960), p. 149; Gardner, *Conjugal Sins*, p. 182. Gardner restates such proto-sublimation in the special context of democratic anxiety described by Tocqueville, Todd (and Jarvis, see note 4 above). "In American life . . . [there] are few whose minds are sufficiently freed from the cares and anxieties of life, from the necessity of earning a

livelihood, with the consequent employment of time and the fatigues of body and brain. The physical energies are too completely used up by these necessities to allow for much excess in pleasure, save at such infrequent intervals as to be comparatively harmless" (p. 85).

53. Freud, *Civilization and Its Discontents*, pp. 50-57; Tocqueville, *Democracy*, vol. 2, bk. 3, ch. 12.

54. Ibid.; John Todd, *Woman's Rights* (Boston: Lee and Shepard, 1867), pp. 26-27.

55. Todd, *Sunset Land*, p. 245.

56. Ibid., p. 26.

57. Ibid., p. 245.

58. Ibid., pp. 226-233.

59. Melville, *Moby Dick*, ch. XCIV.

60. Arthur Moore, *The Frontier Mind* (New York: McGraw-Hill, 1963), p. 127; R. M. Dorson, *Jonathan Draws the Long Bow* (Cambridge, Mass.: Harvard University Press 1946), pp. 14-15; Henry Nash Smith, *Virgin Land* (New York: Vintage Books, 1950), bk. 2.

61. Todd, *Sunset Land*, pp. 66-67.

62. Smith, *Virgin Land*, p. 35; Todd, *Sunset Land*, pp. 28, 241. This is how William Hall described the observation of the advance of the railroad, in a speech to the 1847 Railroad Convention in Chicago: "They saw him pluck out forests, tear up and fling aside the seated hills, and with the rejoicing sound of progress in his train made way into the body of the continent, with the step of a bridegroom going to his chambers or a prince to occupy his throne" ("Speech of William M. Hall of New York in favor of a National Railroad to the Pacific at the Chicago Convention, July 7, 1847," [New York: The Day Book Female Type Setting Establishment, 1853], p. 5).

63. Todd, *Sunset Land*, p.. 74-75.

64. Todd, *Daughter at School*, p. 214.

65. Todd, *Student's Manual*, p. 150.

66. Todd, *Daughter at School*, pp. 208-209.

67. Meyer, *Positive Thinkers*, p. 48.

68. See note 11 above.

69. Jarvis, "Comparative Liability," pp. 154-155, 158.

70. Tocqueville, *Democracy*, 2, bk. 2, ch. 19.

71. For evidence of male concern about women's new life-style, see Anon., *Employment of Females as Practitioners in Midwifery* (Boston: Cummings and Hillard, 1820), pp. 14-15, 22; Cooper, *Notions*, 1: 252-253; A. K. Gardner, "The Physical Decline of American Women," *The Knickerbocker*, 55, no. 1 (January, 1860): 37-52; Marvin Meyers, *The Jacksonian Persuasion* (New York: Vintage Books, 1960), pp. 129-131.

72. Charles D. Meigs, *Woman: Her Diseases and Remedies* (Philadelphia: Blanchard and Lea, 1852 [1st ed., 1848]), p. 54; Horatio Robinson Storer, *The Causation, Course and Treatment of Reflex Insanity in Women* (Boston: Lee and Shepard, 1871), p. 79.

73. Gardner, *Conjugal Sins*, p. 150.

74. Todd, *Woman's Rights*, pp. 18, 37; Gardner, *Our Children*, p. 180; see Benfield, *The Horrors*, pp. 409-411, 574-576 for elucidation.

75. Sims, *Clinical Notes*. "I have seen the inside of an immense number of vaginas, and I never saw two that were in all particulars exactly alike. They are as different from each other as our faces and noses." (p. 18).

76. Gardner, *Our Children*, p. 19; idem; *Conjugal Sins*, p. 143.

77. Sims, *Clinical Notes*, p. 360

78. Gardner, *Sterility*, p. 111; see, too, p. 49.

79. Sims, *Clinical Notes*, p. 360.

80. Gardner, *Sterility*, p. 111.

81. Cooper, *Notions*, 2:263.

82. For examples of the assumption of "positive amorous signs" as disorder, or symptoms of disorder, see B. Sherwood-Dunn, "Conservation of the Ovary: Discussion," *Transactions*

*of the American Association of Obstetricians and Gynecologists.* 10 (1897): 219, 220, 223; George J. Engelmann, "Cliterodectomy" [sic], *The American Practitioner,* 25 (1882): 3, 5; Anon., "Transactions of the Woman's Hospital Society," *American Journal of Obstetrics and Gynecology,* 43 (1901): 721; A. J. Bloch, "Sexual Perversion in the Female," *New Orleans Medical and Surgical Journal,* 22, no. 1 (July, 1894): 7.

83. Gardner, *Conjugal Sins,* p. 147; see, too, Meigs, *Woman,* p. 432.

84. Gardner, *Conjugal Sins,* pp. 17, 145–146.

85. J. Marion Sims, *The Story of My Life,* comp. and ed. H. Marion Sims (New York: D. Appleton, 1885), p. 231; A. K. Gardner, "Treatise on Uterine Haemorrhage," *American Medical Monthly* (June, 1855): 1.

86. Gardner, "Physical Decline," p. 37.

87. Engelmann, "Cliterodectomy," p. 3, passim; E. H. Pratt, "Circumcision of Girls," *Journal of Orificial Surgery,* 6, no. 9 (March, 1898): 390; Anon., "Transactions of the Woman's Hospital Society" (1901): 721–722; Wallace C. Abbott, "The Importance of Circumcision of the Female," *The Medical Council,* 9 (December, 1904): 437–439.

88. Archibald Church, "Removal of Ovaries and Tubes in the Insane and Neurotic," *American Journal of Obstetrics and the Diseases of Women and Children,* 28 (1893): 494–495; ibid., "Discussion," p. 573.

89. Gardner, *Conjugal Sins,* p. 81.

90. Ibid., pp. 72, 78; idem, *Our Children,* pp. 200–201.

91. This is a point *The Horrors* sets out in detail.

92. J. A. Jackson, "Hygiene of Adolescence," *Transactions of the Wisconsin State Medical Society,* 30 (1896): 288; the nocturnal emissions article is cited in note 47 above.

93. A. J. Himel, "Some Minor Studies in Psychology, with Special Reference to Masturbation," *New Orleans Medical and Surgical Journal,* 70 (1907): 442; Holmes is quoted in Ilza Veith, *Hysteria: The History of a Disease* (Chicago: University of Chicago Press, Phoenix Books, 1970), p. 216.

94. See below; see also, Benfield, *The Horrors.*

95. Gardner, "Physical Decline," p. 49; A. K. Gardner, *History of the Art of Midwifery* (New York: Stringer and Townshend, 1852), p. 4.

96. John Todd, *Serpents in the Dove's Nest* (Boston: Lee and Shephard, 1867), pp. 12, 25.

97. Gardner, *Conjugal Sins,* dedication, p. 195. Gardner maintained that subversely sick women should turn their warlike hostility against themselves in the interests of their subordination, and "not only assert their independence, but vindicate their claim to equality, not with chalk powder and balls . . . but by actual attainments over self-degeneracy" (p. 52).

98. Todd, *Young Man,* p. 278. For an account of earlier fears of the same stripe, see Sidney Mead, *The Lively Experiment: The Shaping of Christianity in America* (New York: Harper and Row, 1963), ch. III.

99. Gardner, *Conjugal Sins,* p. 64. These remarks about the body politic have been influenced considerably by Winthrop Jordan, *White Over Black* (Baltimore: Pelican Books, 1969).

100. Freud, *Civilization and Its Discontents,* p. 51.

101. Karl Marx and Friedrich Engels, *Manifesto of the Communist Party* (New York: International Publishers, 1948 [1st ed., 1848]), p. 27

102. See, for example, Louis Hartz, *The Liberal Tradition in America* (New York: Harcourt Brace and World, 1955), pp. 3, 50–64; Leslie Fiedler, *Love and Death in the American Novel* (New York: Stein and Day, 1966 [1st ed., 1960]), p. 76; Jack P. Greene, "Political Mimesis," *The American Historical Review,* 75 (December, 1969): 337–360. The well-known crowings of Daniel Boorstin and lament of Henry James are symptoms of the same phenomenon.

103. Tocqueville, *Democracy,* 2: bk. 2, ch. 2: bk. 3, ch. 17.

104. Ibid.

105. Ibid.

106. Evert A. and George L. Duyckinch, 2 vols., *Cyclopoedia of American Literaure* (Philadelphia: William Rutter, 1880), 1: iii.

107. Robert Wiebe, *The Search for Order* (New York: Hill and Wang, 1967), pp. xiii, 1, 5–6, 8.

108. Ibid., p. 52; Todd, *Serpents*, p. 21.

109. Todd, *Serpents*, p. 16.

110. See Benfield, *The Horrors*, pt. III, ch. 2.

111. Gardner, *Conjugal Sins*, pp. 8, 203.

112. Mark Haller, *Eugenics: Hereditarian Attitudes in American Thought* (New Brunswick: Rutgers University Press, 1963); John Higham, *Strangers in the Land* (New York: Atheneum Publishers, 1968), pp. 150–153. For the rise of drastic surgery see below.

113. Gardner, *Old Wine*, p. 223; Gardner, "Thoughts on Health," *Frank Leslie's Illustrated Newspaper*, 34, no. 876 (July 13, 1872): 283.

114. Gardner, *Old Wine*, pp. 256–257; idem, *Our Children*, pp. 52–53 and passim; see also, idem, *Conjugal Sins*, p. 192.

115. Gardner, *Our Children*, pp. 36, 37, 40.

116. Sources for this are numerous: e.g., David T. Gilliam, "Oophorectomy for the Insanity and Epilepsy of the Female: A Plea for Its More General Adoption," *Transactions of the American Association of Obstetricians and Gynecologists*, 9 (1896): 320–321; Todd, *Woman's Rights*; Gardner, *Conjugal Sins*; Gardner, "Physical Decline."

117. Gardner, *Our Children*, p. 60.

118. Benfield, *The Horrors*, pt. II; Sims, *Clinical Notes*, pp. 131–135; 206–207.

119. These conclusions and the following section of the paper reflect research into nineteenth-century medical journals which are more elaborately documented in *The Horrors*.

120. Abraham Jacobi, "On Masturbation and Hysteria in Young Children," 2 pts., *American Journal of Obstetrics and Diseases of Women and Children*, 8 & 9 (1875, 1876), 9:603.

121. The gradual acceptance of the routine circumcision of male babies seems to have originated as an expression of masturbation phobia (removing the thrill of pulling back the foreskin to urinate or wash). It is a story I give briefly in *The Horrors*.

122. Pierre Lefort, "A Case of Excision of the Clitoris," *Medical Repository*, 4 (1818): 84–87.

123. "Meeting to Consider the Proposition of the Council for the Removal of Mr. I. B. Brown," *British Medical Journal*, 1 (April, 1867): 395–410; Lawson Tait, "Masturbation, *The Medical News*, 53, no. 1 (July 7, 1888): 3; René A. Spitz, "Authority and Masturbation," *Psychoanalytic Quarterly*, 21 (1952): 502.

124. For a chronological and analytical account of clitoridectomy in the United States, see Benfield, *The Horrors*, pt.II.

125. E.g., Robert Morris, "Circumcision in Girls," *International Journal of Surgery*. 25 (1912): 135–136.

126. Frank J. Iiams, "Female Circumcision," *Medical Records and Annals* (Houston, Texas) 31 (1937): 171–173; again, see Benfield, *The Horrors*. This operation was a favorite one of a battery of operations on the lower parts of the body, most frequently the female body, developed from the late 1880s under the auspices of the Orificial Surgery Society, but not in the least limited to "orificialists." These operations, including "the American operation" (removal of the last inch of the rectum), were performed for everything from measles to melancholia, in accordance with a "philosophy" that was nothing more or less than a monistic, monomaniac version of the spermatic economy projected onto women. This philosophy was elaborated into twenty-three rules to guarantee the unobstructed circulation of the bloodstream according to laws of "the waste and supply of the sympathetic nerve." The nerve's energy, and in consequence, the blood flow it supported could become congested in "sphincter openings" which then had to be snipped and trimmed to release the tensions, flush the capillaries and smooth the openings. B. E. Dawson, *Orificial Surgery, Its Philosophy, Application and Technique*, ed. Minnie Elder Dawson (Kansas City, Missouri: Western Baptist Publishing Co., 1925 [1st ed., 1912]) ch. 2, and passim.

127. Norman Himes suggests that contraception was widely accepted in England after the Bradlaugh case of 1879, and not accepted in the United States until after Jacobi's Presidential address to the A.M.A. in 1912, and Margaret Sanger's work in New York in the 1920s.

*Medical History of Contraception* (New York: Schocken, 1970 [1st ed., 1936]), pp. 243, 311–315.

128. See Benfield, *The Horrors*, pt. II.

129. Robert Battey, "Normal Ovariotomy—Case," *Atlanta Medical and Surgical Journal*, 10 (1872): 321–339.

130. For an account of female castration, see Benfield, *The Horrors*, pt. II.

131. Church, "Removal—Discussion," p. 570; Howard A. Kelly, "Conservatism in Ovariotomy," *Journal of the American Medical Association*, 26 (1896): 251.

132. Ely Van de Warker, "The Fetich of the Ovary," *American Journal of Obstetrics and the Diseases of Women and Children* 54 (July-December, 1906): 369.

133. E.g., Robert Morris, "A Cast of Heteroplastic Ovarian Grafting, Followed by Pregnancy, and the Delivery of a Living Child," *Medical Record*, 69 (1906): 697–698.

134. E.g., Kelly, "Conservatism," p. 251.

135. Van de Warker, "Fetich," p. 371.

136. Sims, "Normal Ovariotomy—Battey's Operation," *North Carolina Medical Journal*, 1 (1878): 26–29.

137. See Benfield, *The Horrors*, pt. II.

138. Arnold Praeger, "Is So-Called Conservatism in Gynecology Conducive to the Best Results to the Patient?" *Transactions of the American Association of Obstetricians and Gynecologists*, 8 (1895): 322.

139. Gilliam, "Oophorectomy," pp. 317–320.

140. Tocqueville, *Democracy*, vol. 2, bk. 3, ch. 10.

141. Benfield, *The Horrors*, pt. II.

142. Meyer, *Positive Thinkers*, pp. 52–54.

143. Van de Warker, "The Fetich," p. 372.

144. James W. Cokenower, "A Plea for the Conservative Operations on the Ovaries," *Transactions of the Section on Obstetrics and Diseases of Women of the American Medical Association* (1904): 291.

145. Robert T. Edes, "Points in the Diagnosis and Treatment of Some Obscure Common Neuroses," *Journal of the American Medical Association*, 27 (1896): 1081; idem, "The relations of Pelvic and Nervous Diseases," *Journal of the American Medical Association*, 31 (1898): 1136.

146. Edes, "Points" and "Relations." Gardner expressed such a relation in 1870: "It has been a matter of common observation that the physical status of the women of Christendom has been gradually deteriorating . . . that a numerous class of specialists has arisen within a quarter of a century, devoting their whole energies to the investigation of these [women's] complaints, to the inventing of new instruments for the observation and diagnosis of these physical lesions . . . to remedy these diseases" (*Conjugal Sins*, pp. 13–14). Confusing cause with effect he said "nervous complications," masturbation, contraception, and abortion created "hours of uselessness" and made "of life itself a burden which is worse than valueless" (*Conjugal Sins*, pp. 13–14).

147. W. P. Manton, "Mental Alienation in Women and Abdomino-Pelvic Disease," *Transactions of the Section on Obstetrics and Diseases of Women of the American Medical Association* (1909). This is an argument Donald Meyer makes in his account of the origins of Christian Science and other mind cures, *The Positive Thinkers*, pt. 1.

148. Ray, *Mental Hygiene*, pp. 216, 219. See, also, Jarvis, "Comparative Liability," pp. 150, 156.

149. Again, I must ask the reader to see part II of *The Horrors*.

150. George J. Engelmann, "The Increasing Sterility of American Women," *Transactions of the Section on the Diseases of Women of the American Medical Association* (1901): 271–295; William Goodell, *Lessons in Gynecology* (Philadelphia: D. G. Brinton, 1879), p. 176. See, too, John Higham, *Strangers in the Land* (New York: Atheneum, 1963), pp. 143, 146–148.

151. Sims, *Clinical Notes*, p. 369.

152. Gardner, *History of Midwifery*, p. 31.

153. Ibid.

154. Benfield, *The Horrors*, pp. 534–536.

155. Sims, *Life*, p. 234.

156. E. P. Becton, "Batty [sic] and Batty's Operation," *Texas Courier-Record of Medicine*, 6 (1888–1889): 34.

157. Gardner, *Old Wine*, p. 309; idem, *Conjugal Sins*, p. 110. See Benfield, *The Horrors*, pt. IV for elucidation.

158. Gardner, *Our Children*, pp. 36, 53.

159. Gardner compared gestation to the eating and digesting process (*Old Wine*, pp. 291–292; *Our children*, p. 56). See Benfield, *The Horrors*, pt. IV.

160. E.g., Battey, "Normal Ovariotomy," p. 324; Sims, *Life*, p. 346; Dawson, *Orificial Surgery*, p. 24.

161. Robert Battey, "Normal Ovariotomy," *Atlanta Medical and Surgical Journal*, 11 (1873): 1, 2.

162. Cokenower, "Plea"—Discussion" p. 298.

163. A. Palmer Dudley, "Results of Ovarian Surgery," *Transaction of the Section on Obstetrics and the Diseases of Women* (1901): 198.

164. Smith, *Virgin Land*, ch. X; the work of Todd and Gardner, and medical articles of the same period contain a like fantasy.

165. Edes, "Points," p. 1081.

166. Praeger, "So-Called Conservatism," p. 321.

# 19 | WHAT OUGHT TO BE AND WHAT WAS: WOMEN'S SEXUALITY IN THE NINETEENTH CENTURY

## CARL N. DEGLER

As every schoolgirl knows, the nineteenth century was afraid of sex, particularly when it manifested itself in women. Captain Marryat, in his travels in the United States, told of some American women so refined that they objected to the word "leg," preferring instead the more decorous "limb." Marryat also reported seeing this delicacy carried to extremes in a girls' school where a school mistress, in the interest of protecting the modesty of her charges, had dressed all four "limbs" of the piano "in modest little trousers with frills at the bottom of them!"[1] Women's alleged lack of passion was epitomized, too, in the story of the English mother who was asked by her daughter before her marriage how she ought to behave on her wedding night. "Lie still and think of the Empire," the mother advised.

This view of Victorian attitudes toward sexuality is captured in more than stories. Steven Marcus, writing about the attitudes of English Victorians toward sexuality, and Nathan Hale, Jr., summarizing the attitudes of English Americans on the same subject, both quote at length from Dr. William Acton's *Functions and Disorders of the Reproductive Organs*, which went through several editions in England and the United States during the middle years of the nineteenth century.[2] Acton's book was undoubtedly one of the most widely quoted sexual-advice books in the English-speaking world. The book summed up the medical literature on women's sexuality by saying that "the majority of women (happily for them) are not very much troubled with sexual feelings of any kind. What men are habitually, women are only exceptionally."[3] Theophilus Parvin, an American doctor, told his medical class in 1883, "I do not believe one bride in a hundred, of delicate, educated, sensitive women, accepts matrimony from any desire for sexual gratification; when she thinks of this at all, it is with shrinking, or even with horror, rather than with desire."[4]

Modern writers on the sexual life of women in the nineteenth century have echoed these contemporary descriptions. "For the sexual act was associated by many wives only with a duty," writes Walter Houghton, "and by most husbands with a necessary if pleasurable yielding to one's baser nature; by few, therefore, with any innocent and joyful experience."[5] Writing about late-nineteenth-century America, David Kennedy quotes approvingly from Viola Klein when she writes that "in the whole Western world during the nineteenth century and at the beginning of the twentieth century it would have been not only scandalous to admit the existence of a strong sex urge in women, but it would have been contrary to all observation."[6] Nathan Hale, Jr. sums up his review of the sexual-advice literature at the turn of the century with a similar conclusion: "Many women came to regard marriage as little better than legalized prostitution. Sexual passion became associated almost exclusively with the male, with prostitutes, and women of the lower classes."[7] Most recently Ben Barker-Benfield has argued that male doctors were so convinced that women had no sexual interest that when it manifested itself drastic measures were taken to subdue it, including excision of the sexual organs. "Defining the absence of sexual desire in women as normal, doctors came to see its presence as disease. . . . Sexual appetite was a male quality (to be properly channelled of course). If a woman showed it, she resembled a man."[8]

Despite the apparent agreement between the nineteenth-century medical writers and modern students of the period, it is far from clear that there was in the nineteenth century a consensus on the subject of women's sexuality or that women were, in fact, inhibited from acknowledging their sexual feelings. In examining these two issues I shall be concerned with an admittedly limited yet significant population, namely, women of the urban middle class in the United States. This was the class to which the popular medical-advice books, of which William Acton's volume was a prime example, were directed. It is principally the women of this class upon whom historians' generalizations about women's lives in the nineteenth century are based. And though these women were not a numerical majority of the sex, they undoubtedly set the tone and provided the models for most women. The sources drawn upon are principally the popular and professional medical literature concerned with women and a hitherto undiscovered survey of married women's sexual attitudes and practices that was begun in the 1890s by Dr. Clelia D. Mosher.

Let me begin with the first question or issue. Was William Acton representative of medical writers when he contended that women were essentially without sexual passion? Rather serious doubts arise as soon as one looks into the medical literature, popular as well as professional, where it was recognized that the sex drive was so strong in woman that to deny it might well compromise her health. Dr. Charles Taylor, writing in 1882, said, "It is not a matter of indifference whether a woman live [sic] a single or a married life. . . . I do not for one moment wish to be understood as believing that an unmarried woman cannot exist in perfect health for I know she can. But the point is, that *she must take pains for it.*" For if the generative organs are not used, then "some other demand for the unemployed functions, must be established. Accumulated force must find an outlet, or disturbance first and weakness ultimately results." His recommendation was muscular exercise and education for usefulness. He also described cases of women who had denied their sexuality and even experienced orgasms without knowing it. Some women, he added, ended up, as a result, with impairment of movement or other physical symptoms.[9]

Other writers on medical matters were even more direct in testifying to the presence of sexual feelings in women. "Passion absolutely necessary in woman," wrote Orson S. Fowler, the phrenologist, in 1870. "Amativeness is created in the female head as universally as in the male. . . . That female passion exists, is as obvious as that the sun shines," he wrote. Without woman's passion, he contended, a fulfilled love could not occur.[10] Both sexes enjoy the sexual embrace, asserted Henry Chevasse, another popular medical writer, in 1871, but among human beings, as among the animals in general, he continued, "the male is more ardent and fierce, and . . . the desires of the female never reach that hight [sic] as to impel her to the commission of crime." Woman's pleasure, though it may be "less acute," is longer lasting than man's, Chevasse said. R. T. Trall, also a popular medical writer, counseled in a similar vein. "Whatever may be the object of sexual intercourse," he wrote, "whether intended as a love embrace merely, or as a generative act, it is very clear that it should be as pleasurable as possible to *both parties*."[11]

If one can judge the popularity of a guide for women by the number of its editions, then Dr. George Napheys's *The Physical Life of Woman: Advice to the Maiden, Wife, and Mother* (1869) must have been one of the leaders. Within two weeks of publication it went into a second printing, and within two years 60,000 copies were in print. Napheys was a well-known Philadelphia physician. Women, he wrote, quoting an unnamed "distinguished medical writer," are divided into three classes. The first consists of those who have no sexual feelings, and it is the smallest group. The second is larger and is comprised of those who have "strong passion." The third is made up of "the vast majority of women, in whom the sexual appetite is as moderate as all other appetites." He went on to make his point quite clear. "It is a false notion and contrary to nature that this passion in a woman is a derogation to her sex. The science of physiology indicates most clearly its propriety and dignity." He then proceeded to denounce those wives who "plume themselves on their repugnance or their distaste for their conjugal obligations." Napheys also contended that authorities agree that "conception is more assured when the two individuals who co-operate in it participate at the same time in the transports of which it is the fruit." Napheys probably had no sound reason for this point, but the accuracy of his statement is immaterial. What is of moment is that as an adviser to women he was clearly convinced that women possessed sexual feelings, which ought to be cultivated rather than suppressed. Concerning sexual relations during pregnancy he wrote, "There is no reason why passions should not be gratified in moderation and with caution during the whole period of pregnancy." And since his book is directed to women, there is no question that the passion he is talking about here is that of women.[12]

In 1878 Dr. Ely Van de Warker of Syracuse, a fellow of the American Gynecological Society, described sexual passion in women as "the analogue of the subjective copulative sensations of man, and that the acme of the sexual orgasm in woman is the sensory equivalent of emission in man, observing the distinction necessarily implied between the sexes—that in woman it is psychic and subjective, and that in man it has also a physical element and is objective," that is, it is accompanied by seminal emission. The principal purpose of Van de Warker's article was to deplore the fact that some women lacked sexual feeling, a state which he called "female impotency."[13] What is striking about his article is that he obviously considered such lack of feeling in women abnormal and worthy of medical attention, just as impotency in a man would cause medical concern.

Van de Warker's remarks, as well as his use of the word, make it evident that physicians were well aware that normal women experienced orgasms. Lest there by any doubt that their meaning of the word was the same as ours today, let me quote from a physician in 1883 who described in some detail woman's sexual response. He began by describing the preparatory stage, which, he said,

> may be reached by any means, bodily or mental, which, in the opposite sex, cause erection. Following upon this, then, is a stage of pleasurable excitement, gradually increasing and culminating in an acme of excitement, which may be called the stage of consummation, and the analogue of which in the male is emission. This is followed in both sexes by a degree of nervous prostration, less marked, however, in the female, and . . . by a relief to the general congestion of all the genital organs which has existed, and perhaps increased, from the beginning of the preparatory stage.[14]

All of this evidence, it seems to me, shows that there was a significant body of opinion and information quite different from that advanced on women's sexuality by William Acton and others of his outlook. Now it might be asked how widespread was this counter-Acton point of view? Was it not confined primarily to physicians writing for other physicians? Not at all. Napheys, Chevasse, and Fowler, to name three, were all writing their books for the large lay public that was interested in sexual matters. As we have seen, many of these marriage manuals, particularly Napheys's and Fowler's, were printed in several large editions.

Yet, in the end, there is a certain undeniable inconclusiveness in simply raising up one collection of writers against another, even if their existence does make the issue an open one, rather than the closed one that so many secondary writers have made it. It suggests, at the very least, that there was a sharp difference of medical opinion, rather than a consensus, on the nature of women's sexual feelings and needs. In fact, there is some reason to believe, as we shall see, that the so-called Victorian conception of women's sexuality was more that of an ideology seeking to be established than the prevalent view or practice of even middle-class women, especially as there is a substantial amount of nineteenth-century writing about women that assumes the existence of strong sexual feelings in women. One of the historian's recognized difficulties in showing, through quotations from writers who assert a particular outlook, that a social attitude prevailed in the past is that one always wonders how representative and how self-serving the examples or quotations are. This is especially true in this case where medical opinion can be found on both sides of the question. When writers, however, assume the attitude in question to be prevalent while they are intent upon writing about something else, then one is not so dependent upon the tyranny of numbers in quoting from sources. For behind the assumption of prevalence lie many examples, so to speak. Such testimony, moreover, is unintended and therefore not self-serving. This kind of evidence, furthermore, helps us to answer the second question—to what extent were women in the nineteenth century inhibited from expressing their sexual feelings? For in assuming that women had sexual feelings, these writers are offering clear, if unintended, testimony to women's sexuality.

Medical writers like Acton may have asserted that women did not possess sexual feelings, but there were many doctors who clearly assumed not only that such feelings existed but that the repression of them caused illness. One medical man, for example, writing in 1877, traced a cause of insanity in women to the onset of sexuality. "Sexual development initiates new and extraordinary physical changes," he pointed out. "The erotic and sexual impulse is awakened."[15] Another, writing ten years later, asserted that some of women's illnesses were due to a denial of sexual satisfaction. "Females feel often that they are not appreciated," wrote Dr. William McLaury in a medical journal, "that they have no one to confide in; then they become morose, angular, and disagreeable as a result of continual disappointment to their social and sexual longings. Even those married may become the victims of sexual starvation when the parties are mentally, magnetically, and physically antagonistic."[16] Henry Chevasse, writing for a popular audience, was also impressed by the need for sexual outlets for women. There may be some individuals "of phlegmatic temperament," he conceded, who are not injured by celibacy, but "absolute continence in the sanguine and ardent disposition predisposes to the gravest maladies." His listing of the resulting maladies, of which nymphomania was one, makes it clear that he was referring to women as well as men. These maladies, he went on, "are born as well of extreme restraint as of extreme excess. . . . Females seem to suffer even more than males . . . perhaps because their continence is more complete." (Presumably he was referring here to the absence of nocturnal emissions in women.) As a result, he continued, nunneries were notorious as places of fanaticism. "Hence the old proverb, 'The convent and the confessional are the cradles of hysteria and nymphomania.'"[17]

To Dr. Van de Warker women's sexuality was so obvious that he assumed men required it in order to achieve full sexual satisfaction for themselves. In marriage, he wrote, the husband

> not only demands pleasure and satisfaction for himself, but he requires something much more difficult to give—the appearance, if not the real existence, of satisfaction and pleasure in the object of his attentions. Unhappiness and suspicion are often the result of the absence of this pleasure [in women], and are sure to work to the material disadvantage of the weaker party. To show that this is really the case, I need but to remind physicians how often they are approached by husbands upon this subject; yet further, how often the coldness and indifference of wives are alleged as the excuse for conjugal infidelity.[18]

What is striking in this passage is that husbands complained to doctors about their wives' coldness, a fact that makes it quite evident that passion in wives was not only desired by men, but expected—why, otherwise, would they complain of its lack? Van de Warker, it is worth pointing out, was writing for his fellow physicians, who were in a position to verify his assertions from their own experience with patients.

Van de Warker's explanation for "impotency" in women is revealing, too. Ascribing it to "sexual incompatibility," he went on to say that "so far as my own observation extends, the husband is generally at fault. The more common cause is acute sexual irritability on the part of the husband."[19] Dr. William Goodell, writing in 1887, also asserted that mutual pleasure was essential to successful marital intercourse. In Goodell's mind, as in Van de Warker's, that meant men must recognize women's interests and sexual rhythm. "Destroy the reciprocity of the union," Goodell cautioned, "and marriage is no longer an equal partnership, but a sensual usurpation on the one side and a loathing submission on the other."[20] Another medical writer who also acknowledged women's pleasure in the sex act made the same point as Goodell and Van de Warker. Men must not force themselves upon women or "overpersuade, but await the wife's invitation at this time [during ovulation], when her husband is a hero in her eyes." In this way the husband "would enjoy more and suffer less," the physician predicted.[21] These writers, in short, were not only testifying to their knowledge that women possessed sexual feelings, they were also explaining how those feelings were sometimes denied legitimate satisfaction by inept husbands.

The assumption that women had sexual feelings which required satisfaction also comes through in the course of discussions about contraception. Generally, physicians and other writers on this subject in the nineteenth century strongly opposed contraception, though all recognized that it was widely practiced. One of the methods in common use was *coitus interruptus,* or withdrawal by the male prior to ejaculation. This method was condemned for a variety of reasons, but for our purposes it is significant that among the objections was its harmful effects upon women. This method, wrote Henry Chevasse, is "attended with disastrous consequences, most particularly to the female, whose nervous system suffers from ungratified excitement."[22] Dr. John Harvey Kellogg, a popular writer on medical matters, also warned against the method because of its effects upon women. He quoted at length from a French authority. Whenever this method is practiced, the authority wrote, all of women's genital organs "enter into a state of orgasm, a storm which is not appeased by the natural crisis; a nervous super excitation persists" after the act. The authority then compared the unreleased tension to that evoked in presenting food to a "famished man" and then snatching it away. "The sensibilities of the womb and the entire reproductive system are teased to no purpose." It is evident that in the minds of both writers women were assumed to have sexual feelings that were normally aroused during sexual intercourse.[23] Dr. August Gardner, writing in 1870 also for a popular audience, quoted from the same French authority and for the same purpose as Kellogg.[24]

Anyone who has looked into the sexual history of the nineteenth century is immediately struck by the deep and anxious concern physicians as well as other people felt about masturbation. Although it is often thought that boys were the principal objects of that concern, the fact is that girls were just as much fretted about. That there were such concerns about girls' masturbating is in itself a sign and measure of the recognition of sexual feelings in women. In fact, in 1871 one popular medical writer on women defined masturbation as "the mechanical irritation of the sexual organs in order to excite the same voluptuous sensations attendant upon natural intercourse."[25] Mary Wood-Allen, a leader in the Women's Christian Temperance Union and a writer of advice books for young women, had no doubt that girls could be led into self-abuse. Even girls who would not use any mechanical means "to arouse sexual desire," she pointed out, nevertheless permitted themselves to fantasize or to have mental images that "arouse the spasmodic feelings of sexual pleasure."[26] Indeed, from Wood-Allen's book one receives the message that women's sexual feelings were not only present but dangerously easy to arouse.

Discussion about masturbation in women reveals in another way how widely accepted was the idea that women possessed sexual desires. One physician, in the course of an article on the subject, said that the worst thing about masturbation in women was that a climax and resolution of tension were generally not achieved; hence the vice was persisted in. In response another doctor agreed that masturbation, indeed, gave rise to all the physical harm alleged in the article. But he disagreed with the assertion that in a woman sexual excitation could stop short of orgasm. "A commencement of the act, either of masturbation or coition," the letter writer contended, "*naturally* leads to its consummation, viz., an orgasm." Furthermore, he persisted, if "in the *healthy* female, an orgasm is not produced in the act of coition, she is not satisfied, and either will continue the act herself or with her coadjutor till such consummation does take place."[27]

Women's sexuality is also assumed in another class of medical concerns. When Dr. J. Marion Sims, the "founding father" of American gynecology, published *Clinical Notes on Uterine Surgery* in 1866, conception was only dimly understood. In explaining how it took place Sims revealed, in passing, that most people took for granted that women experienced sexual feelings. "It is the vulgar opinion, and the opinion of many savants," Sims remarked "that, to ensure conception, sexual intercourse should be performed with a certain degree of completeness, that would give an exhaustive satisfaction to both parties at the same moment." This sounds like twentieth-century ideas on optimum sexual performance, for Sims then went on to note, again in passing, that husbands and wives strove for such simultaneity and were unhappy when they failed to have simultaneous orgasms. "How often do we hear husbands complain of coldness on the part of the wives; and attribute to this the failure to procreate. And sometimes wives are disposed to think, though they never complain, that the fault lies with the hasty ejaculation of the husband."[28] Sims's point, of course, was that conception did not depend upon either sexual arousal or satisfaction in the woman. The important point for us, however, is that Sims, the medical readers he was addressing, and the patients he treated, all believed women were naturally capable of sexual feelings. Napheys, in his popular book of advice for women, also alluded to the prevalent idea that conception and pleasure were connected. He said that many people erroneously believed that conception could be known from the "more than ordinary degree of pleasure" on the part of the woman during the sexual act.[29]

In the course of discussing other kinds of women's illnesses, physicians often made it clear that they not only recognized the existence of sexual feelings in women but expected them in normal women. As we have observed already, Dr. Van de Warker considered the lack of sexual feelings in a woman as an abnormality to be cured. He called such women "impotent," just as one would denominate a man who failed to have adequate sexual responses. To Van de Warker, women had to learn how to dislike sex; enjoyment of it was natural.[30] Napheys, too, saw frigidity as abnormal; its removal, he thought, was "so desirable."[31] One physician in 1882, in discussing a case of excessive masturbation, wrote that during an examination his female patient experienced "the most intense orgasm that I have ever witnessed,"[32] implying that he had witnessed others. Another physician listed among the pathological symptoms of one patient "an absence of all sexual desire"[33]—as if its presence were the normal condition of a woman. One medical doctor, in trying to show how intense was the pain a married patient experienced during intercourse, said that both partners had given up sexual relations "although both had unusually violent animal passions."[34] In arguing against birth control Dr. August Gardner told of a wife who, fearing pregnancy since she had borne seven children in seven years, was "otherwise very ardent."[35]

During the 1880s and 1890s, as surgeons became more skillful and antisepsis made abdominal operations safer, a number of doctors sought to alleviate otherwise incurable or obscure pelvic pains and nervous conditions in women through the removal of ovaries. This medical development is a complex one, especially as to the attitudes it might reveal on the part of doctors and society in general. This is not the place to pursue that question, however. It serves to explain, though, why ovariodectomies were a subject of considerable interest among gynecologists. One consequence of that interest was a report in 1890 by a surgeon who had removed forty-six pairs of ovaries. Significantly, he related that "the sexual instinct was always preserved. Three patients, virginal before operation, married later and lived in happy wedlock. The passions persist particularly when the operation is performed early on young persons," he concluded.[36] For us the significance of this report is not whether it is accurate; in fact, I suspect that it is not. For as Dr. Van de Warker remarked on a different occasion, many women who suffered the pain or nervousness that caused them to submit to the operation in the first place probably had never felt any sexual pleasure. Consequently, to ask them after the operation whether there was any diminution in sexual feeling generally brought a denial. Moreover, the removal of the ovaries may well have reduced or eliminated hormonal secretions that may contribute to normal sexual feelings in women. In short, the physician's report suffers from his clear wish to put his series of operations in a good light. But that very wish is revealing, for what it tells us is that women were expected to have sexual feelings and it was undesirable for a surgeon or, presumably, anyone else, to eliminate or even reduce those feelings.

In the light of the foregoing it is difficult to accept the view that women were generally seen in the nineteenth century as without sexual feelings or drives. The question then arises as to how this widely accepted historical interpretation got established? Part of the reason, undoubtedly, is the result of the general reticence of the nineteenth century in regard to sex. The excessive gentility of the middle class has been read by historians as a sign of hostility toward sexuality, particularly in women. The whole cult of the home and women's allegedly exalted place in it was easily translated by some historians into an antisexual attitude.[37] But a good part of the explanation must also be attributable to the simple failure on the part of historians to survey fully the extant sources. The kind of statements quoted from medical writers in this article, for example, was either overlooked or ignored. Another important part of the explanation is that the sources that were surveyed and quoted were taken to be descriptive of the sexual ideology of the time when, in fact, they were part of an effort by some other medical writers to establish an ideology, not to delineate an already accepted one. In other words, the medical literature that was emphasized by Steven Marcus, Oscar Handlin, or Nathan Hale, Jr. was really normative or prescriptive rather than descriptive.

This misinterpretation was easy enough to make since much nineteenth-century medical literature was often descriptive in form even though, in fact, it was seeking to set a new standard of sexual behavior. Sometimes, however, the normative concerns and purposes showed through the ostensible description. A close reading, for example, of William Acton's second edition of *The Functions and Disorders of the Reproductive Organs* reveals in several places his desire to establish a new and presumably "higher" standard of sexual attitude and behavior. After pointing out that publicists strongly condemn sexual relations outside marriage, he asks, "But should we stop there? I think not. The audience should be informed that, in the present state of society, the sexual appetites must not be fostered; and experience teaches those who have had the largest means of information on the matter, that self-control must be exercised." So far, he continues, no one has "dared publicly to advocate . . . this necessary regulation of the sexual feelings or training to continence." Or later, when he discusses women in particular, it is evident that he is arguing for a special attitude, not merely describing common practice. "The *best* mothers, wives, and managers of households know little or nothing of sexual indulgence. Love of home, children, and domestic duties are the only passions they feel," he writes.[38]

American writers of the time who followed the lead of Acton as well as quoting him display a similar mixture of prescription and description. Take Dr. John Kellogg's *Plain Facts for Old and Young*, which sold over 300,000 copies by 1910 and went through five editions. Kellogg, like Acton, made it clear that he thought sex was too dominant in the thoughts of people. As we look around us today, he wrote, "it would appear that the opportunity for sensual gratification has come to be, in the world at large, the chief attraction between the sexes. If to these observations," he continued, "we add the filthy disclosures constantly made in police court and scandal suits, we have a powerful confirmation of the opinion."[39] It was this excess that he warns against, drawing upon quotations from Acton to support his arguments. He is at pains to show, too, that continence, especially in men, is not deleterious to health, as some contended. He admits that the medical profession is not in agreement on the amount of sexual indulgence permitted in marriage. "A very few hold that the sexual act should never be indulged except for the purpose of reproduction, and then only at periods when reproduction will be possible. Others, while equally opposed to the excesses . . . limit indulgence to the number of months in the year." Human beings, he advised, should take their cue from animals, who have intercourse only for procreation and then at widely spaced intervals. Instead of heeding this counsel, he writes, loosely quoting from Acton, "the lengths to which married people carry excesses is perfectly astonishing."[40]

Kellogg's reference to the behavior of animals as a worthy guideline for human behavior was echoed by other writers who sought to control sexuality. William Acton and Orson S. Fowler, for example, also used that standard of sexual behavior. Kellogg even went so far as to make an overt defense of the analogy. He carefully explained to his readers that in the modern age of biology these analogies were extremely helpful in getting at nature's purpose. "It is by this method of investigation," he remarked, "that most of the important truths of physiology have been developed; and the plan is universally acknowledged to be a proper and logical one." Then he launched into a condemnation of those men who use their wives as harlots, "having no other end but pleasure." For it was clear that among animals the end was reproduction only and then only at those one or two times a year when reproduction was possible. But by the time Kellogg reached the place in his book where he defended the analogy with animals he had already revealed that his purpose in invoking the analogy was reformist and normative, not simply scientific and logical. For in the early pages of his book, in making a different normative point—the need to protect children from premature sexuality—he told of a parent whose adolescent children often played games in the nude. When admonished for permitting this practice, the parent replied that it was only natural. "Perfectly harmless; just like little pigs!" Kellogg quoted the parent as saying. Kellogg's comment, however, was quite different from that which he would advise later in his book: "as though pigs were models for human beings!"[41]

In the end Kellogg himself virtually admitted that his "plain facts" were hardly facts at all, but prescriptions and hopes. "There will be many," he wrote, "the vast majority, perhaps, who will not bring their minds to accept the truth which nature seems to teach, which would confine sexual acts to reproduction wholly." And so he was prepared to offer a compromise, that is, a method of contraception. It was not a very effective method, as he admitted—the so-called safe period—but again what is important is his frank recognition that only a minority among his readers confined their sexual activities to reproduction and that he hoped he would be able to induce more to do so.[42]

It would be a mistake, in short, to accept the prescriptive or normative literature, like that of Acton, Kellogg, and others,[43] as revealing very much about sexual behavior in the Victorian era. It may be possible to derive a sexual ideology from such writers, but it is a mistake to assume that the ideology thus delineated is either characteristic of the society or reflective of behavior. On the contrary, it is the argument of this article that the attitudes and behavior of middle-class women were only peripherally affected by that ideology. Not only did many medical writers, as we have seen, encourage women to express their sexuality, but there is a further, even more persuasive reason for believing that the prescriptive literature is not a reliable guide to either the sexual behavior or the attitudes of middle-class women. It is the testimony of women themselves.

Any systematic knowledge of the sexual habits of women is a relatively recent historical acquisition, confined to the surveys of women made in the 1920s and 1930s and culminating in the well-known Kinsey report.[44] Until recently no even slightly comparable body of evidence for nineteenth-century women was known to exist. In the Stanford University Archives, however, are questionnaires completed by a group of women testifying to their sexual habits. The questionnaires are part of the papers of Dr. Clelia Duel Mosher (1863–1940), a physician at Stanford University and a pioneer in the study of women's sexuality. Mosher began her work on the sexual habits of married women when she was a student at the University of Wisconsin prior to 1892. That year she transferred for her senior year to Stanford, where she received an A.B. degree in 1893 and an M.A. in 1894. In 1900 she earned an M.D. degree from Johns Hopkins University. After a decade of private practice she joined the Stanford faculty as a member of the department of hygiene and medical adviser to women students. Her published work dealt with the physical capabilities of women; she was a well-known advocate of physical exercise for women. Mosher's questionnaires are carefully arranged and bound in volume 10 of her unpublished work, "Hygiene and Physiology of Women." Mosher, however, apparently never drew more than a few impressionistic conclusions from the highly revealing questionnaires. She did not even publish the fact of their existence, and so far as can be ascertained no use has heretofore been made of this manuscript source. Yet the amount and kind of information on sexual habits and attitudes of married women in the late nineteenth century contained in these questionnaires are unique.

The project, which spanned some twenty years, was begun at the University of Wisconsin when Mosher was a student of biology in the early 1890s. She designed the questionnaire when asked to address the Mother's Club at the university on the subject of marriage. In later years she added to her cases and used the information when giving advice to women about sexual and hygienic matters.[45] This initiative, as well as the kind of questions she asked, reveals that Mosher was far ahead of her time. She amassed information on women's sexuality that none of the many nineteenth-century writers on the subject studied in any systematic way at all.

The questionnaire itself is quite lengthy, comprising twenty-five questions, each one of which is divided into several parts. Much of the questionnaire, it is true, is taken up with ascertaining facts about the parents and even the grandparents of the respondents, but over half of the questions deal directly with women's sexual behavior and attitudes.[46] The information contained in the questionnaires not only supports the interpretation of women's sexuality that already has been drawn from the published literature, both lay and medical, but it also provides us with a means of measuring the degree to which the prescriptive marriage literature affected women's sexual behavior.

Since the evidence in this questionnaire, which I call the Mosher Survey, has never been used before, it is first worthwhile to examine the social background of the women who answered the questionnaires. All told there are forty-six useable questionnaires, but since two of the questionnaires seem to have been filled out by the same woman at an interval of twenty-three years, the number of women actually surveyed is forty-five.[47] In the aggregates that follow I have counted only forty-five questionnaires. The questionnaires, it ought to be said, were not administered at the same time, but at three different periods at least; moreover the date of administration of nine questionnaires cannot be ascertained. Of those that do provide that information, seventeen were completed before 1900, fourteen were filled out between 1913 and 1917, and five were answered in 1920.

More important than the date of administration of the questionnaires are the birth dates of the respondents. All but one of the forty-four women who provided their dates of birth were born before 1890. In fact thirty-three, or 70 percent of the whole group, were born before 1870. And of these, seventeen, or slightly over half, were born before the Civil War. For comparative purposes it might be noted that in Alfred Kinsey's survey of women's sexuality, the earliest cohort of respondents was only born in the 1890s. In short, the attitudes and practices to which the great majority of the women in the Mosher Survey testify were those of women who grew up and married within the nineteenth century, regardless of when they may have completed the questionnaires.

An important consideration in evaluating the responses, of course, is the social origins of the women. From what class did they come, and from what sections of the country? The questionnaire, fortunately, provides some information here, but not with as much precision as one might like. Since the great majority of the respondents attended college or a normal school (thirty-four out of forty-five, with the education of three unknown), it is evident that the group is not representative of the population of the United States as a whole. The remainder of the group attended secondary school, either public or private, a pattern that is again not representative of a general population in which only a tiny minority of young people attended secondary school. But for purposes of evaluating the impact of the prescriptive or marital-advice literature upon American women this group is quite appropriate. For inasmuch as their educational background identifies them as middle- or upper-class women, it can be said that they were precisely those persons to whom that advisory literature was directed and upon whom its effects ought to be most evident.

In geographical origin the respondents to the Mosher Survey seem to be somewhat more representative, if the location of parents, birthplaces, and colleges attended can be taken as a measure, albeit impressionistic, of geographical distribution. Unfortunately there is no other systematic or more reliable information on this subject. The colleges attended, for example, are located in the Northeast (Cornell [6], Smith, Wellesley, and Vassar [2]), in the Middle West (Ripon, Iowa State University, and Indiana), and in the Far West (Stanford [9], the University of California, and the University of the Pacific). The South is not represented at all among the colleges attended.

Although the emphasis upon prestigious colleges might make one think that these were women of the upper or even leisure class, rather than simply middle class, a further piece of information suggests that, in fact, they were not. One of the questions asked concerned working experience prior to marriage. Although seven of the respondents provided no data at all on this point, and eight reported that they had married immediately after completing their education, thirty of the women reported that they had worked prior to marriage. As a side light on the opportunities available to highly educated women in the late nineteenth century, it is worth adding that twenty-seven of the thirty worked as teachers. On the basis of their working experience it seems reasonable to conclude that the respondents were principally middle- or upper-middle-class women rather than members of a leisure class.

Despite the high level of education of these women, they confessed to having a pretty poor knowledge, by modern standards, of sexual physiology before marriage. Only eleven said that they had much knowledge on that subject, obtained from female relatives, books, or courses in college, while another thirteen said that they had some knowledge. The remainder—slightly over half—reported that they had very little or no knowledge. No guidelines were given in the questionnaire for estimating the amount of knowledge. The looseness of the definition is shown by the fact that three of the respondents who said that they had no knowledge at all named books on women's physiology that they had read. From other titles mentioned in passing it is clear that a number of these women had direct acquaintance with the prescriptive and advisory literature of the time. How did it affect their behavior? Did they repress their sexual impulses or deny them, as some of the prescriptive literature advised? Were they, in fact, without sexual desire? Or were they motivated toward personal sexual satisfaction as the medical literature quoted in this article advised?

The Mosher Survey provides a considerable amount of evidence to answer these and other questions. To begin with, thirty-five of the forty-five women testified that they felt desire for sexual intercourse independent of their husband's interest, while nine said they never or rarely felt any such desire. What is more striking, however, is the number who testified to orgasmic experience. According to the standard view of women's sexuality in the nineteenth century, women were not expected to feel desire and certainly not to experience an orgasm. Yet it is striking that in constructing the questionnaire Dr. Mosher asked not only whether the respondents experienced an orgasm during intercourse but whether "you *always* have a venereal orgasm?" (my italics). Although that form of the question makes quite clear Mosher's own assumption that female orgasms were to be expected, it unfortunately confuses the meaning of the responses. (Incidentally, only two of the forty-five respondents failed to answer this question.) Five of the women, for instance, responded "no" without further comment. Given the wording of the question, however, that negative could have meant "not always, but almost always" as well as "never" or any response in between these extremes. The ambiguity is further heightened when it is recognized that in answer to another question, three of the five negatives said that they had felt sexual desire, while a fourth said "sometimes but not often," and the fifth said sex was "usually a nuisance." Luckily, however, most of the women who responded to the question concerning orgasm made more precise answers. The great majority of them said that they had experienced orgasms. The complete pattern of responses is set forth in Table 1.

**Table 1.** RESPONSE TO THE QUERY: "DO YOU ALWAYS HAVE A VENEREAL ORGASM?"

| Response | Number | Percentage |
|---|---|---|
| No response | 2 | 4.4% |
| "No" with no further comment | 5 | 11.1 |
| "Always" | 9 | 20.0 |
| "Usually" | 7 | 15.5 |
| "Sometimes," "Not Always," or "No" with instances | 18 | 40.0 |
| "Once" or "Never" | 4 | 8.8 |

In sum, thirty-four of the women experienced orgasm, with the possibility that the figure might be as high as thirty-seven if those who reported "no" but said they had felt sexual desire are categorized as "sometimes." (Interestingly enough, of nine women out of the forty-five who said they had never felt any sexual desire, seven said that they had experienced orgasms.) Moreover, sixteen or almost half of those who experienced orgasms did so either "always" or "usually." As we have seen, in the whole group of forty-five, all but two responded to the question asking if an orgasm was always experienced. Of those forty-three, thirty-four were born before 1875. Five answered "no" to that question without any further comment. One other woman responded "never," and two others said "once or twice." If the "noes" and the "never" are taken together, the proportion of women born before 1875 who experienced at least one orgasm is 82 percent. If the "noes" are taken to mean "sometimes" or "once or twice," as they might well be, given the wording of the question, then the proportion rises to 95 percent. For comparative purposes the figures for twentieth-century women provided in Kinsey's study are given in Table 2.

**Table 2.** PERCENTAGE OF WOMEN EXPERIENCING ORGASM DURING INTERCOURSE (BY DECADE OF BIRTH)

| Women Born | Ages 21–25 | Ages 26–30 |
|---|---|---|
| Before 1900 | 72% | 80% |
| 1900–09 | 80 | 86 |
| 1910–19 | 87 | 91 |
| 1920–29 | 89 | 93 |

Source: Alfred C. Kinsey et al., *Sexual Behavior in the Human Female* (Philadelphia, 1953), 397, table 97.

Kinsey's proportions are arranged by age group and chronological period; hence they are not strictly comparable with those derived from Mosher's data. But the comparison is still suggestive, even when made with the women in the age group 26–30.[48]

Much more interesting and valuable than the bare statistics are the comments or rationales furnished by the women, which provide an insight into the sexual attitudes of middle-class women. As one might expect in a population by its own admission poorly informed on sexual physiology, the sexual adjustment of some of these women left something to be desired. Mosher, for example, in one of her few efforts at drawing conclusions from the Survey, pointed out that sexual maladjustment within marriage sometimes began with the first intercourse. "The woman comes to this new experience of life often with no knowledge. The woman while she may give mental consent often shrinks physically." From her studies Mosher had also come to recognize that women's "slower time reaction" in reaching full sexual excitement was a source of maladjustment between husband and wife that could kill off or reduce sexual feelings in some women. Women, she recognized, because of their slower timing were left without "the normal physical response. This leaves organs of women over congested."[49] At least one of her respondents reported that for years intercourse was distasteful to her because of her "slow reaction," but "orgasm [occurs] if time is taken." On the other hand, the respondent continued, "when no orgasm, [she] took days to recover."[50] Another women spoke of the absence of an orgasm during intercourse as "bad, even disastrous, nerve-wracking—unbalancing, if such conditions continue for any length of time." Still a third woman, presumably referring to the differences in the sexual rhythms of men and women, said, "Men have not been properly trained." One of the women in the Mosher Survey testified in another way to her recognition of the differences in the sexuality of men and women. "Every wife submits when perhaps she is not in the mood," she wrote, "but I can see no bad effect. It is as if it has not been. But my husband was absolutely considerate. I do not think I could endure a man who forced it." And her response to a question about the effects of an orgasm upon her corroborate her remark: "a general sense of well being, contentment and regard for husband. This is true Doctor," she earnestly wrote.[51]

Mosher's probing of the attitudes of women toward their sexuality went beyond asking about orgasms. Several of her questions sought to elicit the reactions of women to sexual intercourse. What is the purpose of sex, she asked? Is it a necessity for a man or for a woman? Is it for pleasure, or is it for reproduction?[52] Only two of the women failed to respond in some fashion to these questions. Nine thought sex was a necessity for men, while thirteen thought it was a necessity for both men and women. Fifteen of the respondents thought it was not a necessity for either sex. Twenty-four of the forty-five thought that it was a pleasure for both sexes, while only one thought it was exclusively a pleasure for men. Given the view generally held about sexual attitudes in the nineteenth century, it comes as something of a surprise to find that only thirty marked "reproduction" as the primary purpose of sex. In fact, as we shall see in a moment, some of the women thought reproduction was not as important a justification for intercourse as love.

As one might expect, this particular series of questions was usually answered with a good deal of explanation. One woman who emphasized reproduction as the principal justification took the opportunity to condemn those couples she apparently had heard of who did not want children. "I cannot recognize as true marriage that relation unaccompanied by a strong desire for children." She thought it was close to "legalized prostitution." She admitted that because of her love for her husband she "cultivated the passion to effect the 'compromise' in this direction that must come in every other [area] when people marry." She went on to say that she did not experience orgasm until the fifth or sixth year of her marriage and that even at the time of her response to the questionnaire—the early 1890s—she still did not reach a sexual climax half the time. A second woman was also apparently out of phase with her husband's sexual interests, for she thought a woman's needs for sex occurred "half as often as a man's." It is revealing of her own feelings that though she said "half as often," the figures she used to illustrate her point—twice a week for a man and twice a month for a woman—are actually in the ratio of one to four rather than of one to two as she said. Her true attitude was also summed up in the remark that since she was always in good health and intercourse "did not hurt me, . . . I always meant to be obliging."[53]

But, as the earlier statistical breakdown makes evident, the women who only tolerated intercourse were in a decided minority. A frank and sometimes enthusiastic acceptance of sexual relations was the response from most of the women. Sexual intercourse "makes more normal people," said a woman born in 1857. She was not even sure that children were necessary to justify sexual relations within marriage. "Even if there are no children, men love their wives more if they continue this relation, and the highest devotion is based upon it, a very beautiful thing, and I am glad nature gave it to us." Since marriage should bring two people close together, said one woman born in 1855, sexual intercourse is the means that achieves that end. "Living relations have a right to exist between married people and these cannot exist in perfection without sexual intercourse to a moderate degree. This is the result of my experience," she added. A woman born in 1864 described sexual relations as "the gratification of a normal healthy appetite." The only respondent who was divorced and remarried testified in 1913 that at age fifty-three "my passionate feeling has declined somewhat and the orgasm does not always occur," but intercourse, she went on, was still "agreeable" to her.[54]

Several of the women even went so far as to reject reproduction as sufficient justification for sex. Said one woman, "I consider this appetite as ranking with other natural appetites and like them to be indulged legitimately and temperately; I consider it illegitimate to risk bringing children into the world under any but most favorable circumstances." This woman was born before the Compromise of 1850 and made her comment after she had been married ten years. Another woman, also born a decade before the Civil War, denied that reproduction "alone warrants it at all; I think it is only warranted as an expression of true and passionate love.

This is the prime condition for a happy conception, I fancy." To her, too, the pleasure derived from sexual intercourse was "not sensual pleasure, but the pleasure of love."[55]

A third woman born before 1861 doubted that sex was a necessity in the same sense as food or drink, but she had no doubt that "the desire of both husband and wife for this expression of their union seems to me the first and highest reason for intercourse. The desire for offspring is a secondary, incidental, although entirely worthy motive but could never to me make intercourse right unless the mutual desire were also present." She saw a clear conflict between the pleasure of intercourse and reproduction. "My husband and I," she said in 1893,

> believe in intercourse for its own sake—we wish it for ourselves and spiritually miss it, rather than physically, when it does not occur, because it is the highest, most sacred expression of our oneness. On the other hand, even a slight risk of pregnancy, and then we deny ourselves the intercourse, feeling all the time that we are losing that which keeps us closest to each other.[56]

Another woman, in describing the ideal of sexual relations, said that she did not want intercourse to occur at any time when conception was likely, for conception should not occur by accident. Instead it ought to be the result of

> deliberate design on both sides in time and circumstances most favorable physically and spiritually for the accomplishment of an immensely important act. It amounts to separating times and objects of intercourse into (a) that of expression of love between man and woman (that act is frequently simply the extreme caress of love's passion, which it would be a pity to limit . . . to once in two or three years) and (b) that of carrying on a share in the perpetuation of the race, which should be done carefully and prayerfully.[57]

It seems evident that among these women sexual relations were neither rejected nor engaged in with distaste or reluctance. In fact, for them sexual expression was a part of healthy living and frequently a joy. Certainly the prescriptive literature that denigrated sexual feelings or expression among women cannot be read as descriptive of the behavior or attitude of these women. Nevertheless, this is not quite the same as saying that the marriage handbooks had no effect at all. To be sure, there is no evidence that the great majority of women in the Mosher Survey felt guilty about indulging in sex because of what they were told in the prescriptive literature. But in two cases that literature seems to have left feelings of guilt. One woman said that sexual relations were "apparently a necessity for the *average* person" and that it was "only [the] superior individuals" who could be "independent of sex relations with no evident ill-results." To her, as to St. Paul and some of the marriage-advice books, it was better to indulge than to burn, but it was evidently even better to be free from burning from the beginning. A more blatant sign of guilt over sex came from the testimony of a woman who quite frankly thought the pleasure of sex was a justification for intercourse, but, she added "not necessarily a legitimate one."[58]

Dr. Mosher herself obliquely testified to the effects of the prescriptive literature. She attributed the difficulties some women experienced in

420 | WHAT OUGHT TO BE AND WHAT WAS

reaching orgasm to the fact that "training has instilled the idea that any physical response is coarse, common and immodest which inhibits [women's] proper part in this relation."[59] That was the same point that some of the medical writers in the nineteenth century had made in explaining the coldness of some women toward their husbands.

The advice literature, for men as well as for women, generally warned against excessive sexual activity.[60] This emphasis upon limits is reflected in the remarks of some of the women in the Mosher Survey. One woman said, for example, that "the pleasure is sufficient warrant" for sexual relations, but only if "people are extremely moderate and do not allow it to injure their health or degrade their best feelings toward each other." Another woman had concluded that "to the man and woman married from love," sexual intercourse "may be used temperately as one of the highest manifestations of love granted us by our Creator." A third woman who had no doubt that sexual relations were "necessary to marital happiness," nonetheless said she believed "in temperance in it."[61] But temperance, another one of the women in the Mosher Survey reminds us, should not be confused with repugnance or distaste. Although this respondent did not think the ideal sexual relation should occur more often than once a month, she did think it ought to take place "during the menstrual period . . . and in the daylight." The fact is that this woman, in answer to other questions, indicated that she experienced sexual desire about once a week, but with greatest intensity "before and during menses." She was, in short, restricting her own ideal to what she considered an acceptable frequency of indulgence. Her description of her feelings after orgasm suggests where she learned that limits on frequency might be desirable or expected: "Very sleepy and comfortable. No disgust, as I have heard it described."[62]

This examination of the literature, the popular advice books, and particularly the Mosher Survey makes clear that historians are ill-advised to rely upon the marital-advice books as descriptions either of the sexual behavior of women or of general attitudes toward women's sexuality. It is true that a literature as admittedly popular as much of the prescriptive or normative literature was could be expected to have some effect upon behavior as well as attitudes. But those effects were severely limited. Most people apparently did not follow the prescriptions laid down by the marriage and advice manuals. Indeed, some undoubtedly found that advice wrong or misleading when measured against experience. Through some error or accident the same woman was apparently interviewed twice in the Mosher Survey, twenty-three years apart. As a result we can compare her attitudes at the beginning of her marriage in 1896 and her attitude in 1920. After one year of marriage she thought that sexual relations ought to be confined to reproduction only, but when asked the same question in 1920, she said that intercourse ought not to be confined to reproduction, though she thought it should be indulged in only when not pressed with work and when there was time for pleasure.[63] Another woman in the Mosher Survey changed her mind about sexual relations even earlier in her sexual life. She said,

My ideas as to the reason for [intercourse] have changed materially from what they were before marriage. I then thought reproduction was the only object and that once brought about, intercourse should cease. But in my experience the habitual bodily expression of love has a deep psychological effect in making possible complete mental sympathy, and perfecting the spiritual union that must be the lasting "marriage" after the passion of love has passed away with years.

These remarks were made in 1897 by a woman of thirty after one year of marriage.[64]

Her comments make clear once again that historians need to recognize that the attitudes of ordinary people are quite capable of resisting efforts to reshape or alter them. That there was an effort to deny women's sexual feelings and to deny them legitimate expression cannot be doubted in the light of the books written then and later about the Victorian conception of sexuality. But the many writings by medical men who spoke in a contrary vein and the Mosher Survey should make us doubt that the ideology was actually put into practice by most men or women of the nineteenth century, even among the middle class, though it was to this class in particular that the admonitions and ideology were directed. The women who responded to Dr. Mosher's questions were certainly middle- and upper-middle-class women, but they were, as a group, neither sexless nor hostile to sexual feelings. The great majority of them, after all, experienced orgasm as well as sexual desire. Their behavior in the face of the antisexual ideology pressed upon them at the time offers testimony to the truth of Alex Comfort's comment that "the astounding resilience of human commonsense against the anxiety makers is one of the really cheering aspects of history."[65]

## NOTES

1. Captain Frederick Marryat, *A Diary in America, with Remarks on Its Institutions* (London, 1839), 2: 244–247. The story of the trousers on piano legs is taken seriously in John Duffy, "Masturbation and Clitoridectomy: A Nineteenth-Century View," *Journal of the American Medical Association*, 186 (1963): 246; G. Rattray Taylor, *Sex in History* (New York, 1954), 203; and Peter T. Cominus, "Innocent Femina Sensualis in Unconscious Conflict," in Martha Vicinus, ed., *Suffer and Be Still: Women in the Victorian Age* (Bloomington, 1972), 157.

2. William Acton, *The Functions and Disorders of the Reproductive Organs in Youth, in Adult Age, and in Advanced Life: Considered in Their Physiological, Social, and Psychological Relations* (1857; 2d ed., London, 1858; expanded American ed., Philadelphia, 1865). For references to Acton's writings, see Steven Marcus, *The Other Victorians: A Study of Sexuality and Pornography in Mid-Nineteenth-Century England* (New York, 1966), ch. 1; and Nathan G. Hale, Jr., *Freud and the Americans: The Beginnings of Psychoanalysis in the United States, 1876–1917* (New York, 1971), 36–37.

3. Acton, *Functions and Disorders* (1865), 133.

4. Theophilus Parvin, "Hygiene of the Sexual Functions," *New Orleans Medical and Surgical Journal*, n.s. 11 (1883–1884): 607. Parvin also quotes at length from Acton's book.

5. Walter E. Houghton, *The Victorian Frame of Mind, 1830–1870* (New Haven, 1957),

353. Marcus presents a portrait of Victorian attitudes toward sex similar to that of Houghton, but he disclaims to be talking about behavior: "We need not pause to discuss the degree of truth or falsehood in these assertions. What is of more immediate concern is that these assertions indicate a system of beliefs." *Other Victorians*, 32. Yet it is not clear what point there is in detailing a system of beliefs unless it has some behavioral consequences. Peter T. Cominos also relies upon Acton, in "Late Victorian Sexual Respectability and the Social System," *International Review of Social History*, 8 (1963): 18–48, 217–250. E. M. Sigsworth and T. J. Wyke doubt the pervasiveness in Victorian England of Acton's conception of women's sexuality. They write: "Victorian opinion on the innate sexuality of women was cloudy and divided"—a view about which more will be said in this article. "A Study of Victorian Prostitution and Venereal Disease," in Vicinus, *Suffer and Be Still*, 83.

6. Viola Klein, *The Feminine Character: History of an Ideology* (1946; reprint, Urbana, 1972), 85, as quoted in David M. Kennedy, *Birth Control in America: The Career of Margaret Sanger* (New Haven, 1970), 56–57.

7. Hale, *Freud and the Americans*, 31. Elsewhere Hale sums up the medical view as he sees it: "By 1906 . . . some physicians regarded the asexual female as the norm: 'It may be offered that the sexual appetite in the majority of American females is evoked only by the purest love. In many the appetite never asserts itself and, indeed, the only impulse thereto is in the desire to gratify the object of affection'" (pp. 39–40; quotation from Ferdinand C. Valentine, "Education in Sexual Subjects," *New York Medical Journal*, Feb. 10, 1906, p. 276).

8. Ben Barker-Benfield, "The Spermatic Economy: A Nineteenth-Century View of Sexuality," *Feminist Studies*, 1 (1972): 54.

9. Charles Fayette Taylor, "Effect on Women of Imperfect Hygiene of the Sexual Function," *American Journal of Obstetrics*, 15 (1882): 175–176, 168–171, italics in original.

10. Orson S. Fowler, *Sexual Science; Including Manhood, Womanhood, and Their Mutual Interrelations, etc. . . . as Taught by Phrenology* (Philadelphia, 1870), 680.

11. P. Henry Chevasse, *Physical Life of Man and Woman: or, Advice to Both Sexes* (1866; reprint, New York, 1897), 291–292; quotation from Trall in Michael Gordon, "From an Unfortunate Necessity to a Cult of Mutual Orgasm: Sex in American Marital Education Literature, 1830–1940," in James M. Henslin, ed., *Studies in the Sociology of Sex* (New York, 1971), 58, my italics.

12. George H. Napheys, *The Physical Life of Woman: Advice to the Maiden, Wife, and Mother* (1869; Philadelphia, 1871), 74–75, 180.

13. Ely Van de Warker, "Impotency in Women," *American Journal of Obstetrics*, 11 (1878): 47.

14. J. Milne Chapman, "On Masturbation as an Etiological Factor in the Production of Gynic Diseases," *American Journal of Obstetrics*, 16 (1883): 454.

15. Montrose S. Pallen, "Some Suggestions with Regard to the Insanities of Females," *American Journal of Obstetrics*, 10 (1877): 209.

16. William M. McLaury, "Remarks on the Relation of the Menstruation to the Sexual Functions," *American Journal of Obstetrics*, 20 (1887): 161.

17. Chevasse, *Physical Life of Man and Woman*, 372–373.

18. Van de Warker, "Impotency in Women," 38–39.

19. Ibid., 41. Today the complaint is called premature ejaculation.

20. William Goodell, *Lessons in Gynecology* (Philadelphia, 1887), 567, as quoted in Hale, *Freud and the Americans*, 40.

21. McLaury, "Remarks on the Relation of the Menstruation," 161.

22. Chevasse, *Physical Life of Man and Woman*, 424–425.

23. John Harvey Kellogg, *Plain Facts for Old and Young* (1879; Burlington, Iowa, 1881), 252.

24. Augustus K. Gardner, *Conjugal Sins against the Laws of Life and Health and Their Effects upon the Father, Mother, and Child* (New York, 1870), 98.

25. Chevasse, *Physical Life of Man and Woman*, 33.

26. Mary Wood-Allen, *What a Young Woman Ought to Know* (Philadelphia, 1905), 155.

27. Chapman, "On Masturbation"; letter from S. E. McCully, *American Journal of Obstetrics*, 16 (1883): 844, my italics.

28. James Marion Sims, *Clinical Notes on Uterine Surgery* (London, 1866), 369.

29. Napheys, *Physical Life of Woman*, 104–105. This belief, which other writers also speak of, may well have affected some women's attitudes toward orgasm, for if a woman, under this view, could repress pleasure or climax, conception could be prevented.

30. Van de Warker, "Impotency in Women," 39.

31. Napheys, *Physical Life of Woman*, 86.

32. Horatio R. Bigelow, "Aggravated Instance of Masturbation in the Female," *American Journal of Obstetrics*, 15 (1882): 437.

33. "A Case of Excision of Both Ovaries for Fibrous Tumors of the Uterus, and a Case of Excision of the Left Ovary for Chronic Oöphoritis and Displacement," reported by Dr. E. H. Trenholme in *Canada Lancet*, July 1876, *American Journal of Obstetrics*, 9 (1876–1877): 703.

34. "Case of Vaginismus," reported by Dr. George Pepper, *American Journal of Obstetrics*, 3 (1871): 322–324.

35. Gardner, *Conjugal Sins*, 97.

36. Summary of paper by Dr. Keppler, "The Sexual Life of the Female after Castration," given at the 10th International Medical Congress, *American Journal of Obstetrics*, 23 (1890): 1155–1156.

37. Not all historians, it should be noted, have assumed that nineteenth-century concerns about sex meant hostility toward women's sexuality. In tracing the history of the social- purity movement after 1870, David J. Pivar is careful to distinguish between a concern with the exploitation of women's sexuality and an opposition to women's sexual feelings. See his *Purity Crusade, Sexual Morality, and Social Control: 1868–1900* (Westport, 1973).

38. Acton, *Functions and Disorders* (1858), 8–9; (1865), 134, my italics.

39. Kellogg, *Plain Facts*, 178. Hale gives the figures on Kellogg's sales in *Freud and the Americans*, 37.

40. Kellogg, *Plain Facts*, 206, 209, 247, 225–226, Kellogg also quoted Acton.

41. Ibid., 217, 221–225, 118.

42. Ibid., 265–266.

43. It is true that some of the advice and medical literature that recognized women's sexual feelings and from which I have been quoting was also prescriptive rather than merely descriptive. But for convenience and economy of words in subsequent pages when I refer to "prescriptive or normative literature" I mean only that which minimized or denied women's sexuality.

44. Among the largest and most significant of such surveys were Katharine B. Davis, *Factors in the Sex Life of Twenty-two Hundred Women* (New York, 1929); Robert Latou Dickinson and Lura Beam, *A Thousand Marriages: A Medical Study of Sex Adjustment* (Baltimore, 1931); and Alfred C. Kinsey et al., *Sexual Behavior in the Human Female* (Philadelphia, 1953). The first chapter of Robert Latou Dickinson and Lura Beam, *The Single Woman* (Baltimore, 1934), concerns the sexual life of working girls in the 1890s, but it is based on forty-six cases, the typical patient being born "soon after 1870." I am indebted to David M. Kennedy of Stanford University for this reference.

45. Mosher, "Hygiene and Physiology of Women," 10: xv, Mosher Papers, Stanford University Archives.

46. The principal questions dealing with women's sexual habits are: number of conceptions; number of conceptions by choice and by accident; frequency of intercourse; whether intercourse is participated in during pregnancy; whether intercourse is "agreeable"; whether an orgasm occurs; what effects from orgasm, or from failure to have one; purpose of intercourse; the ideal habit of sexual relations; whether there is desire for intercourse other than during pregnancy; whether contraception is used and method employed; whether wife sleeps in same bed with husband; knowledge of sexual physiology prior to marriage; and the character of menses: age of onset, pain, and amount.

47. The small number of women queried in the Mosher Survey may cause some readers to discount almost entirely the significance of any conclusions drawn from it. While such a response may be understandable as a first reaction, in the end I think it would be unwise. So far as I know, this is the only survey of sexual attitudes and practices in the nineteenth century; historians' standard conception of women's sexual practices and attitudes in the nine-

teenth century has been derived from no previous survey at all. Certainly the systematic questioning of forty-five women at considerable length and their rationales for their answers ought to be at least as significant in shaping historians' conceptions of women's sexuality as the scraps of information from interested writers at the time, novels, and recollections, which have been the bases of our traditional picture of women's sexual attitudes and behavior in the nineteenth century. It is true that we do not know at the present time who these women were or how random their selection was. But there seems little reason to believe that the women were specially chosen by Mosher, if only because the purpose of the original questionnaire as well as the use of the information gained from it were to help her in advising women students. Moreover, as an unmarried woman herself, it is very likely that the information from the questionnaires was Mosher's most valuable source of knowledge on women's sexuality. It is probably true, given the general reluctance of nineteenth-century people to discuss sex, that some women whom Mosher approached refused to answer the questionnaire. But it is worth recalling that the value even of modern sex surveys, including Kinsey's, has been questioned on the grounds that the respondents were largely self-selected. Obviously the Mosher Survey is not the final word on the sexual behavior and attitudes of women in the nineteenth century. But at the same time it ought not to be rejected because of its limited size; that would be applying a methodological standard quite inappropriate for a sensitive subject in which the evidence is always limited and fugitive.

48. A comparison of the sexual responses of the older and younger women in the Mosher Survey did not reveal any greater interest in sex among the younger group, but the numbers involved were too small to be significant. The responses of fourteen women born before 1860 were compared with those of the eight women born after 1875. On the other hand, if the responses to the questions about desire for sex and about orgasmic experience are categorized by date at which the questionnaire was completed, regardless of the age of the respondent, there is a slight, if somewhat ambiguous, difference between the earlier and later respondents. Seventeen women completed the questionnaire before 1900; nineteen did so after 1912. Thirteen of the seventeen completed before 1900 responded to the question of whether they had experienced orgasm; four of the thirteen said they had not. Eighteen of the nineteen who completed the questionnaire after 1912 answered that question; only one out of eighteen failed to experience an orgasm. In themselves these data suggest that women who answered the questionnaire in the twentieth century achieved somewhat more satisfaction in their sexual experience than those who completed the questionnaire in the nineteenth century. But when a similar division by century is made of the questionnaires in regard to another question, that conclusion is not so clear. One of the questions asked whether the respondent felt sexual desire. Fourteen women answered the question prior to 1900, of whom only two said they had failed to feel desire. But of the sixteen who responded to the same question after 1912, three said they lacked any feeling of desire. Here the proportion of sexuality was higher among the nineteenth- than the twentieth-century respondents.

49. Mosher, "Hygiene and Physiology of Women," 10: 1. Twelve of the women were asked how soon after marriage they engaged in intercourse. Six said within the first three days, while six said from ten days to a year after the ceremony.

50. Ibid., case no. 51. The case numbers have been assigned by Mosher herself and appear on each page of each questionnaire. Hereafter the citation of cases will carry only "Hygiene and Physiology of Women" and case number.

51. Ibid., case nos. 47, 40, 41.

52. Since each respondent could legitimately answer "yes" to all three suggested justifications for sexual relations, the totals here can go beyond forty-five, though not all questions were always answered.

53. Ibid., case nos. 24, 19.

54. Ibid., case nos. 41, 18, 2. It is worth noting that here, as elsewhere in the survey, no mention was made of religious reasons for or against intercourse. These women had almost entirely secularized their sexual ideology.

55. Ibid., case nos. 14, 12.

56. Ibid., case no. 15.

57. Ibid., case no. 22.

58. Ibid., case nos. 47, 30. Marcus found a comparable example of guilt arising out of the

prescriptive literature against masturbation. In discussing the Victorian sexual autobiography *My Secret Life*, Marcus observes that the anonymous author gave full credence to the dangers described in the literature, yet he masturbated nonetheless. After doing so, however, the anonymous author reported he suffered from depression, guilt, fatigue, and general feelings of debilitation though he felt none of these symptoms after sexual intercourse. Marcus ascribes these feelings to an internalizing of social attitudes, presumably derived from the prescriptive literature against masturbation. *Other Victorians*, 112. It is significant, however, that the prescriptions did not stop the practice. Why it did not stop is suggested by a more recent study of sexual behavior. Masters and Johnson report that most of their male subjects still believed the old tales of physical and psychical harm from masturbation, especially from "excessive" activity, but none of them desisted from the practice. The authors point out that no matter how active a subject was in this respect, he always defined "excessive" as more active than his own practice, William H. Masters and Virginia E. Johnson, *Human Sexual Response* (Boston, 1966), 201–202.

59. Mosher, "Hygiene and Physiology of Women," 10; 1.

60. Hale cites sources ranging in origin from 1830 to 1910 on the concern for conserving sexual energy. *Freud and the Americans*, 35. Oscar Handlin sums up the advice in this fashion: "Abstinence, repression, and self-restraint thus were the law; and violations were punished by the most hideous natural consequences, described in considerable graphic detail." Handlin's conclusion, however, that the readers of that literature "were overwhelmed by the guilt and shame the necessities of self-control imposed," seems unwarranted on the basis of present evidence. *Race and Nationality in American Life* (Garden City, 1957), 122–123.

61. Mosher, "Hygiene and Physiology of Women," case nos. 33, 10, 13.

62. Ibid., case no. 11.

63. Ibid., case nos. 30, 33. Mosher gives no indication that she knew the two questionnaires were from the same person.

64. Ibid., case no. 22.

65. Alex Comfort, *The Anxiety Makers: Some Curious Preoccupations of the Medical Profession* (London, 1967), 113.

# 20 | THE DATING OF THE AMERICAN SEXUAL REVOLUTION: EVIDENCE AND INTERPRETATION

## DANIEL SCOTT SMITH

Prevailing views of current patterns and recent changes in sexual behavior have been limited by the absence and neglect of systematic historical comparison. The very notion of a "sexual revolution," defined here narrowly as a substantial sustained increase in nonmarital coitus and broadly as a qualitatively more positive evaluation of sex as a human activity, implicitly embodies an attempt at historical periodization. Unfortunately, our understanding of the prerevolutionary phase of the history of sexual behavior rests mainly on ignorance. Sociologists typically place the significant beginnings of a sexual revolution for white American women during the 1920s.[1] Most historians, on the other hand, locate these important changes in values and behavior some ten to twenty years earlier.[2] Other scholars have hinted at cyclical patterns, a constant ongoing revolution since the eighteenth century, or even historical stability in rates of premarital intercourse.[3] Since the attempt to gather historical data about American sexual behavior and attitudes has only recently begun, the overall trends necessarily remain uncertain and confused. What is presently known about the history of sexual attitudes is confined to what may be called "respectable" ideology—extracted from marriage manuals, magazines, novels, and medical literature. What little is available about sexual behavior is concerned with some of the obvious though not inevitable consequences of nonmarital sexual activity—illegitimacy and premarital (or bridal) pregnancy.

This article will be limited to a comparison of the premarital pregnancy indices with other measures of sexual change during the last century in order to specify the dimensions of the complex process commonly labeled the "sexual revolution." Since the last one hundred years are not the most dramatic in the history of American premarital pregnancy, defining the trend is relatively more difficult than for the previous two centuries. The proportion of women pregnant at marriage has varied cyclically, with peaks in the late eighteenth century and in recent years and troughs in the mid-seventeenth and mid-nineteenth centuries (Table 1).[4] Such a long cycle is also apparent in Western European illegitimacy and premarital pregnancy data; however, the major downturn in European nonmarital pregnancy rates came some fifty years or more after the American decline of the early nineteenth century.[5] Since World War II, both illegitimacy and premarital pregnancy have increased significantly in England and Australia as well as in the United States.[6] In order to draw precise inferences about premarital behavior from these data, the alternative possibilities—contraception, fecundability, spontaneous and induced abortion—must be estimated. The biological determinants probably vary within too narrow limits to explain the trends; the social variables appear to be positively correlated over time. For example, illegitimacy, premarital pregnancy, contraceptive use, and perhaps induced abortion have all increased since World War II. Since little is known about the variation in these alternative possibilities for more distant periods, they cannot be definitely excluded.[7]

Relevant information for the study of sexual change during the last century includes data on premarital pregnancy incidence from surveys and the matching of birth and marriage records; illegitimacy for the last half century; premarital coitus for selected samples of twentieth-century women; "respectable" sexual attitudes and values; and other indicators of sociofamilial change such as the divorce rate. By itself, any of the above five sources gives an inadequate and misleading picture of the timing of changes in sexual behavior; considered together, they present a coherent and plausible pattern.

**Table 1.** LONG-TERM HISTORICAL VARIATION IN WHITE AMERICAN PREMARITAL PREGNANCY

| PERIOD | Percentage of first births within nine months of marriage | | Description of sample |
|---|---|---|---|
| | MARRIAGES | AREAS | |
| Before 1701[a] | 11.1% | 9.9% | 1,113 marriages in nine areas (8 in New England) |
| 1701–1760[a] | 23.3 | 19.4 | 1,311 marriages in nine areas (6 in New England) |
| 1761–1800[a] | 33.7 | 34.0 | 1,011 marriages in six areas (5 in New England) |
| 1801–1840[a] | 25.1 | 28.3 | 573 marriages in two areas (1 in New England) |
| 1841–1880[a] | 15.5 | 16.9 | 555 marriages in two areas (both in New England) |
| 1960–1964[b] | 22.5 | | |
| 1964–1966[c] | 19.5 | | |

a. Daniel Scott Smith and Michael S. Hindus, "Premarital Pregnancy in America, 1640–1966: An Overview and Interpretation." (Paper presented at the annual meeting of the American Historical Association, New York City, December 1971).
b. Wilson H. Grabill and Maria Davidson, "Marriage, Fertility and Childspacing: June 1965," U.S. Bureau of the Census, Current Population Reports, series p-20, no. 186 (Washington, 1969), table 17, p. 39. This measure includes births from eight months and zero days to nine months and thirty days after marriage but excludes those born before marriage; the denominator includes all births after forty-eight months of marriage.
c. U.S. Department of Health, Education and Welfare, Public Health Service, "Interval between first marriage and legitimate first birth, United States, 1964-66," *Monthly Vital Statistics Report* 18, no. 12 (March 27, 1970): 2, Table 2. Proportion of first births under eight months of marriage.

**Table 2.** CPS Premarital Pregnancy Rates for Twentieth-Century White Marriage Cohorts

Number of first births within a specified time per 1,000 marriages[a]

| MARRIAGE COHORTS | BEFORE MARRIAGE | | SIX MONTHS | | SEVEN MONTHS | | EIGHT MONTHS | | NINE MONTHS | |
|---|---|---|---|---|---|---|---|---|---|---|
| | 1959 | 1964 | 1959 | 1965 | 1959 | 1965 | 1959 | 1965 | 1959 | 1964 |
| 1900–1909 | n.a. | | 45 | | 57 | | 74 | | 133 | |
| 1910–1919 | n.a. | | 55 | | 69 | | 89 | | 139 | |
| 1920–1924 | n.a. | | 48 | | 59 | | 83 | | 127 | |
| 1925–1929 | n.a. | | 44 | | 56 | | 81 | | 122 | |
| 1930–1934 | n.a. | | 54 | | 69 | | 90 | | 123 | |
| 1935–1939 | n.a. | | 51 | | 68 | | 86 | | 118 | |
| 1940–1944 | n.a. | 22 | 44 | 55 | 61 | 66 | 80 | 87 | 114 | 122 |
| 1945–1949 | n.a. | 23 | 57 | 63 | 77 | 83 | 103 | 108 | 156 | 165 |
| 1950–1954 | n.a. | 25 | 71 | 77 | 96 | 104 | 119 | 130 | 175 | 186 |
| 1955–1959 | n.a. | 37 | 85[b] | 112 | 127[b] | 147 | 160[b] | 183 | 223[b] | 248 |
| 1960–1964 | | 36 | | 129 | | 168[b] | | 205[b] | | 261[b] |

Sources: *1959 survey:* Wilson H. Grabill and Robert Parke, "Marriage, Fertility and Childspacing: August 1959," U.S. Bureau of the Census, *Current Population Reports,* series P-20, no. 108 (Washington, D.C., 1961): 38, table 17.

*1965 survey:* Wilson H. Grabill and Maria Davidson, "Marriage, Fertility and Childspacing: June 1965," U.S. Bureau of the Census, *Current Population Reports,* series P-20, no. 186 (Washington, D.C., 1969): 39, table 17.

a. Based on a question asking for calendar month and year of first marriage and birth. Hence, those born six months after marriage fall in the range from five months and zero days to six months and thirty-one days.

b. Rate adjusted for part of marriage cohort that has not reached stated interval.

## PREMARITAL PREGNANCY

**Survey Data**   In 1959 and 1965 the Current Population Survey (CPS) of the Census Bureau asked national samples of American women the month and year of their first marriage and of the birth of their first child. Between 7 and 9 percent of white women marrying in pre-World War II cohorts had their first child before eight months of marriage; between 10 and 14 percent of white first births born within forty-eight months of marriage came within the first eight months of marriage (Table 2). During 1940–1944 and 1960–1964 both measures doubled, increasing to 20.5 percent and 25.0 percent respectively for the first half of the 1960s. Some 19.5 percent of a national sample of white mothers of legitimate first children born in 1964–1966 reported that they had been married less than eight months.[8] These data, considered alone, suggest that premarital sexual behavior or the outcomes of premarital intercourse have changed significantly only during the last twenty years.[9]

**Record-Matching Data**   This clear picture of a post-World War II sexual revolution becomes questionable when local studies of the interval between marriage and first birth are compared to the CPS national samples.

**Table 3.**   COMPARISON OF CPS AND RECORD-MATCHING DATA ON PREMARITAL PREGNANCY

| MARRIAGE COHORT | Percent within six months* 1959 SURVEY | 1965 SURVEY | Percent within seven months* 1959 SURVEY | 1965 SURVEY | Percent within 196 days* RECORD-MATCHING STUDIES | |
|---|---|---|---|---|---|---|
| 1900–09 | 5.8% | | 7.4% | | 1905–07[a] | 11.9% |
| | | | | | 1913–15[a] | 14.8 |
| 1910–19 | 7.3 | | 9.2 | | 1919–21[b] | 11.9 |
| | | | | | 1918–22[c] | 10.9 |
| 1920–24 | 6.7 | | 8.3 | | 1921–23[a] | 9.6 |
| 1925–29 | 6.4 | | 8.1 | | 1929–31[b] | 8.0 |
| 1930–34 | 8.1 | | 10.4 | | 1929–31[a] | 14.8 |
| 1935–39 | 7.7 | | 10.3 | | 1928–32[c] | 14.1 |
| | | | | | 1939–41[a] | 4.5 |
| 1940–44 | 6.3 | 7.7% | 78.8 | 9.3% | 1939–41[b] | 9.8 |
| 1945–49 | 7.4 | 8.0 | 10.0 | 10.6 | 1939–42[c] | 6.9 |
| 1950–54 | 9.0 | 9.6 | 12.1 | 13.0 | 1949–51[a] | 5.3 |
| 1955–59 | | 13.5 | | 17.7 | | |
| 1960–64 | | 15.7 | | 20.4 | 1957–62[d] | 9.3 |

Sources: *CPS surveys.* See notes for Table 2.

*In order to provide comparability with the measured used in record-matching studies percentages are based on first births occurring within 48 months of marriage.

a. *Utah County, Utah:* Harold T. Christensen, "Child-Spacing Analysis via Record Linkage," *Marriage and Family Living* 35 (1963): 275.

b. *Tippecanoe County, Indiana:* Ibid., p. 275.

c. *Defiance County, Ohio:* Ibid., p. 275.

d. *Wood County, Ohio:* Samuel H. Lowrie, "Early Marriage, Premarital Pregnancy and Associated Factors," *Journal of Marriage and the Family* 27 (1965): 50.

No trend is apparent from the first decade of the twentieth century to the early 1960s (Table 3). Using a long interval, ranging from 251 to 265 days, or allocating uncertain cases by birth weight, between 17 and 30 percent of first births occurring in the same geographical location as the marriage were conceived before marriage in these twentieth-century samples. In the most recent data, the record-matching method produces a figure comparable to the CPS surveys. The 18.8 percent figure for Wood County, Ohio, for 1957–1962 and the 19–20 percent indicated for Detroit couples in the early 1960s are sufficiently close to the national survey of mothers of 1964–1966 legitimate first births (19.5 percent) to be considered identical.[10] For the pre-1940 samples, record-matching consistently produces a higher incidence than the retrospective CPS cohorts surveyed in 1959.

At first glance one might dismiss the narrow, unrepresentative local samples, such as the Mormon Utah study, as reflecting special circumstances. Since a substantial proportion of marriages cannot be linked to a first birth because of such factors as geographically exogamous marriage, migration of the couple after marriage but before childbearing, and infertility of the couple, record-matching provides an index but perhaps not a precise measure of the absolute level of premarital pregnancy. For assessing trends the key issue is the stability of the ratio of migratory pregnant couples to those who migrate nine or more months after marriage but before they have their first child. Since it seems unlikely that social censure of the premaritally pregnant has increased during the twentieth century, the record-matching index of premarital pregnancy should exhibit an upward movement similar to the CPS trend.

The reliability of the CPS curve as an index of change depends on the absence of an age bias in response to the survey. The women surveyed in 1959 who were first married before 1940 were all over forty; their answers may reflect to some extent their current attitudes, especially with regard to the premarital sexual behavior of their daughters, and not their actual experience several decades earlier.[11] If sexual attitudes have actually become progressively more liberal in recent years, younger women should be less concerned than their elders with suppressing the fact of a premarital conception. Supporting this hypothesis of increasing honesty about the subject is the higher reported incidence (0.7 percent, 0.5 percent, 1.1 percent and 2.3 percent for the 1940–1944, 1945–1949, 1950–1954 and 1955–1959 marriage cohorts) of children born within eight months of marriage in the 1965 survey as compared to the group sampled in 1959 (see Table 2). Thus, it is quite likely that the upward trend since 1945 in the CPS premarital pregnancy curve is exaggerated. Nevertheless, the upsurge is not entirely a statistical mirage. Since premarital pregnancy and early marriage are related, the decline in the age at first marriage between 1940 and 1960 implies an increasing number of brides pregnant at marriage. Since World War II, women marrying at age twenty-two or over have been only three-fourths as likely to have a birth within seven months of marriage as those women marrying under that age.[12] Without any increase in age-specific premarital pregnancy rates, the overall proportion of women pregnant at marriage would increase somewhat. The shape of the national trend for the first forty years of the twentieth century is not necessarily flat. In Australia, for example, just over 30 percent of women married in 1911 were pregnant at marriage; by 1942 a mere 11.7 percent were, while in 1965, 23.6 percent of all brides were pregnant.[13]

## ILLEGITIMACY

Further evidence of a substantial increase in white premarital sexual activity since 1940 is found in the striking rise in illegitimacy, that is the conception and birth of children outside marriage. Following two decades of stability, the white illegitimacy rate leaped 250 percent between 1940 and 1967 (Table 4). The general increase in illegitimacy for women of all ages reflects mainly an increase in the incidence of premarital coitus. If the CPS post-1940 trend in premarital pregnancy is biased upward, then a decreasing proportion of white nonmarital pregnancies are now being terminated within marriage.[14] This relative shift from bridal pregnancy to illegitimacy is also apparent in national data for England and Australia.[15] Consistent with this development is the reported lesser emotional commitment required for coitus by modern college coeds.[16] The qualitative context as well as the quantitative incidence of premarital sexual activity has been modified since World War II.

**Table 4.**    AGE-SPECIFIC ILLEGITIMACY RATES FOR WHITE AMERICAN WOMEN (BIRTHS PER 1,000 OF UNMARRIED WOMEN)

| | Age of women | | | | | | |
|---|---|---|---|---|---|---|---|
| YEAR | 15–44 | 15–19 | 20–24 | 25–29 | 30–34 | 35–39 | 40–44 |
| 1940 | 3.6 | 3.3 | 5.7 | 4.0 | 2.5 | 1.7 | 0.7 |
| 1950 | 6.1 | 5.1 | 10.0 | 8.7 | 5.9 | 3.2 | 0.9 |
| 1960 | 9.2 | 6.6 | 18.2 | 18.2 | 10.8 | 3.9 | |
| 1965 | 11.6 | 7.9 | 22.1 | 24.3 | 16.6 | 4.9 | |
| 1967 | 12.5 | 9.0 | 23.1 | 22.7 | 14.0 | 4.7 | |
| Increase 1940–67 | 247% | 273% | 305% | 467% | 460% | 292%- | |

Sources: U.S. Department of Health, Education and Welfare, Public Health Service, Vital and Health Statistics, series 21, no. 15, "Trends in Illegitimacy, United States, 1940-1965" (Washington, D.C., 1968), p. 4, table B; Vital and Health Statistics, series 21, no. 19, "Natality Statistics Analysis, United States, 1965-1967," (Rockville, Maryland, 1970), p. 33, table 23.

## PREMARITAL COITUS

The behavioral evidence for the dating of the sexual revolution in the 1920s consists of surveys of the premarital coital experience of selected groups of American women. Although sociologists allow for an important liberalization of attitudes and an increase in noncoital sexual activity such as petting, they have cautiously concluded that between the 1920s and the early 1960s no marked increase in premarital coitus occurred. With evidence indicating a jump in the level of premarital intercourse during the late 1960s, a new phase of the sexual revolution is apparently now in progress.[17] While the increase in illegitimacy and premarital pregnancy in the late 1940s and 1950s may cast some doubt on the timing of this second take-off, the dating of the first phase relies on the small minority of women who attended college. Between two-thirds and three-fourths of the women in the three most important historical studies of premarital coitus had some college experience, while only 10.2 percent and 13.1 percent of native-born women born, respectively, between 1891 and 1900 and between 1901 and 1910 went beyond high school. While nearly half of all native-born white women terminated their formal education before the ninth grade, a mere 2.3 percent to 4.5 percent in the three studies had less than a high school education.[18] For this college-educated minority, the sexual revolution may have originated in the 1920s or, as the Terman sample suggests, during the preceding decade (Table 5).[19] Furthermore, it is not clear *which* college-educated women appear in these studies; it is possible that the older women interviewed by Kinsey and associates were drawn more heavily from religious groups instead of universities and clubs.[20]

Since late nineteenth- and early twentieth-century premarital pregnancy ratios are very close to the reported pre-1900 levels of premarital coitus, a downward bias of the pre-1900 reported intercourse incidence is likely. While 7 percent of the Davis sample, 13 percent of the pre-1890 and 26 percent of the 1890–1899 birth cohorts in the Terman study, and 27 percent of the pre-1900 Kinsey birth cohort had premarital intercourse, 16 percent of first births were conceived before marriage in Hingham, Mass. (1861–1880), 19 percent in Lexington, Mass. (1885–1895), 20 percent (1905–1907) and 29 percent (1913–1915) in Utah County, Utah, and 20 percent in Tippecanoe County, Indiana (1919–1921).[21] As every school girl should know, intercourse is a necessary though not sufficient prerequisite to pregnancy. The absence of a larger differential between premaritally conceived first births and the incidence of premarital coitus suggests that the timing of the first phase of the sexual revolution varied for dif-

**Table 5.** INCIDENCE OF PREMARITAL COITUS FOR WHITE AMERICAN WOMEN: THE SEXUAL REVOLUTION OF THE 1920S?

| Authors of study | Birth dates of women in study | Percent with premarital coitus |
|---|---|---|
| Davis[a] | before 1900 | 7.2% |
| Terman[b] | before 1890 | 13.5% |
| | 1890–1899 | 26.0 |
| | 1900–1909 | 48.8 |
| | 1910–later | 68.3 |
| Kinsey et al[c] | before 1900 | 26.6 |
| | 1900–1909 | 51.3 |
| | 1910–1919 | 56.1 |
| | 1920–1929 | 51.2 |

a. Katherine B. Davis, *Factors in the Sex Lives of Twenty-Two Hundred American Women* (New York, 1929), p. 19.

b. Lewis M. Terman, *Psychological Factors in Marital Happiness* (New York, 1938), p. 321.

c. Ira L. Reiss, "Standards of Sexual Behavior," in Albert Ellis and Albert Abarbanel, *The Encyclopedia of Sexual Behavior* (New York, 1961), 2: 999. Calculated from unpublished data from the Institute for Sex Research.

ferent social strata in the white population. College-educated women, largely of middle- and upper-middle-class backgrounds, maintained conservative sexual standards longer than the remainder of the population. The premarital pregnancy ratio in Hingham increased from 8.5 percent (1841–1860) to 16.0 percent (1861–1880), and in Lexington the comparable index jumped from 3.6 percent (1854–1866) to 19.3 percent (1885–1895). For the general population of women, important changes in premarital sexual behavior already were under way during the late nineteenth century.

Very recent data from the first national probability sample of the incidence of teenage premarital coitus helps define more precisely the magnitude of change in sexual behavior since the 1940s. Today's teenagers from fifteen to nineteen are at least twice as likely to have had coital experience as the Kinsey women born during the 1920s. Two-fifths of single white nineteen-year-old women have experienced coitus while only 23 percent in the 1910–1919 and 21 percent in the 1920–1929 Kinsey birth cohorts had such experience by the age of twenty.[22] It is possible that this doubling of teenage coital incidence rates merely represents a lowering of the age of sexual participation, which may be attributed to the declining age at menarche and earlier socio-sexual maturity.[23] The incidence figures for sixteen and eighteen year olds in the recent survey are only slightly above the Kinsey figures for women marrying between sixteen and twenty (17.5 percent and 33.5 percent versus 15 percent and 30 percent, respectively).[24] However, the illegitimacy rate has increased more for women between twenty-five and thirty-four than for those between fifteen and twenty-four (bottom row of Table 4), and the concentration of premarital pregnancy among younger women has not increased between 1945–1949 and 1960–1964.[25] While the Kinsey sample is not a representative benchmark, the apparent increase in teenage premarital coitus is consistent with the other indicators of change in sexual behavior. Finally, of course, this focus on the significance of the past decade or so as a period of comparatively rapid sexual change does not contradict the obvious manifestations of changing social attitudes and increasing *public* interest concerning sexuality.

## ATTITUDES

Since sexual standards are largely maintained by the family, the most impenetrable social institution, the connection between shifts in behavior and public attitudinal change is not automatic or inevitable, especially in the short run. However, the investigation of ideal sexual standards does supplement the tentative conclusions with regard to behavior. Following a more general trend in American historiography that focuses on the internal dissolution of Victorian bourgeois culture, the emergence of new, more liberal sexual attitudes is now being dated before the First World War.[26] The origins of these changes, like the increase in premarital pregnancy in the two Massachusetts towns with available data, lie in the last decades of the nineteenth century. By 1900 the ideal conception of woman as frail, dependent, and virtuous was being challenged by a small but vocal group of feminists.[27] By the beginning of World War I the "newness" of non-Victorian attitudes was wearing off.[28] Articles on birth control, prostitution, divorce, and sexual morals between 1910 and 1914 were more numerous than articles indexed by the *Reader's Guide* for either 1919–1924 or 1925–1928.[29] During the last two decades of the nineteenth century authors of marriage manuals for middle-class educated readers were beginning to endorse pleasure as a positive aspect of marital sexuality; during the first two decades of this century this shift continued but was not complete until the 1920s.[30]

The movement for legal sexual repression associated with the work of Anthony Comstock and state anticontraception laws during the last third of the nineteenth century is consistent with the hypothesis that the Victorian moral order was already in crisis before 1900.[31] By the end of the century the conservative defenders of premarital continence were becoming more defensive and frenetic. During the early twentieth century their efforts met with both ridicule and support.[32] If public opinion and individual internalization of morality were operative, official repression of deviant sexual activity would have been superfluous and unnecessary. The official response to what was considered sexual deviancy resulted from an objective increase in "deviant" behavior.

## DIVORCE

Changes in attitudes and behavior must be considered simultaneously to ascertain if *significant* change is occurring. In as sensitive an area as sexual behavior before marriage, considerable divergence is to be expected. Hence, information on another aspect of family change is quite relevant to this discussion of the dating of the sexual revolution. The conceptual rationale for divorce as an integral part of a marriage system based on affection was established in the late nineteenth century.[33] Since divorce is an indicator of the social meaning of marriage, time-series data on the divorce rate provide a suggestive supplement to this periodization of sexual change. The number of divorces per 1,000 existing marriages increased 102 percent between 1860–1864 and 1880–1884, 79 percent between 1880–1884 and 1900–1904, 71 percent between 1900–1904 and 1920–1924, and 43 percent between 1920–1924 and 1940–1944. However, the absolute increases were greatest during the twentieth century with upward increments of 1.2, 1.9, 3.0, and 3.1 per 1,000 existing marriages, respectively, for the above periods.[34] Although the absolute change increases, the rate of change declines over time. A parallel conclusion with regard to changes in the incidence of premarital sexual behavior seems plausible for the period between the Civil War and World War I.

## CONCLUDING SCENARIO OF THE "SEXUAL REVOLUTION"

Clearly, more research is needed on both behavior and attitudes before firm conclusions can be drawn about the history of American sexuality and the dating of the sexual revolution. Considerable and surprising variation is obvious, particularly in the premarital pregnancy boom of the eighteenth century and the bust of the nineteenth. For the sexual revolution since the Victorian nadir, the following conclusions may be tentatively advanced:

(1) The "revolutionary" character of the sexual revolution can easily be overstated. The trend toward increasing nonmarital sexual intercourse has been ongoing for nearly a century from a level which was not fully restrictive. Even in respectable sexual ideology, mid-nineteenth-century women were not typically considered to be asensual.[35] Two-thirds of all women in the most conservative pre-1900 birth cohort in the Kinsey study experienced orgasm during the first year of marriage, compared to 78 percent of those born in the 1920s.[36] Clearly there was an increase, but equally clearly "sexlessness" was nowhere near being a majority experience for American women before the sexual revolution began. The qualitative meaning of the sexual revolution in behavior is not promiscuity; for the great majority of American women, premarital sexual permissiveness is intimately related to affection, mutuality, and a positive choice for the close interpersonal relationship. Half of the sexually experienced teenagers surveyed by Zelnik and Kantner said they intended to marry their lovers.[37] A substantial minority are pregnant at marriage but only a tiny fraction bear an illegitimate child.

(2) Change in sexual behavior has probably not been linear and continuous. Little or no change in premarital pregnancy, illegitimacy, or premarital coitus occurred between the 1920s and the 1940s. Both quantitatively and qualitatively, the most significant phase of the sexual revolution has occurred during the last two decades.

(3) The timing of the first wave of the sexual revolution has probably varied markedly for different groups in the white population. If one particular period can be labeled the "origins," the last third of the nineteenth century probably encompassed a larger proportion of the population than either the 1920s or the decade before World War I. During the late nineteenth century the intellectual basis for a more positive evaluation of human sexuality was established. The first three decades of this century may be characterized as an era in which the behavior of the educated minority of women converged upon the behavior of the less-educated majority. During the same three decades the sexual attitudes of the younger educated strata were significantly liberalized. Then from the 1920s to the 1950s the higher level of premarital coitus was increasingly supported by a further democratization of this more tolerant ideology. When this convergence of attitudes and behavior neared completion during the 1950s, the stage was set for the most recent transformation in both behavior and attitudes.

## NOTES

1. Ira L. Reiss, "The Sexual Renaissance: A Summary and Analysis," *Journal of Social Issues* 22, no. 2 (1966): 123–137. Erwin O. Smigel and Rita Seiden, "The Decline and Fall of the Double Standard," *The Annals of the American Academy of Political and Social Science* 376 (1969): 6–17.

2. James R. McGovern, "The American Woman's Pre-World War I Freedom in Manners and Morals," *Journal of American History* 55, no. 2 (1968): 315–333. David M. Kennedy, *Birth Control in America: The Career of Margaret Sanger* (New Haven, 1970). William L. O'Neill, *Divorce in the Progressive Era* (New Haven, 1967). Nathan G. Hale, Jr., *Freud and the Americans: The Beginnings of Psychoanalysis in the United States, 1876–1917* (New York, 1971).

3. For an implied cyclical view, see Robert R. Bell, *Premarital Sex in a Changing Society,* (Englewood Cliffs, N.J., 1966), pp. 17–40; and Paul Woodring, "Some Thoughts on the Sexual Revolution," in Gerald D. Winter and Eugene M. Nuss, *The Young Adult: Identity and Awareness* (Glenview, Ill., 1969), pp. 116–119. Winter and Nuss claim in their introduction to the Woodring essay that "it would appear that America has been the scene of a continuous sexual revolution from at least as early as the beginning of the eighteenth century." More commonly, evidence of high levels of premarital sexual activity in the distant past has been used to conclude that little change has occurred in the course of American history. For this inference, see Thomas P. Monahan, "Premarital Pregnancy in the United States: A Critical Review and Some New Findings," *Eugenics Quarterly* 7, no. 3 (1960): 133–147; and Ira L. Reiss, *Premarital Sexual Standards in America* (New York, 1960), p. 132.

4. A speculative explanation and more detailed examination of this long cycle is provided in Daniel Scott Smith and Michael S. Hindus, "Premarital Pregnancy in America, 1640–1966: An Overview and Interpretation" (paper presented at the annual meeting of the American Historical Association, December 1971).

5. Edward Shorter, "Illegitimacy, Sexual Revolution and Social Change in Modern Europe," *Journal of Interdisciplinary History* 2, no. 2, (1971): 237–272. P. E. H. Hair, "Bridal pregnancy in rural England in earlier centuries," *Population Studies* 20 (1966): 233–243 and "Bridal pregnancy in earlier England further examined," *Population Studies* 24 (1970: 59–70. Edward Shorter, John Knodel, and Etienne van de Walle, "The Decline of Non-Marital Fertility in Europe, 1880–1940," *Population Studies* 24 (1971), 375–393.

6. Phillips Cutright, "Illegitimacy: Myths, Causes and Cures," *Family Planning Perspectives* 3, no. 1 (1971): 26. Shirley M. Hartley, "The Amazing Rise of Illegitimacy in Great Britain, *Social Forces* 44, no. 4 (1966): 533–545. K. G. Basavarajappa, "Pre-marital Pregnancies and Ex-Nuptial Births in Australia, 1911–66," *Australian and New Zealand Journal of Sociology* 4, no. 2 (1968): 126–145.

7. On the alternative possibilities, see Kingsley Davis and Judith Blake, "Social Structure and Fertility: An Analytic Framework," *Economic Development and Cultural Change* 4, no. 3 (1956): 211–235, and Cutright, "Illegitimacy," pp. 26–28.

8. U.S. Department of Health, Education, and Welfare, Public Health Service, "Interval Between First Marriage and Legitimate First Birth, United States, 1964–66," *Monthly Vital Statistics Report* 18, no. 12, supplement (March 27, 1970): 2, table 2.

9. In an important analysis of the components of the increase in teenage illegitimacy, Phillips Cutright allocates 77 percent of the white increase in premarital pregnancy and illegitimacy to higher rates of premarital intercourse and 23 percent to improved fecundity and health. "The Teenage Sexual Revolution and the Myth of an Abstinent Past," *Family Planning Perspectives* 4, no. 1 (1972), table 3, col. 6.

10. Samuel H. Lowrie, "Early Marriage, Premarital Pregnancy and Associated Factors," *Journal of Marriage and the Family* 27 (1965): 50. Lolagene C. Coombs, Ronald Freedman, Judith Friedman, and William F. Pratt, "Premarital Pregnancy and Status before and after Marriage," *American Journal of Sociology* 75, no. 5 (1970): 804.

11. Reiss has found that the social roles associated with age are important determinants of attitudes toward premarital sexual permissiveness. Some 21 percent of persons between 21 and 34, 20 percent of those 35–49, but only 13 percent of persons over 50 expressed "highly permissive" views on the subject. Similarly, people with teenage children were less permissive than those with preteenagers or no children. Reiss, *The Social Context of Premarital Sexual Permissiveness* (New York, 1967), pp. 141–143.

12. Wilson H. Grabill and Maria Davidson, "Marriage, Fertility and Childspacing: June 1965," U.S. Bureau of the Census, *Current Population Reports,* series P-20, no. 186 (Washington, 1969), p. 47, table 21.

13. Basavarajappa, "Pre-marital Pregnancies," p. 143, table A.

14. Accepting the accuracy of the CPS premarital pregnancy series, Reynolds Farley and Albert I. Hermalin have calculated that 55 percent, 63 percent, and 60 percent, of the offspring of all white first premarital pregnancies were born after marriage in the 1940–1949, 1950–1959, and 1960–1964 marriage cohorts. See "Family Stability: A Comparison of Trends between Blacks and Whites," *American Sociological Review* 36, no. 1 (1971): 12–13.

15. Hartley, "The Amazing Rise," p. 540, table 3. Basavarajappa, "Pre-marital Pregnancies," p. 141.

16. Compared to 1958 the percentages of coeds having intercourse in 1968 in a "dating" situation has increased from 10 percent to 23 percent, in a "going steady" context from 15 percent to 28 percent, but in an "engagement" relationship the rise has only been from 31 percent to 39 percent. Furthermore, the proportion feeling they "went too far" has been cut in half in all three contexts. Robert R. Bell and Jay B. Chaskes, "Premarital Sexual Experience among Coeds, 1958–1968," *Journal of Marriage and the Family* 23, no. 1 (1970): 83. For a general review of recent events, see Kenneth L. Cannon and Richard Long, "Premarital Sexual Behavior in the Sixties," *Journal of Marriage and the Family* 53, no. 1 (1971): 36–49.

17. Reiss, "The Sexual Renaissance," p. 127.

18. Lewis M. Terman, *Psychological Factors in Marital Happiness* (New York, 1938), p. 43. Katherine B. Davis. *Factors in the Sex Life of Twenty-Two Hundred American Women* (New York, 1929), p. 3. Paul H. Gebhard, Wardell B. Pomeroy, Clyde E. Martin, and Cornelia V. Christenson, *Pregnancy, Birth and Abortion*, (New York, 1958), p. 24. Data for native-born white women from Wilson H. Grabill, Clyde V. Kiser, and Pascal K. Whelpton, *The Fertility of American Women* (New York, 1958), p. 191.

19. Coital incidence and educational level are not related in the Kinsey sample, once age at marriage is controlled. However, there are only 97 single women over twenty with less than a high-school education. Alfred C. Kinsey, Wardell B. Pomeroy, Clyde E. Martin, and Paul H. Gebhard, *Sexual Behavior in the Human Female*, (New York, 1965), p. 333, table 75.

20. How Kinsey prodigiously collected his sexual histories is related by Wardell B. Pomeroy, *Dr. Kinsey and the Institute for Sex Research* (New York, 1972), pp. 106–137, 369–371; and Cornelia V. Christenson, *Kinsey: A Biography* (Bloomington, Ind., 1971), pp. 103–110, 134–135. On the inadequacies and the considerable relative merits of the Kinsey population, see the analysis of the male volume by William C. Cochran, Frederick Mosteller, and John W. Tukey, *Statistical Problems of the Kinsey Report* (Washington, 1954), pp. 21–29, 44–65.

21. Smith and Hindus, "Premarital Pregnancy," pp. 55–56, 67. A measure of 8 1/2 months was used for the Massachusetts towns and 251 days for the samples in Table 3.

22. Report on the study undertaken by Melvin Zelnik and John F. Kantner for the Commission on Population Growth and the American Future, *New York Times*, May 10, 1972, p. 9.

23. Cutright, "The Teenage Sexual Revolution," pp. 25–26. J. M. Tanner, "Earlier Maturation in Man," *Scientific American* 218, no. 1 (1968): 24–27.

24. *New York Times*, May 10, 1972, p. 9. Kinsey et al., p. 337, table 79.

25. Grabill and Davidson, "Marriage, Fertility and Childspacing: June 1965," p. 47, table 21.

26. The pioneering revisionist study is Henry F. May, *The End of American Innocence: A Study of the First Years of our Time, 1912–1917* (New York, 1959), esp. pp. 334–347.

27. Kennedy, *Birth Control in America*, pp. 53–63.

28. Ibid., p. 71.

29. McGovern, "American Woman's Pre-World War I Freedom," p. 316.

30. Michael Gordon, "From an Unfortunate Necessity to a Cult of Mutual Orgasm: Sex in American Marital Education Literature, 1830–1940," in James Henslin, ed., *Studies in the Sociology of Sex* (New York, 1971), pp. 53–77.

31. Carol Flora Brooks, "The Early History of the Anti-Contraceptive Laws in Massachusetts and Connecticut," *American Quarterly* 18 (1966): 3–23. Robert Bremner, ed., *Traps for the Young by Anthony Comstock* (Cambridge, 1967), pp. vii–xxxi.

32. Hale, *Freud and the Americans*, p. 26. Bremner, *Traps for the Young*, pp. xxix–xxxi and cartoons following p. 130.

33. O'Neill, *Divorce in the Progressive Era*, pp. 89–167.

34. Paul H. Jacobson, *American Marriage and Divorce* (New York, 1959), estimated rates on p. 90, table 42.

35. Gordon, "Sex in American Marital Education Literature," pp. 53–77.

36. Kinsey et al., p. 403, table 104.

37. *New York Times*, May 10, 1972, p. 9.

# SELECTED READINGS FOR PART FIVE

FLAHERTY, DAVID H. *Privacy in Colonial New England.* Charlottesville: University of Virginia Press, 1972.

FLANDRIN, J. L. "Repression and Change in the Sexual Life of Young People in Medieval and Early Modern Times," *Journal of Family History*, 2 (1977), 196–210.

GORDON, MICHAEL. "From an Unfortunate Necessity to a Cult of Mutual Orgasm: Sex in American Marital Education Literature, 1830–1940." In *Studies in the Sociology of Sex.* Ed. James Henslin. New York: Appleton-Century-Crofts, 1971.

HALLER, JOHN S., AND ROBIN M. HALLER. *The Physician and Sexuality in Victorian America.* Urbana: University of Illinois Press, 1974.

KINSEY ALFRED C. et al. *Sexual Behavior in the Human Male.* Philadelphia: Saunders, 1948.

_____. *Sexual Behavior in the Human Female.* Philadelphia: Saunders, 1953.

ROBINSON, PAUL. *The Modernization of Sex.* New York: Harper & Row, 1976.

ROSENBERG, CHARLES. "Sexuality, Class and Role in Nineteenth-Century America." *American Quarterly*, 25 (1973), 131–153.

SHORTER, EDWARD. "Illegitimacy, Sexual Revolution, and Social Change in Modern Europe." *Journal of Interdisciplinary History*, 2 (1971), 237–272.

SMITH, DANIEL SCOTT, AND MICHAEL HINDUS. "Premarital Pregnancy in America, 1640–1971: An Overview and Interpretation." *Journal of Interdisciplinary History*, 4 (1975), 537–570.

STRONG, BRYAN. "Ideas of the Early Sex Education Movement in America, 1890–1920." *History of Education Quarterly*, 12 (1972), 129–161.

THOMAS, KEITH. "The Double Standard," *Journal of the History of Ideas*, 20 (1959), 195–216.

WALTERS, RONALD G. "The Erotic South: Civilization and Sexuality in American Abolitionism." *American Quarterly*, 25 (1973), 177–201.

# PART SIX |

# ETHNICITY

The three papers in this section focus on the experience of black Americans, and the one by Pleck introduces data on Italian-Americans as well. As noted in the introductory essay, the family life of black Americans during and after slavery has been one of the fastest growing and most controversial research areas dealt with in this volume. In brief, the issue that has caused the furor is the ways in which the experience of slavery impinged on black family structure both before and after the Civil War. Much of the new literature can be characterized as revisionist because it attempts to correct the notion frequently encountered in the older literary histories that the black family has been effectively destroyed under slavery both because of the cavalier attitude shown by plantation owners toward the integrity of the family unit and by their sexual exploitation of black women. The new historians do not minimize the moral and physical horrors of slavery; rather, they show why, under certain circumstances, it was beneficial for slave owners to support black family structure and not vent their lust on women slaves. More importantly, the new historians also demonstrate how black Americans were able to create family structures that enabled them to survive in the face of slavery.

Allan Kulikoff's work "The Beginnings of the Afro-American Family in Maryland" allows us to look intensively at an issue which has been painted with the broadest of brushes in most other studies of slavery. Moreover, it deals with the eighteenth century—a period which has been neglected—though its focus is only on one region. Much of the debate over slavery concerns its impact on the family; this paper highlights the complexity of the question and shows how easily it is subject to different interpretations. Kulikoff demonstrates the necessity of phrasing questions about family cohesiveness in terms of setting—plantation or farm—and life cycle. We see that two-parent households were more common on large plantations than on small farms. In the former more than half of the children aged ten to fourteen were living in two-parent households. In addition, Kulikoff suggests that by the middle of the eighteenth century a progression of different household structures can be observed in association with various phases of the life cycle. In a manner not unlike that then current among white colonists in New England, we see children between ten and fourteen leaving the parental home and going to live in a number of different settings. Whether this pattern of child placement resembles that of New England in intent as well as in structure is not known at present. To a great extent the decision regarding child placement was controlled by slave owners, especially when children were sold away from the plantation, so we must tread lightly in making too facile comparisons with white New Englanders. There are a number of other interesting and important findings in the Kulikoff paper, such as how changing sex ratios during the eighteenth century were a factor affecting marriage patterns and how it took time for the slaves to build up kin networks to replace those from which they had been torn in Africa by the slave traders.

Herbert G. Gutman's paper "Persistent Myths about the Afro-American Family" is based on a number of data sets covering the 1855 to 1880 period and is separated in time rather dramatically from Kullikoff's. Yet the question they are both asking is very similar. Gutman phrases it more or less as follows: if slavery did, in fact, have the insidious effect on black-American family structure that has previously been believed, would we not expect to find evidence of this in the residential patterns of free men and women before the Civil War and other blacks after it? Gutman's data reveal that—whether the community was St. Helena's Township, South Carolina, in 1880 (a poor rural area) or Buffalo, New York, in 1855 or 1875—the overwhelming majority of black households were ones in which a male was present. Moreover, when Gutman directs his attention toward those households that were headed by females (aged twenty to twenty-nine) in a number of southern areas in 1880, he discovers that communities such as Natchez, Mobile, and Richmond had sex ratios of the order of fifty-seven males for every one hundred black women in this age group. Given such a ratio, Gutman notes that one might really ask "why were there so *few* female-headed Negro households?" Gutman also considers the economic situation encountered by blacks in antebellum cities which may have affected black family structure. However, he is loathe to accept a totally reactive model of black culture; he rejects the traditional stance of interpreting the lives of black Americans without allowing them credit for creating and sustaining their own structures. The fact that such large numbers of black families maintained themselves in two-parent form both before and after the Civil War is evidence of the strength of black culture in the face of a cultural context which put economic considerations above all else, including the integrity of the black family.

"A Mother's Wages: Income Earning among Italian and Black Women, 1896–1911" by Elizabeth H. Pleck carries us into the twentieth century. It compares the employment pattern of black and immigrant Italian women in a number of different cities in 1896 and 1911. While the focus of the study is narrow, its implications are quite broad. In order to explain why married black women were more likely to be employed than their Italian counterparts, Pleck explores various aspects of family life among these two ethnic groups. In the process she gives us an appreciation of the similarities shared as a result of their common poverty and the distinctiveness stemming from cultural differences.

What gives Pleck's work a special quality is the effective way in which she investigates various hypotheses that might account for the greater proclivity to seek employment shown by the black wives. By controlling, in effect, each variable she shows that when income, children at home, and other relevant factors are considered, the differences between blacks and Italian Americans remain, forcing us to adopt a cultural rather than a structural explanation.

Pleck's paper should be read in conjunction with Gutman's because, to a degree, they illuminate each other. Pleck does attempt, however briefly, to explore the relationship between the unemployment of the husband and the wife's subsequent desertion. Moreover, like Gutman, she is committed to an interpretation of black family behavior—in this case, female employment rather than two-parent households—in terms of the nature of black-American culture rather than as a response to white-American culture.

These three papers hardly represent the total range of studies carried out on the black family during the 1970s, but they do convey the major themes and methodological advances while giving the reader a broad sense of black family experience during the total period covered by this book. When read in collaboration with studies of the black family today, we can see the historical continuity as well as the differences. For instance, it is worth reflecting on the pattern of child placement in mid-eighteenth-century Maryland as discussed by Kulikoff and those described by Stack* in her 1974 study of a black ghetto in a contemporary American city. While this is only one example, it illustrates the importance of historical perspective in the study of the family.

*A complete citation is in the selected readings on p. 511.

# 21 | THE BEGINNINGS OF THE AFRO-AMERICAN FAMILY IN MARYLAND

## ALLAN KULIKOFF

Sometime in 1728, Harry, a recently imported African, escaped from his master in southern Prince George's County, Maryland, and joined a small black community among the Indians beyond the area of white settlement. The following year, Harry returned to Prince George's to urge his former shipmates, the only "kinfolk" he had, to return there with him. Over forty years later, another Harry, who belonged to John Jenkins of Prince George's, ran away. The Annapolis newspaper reported that "he has been seen about the Negro Quarters in *Patuxent*, but is supposed to have removed among his Acquaintances on Potomack; he is also well acquainted with the Negroes at Clement Wheeler's Quarter on Zekiah, and a Negro Wench of Mr. Wall's named Rachael; a few miles from that Quarter is his Aunt, and he may possibly be harboured thereabouts."[1]

These two incidents, separated by two generations, are suggestive. African Harry ran away *from* slavery to the frontier; Afro-American Harry ran *to* his friends and kinfolk spread over a wide territory. The Afro-American runaway could call on many others to hide him, but the African had few friends and seemingly, no wife. These contrasts raise many questions. How did Afro-Americans organize their families in the Chesapeake colonies during the eighteenth century? Who lived in slave households? How many Afro-American fathers lived with their wives and children? What was the impact of arbitrary sale and transfer of slaves upon family life? How did an Afro-American's household and family relationships change through the life cycle?

This paper attempts to answer these questions.[2] While literary documents by or about slaves before 1800, such as runaway narratives, WPA

Allan Kulikoff is an asst. Prof. & Research Associate, office Social & Dem. Hist. Univ. of Ill., Chicago Circle. He would like to thank Ira Berlin, Lois Green Carr, John P. Demos, David H. Fischer, Rhys Isaac, Aubrey C. Land, Elizabeth Pleck, and the staff of the Institute of Early American History and Culture for their perceptive comments on earlier versions of this paper and, especially, Russell R. Menard for his many useful suggestions and Herbert G. Gutman for his valuable critique. Research for this essay was supported by Brandeis University through a Rose and Irving Crown fellowship and research grant and by the National Science Foundation (GS35781).

This is a revised version of the article in *Law, Society and Politics in Early Maryland,* edited by A. C. Land, L. G. Carr, and E. C. Papenfuse (Baltimore: Johns Hopkins Press, 1977).

freed-slave interviews, black autobiographies, or detailed travel accounts are very infrequently available to historians of colonial slave family life, they can gather age and family data from probate inventories, personal information from runaway advertisements, and depositions in court cases. These sources, together with several diaries and account books kept by whites, provide a great deal of material about African and Afro-American family life in the Chesapeake region.

Almost all the blacks who lived in Maryland and Virginia before 1780 were slaves. Because his status precluded him from enjoying a legally secure family life, a slave's household often excluded important family members. Households, domestic groups, and families must therefore be clearly distinguished. A household, as used here, is a coresidence group that includes all who shared a "proximity of sleeping arrangements," or lived under the same roof. Domestic groups include kin and nonkin, living in the same or separate households, who share cooking, eating, childrearing, working, and other daily activities. Families are composed of people related by blood or marriage. Several distinctions are useful in defining the members of families. The immediate family include husband and wife or parents and children. Near kin include the immediate family and all other kin, such as adult brothers and sisters or cousins who share the same house or domestic tasks with the immediate family. Other kinfolk who do not function as family members on a regular basis are considered to be distant kin.[3]

The process of family formation can perhaps best be understood as an adaptive process. My ideas about this process owe much to a provocative essay by Sidney Mintz and Richard Price on Afro-American culture. Blacks learned to modify their environment, learned from each other how to retain family ties under very adverse conditions, and structured their expectations about family activities around what they knew the master would permit. If white masters determined the outward bounds of family activities, it was Africans, and especially their descendants, who gave meaning to the relationships between parents and children, among siblings, and with more distant kinfolk. As a result, black family structure on the eve of the Revolution differed from both African and white family systems.[4]

Africans who were forced to come to the Chesapeake region in the late seventeenth and early eighteenth centuries struggled to create viable families and households, but often failed. They suffered a great loss when they were herded into slave ships. Their family and friends, who had given meaning to their lives and structured their place in society, were left behind and they found themselves among strangers. They could never recreate their families and certainly not devise a West African kinship system in the Chesapeake. The differences between African communities were too great. Some Africans lived in clans and lineages, others did not; some traced their descent from women but others traced descent from men; mothers, fathers, and other kin played somewhat different roles in each community; initiation ceremonies and puberty rites, forbidden marriages, marriage customs, and household structures all varied from place to place.[5]

Though African immigrants did not bring a unified West African culture with them to the Chesapeake colonies, they did share important beliefs about the nature of kinship. Africans could modify these beliefs in America to legitmate the families they eventually formed. They saw kinship as the principal way of ordering relationships between individuals. Each person in the tribe was related to most others in the community. The male was father, son, and uncle; the female was mother, daughter, and aunt to many others. Because their kinship system was so extensive, Africans included kinfolk outside the immediate family in their daily activities. For example, adult brothers or sisters of the father or mother played an important role in childrearing and domestic activities in many African societies.[6]

Secondly, but far less certainly, African immigrants may have adapted some practices associated with polygyny, a common African marital custom. A few men on the Eastern Shore of Maryland in the 1740s, and perhaps others scattered elsewhere, lived with several women. However, far too few African women (in relation to the number of men) immigrated to make polygynous marriages common. Nevertheless, the close psychological relationship between mothers and children, and the great social distance between a husband and his various wives and children found in African polygynous societies might have been repeated in the Chesapeake colonies. In any event, African slave mothers played a more important role than fathers in teaching children about Africa and about how to get along in the slave system. Both African custom and the physical separation of immigrant men and women played a role in this development.[7]

Africans faced a demographic environment hostile to most forms of family life. If African men were to start familes, they had to find wives, and that task was difficult. Most blacks lived on small farms of less than 11 slaves; and the small black population was spread thinly over a vast territory. Roads were rudimentary. Even where concentrations of larger plantations were located, African men did not automatically find wives. Sex ratios in southern Maryland rose from 125 to 130 (men per 100 women) in the mid-seventeenth century to about 150 in the 1710s and 1720s, and to around 180 in the 1730s. In Surry County, Virginia, the slave sex ratio was about 145 in the 1670s and 1680s, but over 200 in the 1690s and 1700s. Wealthy slaveowners did not provide most of their African men with wives; the larger the plantation, the higher the sex ratio tended to be.[8]

Africans had competition for the available black women. By the 1690s, some black women were natives, and they may have preferred Afro-American men. White men were also competitors. Indeed, during the seventeenth and early eighteenth centuries, white adult sex ratios were as high (or higher) than black adult sex ratios. At any period whites possessed a monopoly of power and some of them probably took slave women as their common-law wives. African men competed for the remaining black women who were mostly recently-enslaved Africans. These immigrant women often waited two or three years before marrying. Since the number of women available to African men was so small, many probably died before they could find a wife. In 1739 African men planned an uprising in Prince George's County partly because they could not find wives.[9]

Foreign-born male slaves in Maryland and Virginia probably lived in a succession of different kinds of households. Newly imported Africans had no black kin in the Chesapeake. Since sex ratios were high, most of these men probably lived with other, unrelated men. African men may have substituted friends for kin. Newly enslaved Africans made friends with their nearest shipmates during the middle passage, and after their arrival in Maryland, some of them lived near these men. New Negroes could live with other recent African immigrants because migration from Africa occurred in short spurts from the 1670s to the late 1730s. The high sex ratios of large plantations indicate that wealthy men bought many of these Africans. Even if his shipmates lived miles away, the new immigrant could share the experiences of others who had recently endured the middle passage.[10]

Despite the difficulties, most Africans who survived for a few years eventually found a wife. In societies with high sex ratios, women tend to marry young, but men have to postpone marriage. This increases the opportunity of older men to marry by reducing the sexual imbalance. (That is, there are as many younger women as older men.) By the 1690s, large numbers of Afro-American women entered their midteens and married Afro-American and African men.[11] Because the plantations were small, and individual farm sex ratios likely to be uneven, the wives and children of married African men very often lived on other plantations. These men still lived mainly with other unrelated men, but at least they had begun to develop kin ties.[12] A few African men lived with their wives and children, and some limited evidence suggests that the longer an African lived in the Chesapeake, the more likely he was to live with his immediate family.[13]

Unlike most African men, African women commonly lived with their children. Some African women may have been so alienated that they refused to have children, but the rest bore and raised several offspring, protected by the master's reluctance to separate very young children from their mothers. Since the children were reared by their mothers and eventually joined them in the tobacco fields, these households were domestic groups although incomplete as families.[14]

A greater proportion of African women than African men lived with both spouses and children. These opportunities usually arose on large plantations. There was such a surplus of men on large plantations that African women who lived on them could choose husbands from several African or Afro-American men. The sex ratio on large plantations in Prince George's during the 1730s, a period of heavy immigration, was 249. This shortage of women prevented most recently arrived African men from finding a wife on the plantation. For them the opportunity to live with a wife and children was rare. More Africans probably lived with their immediate families in the 1740s; immigration declined, large planters bought more African women, and the sex ratio on big plantations fell to 142.[15]

Because African spouses were usually separated, African mothers reared their Afro-American children with little help from their husbands. Even when the father was present, the extended kin so important in the lives of African children was missing. Mothers probably taught them the broad values they brought from Africa and related the family's history in

Africa and the Chesapeake. When the children began working in the fields, they learned from their mothers how to survive a day's work and how to get along with master and overseer.

Each group of Africans repeated the experiences of previous immigrants. Eventually, more and more Afro-American children matured and began families of their own. The first large generation of Afro-Americans in Maryland probably came of age in the 1690s; by the 1720s, when the second large generation had matured, the black population finally began increasing naturally.[16]

The changing composition of the black population combined with other changes to restructure Afro-American households and families. Alterations in the adult sex ratio, the size of plantations, and black population density provided black people with opportunities to enjoy a more satisfying family life. The way masters transferred slaves from place to place limited the size and composition of black households, but Afro-American family members separated by masters managed to establish complex kinship networks over many plantations. Afro-Americans used these opportunities to create a kind of family life that differed from African and Anglo-American practices.

Demographic changes led to more complex households and families. As the number of adult Africans in the population decreased, the sex ratio in Maryland declined to between 100 and 110 by the 1750s. This decline gave most men an opportunity to marry by about age thirty. The number of slaves who lived on plantations with more than twenty blacks increased; the density of the black population in tidewater Maryland and Virginia rose; the proportion of blacks in the total population of Prince George's County, in nearby areas of Maryland, and throughout tidewater Virginia rose to half or more by the end of the century; and many new roads were built. The number of friends and kinfolk whom typical Afro-Americans saw every day or visited with regularity increased, while their contact with whites declined because large areas of the Chesapeake became nearly black counties.[17]

How frequently masters transferred their Afro-American slaves, and where they sent them, affected black household composition. Surviving documents do not allow a systematic analysis of this point, but several conclusions seem clear. First, planters kept women and their small children together but did not keep husbands and teenage children with their immediate family. Slaveowner after slaveowner bequeathed women and their "increase" to sons or daughters. However, children of slaveowners tended to live near their parents; thus, even when members of slave families were so separated, they remained in the same neighborhood.[18] Secondly, Afro-Americans who lived on small farms were transferred more frequently than those on large plantations. At their deaths small slaveowners typically willed a slave or two to their widows and to each child. They also frequently mortgaged or sold slaves to gain capital. If a slaveowner died with many unpaid debts, his slaves had to be sold.[19] Finally, relatively few blacks were forced to move long distances. Far more blacks were affected by migrations of slaves from the Chesapeake region to the new Southwest in the nineteenth century than by long-distance movement in the region before the Revolution.[20] These points should not be misunderstood. Most Afro-Americans who lived in Maryland or Virginia during the eighteenth century experienced separations from members of their immediate families sometime in their lives. Most, however, were able to visit these family members occasionally.

These changes led to a new social reality for most slaves born in the 1750s, 1760s, and 1770s. If unrelated people and their progeny stay in a limited geographic area for several generations, the descendants of the original settlers must develop kin ties with many other people who live nearby. Once the proportion of adult Africans declined, this process began. African women married and had children; the children matured and married. If most of them remained near their first homes, each was bound to have siblings, children, spouses, uncles, aunts, and cousins living in the neighborhood. How these various kinspeople were organized into households, families, and domestic groups depended not only upon the whims of masters but also upon the meaning placed on kinship by the slaves themselves.

The process of household and family formation and dissolution was begun by each immigrant woman who lived long enough to have children. The story of Ann Joice, a black woman who was born in Barbados, taken to England as a servant, and then falsely sold into slavery in Maryland in the 1670s, may have been similar to that of other immigrant women once she became a slave. The Darnall family of Prince George's owned Ann Joice. She had seven children with several white men in the 1670s and 1680s; all remained slaves the rest of their lives. Three of her children stayed on the Darnall home plantation until their deaths. One was sold as a child to a planter who lived a few miles away; another was eventually sold to William Digges, who lived about five miles from the Darnall farm. Both the spatial spread and the local concentration of kinfolk continued in the next generation. Peter Harbard, born between 1715 and 1720, was the son of Francis Harbard, who was Ann Joice's child. Peter grew up on the Darnall farm, but in 1737 he was sold to George Gordon, who lived across the road from Darnall. As a child, Peter lived with or very near his grandmother Ann Joice, his father, and several paternal uncles and aunts. He probably knew his seven cousins (father's sister's children), children of his aunt Susan Harbard, who lived on William Digges's plantation. Other kinfolk lived in Annapolis but were too far away to visit easily.[21]

As Afro-American slaves were born and died, and as masters sold or bequeathed their slaves, black households were formed and reformed, broken and created. Several detailed examples can illustrate this process. For example, Daphne, the daughter of Nan, was born about 1736 on a large plantation in Prince George's owned by Robert Tyler, Sr. Until she was two, she lived with her mother, two brothers, and two sisters. In 1738, Tyler died and left his slaves to his wife, children, and grandchildren. All lived on or near Tyler's farms. Three of Daphne's siblings were bequeathed to granddaughter Ruth Tyler, who later married Mordecai Jacob, her grandfather's next-door neighbor. Daphne continued to live on the Tyler plantation. From 1736 to 1787, she had six different masters, but she still lived where she was born. Daphne lived with her mother until her mother died, and with her ten children until 1779. Children were eventually born to Daphne's daughters; these infants lived with their mothers and near their maternal grandmother. When Robert Tyler III, Robert senior's grandson and Daphne's fifth master, died in 1779, his will divided Daphne's children and grandchildren between his son and daughter. Daphne was thus separated from younger children, born between 1760 and 1772. They were given to Millicent Beanes, Robert III's daughter, who lived several miles away. Daphne continued to live on the same plantation as her four older children and several grandchildren. An intricate extended family of grandmother, sons, daughters, grandchildren, aunts, uncles, nieces, nephews, and cousins resided in several households on the Tyler plantation in 1778, and other more remote kinfolk could be found on the neighboring Jacob farm.[22]

Family separations might be more frequent on smaller plantations. Rachael was born in the late 1730s and bore ten children between 1758 and 1784. As a child she lived on the plantation of Alexander Magruder; a large slaveowner in Prince George's; before 1746, Alexander gave her to his son Hezekiah, who lived on an adjoining plantation. Hezekiah never owned more than ten slaves, and when he died in 1769, he owned only two—including one willed to his wife by her brother. Between 1755 and 1757, he mortgaged nine slaves, including Rachael, to two merchants. In 1757, Samuel Roundall (who lived about five miles from the Magruders) seized Rachael and six other slaves mortgaged to him. This and subsequent transfers can be seen on Figure 1. In 1760 Roundall sold Rachael and her eldest daughter to Samuel Lovejoy, who lived about nine miles from

**Figure 1.** SALE AND LATER TRANSFER OF HEZEKIAH MAGRUDER'S SLAVES, 1755–1780

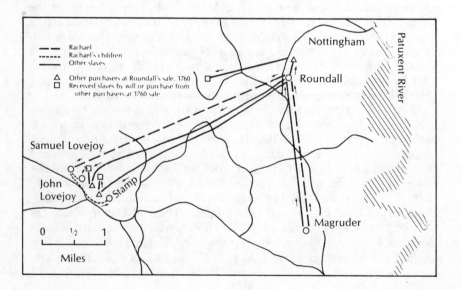

Roundall. At the same time, four other former Magruder slaves were sold: two to planters in Lovejoy's neighborhood, one to a Roundall neighbor, and one to a planter living at least fifteen miles away in Charles County. Rachael's separation from friends and family members continued. In 1761, her eldest child was sold at age three to George Stamp, a neighbor of Lovejoy. By the time Samuel Lovejoy died in 1762, she had two other children. She and her youngest child went to live with John Lovejoy, Samuel's nephew and near-neighbor, but her second child, about age two, stayed with Lovejoy's widow. Her third child was sold at age six, but Rachael and her next seven children lived with John Lovejoy until at least 1787.[23]

These three examples suggest how Afro-American households and families developed in the eighteenth century. Husbands and wives and parents and children were frequently separated by the master's transfers of family members. At the same time, as generation followed generation, households, or adjacent huts, became increasingly complex, and sometimes included grandparents, uncles, aunts, or cousins, as well as the immediate family. Since other kin lived on nearby or distant plantations, geographically concentrated (and dispersed) kinship networks that connected numbers of quarters emerged during the pre-Revolutionary era.

How typical were the experiences suggested by the examples? How were families organized into households and domestic groups on large and small quarters? Data from three large planter's inventories taken in 1759, 1773–1774, and 1775, and from a Prince George's census of 1776 permit a test of the hypotheses concerning changes in household structure, differences between large and small units, and the spread of kinfolk across space. Table 1 details household structure on large quarters of over twenty

**Table 1** AFRO-AMERICAN HOUSEHOLD STRUCTURES ON THREE LARGE PLANTATIONS IN PRINCE GEORGE'S AND ANNE ARUNDEL COUNTIES, MARYLAND, 1759–1775

| HOUSEHOLD TYPE | Percentage in Household Type | | | | Percentage Total in Household Types |
| | MALES 15+ | FEMALES 15+ | CHILDREN 0–9 | CHILDREN 10–14 | |
| --- | --- | --- | --- | --- | --- |
| Husband-wife-children | 40 | 43 | 55 | 44 | 47 |
| Mother-children | 2 | 17 | 22 | 10 | 14 |
| Mother-children-other kin | 4 | 14 | 8 | 13 | 9 |
| Siblings | 7 | 4 | 6 | 12 | 7 |
| Husband-wife-children-other kin | 2 | 2 | 2 | 2 | 2 |
| Father-children | 5 | 0 | 3 | 5 | 3 |
| Husband-wife | 2 | 2 | 0 | 0 | 1 |
| Three generation | 1 | 2 | 2 | 3 | 2 |
| Unknown or mixed | 36 | 16 | 3 | 12 | 15 |
| Total percentage | 99 | 100 | 101 | 101 | 100 |
| Number people | 142 | 129 | 178 | 77 | 526 |

Sources: PG Inventories, GS No. 1, f. 73 (1759; James Wardrop's, 32 slaves); and GS No. 2, ff. 334–336 (1775; Addison's 3 plantations, 109 slaves) and Charles Carroll Account Book, Maryland Historical Society (rest of slaves). The three-generation households include grandparents and grandchildren but not the generation in between. The unknown or mixed category includes all those apparently living away from all kinfolk but perhaps living near them. Some of the slaves in this category probably belong in the others, but the sources (especially the Addison and Wardrop documents) do not permit location of them.

**Table 2**  AFRO-AMERICAN HOUSEHOLD STRUCTURES ON SMALL PLANTATIONS (1–8 SLAVES). PRINCE GEORGE'S COUNTY, MARYLAND, 1776

| HOUSEHOLD TYPE | Percentage in Household Type | | | | Percentage of Total in Household Types |
| | MALES 15+ | FEMALES 15+ | CHILDREN 0–9 | CHILDREN 10–14 | |
| --- | --- | --- | --- | --- | --- |
| Husband-wife-children | 17 | 18 | 22 | 10 | 18 |
| Mother-children | 2 | 35 | 56 | 29 | 32 |
| Father-children | 2 | * | 4 | 1 | 2 |
| Siblings | 7 | 5 | 6 | 17 | 8 |
| Mixed | 72 | 42 | 12 | 43 | 41 |
| Total percentage | 100 | 100 | 100 | 100 | 101 |
| Number of people | 275 | 276 | 325 | 162 | 1038 |

, *Source:* 1776 Census. The household types were assumed from black age structures on individual farms. The statistics must be treated as educated guesses. For a detailed explanation of the biases of this table, see the original article in *Law, Society and Politics in Early Maryland.* Land et al., eds., (Baltimore: John Hopkins Press, 1977).

* = less than ½%.

and Table 2 shows the kinds of households on small farms. About half of all slaves probably lived on each plantation type.[24] This evidence provides a good test, because by the 1770s most Afro-Americans could trace a Chesapeake genealogy back to immigrant grandparents or great-grandparents.[25]

Kinfolk (immediate families and near kin) on large plantations were organized into three kinds of residence groups. Most of the slaves of some quarters were interrelated by blood or marriage. Domestic groups included kinfolk who lived on opposite sides of duplex slave huts and who shared a common yard and eating and cooking arrangements. Finally, most households included members of an immediate family.

The kinship structure of large plantations is illustrated by a household inventory taken in 1773–1774 of 385 slaves owned by Charles Carroll of Carrollton on thirteen different quarters in Anne Arundel County. Because Carroll insisted that the inventory be "taken in Familys with their Ages," the document permits a detailed reconstruction of kinship networks.[26] Though the complexity and size of kinship groups on Carroll's quarters were probably greater than on other large plantations, the general pattern could easily have been repeated elsewhere.[27]

The ten men and three women who headed each list were probably leaders of their quarters. Five of the quarters were named for these individuals.[28] They tended to be old slaves who had been with the Carroll family for many years. While the mean age of all adults was thirty-seven years, the mean age of the leaders was forty-nine, and six of the thirteen were over fifty-five.[29] The leader often lived with many kinfolk; he or she was closely related to about 36 to 38 percent of all the other slaves on the quarter. For example, Fanny, sixty-nine years of age, was surrounded by at least forty near kinfolk on the main plantation at Doohoregan, and Mayara James, sixty-five years of age, lived with twenty-three relatives on his quarter.[30]

The two slaves' genealogies presented in Figures 2 and 3 provide detailed examples of the kinds of kinship networks that could develop on quarters after several generations of relative geographic stability. Because most slave quarters had between fifteen and thirty slaves, the network included just two or three households. The kin group shown in Figure 2 may have been typical. Thirteen of the seventeen slaves who lived at Annapolis Quarter in 1774 were descendants of Iron Works Lucy. Ten were children and grandchildren of Sall. One of Sall's sons-in-law and his brother also lived there. Peter and Charles, other descendants of Lucy, lived on the quarter but had families elsewhere.

Nearly half the slaves who resided on Riggs Quarter, Carroll's main plantation, were kinfolk (63/130). A network of this size could develop only on the home plantation of the largest Chesapeake planters.[31] Each of the members of the group was either a direct descendant or an affine (in-law) of old Fanny. She was surrounded on her quarter by five children, nineteen grandchildren, nine great-grandchildren, four children-in-law, and three grandchildren's spouses. The network grew through the marriage of Fanny's children and grandchildren to children of other residents of the quarter. For example, Cooper Joe, his wife, and thirteen children and grandchildren were closely related to Fanny's family. By the early 1750s Cooper Joe had married Nanny of Kate, and about 1761 Fanny's son Bob married Frances Mitchell of Kate. Joe and Nanny's children were first cousins of the children of Bob and Frances, and thereby more remotely connected to all the rest of Fanny's descendants. The alliance of the two families was cemented in 1772, when Dinah, the daughter of Kate of Fanny married Joe, the son of Cooper Joe.[32]

The intraquarter kinship network was also a work group. Fanny's and

**Figure 2.** KINSHIP TIES AMONG CHARLES CARROLL'S SLAVES AT ANNAPOLIS QUARTER, 1774

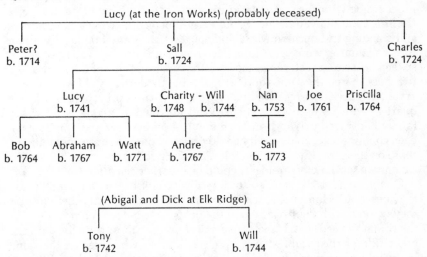

Lucy (at the Iron Works) (probably deceased)

Peter?
b. 1714

Sall
b. 1724

Charles
b. 1724

Lucy
b. 1741

Charity - Will
b. 1748    b. 1744

Nan
b. 1753

Joe
b. 1761

Priscilla
b. 1764

Bob
b. 1764

Abraham
b. 1767

Watt
b. 1771

Andre
b. 1767

Sall
b. 1773

(Abigail and Dick at Elk Ridge)

Tony
b. 1742

Will
b. 1744

*Source:* Charles Carroll Account Book, Maryland Historical Society.

*Note:* Will, son of Abigail and Dick and Charity's husband, appears twice. Peter may not be Lucy's son, but it seems probable. Mark (b. 1758) and Jem (b. 1754) apparently were not related to others on the quarter but had relatives elsewhere on Carroll's plantations.

Lucy's adult and teenage kinfolk worked together in the fields. Masters separated their slaves by sex, age, and strength, and determined what each would do, but blacks judged each other in part by the reciprocal kinship obligation that bound them together. Afro-Americans worked at their own pace and frequently thwarted their masters' desires for increased productivity. Part of this conflict can be explained by the Afro-American's preindustrial work discipline, but part may have been due to the desires of kinfolk to help and protect each other from the master's lash, the humid climate, and the malarial environment.[33]

Landon Carter's lament upon the death of his trusted old slave Jack Lubbar suggests the dimensions of kinship solidarity in the fields. Lubbar had been a foreman over many groups of slaves. In his old age, he worked at the Fork quarter "with 5 hands and myself; in which service he so gratefully discharged his duty as to make me by his care alone larger crops of Corn, tobacco and Pease twice over than ever I have had made by anyone. . . . " Other blacks did not share Lubbar's desire to produce a large crop for Carter. "At this plantation," Carter writes, "he continued till his age almost deprived him of eyesight which made him desire to be removed because those under him, mostly his great grandchildren, by the baseness of their Parents abused him much." Lubbar's grandchildren and great-grandchildren, who worked together, were related in intricate ways: parents and children, maternal and paternal cousins, uncles and aunts, and brothers and sisters. They united against Lubbar to slow the work pace and conserve their energy.[34]

When Afro-Americans came home each night from the fields, they broke into smaller domestic groups. Their habitat set the scene for social intercourse. On large plantations "a Negro quarter is a Number of Huts or Hovels, built at some distance from the Mansion House; where the Negroes reside with their wives and Families, and cultivate at vacant times the little spots allow'd them."[35] Four early-nineteenth-century slave houses still standing in Southern Maryland suggest that slave families living on the same quarter were very close. Each house included two rooms of about sixteen-by-sixteen feet, separated by a thin wall. In three of the homes, the two huts shared the same roof but had separate doorways. Two had separate fireplaces, the residents of one duplex shared a fireplace, and one quarter (which was over a kitchen) did not have a fireplace.[36] Neither family had much privacy, and communication between them must have been commonplace. No activity could occur on one side of the hut without those on the other knowing about it. And the two halves of the hut shared a common yard, where residents could talk, eat, or celebrate.

On the quarters the smallest local residence unit to contain kinfolk was the household. Household members were not isolated from other kinfolk; they worked with their relatives in the fields, associated with neighbors in the common yard, and cooked meals or slept near those who lived on the other side of their duplex. Nevertheless, kinfolk who lived in the same household were spatially closer when at home than any other group of kin. Who lived in typical households on slave quarters? How many husbands lived with their wives and children? How many children were separated from their parents? Did kin other than the immediate family live in many households?

**Figure 3.** FANNY AND SOME OF HER KINFOLK ON DOOHOREGAN MANOR, 1773

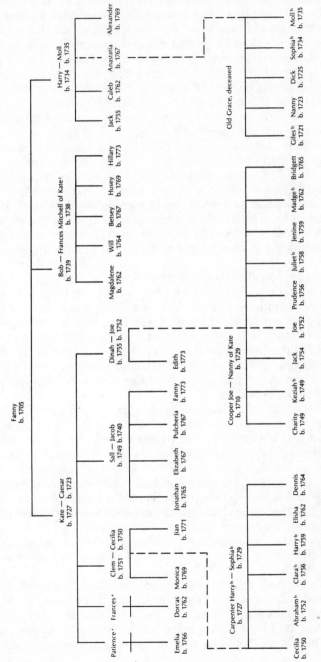

*Source:* Charles Carroll Account Book, Maryland Historical Society:

a. Those without a birthdate not resident on any Carroll farm.

b. Did not live at Rigg's Quarter (Fanny's Quarter).

c. This family lived at the sawmill at the main quarter of Doorhoregan Manor. Frances Mitchell was a sister of Nanny, who was the wife of Cooper Joe.

Nearly half of all the Afro-Americans who lived on the three large plantations described in Table 1 resided in households that included both parents and at least some of their children. Over half of the young children on all three plantations lived with both parents, but a far higher proportion of adults and children ten to fourteen years of age lived in two-parent households on the Carroll quarters than on the three Addison farms and Wardrop's plantation in Prince George's. While 49 percent of the women, 51 percent of the men, and 52 percent of children between ages ten and fourteen on Carroll's farms lived in two-parent households, only 28 percent of the women, 24 percent of the men, and 30 percent of those ten to fourteen years old could be found in two-parent homes on the other farms. Almost all the other children lived with one parent, usually the mother; but over a quarter of those ten to fourteen years of age lived with siblings or with apparently unrelated people.

The differences between Carroll and the other two large slaveowners is striking. Carroll, unlike all but a few other Chesapeake gentlemen, was able to provide his people with spouses from his own plantations and chose to keep adolescent children with their parents. Over six-tenths of the men (62 percent) and 28 percent of the women on Addison's and Wardrop's plantations lived with siblings, were unmarried, or lived away from spouses and children. On Carroll's quarters only 27 percent of the men and 12 percent of the women were similarly separated from wives and children.

Many blacks on these three large farms lived with or near kin other than their parents or children. About 7 percent were in the household of a brother or sister, and over a tenth (13 percent) of parents and children shared their homes with another kinsperson. There were several types of these extended households: seven included parent(s), children, and sibling(s) of the mother; two included grandmother living with her children and grandchildren; in one household grandparents took care of two young grandchildren; and in one hut, an adult brother and sister lived with her children and one grandchild.

Far less can be learned about families on small plantations. On these farms, the slave quarter could be in an outbuilding or in a small hut.[37] All the slaves, whether kin or not, lived together, cooked together, reared children together, and slept in the same hut. Table 2 very roughly suggests the differences in household composition of large plantations and small farms. Only 18 percent of the blacks on small units lived in two-parent households. About a third resided in mother-child households, and that included over half the young children and three-tenths of those ten to fourteen years of age. Nearly three-quarters of the men and two fifths of the women—some unmarried—lived with neither spouse nor children. Over two-fifths of the youths ten to fourteen years of age lived away from parents and siblings.

By the 1750s, a peculiar Afro-American life cycle had developed. Afro-Americans lived in a succession of different kinds of households. Children under ten years almost always lived with their mothers, and over half on large plantations lived with both parents. Between ten and fourteen years of age, large numbers of children left their parents' home. Some stayed with siblings and their families, others were sold, the rest lived with other kin or unrelated people. Women married in their late teens, had children, and established households with their own children. Over four-tenths of the women on large plantations and a fifth on small farms lived with husbands as well as children. The same proportion of men as women lived with spouses and children, but because children of separated spouses usually lived with their mothers, large numbers of men, even on big plantations, lived with other men.

These life-cycle changes can perhaps best be approached through a study of the critical events in the lives of Afro-Americans. Those events probably included the following: infancy, leaving the matricentral cell, beginning to work in the tobacco fields, leaving home, courtship and marriage, chidrearing, and old age.[38]

For the first few months of life, a newborn infant stayed in the matricental cell, that is, received his identity and subsistence from his mother.[39] A mother would take her new infant to the fields with her "and lay it uncovered on the ground . . . while she hoed her corn-row down and up. She would then suckle it a few minutes, and return to her labor, leaving the child in the same exposure." Evenutally, the child left its mother's lap and explored the world of the hut and quarter. In the evenings, he ate with his family and learned to love his parents, siblings, and other kinfolk. During the day the young child lived in an age-segregated world. While parents, other adults, and older siblings worked, children were "left, during a great portion of the day, on the ground at the doors of their huts, to their own struggles and efforts."[40] They played with age-mates or were left at home with other children and perhaps an aged grandparent. Siblings or agemates commonly lived together or in nearby houses. On the Potomac side of Prince George's County in 1776, 86 percent of those zero to four years of age, and 82 percent of those five to nine years of age lived on plantations with at least one other child near their own age. Many children lived in little communities of five or more children their own age. Children five to nine years old, too young to work full-time, may have cared for younger siblings; in Prince George's in 1776, 83 percent of all children zero to four years of age lived on a plantation with at least one child five to nine years of age.[41]

Black children began to work in the tobacco fields between seven and ten years of age. For the first time they joined fully in the daytime activities of adults.[42] Those still living at home labored beside parents, brothers and sisters, cousins, uncles, aunts and other kinfolk. Most were trained to be field hands by white masters or overseers and by their parents. Though these young hands were forced to work for the master, they quickly learned from their kinfold to work at the pace that black adults set and to practice the skills necessary to "put massa on."

At about the same age, some privileged boys began to learn a craft from whites or (on the larger plantations) from their skilled kinfolk. Charles Carroll's plantations provide an example of how skills were passed from one generation of Afro-Americans to another. Six of the eighteen (33 percent) artisans on his plantations under twenty-five years of age in 1773 probably learned their trade from fathers and another four (22 percent) from other kinfolk skilled in that occupation. For example, Joe, twenty-one, and Jack, nineteen, were both coopers and both sons of Cooper Joe, sixty-three. Joe also learned to be a wheelwright, and in turn probably helped train his brothers-in-law, Elisha, eleven, and Dennis, nine, as wheelwrights.[43]

Beginning to work coincided with the departure of many children from their parents, siblings, and friends. The fact that about 54 percent of all slaves in single slave households in Prince George's in 1776 were between seven and fifteen years of age suggests that children were typically forced to leave home during those ages. Young blacks were most frequently forced from large plantations to smaller farms.[44] The parents' authority was eliminated, and the child left the only community he had known. Tension and unhappiness often resulted. For example, Hagar, age fourteen, ran from her master in Baltimore in 1766. "She is supposed to be harbor'd in some Negro Quarter," he claimed, "as her Father and Mother Encourages her in Elopements, under a Pretense she is ill used at home."[45]

Courtship and marriage were highly significant *rites de passage* for many Afro-American men and women. The process began earlier for women: while men probably married in their mid- to late twenties, women usually married in their late teens.[46] Men initiated the courtship. They typically searched for wives, visiting numbers of neighboring plantations, and often found a wife near home, though not on the same quarter. Some evidence for this custom, suggestive but hardly conclusive, can be seen in the sex and age of runaways. Only 9 percent (22/233) of all Southern Maryland runaways, 1745–1779, were women. Few men (in terms of the total population) ran away in their late teens, but the numbers rose in the early twenties when the search for wives began, and crested between twenty-five and thirty-four when most men married and began families. Courtship on occasion ended in a marriage ceremony, sometimes performed by a Roman Catholic or Anglican clergyman, sometimes celebrated by the slaves themselves.[47] (See Table 3.)

Marriage was more important for women than men. After the relationship was consummated, the woman probably stayed with her family (par-

**Table 3**    AGES OF RUNAWAY MEN, 1770–1779, SOUTHERN MARYLAND

| Age Group | Number in Group | Percentage in Group | Percentage, 1776 Census |
|---|---|---|---|
| 15–19 | 4 | 6 | 19 |
| 20–24 | 22 | 31 | 19 |
| 25–29 | 22 | 31 | 15 |
| 30–34 | 17 | 24 | 11 |
| 35–39 | 3 | 4 | 8 |
| 40–49 | 4 | 6 | 13 |
| 50– | 0 | 0 | 15 |
| Totals | 72 | 102 | 100 |

*Source:* All runaway slave ads published in the *Maryland Gazette,* 1745–1779, the *Maryland Journal,* 1773–1779, and *Dunlap's Maryland Gazette,* 1775–1779, from Prince George's, Charles, Calvert, Frederick (south of Monocacy River), and Anne Arundel (south of Severn River, excluding Annapolis) counties, and any slave born in or traveling to those areas. Each slave runaway equals a single observation, but when the same slave ran away twice during the same time period, he was counted only once. The fourth column is from Prince George's County Census, 1776, and is included to provide a rough test of the likelihood that slaves of particular ages will run away.

ents and siblings) until a child was born, unless she could form a household with her husband.[48] Once she had a child, she moved from her parents' home into her own hut. Though almost all women were field laborers, their role as wives and mothers gave them a few privileges. Masters sometimes treated pregnant women—and their children after birth—with greater than usual solicitude. For example, Richard Corbin, a Virginia planter, insisted in 1759 that his steward be "Kind and Indulgent to pregnant women, and not force them then with Child upon any service or hardship that will be injurious to them." Children were "to be well looked after."[49]

There was less change in the life of most new husbands. Many continued to live with other adult men. Able to visit his family only at night or on holidays, the nonresident husband could play only a small role in childrearing. If husband and wife lived together, however, they established a household. The resident father helped raise his children, taught them skills, and tried to protect them from the master. Landon Carter reacted violently when Manuel tried to help his daughter. "Manuel's Sarah, who pretended to be sick a week ago, and because I found nothing ailed her and would not let her lie up she ran away above a week and was catched the night before last and locked up; but somebody broke open the door for her. It could be none but her father Manuel, and he I had whipped."[50]

On large plantations, mothers could call upon a wide variety of kin to help them raise their children: husbands, siblings, cousins, and uncles or aunts might be living in nearby huts. Peter Harbard learned from his grandmother, father, and paternal uncles how his grandmother's indentures were burned by Henry Darnall and how she was forced into bondage. He "frequently heard his grandmother Ann Joice say that if she had her just right that she ought to be free and all her children. He hath also heard his Uncles David Jones, John Wood, Thomas Crane, and also his father Francis Harbard declare as much." Peter's desire for freedom, learned from his kinfolk, never left him. In 1748, he ran away twice toward Philadelphia and freedom. He was recaptured, but later purchased his freedom.[51]

As Afro-Americans grew older, illness and lack of stamina cut into their productivity, and their kinfolk or masters were forced to provide for them. On rare occasions, masters granted special privileges to favored slaves. When Thomas Clark died in 1766, he gave his son Charles "my faithful old Negro man Jack whom I desire may be used tenderly in his old age." Charles Ball's grandfather lived as an old man by himself away from the other slaves he disliked. Similarly, John Wood, Peter Harbard's uncle, was given his own cabin in his old age.[52]

Many old slaves progressed through several stages of downward mobility. Artisans and other skilled workers became common field hands. While 10 percent of men between forty and fifty-nine years of age were craftsmen, only 3 percent of men above sixty years of age held similar positions.[53] Mulatto Ned, owned by Gabriel Parker of Calvert County, was a carpenter and cooper most of his life, but he had lost that job by 1750 when he was sixty-five. Abraham's status at Snowden's Iron Works in

Anne Arundel County changed from master founder to laborer when he could not work full-time. As slaves became feeble, some masters refused to maintain them adequately, or sold them to unwary buyers. An act passed by the Maryland Assembly in 1752 complained that "sundry Persons in this Province have set disabled and superannuated Slaves free who have either perished through want or otherwise become a Burthen to others." The legislators uncovered a problem: in 1755, 20 percent of all the free Negroes in Maryland (153/895) were "past labour or cripples," while only 2 percent (637/29,141) of white men were in this category. To remedy the abuse, the assembly forbade manumission of slaves by will, and insisted that masters feed and clothe their old and ill slaves. If slaveholders failed to comply, they could be fined £ 4 for each offense.[54]

As Afro-American slaves moved from plantation to plantation through the life cycle, they left behind many friends and kinfolk, and established relationships with slaves on other plantations. And when young blacks married off their quarter, they gained kinfolk on other plantations. Both of these patterns can be illustrated from the Carroll plantations. Sam and Sue, who lived on Sam's quarter at Doohoregan Manor, had seven children between 1729 and 1751. In 1774, six of them were spread over four different quarters at Doohoregan: one son lived with his father (his mother had died); a daughter lived with her family in a hut near her father's; a son and daughter lived at Frost's; one son headed Moses' quarter; and a son lived at Riggs. Figure 3 shows how marriages increased the size and geographic spread of Fanny's relations. A third of the slaves (85/255) who lived away from Riggs Quarter (the main plantation) were kin to Fanny or her descendants. Two of Kate's children married into Fanny's family; Kate and one son lived at Frost's and another son lived at Jacob's. Cecilia, the daughter of Carpenter Harry and Sophia married one of Fanny's grandchildren. Harry and Sophia lived with three of their children at Frost's, and two of their sons lived at Riggs, where they were learning to be wheelwrights with kinsperson Joe, son of Cooper Joe.[55]

Since husbands and wives, fathers and children, and friends and kinfolk were often physically separated, they had to devise ways of maintaining their close ties. At night and on Sundays and holidays, fathers and other kinfolk visited those family members who lived on other plantations. Fathers had regular visiting rights. Landon Carter's Guy, for instance, visited his wife (who lived on another quarter) every Monday evening.[56] Kinfolk, friends, and neighbors gathered in the yard around the slave cabins and talked, danced, sang, told stories, and drank rum through many an evening and special days on larger plantations.[57] These visits symbolized the solidarity of slave families and permitted kinfolk to renew their friendships but did not allow nonresident fathers to participate in the daily rearing of their children.

The forced separation of Afro-American kinfolk by masters was not entirely destructive. Slave society was characterized by hundreds of interconnected and interlocking kinship and friendship networks that stretched from plantation to plantation and from county to county. A slave who wanted to run away would find kinfolk, friends of kinfolk, or kinfolk of friends along his route who willingly would harbor him for a while.[58] As Afro-American kinship and friendship networks grew ever larger, the proportion of runaways who were harbored for significant periods of time on slave quarters seemed to have increased in both Maryland and Virginia.[59]

There were three different reasons for slaves to use this underground. Some blacks, like Harry—who left his master in 1779, stayed in the neighborhood for a few weeks and then took off for Philadelphia—used their friends' and kinfolk's hospitality to reach freedom.[60] Others wanted to visit. About 27 percent of all runaways from southern Maryland mentioned in newspaper advertisements from 1745 to 1779 (and 54 percent of all those whose destinations were described by masters) ran away to visit. For example, Page traveled back and forth between Piscataway and South River in 1749, a distance of about forty miles, and was not caught. He must have received help at many quarters along his route. And in 1756, Kate, thirty years old, ran away from her master, who lived near Georgetown on the Potomac. She went to South River about thirty miles distant, where she had formerly lived. Friends concealed her there. Her master feared that since "she had been a great Rambler, and is well known in *Calvert* and *Anne Arundel* Counties, besides other parts of the Country," Kate would "indulge herself a little in visiting her old Acquaintances," but spend most of her time with her husband at West River.[61]

Indeed, 20 of 233 Maryland runaways (9 percent) left masters to join their spouses. Sue and her child Jem, eighteen months old, went from Allen's Freshes to Port Tobacco, Charles County, a distance of about ten miles, "to go and see her husband." Sam, age thirty, lived about thirty miles from his wife in Bryantown, Charles County, when he visited her in 1755. Will had to go over a hundred miles, from Charles to Frederick County, to visit his wife, because her master had taken her from Will's neighborhood to a distant quarter.[62]

This essay has pointed to the basic cultural and demographic cleavage between African and Afro-American families. African immigrants, like free and servant immigrants from Britain, remembered their native land but had to adjust to the new conditions of the Chesapeake. As free Africans they had lived among many kinfolk; in the Chesapeake, kin ties were established with difficulty. Because most immigrants were young adult males and because plantations were small, two-parent households were rare. Mothers, by default, became the major black influence upon Afro-American children.

After immigration from Africa slowed, the sex ratio declined, and plantation sizes increased. As generation followed generation, Afro-Americans in Maryland and Virginia created an extensive kinship system. More households, especially on large plantations, included two parents and their children. Although most households did not include kinfolk other than the immediate family, other relations lived in adjacent huts. Mothers and children worked in the tobacco fields with kinfolk, ate and celebrated with many relations, and invited kin who lived elsewhere to share in the festivities. Afro-Americans forcibly separated from relatives managed to maintain contact with them. And finally, slave resistance—whether expressed in the fields or by running away—was fostered and encouraged by kinfolk.

This article has attempted to portray African and Afro-American family life among slaves in the eighteenth-century Chesapeake. It is based upon all the available evidence and upon speculations from that evidence. Many important questions about black family life in the colonial period remain to be answered. In the first place, we need to know more about household and family structure. Could the same structures be found in other parts of the region? In South Carolina? In the northern and middle colonies? Was the pattern of change described here repeated in other areas? Secondly, we must go beyond this essay and describe in greater detail the nature of the Afro-American developmental cycle and the emotional content of relationships among kinfolk in various places at different times.

## NOTES

1. Prince George's County Court Record O, f. 414, ms., Hall of Records, Annapolis, Md., hereafter cited as PG Ct. Rec.; *Maryland Gazette* (Annapolis), 12 March 1772. All manuscripts, unless otherwise noted, can be found at the Hall of Records.

2. Pioneering essays by Russell Menard, "The Maryland Slave Population, 1658-1730: A Demographic Profile of Blacks in Four Counties," *William and Mary Quarterly*, 3d ser. 32 (1975):29-54, and Peter Wood, *Black Majority: Negroes in Colonial South Carolina through the Stono Rebellion* (New York, 1974), ch. 5, suggest some characteristics of colonial black families. Much more is known about slave families in the nineteenth century. Herbert G. Gutman, *The Black Family in Slavery and Freedom, 1750-1925* (New York, 1976) is the standard reference. Other studies include Eugene D. Genovese, *Roll, Jordan Roll: The World the Slaves Made* (New York, 1974), pp. 443-524; E. Frank Frazier, "The Negro Slave Family," *Journal of Negro History* 15 (1930): 198-266; John Blassingame, *The Slave Community: Plantation Life in the Ante-Bellum South* (New York, 1972), ch. 3; George P. Rawick, *From Sundown to Sunup: The Making of the Black Community* (New York, 1972), ch. 5.

3. There are no standard definitions of household, domestic group, and family. I have borrowed my definitions of household and domestic group from Donald R. Bender, "A Refinement of the Concept of Household: Families, Co-residence, and Domestic Functions." *American Anthropologist* 69 (1967):493-504, quote on p. 498. The use of "immediate family," "near kin," and "distant kin" were suggested to me by Herbert Gutman.

4. Sidney W. Mintz and Richard Price, *An Anthropological Approach to the Afro-American Past: A Caribbean Perspective*, ISHI Occasional Papers in Social Change, #2 (Philadelphia, 1976). A more systematic application of these hypotheses to the colonial Chesapeake will be found in Allan Kulikoff, "The Origins of Afro-American Society in Tidewater Maryland and Virginia, 1700-1790," *William and Mary Quarterly*, forthcoming.

5. It is difficult to be more precise because most data on African kinship systems comes from twentieth-century anthropological works. The following works suggest variations in African kinship patterns: A. R. Radcliffe-Brown, "Introduction" to *African Systems of Kinship and Marriage*, ed. Radcliffe-Brown and Daryll Ford (London, 1950), pp. 1-85: Meyer Fortes, "Kinship and Marriage among the Ashanti," ibid., pp. 252-284; Jack Goody, *Comparative Studies in Kinship* (Stanford, 1969), ch. 3; Robert Bain, *Bangwa Kinship and Marriage* (Cambridge, England, 1972); William J. Goode, *World Revolutions and Family Patterns* (New York, 1963), pp. 167-200.

6. Mintz and Price, "Afro-American Culture History," pp. 56–78 but esp. pp. 61–62; John S. Mbiti, *African Religions and Philosophy* (New York, 1969), pp. 104–109.

7. Goode, *World Revolutions*, pp. 167–168, 196; Mbiti, *African Religions*, pp. 142–145. Women in polygynous societies also nursed infants for three to four years and abstained from intercourse during part of that period. If this pattern was repeated in the Chesapeake, it was partially responsible for the low gross birth rate among blacks in seventeenth-century Maryland; see Kulikoff, "Tobacco and Slaves," ch. 4; Menard, "Maryland Slave Population," p. 41; Mbiti, *African Religions*, p. 111. For polygyny on the Eastern Shore, see "Eighteenth-Century Maryland as Portrayed in the 'Itinerant Observations' of Edward Kimber," *Maryland Historical Magazine* 51 (1956):327.

8. For sex ratios, see Menard, "Maryland Slave Population," p. 32 and Allan Kulikoff, "A 'Prolifick' People: Black Population Growth in the Chesapeake Colonies, 1700–1790," *Southern Studies*, forthcoming; for plantation sizes, see Kulikoff, "Origins of Afro-American Society."

9. For the conspiracy of 1739 and evidence concerning the competition Africans faced when searching for wives, see Kulikoff, "Tobacco and Slaves," 197 and Kulikoff, "Origins of Afro-American Society."

10. Mintz and Price, *Anthropological Approach*, 22–23; Kulikoff, "'Prolifick' People;" PG Inventories, 1730–1769, mss. Large plantations were those with ten or more adult slaves.

11. Menard, "Maryland Slave Population," pp. 42–47; Kulikoff, "'Prolifick' People," table 5 shows mean age at conception of first child of slave women born 1710–1739 to be about 17.6.

12. These statements are based upon PG Wills, mss., for the 1730s and 1740s.

13. See the inventory of the plantation of Daniel Carroll of Duddington found in the Charles Carroll of Annapolis Account Book, ms 220, Maryland Historical Society, Baltimore (the inventory was never probated). The inventory was taken in 1735, a time of high slave imports, but Carroll sold rather than bought slaves. There were only two men between 15 and 29 years of age (but 12 twelve women) on his plantations, and seven above 60; two of the four men in their 40s, two of the three in their 50s, and six of seven in their 60s or older lived with wives and children.

14. White common-law husbands found open cohabitation with black women socially undesirable. When William Hardie of Prince George's accused Daniel Carroll of Upper Marlborough, a wealthy merchant of the same county, of buggery and of keeping mulattoes, since "he . . . could use them as he pleased," Carroll sued him for slander, finding both charges equally harmful; see Clinton Ashley Ellefson, "The County Courts and the Provincial Courts of Maryland, 1733–1764" (Ph.D. diss., University of Maryland, 1963), pp. 544–546.

15. PG Inventories, 1730–1744.

16. Menard, "Maryland Slave Population," pp. 42–46; Kulikoff, "'Prolifick' People."

17. These points are fully developed in Kulikoff, "Origins of Afro-American Society."

18. These statements are based upon PG Wills, 1730–1769 and court cases discussed below.

19. PG Wills, 1730–1769; mortgages in PG Land Records, libers T, Y, and PP, mss. Estate sales were sometimes advertised in the *Maryland Gazette*. Slaves could not be sold from an estate until all other moveable property had been used to pay debts. Elie Valette, *The Deputy Commissary's Guide within the Province of Maryland* (Annapolis, 1774), pp. 91, 134–35.

20. Eighteenth-century migrations of slaves are discussed in Kulikoff, "Tobacco and Slaves: Population, Economy and Society in Eighteenth-Century Prince George's County, Maryland," (Ph.D. diss., Brandeis University, 1976), ch. 6 and slave migrations in the nineteenth century are analyzed in idem, "Black Society and the Economics of Slavery," *Maryland Historical Magazine* 70 (1975):208–10.

21. Court of Appeals of the Western Shore, BW no. 10(1800–1801), ff. 456–583, but esp: ff. 459–460, mss.

22. Chancery Papers no. 5241 (1788) mss.; PG Wills 1:280–5; PG Original Wills, box 7, folder 66, and box 13, folder 51, mss.; PG Inventories DD no. 1, ff. 22–24; DD no. 2, ff. 379–386; GS no. 1 ff. 246–248; and ST no. 1, ff. 96–100.

23. Chancery Records 16:298–304, ms.; PG Land Record PP (second part) 4; NN, f. 407; PG Original Wills, box 7, folder 3, and box 9, folder 52; PG Inventories DD no. 1, ff. 438–441, and GS no. 2, ff. 111–112.

24. About 40 percent of Prince George's slaves lived on large units from 1750 to 1779 (estimate based upon probate inventories), and 52 percent of the slaves in that county lived on big units in 1790 (federal census); see Kulikoff, "Tobacco and Slaves," table 6-1 for references.

25. Large in-migrations of Africans to the Chesapeake region occurred in the 1670s and 1690s (see Kulikoff, "Tobacco and Slaves," ch. 4, and references there). The great-grandmother of a man born in 1755 could have immigrated from Africa as a young woman in the 1690s.

26. "A List of Negroes on Doohoregan Manor taken in Familys with their Ages Dec. 1 1773." and other lists of slaves at Popular Island, Annapolis Quarter, and Annapolis taken in February and July 1774, Carroll Account Book. There were ten quarters on the 10,500 acres of Doohoregan. I am greatly indebted to Edward Papenfuse for calling this list to my attention.

27. Only a handful of people in the Chesapeake colonies owned as many slaves as Carroll. He could therefore afford to keep most of his slave families together, an option not open even to the very large slaveowner with several children and 100 slaves. Nevertheless, two-thirds of Carroll's slaves lived on units with less than 40 people, and 57 percent of them on quarters with less than 30. Only the 130 slaves who lived at Riggs (the main plantation at Doohoregan) developed more extensive kinship networks on a single quarter than was possible for slaves who lived on other large Chesapeake quarters of 15 to 30 slaves.

28. See Menard, "Maryland Slave Population, pp. 35–36 for seventeenth-century examples of quarters named for slave residents.

29. There were 139 married adults (all ages ) and single people 21 years and over in the group. While 46 percent of the leaders were over 55, only 11 percent (15/138) of all adults were over 55. The oldest member of a quarter kin group did not necessarily head the list. For example, Carpenter Harry, 46, headed Frost's Quarter even though his mother, Battle Creek Nanny, 78, was also living there.

30. The statistics are means: 36 percent of all slaves counted together, 38 percent with each quarter counted separately (sum of means). For a complete accounting of the kin ties of quarter leaders on farms where they lived, see the original article in *Law, Society and Politics in Early Maryland,* Land et al. (eds,) (Baltimore: Johns Hopkins, 1977).

31. Only a maximum of 6 percent of all the slaves in Prince George's, Anne-Arundel, Charles, and St. Mary's Counties, Md., in 1790, lived on units of more than 100. (The 6 percent is a maximum number because the census taker sometimes put slaves from several of the same master's quarters in the same entry) *Heads of Families at the First Census of the United States Taken in the Year 1790; Maryland* (Washington, 1907), pp. 9–16, 47–55, 92–98, 104–109.

32. Joe married his mother's sister's husband's mother's grandchild.

33. See Kulikoff, "Tobacco and Slaves," ch. 7.

34. Jack Greene, ed., *The Diary of Landon Carter of Sabine Hall, 1752–1778* (Charlottesville, 1965), p. 840 (27 July 1775).

35. Kimber, "Itinerant Observations," p. 327. See Kulikoff, "Tobacco and Slaves," ch. 6, for a fuller description of slave quarters.

36. Three of the structures are in St. Mary's; the other once stood in Prince George's. I am indebted to Cary Carson, coordinator of research, St. Mary's City Commission, for sharing the data on St. Mary's with me, and to Margaret Cook (a local historian, who lives in Oxon Hill, Md.) for her descriptions and slides of the Prince George's hut.

37. On a small plantation a slave quarter located in a kitchen is described in Provincial Court Judgments, El no. 4, ff. 110–112, ms.

38. For a similar perspective on the succession of households and on life cycles, see Lutz Berkner, "The Stem Family and the Developmental Cycle of the Peasant Household: An Eighteenth-Century Austrian Example," *American Historical Review* 77 (1972):398–418.

39. For the matricentral cell, see Meyer Fortes, "Introduction," to *The Developmental Cy-*

cle in *Domestic Groups*, ed. Jack Goody, Cambridge Papers in Social Anthropology, no. 1 (Cambridge, 1958), pp. 1-14, but esp. p. 9, and Sidney W. Mintz, "A Final Note," *Social and Economic Studies* 10 (1961):528-535, but esp. pp. 532-533.

40. Samuel Stanhope Smith, *An Essay on the Causes of the Variety of Complexion and Figure in the Human Species* (Philadelphia, 1787), p. 35; ibid., ed. Winthrop D. Jordan (Cambridge, Mass., 1965 [reprint of 1810 ed.]), pp. 61-62, 156-157.

41. Prince George's County Census, 1776, found in Gaius Marcus Brumbaugh, ed., *Maryland Records, Colonial Revolutionary, County, and Church*, 2 vols. Lancaster, Pa., 1915-28), 1-88. For the distribution of children on plantations see the original article.

42. Kulikoff, "Tobacco and Slaves," pp. 251-254.

43. Carroll Account Book. Elisha and Dennis were sons of Carpenter Harry and Sophia. Joe married Dinah of Kate and Caesar; her brother married Cecilia of Harry and Sophia. Elisha and Dennis were therefore Joe's wife's brother's wife's brothers.

44. Only the children of slaveowners or those who had just bought their first slave were likely to have only one slave, so this data is a useful indicator of the age children were first sold. The transfers from large to small plantations can be seen in the fact that 12 percent of all slaves 10 to 14 years of age on large plantations, but 43 percent on small farms, lived away from parents and kinfolk (see tables 1 and 2). A distribution of the ages of slaves in single person households can be found in the original article.

45. *Maryland Gazette*, 1 Oct. 1766.

46. Kulikoff, "Tobacco and Slaves," table 4-1, shows that the median age at first conception for slave women born 1710-1759 was 17 years. Age at marriage cannot be determined with precision but can be approximated from the age differences of husbands and wives. On the Carroll, Addison, and Wardrop plantations, 47 husbands were 6.8 years (mean) older than their wives, Carroll Account Book; PG Inventories GS no. 1, f. 73; GS no. 2, ff. 334-336.

47. Thomas Hughes, *History of the Society of Jesus in North America Colonial and Federal*, 4 vols. (London, 1910-1917), *Text, 1645-1773*, 2:560-61; William Stevens Perry, ed., *Historical Collections Relating to the American Colonial Church*, 4 vols. (Davenport, Iowa, 1870), 4:306-7; Thomas Bacon, *Four Sermons upon the Great and Indispensible Duty of All Christian Masters and Mistresses to Bring Up Their Negro Slaves in the Knowledge and Fear of God* (London, 1750), pp. v-vii.

48. Seventy percent of all marriages of slave women, 1720-1759 birth cohorts, took place before age 20 (marriages defined as first conception). Kulikoff, " 'Prolifick' People." Substantial numbers of these teenage girls should have been pregnant with their first children between ages 16 and 19. If they were living with husbands, then their households would include only a husband and wife. On the three large plantations analyzed in Table 1, there were only three husband-wife households, and the women in them were 19, 27, and 56 years old. There is evidence that five of the sixteen women, 16 to 19 years old, were married—three who had children lived with sisters; one lived with her husband; one was separated from her husband but had no children; and the other lived with her husband and children. Ten of the other eleven lived with their parents.

49. For female occupations, see Kulikoff, "Tobacco and Slaves," ch. 7; quote from William Kauffman Scarborough, *The Overseer: Plantation Management in the Old South* (Baton Rouge, 1966), pp. 183-184.

50. Green, *Diary of Landon Carter*, p. 777 (22 Sept. 1773).

51. Court of Appeals of the Western Shore, BW no. 10 (1800-1801), ff. 459-460; *Maryland Gazette*, 2 Nov. 1748.

52. PG Original Wills, box 10, folder 35; Charles Ball, *Fifty Years in Chains* (1836; New York, 1970), pp. 21-22; Court of Appeals of the Western Shore, BW no. 10, f. 549 (1802). These were the only examples I found in all the wills and court records I examined.

53. Kulikoff, "Tobacco and Slaves," table 7-6. Ages were collected from PG Inventories, 1730-1769.

54. Snowden Account Book, Private Accounts, ms.; Inventories 43:320, ms.; Chancery Records, 7:2-12, 25-34, 50-52; William Hand Browne, et al., eds. *Archives of Maryland*, 72 vols. (Baltimore, 1883-), 50:76-78; *Gentleman's Magazine* 34 (1764):261. For two examples

of ill slaves sold from master to master, see *Maryland Journal*, 28 Sept. 1778, and Chancery Records 16:469–78 (1789).

55. Carroll Account Book.

56. Greene, *Diary of Landon Carter*, pp. 329, 348, 648, 845, 1109–1110; *Maryland Gazette*, 11 July 1771.

57. See references cited in Kulikoff, "Tobacco and Slaves," ch. 6, note 44.

58. My work on slavery owes much to the pioneering book of Gerald Mullin, *Flight and Rebellion: Slave Resistance in Eighteenth-Century Virginia* (New York, 1972), but my perspective on runaways differs from the ones he presents in chapters 3 and 4 of his book. Mullin has, I believe, missed the significance of kin networks in helping most runaways.

59. See Kulikoff, "Tobacco and Slaves," table 6-4; Mullin, *Flight and Rebellion*, p. 129, shows that the proportion of visitors (as defined in table 8.5) increased from 29% before 1775 to 38% of all runaways whose destinations can be determined from 1776 to 1800. The major problem with this data and Mullin's is the large number of unknowns (52% in Maryland and 40% in Virginia).

60. *Maryland Gazette*, July 6, 1779. Other examples of slaves using the underground to escape slavery are found in ibid., April 28, 1757, and July 11, 1771. A profile of slaves from Southern Maryland who ran away from 1745 to 1779 follows. A distribution of destinations of slaves broken down into five-year groups and a discussion of the method of computing the data can be found in the original article:

MOTIVE OF RUNAWAY SLAVE

|  | To Visit Spouse | To Visit Other Kinfolk | To Visit Friends | Number of Runaways |
|---|---|---|---|---|
|  | 20 | 9 | 34 | 233 |
| % All Runaways | 9 | 4 | 15 | 27 |
| % All Visitors | 32 | 14 | 54 | 100 |

61. Ibid., 4 Oct. 1749; Nov. 1756; for other extensive visiting networks, see ibid., 11 Aug. 1751; 12 March 1772; 30 Jan. and 22 May 1777.

62. Ibid., 9 March 1758; 6 Feb. 1755, and 12 Aug. 1773; table 8.7. John Woolman claimed that husbands and wives were often separated, *The Journal of John Woolman* (Corinth ed., New York, 1961), p. 59.

# 22 | PERSISTENT MYTHS ABOUT THE AFRO-AMERICAN FAMILY

## HERBERT G. GUTMAN

We start with Alexander Hamilton. He was neither a historian nor a sociologist. Surely he would not be classified as an expert on the history of the Afro-American family. But a single sentence of his remains relevant to the theme of this paper. "The contempt we have been taught to entertain for the blacks," Hamilton observed nearly two centuries ago, "makes us fancy many things that are founded neither in reason nor in experience."[1] Just now, such "things" and much else in the Afro-American past are being subjected to fresh examination by persons dissatisfied with inadequate but widely approved "explanations." Controversy and polemic range over many subjects. There is dispute about the "docility" of the slaves, the origins of segregation, the personality of Nat Turner, the content of Radical Reconstruction, the objectives of Booker T. Washington, and much else. One subject essential to an enriched and deepened understanding of historic Afro-American subculture has remained thus far immune from serious discussion and controversy. That is the history of the Afro-American family. This paper reopens that subject on two separate but also connected levels: first, by a reexamination of certain major themes in E. Franklin Frazier's classic study, *The Negro Family in the United States*, and second, by the presentation of a sample of much new evidence concerning Afro-American family and household composition at a given moment in several parts of the United States but especially in the South between 1860 and 1880 and in one northern city, Buffalo, New York, between 1855 and 1925.

Although the data have not yet been entirely analyzed, preliminary study casts serious doubt on several central theoretical conceptions that guided Frazier's approach to the Afro-American family's past. Much is at issue that cannot adequately be discussed in these few pages: the anthropological distinctions between "folk culture" and "urban culture" common in the 1920s and 1930s; the relationship between economic structure and social and cultural change; and, especially, the sociological "models" shaped by Park and other University of Chicago social scientists, which profoundly affected Frazier's work.[2] Here we shall focus on Frazier's central arguments that two streams of Afro-American family life developed out of the slave experience, that one of them—the "matriarchy"—was the more important in the nineteenth century, and that "class" affected family structure in a simple and direct way. This new evidence suggests, furthermore, the pressing need for a full reexamination of the Afro-American's family history, slave as well as free, and, perhaps even more importantly, a reconsideration of the social and class structure of varied nineteenth- and early twentieth-century black urban and rural communities.

Much has been written about the history of the Afro-American family, but little, in fact, is really known about its composition and household at given historical moments, and even less is known about how and why it changed over time. Without such knowledge, it is difficult to assess historic family roles or the changing relationship between family life and the larger culture that shaped it. Despite such deficiencies, most historians and sociologists consider these questions closed and settled. Moynihan and his critics, for example, quarreled bitterly over the contemporary structure of the "Negro family," but all shared a common view of its recent and distant history.[3] They did not dispute about Afro-American family life 100 or even 50 years ago but shed angry words over the relationship between past patterns of black family life and present conditions in the black ghetto. The past remained fixed in their bitter arguments. For instance, Hauser, a sociologist, summed up the conventional wisdom that informed this dispute and much else written about the history of the Negro family:

> Family disorganization and unstable family life among Negro Americans is a product of their history and caste status in the United States. During slavery and for at least the first half century after emancipation, the Negro never had the opportunity to acquire the patterns of sexual behavior and family living which characterize middle-class white society. African family patterns were, of course, destroyed during slavery, when it was virtually impossible to establish any durable form of family organization. This historical tendency toward a matrifocal family structure has been reinforced by the continued inability of the Negro male, because of lack of opportunity and discriminatory practices, to assume the role of provider and protector of his family in accordance with prevailing definitions of the role of husband and father. The Negro male has, in a sense, been the victim of social and economic emasculation which has perpetuated and reinforced the matriarchal Negro family structure created by slavery.[4]

Such views draw in a somewhat distorted fashion upon Frazier's major arguments. They are not serious historical and sociological analyses; instead, they serve as mere diachronic speculation about the relationship between slavery and twentieth-century Afro-American life.

Despite my quarrel with Frazier's work as a *historian* of the black family, his reputation as a distinguished sociologist and pioneer student of Afro-American family life remains secure—for good reason. His scholarship and that of W. E. B. DuBois were the most significant in refuting widely approved racial "explanations" of Afro-American marital and family institutions. "In a long and intimate connection with this folk," Shaler, who rose to head Harvard's Lawrence Scientific School, said, "I have never heard a [Negro] refer to his grandfather and any reference to their parents is rare. The Negro must be provided with these motives of the household; he must be made faithful to the marriage bond, and taught his sense of ancestry."[5] Such views were regularly repeated by "social scientists" and popular writers on the black family before Frazier tackled the subject. A single illustration suffices to explain why much of this literature, quite properly, now is read by students of racial prejudice, not students of the black family. Odum's highly-praised study of the *Social and Mental Traits of the Negro* insisted that "in his home life, the Negro is filthy, careless, and indecent, . . . as destitute of morals as many of the lower animals, . . . [and with] little knowledge of the sanctity of home or marital relations."[6] Frazier was the first to challenge seriously the work of Odum, Hoffman, Tillinghurst, Elwang, Weatherford, Thomas, and others of similar persuasion.[7]

Burgess did not exaggerate when he called Frazier's 1939 study "indispensable" because it "explodes completely, and it may be hoped once and for all, the popular misconception of the uniformity of behavior among Negroes. It shows dramatically the wide variation in conduct and in family life by social classes."[8] More than this, when we search for comparative material on the history of white lower-class families, we cannot find a single study that compares in scope or detail with Frazier's work on the black family. It remains the best single historical study of the American family, black or white, published to date.

To say this, however, is not to insist that Frazier's history was without serious fault. Quite the contrary. Frazier did not use careful methods in developing a historical explanation for the condition of the black family in the 1920s and the 1930s. Instead, he read that "condition" back into the past and linked it directly to the nineteenth-century slave experience. His most significant contributions included an analysis of the development of a "matriarchal" family structure as an adaptation to the conditions of slavery and those of post-emancipation rural and urban southern life together with a detailed examination of the interplay between that "way of life" and the urban experience of migrating blacks between 1910 and 1940. Frazier respected the historical record, so he also described the presence of a two-parent, male-centered household among certain nineteenth-century free blacks, North and South. But his evidence concerning these two strands was quite limited. He depended largely upon the testimony of white travelers and missionaries, the writings of ex-slaves, the oral recollections of blacks many decades after that time, and a printed historical record heavily colored by racial and class preconceptions and biases.

In essence, Frazier found two streams of historic Afro-American family life—one more important than the other. The more dominant stream was nurtured by slavery and the conditions of rural southern life; a "matriarchal family" was its most characteristic form. A subordinate "stream" was the two-parent, male-headed household that existed among a small minority of Afro-Americans who owned property, enjoyed middle-class occupations, or had independent artisan and craft skills. Thus, Frazier directly linked the two-parent, Afro-American household to property ownership, and skill to "class." Since so few Afro-Americans owned property or retained traditional skills, Frazier found the first stream to be the more important of the two trends and drew large conclusions from his two-stream theory. He rooted much of Afro-American difficulty in family life in the dominance of the one pattern:

The widespread disorganization of family life among Negroes has affected practically every phase of their community life and adjustments to the larger white
world. Because of the absence of stability in family life, there is a lack of traditions. Life among a large portion of the urban Negro populaton is casual, precarious, and fragmentary.

"It lacks," Frazier concluded, "continuity, and its roots do not go deeper
than the contingencies of daily living."[9]

Since the appearance of Frazier's work, little else of value has been written about the history of the Afro-American family. Impressed by it,
Myrdal and his coworkers gave little space to the black family in *An
American Dilemma*; instead, they advised readers to study Frazier's
book.[10] Historians of slavery in recent decades have added little to the traditional picture of the slave family because they have not yet studied slave
culture fully.[11] Superior studies of the antebellum southern and northern
free blacks such as those by Franklin and Litwack say little about family
relations. The same is true of such penetrating monographs about postbellum southern blacks as the works of Taylor, Wharton, and Tindall. In
their recent books on South Carolina during Reconstruction, Rose and
Williamson have broken the silence about the Afro-American family and
added significant new data, but these are exceptions to the rule.[12] More
common is the general view put forth in the late Gilbert Osofsky's *Harlem*.
What happened to the black migrant family is summed up in a single sentence: "Slavery initially destroyed the entire concept of family for
American Negroes and the slave heritage, bulwarked by economic conditions, continued into the twentieth century to make family instability a
common factor in Negro life." A similar argument threads two recent
general studies of the Afro-American family by Billingsley and by Bernard. The former deals with the Afro-American family between 1865 and
the great migration in fewer than three pages; Bernard's volume is a tangle
of sociological jargon and misused historical evidence. In truth, historians
and sociologists have said little new about the history of the Negro family
since Frazier published his work thirty-five years ago. Glazer was correct
to write: "We have the great study of E. Franklin Frazier, *The Negro Family in the United states*—aside from that precious little."[13]

If, as Frazier and others insisted, the slave household developed a "fatherless," matrifocal pattern sufficiently strong to become self-sustaining over
time and to be transmitted from generation to generation among large
numbers of blacks, such a condition necessarily must have been common
among those Afro-Americans closest in time and in experience to actual
chattel slavery. Subnuclear and, generally, matrifocal family ties rather
than conjugal and nuclear bonds should regularly appear in the quantitative data that describe family and household composition among antebellum northern and southern free blacks and among rural and urban freedmen during and just after Reconstruction. For this reason, my larger study
focuses intensely on the years between 1850 and 1880. It is there that the
effects of chattel slavery on personality and family structure should have
been most severe. By starting with these decades, my study tells nothing
*directly* about either slave family life or the family arrangements among

post-Reconstruction blacks. But the findings *indirectly* call into question many views on both of these subjects.

We turn first to the dominant historical view of the Afro-American family between 1850 and 1880 and especially the way in which most historians and sociologists saw it in the aftermath of emancipation. Frazier's argument deserves attention at the start. Afro-American family patterns following freedom offered a critical test for his "two-stream" theory. Frazier insisted that "normal" family patterns had developed among small groups of antebellum free blacks, especially those of "mixed color" who had some economic opportunity in northern and southern cities or who lived in isolated "racial islands." Although Frazier admitted that emancipation increased their numbers, especially with those among ex-slaves who had been house servants or artisans and found in freedom the occasion to build stable, two-parent households, his major argument took exactly the opposite direction: the slave experience blocked "normal" family life for most freedmen. In the 1930s, readers of *The Negro Family in Chicago* learned from Frazier that "the Negro family, which was at best an accomodation to the slave order, went to pieces in the general break-up of the plantation."[14] Frazier later expanded this point:

> What authority was there to take the place of the master's in regulating sex relations and maintaining the permanency of marital ties? Where could the Negro father look for sanction of his authority in family relations which had scarcely existed in the past? . . . Emancipation was a crisis in the life of the Negro that tended to destroy all his traditional ways of thinking and acting. . . . The mobility of the Negro population after emancipation was bound to create disorder and produce widespread demoralization. . . . When the yoke of slavery was lifted, the drifting masses were left without any restraint upon their vagrant impulses and wild desires. The old intimacy between master and slave, upon which the moral order under the slave regime had rested was destroyed forever. . . . Promiscuous sexual relations and constant changing of spouses became the rule with the demoralized elements in the freed Negro population. . . . Marriage as formal and legal relation was not a part of the mores of the freedmen.[15]

Similar but briefer arguments appeared a decade later in *The Negro in the United States.* "The Civil War and Emancipation," Frazier concluded, "destroyed the discipline and the authority of the masters and uprooted the stable families from their customary mode of living."[16]

Frazier was neither the first nor the last to put forth such views. Contemporary enemies and even many friends of the freedman saw nothing but chaos and breakdown in his postbellum family life. Historians at the turn of the century joined to stamp final approval on this "truth." Unlike Frazier, however, their explanations turned on "race." "Negro he is, negro he always has been, and negro he always will be," said George Fitzhugh in 1866. Fitzhugh believed that racial inferiority and the withdrawal of paternal protection together doomed blacks.

> They [Negro orphans] lost nothing in losing their parents, but lost everything in losing their masters. Negroes possess much amiableness of feeling, but not the least steady, permanent affection. "Out of sight, out of mind" is true for them all. They never grieve twenty-four hours for the death of parents, wives, husbands, or children. . . . [17]

Others echoed Fitzhugh. A rural Georgia newspaper (1865) mockingly approved a reader's suggestion that Negro marriages be legalized: "If *he can*, let him confer upon them the sanctity of the marriage relation; let him make them all virtuous and chaste and continent; let him teach them to read the Bible and Shakespeare and then let him confer upon them liberty and white skin." Robert Toombs was no less direct. "Now," he asked *Atlanta Consitution* readers in 1871, "what does the negro know about the obligations of the marriage relation? No more, sir, than the parish bull or village heifer."[18] Toombs' animal analogy found a resonant friend in Bruce whose *Plantation Negro as Freeman* Frazier quoted as an authoritative source on Negro social life. Planters, Bruce insisted, could no longer "compel" black "parents to prevent their offspring from running wild like so many young animals." Whatever its deficiencies, moreover, slavery had offered more protection against "promiscuous intercourse" than freedom. "Marriage under the old regime," said Bruce, "was very like unlawful cohabitation under the new, only that the master, by the power he had, compelled the nominal husband and wife to live together permanently."[19] Fleming shared this belief and helped to legitimize it as historical "fact". The absence of a single shred of evidence did not prevent Fleming from insisting that in 1865 and 1886 "the fickle negroes, male and female, made various experiments with new partners" so that soon thousands "had forsaken the husband and wife of slavery times and 'taken up' with others." Again, without evidence of any sort, Fleming told that black "foeticide and child murder were common crimes." Not surprisingly, he concluded that "the marriage relations of the negroes were hardly satisfactory, judged by white standards."[20]

We cite these *opinions* not to say that Frazier shared them but to show instead that persons of quite different perspectives accepted as "fact" that chaos and disorder typified family life and marital relations among "freedmen" of both sexes. And this view continues to saturate historical and sociological writing and therefore smothers the past. Richardson wrote of Florida blacks during Reconstruction: "Through no fault of their own some of the freedmen had little conception of marital and family obligations. . . . The ex-slaves saw no particular reason for changing the practices by which they had always lived." Billingsley admits that "Emancipation had some advantages for the Negro family" but calls it "a catastrophic social crisis for the ex-slave" and finds "Reconstruction . . . a colossal failure." Mostly racist sources convinced Donald that freedmen and women had "no traditions or experience of marriage and family mores" and "had not yet developed that feeling of concern and sympathy which kinsmen ordinarily have for one another." Sociologists Broom and Green put it differently when they asserted that "many Negro males used their new freedom of movement to desert their wives and children, and some demoralized mothers abandoned their children." Bernard wants us to believe that "so far as *anomie* is concerned, there does seem to be one period in American history when this term could adequately serve: the tragic Reconstruction Era." Then, "the Negro male was put in a situation which forbade his becoming a mature human being, and then was both rewarded and punished for not becoming one. The result was a classic case of the self-fulfilling prophecy. . . . For over a generation after emancipation, the Negro obliged his detractors by acting out the prophecy." Lincoln says the same: "Freedom did not improve the image of the Negro male or give him a sense of security as the head of the family. He remained a semi-slave. . . ." What matters is not the truth of these observations but the fact that they reinforce and strengthen Frazier's conception of two streams of historic Afro-American family life.[21]

New evidence lets us test in significiant ways the conventional picture of the Afro-American family composition between 1850 and 1880. But, first, a few words about the data. The discrete pieces of information gathered about individual blacks and their families from manuscript state, federal, and Freedmen's Bureau censuses number in the tens of thousands because nearly every Afro-American household has been reconstructed in twenty-one distinct urban and rural communities.[22] In each city and rural area, percentage distributions have been calculated for thirty types of Afro-American families, ranging from an augmented-extended family headed by a black father, to a subnuclear family headed by a black mother living in a white household. Five major types have been studied: nuclear, extended, augmented, households, and subfamilies living with either other black or white families. Each of these larger types has been broken down into subsets to tell just how many nuclear families, for example, were composed of a husband and wife, a husband, wife and their children, a father and his children, or a mother and her children. In addition, the age, sex, occupation, and, where available, real and personal property have been recorded for each individual black.

The scope of the study has widened over time. In a preliminary but unpublished study, Glasco and I reconstructed the household structure for the entire black population in Buffalo in 1855 and 1875, and sampled households in 1905 and 1925 (in all 684 households).[23] A comparison of all items of significance between the 1855 black population and more than 15,000 natives and Irish and German immigrants followed. In addition, comparative materials were collected for portions of the 1860 New York City (128 households) and Brooklyn (191 households) black community, and for the entire 1860 free black community in Mobile, Alabama (212 households). Critics of this early study worried because the 1860 manuscript census failed to delineate exact family relationships. They also correctly argued that its selection was biased because free blacks, North and South, however close in time to slavery, nevertheless may have been distinct from the slaves and later freedmen in their aspirations. Thus, the study was expanded to confront the ex-slave and much else more directly. From his own unpublished work, Daniel Walkowitz supplied full demographic data on the Troy, New York, black community in 1860 and 1880 (253 households). Despite its limitations, full census data were gathered for the 1860 free black community in Richmond, Virginia (633 households), and Charleston, South Carolina (623 households). And, more important, the 1880 federal manuscript census permitted the reconstruction of thousands of rural and urban southern households inhabited by mostly ex-slaves: St. Helena's Island (904 households), St. Helena's Township

(491 households), and the town of Beaufort, South Carolina (491 households); Natchez, Mississippi (769 households); all of rural Adams County, Mississippi (3,093 households); Mobile, Alabama (3,235 households); and finally, Richmond, Virginia (5,670 households).[24]

Additional material of unusual significance gathered from the Freedman's Bureau records in the National Archives added independent evidence. These data fell into two categories. First, exceedingly detailed manuscript censuses of the freedmen were gathered by Virginia Bureau officials in 1865 and 1866. Those for York (994 households), Montgomery (500 households), and Princess Anne (375 households) counties permitted careful examination of the household composition among Virginia blacks just after emancipation. In addition, marriage registers kept by Bureau officials revealed otherwise inaccessible information about prior family arrangements among more than 800 couples in Rockbridge and Nelson counties, Virginia; a similar number in Washington, D.C.; and more than 2,000 black men and women in and near Vicksburg, Mississippi.

In all, but not including the marriage registers or the 1905 and 1925 Buffalo census data, information has been gathered about the composition of nearly 19,000 Afro-American households between 1855 and 1880. It is a more than adequate sample. Only the time factor is held constant. The range is far-reaching and covers distinct social and economic environments that affected Afro-American life differently. Virginia counties that sold off "surplus" slaves before the Civil War are included. So are northern industrial (Troy) and port (Buffalo) cities. Charleston was a decaying southern city in 1860. That year and twenty years later, Mobile was a booming Gulf port. Richmond in the same years allowed an examination of the family life of black factory workers. Beaufort and Natchez told about the small town: one a river port and the other, a predominantly black village. The South Carolina Sea Island townships were densely black in population and a repository of African "survivals." Only 59 whites, for example, lived among St. Helena Island's 4,267 Negroes. And rural Adams County was Deep South and had its own particular social structure. So diverse a setting allows us to ask and answer many questions. We can compare the household composition of antebellum free blacks in northern and southern cities and contrast particular southern cities. Rural and urban patterns among the freedmen and women can be distinguished. So can differences within a city: for example, the densely black wards in Richmond (Marshall and Jackson wards) and in Mobile (the seventh ward) show a more regular two-parent household than the "integrated" wards in these cities. Most important for this article are the answers to the questions posed earlier. Were there two streams of Afro-American family life? How widespread was the matriarchal household? What were the relationships between class and household composition?

The findings in this study dispute vigorously the general view of the black family and household composition between 1850 and 1880 because most antebellum free blacks, North and South, lived in double-headed households, and so did most poor rural and urban freedmen and women. Female-headed households were common but not typical. Some of the evidence for these conclusions may be summarized briefly.

The communities studied consisted overwhelmingly of urban and rural lower-class families; an occupational analysis of male and female income earners makes this fact clear. In rural Adams County, only 141 of 2,971 Mississippi black males had occupations other than farmer, farm laborer, farm worker, or laborer. Of these, only twenty-two were nonworkers, including the coroner and the sheriff. The same was true for the Sea Island rural blacks. Only 26 of St. Helena's 850 adult males were neither farmers nor farm laborers. In the cities, except for the antebellum southern towns, black males worked mostly as unskilled laborers or domestic servants. The free black males of Charleston, Mobile, and Richmond counted many artisans and craftsmen among them: 32 percent in Richmond, 43 percent in Mobile, and 70 percent in Charleston. A quite tiny percentage held "middle-class" occupations (1 per cent in Mobile and Richmond and 4 percent in Charleston).

Northern cities showed the opposite picture. There, the typical black male was an unskilled laborer or a service worker: The percentages in these occupational categories in Buffalo (1855 and 1875), Troy (1860 and 1880), and New York and Brooklyn (1860) ranged from 68 percent to 81 percent. Mostly unskilled male laborers also worked in the reconstructed southern cities. Only Beaufort had a substantial nonworking class, 12 percent of adult males. Half of one percent of Natchez's black males fell into this category; the percentage was a bit higher in Richmond and Mobile. Three of five Beaufort males worked as unskilled laborers or as domestics; in Natchez, four of five; in Mobile, nearly nine of ten. Richmond's factories made its black labor force more complex. One of every five adult males was a factory worker, and, including them, at least 80 percent of Richmond's male workers were dependent wage earners.

Such occupational information together-with scattered but still useful data on income and property ownership casts serious doubts on the simple proposition that "class" factors *alone*—income, skill, property, and middle-class occupations—*determined* the presence of a two-parent household. To say this is not to minimize the importance of such factors but rather to assess their significance and to reject Frazier's crude economic determinism. To cite an example: the typical male head of an antebellum northern black family was an unskilled laborer or a domestic servant; his southern counterpart more probably was a skilled artisan. But a much higher percentage of Negro children younger than eighteen in 1860 lived in male-present households in Buffalo, Troy, and Brooklyn than in Charleston and Richmond. Not just "economic" factors affected the shape of these households. For the entire period studied, a large proportion of the families and households analyzed had at their head poor, unskilled rural and urban laborers and domestic servants. Black males with artisan skills or real and personal property obviously had a better chance to build stable, two-parent households than others less fortunate. But it does not follow that unskilled black males, despite numerous obstacles, found it impossible to build and sustain such households. Actually, since most black households were headed by just such persons, it seems clear that the composition of the black household was affected by, but independent of, income, skill, and property. If most black families studied were male-present households, then it follows that that kind of household belonged to other nineteenth-century blacks than just a small black "elite"—those whom Frazier called the "favored few" who had "escaped from the isolation of the black folk."[25] As a result, the concept of two separate "streams" of Afro-American family life developing quite separately over time is, at best, misleading.

We therefore disregard the two-stream theory and instead ask a simple question: how *common* was the two-parent household among the thousands of Afro-American households examined between 1855 and 1880? Percentages vary for fourteen different northern and southern black communities but reveal a consistent pattern everywhere. Depending upon the particular setting, no fewer than 70 percent and as many as 90 percent of the households contained a husband and wife or just a father (Table 1). In the Virginia counties surveyed by the Freedmen's Bureau in 1865 and 1866, male-present households ranged from 78 percent to 85 percent. Northern cities did not fall below 85 percent (and in Buffalo, significantly, the percentage remained that high in 1905 and 1925). The southern towns and cities revealed the lowest percentage of male-present households, but Beaufort, Natchez, Mobile, and Richmond all ranged between 70 percent and 74 percent. Southern rural two-parent households were more common, ranging from 81 percent to 87 percent in Mississippi and in South Carolina. Not surprisingly, most black children lived in two-parent households. In 1880, for example, 69 percent of black Natchez children younger than six lived with a father; the percentage was even higher, 77 percent each, in Richmond and Mobile.

To turn from the male-present household to the types of households that blacks lived in (whether or not an adult male was present), means again to unearth new findings that upset conventional views. Black households and family systems were exceedingly complex in the aftermath of

**Table 1.** PERCENTAGE OF MALE-PRESENT NEGRO HOUSEHOLDS, 1855–1880

| Place and Date | Number of Households | Male-Present Households (%) | Male-Absent Households (%) |
|---|---|---|---|
| Buffalo, N.Y., 1855 | 145 | 90 | 10 |
| Buffalo, N.Y., 1875 | 159 | 85 | 15 |
| Troy, N.Y., 1880 | 128 | 85 | 15 |
| York County, Va., 1865 | 994 | 85 | 15 |
| Montgomery County, Va., 1866 | 500 | 78 | 22 |
| Princess Anne County, Va., 1865 | 375 | 84 | 16 |
| Natchez, Miss., 1880 | 769 | 70 | 30 |
| Beaufort, S.C., 1880 | 461 | 70 | 30 |
| Richmond, Va., 1880 | 5670 | 73 | 27 |
| Mobile, Ala., 1880 | 3235 | 74 | 26 |
| Rural Adams County, Miss., 1880 | 3093 | 81 | 19 |
| St. Helena's Township, S.C., 1880 | 491 | 87 | 13 |
| St. Helena's Island, S.C., 1880 | 904 | 86 | 14 |

emancipation. Arrangements within them varied greatly, but "chaos" and "disorder" are not useful concepts in understanding them. Only the 1880 manuscript census, however, is precise enough in defining family relationships to allow us to reconstruct some of this complexity. And even that source is deficient because it tells nothing about kinship ties between separate households. Yet, it reveals a great deal when sorted according to nuclear, extended, and augmented households as well as subfamilies living either with other black or white families (Table 2). The patterns are clear. Except for Richmond, very few black families lived in white households. One of every nine or ten urban black families lived with another black family. Together, extended and augmented families never accounted for more than 30 percent of the households in any area. Most black households were *nuclear* in composition: the range spreads from 50 percent in Natchez to 80 percent in St. Helena's Township; Richmond, Mobile, Beaufort, rural Adams County, and St. Helena's Island fall in between.

That so large a percentage of southern black households had two parents and were nuclear in composition tells more than that the double stream is a fiction. Most adults in these families were illiterate, and unless we give unwarranted credit to northern evangels, their behavior had to be profoundly shaped by tradition and custom. So it becomes clear that the new data pose significant questions about the consciousness, the culture, and the family life of enslaved Afro-Americans. Unless we are prepared to believe that most slave owners taught their chattel the value of a two-parent nuclear household and sustained it in practice, then we must reject Elkins' conception of American slavery as a "closed system" that let masters remake slaves in their image. Elkins' "significant other" may have been a husband or a father, not just a master. That so many rural South Carolina and Mississippi blacks lived in two-parent nuclear families is hard to reconcile with Stampp's conclusion that slave family life was "a kind of cultural chaos," was "highly unstable," and often revealed "the failure of any deep and enduring affection to develop between some husbands and wives." Similarly, there is difficulty in agreeing with Wade that urban slave marriage involved "a great deal of fiction" and that "family ties were weak at best." "Male and female slaves found their pleasure and love," Wade argues, "wherever they could. . . . Generally, relations were neither prolonged nor monogamous. . . . The very looseness of their mating . . . made a meaningful family unit even more difficult. . . . For the children of such a marriage, there could be no ordinary family life."[26] Such

**Table 2.**  TYPES OF AFRO-AMERICAN HOUSEHOLDS BY PERCENTAGES, 1880

| Place | Nuclear | Extended | Augmented | Sub-Black | Sub-White |
|-------|---------|----------|-----------|-----------|-----------|
| Richmond, Va. | 52 | 10 | 19 | 9 | 10 |
| Mobile, Ala. | 60 | 14 | 11 | 10 | 5 |
| Natchez, Miss. | 50 | 17 | 20 | 10 | 3 |
| Beaufort, S.C. | 63 | 17 | 10 | 9 | 1 |
| Rural Adams County, Miss. | 58 | 15 | 15 | 10 | 2 |
| St. Helena's Island, S.C. | 76 | 14 | 2 | 8 | 0 |
| St. Helena's Township, S.C. | 80 | 12 | 4 | 4 | 0 |

arguments do not square easily with the fact that fifteen years after slavery's end three of every four Richmond and Mobile black families, nearly all headed by adult ex-slaves, were two-parent households.

It is hazardous to read history backward, but such data indicate that the final word has yet to be written about slave family life and culture in the cities and on the farms and plantations. Important new evidence about the attitudes of freedmen and women toward marriage and family life as well as their marital condition as slaves is found in the Freedmen's Bureau manuscripts. Registers that listed the marriages of former slaves in Washington, D.C., and Rockbridge and Nelson counties, Virginia, between 1865 and 1867 show that models of stable marriages existed among the slaves themselves, not just among their masters, other whites, or free blacks. Some had lived together as husband and wife for more than forty years in slavery. In all, registers recorded the dates of 1,721 marriages: 46 percent in the Nelson county, 43 percent in Rockbridge county, and 36 percent in Washington, D.C., had resided together at least ten years. The Washington register tells even more. It listed 848 marriages, and of them only 34 were between men and women who had lived in the District before emancipation. The rest had moved there, probably as families, mostly from nearby rural counties in Maryland and Virginia. Asked by the registrar who had married them, some did not know or could not remember. Others named a minister, a priest, or, more regularly, a master. Most important, 421, nearly half, responded, "no marriage ceremony," suggesting clearly that slaves could live together as husband and wife in a stable (though hardly secure and ideal) relationship without formal religious or secular rituals. The Vicksburg, Mississippi, marriage registers for 1864 and 1865 give even more significant information. Freedmen and women whose slave marriages had been disrupted told how long they had lived together in an earlier marriage, the cause for its termination, and the number of children resulting from a prior marriage. Although these registers have not yet been fully analyzed, they have already yielded valuable information. Answers given by more than 2,100 ex-slaves who were taking new spouses show that 40 percent of the men and 35 percent of the women had been married for at least five years, and some for more than twenty years. "Death" (40 percent for the men and 57 percent for the women) and "force" (i.e., physical separation) (48.5 percent for the men and 31 percent for the women), explained the rupture of most of these marriages, but one of every twenty men and women gave as the reason "mutual consent."

Death and force broke up many slave marriages, but it does not follow that such severe disruption shattered slave *consciousness* of normal slave marriage relations and of the value of a two-parent household. The 1866 Freedmen's Bureau census in Princess Anne County, Virginia, sheds clear light on the consciousness. Bureau officials gathered detailed demographic data on 1,796 black men, women, and children. Only the occupational data were limited in use (all of the employed adult males were listed simply as "laborers"). Of these blacks, 1,073 were fifteen years and older, and of them 2 percent were of "mixed color," 6.3 percent had been free before 1863, and 3.5 percent could read. In other words, the adult population consisted almost entirely of black, illiterate ex-slaves. The census also recorded the names of former owners and where each person had lived before emancipation. Sixty-three percent, nearly two-thirds, of the entire population had not resided in Princess Anne County before emancipation. Most migrants had lived nearby in Virginia and North Carolina counties; a few came from Maryland and three from as far as Kentucky, Georgia, and Texas. Despite such extraordinary mobility, no more than one in ten lived apart from a larger black household. Ninety percent of the migrants and local residents lived in 375 families, 84 percent of which housed a husband and his wife. Part of the reason for so much physical movement was the reconstitution of former slave families. Not one of the female-headed households was composed of persons who had belonged to different owners. The two-parent households tell a different story. Of 291 households headed by a former male slave, 193, two-thirds in all, came from separate owners. Some came together from more than two owners, but in most instances the wife and children were from a single master and the husband from another master. Just how many of these families were reconstituted and how many were new marriages cannot be known without additional information, but even by itself these data help to explain the geographical mobility of so many freedmen in 1865 and 1866, movement widely misinterpreted by white contemporaries and, until quite recently, by historians. What many white contemporaries thought of such behavior often drew upon sources other than the behavior itself. So we are not surprised to read in the *New York Times* in 1865: "The Negro misunderstands the motives which made the most laborious, hard-working people on the face of the globe clamour for his emancipation. You are free, Sambo, but you must work. Be virtuous, too, oh, Dinah! 'Whew! Gor Almighty! bress my soul!' "[27] It may be in reexamining the consciousness, culture, and family life of slaves and freedmen, marriage registers and census tracts will prove more valuable than the *New York Times* and other traditional sources.

Let us turn finally to a portion of another world which figured so prominently in Frazier's sociohistorical model: the female-headed black household in the rural and urban South between 1855 and 1880. In this period and for still another generation, Frazier argued, the "Matriarchate" ("the House of the Mother") flourished. Property-owning Negro farmers became black Puritan fathers, and small numbers of Negro males headed households in the South's urban bourgeois enclaves, but these did not count as much as the "matriarchal" households that surrounded them. Five chapters argued that matriarchy became a *legitimized counter-norm*. "Motherhood outside of institutional control was accepted by a large group of Negro women with an attitude of resignation as if it were nature's decree." Such were "the simple folkways of . . . peasant folk." "In the rural areas of the South," Frazier said again, "we find the maternal family functioning in its most primitve form as a natural organization." The three-generation female household—grandmother-daughter-and grandchildren—counted for much in this construct and Frazier insisted that the older Negro woman headed "the maternal family among a primitive peasant people."[28]

It is difficult to dispute when Frazier writes that "the maternal-family organization, a heritage from slavery, . . . continued on a fairly large scale" because this critical assertion rested on almost no historical evidence. Seventy pages of text on the post-slavery "matriarchy" include just six pieces of historical data on the critical decades between 1870 and 1900: a letter, from Elizabeth Botume; an extract from A. T. Morgan's *Yazoo* (Washington, D.C., 1884); and two quotations each from Philip Bruce and J. Bradford Laws, a Department of Labor investigator who studied two small Louisiana plantations at the turn of the century. (Frazier neglected Laws' comments that the plantation Negroes were "grossly animal in their sexual relations" and that "very few . . . appear capable of deep emotion; sorrow over the dead dies with the sun. . . . ")Despite the lack of evidence, Frazier's arguments about matriarchy have gained widespread approval. Glazer for example, writes in 1966 that Frazier's main proposition "remains solid and structures all our thinking on the Negro family." Glazer even wants readers to believe that an "extension of the matriarchy" took place after emancipation.[29] Although these and similar propositions remain unproven, they nevertheless need to be seriously tested.

Three objective measures of matriarchy as a form of household and family organization are available: male presence, the presence of older female relatives in the household, and the earning power of women as contrasted with men. Males, as seen, most usually husbands, were found in at least 70 percent of the households examined. That so few were extended households suggests the infrequency of older female relatives as household members. Income is another matter. Unskilled black laborers earned two or three times more a week than female servants or washerwomen, but little is yet known of the regularity of male employment, so that this question remains open.

There are other ways to examine these female-headed households in order to see them in historical perspective. We do not regularly find large numbers of children in female-headed households (Table 3). In 1880, for example, female-headed households among women aged thirty to forty-nine usually had one or two children younger than eighteen. Furthermore, the overall age distribution of all female household heads studied in 1880 suggests that a good portion of them were heads because their husbands had died and for no other reason. Between 23 percent and 30 percent of the households studied in each rural and urban area had as its head a woman of at least age fifty. An even more significant test of the matriarchal ethos and of the conceptions of family and marriage held by black men and women can be constructed by asking how many women aged twenty to

**Table 3.** SIZE OF FEMALE-HEADED BLACK HOUSEHOLDS, INCLUDING ALL CHILDREN YOUNGER THAN 18 FOR MOTHERS AGED 30–49, 1880

| Place | Total | One or Two Children (%) | Three or More Children (%) |
|---|---|---|---|
| Beaufort, S.C. | 50 | 72 | 28 |
| St. Helena Island and St. Helena Township, S.C. | 85 | 65 | 35 |
| Richmond, Va. | 658 | 72 | 28 |
| Natchez, Miss., Wards I–III | 92 | 61 | 39 |

twenty-nine in 1880 headed households in relationship to all black women of that age. They are a good group to examine. Born between 1851 and 1860, they grew up as slave children and matured as young women in the "chaos" and "disorder" of the Reconstruction era. They fall into three categories: those married, with or without children; those with children and heading households; and single women boarding with white or black families or living with their parents (Table 4). Except in rural Adams County, single women far outnumbered those who headed households with children. More than this, four times as many Richmond and Mobile women were married, with or without children, than headed households with children. The proportions were higher in the rural Sea Islands and somewhat lower in Natchez, Beaufort, and rural Adams County. These relationships take on even greater significance when the extremely unfavorable female sex ratio is considered. For reasons as yet not entirely clear, black women between the ages of fifteen and forty far outnumbered males in the same age group. This imbalance was not nearly as marked in the southern rural areas as in the southern cities where it was astonishing. For every 100 Negro women aged twenty to twenty-nine in Beaufort, Natchez, Mobile, and Richmond, there were only 57 black males! In any modern social system, such a ratio weakens the position of the woman and, by itself, spawns prostitution and illegitimacy. When we realize that this unfavorable sex ratio existed in the "'redeemed" and "Bourbon" southern cities, then the matriarchy ethos loses more of its "potency" and we ask ourselves, instead, why were there so *few* female-headed Negro households?

Similar computations about the household status of all black women older than fifty test Frazier's notion of the three-generation matriarchal household, the "classic" grandmother-daughter-grandchildren arrangement. If we ask in 1880 what percentage of black women aged fifty and older headed such households or cared alone for their grandchildren, we find a relatively significant number only in Beaufort where 16 percent (21 of 134 women) headed such households. The percentage dwindles in all

**Table 4.**  HOUSEHOLD STATUS OF ALL BLACK WOMEN, AGED 20–29, IN 1880

| Area | Number | Married With/ Without Children (%) | Head of Household With Children (%) | Single, Boarder, or Daughter (%) |
|---|---|---|---|---|
| Beaufort, S.C. | 243 | 54 | 18 | 28 |
| Natchez, Miss. | 227 | 31 | 14 | 55 |
| Mobile, Ala. | 1570 | 52 | 13 | 35 |
| Richmond, Va. | 3400 | 39 | 9 | 52 |
| St. Helena's Island, S.C. | 393 | 70 | 9 | 21 |
| St. Helena's Township, S.C. | 172 | 80 | 8 | 12 |
| Kingston and Washington Township, Adams Co., Miss. | 478 | 68 | 21 | 11 |

other places: 9 percent each in St. Helena's Island and Natchez, 6 percent each in St. Helena's Township and rural Adams County, and 5 percent in Richmond. Everywhere, the number of black widows aged fifty and more living just with their children was greater, but an even larger proportion lived alone with a husband or still shared full family life with a husband and their children. The total picture in rural Adams County is revealing for other places, too. Of 843 women aged fifty and older who resided there, half lived with husbands, with or without children and other relatives; another 15 percent, widowed, lived with married children; 19 percent boarded with relatives and nonrelatives or lived alone; 10 percent headed households that contained just their children or their children and distant kin; just 6 percent fit the "classic" model sketched by Frazier and so many others. None of this is surprising in light of the larger pattern uncovered.

Because so many black women worked, the relationship between their occupation and family position tells something important about the question of "matriarchy." We concentrate only on the cities and, in particular, on Richmond washerwomen and domestic servants. The data are still raw, but certain tentative observations can be reported. Not all women worked; mostly married women with children did not work. But still, slightly more than 6,000 Richmond women labored. Fewer than expected worked in the tobacco factories; one of every five was a washerwoman; two of every three were domestic servants. Married women, with or without children, and female heads of households worked more as washerwomen; 37 percent of Richmond's washerwomen were married and most often mothers; 28 percent headed households. Only 12 percent of the nearly 4,000 servants were married women. Fifty-three percent of all servants lived as individuals with white families. When we study their ages, patterns emerge. Washerwomen tended to be older as a group than servants. They may have preferred to toil over the tub and the dignity of their own poor homes to daily demeaning servant relationships outside the home. The typical black servant was an unmarried young woman. Just as many girls younger than age fifteen worked as house servants as women aged sixty and older. Only 13 percent of Richmond's servants were aged fifty and older; 57 percent were less than thirty. As "single" women, most servants either supported themselves or contributed to family incomes. Few black female servants fit the classic "Mammy" stereotype. Either whites preferred younger black women, or older black women stayed away from such work.

So much for an obsolete sociohistorical model that has told much about the history of the Afro-American family but nevertheless confused or blinded scholars as well as citizens. To dispute this model, however, is not the same as to offer another. Before that is done, new questions have to be answered and much material examined in fresh, systematic ways. The slave family is just one example. *Historical* comparisons with white lower-class families, immigrant and native-born, as well as with black families in other cultures are needed. Glasco and I compared the 1855 Buffalo Negro family with that of Irish and German immigrants and native whites and found significant similarities and differences, and strengths as well as weaknesses. But this is just a start.[30] More importantly, the quality of culture and family life cannot be constructed by a desk calculator. Whole ranges of nonquantitative data must be examined. But there are difficulties. Few nineteenth-century white Americans reported findings consistent with the data in these pages. When they did, they expressed "surprise," even shock. Why so few whites saw the Afro-American family as, in fact, it existed is a significant and complex question. Part of the reason reflects a curious coincidence between antislavery and proslavery arguments. White abolitionists denied slaves a family life or *even* a family consciousness because for them marriage depended only on civil law, not on culture. Proslavery apologists said free blacks could not build wholesome marriages for racial reasons. Together, these arguments blurred white perception of black families. Race and slavery were involved, but so was class.

Plumb has reminded us that racial stereotypes of Negroes had their counterpart in eighteenth- and nineteenth-century England. "Even the Sambo mentality," Plumb notes, "can be found in the deliberately stupid country yokel or in the cockney clown of later centuries. So, too, the belief, as with Negroes, that they were abandoned sexually, given to both promiscuity and over-indulgence." Slaves and free workers "were the objects of exploitation. . . . Hence we should not be surprised to find similar attitudes."[31] Race and class, however, mixed together so meanly for many whites that what they believed had little connection to what they saw. A single example from many serves this point. During Reconstruction, a British traveler heard a Macon, Georgia, black condemn a former master whom others praised:

> I was dat man's slave; and he sold my wife, and he sold my two chill'un; yes, brudders, if dere's a God in heaven, he did. Kind! yes, he gib me corn enough, and he gib me pork enough, and he neber gib me one lick wid de whip, but whar's my wife?—whar's my chill'un? Take away de pork, I say; take away de corn, I can work and raise dese for myself, but gib me back de wife of my bosom, and gib me back my poor chill'un as was sold away.

The same writer who reported these words said most freedmen and women "have no conception of the sacredness of marriage" and lived "in habitual immorality." He and others like him further validate Gramsci's dictum that "for a social elite the features of subordinate groups always display something barbaric and pathological."[32]

So we must use traditional historical sources with great care. In addition, we must not isolate the Afro-American family from both the black and the larger white social and class structure that profoundly affected it. Even though his application of it was faulted, Frazier's insistence upon such approaches must be retained. Take the question of occupational mobility. Glasco and I have completed an occupational analysis of the Buffalo black community in 1855, 1875, 1892, 1905, and 1925. The trend between 1855 and 1905 was not encouraging. Occupational opportunities narrowed relatively and absolutely for Buffalo blacks over time (Table 5). They could not penetrate the city's dynamic industrial and construction sectors. Although the number of black males older than fifteen increased

Table 5. SELECTED OCCUPATIONS OF BLACKS IN BUFFALO, N.Y., 1855–1925

| Occupation | 1855. N:133 | | 1875. N:188 | | 1892. N:346 | | 1905. N:425 | | 1925. N:211[c] | |
|---|---|---|---|---|---|---|---|---|---|---|
| | N | % Negro Males 1855 | N | % Negro Males 1875 | N | % Negro Males 1892 | N | % Negro Males 1905 | N | % Negro Males 1925 |
| Barbers | 21 | 16.0 | 16 | 8.5 | 9 | 2.6 | 6 | 1.4 | 3 | 1.4 |
| Sailors | 11 | 8.0 | 7 | 3.7 | 3 | 0.9 | 0 | 0.0 | 0 | 0.0 |
| Musicians | 1 | 0.8 | 3 | 1.5 | 10 | 3.0 | 18 | 4.2 | 0 | 0.0 |
| Building Trades | 8 | 6.0 | 8 | 4.3 | 7 | 2.0 | 7 | 1.6 | 10 | 4.7 |
| Masons | 1 | 0.8 | 0 | 0.0 | 2 | 0.6 | 14 | 3.3 | 2 | 1.0 |
| "Crafts"[a] | 6 | 4.5 | 5 | 2.7 | 6 | 1.7 | 10 | 2.4 | 25[b] | 11.8 |
| Factory Labor | 0 | 0.0 | 0 | 0.0 | 0 | 0.0 | 2 | 0.5 | 47 | 22.0 |
| Clerk, Messenger | 0 | 0.0 | 0 | 0.0 | 13 | 3.7 | 7 | 1.6 | 1 | 0.5 |
| Storekeeper | 0 | 0.0 | 0 | 0.0 | 0 | 0.0 | 0 | 0.0 | 1 | 0.5 |
| Professional | 6 | 4.5 | 3 | 1.5 | 5 | 1.4 | 4 | 0.9 | 3 | 1.4 |

a. Some of those listed under particular crafts must have labored in factories or workshops, but the census did not make such distinctions.
b. Does not include railroad firemen and brakemen.
c. The 1925 data are a sample that drew all Negro males older than 15 residing in every twentieth Negro-headed household in wards 6, 7, and 8.

by more than 300 percent, the number of barbers fell from twenty-two to six, sailors from eleven to none, building-trades craftsmen from eight to seven, and so forth. In 1855, barbers were 16 percent of all employed black males; in 1905, 1.4 percent. Skilled building-trades workers fell from 6 percent to 1.6 percent in the same years. Factory labor was not available to black males: in 1855, 1875, and 1892, census takers did not record a single black factory worker; in 1905, only 2 of 425 males were listed as factory workers. Just as black males were closed off from the building trades and factory labor between 1855 and 1905, so, too, were they blocked from occupations with a higher status. Black professionals, usually ministers and doctors, fell from six (4.5 percent) to four (0.9 percent) between 1855 and 1905, and the retail trades found no blacks at all in these years.

Such occupational depression and disadvantage were not isolated trends that happened only in Buffalo. In Troy, of 162 black males employed in 1880, 123 were menial workers or laborers; only two were iron workers. And this in a city that gave employment to several thousand immigrant and native white iron workers. Occupational exclusion of blacks actually began *before the Civil War*. In an unpublished study, Weinbaum has demonstrated conclusively such exclusion and decline for Rochester, New York, blacks between 1840 and 1860.[33] My own work shows a similar decline in Charleston, South Carolina, between 1850 and 1860. And these trends continued in the southern cities during Reconstruction: a crucial story that has yet to be told. The 1870 New Orleans city directory, Woodward pointed out, listed 3,460 black carpenters, cigarmakers, painters, shoemakers, coopers, tailors, bakers, blacksmiths, and foundry hands. By 1904, less than 10 percent of that number appeared even though the New Orleans population had increased by more than 50 percent.[34] The process of enclosing ex-slaves began during Reconstruction and is part of any larger study of the Afro-American family. Mobile, Alabama, for example, had among its 1,880 residents 139 black carpenters. Only 29 percent were younger than forty years of age. What matters is that 56 percent of Mobile's native white carpenters and 76 percent of its carpenters who were sons of European immigrants were younger than forty. Thirteen percent of Mobile's black carpenters were younger than thirty; 58 percent of the same city's black male servants were younger than 30. Because similar patterns emerge in other crafts *and* in other 1880 southern cities, it is clear that Afro-American fathers were not able to pass accumulated skills to their sons at this early date. The Buffalo study also shows the absence of a local entreprenurial and professional class among the blacks. Although the occupational structure was more diverse in southern cities, few blacks were nonworkers. More than 6,500 black males earned income in Richmond in 1880: among them, a single physician, a single lawyer, twelve teachers, thirteen clergymen, and sixteen store clerks. Artisans made up the "elite" among blacks in the northern and southern postbellum cities. But institutional racism shattered that "elite" in these years.

The implications of these findings are significant for the reconstruction of the history of the Afro-American family. Such occupational patterns may be a clue to an American variant of what Smith found in his outstanding study of Negro family life in British Guiana:

In rigidly stratified societies such as that of British Guiana, where social roles are largely allocated according to ascriptive criteria of ethnic characteristics, the lower-class male has nothing to buttress his authority as husband-father except the dependence upon his economic support. The uncertainty of his being able to carry out even this function adequately, because of general economic insecurity, undermines his position even further.[35]

But occupational segregation undermined more than the male's position in the household. The absence of a complex occupational hierarchy may have so weakened the Afro-American community as to prevent it from successfully organizing to compete with native whites and immigrant groups. At best, the Afro-American structure was "two-dimensional." Its width was a function of the numbers of blacks in the entire community; its depth a function of a complex family system. But it was denied the "height" derived from a complex class structure based on occupational diversity. As a result, the family system *may* have been more important in giving cohesion to the black than to the white lower-class community. Significantly, the occupational disability that victimized Buffalo blacks did *not* shatter their family system. In 1905, for example, 187 of Buffalo's 222 black households, 85 percent, were headed by males. Nevertheless, the decline of the black artisan and the absence of a significant middle class in all cities studied had significant implications that distinguish the black lower class from the white lower class, immigrant and native-born alike. Among the lower classes in the nineteenth and early twentieth centuries, the artisans were the dynamic and organizing element. Some became manufacturers, others became factory workers. Voluntary associations found leaders among them. Local politicians came from the artisans and skilled workers, so did leaders of trade unions and reform and radical movements. But the black skilled worker was blocked from playing these roles. Before that enclosure occurred, he had held a significant place in such movements. Unpublished studies demonstrate this fact in important ways. White has shown that black artisans led a protest movement against Buffalo's segregated school system between 1839 and 1868. Even more important Magdol has recently uncovered a pattern of artisan and craft leadership among the rural, town, and village blacks of the South between 1865 and 1870.[36] The destruction of artisan traditions wiped out such leadership and distorted the black community structure *above* the level of its family organization. Much that flows from this fact may help us in understanding black political and social behavior between 1870 and 1910.

We return to the beginning. Let us follow Alexander Hamilton's advice and set aside views about blacks "founded neither in reason nor in experience." Evidence from Buffalo, other northern cities, and, more important, southern rural regions, towns, and cities refutes the argument that makes of black family life little more than a crude speculation about the relationship between slavery and twentieth-century black experience. Such theorizing rests on faulty historical knowledge. Silberman, for example, said:

> Slavery had emasculated the Negro males, had made them shiftless and irresponsible and promiscuous by preventing them from asserting responsibility, negating their role as husband and father, and making them totally dependent

on the will of another. There was [after emancipation] no stable family structure to offer support to men or women or children in this strange new world. With no history of stable families, no knowledge of even what stability might mean, huge numbers of Negro men took to the roads as soon as freedom was proclaimed. . . . Thus there developed a pattern of drifting from place to place and woman to woman that has persisted (in lesser degrees, of course) to the present day.[37]

There is no reason to repeat such nonsense any longer. Ellison has answered the assumptions on which it rests in an eloquent and authoritative fashion: "Can a people . . . live and develop over 300 years by simply reacting?" he asks. "Are American Negroes simply the creation of white men, or have they at least helped create themselves out of what they found around them? Men have made a way of life in caves and upon cliffs, why can not Negroes have made a life upon the horn of the white man's dilemma?"[38]

Slavery and quasifreedom imposed countless burdens upon American blacks, but the high proportion of two-parent households found among them between 1855 and 1880 tells how little is yet known about the slave family, its relationship to the dominant white family structure, and the ways in which freedmen and freedwomen adapted, transformed, retained, or rejected older forms of family life. Finally, if the family transmits culture from generation to generation, then black subculture itself needs to be reexamined. It is too simple to say with Frazier: "Because of the absence of stability in [Negro] family life, there is a lack of traditions."[39] The composition of the Afro-American family and household between 1855 and 1880 suggests compelling reasons to reexamine historic Afro-American community life and the very meaning of American black culture.

## NOTES

1. Quoted in W. E. B. DuBois, *Negro-American Family* (Atlanta, 1909), opposite title page.

2. See, for example, Robert E. Park, "The Conflict and Fusion of Cultures with Special Reference to the Negro," *Journal of Negro History*, IV (1919), 111–133.

3. The most convenient collection of materials on this report—a volume which includes the full text of Daniel Patrick Moynihan's *The Negro Family: The Case for National Action* (Washington, D.C., 1965), and the responses of diverse critics—is Lee Rainwater and William L. Yancey, *The Moynihan Report and the Politics of Controversy* (Cambridge, Mass., 1967).

4. Philip M. Hauser, "Demographic Factors in the Integration of the Negro," *Daedalus* XCIV (1965), 854.

5. Nathaniel Shaler, "The Nature of the Negro" and "The African Element in America," *Arena*, II, III (1890), 664–665, 23–35.

6. Howard Odum, *Social and Mental Traits of the Negro: Research into the Basic Condition of the Negro Race in Southern Towns* (New York, 1910), *passim*, but esp. 36–42, 150–176, 213–237.

7. See, for example, Frederick L. Hoffman, *Race Traits and Tendencies of the American Negro* (New York, 1896); Joseph A. Tillinghurst, *The Negro in Africa and America* (New York, 1902); William W. Elwang, *The Negroes of Columbia, Missouri: A Concrete Study of the Race Problem* (Columbia, 1904); William H. Thomas, *The American Negro, What He*

*Was, What He Is, and What He May Become* (New York, 1904); W. D. Weatherford, *The Negro from Africa to America* (New York, 1924).

8. Ernest Burgess, "Introduction," in E. Franklin Frazier, *The Negro Family in the United States* (Chicago, 1939).

9. Frazier, *The Negro in the United States* (New York, 1949), 636.

10. Gunnar Myrdal, *An American Dilemma: The Negro Problem and Modern Democracy* (New York, 1944), 930–935.

11. Since this article was written, the following works dealing with various aspects of the slave family have appeared: John W. Blassingame, *The Slave Community: Plantation Life in the Antebellum Community* (New York, 1972); Robert W. Fogel and Stanley L. Engerman, *Time on the Cross: The Economics of American Negro Slavery* (Boston, 1974), 2v.; Eugene D. Genovese, *Roll, Jordan, Roll: The World the Slaves Made* (New York, 1974). These works differ significantly in their treatment of the slave family, but all are "positive" in their emphasis. These works, however, contain inadequate explanatory "models" in describing slave familial life and behavior. All revise the "traditional picture of the slave family," but the evidence offered is largely descriptive and not analytic.

12. See, for examples, John Hope Franklin, *The Free Negro in North Carolina, 1790–1860* (Chapel Hill, 1943); Leon F. Litwack, *North of Slavery: The Negro in the Free States, 1790–1860* (Chicago, 1961); Alrutheus A. Taylor, *The Negro in South Carolina during the Reconstruction* (Washington, D.C., 1924), *The Negro in the Reconstruction of Virginia* (Washington, D.C. 1926) *The Negro in Tennessee, 1865–1880* (Washington, D.C., 1941); Vernon Lane Wharton, *The Negro in Mississippi, 1865–1890* (Chapel Hill, 1947); George Tindall, *South Carolina Negroes, 1877–1900* (Columbia, 1952); Willie Lee Rose, *Rehearsal for Reconstruction: The Port Royal Experiment* (Indianapolis, 1964); Joel Williamson, *After Slavery: The Negro in South Carolina during Reconstruction, 1861–1867* (Chapel Hill, 1965). The following important more recent studies have shed additional light on the Afro-American family in the aftermath of the general emancipation: Robert H. Abzug, "The Black Family during Reconstruction," in Daniel Fox, Nathan Huggins, and Martin Kilson (eds.), *Key Issues in the Afro-American Experience* (New York, 1971), II, 26–41; Peter Kolchin, *First Freedom: The Responses of Alabama's Blacks to Emancipation and Reconstruction* (Westport, Conn., 1972), 56–79; John Blassingame, *Black New Orleans, 1800–1880* (Chicago, 1973), 79–106.

13. Gilbert Osofsky, *Harlem: The Making of a Ghetto (Negro New York, 1890–1930)* (New York, 1963), 133–134. Andrew Billingsley, *Black Families in White America* (Englewood Cliffs, N.J., 1968), 69–71; Jessie Bernard, *Marriage and Family among Negroes* (Englewood Cliffs, N.J., 1966), *passim*; Nathan Glazer, "Introduction," in Stanley M. Elkins, *Slavery: A Problem in American Institutional and Intellectual Life* (New York, 1963), xv.

14. Frazier, *The Negro Family in Chicago* (Chicago, 1932), 33–34.

15. Frazier, *The Negro Family in the United States*, 89.

16. Frazier, *The Negro in the United States*, 627.

17. George Fitzhugh, "Camp Lee and the Freedmen's Bureau," *DeBow's Review*, II (1866), 346–355.

18. Quoted in Allan Conway, *Reconstruction of Georgia* (Minneapolis, 1966), 65–66.

19. Philip A. Bruce, *The Plantation Negro as Freeman* (New York, 1889), 4, *passim*.

20. Walter L. Fleming, *Civil War and Reconstruction in Alabama* (New York, 1905), 763–764.

21. Joe M. Richardson, *The Negro in the Reconstruction of Florida, 1865–1867* (Tallahassee, 1965). Billingsley, *Black Families in White America*, 69–71; Henderson H. Donald, *The Negro Freedman* (New York, 1952), 56–75; Leonard Broom and Norval Glenn, *The Transformation of the Negro American* (New York, 1967), 15–21; Jesse Bernard, *Marriage and Family Among Negroes*, 70–75; C. Eric Lincoln, "The Absent Father Haunts the Negro Family," *New York Times Magazine* (Nov. 28, 1965), 60, 172–176.

22. Data also have been gathered on all single blacks who lived alone or in white households.

23. Herbert G. Gutman and Laurence A. Glasco, "The Buffalo, New York, Negro, 1855–1875: A Study of the Family Structure of the Free Negroes and Some of Its Implications," un-

pub. paper prepared for the Wisconsin Conference on the History of American Political and Social Behavior (May, 1968); *idem*, "The Negro Family, Household, and Occupational Structure, 1855–1925, with Special Emphasis on Buffalo, New York, but Including Comparative Data from New York City, Brooklyn, Mobile, and Adams County, Mississippi," unpub. paper prepared for the Yale Conference on Nineteenth-Century Cities (Nov., 1968).

24. In gathering data from the 1880 federal census, the author was greatly assisted by Elizabeth Ewen, Ursula Lingies, and Mark Sosower.

25. Frazier, *Negro Family in the United States*, 479.

26. Elkins, *Slavery* (Chicago, 1959), 81–88, 115–139; Kenneth M. Stampp, *The Peculiar Institution: Slavery in the Antebellum South* (New York, 1956), 340–349; Richard C. Wade, *Slavery in the Cities: The South, 1820–1860* (New York, 1964). 117–120.

27. *New York Times* (May 17, 1865), quoted in Myrta L. Avery, *Dixie After the War* (New York, 1906), 210.

28. Frazier, *Negro Family in the United States*, 106–107, 121, 127; see, esp., chs. 5–8.

29. J. Bradford Laws, *The Negroes of Cinclaire Central Factory and Calumet Plantation, Louisiana* (Washington, D.C., 1903), 120–121. Nathan Glazer, "Foreword" to revised and abridged edition, Frazier, *The Negro Family in the United States* (Chicago, 1966), viii.

30. See note 23.

31. J. H. Plumb, "Slavery, Race, and the Poor," *New York Review of Books*, XII (March 13, 1969), 3–5.

32. William Macrae, *Americans at Work*, 316–320. Antonio Gramsci quoted in Charles Tilly, "Collective Violence in European Perspective," in Hugh Graham and Ted R. Gurr (eds.), *Violence in America* (New York, 1969), 12.

33. Unpublished paper, by Paul Weinbaum, "Rochester, New York, Blacks Before the Civil War," 1968, in the author's possession.

34. C. Vann Woodward, *Origins of the New South, 1877–1913* (Baton Rouge, 1951), 361.

35. Raymond T. Smith, *Negro Family in British Guiana* (New York, 1956), 73.

36. Arthur White, "Antebellum School Reform in Boston: Integrationists and Separatists," *Phylon*, XXXIV (1973), 203–219; Edward Magdol, "Local Black Leaders in the South, 1867–75: An Essay Toward the Reconstruction of Reconstruction History," *Societas*, IV (1974), 81–110.

37. Charles E. Silberman, *Crisis in Black and White* (New York, 1964), 94–95.

38. Ralph Ellison, *Shadow and Act* (New York, 1964), 315.

39. Frazier, *Negro in the United States*, 636.

# 23 | A MOTHER'S WAGES: INCOME EARNING AMONG MARRIED ITALIAN AND BLACK WOMEN, 1896-1911

## ELIZABETH H. PLECK

In rural areas black as well as white wives were productive laborers, often working in the fields alongside their husbands. In urban areas white wives labored in their homes but did not earn wages; black wives did both. A far higher proportion of black wives were earning wages than any other group of married women: even with her husband at work, a black wife often continued to earn a living. In 1900 the rate of wage earning was 26 percent for married black women and 3.2 percent for married white women.[1] Nor does the contrast of black and immigrant wives narrow this difference. In nearly all American cities in 1900, the rate of employment for black married women was anywhere from four to fifteen times higher than for immigrant wives.[2]

A host of diverse economic, cultural, and demographic grounds have been given in accounting for the high rate of labor-force participation among black married women.[3] Many argue that slavery destroyed any vestige of domesticity and left in its place a black wife and mother hardened to back-breaking drudgery. Others refer to the menial jobs and frequent unemployment of black husbands. Because these men could not find work, it has been said, black wives had to secure jobs as domestics, laundresses, or cooks. As a result of this imbalance, many marriages broke up: husbands separated or deserted and wives were forced to support the family. Then, too, it is claimed that black mothers could easily accept paid jobs because of the availability of grandmothers or other elderly relatives as child caretakers.

Another set of explanations has been given for the absence of immigrant wives from the urban labor market. Among the immigrants Italian women have received particular attention. Italian wives rarely earned wages, despite low incomes and severe unemployment among their husbands. In her study of Italian families in early twentieth-century Buffalo, Virginia Yans-McLaughlin found very few single or married Italian women took jobs. She argued that Italian culture prohibited these women from working, even at the price of family economic well-being.[4] On the other hand, Louise Tilly suggested alternative economic and demographic explanations, such as the large number of mothers with young children or the absence of demand for women workers in Buffalo.[5]

On this subject opinions are strongly held; alas, with little empirical investigation. Survivals of peasant customs can encourage, limit or prohibit specific behavior; old cultural patterns can be enlivened by new economic circumstances or destroyed in the process.[6] Two cultures may respond in a different manner to similar economic circumstances, and a particular culture may also vary its response as economic circumstances change. Too often in recent historical writing family norms have been pitted against economic imperatives without appreciating the context of family needs and economic choices.[7] It is not a question of choosing between economic, demographic and cultural factors but of showing the interaction between these factors. A systematic comparison of groups roughly similar in economic condition is required. Because of the large body of available information and the extent of historical writing, Italians have been compared with blacks, although another European immigrant group could have been selected. Before making the comparison, some background is provided. First, special surveys of Italian and black families around the turn of the century form the basis of the comparison. A portrait of the general economic condition among blacks and Italians demonstrates that both groups lived in desperate poverty. Differences in the higher rate of wage earning for black than for Italian wives are examined in the context of similar as well as changing family conditions and economic opportunities. Finally, some of the reasons for this difference are suggested. Taken together, a black wife faced economic need and found cultural support for working; an Italian wife, often at the edge of poverty, encountered cultural barriers toward her employment which could only be offset by the offer of higher wages.

I

Several government documents permit a direct contrast of urban black and Italian wives. The U. S. Bureau of Labor in 1896 surveyed 6,773 Chicago Italians near Hull House. The same year the Bureau assigned black investigators to study living conditions among 2,748 blacks in Atlanta, Cambridge, Massachusetts, and Nashville. Fifteen years later Senate investigators conducted another survey asking similar questions. The subsequent report, issued by the Senate Committee on the Investigation of the Condition of the Immigrants, known as the Dillingham Commission, ran into forty-six volumes. Two volumes concerned black and immigrant families in seven cities: these seven differed in size, ethnic composition, and most importantly, economic opportunities for working women. Whether it was Cleveland, Boston, or any of the large cities, there was always some demand for women workers as servants. But, in addition, in four of these cities—Philadelphia, Chicago, Boston, and New York—garment industries employed many women workers. The other three—Milwaukee, Cleveland and Buffalo—dominated by aluminum and steel industries, breweries or oil refineries, offered few jobs other than service for women workers.

A comprehensive profile of women's work can be drawn from these documents. Compared with the federal census for the same period, these surveys were far more complete in delineating women's work. The federal census inquired about boarders in the household and women's paid employment but failed to inquire about wages (for women or men) and piece work performed at home. These surveys in 1896 and 1911 included these questions and much more: data concerning hours of work, weeks of unemployment, and family income. By combining three separate pieces of information from the surveys—paid employment, taking boarders, and piece work—we are able to more accurately contrast wage earning among black and Italian wives.

One can always doubt the accuracy of this information. Surveys have rarely recorded the full range of women's work, but there is little reason to conclude that the wage earning of Italian wives was more carefully noted than for blacks. In 1896 the Bureau of Labor employed black men and women, at least one a lawyer, another a college professor, as surveyors. They asked questions similar to those in the Bureau of Labor report on Chicago's Italians the same year. Blacks have often been underenumerated in surveys, but the absent group generally consists of young black men, not married women. If, for any reason, these surveys failed to count many impoverished black wives, the percentages reported here represent conservative estimates of black women's rate of working: missing women were just as likely, if not more likely to work, as other black women.

Seen from a distance, one might have suspected that Italian wives were more tradition bound and less likely to earn a living than other immigrant women. They were raised in a Catholic, Mediterranean culture which circumscribed a woman's dress and demeanor.[8] A man's honor was a precious but fragile commodity: in her daily actions a wife had to avoid bringing shame on her husband.[9] As recent arrivals in American cities, such wives spoke no English and knew very little about finding employment. Then, too, Italian migration consisted mostly of men. Because this was so, Italian women were likely to marry, often at a young age, and if their husbands found work, it was less necessary for them to do so.

Closer scrutiny of documents for 1896 and 1911 shows that Italian wives were no more confined to the home than other immigrant wives. Peasant wives in Italy were expected to contribute to the family by field work as well as their performance of traditional female tasks. In the blistering Mediterranean sun, Italian wives picked grapes at harvest time and mowed, winnowed, bundled, and hauled sheaves of grain. In a contemporary account about women in Sicily, only the poorest wives worked alongside their husbands in the fields, yet most of the women carried heavy bags of water to the men.[10] Even in Sicily, the wives planted vegetable gardens and sold the surplus, slaughtered pigs, cut wood, dug and weeded mattock.

In American cities few married women from any immigrant background were employed, according to the survey in 1911. Italian wives were as likely to work as German or Irish wives and more often employed than Polish or Russian Jewish married women (Table 1). Nor did Italian traditionalism prevent daughters from working in American sweatshops and factories, generally with parental approval. In depression-ridden Chicago in 1896, the one city for which information is available, about half of unmarried Italian girls between the ages of fifteen and nineteen were employed.[11] Ruth True, a New York City social reformer, recognized that Italian values, the importance of the family above individual preference, actually encouraged the employment of teenage daughters. She noted: "The girl herself is as eager to go to work as her parents are to have her. She takes it for granted that she should help in the family income. Carlotta gets a job not because she feels the need of self-support as an expression of individuality, or self-dependence, but because she feels so strongly the sense of family obligation."[12] A New York Italian daughter who quit parochial school at age twelve echoed these conclusions: "My father was a stone mason, you know how it is. He didn't have steady work and my mother used to talk all the time about how poor we were. So I had my mind on work all the time. I was thinking how I could go to work and bring money home to my mother."[13]

There are additional reasons for doubting the uniqueness of the Italian situation. Unfamiliarity with a city or with American life was never an effective barrier to employment; the level of employment rose only slightly as Italian wives became accustomed to America. For those Chicago Italian wives in 1896 residing in the city more than ten years, 16 percent were employed, only 3 percentage points higher than for wives resident in Chicago six to ten years, or 6 points higher than for wives in America less than six years.[14] Knowledge of spoken English was never a prerequisite for paid employment, at least in the kind of jobs immigrant wives were forced to accept. The typical Italian wife from any one of seven American cities in 1911 was far less likely to speak English than the Jewish, Polish, or German wife, but she was just as likely and sometimes even more likely to be employed than these women.[15] Even within the Italian community, the ability to speak English was not a necessary job qualification. Among Chicago Italian wives in 1896 the rate of labor-force participation was only 2 percentage points higher for wives speaking English compared with non-English-speaking wives (10 percent vs. 8 percent).[16] Finally, the excess of men failed to alter the rate of working women among Italians. For instance, there were 132 Italian men for every 100 New York City Italian women in 1905.[17] Nonetheless, the rate of labor-force participation among Italian wives was higher there than in any other American city in 1911— almost a third of Italian wives were employed.[18] Since single women were removed as competitors for New York City jobs, it may have been slightly easier for Italian wives to find work. Or, more likely, the balance of the sexes may have had less bearing on the employment of wives than the economic demand for women in New York's garment industry.

## II

Three dimensions of poverty—low family income, chronic male unemployment, and unskilled labor for men—plagued Italian as well as black families. In these conditions, Italians suffered as much as blacks from low incomes and more from severe unemployment, but they were less concentrated in dead-end and demeaning jobs. Working women from both groups were employed in low wage, low skill jobs, but black women were largely excluded from factory employment. In terms of family income,

Italian poverty matched that of blacks. For Chicago Italians in 1896 the median income for a male-present family was $235 compared with black family incomes that year of $393.50 in Nashville, $374 in Atlanta, and $584 in Cambridge.[19] Fifteen years later, despite an increase in real wages, both groups continued near subsistence. Philadelphia's Italians in 1911 earned ten or twenty dollars less than blacks, and New York City's Italians earned virtually the same as blacks.[20]

Severe male unemployment was even more pronounced among Italians than blacks. During a national depression in 1896, a black father in any of eighteen northern or southern cities was out of work an average of 11.7 weeks.[21] Chicago Italian fathers, unemployed on the average thirty-six weeks during the year in 1896,[22] spent the rest of the time in "idleness and almost absolute inactivity in poorly ventilated rooms."[23] Pursuing the question of how families subsisted during hard times, the Bureau of Labor found no unemployed Italian fathers who depended on their wives' wages and only a few who relied on their children. Instead, most Italian families were living on savings or a combination of savings and credit.[24] "When no more money," one Italian father in New York City made plain, "me take out trust at grocery man."[25] An Italian daughter in New York City stated simply: "If there is no money, we eat less."[26] Asked about their means of subsistence, black families also listed savings or credit, but in addition, eleven families in Atlanta, ten in Cambridge, and seventeen in Nashville mentioned the wife's earnings.[27]

Italian as well as black husbands were heavily concentrated in unskilled labor. About one quarter of Italian husbands in Chicago or black men in Atlanta, Nashville, or Cambridge were common laborers.[28] In the other jobs available, Italians differed from blacks: they had access to jobs which in the present offered low wages and high unemployment but which held some promise for the future. Aside from unskilled labor, Italian men earned their livings as tailors, carpenters, barbers, and fruit peddlars. Among New York City Italian male workers in 1905, the racial gap is clear: almost two out of ten Italians were employed in the garment industry and another three out of ten in skilled trades; in contrast, only one out of ten employed black men was in one of these two types of work.[29] Most black husbands not employed as unskilled laborers were servants and waiters and elevator operators: in sum, low-wage jobs, paying almost half what one made in unskilled labor.

An unskilled but racially segregated labor market was even more apparent among the women. Italian daughters, not their fathers, entered factories, mostly sewing pants, shirts, dresses, and gloves, and making boxes, candy, and artificial flowers.[30] More Italian than black women found work in Philadelphia clothing factories; the few black women in this industry were confined to low-paying jobs as pressers, or they sewed the cheaper garments like middy blouses, overalls, and housedresses.[31] Most black women were excluded from factories in the North except as strike breakers or as extra laborers during wartime. Social worker Mary White Ovington summarized the difference between white and black women's work in New York City around the turn of the century:

She [the black woman] gets the job that the white girl does not want. It may be that the white girl wants the wrong thing, and that the jute mill and tobacco shop and flower factory are more dangerous to health and right living than the mistress' kitchen, but she knows her mind and follows the business that brings her liberty of action when the six o'clock whistle blows.[32]

Two jobs were the mainstay of black women workers: laundry work and domestic service. At these two occupations eight out of ten black wives were employed in 1900. Laundry work was largely the preserve of black mothers. These women, who wanted to remain at home, worked "at their tubs or ironing boards from Monday morning until Saturday night,"[33] often at wages lower than in service. This condition, Mary White Ovington noted, "makes the tenement rooms, tiny enough at best, sadly cluttered, but it does not deprive the children of the presence of their mother, who accepts a smaller income to remain at home with them."[34] Single as well as married black women disliked service. Philadelphia black working women, interviewed in 1919, preferred their work in a rag factory to domestic service because they could enjoy free evenings, holidays, and Sundays.[35] If all else failed, a black mother entered service: five times as many black as foreign-born domestics in 1900 were married.[36] When mothers were compelled to become maids, they often left their children with "babytenders." Although some of these caretakers must have had years of experience; others were unable to properly supervise children and incapable of giving sufficient milk to infants.[37]

Despite the many similarities in economic need for both Italian and black families, there was one defining difference: black wives were far more often breadwinners than Italian wives. There is no mistaking the extent of this racial difference. First of all, the rate of black wives at work was 44 percent in Cambridge, 55 percent in Nashville, and 65 percent in Atlanta in 1896; the rate of Chicago Italian wives at work that year was 15 percent. Fifteen years later, it appears from Table 1, over half of Philadelphia and New York City black wives were employed, but just one out of six Italian wives in these cities were working.

Black mothers were also more likely to supplement the family budget by doing paid work at home.[38] The Dillingham Commission of 1911, which inquired about the number of wives working in the family's quarters, found about one in five black wives in New York City and Philadelphia working at home, usually as laundresses. The photographic record of New York City Italian mothers making artificial flowers or sewing shirts around the kitchen table harmonizes with the statistical reality. In 1911 one-third of Italian wives in New York City were earning wages at home, mostly as tailoresses. But these women were the exception for Italian immigrants: few Italian wives elsewhere were doing piece work, whether in Buffalo or Boston, Chicago or Milwaukee (Table 2).

Black and Italian wives were probably equally as likely to earn money by a third method, taking lodgers. From the percentages in Table 1, it is impossible to give the edge to blacks or Italians in this regard. The number of lodgers varied between years and between cities, perhaps coinciding with the waves of migrants reaching each locale. It is also puzzling to ex-

**Table 1.** PROPORTION OF BLACK AND ITALIAN FAMILIES WITH INCOME CON-
TRIBUTED BY WIVES, CHILDREN, AND LODGERS[a]

| Group, City and Date | % with Wives Working | % with Children Working | % with Lodgers | N |
|---|---|---|---|---|
| Blacks, Atlanta, 1896 | 65 | 10 | 8 | 240 |
| Blacks, Nashville, 1896 | 55 | 12 | 6 | 199 |
| Blacks, Cambridge, 1896 | 44 | 8 | 8 | 88 |
| Blacks, New York, 1905 | na | na | 42 | 3014 |
| Blacks, New York, 1911 | 51 | 10 | 27 | 145 |
| Blacks, Philadelphia, 1911 | 54 | 13 | 41 | 71 |
| Italians, Chicago, 1896[b] | 15 | 36 | 16 | 1227 |
| Italians, Chicago, 1911 | 19 | 25 | 17 | 219 |
| Italians, Buffalo, 1905 | 14 | 19 | na | na |
| Italians, Buffalo, 1911 | 0 | 9 | 37 | 115 |
| Italians, New York, 1905 | na | na | 21 | 2945 |
| Italians, New York, 1911 | 36 | 19 | 20 | 333 |
| Italians, Philadelphia, 1911 | 8 | 23 | 16 | 195 |
| Italians, Boston, 1911 | 16 | 25 | 39 | 210 |
| Italians, Cleveland, 1911 | 10 | 22 | 41 | 111 |
| Germans, New York, 1911 | 30 | 35 | 0 | 308 |
| Germans, Chicago, 1911 | 8 | 44 | 11 | 208 |
| Germans, Milwaukee, 1911 | 5 | 28 | 14 | 163 |
| Poles, Chicago, 1911 | 7 | 21 | 43 | 410 |
| Poles, Philadelphia, 1911 | 7 | 10 | 60 | 159 |
| Poles, Boston, 1911 | 11 | 4 | 61 | 95 |
| Poles, Cleveland, 1911 | 4 | 4 | 43 | 131 |
| Poles, Buffalo, 1911 | 2 | 28 | 9 | 178 |
| Poles, Milwaukee, 1911 | 5 | 24 | 17 | 150 |
| Russian Jews, New York, 1911 | 1 | 31 | 56 | 452 |
| Russian Jews, Chicago, 1911 | 8 | 30 | 38 | 187 |
| Russian Jews, Boston, 1911 | 15 | 41 | 40 | 226 |
| Irish, New York, 1911 | 5 | 18 | 20 | 272 |
| Irish, Philadelphia, 1911 | 28 | 50 | 19 | 98 |
| Irish, Boston, 1911 | 27 | 49 | 18 | 197 |
| Irish, Cleveland, 1911 | 5 | 36 | 10 | 122 |

Sources: computed from data in "Condition of the Negro in Various Cities," *Bulletin of the Department of Labor,* Vol. II, No. 10, (May, 1897), pp. 257–360; Carroll D. Wright, *The Italians in Chicago: A Social and Economic Study,* (Washington, D.C., 1897), Table I, pp. 52–273; Virginia Yans-McLaughlin, "Patterns of Work and Family Organization: Buffalo's Italians," *Journal of Interdisciplinary History,* Vol. II, No. 2, (Autumn, 1971), pp. 111–126; U.S. Senate Reports, 62nd Cong. 1st sess., *Immigrants in Cities,* Vol. 2, (Washington, D.C., 1911), Table 401, pp. 546–548; Herbert G. Gutman, *The Black Family in Slavery and Freedom, 1750–1925* (New York, 1976), Table B-4, p. 530.
a. Data pertains to families with both husband and wife present.
b. All evidence for Italians is for South Italians only.

plain the relative absence of lodgers from black homes in Atlanta, Nashville, or Cambridge for 1896. Nevertheless, among black and Italian
families in the same city, there was a tendency for blacks to house lodgers
more often than Italians. Lodgers were twice as common among black
than Italian New York City households in 1905,[39] although six years later
the gap between the groups was erased. For Philadelphia in 1911, lodgers
were almost three times as common in black as Italian households.

By any measure of income earning, black wives were more often bread-

**Table 2.** PERCENTAGE OF ALL ITALIAN AND BLACK WIVES EMPLOYED AT HOME, 1911

|  | % | N |
| --- | --- | --- |
| Blacks, New York City | 23 | 273 |
| Blacks, Philadelphia | 17 | 139 |
| South Italians, New York City | 22 | 402 |
| South Italians, Philadelphia | 3 | 349 |
| South Italians, Boston | 5 | 309 |
| South Italians, Buffalo | 1 | 205 |
| South Italians, Chicago | 3 | 349 |
| South Italians, Milwaukee | 1 | 145 |

Source: U.S. Immigration Commission, *Immigrants in Cities,* Vol. II, Tables 24, 78, 126, 290, 340, pp. 39, 83, 127-129, 239, 293–298, 350–352.

winners than Italian wives. They often took lodgers, earned money doing laundry in their homes, and worked as domestics or cooks. Italian wives frequently housed lodgers, avoided piece work (except in New York City), and very rarely held paid employment.

# III

Common sense explanations for why black wives were so often breadwinners have rarely been subjected to systematic comparison. The idea is that some hidden difference in group composition between Italians and blacks accounted for the difference in the rate of wage earning. One by one, seven possible reasons are evaluated: that Italians differed from blacks in terms of income, male unemployment, the presence of young children at home, attitudes toward children's schooling, reliance on child labor, availability of childcare, or marital stability. Any of these seven differences may have produced the lower rate of wage earning among Italian than black wives. The research method examines differences in wage earning, holding each of these factors constant.

First of all, even with husbands earning identical incomes, a black wife was more likely to work than an Italian wife. Among the poorest families in 1896, those with husbands earning less than $200 a year, almost all black wives in Atlanta, Nashville, or Cambridge were working, whereas the same desperation sent only a fifth of Italian wives in Chicago to work. At all income levels, Table 3 demonstrates that black wives were far more likely to work than Italian wives. One also needs to include taking boarders as women's income, information which is only available for 1911 (Table 4). The inclusion of this additional income does not alter the basic difference. For every income category, black wives were still more likely to earn wages *and* admit boarders.

When her husband became unemployed, a black wife was more likely to work than an Italian wife.[40] Since the 1911 study by the Dillingham Commission did not include information on unemployment, this comparison depends on computations for 1896. Among Italian wives whose husbands were unemployed at least twenty-one weeks a year, only one in six wives earned wages. For Nashville, Cambridge, and Atlanta black wives in this

**Table 3.** PERCENTAGE OF WIVES IN PAID EMPLOYMENT ACCORDING TO HUSBAND'S INCOME, AMONG CHICAGO'S ITALIANS AND BLACKS IN ATLANTA, NASHVILLE, AND CAMBRIDGE, 1896

|  | $0–100 (%) | N | $101–200 (%) | N | $201–300 (%) | N | $301–400 (%) | N | $401–500 (%) | N | $501+ (%) | N |
|---|---|---|---|---|---|---|---|---|---|---|---|---|
| Italians, Chicago | 20 | 334 | 12 | 379 | 12 | 178 | 9 | 89 | 5 | 55 | 7 | 43 |
| Blacks, Cambridge | 100 | 2 | 100 | 3 | 25 | 8 | 64 | 11 | 41 | 17 | 29 | 38 |
| Blacks, Atlanta | 80 | 10 | 77 | 39 | 66 | 62 | 40 | 42 | 36 | 14 | 28 | 32 |
| Blacks, Nashville | 60 | 15 | 68 | 19 | 56 | 43 | 48 | 48 | 11 | 19 | 41 | 27 |

Sources: Carroll D. Wright, *The Italians in Chicago: A Social and Economic Study* (Washington D.C., 1897), Table 1, pp. 52–273; "Condition of the Negro in Various Cities," *Bulletin of the Department of Labor,* Vol. II, No. 10 (May 1897), pp. 257–360.

predicament, the percentage of working wives was at least three times greater. The racial gap appeared whether a husband was unemployed a few weeks or most of the year; in either of these circumstances, a black wife was more likely to work than an Italian wife.

Even with young children at home, black mothers more often took paid jobs than Italian mothers.[41] It is almost a universal condition that mothers of young children find it too difficult to accept paid work; yet the presence of young children was less of a barrier to the employment of black than Italian mothers. For mothers with preschool children, probably youngsters under age six in 1896, the data in Table 5 indicates that black mothers in Atlanta, Nashville, and Cambridge were almost four times as likely to earn wages as Italian mothers of young children.

It might be thought that black mothers accepted jobs because they could depend on their kin for childcare. In *The Black Family in Slavery and Freedom,* Herbert Gutman demonstrated the importance of kin networks among slave and emancipated black families. In cities kin were not always available; the evidence suggests female kin were far more frequent in Italian than black urban households. One approximate measure of the availability of female caretakers was the residence of adult women relatives in the household. Yet the odds were one and a half times greater that an Italian household in Chicago included a female relative compared with a black household in Cambridge, Atlanta, or Nashville for 1896.[42] In 1905

**Table 4.** PERCENTAGE OF WIVES EARNING WAGES OR TAKING IN BOARDERS BY HUSBAND'S INCOME FOR BLACK AND ITALIAN FAMILIES 1911

|  | Husband's Income | | | | | |
|---|---|---|---|---|---|---|
|  | 0–$399 | N | $400–$599 | N | $600+ | N |
| Blacks, New York City | 90% | 42 | 71% | 38 | 61% | 28 |
| Blacks, Philadelphia | 72 | 29 | 60 | 20 | 83 | 6 |
| Italians, New York City | 47 |  |  |  | 71 |  |
| Italians, Philadelphia | 25 | 130 | 16 | 43 | 8 | 13 |

Source: U.S. Senate Reports, 62nd Cong., 1st sess., *Immigrants in Cities,* Vol. I, Table 69, p. 230, 410.

**Table 5.** RELATIONSHIP OF MOTHER'S WAGE EARNING TO THE PRESENCE OF CHILDREN AMONG ITALIANS IN CHICAGO, AND BLACKS IN ATLANTA, NASHVILLE, AND CAMBRIDGE, 1896

| | Percentage of Mothers at Work | | | | | | | |
| | NO CHILDREN AT HOME | N | CHILDREN AT HOME | N | CHILDREN AT SCHOOL | N | CHILDREN AT WORK | N |
| --- | --- | --- | --- | --- | --- | --- | --- | --- |
| Italians, Chicago | 15% | 180 | 12% | 848 | 18% | 124 | 23% | 75 |
| Blacks, Cambridge | 48 | 25 | 41 | 32 | 43 | 14 | 67 | 3 |
| Blacks, Atlanta | 49 | 65 | 60 | 108 | 61 | 31 | 50 | 8 |
| Blacks, Nashville | 51 | 51 | 44 | 89 | 57 | 37 | 65 | 17 |

Sources: Carroll D. Wright, *The Italians in Chicago: A Social and Economic Study* (Washington, D.C., 1897), Table I, pp. 52–273; "Conditions of the Negro in Various Cities," *Bulletin of the Department of Labor*, Vol. II, No. 10 (May 1897), pp. 257–360.

the likelihood was that a New York City Italian rather than black household included relatives (23 percent for Italians, 16 percent for blacks).[43] Even when Italian kin did not occupy the same living quarters, they often lived nearby. In studying Italian families of Providence, Rhode Island, in 1915, Judith Smith found that three out of five Italian families were related to at least one other household in the city, and almost all of these kin lived less than eight blocks from their families.[44]

Another possible source of the difference might lie in parental attitudes toward schooling. There is at least substantial reason to think that black parents held more favorable attitudes toward children's education than Italians. If a black mother chose to keep her older children in school rather than sending them to work, she may have been compelled to earn the extra income for her family. To be sure, black children were more likely to attend school than Italian youngsters. The rate of school attendance was almost twice as great for black sons in Atlanta, Cambridge, or Nashville compared with Chicago Italian sons (aged ten to fourteen) in 1900. Similar disparities appeared in the rate of school attendance among schoolage Italian and black daughters in those cities.[45] Beyond the legal age requirements for school attendance, the pattern of difference held true. Black teenagers of both sexes in Atlanta, Cambridge, and Nashville in 1900 were more likely to attend high school than Italian adolescents. Nonetheless, there is reason to doubt that keeping children in school was the motive behind more black than Italian mothers working. If this had been the case, then one might expect such mothers to quit their jobs when their children finished school. The exact opposite situation occurred for both black and Italian mothers. Both groups of women (with the exception of black wives in Atlanta) were more inclined to work than mothers with school children.

Italian youngsters, who often dropped out of school at an early age, were contributing their wages to the family. In city after city, child labor was more common among Italians than blacks. Can we then conclude that black wives worked because the family could not rely on child labor? To test this suggestion, we can compare Italian and black mothers of child laborers. Even black mothers who could send their children to work still earned wages. Only a quarter of Chicago Italian mothers in 1896 with working children were employed, whereas between one-half and two-thirds of the black mothers of employed children in Cambridge, Atlanta, or Nashville in 1896 still earned a living.

A final explanation for black women's greater participation in the work force is rooted in the short-lived duration of many black marriages. Households with a missing (dead, deserted, or separated) husband were far more common among blacks than Italians, according to a New York City sample from the state census in 1905. In studying two Italian and black neighborhoods in New York City, one in Greenwich Village and the other in San Juan Hill, Herbert Gutman found such female-headed households were almost four times as common among blacks as Italians.[46] Given these differences, it might be argued that black wives anticipated an end to their marriages, and therefore held jobs as a form of economic insurance for the future. Evidence from my research on blacks in late-nineteenth-century Boston is relevant to this argument. The rate of marital dissolution was determined for black couples listed in the manuscript census schedules of the federal census for 1880 who were traced to the same records for Boston twenty years later. (If one or both spouses had died in the intervening period, as certified by Boston death records, they were eliminated from the trace.) Boston black wives whose husbands had left them by 1900 were no more likely to have been employed in 1880 than black wives in stable marriages lasting the two decades, but the 7 percent difference was not statistically significant. In sum, a wife's wage earning bore little connection to her husband's subsequent absence. It is still possible that taking paid employment expressed a wife's doubt about the future of her marriage, but if that was the case, her calculations were inaccurate.

To summarize these comparisons, we have seen that no single economic or demographic condition accounts for the higher rate of wage earning among black than Italian wives. Even if her husband was unemployed or earning very low wages, an Italian wife generally decided against employment, whereas her black counterpart generally took a job. More black than Italian mothers of young children went to work, despite the fact that the supply of female relatives as caretakers was greater in Italian than black households. As Italian children entered the labor force, a mother became the manager of the family finances; even after her working children contributed to the household, a black mother continued to earn an income as well as oversee family affairs. When an Italian mother could rely on the wages of her working children, she did not enter the labor market, while black mothers of working children remained in the labor force. It is true that black wives, who were more often living without husbands than Italian wives, needed to work. But there is no reason to conclude that uncertainty about the future of a marriage was the impetus behind a black wife working.

IV

Faced with similar conditions, blacks and Italian wives acted differently. Confronted with changing conditions, how did they respond? Evidence from Tables 1 through 6 illustrate the effect of changes in the economics of family environment on the labor-force participation of Italian and black wives. Three factors—family economic need, the composition of the household, and the wage rate for women workers—led to higher rates of working among black as well as Italian wives.

As a first principle, growing immiserization was an inducement to work. The poorer her husband, the more likely that a black wife sought employment in Cambridge, Atlanta, or Nashville in 1896 or in New York City in 1911. Perhaps due to the small number of families studied, this was not true for Philadelphia black wives in 1911: there the wives of wealthier husbands were even more likely to work than more impoverished married women. The same economic squeeze compelled Italian wives to work, whether in Chicago in 1896 or New York and Philadelphia in 1911. A glance at Tables 3 and 4 demonstrates that wage earning for the Italian wife increased as her husband's wage decreased.

The evidence from Table 6 suggests a second conclusion: that chronic unemployment for either the Italian or black husband sent his wife to work. As the number of weeks a husband was unemployed mounted, the wife's rate of employment climbed. Cambridge black wives in 1896, whose incomes were higher, rarely sought work until a husband lost his job. Once that happened, they, like black wives elsewhere, entered the labor force in large numbers. Sustained unemployment for an Italian husband also increased the likelihood of a wife working. For Chicago in 1896, Italian wives with husbands unemployed at least twenty-one weeks a year were twice as likely to work as wives with fully employed husbands.

The age of her children also influenced a mother's willingness to work. All mothers of young children were more likely to remain at home before reentering the work force when their children were grown. Black mothers from Cambridge or Nashville in 1896 slightly decreased their participation in the labor market during the child-bearing years but later reentered the

**Table 6.** PERCENTAGE OF WIVES WORKING DUE TO HUSBAND'S UNEMPLOYMENT, AMONG CHICAGO'S ITALIANS AND BLACKS IN ATLANTA, NASHVILLE, AND CAMBRIDGE, 1896

|  | FULLY EMPLOYED | N | UNEMPLOYED FOR SOME TIME DURING THE YEAR | N | Number of Weeks Husband Unemployed | | | | | |
|---|---|---|---|---|---|---|---|---|---|---|
|  |  |  |  |  | 1-10 | N | 11-20 | N | 21-52 | N |
| Italians, Chicago | 10% | 370 | 17% | 767 | 15% | 66 | 9% | 68 | 18% | 633 |
| Blacks, Cambridge | 16 | 30 | 53 | 49 | 42 | 26 | 53 | 13 | 80 | 10 |
| Blacks, Atlanta | 50 | 134 | 64 | 66 | 58 | 38 | 63 | 16 | 83 | 12 |
| Blacks, Nashville | 48 | 127 | 47 | 53 | 43 | 21 | 38 | 16 | 63 | 16 |

Sources: Carroll D. Wright, *The Italians in Chicago: A Social and Economic Study* (Washington D.C., 1897), Table I, pp. 52-273; "Condition of the Negro in Various Cities," *Bulletin of the Department of Labor*, Vol. II, No. 10 (May 1897), pp. 257-360.

work force in large numbers. Atlanta black mothers never dropped out of the labor force even as young matrons. Freedom from childcare responsibilities also made it easier for Italian mothers to take paid jobs. The tendency to work among Chicago Italian mothers was twice as strong for mothers of adult children compared with mothers of preschoolers.[47]

Outside of the family's circumstances, the offer of "higher wages" persuaded more Italian as well as black wives to work.[48] A fair comparison must exclude the black women in southern cities, working at disastrously low wages. In northern cities the offer of higher wages led to expanded levels of paid employment for both sets of wives. For instance, in Philadelphia where black women in 1911 made an average of $170 a year, about half of black wives were earning wages; in New York City that year, where the median wage was $215 a year, seven out of ten black wives worked. When offered slightly higher wages, Italian wives in 1911 were also more willing to work. At a wage of $100 a year, the average for Italian working women in Cleveland and Philadelphia, one out of ten wives worked. With a twenty-dollar increase in pay, the rate in Chicago, two out of ten wives worked. An additional sixty dollars in pay persuaded one-third of New York City Italian wives to work. Just taking the two cities where comparable information was available, Philadelphia and New York, shows that both black and Italian wives responded to economic incentives. An additional sixty-five dollars in wages increased the Italian woman's rate of working by 14 points; a slightly smaller wage increase raised the black woman's rate of working about the same level.[49]

## V

A number of possible reasons often advanced to explain the higher rate of employment among black than Italian married women have been eliminated. However, no clear alternative has emerged. There remains one suggestive economic difference: that black women's wage earning was a means of coping with long-term income inadequacy. Like black husbands, Italian men suffered from low wages and chronic unemployment, but their jobs in skilled crafts, the expanding garment industry, or in retail trade offered more future promise: better pay, on-the-job training, and promotions. The jobs of black men as waiters, cooks, and elevator operators were more often dead ends. From the available evidence one can neither confirm nor deny the possibility of this kind of economic difference. However, short of this kind of proof, and having eliminated a large number of economic and demographic explanations, we are forced to consider a residual factor: cultural differences between Italians and blacks.

For Italians cultural attitudes acted as a barrier to the employment of married women. This barrier was less a high stone wall than a low chain fence. Prohibitions applied to married women, especially mothers, but did not extend to daughters. Prior to marriage, Italian daughters often earned wages: after marriage, Italian wives managed finances, cared for the home, gave birth to children, and looked after youngsters. Yet even Italian cultural prohibitions could be overcome with the offer of higher wages, especially for wives doing piece work at home or employed along with other women in neighborhood factories.

For black women the natural tendency is to trace their pattern of wage earning to the legacy of slavery. If bondage fundamentally reshaped the role of slave women, then we would expect to find nearly all of them in the labor force a generation or two after emancipation. This was clearly not the case. Nor was it true that black married women behaved in a manner similar to poverty-stricken white married women. There was a fundamental cultural difference. We need to identify the connection between the slave experience and black attitudes about the involvement of wives in productive labor and in the family. Despite the magnificent new research on slave culture, consciousness, and family life, we are still far from answering this question. What follows are suggestions about how slave culture (defined here as ways of living) related to the wage earning of black married women. It is beyond the scope of this paper to analyze the *origins* of this slave culture (in West African tradition, learning from whites, or the blending of the two experiences admist generations of life as slaves); rather what concerns us here is to pinpoint the slave ways of life which support black women's wage earning after emancipation. More specifically, we can suggest that black women's wage earning was influenced by three patterns, husband-wife relations, child-rearing, and the emphasis on children's schooling. However, for all the cultural support favoring women's employment, black husbands and wives approached this subject with considerable ambiguity. In fact, these three cultural elements were necessary to offset strong objections to paid employment.

Among black husbands slavery left as its first legacy negative attitudes toward the employment of wives. It is true that contemporary studies, such as a 1970 survey, indicate more favorable opinions toward working wives among black than white men.[50] Another survey in 1966 also found that black husbands, even those born prior to 1911, were less opposed to the employment of mothers with school-age children than white husbands.[51] Nonetheless, contemporary surveys cannot be grafted onto the past. During Reconstruction black husbands vehemently prevented their wives from working in the fields.[52] All over the South freedmen, who demanded a man's wage to support their families, believed their wives should remain at home with the children. One Louisiana plantation mistress noted in 1865 that "Pete is still in the notion of remaining but chooses to feed his wife out of his wages rather than to get her fed for her services."[53] A cotton planter lost money because he had to support "on an average twenty-five to thirty negro (*sic*) women and children in idleness, as the freedmen will not permit their wives and children to work in the fields."[54] This idleness would continue, according to an Alabama cotton grower, because "it is a matter of pride with the men to allow exemption from labor to their wives . . . "[55] Long after Reconstruction black husbands refused to allow their wives to work for white families. One ex-slave father in the South confessed his ambition "to support his family by his own efforts; never to allow his wife and daughters to be thrown in contact with Southern white men in their homes."[56] In the early twentieth century, an Alabama sharecropper kept his wife from doing laundry for whites. He said, "I didn't want any money comin into my house from that. My wife didn't wait on white folks for their dirty laundry. There was plenty of em would ask her and there'd be an answer ready for em."[57]

Three countervailing cultural tendencies were necessary to set aside these attitudes. The first of these was the pattern of relations between husbands and wives which arose out of slavery. These patterns of interaction were not simple character traits but rather a bundle of contradictions: belief in the husband's responsibility to support his family but doubts about his ability to do so, forthright self-assertion as well as subtle influence and crafty manipulation. The small body of evidence available indicates exslave wives also believed in the husband's role as family breadwinner. In the early years of emancipation, freed wives on Henry Watson's Alabama plantation refused to work. They told him "they never mean to do any more outdoor work, that white men support their wives, and they mean that their husband shall support them."[58] Throughout the South the Freedman's Bureau received complaints about black wives who "would not work at all" or others, like the freedwomen in Wharton, Texas, who left their cabins late and quit the field early."[59] At the same time slavery also taught black women that a husband could not always provide for his family. Many slave fathers died or were sold: perhaps as many as one out of every four husbands or wives were separated by sale.[60] Even when separation did not occur, the slave family did not by itself provide for its needs. Slaves realized that the work of fathers, mothers and children contributed to food and clothing, but the master was the middleman: he not only distributed food and clothing, but also made crucial decisions about the family's future. At the same time the slave wife, who labored in the fields and often cared for her family in her husband's absence, developed more respect for her own ability to assist the family.

Given that freed women did not want to work outside their homes during Reconstruction, how do we explain their unusually high rate of wage earning by 1900? One can only speculate about how this reconciliation occurred. It appears that a black wife recognized the need for more income for the family (which probably was used to purchase food) and then identified her own responsibility for providing some of the cash for the family's needs. Even if a wife decided to seek employment, she often encountered objections from her husband. Most black wives, it appears, successfully overcame their husband's doubts. One cannot uncover this entire process of decision making in black families, except at the final stage: when a wife tried to overcome her husband's objections to her employment. Wives often defined their role in terms of "helping out." As a young girl, Hannah Shaw chopped and picked cotton and milked cows. When she married, her husband insisted she quit working in the field. But she persisted, as he recalled.

"I'd be in the field at work and my wife—I'd look around, see her comin out there with a hoe. I'd say, "what you comin out here for."
"I thought I'd come out here and help you."[61]

Years later the testimony of Hannah Shaw's husband demonstrates the success of her strategy: "Every step she took, to my knowledge, was in my favor."[62] Martha Harrison, an ex-slave mother, was equally successful in overcoming her husband's objections to her employment. She confessed her tactics:

My husband never did like for me to work: he used to ask me how come I work; he was doing all he could to give me what I wanted. "Looks like you don't appreciate what I'm trying to do for you." But I'd say, "Yes, I do honey I just help you cause I don't want you to break down. If you put a load on a horse it will pull him down but two horses can pull it jest as easy."[63]

Since there are no parallel examples of black husbands persuading their wives to work, we can assume that black women changed their own minds about employment and then persuaded their husbands. Identifying this process may also reveal what kept Italian wives outside the labor force. To begin with, it might have been the case that they did not define a higher standard of living as a family goal or that they did so, but saw wage earning as the responsibility of the husband and children. Or they may have defined their economic responsibilities in a manner similar to black wives, but simply have been unable to overcome a husband's objection to their employment. The research task is to identify where in this process Italian wives differed from blacks, but so far no documentary material has been uncovered which makes this clear.

The pattern of child rearing in black families was a second reason black mothers found it easier to work than Italian mothers. Italians believed in close supervision of children, blacks in training for independence. Properly raised Italian children (*ben educati*) were never left alone. Mothers told their children to play with siblings and other relatives rather than with neighbors. The extent of supervision probably increased in the New World not only because of dangerous living conditions but also for fear "America . . . will take our children."[64] Far different patterns of child rearing for blacks were the result of slavery. Because mothers as well as fathers worked in the fields, elderly black nurses sometimes cared for children, but more often older older siblings supervised the young. It seems plausible to suggest that slave parents rarely connected their physical presence with good parenting; an obedient youngster remained out of trouble when left alone. However, the withdrawal of women from field labor in Reconstruction again suggests that ex-slave mothers wanted to invest more time in child rearing. It seems it was with some reluctance that black families devised patterns of child rearing which taught self reliance at an early age. A working mother was forced to train her children to care for themselves and for each other. One home economist, studying the budgets of Philadelphia blacks between 1916 and 1918, observed that black children often prepared the meals and purchased food for the family at the corner store.[65] In *The Philadelphia Negro* DuBois noted that the chief employment of black children was in "helping about the house while the mother was at work."[66]

A third cultural underpinning for black women's work consisted of parental attitudes towards children's education. Even as slaves blacks desperately sought to read and write. They connected literacy with being able to read the Bible; they gave their greatest respect to fellow slaves who could read aloud passages from Scripture. Ex-slave parents reacted to their deprivations on the plantation: they wanted to read the Bible, write their names, correspond with relatives, keep accounts and much more. In the first years after emancipation, children of the slaves flocked to the newly opened missionary schools and sometimes their parents accompanied them. The belief in education persisted among black parents. We have already seen that even in 1900 the rate of school attendance was far higher among blacks than Italians. But the value of education for children operated within an economic context: because of racial discrimination in hiring, black children found it difficult to secure employment. Moreover, it is too simple to conclude that keeping children in school was the major reason a mother worked. As we have observed, mothers continued to earn wages, even when their children were grown. Instead, the importance of education for children helped mother overcome doubts about women's wage earning.

This emphasis on children's education was imbedded within a family's plans for its survival. Both groups may have shared the same parental concern for provision in old age, but expressed the concern through different strategies: for Italians, through the continued presence of at least one adult child as a wage earner in the household; for blacks, through the education and social mobility for the children. Both groups tried to plan for the future, but a black family may have placed greater emphasis on a child's schooling as the means of meeting long-term family needs. Thus, both Italians and blacks believed in self-sacrifice, but with a difference. Whereas Italian children often submerged their needs to those of their parents, especially their mothers, black mothers deprived themselves of necessities for the sake of their children. According to a New York City social investigator, the Italian daughter was taught to "subordinate her individual desire" to family needs.[67] Such children, when they went out to work, knew their wages belonged to the family. In contrast, black mothers worked extra hours to help educate their children. Ex-slave mothers in the South "make great sacrifices to spare their own children during school-hours."[68] Mothers in demeaning jobs justified their work in terms of the dignity conferred by educating one's children. One Raleigh, North Carolina, black mother in 1869 stated proudly, "I don't care how hard I has to work if I can only send Sallie and the boys to school looking respectable."[69] We can suggest that in their relations with their husbands, their training of independent children, and their self-sacrifice for children's education, black wives and mothers found strength and support for their wage earning, but at this stage of research, these remain tentative ideas which can only be demonstrated by reexamining how black families in slavery and in the early years of emancipation made choices about women's involvement in work and in the family.

## NOTES

A previous version of this paper was presented at the Newberry Library Colloquium on Family and Community History, November, 1975. The author wishes to acknowledge the helpful criticisms of this paper from Miriam Cohen, Leonore Davidoff, Douglas L. Jones, Claudia Goldin, Maurine Greenwald, Nancy Hafkin, Karen Mason, Leslie Page Moch, John Modell, Joseph Pleck, and Sheila Rowbotham.

1. U. S. Bureau of the Census, *Twelfth Census of the United States: 1900, Supplementary Analysis and Derivational Tables* (Washington, D. C., 1906).

2. U. S. Bureau of the Census, *Statistics of Women at Work* (Washington, D.C., 1900), Table 29, pp. 311, 315, 323, 325, 353–354, 359, 363–364, 373–374, 387; U. S. Bureau of the Census, *Population*, II (Washington, D.C., 1902), Table 32, pp. 311–314, 325, 337, 342.

3. Studies concerned with the higher rate of wage earning among black women include Glen C. Cain, *Married Women in the Labor Force: An Economic Analysis* (Chicago, 1966); William G. Bowen and T. Aldrich Finegan, *The Economics of Labor Force Participation* (Princeton, 1969); Duran Bell, "Why Participation Rates of Black and White Wives Differ," *Journal of Human Resources*, Vol. 9, No. 4 (Fall, 1974), pp. 465–479; Claudia Dale Goldin, "Female Labor Force Participation: The Origin of Black and White Differences, 1870 and 1880," *Journal of Economic History*, v. xxxvii, No. 1 (March, 1977), pp. 87–112; Edwin Harwood and Claire C. Hodge, "Jobs and the Negro Family: A Reappraisal, *The Public Interest*, No. 23 (Spring, 1971), pp. 125–131.

4. Virginia Yans-McLaughlin, "A Flexible Tradition: South Italian Immigrants Confront a New Work Experience," *Journal of Social History*, Vol. 7, No. 4 (Summer, 1974), pp. 442–445. See also Virginia Yans-McLaughlin, "Italian Women and Work: Experience and Perception," in *Class, Sex, and the Woman Worker*, ed. Milton Cantor and Bruce Laurie (Westport, Connecticut, 1977), pp. 101–119.

5. Louise A. Tilly, "Comments on the Yans-McLaughlin and Davidoff Papers," *Journal of Social History*, Vol 7, No. 4 (Summer, 1974), pp. 452–459. An excellent analysis of Italian women's work that emphasizes changes in the economy is Miriam Cohen, "Italian-American Women in New York City, 1900-1950: Work and School," in *Class, Sex and the Woman Worker*, pp. 120–143.

6. John Bodnar, "Immigration and Modernization: The Case of Slavic Peasants in Industrial America," *Journal of Social History*, Vo. 10, No. 1 (Fall, 1976), pp. 44–71.

7. A more balanced approach, emphasizing family needs as well as the demands of the industrial environment, is presented in Tamara K. Hareven's, "Family Time and Industrial Time: Family and Work in a Planned Corporation Town, 1900-1974," *Journal of Urban History*, Vol. 1, No. 3 (May, 1975), pp. 365–389.

8. Since Sicilian wives were more home bound than other Italian immigrants, their presence in certain cities may have accounted for the absence of Italian married women from the labor market. In point of fact, low rates of wage earning characterized Chicago and Philadelphia Italian women, despite the fact that 8 percent of Chicago's Italians and 12 percent of Philadelphia's Italians were born in Sicily, and high rates of wage earning prevailed among New York City's Italians, about half of whom were Sicilian. Carroll D. Wright, *The Italians in Chicago: A Social and Economic Study* (Washington, D.C., 1897), Table V, p. 372; U. S. Senate Reports, 62nd Cong., 1st sess., *Immigrants in Cities*, Vol. 1 (Washington, D.C., 1911), Table 13, p. 358 and Table 17, p. 175.

9. Jane Schneider, "Of Vigilance and Virgins: Honor, Shame and Access to Resources in Mediterranean Society," *Ethnology*, Vol. 10 (January, 1971), pp. 1–24. This tradition applied especially to Italian women from the South.

10. Leonard Covello, *The Social Background of the Italo-American School Child* (Totawo, New Jersey, 1972), p. 296.

11. Computed from data in Ninth Special Report of the Commissioner of Labor, *The Italians in Chicago: A Social and Economic Study* (Washington, D.C., 1897), Table I, pp. 52–273.

12. Ruth S. True, *The Neglected Girl* (New York, 1914), p. 109.

13. Louise C. Odencrantz, *Italian Women in Industry* (New York, 1919), pp. 175–176.

14. Computed from data in Commission of Labor, *Italians in Chicago*, Tables I and II, pp. 52–351.

15. U. S. Senate, *Immigrants in Cities*, Vol. 2, Table 401, pp. 546–548.

16. Computed from data in Commission of Labor, *Italians in Chicago*, Tables I and II, pp. 52–351.

17. Herbert G. Gutman, *The Black Family in Slavery and Freedom, 1750-1925* (New York, 1976), Table B-1, p. 527.

18. U. S. Senate, *Immigrants in Cities*, Vol. 2, Table 401, pp. 546–548.

19. Computed from data in Commissioner of Labor, *The Italians in Chicago*, Table I, pp. 52–273 and "Condition of the Negro in Various Cities," *Bulletin of the Department of Labor*, Vol. II, No. 10 (May, 1897), pp. 257–360. In weekly wages Italian male laborers earned less than blacks in Cambridge, Nashville, or Atlanta. Italian wives heading households were also poorer than similar black wives.

20. U. S. Senate, *Immigrants in Cities*, Vol. I, Table 64, p. 226.

21. Computed from data in Department of Labor, "Condition of the Negro in Various Cities," pp. 257–360.

22. Computed from data in Commissioner of Labor *Italians in Chicago*, Table I, pp. 52–273.

23. Ibid., p. 722.

24. Ibid., pp. 52–273.

25. Odencrantz, *Italian Women in Industry*, p. 163.

26. Ibid.

27. Computed from data in Department of Labor, "Condition of the Negro in Various Cities," pp. 257–360.

28. U. S. Senate, *Immigrants in Cities*, Vol. 1, Table 55, p. 216 and Table 52, p. 396; U. S. Bureau of the Census, *Occupations*, Table 43, pp. 486–489, 506–509, 618–621.

29. Gutman, *Black Family*, Table B-2, p. 527.

30. Commissioner of Labor, *Italians in Chicago*, pp. 379–380

31. Barbara Klaczynska, "Why Women Work: A Comparison of Various Groups—Philadelphia, 1910–1930," *Labor History*, Vol. 17, No. 1 (Winter, 1976), pp. 73–87.

32. Mary White Ovington, *Half A Man: The Status of the Negro in New York* (New York, 1911; New York 1969), p. 162.

33. Ibid., p. 62.

34. Ibid.

35. Ibid.

36. U. S. Bureau of the Census, *Statistics of Women at Work*, Table 27, pp. 215–217.

37. Ovington, *Half A Man*, p. 58.

38. In New York City large numbers of Italian women were occupied earning wages, generally sewing in their apartments, and fewer wives took in lodgers. This substitution of a mother's wages for a lodger's income was true only in New York City. In other cities wives earned wages as well as taking in lodgers, and elsewhere wives did not work and did not accept lodgers.

39. Gutman, *Black Family*, Table B-4, p. 530.

40. In modern American cities male unemployment depresses the rate of female participation in the labor market, but around the turn of the century, male unemployment led to increases in the number of women working. The contemporary evidence is summarized in James Sweet, *Women in the Labor Force* (New York, 1973), p. 23.

41. Was the absence of other wage earners the reason a black wife had to work? Taking into account the number of wage earners in the family, black wives were still more likely to work than Italian wives. When an Italian family relied on one other income source, generally the husband's wage, one out of ten Chicago Italian wives worked in 1896, compared with one-third to one-half of black wives in Atlanta, Cambridge, and Nashville. With three additional incomes, about seven in ten black wives in Cambridge, Atlanta, and Nashville worked, compared with two out of ten of Chicago's Italian wives in 1896.

42. Wright, *Italians in Chicago*, Table VII, p. 374; Department of Labor, "Condition of the Negro in Various Cities," Table I, pp. 287–288.

43. Gutman, *Black Family*, Table B-4, p. 530.

44. Judith Smith, "Work and Family Patterns of Southern Italian Immigrant Women in Providence, Rhode Island, 1915," unpublished paper delivered at the Berkshire Conference on Women's History, June, 1976.

45. For school attendance figures among black children, I substituted data from the 1900 federal census, which employed a division by age unavailable in the Bureau of Labor survey.

Wright, *Italians in Chicago*, Table XVI, p. 385; U.S. Bureau of the Census, *Population*, Part II, Table 54, pp. 396–397, Table 9, pp. 122–136.

46. Gutman, *Black Family*, Table B-4, p. 530.

47. The greater the number of contributors to the family's economy, the higher the rate of wives at work. If just one additional member of an Italian family was employed, then only 10 percent of the wives worked. If at least three other members of the family worked, 17 percent of Italian wives did so. Black wives also increased their rate of working as more family members entered the labor force. For Cambridge black wives, the rate of labor-force participation rose from 36 percent with one additional income earner to 60 percent in families with at least three extra incomes. The rate of working increased from 43 percent to 63 percent for Atlanta wives, and from 53 percent to 67 percent for Nashville wives.

48. A working wife could never expect to match her husband's income: hence, the availability of work for women never adequately replaced a man's wages. Nevertheless, the ratio of male to female wages was higher for blacks than Italians. In Philadelphia the wages of a black wife in 1911 were 42 percent those of her husband, and 71 percent in New York City. By contrast, among New York and Philadelphia Italians, a wife earned one-third what her husband made. U. S. Senate, *Immigrants in Cities*, Vol. 1, Tables 66–67, pp. 228–229, 408–409.

49. U. S. Senate, *Immigrants in Cities*, Vol. 1. Table 57, p. 64; Table 65, p. 448; Table 67, p. 229, p. 409, Table 70, p. 583, Table 72, p. 746; Table 76, p. 324.

50. Karen Oppenheim Mason and Larry L. Bumpass, "U.S. Women's Sex Role Ideology, 1970," *American Journal of Sociology*, Vol. 80, No. 5, (March, 1975), pp. 1212–1219.

51. James Morgan, I. Sirageldin, and Nancy Baerwaldt, *Productive Americans: A Study of How Individuals Contribute to Economic Progress* (Ann Arbor, 1966), Figure 19-4 p. 330. Consult also John Scanzoni, "Sex Roles, Economic Factors and Marital Solidarity in Black and White Marriages," *Journal of Marriage and the Family*, Vol. 37, No. 1, (February, 1975), pp. 130–144; Leland J. Axelson, "The Working Wife: Differences in Perception Among Negro and White Males," *Journal of Marriage and the Family*, Vol. 32, No. 3 (August, 1970), pp. 457–464; D. D. Lewis, "The Black Family: Socialization and Sex Role," *Phylon*, Vol. 36, No. 3, (1975), pp. 221–237.

52. Eugene D. Genovese, *Roll, Jordan, Roll*, p. 490; Vernon Burton, "Black Household Structure in Edgefield County, South Carolina," unpublished paper, 1976; Robert Abzug, "The Black Family during Reconstruction," in *Key Issues in the Afro-American Experience*, ed. Nathan I. Huggins, Martin Kilson, and Daniel M. Fox Vol. 2, (New York, 1971), pp. 26–41.

53. Gutman, *Black Family*, p. 168.

54. Ibid.

55. Ibid.

56. Gerda Lerner, *Black Women in White America: A Documentary History* (New York, 1973), p. 292.

57. Theodore Rosengarten, *All God's Dangers: The Life of Nate Shaw* (New York, 1974), p. 128.

58. Gutman, *Black Family*, p. 168.

59. Ibid.

60. Ibid, pp. 146–155; John Blassingame, *the Slave Community: Plantation Life in the Ante-Bellum South* (New York, 1972), p. 90; Herbert Gutman and Richard Sutch, "The Slave Family: Protected Agent of Capitalist Masters or Victim of the Slave Trade," in Paul A. David, Herbert G. Gutman, Richard Sutch, Peter Temin, and Gavin Wright, *Reckoning with Slavery: A Critical Study in the Quantitative History of American Negro Slavery* (New York, 1976), Table 3, p. 129.

61. Rosengarten, *All God's Dangers*, p. 127.

62. Ibid., p. 475.

63. Lerner, *Black Women*, p. 15.

64. Covello, *The Social Background of the Italo American School Child*, p. 296.

65. Sadie Tanner Mossell, "The Standard of Living Among One Hundred Negro Migrant

Families in Philadelphia," *Annals of the America Academy of Political and Social Science*, v, XCVIII, No. 187 (November, 1921), p. 186.

66. W. E. B., DuBois, *The Philadelphia Negro: A Social Study* (Philadelphia, 1899, New York, 1967), p. 111.

67. Mary Van Kleeck *Artificial Flower Makers* (New York, 1913), p. 86, as quoted in Miriam J. Cohen "The World of Work and the Family: New York City Italians, 1900–1950," unpublished paper, 1977.

68. Lerner, *Black Women*, p. 246.

69. Ibid., p. 102.

# SELECTED READINGS FOR PART SIX

BLASSINGAME, JOHN W. *The Slave Community.* New Haven: Yale University Press, 1972.

DUBOIS W. E. B. *The Philadelphia Negro.* 1899. Reprint. New York: Schocken Books, 1967.

FOGEL, ROBERT W., AND STANLEY L. ENGERMAN. *Time on the Cross.* Boston: Little, Brown, 1974.

FURSTENBERG, FRANK F., JR., THEODORE HERSHBERG, AND JOHN MODELL. "The Origins of the Female-Headed Black Family: The Impact of the Urban Experience." *Journal of Interdisciplinary History,* 2 (1975), 211–233.

GENOVESE, EUGENE V. *Roll, Jordan Roll.* New York: Pantheon, 1975.

GLASCO, LAURENCE A. "Life Cycles and Household Structure of American Ethnic Groups: Irish, Germans, and Native-born Whites in Buffalo, New York, 1855." *Journal of Urban History,* 1 (1975), 339–364.

GUTMAN, HERBERT G. *The Black Family in Slavery and Freedom.* New York: Pantheon, 1976.

HAREVEN, TAMARA K. "The Laborers of Manchester, New Hampshire, 1912–1922: The Role of the Family and Ethnicity in Adjustment to Industrial Life." *Labor History,* 16 (1975), 249–265.

HERSHBERG, THEODORE. "Free Blacks in Ante-Bellum Philadelphia." *Journal of Social History,* 5 (1971–1972), 183–209.

LAMMERMEIER, PAUL J. "The Urban Black Family of the Nineteenth Century: A Study of Black Family Structure in the Ohio Valley, 1850–1880." *Journal of Marriage and the Family,* 35 (1973), 440–456.

MCLAUGHLIN, VIRGINIA YANS. "Patterns of Work and Family Organization: Buffalo's Italians." *Journal of Interdisciplinary History,* 2 (1971), 299–314.

PLECK, ELIZABETH H. "The Two-Parent Household: Black Family Structure in Late Nineteenth-Century Boston." *Journal of Social History,* 6 (1972), 1–31.

RAWICK, GEORGE P. *From Sundown to Sunup.* Westport, Conn.: Greenwood, 1972.

SHIFFLETT, CRANDALL A. "The Household Composition of Rural Black Families: Louisa County, Virginia, 1880." *Journal of Interdisciplinary History,* 2 (1975), 235–260.

STACK, CAROL B. *All Our Kin.* New York: Harper & Row, 1974.

# PART SEVEN

# DEMOGRAPHY: BIRTHS, DEATHS, AND MIGRATION

Demographic research is the source from which the new family history has sprung and it retains an important place in this field. The articles in this section are by three people who have made important contributions to American historical demography. Each selection gives the reader a general background in the field as well as some sense of the issues being debated.

Robert V. Wells's article "Family History and Demographic Transition" reconsiders what is probably the most influential and controversial theory of demographic change to be developed since World War II. Demographic Transition theory holds that the premodern population was characterized by high levels of fertility and mortality which acted to counterbalance each other and keep population size relatively stable. The coming of industrialization saw the improvement of life expectancy because of better diet and preventive medicine at the same time that people were continuing to reproduce at traditionally high levels. This created a period of "transition" during which the population grew rapidly and did not fall until, slowly but surely, family limitation was practiced, returning population growth to less explosive levels. Criticisms of this theory have rested largely on its supposed inability to deal with current third-world patterns and the inadequacy of its proponents' explanations of why and how various aspects of change took place.

Wells maintains that any explanation of change in fertility behavior—the element of transition theory which is most subject to conscious choice—must ultimately look to the *values* of the people involved. If we are to understand why people began imposing limits on their reproductive capacities, we must not fall prey to explanations which place too much weight on contraceptive technology—withdrawal having long been a reasonably effective contraceptive—but, rather, we must learn what inspired people to employ the techniques available to them. Did modernization cause fatalism to be replaced with a rationality that enabled people to adopt an outlook that involved conscious planning and behavior oriented toward the future? Such an outlook certainly would have been conducive to family planning. These are some of the issues raised by Wells.

Richard A. Easterlin's work "Factors in the Decline of Farm Family Fertility in the United States: Some Preliminary Results" looks at the decline in American fertility during the nineteenth century. While there are scattered instances of fertility falling in the United States before 1800, nationally the figures did not begin to drop until that time. Easterlin focuses on the decline among the rural population because he sees this as problematic, given the abundance of farm land in this country. His initial assumption is that if land were available, there would be no need for people to limit their fertility. This interpretation seems to differ greatly from the one offered by Wells to the extent that it stresses material considerations (in other words, land) at the expense of "values," but before Easterlin's paper is finished there are some modest signs of convergence.

In looking at statistics from a sample of rural American households in 1860, Easterlin discovered that fertility decline was not distributed equally through the country. Rather, as one moved from older to newer areas (for example, from New Hampshire to Kansas), fertility increased except in extreme frontier regions where it was slightly lower than in the settled areas just behind them. After exploring and testing a number of different hypotheses to explain this phenomenon, Easterlin tentatively concludes that the declining availability of land made it increasingly difficult for parents to settle their children on land near them; thus they reduced their fertility to enable children to remain nearby without experiencing downward social mobility between generations. In subsequent papers (see the selected readings at the end of this section) Easterlin has tested this hypothesis further and found some indirect confirmation. While the emphasis is clearly economic, readers should realize that Easterlin's explanation draws as much on values as it does on land. For example, he assumes that: (1) parents want their children to settle near them, and (2) they want their children to maintain a life-style at least as good as the one they experienced while growing up. In certain respects this resembles Banks's "Standard of Living" argument (1954).* Nevertheless, the focus on land availability does set this work apart from Wells's concern with people's orientations as an explanation of fertility. Not surprisingly, Easterlin's works have been criticized by less economically oriented demographers and historians, but the care with which he executed his research and the implications of his findings require that we give his work serious attention.

The final article in this section shifts us from birth to death. Maris A. Vinovskis looks at two questions in "Angels' Heads and Weeping Willows: Death in Early America": (1) life expectancy in colonial America and (2) attitudes toward death during that period. In considering the first issue he presents data that may surprise some readers. Until fairly recently there was widespread belief that life expectancy in colonial America was rather low when compared to modern rates. Demographic research carried out since the 1960s reveals that while death rates were high in *urban* New England during the seventeenth and eighteenth centuries, cities like Boston and Salem were not typical of the country as a whole. On the contrary, the death rates in smaller rural communities such as Andover, Hingham, and Dedham averaged about half those found in more urban communi-

*Complete citations for works referred to are in the selected readings on pp. 564.

ties. Vinovskis makes a point that seems terribly obvious but which, unfortunately, has only recently been made; namely, most of the difference in life expectancy between Americans living in the last quarter of the twentieth century and those living two and three centuries earlier is related to differentials in infant and child mortality. Once a male colonial New Englander had survived to twenty-one, he had a life expectancy of only one year less than a male living today; females, because of the high incidence of death during childbearing, did not fare as well—their expectancy being six years less than today's women. However, rates of infant and child mortality were *very* high and posed a great social and medical problem; it was the exceptional family that did not lose at least one of its children.

Given the fact that those who survived childhood could expect a reasonably long life, why, Vinovskis asks, do we find a morbid preoccupation with death among colonial New Englanders? Apart from a religious preoccupation with mortality, he feels the answer lies in the fact that people were not shielded from death. Death occurred at home rather than in hospitals, and the absence of funeral parlors meant that the body was viewed at home. Moreover, cultural expectations required that all members of colonial villages attend the funeral of a townsperson. Finally, burial places often were on the family land or in a nearby communal plot. Unlike today's population, people were not able to keep the details and reminders of death at a distance.

# 24 | FAMILY HISTORY AND DEMOGRAPHIC TRANSITION

## ROBERT V. WELLS

In recent years, the family has emerged as a major subject of historical inquiry.[1] Numerous books and articles have appeared describing, among other things, the composition, kinship, and other interpersonal relationships, economic functions, and political importance of families.[2] In addition, other works have dealt with values and attitudes toward the family and its members.[3] Venturous scholars have even tried to relate family matters to such subjects as the Salem witchcraft trials, the development of a revolutionary milieu in eighteenth-century New England, and the nature of British politics in the seventeenth and eighteenth centuries, or in the case of the *Annales* school, to the total environment of a locality.[4]

Characterized by a wide range of approaches, these efforts have produced an extraordinary number of interesting findings. However, on the surface at least, historical research on the family has lacked unity and a common sense of direction. Not only have individual scholars often pursued answers to their own idiosyncratic questions, using their own definitions, but the appearance of disunity also has been fostered by the wide temporal and geographic distribution of work on the family. Thus, while our knowledge about families in the past has been increasing rapidly, it has generally been difficult to relate the results of one investigation to conclusions reached in other studies.[5]

Certainly this broad attack on the history of the family is to be encouraged. To study only one aspect of the family or families of only one time or place would be unnecessarily limiting. Furthermore, it is important to recognize that current methodologies available to historians of the family tend to focus on the details of the lives of relatively few persons. In such a situation generalization becomes possible only after a reasonably large number of similar studies have been done. Nonetheless, it seems desirable that historians of the family, of whatever persuasion, try to approach their work with at least some reference to a broader picture.

It is easy to call for some organizing theme to give unity and direction to work on families of the past; it is more difficult to suggest what such a theme should be. At the risk of being presumptuous, however, my purpose here is to do exactly that.

Perhaps the most popular theory among demographers today is the theory of Demographic Transition, which describes (and often attempts to explain) the historic decline of both death and birth rates in the industrialized nations of the world.[6] However, in the light of recent work on the history of the family, this theory (which we will consider in more detail shortly) needs to be recast if it is to make any sense. When I attempted to do this, it became apparent that not only could history help to reshape the theory of Demographic Transition but that the altered version of the theory also gave coherence to many of the hitherto remotely connected studies in the history of the family.

Thus, the purpose of this paper is fourfold. First, I want to offer a critique of the theory of Demographic Transition as it currently stands. Second, I want to suggest in abstract how the theory might be reformulated to account for the historical evidence which challenges the current model. Third, by surveying families in American history, I will try to relate the revised theory to the facts of the past. I will conclude by indicating some areas of research in family history which appear to be worth further study. In so doing, I hope to show how closely integrated much of the research in family history has been in the past, and how unified it can be in the future.

Because my own special area of competence happens to be American history, I shall rely heavily on evidence from this country, especially in testing the revised hypothesis. However, I shall attempt to indicate how data from other countries also seem to fit the new model. If the evidence appears scattered sometimes, that is in part the result of my own knowledge (or lack thereof), but is more the result of the sizeable gaps in our knowledge of the relevant areas of history. In any case, it should be emphasized that I am putting forth this model of the Demographic Transition with the awareness that future research will probably revise it. My main concerns, then, involve both the accuracy of the theory as revised here and a hope that this paper will serve to give a greater sense of common purpose to students of family history.

The theory of Demographic Transition can be usefully divided into two parts for purposes of analysis and criticism. The first area which we will consider *describes* the general decline in birth and death rates in industrialized countries. The second part deals with *attempts to explain* why the change occurred.

In the past, according to Transition theory, all populations were characterized by birth and death rates which were much higher than those found in industrialized countries today. Although these rates might vary over the short term, over a long period of time they tended to be rather closely balanced, with the result that natural increase was small and population growth was slow. Starting in France, and possibly Scandinavia, in the late eighteenth and early nineteenth centuries the death rate began to decline noticeably. Since the birth rate did not fall until later, there was a transitional period (hence the name of the theory) of rapid population growth as births exceeded deaths by a considerable margin. However, in the long run the birth and death rates once again came into rather close balance, though at much lower levels than before, and rapid growth ceased. While France was the first nation to experience this transition, other nations (all industrialized) have followed much the same path, although the timing of the change, the rate of decline of fertility and mortality, and the extent to which the transition has been completed vary considerably from one nation to another. Much of the current interest in this theory stems from the fact that in many of the nonindustrialized countries of the world, death rates have fallen remarkably since World War II, leading to rather rapid transitional growth at the present. Obviously, demographers are interested if and when fertility will fall in these parts of the world, slowing the growth rate and bringing the birth and death rates into balance at a relatively low level.

In the light of recent historical investigations, about the only parts of this theory which are clearly beyond question are that rapid growth occurred during the demographic transition and that birth and death rates are now lower in some parts of the world than they ever have been for any extended period in the past. The assumption that relatively slow growth was universal before the transition began needs to be qualified in light of recent findings suggesting rather remarkable oscillations of population in Egypt between about 700 B.C. and the present, the depopulation of Europe during the plague of the fourteenth century and its ultimate recovery, and the rather remarkable short-term variations found in the populations of some British colonies in America around 1700.[7]

Interestingly, when most demographers and historians deal with the demographic transition, they make remarkably few clearcut statements about the cause of the change. Almost all demographers note carefully that the decline in mortality and fertility always is well under way wherever literacy is high, over half the labor force is employed in nonagricultural pursuits, and the majority of the people live in urban areas. Although few specify the exact relationships, it seems to be a common assumption that these trends (whether called development, industrialization, or modernization) have caused both mortality and fertility to decline.

The explanation for why death rates might have fallen in such a situation is quite plausible. It seems safe to say that the changes noted above were generally accompanied by better and more available medical aid. In addition, standards of living tended to improve as well, producing better diets and more healthful environments.

The reasons why the birth rate should have declined as well are less obvious. Perhaps the best summary of the possible causes behind falling fertility have been given by David Heer in his article, "Economic Development and the Fertility Transition."[8] Heer notes first that the decline in infant mortality accompanying rising living standards may reduce the need for parents to have large numbers of children in order to have a few reach maturity. The change from agriculture to industry, and from rural to urban, also may have led to reduced childbearing according to Heer, simply because children were no longer economically valuable in a new environment. Closely related to these factors was the emergence of governmental care for the aged, which meant that parents no longer needed children to care for them when they grew old. Finally, social attitudes stressing education and achievement in an industrial society and recognizing birth control as acceptable may also have fostered decreased fertility. Put simply, Heer and others stress the fact that in an urban, industrial environment children are no longer benefits but may actually be detrimental to parental aspirations, and hence fertility declines.

In spite of the plausibility of the theory, historical evidence suggests that these causal relationships may not have existed. One assumption which seems common to most advocates of Transition theory is that urbanization and industrialization occurred *before* fertility began to decline. Yet, we have evidence of family limitation being practiced by English and Genevans in the seventeenth century and by some French, American, and Japanese people in the eighteenth and early nineteenth centuries.[9] In every case, these fertility declines predated any significant industrial development. Ironically, in England and possibly elsewhere as well, the move to industry and the cities was associated with an *increase* in the birth rate, quite in contrast to what Transition theory would lead us to expect.[10] Finally, the baby boom which followed World War II is an extraordinarily puzzling phenomena from the perspective of the theory of Demographic Transition. The explanations cited by Heer implicitly assume that once the birth rate declined it would probably stay low. Certainly it should not increase during times of rising prosperity and movement into cities. In fact, so inconsistent was behavior with theory that the prosperous United States had a much greater surge in fertility than did Europe, where war devastation might presumably have led to a reversion to early patterns of reproduction.

Two questions thus arise. The first is, why did fertility fall in the historical change known as the Demographic Transition? The second is, does any connection remain between this decline and the processes known as industrialization or modernization?

In order to answer these two questions we should look at four possible models which might explain a widespread decline in fertility. First of all, it is possible for birth rates to drop for unintended reasons. Changes in health, sexual customs, or marriage patterns all can depress fertility, even though reduced childbearing may not have been the purpose of the initial change. It is clear, however, that the demographic transition involved a deliberate reduction in fertility, and so we must concentrate on conscious efforts to reduce the birth rate. The second model (and first one positing a conscious effort to control reproduction) assumes that when the birth rate was high, there was neither the knowledge of how to limit families nor any desire to do so. Within this framework, the demographic transition is seen as the result of new environments which lead to pressures to control childbearing for the first time, as well as make available the knowledge which allows these desires to be put into effect. Once again, however, the historical evidence makes it difficult to accept this possibility. We noted above that several populations in various parts of the world seem to have practiced family limitation well before industrialization and urbanization introduced new life styles which might have altered the desires of parents to have children. In addition, this evidence and the extraordinary study by Norman Himes on the *Medical History of Contraception* make it clear that knowledge that births could be limited was reasonably widespread before industrial societies began to emerge.[11]

The third model of why fertility falls is a variation of the second. In this case, the assumption is that people wanted to limit their families but could not because they did not know how to. The appeal of this explanation is that it offers some reason why the educated upper classes generally controlled their fertility before the less knowledgeable lower classes. Likewise, it would also seem to explain why highly literate nations generally have much lower fertility than nations where the educational level is low. However, the evidence suggests that this model too may be invalid. In England in the seventeenth century, both peers and the peasants of Colyton were limiting the size of their families.[12] While their motives may have been different than those of the peers, the residents of Colyton did not have to wait until the industrial revolution to share in the knowledge that births could be limited. Furthermore, among the Colyton residents and the Quakers of the middle colonies whom I have studied, the onset of family limitation was rapid.[13] The speed at which family size fell seems to preclude any slow spread of the knowledge of birth control. I have found no evidence suggesting that the Quakers either gradually or suddenly became aware of methods of limiting births. In fact, the only specific mention of family limitation I have found suggested the adoption of an old method of restricting births (nursing) to a woman who had had a difficult pregnancy and wanted to avoid another.[14] Regardless of the effectiveness of nursing as a long-term means of family limitation, the important point is that, in this instance, it was motivation for and not knowledge about birth control which changed.

The fourth model is very closely connected to the experience of the Quaker wife cited above. It assumes that most populations have at least some notions of how to control fertility (if not by contraception, then certainly by practicing abortion, infanticide, or abstention). Thus, fertility declines occur primarily because the motivation is strong enough for a people to practice one or more of these methods, rather than because they suddenly learn some new technique. Given the rapidity of change in Colyton and among the Quakers, and the fact that major declines in fertility had occurred long before rubber condoms or diaphragms (let alone pills or IUDs) became available, there can be little doubt that at least the initial stages of the demographic transition occurred because people began frequent use of traditional forms of family limitation.[15] It is of interest to note here, incidentally, that Kingsley Davis, a prominent demographer, has issued a telling criticism of current birth-control programs, stressing that they are failing not because of lack of knowledge or techniques but rather because people see no reason to reduce their fertility.[16]

Emphasizing the importance of motivation in the reduction of fertility is certainly not in conflict with the theory of Demographic Transition. Where this paper does differ from the theory is in the suggestion that motivation to have few children did not result from the economic and social changes accompanying industrialization. Rather, I wish to hypothesize that fertility fell for reasons which *also* produced a decline in the death rate as well as changes in family structure and interpersonal relations and in economic development. Thus, industrialization and the demographic transition continue to be associated, but as two effects of the same cause, rather than one causing the other.

Central to this hypothesis is the assumption that human beings have sets of values which are generally well integrated.[17] If this is true, then the demographic transition may be seen as only one manifestation of a major change in value orientation, a change which can conveniently be typified as the shift from a traditional to a modern world view.[18]

The nature of this change in values has been portrayed effectively in an article by Laila El-Hamamsy entitled, "Belief Systems and Family Planning in Peasant Societies."[19] In an analysis of peasant cultures in both Egypt and Latin America, El-Hamamsy found that persons in such societies were generally characterized by a sense of powerlessness over their own lives and over the world around them. Both nature and human affairs were seen as capricious, hard, and uncontrollable. God had ordered the world according to some mysterious laws, and it was not within the province of men to interfere. As a result, most peasants either do not think about the future or else feel that the future will be the same as the past. Fear, fatalism, and a sense that contentment with the status quo is desirable to avoid disappointed ambitions have led most peasants to conclude that they can do little to alter the course of their lives. Within this framework, there is no apparent reason why few children would be preferable to many (in fact, interfering with conception might anger God), just as there is no apparent reason for altering any other social or economic traditions.

These views are strikingly different from attitudes (which we shall call modern here) which have emerged in Western European society since the sixteenth century. According to E. A. Wrigley, the best way to sum up modern attitudes is with the concept of rationality.[20] Wrigley defines a modern society as one in which recruitment to roles is done on the basis of achievement rather than birth, social roles are more clearly and narrowly defined, and where the rule of law is substituted for arbitrary and capricious behavior. Furthermore, self-interest (or, at most, interest in the nuclear family) is seen as replacing any willingness by individuals to submit to broader social or institutional needs. Thus, in contrast to the traditional view, persons with modern values believe not only that the world is knowable and controllable but that it is also to an individual's advantage to plan his or her life and attend to the future, as well as to the present and past. To merely avoid trouble is no longer enough (as it was in traditional society) for the modern individual; such a person wants to advance and often measures advancement in terms of his or her material well-being.

It is easy to see how at least some demographic patterns and forms of family structure might readily have been altered once modern attitudes began to prevail. The reduction of mortality , for example, may well have resulted from the emergence of attitudes that misery did not have to be accepted after all. Such notions would have been conducive to both medical experimentation and the acceptance of new techniques. Similarly, in situations where children came to be seen as burdens, modern values might permit and promote the use of family limitation to protect or enhance one's position in the world. Likewise, the movement into cities, frequently seen as a cause of falling fertility, may actually only be another manifestation of modern attitudes. Urban immigrants may well have been those people who first came to believe that by individual actions (such as migration, or learning industrial skills) it was possible for a person to improve his lot. As we shall see shortly, attitudes toward both women and children changed during the course of the demographic transition, reflecting perhaps a modern emphasis on the worth of the individual and a denial of the unchangeable order of the world. Finally, industrialization and economic development may well be related to the demographic transition. But, instead of one causing the other, the habits of saving, investment, and experimentation and the adoption of new technology necessary to industrial society may have been a response to the sense that the future could be controlled, much as family limitation may have been a different reaction to the same concern for the future.

Certainly the relationships outlined here are plausible. The historical evidence that we have tends to support this line of argument. But before we turn to the data, one last point needs to be made. It is obvious that my argument rests on the assumption that values help to shape the decisions that individuals make. It is not, however, my contention that a shift in values alone will be sufficient to change behavior. Thus, while the hypothesis advanced here asserts that the demographic transition (and related phenomena) could only occur after modern attitudes appear, it does not imply that such changes would have been an automatic result of the adoption of new ideas.

Having put forth a new hypothesis, it is now necessary to begin to test its merits. I shall attempt to do this by drawing on historical evidence for families in America. As was noted earlier, this focus on America is primarily because my expertise lies there. However, as I shall indicate from time to time, evidence from other countries also appears to fit the hypothesis advanced above.

The obvious place to begin is to show that modern ideas were emerging in America before the demographic transition or any of its economic or social correlates were apparent. Although some would say that the emergence of modern attitudes began as early as the sixteenth century, it is clear that at least some of the first colonists had attitudes which were similar to those found in the peasant societies discussed earlier. Edmund Morgan has found a remarkable fatalism and willingness to accept misery among the early settlers of Virginia.[21] The Puritans who settled in New England also shared many traditional attitudes. Nature was seen as mysterious and fearful. Any deviance from the proper path could bring God's wrath upon individuals or a whole people. A theology which stressed predestination and order was certainly not conducive to notions of the individual improving himself. In fact, residents of Massachusetts Bay who were so bold as to advance ideas of human equality, the rule of the law, or the capacity of people to improve themselves were often accused of heresy and driven from the colony.[22] To the extent that the early settlers worried about the future, they were concerned with the next world rather than this one. Life on earth was merely a brief prelude to an eternity in heaven or hell.

In some ways, the surprising thing about colonial society is how quickly modern attitudes began to appear. Richard Brown has recently shown that such values were clearly present in America by the end of the seventeenth century.[23] By the time of the American Revolution, modern attitudes seem to have been quite prevalent in the colonies. According to E. A. Wrigley, "a government which . . . levies large extractions arbitrarily and without due notice . . . is incompatible" with modern, rational attitudes toward life.[24] Thus, the American resistance to Parliamentary interference stands as partial proof of the presence of modern values in society. The colonists were asserting not only constitutional principles but also an attitude that life was controllable and misfortune need not be passively accepted. Anyone who reads the biographies of the Hancock or Otis families in Massachusetts, the Browns of Providence, Rhode Island, or the Beekmans in New York will certainly be struck by the fact that these people were concerned with this world and with controlling as much of their lives as possible.[25] A man like Benjamin Franklin may have expressed the new ideas better than most of his contemporaries, but the values he articulated were shared by many others.

According to the hypothesis advanced earlier, the emergence of new attitudes should have had an effect on population in general and on the family in particular. Perhaps the earliest evidence of modern ideas affecting population trends in America was the adoption of smallpox inoculation in Boston and elsewhere in the colonies during the eighteenth century.[26] It is possible to debate at length the motives and scientific attitudes which led Dr. Boylston and Cotton Mather to introduce inoculation in Boston in 1721. Nonetheless, the careful tabulation of statistics regarding the effectiveness of the treatment and the wholehearted adoption of inoculation after 1750 seems to be indicative of an attitude that disease could be understood and controlled, and that death need not be always accepted passively.[27] In fact, the last quarter of the eighteenth century saw considerable interest in the scientific study of the patterns and causes of death.[28] Richard Shryock has shown how professionalism, education, and scientific attitudes began to characterize the medical profession by the late eighteenth century.[29] Although these changes did not have a significant impact on health until the nineteenth century, when accurate findings finally began to accumulate, they too reflect a modern outlook on the world.

As with the death rate, the Americans' growing sense of an individual's worth and his influence over his life may have affected family size and structure well before industrialization and urbanization played a prominent role in our society. About the time of the American Revolution, at least some Quaker couples living in the middle colonies began to limit their families deliberately.[30] Although we cannot be sure, it seems plausible that these Friends were responding to the dislocations of wartime by postponing some of the births they might otherwise have had. At present we do not know why individual Quaker couples decided to limit their childbearing. We can suggest, however, that the military campaigns in the middle colonies, the pressure of being pacificsts in a time of conflict, severe inflation, and the withdrawal of Quakers from political affairs after 1750 may have made the future uncertain for many Friends. In such a milieu, a reduction of childbearing would make good sense. It is of interest to note here that times of severe crisis seem also to have produced a similar response in Colyton, England, in the 1640s, in France at the time of her Revolution, and in Japan following World War II.[31] It would be wrong, however, to assume on the basis of this evidence that catastrophies generally lead to a durable reduction of fertility. Without modern attitudes to give people the feeling that they need not passively accept their fate, and without a clear sense that a smaller family would improve prospects for the future, such change would not be likely to occur.

While the American Revolution may have triggered the adoption of family limitation among the Quakers, a crisis which evolved more slowly may have led other parts of the American population to reduce their fertility. In the early years of settlement, land had been abundantly available. But, by the middle of the eighteenth century, at least some of the older settlements were beginning to feel the pressure of population on natural resources. As a result, fertility began to change. Kenneth Lockridge has shown that overpopulation was becoming a legitimate concern in New England by the second half of the eighteenth century.[32] Thus, it is of considerable interest to find that the proportion of children in the total population in New England in 1790 was generally lower than in the other states.[33] The age distribution indicates clearly that childbearing was lower there than in any of the other colonies.

Increasing population density and declining economic opportunities may have led to reduced fertility in New England first. But by the early nineteenth century, the same phenomenon was appearing elsewhere. A recent book by Colin Forster and G. S. L. Tucker, *Economic Opportunity and White American Fertility Ratios*, has shown that between 1800 and 1860 substantial reductions in fertility occurred wherever farmland became scarce.[34] This was true from one section of the United States to another. It was also true as a given region became more densely populated over time. Yet density alone may not have produced the change. Evidence from the present indicates that population density does not necessarily cause a decline in the birth rate. Thus, if my hypothesis is correct, it was not only greater density which mattered but also the perception that reduced fertility would aid individuals in either protecting or advancing their economic well-being.[35]

The ways by which fertility was controlled, at least in these early stages of the transition from high to low birth rates, are not certain. We do know that deliberate family limitation was practiced by at least one part of the American population by 1800. There is no reason why other groups were not capable of the same behavior given proper motivation. There can be little doubt that family limitation within marriage became widespread during the nineteenth century, but it is also possible that part of the reduction in the birth rate from about 50 per 1,000 in 1800 to 18.5 per 1,000 in 1900 was the result of altered marriage patterns.[36] Etienne van de Walle has shown that in nineteenth-century France, both late marriage and family limitation within marriage were used to control childbearing, though generally only one method or the other was used in a particular locality.[37] Thus, it is plausible that both marriage patterns and marital fertility could have been altered by residents of the United States to ensure their future well-being by limiting births. Unfortunately, our knowledge of nineteenth-century marriage patterns does not allow us to determine which means of control was more prevalent at that time. Suffice it to say that both may be rational responses to a perceived problem and hence either means of control would fit the hypothesis as stated earlier.

The decline in the birth rate which began around 1800 (if not before) continued until 1933 when it leveled off. After several years of minor fluctuation, the birth rate began to climb slowly after 1938, and spurted upwards between 1940 and 1947. Had it not been for peculiarities in the age composition, the birth rate would have continued to climb until 1957, at which point it once again would have declined.[38] This baby boom, which occurred primarily after World War II, has been extremely difficult for Transition theory to explain. At a time when America was more urbanized and industrialized than ever before, fertility should have decreased rather than risen. As the theory has been reformulated here, however, the baby boom makes more sense. Often reduced fertility involves the postponement of children who might be desired if circumstances permitted. In such a situation, any favorable change in the environment might lead to a sudden surge in fertility. As Richard Easterlin has suggested, this seems to be exactly what happened after World War II.[39] For a variety of reasons, persons in the prime childbearing years were unusually prosperous. This alone might well have increased the birth rate, for the same reaction may have occurred in England in the late eighteenth and early nineteenth centuries as rising incomes were accompanied briefly by rising births, much to Malthus' dismay.[40] However, the perception of well-being in post-World War II America must certainly have been accentuated by the contrast with the decade of the 1930s, a recent and vivid memory to those who had the boom babies. Why the boom came to an end is not clear, though we can surmise that a decade of high fertility was enough once again to emphasize the high costs of children, even in times of prosperity.

So far we have seen how the modified version of Transition theory can help to explain variations in fertility patterns in American history which were inconsistent with the earlier theory. It is now time to turn our attention to the way in which the hypothesis advanced above may help to connect demographic change with altered kinship relationships and attitudes toward women and children.

Recall that traditional societies place an emphasis on order and stability. Everyone has a place in society and is expected to stay there until death. Human dignity and individual development are not considered important in such societies. In contrast, modern values place an emphasis on achievement (often monetary) and equality before the law. Although the evidence is scarce, it is possible to suggest that as modern values replaced traditional ones in America, attitudes toward family, women, and children altered significantly.

It is convenient to look first at the studies of colonial families in Andover and Dedham, Massachusetts done by Philip Greven and Kenneth Lockridge respectively.[41] Both these works show that in the seventeenth century, families were well ordered and controlled. The ideals described by Edmund Morgan in *The Puritan Family* were being practiced there.[42] Perhaps the most remarkable finding was the extraordinary authority exercised by parents over their older children. Of course, the desire to inherit the farm may have had some influence on keeping sons dutiful, but in a land of abundant acreage, it seems implausible that such control could have worked without a system of values which encouraged duty and suppressed any thoughts of individual advancement. Interestingly enough, in both Dedham and Andover control broke down in the eighteenth century, precisely the time when newer attitudes were emerging. John Demos' study of Plymouth indicates a rather high degree of mobility there, suggesting that modern attitudes may have emerged slightly earlier among the Separatists than among the Puritans.[43] However, even among the Plymouth inhabitants authority within the family was important.

I have argued elsewhere that attitudes regarding the family had changed noticeably by the time of the American Revolution.[44] No longer were marriage and life in a family deemed necessary for all individuals. Alternative roles and alternative living arrangements became more acceptable by the end of the eighteenth century. By the nineteenth century, family ties seem to have loosened even further. Mobility was common as a series of recent community studies have shown.[45] No longer did individuals wait at home to inherit the family farm. Rather, Americans set out to improve their lot. And, if the evidence is to be believed, they kept on moving until they established themselves economically. Clearly, attitudes by this time favored individual advancement rather than passive acceptance of fate—a plot made famous by Horatio Alger. One hardly need add that migration for personal betterment is still a prominent feature of American life.

When we look at the actual structure of families, the evidence appears somewhat confusing as to whether nuclear or extended families prevailed. On the one hand, we find nuclear families common before 1800; on the other hand, kinship ties today are still important to many groups in our society. In the end, this debate over whether extended or nuclear families prevailed may miss the point. Instead of worrying over whether an individual had only immediate relatives or a large family to associate with, perhaps we should concern ourselves with the quality of those relationships. Michael Anderson has shown, for example, that in nineteenth-century Lancashire, extended families existed in towns, but on the basis of mutual aid and for calculated advantage.[46] Families were to be used for protection and advancement. They were not designed to control an individual and keep him in his place. The kinship ties among various American ethnic groups seem remarkably similar to this pattern, encouraging rather than restricting individual advancement.[47] However typical the Andover families of the seventeenth century may have been at that time, such relationships seem to have dissolved as modern values became more prevalent.

As traditional values gave way to modern, we might expect parental attitudes toward children to shift—and that they did. Studies of both Puritan and Quaker attitudes toward children show that before the middle of the eighteenth century, parents felt their main duties were controlling the child until he was responsible and trying to protect the state of his soul.[48]

Little emphasis was placed on the development of individuality; life after death was considered more important than life on earth. Gradually, these attitudes changed. Parents began to respect, rather than fear, the unique qualities of their children. Discipline remained important, but by the first half of the nineteenth century it was important to insure success in this world rather than the next. Parents came to feel that they had a significant role to play in shaping their children's future; not all had been predestined or would be decided by fate.[49] The childrearing literature of the early twentieth century was much like that found a hundred years before, with one exception. In addition to being taught that they could influence a child's success, parents were told they could shape his health as well. In the 1830s death was still only partly predictable and controllable; by the 1930s disease was something to be prevented or cured, not endured.[50] Thus, rather than viewing attitudes toward children as either cause or effect of variations in fertility or infant mortality, or as the result of an urban-industrial society, it seems more useful to see lower fertility, attempts to improve health, and notions of a child's unique qualities all as recognitions that the future on earth has some promise, especially if people work at improving it.

The role of women also seems to have evolved as modern values came to replace traditional attitudes. In the seventeenth century legal and social pressures combined to limit women's roles outside of marriage. By the time of the Revolution, however, legal changes began to indicate a recognition that women had equal rights before the law as property holders, an essential characteristic of modern society.[51] Furthermore, attitudes toward marriage changed at the same time. No longer were unwed women oddities; those who married were able to choose a husband more on the basis of love, rather than for economic considerations. Individual happiness increasingly played a part in a woman's choices—in fact, women had choices by 1800 in a way they had not apparently had a century earlier.[52]

The nineteenth century was a time of paradox for women in America. On the one hand, women joined in various reform movements as never before, expressing, it seems to me, the notion that the future could be improved. On the other hand, women were seen as the unchanging repositories of purity and virtue, who, among other things, suffered with great patience.[53] This latter attitude sounds remarkably traditional, but given the extent of reform activity on the part of nineteenth-century women, it is hard to believe that they felt no chance to alter the future. Rather, I would suggest, many of the notions of purity and suffering were related to sex. Women were not supposed to enjoy sex, while at the same time they were to understand the animal drives of their husbands and sons, especially when they strayed to prostitutes. While these attitudes may seem strangely out of place today, they may have made good sense in the nineteenth century. At a time when people wanted to limit births but had only crude means available, it may have been useful to deny a woman's interest in sex. *Coitus interruptus* could not have been terribly satisfying to many women. Likewise, prostitution, whatever its evils, served as one means of reducing the risk of pregnancy for wives.

It is of interest to note that the admission that women, like men, have a sexual side corresponds nicely to the development of more efficient and less obtrusive forms of birth control.[54] The twentieth century has seen a greater concern for the development of a woman's full personality than ever before. It may well be that this has happened not only as a result of modern attitudes but also because more effective birth-control methods have allowed these attitudes to prevail, whereas in the nineteenth century the desire to control fertility worked at cross purposes to any tendency to liberate women.

One last point deserves mention before we examine what future research on the family should entail. Not all parts of the American population have experienced changes in mortality and fertility at the same rate. Undoubtedly some of the variations can be explained by different preferences for the ideal family size, by different promises for the future, and by different access to the best birth-control methods. At the same time, at least parts of the population may simply have maintained traditional attitudes much longer than others. Blacks, for example, seem to have had levels of fertility and mortality in the late nineteenth century which were unchanged from the colonial period, when their experience was much the same as the whites.[55] Undoubtedly some of this can be explained by the denial of medical services to blacks, but we should not overlook the possibility that under slavery and the Jim Crow laws there was little reason to hope for the future. For many blacks, the world was uncontrollable and uncertain, much as it is for many peasant cultures today. Interestingly, once blacks began to move out of the South (an action which in itself is indicative of a sense that the future can be improved) and into the cities, the demographic differences between the races narrowed noticeably.[56] Although differences still exist, the trends since the 1930s have been remarkably similar, suggesting that many of the factors which determine fertility and mortality are color blind, even if much of the rest of our society is not.

In contrast to the black experience, the Hutterites, a religious group in the northern plains states, continue to have children at a rate that only the colonists could match.[57] This is noteworthy because the religious values of this group are extremely conservative and very traditional. Order, discipline, and the submission of the individual are important values to these people. While they are aware that the future can be controlled, they are more concerned with the success of the group than with the development of the individual. Unlike immigrant groups who fostered kinship ties to protect and advance the individual, the Hutterites use kinship ties to subordinate individual success to the good of the whole, a very traditional attitude.

As projected here, the new version of the theory of Demographic Transition appears to make better sense of the historical facts of fertility and mortality changes. In addition, the emphasis on a revolution in values serves to integrate many of the disparate approaches to the study of families in the past. Nonetheless, what I have said here is only an hypothesis, and as such must be tested and presumably revised. It is my hope that historians of the family will find this task worthwhile, not only because it has some significance in a world faced with problems of implementing large-scale reductions in fertility, but also because this hypothesis can provide some unity to research on the family.

What needs to be done? First, we need to know more precisely when fertility, mortality, and migration patterns changed in the past. These patterns must be connected with the revolution in values I have assumed to have occurred. If modern attitudes do not predate or at least overlap with new forms of demographic behavior, then the whole hypothesis falls. Likewise, it is important to determine how the changes occurred. In part this is important because we need to know which changes were deliberate and controlled and which were accidental results of other changes in behavior. In the case of fertility, it is useful to know, for example, that a falling birth rate came from birth control rather than new marriage patterns, because the attitudes toward women and children and the future trends of childbearing may be determined by which method is used.

Of considerable interest here are comparative studies. Such comparisons would be cross-national, cross-cultural, or based on socioeconomic differences within a society. The theory, as outlined here, seems to fit the American experience. But does it hold in Europe or Japan? Furthermore, do regions which have still to experience the demographic transition all have traditional attitudes? Have recent declines in mortality been the result of the acceptance of modern attitudes, or have they been imposed from above by an imported medical technology?

Obviously most students of family history will continue to have more interest in one aspect of the family than another. This is understandable and is probably the most practical approach to the immediate problem of finding out what families in the past have been like. At the same time, I would hope that no longer would one definition of or approach toward the family be considered the only appropriate one. Studies of the family should no longer focus exclusively on kinship, or fertility rates, or child-rearing practices, or the role of women. Rather, they should seek to incorporate all relevant changes in values and behavior which may have affected the family. We must accept the idea that as a subject, the family is a complex but highly interrelated entity. A satisfactory approach to the history of the family must involve a study of all aspects of behavior within the family setting, as well as recognizing that family patterns are closely related to more general attitudes and behavior patterns of the society under study.[58]

## NOTES

1. Several older studies do exist. One of the first was Arthur W. Calhoun, *A Social History of the American Family*, 3 vols. (Cleveland, 1917). More useful are the works by Philippe Ariès, *Centuries of Childhood* (New York, 1965); and Edmund S. Morgan, *The Puritan Family*, rev. ed. (New York, 1966).

2. See, for example, Bernard Bailyn, *The New England Merchants in the Seventeenth Century* (New York, 1964); John Demos, "Families in Colonial Bristol, Rhode Island; An Exercise

in Historical Demography," *William and Mary Quarterly* 25 (1968): 40–57; Philip Greven, *Four Generations* (Ithaca, 1970); and Leonard Labaree, *Conservatism in Early America* (Ithaca, 1948), pp. 1–31. At least two journals have devoted whole issues to the family in history; see *Journal of Interdisciplinary History* 2 (1971), and *Journal of Marriage and the Family*, Vol. 35 (1973).

3. Mary S. Benson, *Women in Eighteenth-Century America* (New York, 1935); Edward Shorter, "Female Emancipation, Birth Control, and Fertility in European History," *American Historical Review* 78 (1973): 605–640; Bernard Wishy, *The Child and the Republic* (Philadelphia, 1968).

4. John Demos, "Underlying Themes in the Witchcraft of Seventeenth-Century New England," *American Historical Review* 75 (1970): 1311–1326; Pierre Goubert, *Beauvais et la Beauvaisis de 1600 – 1730* (Paris[?], 1960); Kenneth Lockridge, *A New England Town* (New York, 1970); Lewis Namier, *The Structure of Politics at the Accession of George III*, 2nd ed. (London, 1957); Lawrence Stone, *The Crisis of the Aristocracy* (Oxford, 1965), pp. 589–671.

5. The studies published in *Annales: Economies, Sociétés, Civilisations* and under the auspices of L'Institut national d'études démographiques are clear exceptions as the French scholars quite clearly build on each others' work.

6. Reference to the demographic transition appears in virtually all major texts on population; see, for example, Donald Bogue, *Principles of Demography* (New York, 1969) or William Peterson, *Population*, 2nd ed. (London, 1969). It also plays a prominent role in such recent studies as Ita I. Ekanem, "A Further Note on the Relation between Economic Development and Fertility," *Demography* 9 (1972); 383–398; H. J. Habakkuk, *Population Growth and Economic Development Since 1750* (New York, 1971); Donnella H. Meadows et al., *The Limits to Growth* (New York, 1972); and E. A. Wrigley, *Population and History* (New York, 1969).

7. T. H. Hollingsworth, *Historical Demography* (Ithaca, 1969), pp. 307–311, 355–388. The data on growth rates in the British colonies are contained in Robert V. Wells, *The Population of the British Colonies in America Before 1776: A Survey of Census Data* (Princeton, 1975).

8. Published in D. V. Glass and Roger Revelle, eds., *Population and Social Change* (New York, 1972), pp. 99–114. Many of the articles in this book first appeared in *Daedalus* 97 (1968), an issue of the journal devoted to historical population studies.

9. Jean Ganiage, *Trois Villages de l'Ile-de-France* (Paris, 1963); Akira Hayami, "The Demographic Analysis of a Village in Tokugawa Japan," *Keio Economic Studies* 5 (1967–1968): 50–88; Louis Henry, *Anciennes Familles Genevoises* (Paris, 1956); T. H. Hollingsworth, *The Demography of the British Peerage*, supplement to *Population Studies* 18 (1964); R. V. Wells, "Family Size and Fertility Control in Eighteenth-Century America," *Population Studies* 25 (1971): 73–82; E. A. Wrigley, "Family Limitation in Pre-industrial England," *Economic History Review*, 2nd Ser., 19 (1966): 82–109.

10. Wrigley, *Population and History*, pp. 179–184.

11. First published in 1936 in Baltimore. Himes argues that birth-control knowledge was not widespread and that fertility fell because it was diffused. His evidence seems to me to support the contrary position just as well, if not better.

12. Hollingsworth, *British Peerage*; Wrigley, "Family Limitation."

13. Wells, "Family Size and Fertility Control."

14. Cecil K. Drinker, *Not So Long Ago* (New York, 1937), pp. 55, 59.

15. Himes, *Medical History of Contraception*, pp. 201–206.

16. Kinglsey Davis, "Population Policy: Will Current Programs Succeed?" *Science* 158 (1967): 730–739.

17. Several studies from various parts of the world deal not only with this issue but also show that values play an important role in determining demographic behavior. See J. A. Banks, *Prosperity and Parenthood* (London, 1954); J. A. and Olive Banks, *Feminism and Family Planning in Victorian England* (New York, 1964); William B. Clifford, II. "Modern and Traditional Value Orientations and Fertility Behavior," *Demography* 8 (1971): 37–48; Eva Mueller, "Economic Motives for Family Limitation: A Study Conducted in Taiwan," *Population Studies* 26 (1972): 383–403; and Shorter, "Female Emancipation."

18. After considerable thought I have decided to use the terms "traditional" and "modern"

here. There is an immense literature on these terms, much of it reflecting the peculiar interests of the authors. Hopefully my use of these terms will be made clear in the definitions which follow.

19. Included in Harrison Brown and Edward Hutchings, Jr., eds., *Are Our Descendants Doomed?* (New York, 1970), pp. 335–357.

20. E. A. Wrigley, "The Process of Modernization and the Industrial Revolution in England," *Journal of Interdisciplinary History* 3 (1972): 225–259.

21. Edmund S. Morgan, "The Labor Problem at Jamestown, 1607–1618," *American Historical Review* 76 (1971): 595–611.

22. Perry Miller's two volumes on *The New England Mind* (Cambridge, Mass., 1953) are the obvious place to begin an understanding of Puritan attitudes. But Edmund S. Morgan, *The Puritan Dilemma* (Boston, 1962) offers an excellent, short introduction.

23. Richard D. Brown, "Modernization and the Modern Personality in Early America, 1600–1865: A Sketch of a Synthesis," *Journal of Interdisciplinary History* 2 (1972): 201–228. Richard Dunn's study of the Winthrop family, *Puritans and Yankees* (Princeton, 1962) offers an interesting illustration of this change occurring within one family.

24. Wrigley, "Process of Modernization," p. 230.

25. W. T. Baxter, *The House of Hancock* (Cambridge, Mass., 1945); James B. Hedges, *The Browns of Providence Plantations*, vol. 1 (Cambridge, Mass., 1952); John J. Waters, Jr., *The Otis Family in Provincial and Revolutionary Massachusetts* (Chapel Hill, N.C., 1968); Philip L. White, *The Beekmans of New York in Politics and Commerce, 1647–1877* (New York, 1956).

26. John Duffy, *Epidemics in Colonial America* (Baton Rouge, La., 1953), pp. 16–106.

27. Otho T. Beall, Jr., "Cotton Mather, the First Significant Figure in American Medicine," *Bulletin of the History of Medicine* 26 (1952): 103–116, discusses some of Mather's motives; the statistics produced during the eighteenth century may be found in Massachusetts Historical Society, *Collections*, 1st Ser., vol. 3 (1794), p. 292.

28. Two of the notable results of this interest are Edward Wigglesworth, "A Table Showing the Probability of the Duration, the Decrement, and the Expectation of Life in the States of Massachusetts and New Hampshire, formed from sixty-two Bills of Mortality on the Files of the American Academy of Arts and Sciences in the year 1789," *Memoirs* of the American Academy of Arts and Sciences, vol. 2, pt. 1 (1791): 131–135; and Joseph McKean, "Synopsis of Several Bills of Mortality," *Memoirs*, A.A.A.S., vol. 2, pt. 2 (1804): 62–65.

29. Richard H. Shryock, *Medicine and Society in America, 1660–1860* (New York, 1960).

30. Wells, "Family Size and Fertility Control."

31. Wrigley, "Family Limitations"; Ganiage, *Trois Villages;* Menoru Muramateu, "Changing Attitudes Toward Population Growth in Japan," in Brown and Hutchings, eds., *Are Our Descendants Doomed?*, pp. 266–277.

32. Kenneth Lockridge, "Land, Population, and the Evolution of New England Society, 1630–1790," *Past and Present* no. 39 (1968): 62–80. This pattern is also apparent in Charles Grant, *Democracy in the Connecticut Frontier Town of Kent* (New York, 1961), especially pp. 83–103; and Greven, *Four Generations.*

33. U. S. Bureau of the Census, *A Century of Population Growth* (Washington, 1909), pp. 96, 100.

34. Published in New Haven in 1972, this work elaborates on Yasukichi Yasuba, *Birth Rates of the White Population in the United States, 1800–1860* (Baltimore, 1962).

35. In addition to Banks, *Prosperity and Parenthood;* and Mueller, "Economic Motives;" see David M. Kennedy, *Birth Control in America* (New Haven, 1970), pp. 45–50 for evidence that fertility is often controlled for economic reasons.

36. Estimates of the birth rate vary. This author has used those in Ansley J. Coale and Melvin Zelnik, *New Estimates of Fertility and Population in the United States* (Princeton, 1963), pp. 21–22, 34. The only major study of marriage patterns, Thomas P. Monahan, *The Pattern of Age at Marriage in the United States* (Philadelphia, 1951) offers little help on this subject.

37. Etienne van de Walle, "Marriage and Marital Fertility," in Glass and Revelle, eds., *Population and Social Change*, pp. 135–151.

38. Coale and Zelnik, *New Estimates,* pp. 23, 36.

39. Richard Easterlin, *The American Baby Boom in Historical Perspective* (New York, 1962).

40. This change is rather complex as is evident in Wrigley, "Modernization," pp. 250–256. Malthus' reaction to these phenomena is, of course, to be found in T. R. Malthus, *An Essay on the Principle of Population, as It Affects the Future Improvement of Society* (London, 1798; reprinted with the 7th edition, New York, 1960).

41. Greven, *Four Generations;* Lockridge, *A New England Town.*

42. See note 1.

43. John Demos, *A Little Commonwealth* (New York, 1970).

44. Robert V. Wells, "Quaker Marriage Patterns in a Colonial Perspective," *William and Mary Quarterly* 29 (1972): 436–439.

45. There are a number of such studies; among the most prominent are Merle Curti, *The Making of an American Community* (Stanford, 1959); Richard J. Hopkins, "Occupational and Geographic Mobility in Atlanta, 1870–1896," *Journal of Southern History* 34 (1968): 200–213; and Stephan Thernstrom and Peter R. Knights, "Men in Motion: Some Data and Speculations about Urban Population Mobility in Nineteenth-Century America," in Tamara Hareven, ed., *Anonymous Americans* (Englewood Cliffs, N.J., 1971), pp. 17–47.

46. Michael Anderson, *Family Structure in Nineteenth-Century Lancashire* (Cambridge, Eng., 1971).

47. The literature on immigrants is immense, but among the most helpful places to start is Philip Taylor, *The Distant Magnet* (New York, 1971), especially chapters 9–12. Two other works of some interest are John J. Appel, ed., *The New Immigration* (New York, 1971); and, of course, Oscar Handlin, *The Uprooted* (Boston, 1951).

48. Sandford Fleming, *Children and Puritanism* (New Haven, 1933); Jerry W. Frost, "As the Twig is Bent: Quaker Ideas of Childhood," *Bulletin* of the Friends Historical Association (Autumn, 1971): 67–87; Walter J. Homan, *Children and Quakerism* (Berkeley, 1939).

49. For evidence that these changes occurred in other groups, see David J. Rothman, *The Discovery of the Asylum* (Boston, 1971), chs. 2, 3, 9; and Wishy, *Child and the Republic.*

50. Compare, for example, John S. C. Abbot, *The Mother at Home* (London, 1834), or Lydia Child, *The Mother's Book* (Boston, 1831), with *The Child Rearing Literature of Twentieth Century America* (New York, 1972), compiled and published by Arno Press.

51. Richard B. Morris, *Studies in the History of American Law* (New York, 1930), ch. 3, "Women's Rights in Early American Law."

52. Herman R. Lantz et al., "Pre-Industrial Patterns in the Colonial Family in America," *American Sociological Review* 33 (1968): 413–426; Wells, "Quaker Marriage Patterns," pp. 428–439.

53. The clearest statement of this position is Barbara Welter, "The Cult of True Womanhood: 1820–1860," *American Quarterly* 18 (1966): 151–174. A more complex view is given in Charles E. Rosenberg, "Sexuality, Class and Role in 19th-Century America," *American Quarterly* 25 (1973): 131–153.

54. Kennedy, *Birth Control in America,* pp. 36–135; Page Smith, *Daughters of the Promised Land* (Boston, 1970), pp. 227–252.

55. Reynolds Farley, "The Demographic Rates and Social Institutions of the Nineteenth-Century Negro Population," *Demography* 2 (1965): 386–398.

56. The movement into the cities and the motives behind this migration are presented clearly in Clyde Kiser, *Sea Island to City* (New York, 1932); for recent trends in fertility and mortality see Irene B. and Conrad Taeuber, *People of the United States in the 20th Century* (Washington, 1971, a census monograph), pp. 443–453, 500–517.

57. J. W. Eaton and A. J. Mayer, "The Social Biology of Very High Fertility among the Hutterites," *Human Biology* 25 (1953): 206–264.

58. Since this article was written, a number of works on various aspects of family history have appeared. Because the original notation was illustrative rather than exhaustive I have chosen not to revise the manuscript to include the more recent examples. More important, my ongoing reading has only reenforced my belief in the hypothesis offered above.

# 25 | FACTORS IN THE DECLINE OF FARM FAMILY FERTILITY IN THE UNITED STATES: SOME PRELIMINARY RESEARCH RESULTS

## RICHARD A. EASTERLIN

Great movements in the history of world population have often been a source of conjecture among historians.[1] The most spectacular population development has been the surge and subsequent slowdown in population growth in industrializing countries during the modern era, the so-called "demographic transition." Early scholars viewed the demographic transition, and particularly the decline in fertility that caused the slowdown in population growth, as a result of urbanization and industrialization, though the specific links between these processes and fertility were unclear.[2] Recent work, however, has suggested the importance of decreasing fertility of the rural population in the total fertility decline.

Nowhere has the role of the rural population been more evident than in the United States. The level of American fertility in the eighteenth century was one of the highest ever recorded. For the early part of the nineteenth century, however, when the population was 90 to 95 percent rural, there is unmistakable evidence of a downtrend, and there are indications of declines in rural fertility even before 1800.[3] By 1900, the fertility of the rural white population was only about 60 percent of that a century earlier. This decline occurred in all geographic areas of the country, although it varied in magnitude.[4]

The decline in rural fertility took place in a country where good farm land was cheaper and more abundant perhaps than anywhere in the world. Environmental constraints on population growth were seemingly at a minimum, a point that Thomas R. Malthus was quick to note.[5] Yet despite seemingly abundant agricultural opportunities, a substantial and persistent downtrend in the fertility of the American farm population set in quite early.

Why, in view of the apparent absence of pressures for reduction, did such an early and continuous fertility decline take place? This question is the genesis of the investigation of American farms and farm families on which this paper provides a preliminary report.[6] Although no definite

Richard A. Easterlin is professor of economics in the University of Pennsylvania. The author acknowledges the financial assistance of the National Institute of Child Health and Human Development.

533

answer can yet be given, the results so far help to distinguish between more and less plausible explanations. The results also open up more general questions on which new research, particularly by historians, is needed.

The methodology used in this research can be labeled collective biography. The basic data set is comprised of a massive sample of rural households taken by Fred Bateman and James D. Foust from the 1860 federal manuscript censuses. The sample covers all households living on farms or in rural villages in each of 102 townships scattered across sixteen northern states from New Hampshire to Kansas.[7] Households living in towns or cities in these townships are excluded. In all there are 20,664 households, almost all of which are white. Over half of the household heads—those on whom the present paper chiefly focuses—lived and worked on farms, but even among those not living on farms, probably as many as half or more worked on farms.

The data for each household in the sample include almost all information from the free population census schedule, and, for each farm household, information from the agricultural schedule as well. The availability for farm households of matched demographic and economic data and the unusually large sample size offer exceptional analytical opportunities.

The present approach follows the line of inquiry opened up by the studies of Yasukichi Yasuba and Colin Forster and G. S. L. Tucker, among others.[8] These scholars, noting the much higher fertility levels in newer western states than in older eastern states, both in the North and the South, sought clues to the rural fertility decline in factors associated with a regional differential. But the depth of their studies was limited by an inability to go beyond the aggregative published census data. In contrast, the data used here permit singling out and comparing the demographic and economic circumstances of individual farm households.

Initially, households have been grouped according to the stage of settlement of the townships in which they lived, as measured by the ratio of improved agricultural land in 1860 to the maximum ever improved.[9] "New" areas are those where a high proportion of agricultural land was unimproved by 1860, conversely, for "old" areas. The data for all households falling in each of five settlement classes from new to old were combined to obtain measures of average family fertility, average farm size and value, and so on (see Table 1).

The measure of fertility used in most previous studies is the "child-woman ratio," that is, the ratio of children under ten to women of reproductive age, computed from published census data on the sex and age distribution of the population, usually by state. The authors of earlier studies were well aware that differences of fertility between old and new states shown by such a measure might be caused by differences in the composition of the population by marital status, age, and place of residence. Attempts to test for these influences showed that the child-woman ratio tended to be lower in older compared with newer states because of a lower proportion of married females and a larger share of lower fertility urban-industrial persons in the population. Differences in the age distribution of reproductive-aged women had little, if any, systematic effect on the child-woman ratio in older versus newer states.[10] Most importantly, however,

**Table 1.** MEAN VALUE OF SPECIFIED ITEM FOR FARM HUSBAND-WIFE HOUSE-
HOLDS WITH WIFE AGED 30–39, BY SETTLEMENT CLASS, BATEMAN-FOUST NORTHERN
FARM SAMPLE, 1860

| ITEM | Farm Settlement Class[a] | | | | | |
|------|----------------|---------|------|-----|-----|--------|
| | ALL CLASSES | I (OLD) | II | III | IV | V (NEW) |
| Number of households | 2,870 | 757 | 766 | 470 | 565 | 312 |
| Children 0–9 per woman 20–49 | 2.11 | 1.77 | 2.01 | 2.40 | 2.42 | 2.22 |
| Percent of heads born abroad | 15 | 11 | 13 | 17 | 16 | 28 |
| Age of wife | 34.3 | 34.5 | 34.2 | 34.2 | 34.2 | 34.3 |
| Age of mother at first birth | 22.7 | 23.3 | 22.8 | 21.8 | 21.9 | 23.7 |
| Age of mother at latest birth | 29.6 | 28.9 | 29.2 | 30.2 | 30.3 | 29.9 |
| Persons under 15 per household | 3.40 | 2.99 | 3.25 | 3.80 | 3.80 | 3.42 |
| Persons 55 and over per household | .13 | .18 | .18 | .10 | .09 | .04 |
| Percent literate: | | | | | | |
| a. Husbands | 94 | 96 | 96 | 93 | 89 | 93 |
| b. Wives | 91 | 97 | 96 | 87 | 84 | 86 |
| Percent attending school | | | | | | |
| a. Males 10–14 | 84 | 85 | 87 | 88 | 81 | 71 |
| b. Females 10–14 | 82 | 84 | 86 | 86 | 81 | 61 |
| Percent of heads with real property | 88 | 87 | 90 | 91 | 88 | 76 |
| Total acres per farm | 126 | 109 | 113 | 134 | 152 | 142 |
| Improved acres per farm | 67 | 78 | 71 | 69 | 60 | 37 |
| Value of farm, dollars | 2,607 | 3,316 | 2,863 | 2,527 | 2,017 | 1,446 |
| Percent of migrants with all children born in state of residence[b] | 74 | — | 87 | 84 | 79 | 35 |

Source: Easterlin, Alter, and Condran, "Farms and Farm Families in Old and New Areas."

a. Households are grouped according to the farm settlement class of the township in which they reside. Settlement classes, consisting of quintiles from 0 to 100 percent, are established by computing for each county containing a sample township the percentage of ever-improved agricultural land not improved by 1860.

b. For migrants with at least two children and head born in north central or southern states.

these tests indicate that after controlling for differences in population composition there were real and sizeable fertility differences between old and new states.

The data for individual households used here—rather than the standardization procedures customarily used in analyzing published census data—enable one to look more closely at the differences in fertility between old and new areas. There was a marked difference between old and new areas in the reproductive performance of households living on farms and in which the wife was in her thirties and living with her husband.[11] On the average, the child-woman ratio of farm women in the oldest area— that where most of the land is already improved—was about 25 percent less than that in the area of highest fertility.[12] The difference was about the same as that shown by published census data for approximately the same geographic areas.[13] Fertility rises consistently as one moves from older to newer settlement areas, with one exception. Average fertility in the "frontier townships," while higher than in the oldest area, was perhaps 5 to 10 percent lower than in the newly settled areas slightly behind the frontier, those with approximately 20 to 40 percent of their land improved.

It is possible that fertility differences between older and newer areas reflect variations in the native and foreign-born composition of the farm population. Higher fertility in newer areas perhaps reflects a disproportionate share in those areas of high fertility immigrants. The data do show somewhat higher fertility rates for foreign-born than native-born Americans in rural areas: on the average, the excess was about 13 percent. Thus, the Forster and Tucker speculation that the foreign-native-born differential at midcentury might show an excess for native-born Americans over immigrants is not supported by these data, although it should be noted that this sample excludes southern states, which generally had a higher level of fertility.[14] Nevertheless, variations among areas in the relative importance of foreign-born account for a negligible share of the fertility difference between older and newer areas. This is because the relative importance of the foreign-born population is quite similar in older and newer areas; for example, the proportions of foreign-born in the population in the lowest and highest fertility areas are, respectively, 13 and 16 percent.[15] A search for the causes of lower fertility in more settled areas must center, therefore, on the factors shaping the behavior of native-born Americans.

Analogous reasoning might be applied to the composition of the native-born population. The fertility of natives born in the South and Midwest was higher than that of those born in the Northeast. Perhaps lower fertility in older areas was due to a disproportionately high share of low-fertility northeasterners. In this case, the composition of the population does tend to raise the child-woman ratio in newer versus older areas. The shares of northeasterners in the population of the lowest and highest fertility areas are, respectively, 78 and 18 percent. However, this compositional factor is not the dominant source of the fertility differential between older and newer areas. If one segregates in the sample those born in the Northeast and compares their fertility by area of residence, one finds that the fertility of northeasterners living in the highest fertility area is 20 percent above that of those living in the lowest fertility area. It appears, therefore, that there was a substantial fertility difference between newer and older areas that cannot be explained in terms of the origins of the population of these areas.

Before turning to an examination of substantive hypotheses, one must ask whether the observed differences in fertility arise from deficiencies in the basic census data or the particular measure of fertility used. At least three problems merit attention: child and maternal mortality, children absent from the household, and deficiencies in census enumeration. The question is whether the problem may have a differential incidence between older and newer areas of a type that might produce the observed variation in child-woman ratios.

Mortality takes its toll both of children and mothers and thus influences both numerator and denominator of the child-woman ratio. Since rates of infant and child mortality are much higher than maternal mortality, the principal concern relates to possible biases in the numerator of the ratio. Clearly the child-woman ratio understates the number of births per woman over the preceding ten years because of the omission of children who die prior to the census enumeration date. For the present purpose, the question is whether this downward bias is greater in older areas than newer areas: is it possible that the lower child-woman ratio in older areas may reflect, not lower fertility, but higher infant and child mortality? The scarcity of systematic research on nineteenth-century American mortality makes it difficult to answer this question. The safest generalization is that urban mortality was much higher than rural.[16] Clearly this would depress state-wide child-woman ratios in eastern versus western states. But the child-woman ratios for farm households in the present analysis exclude the high mortality urban population and thus are not subject to this bias. One might argue, of course, that even on farms mortality in eastern areas was greater than in western areas because of greater contact with urban centers in the East. As an offsetting influence, however, one might suppose that the hardships of childbearing under isolated circumstances were felt more heavily in western areas. The one bit of evidence presently at hand is Yasuba's analysis of the 1850 census returns on mortality. His calculation of the death rate for white children under ten years old shows, for the states included in this sample, somewhat higher mortality in the East than in the West.[17] This difference appears to be largely or wholly due, however, to differences in urbanization: the most urbanized western states, Ohio and Missouri, have mortality rates much like those of New York, New Jersey, and Pennsylvania. While much remains to be done on this question, it is unlikely that infant and child mortality differences by geographic area within the farm population could account for variation in the child-woman ratio of the magnitude observed.

The present estimates of child-woman ratios include only children present in the farm household at the time of enumeration. Children of the nuclear family who live away from home were counted in their place of residence. If these children lived on nearby farms, no bias would occur in the regional average. Higher out-migration, however, from eastern farms to urban areas or the frontier would produce a differential downward bias in the child-woman ratio in the eastern areas. There is internal evidence in the present data of the absence of nuclear children from the household, but this appears chiefly to be true of children fifteen years of age and over.[15] Since the fertility measure relates to children under ten, it should be largely free of bias from this source. Of course, younger children might go to live elsewhere with older teenage siblings, but the present fertility comparisons relate chiefly to women under forty, and this group had relatively few older teenagers.[19] Altogether, it seems unlikely that this problem accounts for the substantial fertility variation observed here.

As for the problem of deficiencies in census enumeration, one might speculate that the likelihood of missing whole families would be greater in frontier areas than in long established farm areas. It seems likely too that children, especially infants, are undercounted, and that this undercount is considerably larger in relative terms than for other age-sex groups, including women of reproductive age.[20] For the present purpose, however, these observations are not particularly pertinent; the real issue is whether the underenumeration of children relative to reproductive women would be greater in eastern areas, biasing downward the child-woman ratio for these areas compared with the West. Although there is no evidence to go on, this seems doubtful. One would suppose that children would be less likely to be missed in eastern areas because the enumerators were probably more experienced and because parents were less likely to omit mention of new offspring if families were smaller.

The assessment of possible statistical biases points to the conclusion that these factors cannot account for the observed variation in child-woman ratios. There are, in short, real fertility differences between farm households in older and newer areas.

Since it is doubtful that biological constraints limited the fertility of eastern more than western farm wives, the next question is whether lower fertility in the East resulted from marriage practices that led to more limited exposure to the possibility of childbearing, or to the deliberate restriction of fertility within marriage, or both.[21] The answer appears to be "both." The age at marriage for women in the sample cannot be determined, but one can compute a reasonable proxy—age at first birth, computed at the age of wife less age of oldest nuclear child. For farm wives in their thirties, median age at first birth in the oldest settlement areas was 23.3 years, almost one and a half years higher than that in the highest fertility area (see Table 1). This creates a strong presumption that wives on farms in the older areas married later than those in the newer areas.

The only measure so far used to test for the use of deliberate fertility control is median age of mother at most recent birth. For farm wives in their thirties, the median age at most recent birth is lower for wives in the oldest eastern area compared with the highest fertility western area by almost a year and a half, despite the fact that the median age of the wives in the two areas is virtually the same. For women in their forties, the gap between wives in the two areas widens to over two years.[22] It thus appears that eastern wives not only started their childbearing later but terminated it earlier, presumably, at least for some wives, by the deliberate limitation of fertility. The methods of deliberate fertility control cannot be determined, but coitus interruptus and perhaps abortion may be the most likely candidates.

In considering hypotheses about the causes of reduced fertility in older farm areas, focus will be on explaining marital fertility rather than marriage behavior, although the same arguments are sometimes pertinent to both.

A possible source of pressure for reduced childbearing in older areas might be a greater burden of aged dependents. Families settling in newer areas may be freer from the worry of supporting aging relatives and thus more willing to have children. The present data give little support to this hypothesis. Dependency, including both children and aged persons, is much higher in newer areas.[23] This reflects the higher fertility of newer areas, for the dependency ratio is dominated by geographic difference in children per household, not older persons per household (see Table 1). If one looks only at older persons per household, one does find a greater number in the more settled eastern areas. The average number per household is low, however, and not much above that in newer areas. For example, the proportion with no persons fifty-five and over is about 82 percent in the lowest fertility area compared with 91 percent in the highest (see Table 1). Thus most childbearing households, both in the older and newer areas, were free of aged dependents. Some aged dependents might not be living on the farm at the time of enumeration. When one takes account of the sharply sloped age pyramid that is created by a population with recent or current high fertility, the indication of the data that there are not enough aged persons relative to prime-age working adults to create a widespread dependency problem seems correct. Dependency is not a promising lead for explaining the emergence of lower fertility levels in older areas.

Education is often cited as a factor inducing lower fertility, enabling better information about or better practice of ways of limiting fertility. It is further suggested that education changed household tastes or attitudes toward lower fertility and raised the costs of children by widening the job opportunities available to women. The indicators of education, though imperfect, do not show very important differences between newer and older areas. Literacy rates were high throughout the farm population: among wives in the lowest fertility area the literacy rate was over 95 percent, and in the highest fertility areas between 85 and 90 percent (see Table 1). School attendance rates of children aged ten to fourteen were over 75 percent in both the highest and lowest fertility areas, and only slightly lower in the former than the latter (see Table 1). Although these indicators of education are crude, there is reason to suppose that even better measures would not show greatly magnified regional differences in education. This is because the high fertility populations in the newer areas are overwhelmingly native-born migrants. It is reasonable to suppose that these migrants in their new areas of residence tended to create educational arrangements much like those which they had experienced in their area of origin. Therefore, educational differentials are a doubtful cause of the fertility variations between older and newer areas.

A hypothesis currently enjoying some vogue in the economic-demographic literature is that lower fertility is induced by an increasing opportunity cost of women's time. It is supposed that as the education of women advances and their labor market qualifications correspondingly grow, more of them are attracted into paid employment at the expense of childbearing. This hypothesis can be safely rejected for the farm wives in the sample. It has already been shown that the educational differential between older and newer areas was not very great. More important, both in older and newer areas almost no farm wives reported an occupation outside the home. It seems clear that farm wives in older areas were not curtailing their fertility because they had other, more monetarily rewarding things to occupy their time.

While wives in older and newer areas may have differed little in paid employment opportunities, perhaps there were important differences in the need for child labor on farms. Perhaps a farm child's net contribution to family income was lower in older areas and this reduced the incentive for childbearing. The basic premise of the argument—that child labor opportunities were greater in newer areas—is not clearly supported by the available evidence. If one takes the wage rates of adult male farm laborers as one indicator of labor scarcity, one finds the highest wage rates in both the newest and oldest states. In the highest fertility areas—those somewhat behind the frontier—farm wage rates were, in fact, among the lowest in the northern states.[24] The special labor requirements on the frontier related chiefly to adult males, not to children, since the work involved was that of farm making—clearing and breaking land, laying drainage tiles, fencing, and so on.[25] The sample data show that children in farm households on the frontier were typically quite young, and one may question whether their contribution to such tasks was in excess of their costs of rearing. In the highest fertility areas behind the frontier, there were doubtless jobs to which children could contribute, but it is far from clear that such jobs were more plentiful than on eastern farms. Consider the tasks at which children could be especially helpful—hoeing and weeding field crops, milking cows, making butter and cheese, feeding pigs and poultry, tending gardens, collecting eggs, and so on. Aside from the first, these tasks relate especially to work that was likely to be more plentiful on farms producing items for urban markets, such as dairy products and garden vegetables, in short, to farms more likely to be found in the East. Thus, it is far from clear that the child-labor incentive to fertility was lower on farms in older areas than in newer. If one is to explain the lower fertility in older farm areas, one must look primarily to considerations other than the employment opportunities for women and children.

In writing of eighteenth-century New England, Kenneth Lockridge argued that there was a trend toward overcrowding in rural areas and the consequent emergence of a rural proletariat living under adverse conditions.[26] Perhaps such processes were at work more generally in older farm areas in nineteenth-century America and led to pressures to curtail fertility.

The present data give little indication of the growth of a sizeable farm proletariat. On farms in older areas there were .65 to 1.04 additional agricultural workers per farm head; in the highest fertility area this figure ranges between .66 and .84.[27] Most of these workers were young and therefore probably in a transitory stage prior to taking over their own farm. Moreover, the data show that lower fertility in older areas characterized the households of farm operators, not just those dependent on others for employment.

It might be that farm operators were disproportionately tenants in the East. Again, however, this is not supported by the data. The percent of farm heads reporting real property ownership is high and almost identical in the lowest and highest fertility areas, close to 90 percent (see Table 1).

It is true that the average size of farms was smaller in eastern areas, but improved acres per farm were larger (see Table 1). And, average farm value—the best indicator of the income generated by the farm—was more than 50 percent higher in the lowest than in the highest fertility area (see Table 1). It is possible that the farm value figures do not fully reflect the expectations of farmers in newer areas of greater growth in farm income or capital gains from land sales. This qualification aside, it appears that farm households in older areas were having fewer children, despite a greater capacity to support them.

It might be argued that people migrated to newer areas because of higher present or prospective fertility, in which case selective migration would account for higher fertility in newer versus older areas. This argument might be based on natural fertility considerations: for example, those with greater fecundity find their families growing rapidly relative to those with lower fecundity, and, other things equal, feel a greater pressure to move. Or the argument might be based on desired family size: those who want larger families are more likely to move to the frontier.

One problem with this argument is that it leaves unanswered the question of why parents would choose the frontier as a better place for raising a large family. Thus, it leads back to questions of the sort discussed in previous sections, such as whether labor needs were greater in newer areas. A second problem arises when, as logical consistency requires, an analogous argument is applied to farm-nonfarm migration. Since nonfarm fertility was lower than farm, in the case of farm-nonfarm migration the hypothesis would be that nonfarm migration is selective of those prone to lower fertility. But since farm-nonfarm migration was higher in older than newer areas, the farm population in older areas would be relatively depleted of low fertility households, and farm fertility would be raised in older compared with newer areas, an effect contrary to the observation we seek to explain. Finally, the argument is called into doubt by the present evidence. The highest fertility group was not adult migrants on the frontier but those in the area behind the frontier, who although usually born out of state were probably raised from childhood in their current state of residence. It is hard to believe that the childhood migration of this group had anything to do with concerns on their part about family size. Rather, their fertility behavior is more plausibly viewed as a response to their current environment.

Before proceeding to the next hypothesis, it seems useful to pursue further the pattern of fertility change as a farming area undergoes settlement. A distinction may be drawn between: first generation settlers, recent migrants who have often had at least some of their children somewhere else than their current place of residence; second generation settlers, those born in their place of residence or brought there by parents; and third or later generation settlers. The implication of the present data is that as a given area moves through these successive generations of settlers, marital fertility occurs with the second generation, the first group of "home grown" residents.

The probable course of marital fertility during settlement suggests that the problem of explaining differential fertility between older and newer areas is properly conceived as a search for antifertility pressures that emerge as an area become more settled, pressures to which the first wave of "home grown" settlers are largely oblivious but which become increasingly apparent to their successors. This leads to the final hypothesis to be considered here, the one for which the most support has been advanced:

that declining land availability in older areas created pressures for reduced fertility. In cross-section analyses of nineteenth-century data this relationship has been found to hold in one form or another among states of the United States, counties within the states of New York and Ohio, counties in Ontario and Quebec, and townships within New York state.[28] The fertility difference between older and newer areas in the present data provide further support for the hypothesis, since these areas are differentiated in terms of a measure of land availability, the percentage of cultivable land not yet improved. As was noted, the frontier townships in the sample constitute something of an exception to the rule, since fertility in these townships is somewhat less than in the settlement area just behind the frontier. However, this is probably because a disproportionately large number of those on the frontier built their families, not under frontier conditions, but in the more constraining environmental circumstances of their area of origin (see Table 1).

Although the land availability hypothesis seems generally to be consistent with the evidence presented here, the theory of how the pressure of land scarcity makes itself felt is not clear. If it is a factor in fertility decisions, land scarcity should exert its effect through taste, cost, or income considerations. Consider, however, the implications of the previous discussion for the situation of a typical young married couple with their own farm in a long-settled area. The prospective net return from child labor on farms in long-settled areas is not clearly inferior to that in newer areas. Moreover, the income generated by the farm is likely to be greater, and there is little added burden from aged dependents. Why, then, should limited land availability in the local area serve to discourage childbearing? Why not have children as freely as young farm households in newer areas?

One answer to this is that one component of child cost, not heretofore considered and tied directly to land availability, is actually much higher in older areas, namely, the cost of establishing children on nearby farms when they reach adulthood. This cost mounts rapidly as land is progressively taken up in older areas, and increasingly serves as a deterrent to unrestricted fertility. This argument rests on several key assumptions, evaluations of which go beyond the data presently at hand. American historians, who know the basic sources—qualitative and quantitative— better than other social scientists, may be able to provide valuable help in testing the validity of these assumptions. A summary of some of the research needs in regard to the land availability argument may therefore provide an appropriate ending to the present paper.

The argument assumes that there was among most parents at this time what Philip J. Greven describes as a "consuming concern . . . to see that their sons were settled upon land. . . . "[29] There is some fragmentary evidence of this concern among farm households in the nineteenth century, but the documentation should be much fuller.[30]

The argument assumes further that farmers were reluctant to subdivide their property, at least beyond some minimum point. If not, then a farmer in an older area could have as many children as one in a newer area and assure that they were settled locally by splitting up the farm. There is some evidence of reluctance to subdivide, but, again, it is not nearly as much as one would like.[31] It would be of interest to know whether this resistance sprang from scale considerations—for example, halving the farm would more than half output—or a reluctance to see lower living levels imposed on children by subdividing farms.

Finally, the argument assumes that the higher cost of establishing children on farms in older areas was not counterbalanced by higher farm income in those areas. It does seem that land in older areas was more costly not just in absolute terms but also relative to ability to buy. Again, however, scholars need to collect more evidence on this score.

These remarks reflect the distressing lack of information on inheritance arrangements in nineteenth-century rural America, on the manner in which farms and farm land passed from hand to hand in the course of the settlement process, and on the extent to which farm parents felt responsible for giving their children a start in life, whether in farming or not. If this gap in knowledge could be bridged, it would help to clarify trends and differentials in farm family building in nineteenth-century America and provide new insight into the mechanisms shaping the social structure.

# NOTES

1. See, for example, William L. Langer, "Europe's Initial Population Explosion," *American Historical Review*, LXIX (Oct. 1963), 1–29

2. Richard Tilly and Charles Tilly, "Agenda for European Economic History in the 1970s," *Journal of Economic History*, XXXI (March 1971), 190.

3. Robert V. Wells, "Demographic Change and the Life Cycle of American Families," *Journal of Interdisciplinary History*, II (Autumn 1971), 273–282; Robert V. Wells, "Family Size and Fertility Control in Eighteenth-Century America: A Study of Quaker Families," *Population Studies*, XXV (March 1971), 73–82; Yasukichi Yasuba, *Birth Rates of the White Population in the United States, 1800–1860: An Economic Study* (Baltimore, 1962).

4. Colin Forster, G. S. L. Tucker, and Helen Bridge, *Economic Opportunity and White American Fertility Ratios, 1800–1860* (New Haven, 1972), 3–10; Wilson H. Grabill, Clyde V. Kiser, and Pascal K. Whelpton, *The Fertility of American Women* (New York, 1958), 16–19.

5. Thomas R. Malthus, *First Essay on Population, 1789* (London, 1926), 104–110.

6. The project is a joint one with R. Marvin McInnnis, who is conducting a parallel analysis of Canadian fertility. See R. Marvin McInnis, "Birth Rates and Land Availability in Nineteenth Century Canada," prepared for the annual meeting of the Population Association of America, 1972; R. Marvin McInnis, "Farm Households, Family Size and Economic Circumstances in Mid-Nineteenth Century Ontario," prepared for the Cliometrics Conference, 1974.

7. For sampling procedures and tests of representativeness, see Fred Bateman and James D. Foust, "A Sample of Rural Households Selected from the 1860 Manuscript Censuses," *Agricultural History*, XLVIII (Jan. 1974), 75–93.

8. Forster, Tucker, and Bridge, *Economic Opportunity and White American Fertility Ratios;* Yasuba, *Birth Rates of the White Population*. An as yet unpublished study by Peter Lindert explores some of the same questions for a later period but is much wider ranging in both its theoretical and empirical scope. Peter Lindert, "Fertility and Scarcity in America" (1974).

9. Because data at the township level were not available, the ratio is computed for the county in which each township is located.

10. Yasuba, *Birth Rates of the White Population*, 102–185.

11. Unless otherwise indicated, results of the analysis of the census sample cited throughout this paper will be for this same group—farm husband-wife households with the wife in her thirties.

12. See Table 1. A similar difference appears in a fertility measure specific to farm wives, number of own children under ten per farm wife.

13. For this comparison, child-woman ratios were computed from the published census data for the counties in which the sample townships were located. The ratios for the counties in each of the five settlement classes were then averaged according to the counties' shares in the sample number of farm households in that settlement class. The measure thus includes nonfarm as well as farm population and reflects area differences in proportions marrying and the age distribution of reproductive females.

14. Forster, Tucker, and Bridge, *Economic Opportunity and White American Fertility Ratios*, 71–86.

15. See Table 1, line 3. The newest settlement areas had a somewhat higher share of foreign born than the other areas, almost 28 percent, but its fertility level was actually lower than that in the highest fertility areas, that slightly behind the frontier.

16. Conrad Taeuber and Irene B. Taeuber. *The Changing Population of the United States* (New York, 1968), 274; Yasuba, *Birth Rates of the White Population*, 73–101.

17. Yasuba, *Birth Rates of the White Population*, 80.

18. Richard A. Easterlin, George Alter, and Gretchen A. Condran, "Farms and Farm Families in Old and New Areas: The Northern States in 1860," prepared for the Mathematical Social Science Board Summer Conference in Historical Demography, 1974, p. 15.

19. The median age, for example, of farm wives in their thirties for whom child-woman ratios were cited earlier is a little over thirty-four years (see Table 1, line 4).

20. Grabill, Kiser, and Whelpton, *Fertility of American Women*, 406–413.

21. The concern here is with the fertility of married women. It was noted earlier that the child-woman ratio was also reduced in the East compared with the West because of a lower proportion marrying.

22. Easterlin, Alter, and Condran, "Farms and Farm Families in Old and New Areas," Table 16.

23. Ibid., Table 6.

24. Stanley Lebergott, *Manpower in Economic Growth: The American Record since 1800* (New York, 1964), 539.

25. Martin L. Primack, "Farm Construction as a Use of Farm Labor in the United States, 1850–1910," *Journal of Economic History*, 25 (March 1965), 114–125; Martin L. Primack, Farm Fencing in the Nineteenth Century," *Journal of Economic History*, 29 (June 1969), 287–289; Martin L. Primack, "Farm Formed Capital in American Agriculture, 1850–1910" (doctoral dissertation, University of North Carolina, 1963).

26. Kenneth Lockridge, "Land, Population and the Evolution of New England Society, 1630–1790," *Past and Present*, 39 (April 1968), 62–80; Kenneth A. Lockridge, "The Population of Dedham, Massachusetts, 1636–1736." *Economic History Review*, Second Series, XIX (1966), 318–344.

27. Easterlin, Alter, and Condran, "Farms and Farm Families in Old and New Areas," Table 26.

28. Wendell H. Bash, "Changing Birth Rates in Developing America: New York State 1840–1875," *The Milbank Memorial Fund Quarterly*, XLI (April 1963), 161–182; Forster and Tucker, *Economic Opportunity and White American Fertility Ratios*; Don R. Leet, "The Determinants of the Fertility Transition in Ante-Bellum Ohio," prepared for the annual meeting of the Population Association of America, 1974; Don R. Leet, "Human Fertility and Agricultural Opportunities in Ohio Counties: From Frontier to Maturity, 1810–1860," David C. Klingaman and Richard K. Vedder, eds., *Essays in Nineteenth Century Economic History: The Old Northwest* (Athens, Ohio, 1975); McInnis, "Birth Rates and Land Availability in Nineteenth Century Canada"; McInnis, "Farm Household, Family Size and Economic Circumstances in Mid-Nineteenth Century Ontario"; Yasuba, *Birth Rates of the White Population*. John Modell's failure to obtain supporting results is doubtless due to his concentration on frontier counties. There are no "older areas" in his analysis. John Modell, "Family and Fertility on the Indiana Frontier, 1820," *American Quarterly*, 23 (Dec. 1971), 615–634.

29. Philip J. Greven, Jr., *Four Generations: Population, Land, and Family in Colonial Andover, Massachusetts* (Ithaca, 1970), 254.

30. Clarence H. Danhof quotes at length from an account of Connecticut farming in an agricultural periodical of the 1850s that states: "that liberal expenditure in improvement which would render farming in the highest degree pleasant and profitable is prevented. The education of children and their establishment employs the surplus funds." Clarence H. Danhof, *Change in Agriculture: The Northern United States, 1820–1870* (Cambridge, 1969), 110. Danhof is one of the few scholars who has taken up at some length some of these issues noted in the paragraphs above. Ibid., 101–180. Allan G. Bogue and Merle Curti also provide helpful information. Allan G. Bogue, *From Prairie to Cornbelt: Farming on the Illinois and Iowa Prairies in the Nineteenth Century* (Chicago, 1963). Merle Curti, Robert Daniel, Shaw Livermore, Jr., Joseph Van Hise, and Margaret W. Curti, *The Making of an American Community: A Case Study of Democracy in a Frontier Community* (Stanford, 1959). Pertinent studies for a later period are Marian Deininger and Douglas Marshall, "A Study of Land Ownership by Ethnic Groups from Frontier Times to the Present in a Marginal Farming area in Minnesota," *Land Economics,* 31 (Nov. 1955), 351–360; W. J. Spillman, "The Agricultural Ladder," *American Economic Review,* Supplement IX (March 1919), 170–179; James D. Tarver, "Intra-Family Farm Succession Practices," *Rural Sociology,* 17 (Sept. 1952), 266–271.

31. Danhof states: "Most of our farmers begin with small means. The ancestral farm if subdivided would be too small to meet their views," Danhof, *Change in Agriculture,* 110. The courts served to prevent fragmentation. See Kenneth H. Parsons, Raymond J. Penn, and Philip M. Raup. eds., *Land Tenure: Proceedings of the International Conference on Land Tenure and Related Problems in World Agriculture Held at Madison, Wisconsin, 1951* (Madison, 1956), 573.

# 26 | ANGELS' HEADS AND WEEPING WILLOWS: DEATH IN EARLY AMERICA

## MARIS A. VINOVSKIS

Most recent studies of America's past can be placed into one of two distinct and sometimes hostile camps. Traditional historians have continued to rely almost exclusively on literary sources of information. As a result, their work has focused on the ideology and attitudes of early Americans. On the other hand, a small group of historians, borrowing heavily from the other social sciences, have undertaken to recreate the behavioral patterns of American society in the past. Though these two approaches are potentially complementary to each other, there has been very little effort made to integrate them.

This bifurcation of approaches to the study of American history is quite evident in the recent efforts to analyze the role of death in America. Traditional historians have begun to examine the writings of early Americans in order to recreate their attitudes and images of death. Historical demographers have exploited the censuses and vital records to calculate the incidence and timing of death in early America. But no one has attempted to explore systematically the relationship between attitudes toward death and the actual levels and trends in mortality in early America. In part, this is the result of the assumption by most historians that the attitudes toward and the incidence of death in America were identical.

In this essay we will demonstrate that most colonists did not accurately perceive the extent of mortality in their society. We will suggest some of the reasons for their misperception. Hopefully this essay will encourage other scholars to integrate attitudinal and behavioral approaches to the study of American history.

Most of us have certain preconceived notions about death in colonial America. We envision the early settlers of our country facing such a multitude of hazards that death at a fairly early age was practically inevitable. We also imagine that persons surviving to old age were quite rare and extremely fortunate in having escaped the continuous waves of famine

This paper was presented as a public lecture at the American Antiquarian Society on May 22, 1974, while the author was the Rockefeller Fellow in the History of the Family Program at Clark University and AAS. The author is deeply indebted to Andrew Achenbaum, Georgia Bumgardner, Ronald Formisano, Tamara Hareven, John Hench, Kathryn Sklar, Mary Vinovskis, and John Zeugner for their helpful comments and suggestions.

and pestilence which swept through the population. The idea that high mortality rates prevailed in colonial America has been reinforced by the numerous instances of entire families or communities perishing in the hostile environment of the New World.

Nearly all of us are familiar with the tragic experiences of the Pilgrims who landed at Plymouth on November 11, 1620. Though only one of the 102 passengers aboard the *Mayflower* perished at sea, the eleven-week journey had left the rest of them weak, exhausted, and unprepared for the coming winter. Bradford noted their ordeal in his diary: ". . . But that which was most sadd & lamentable was, that in 2. or 3. moneths time halfe of their company dyed, espetialy in Jan: & February, being the depth of winter, and wanting houses & other comforts; being infected with the scurvie & other diseases, which this long vioage & their inacomodate condition had brought upon them; so as ther dyed some times 2. or 3. of a day, in the foresaid time; that of 100 & odd persons, scarce 50 remained. . . ."[1]

Even those settlers who survived the rigors of the first year in the New World faced unforeseen epidemics which took very heavy tolls of the inhabitants—especially in urban areas such as Boston and Salem. In 1721 there was an outbreak of smallpox in Boston in which over 50 percent of its 11,000 inhabitants contracted the disease. In that year the Boston death rate soared to an incredible 103 deaths per thousand population. Thus, over 10 percent of the city's population died within the space of one year.[2] Only the very small percentage of the people daring enough to try the new technique of inoculation managed to escape the high death rate among those who had smallpox.[3]

Smaller communities were not safe from the terrors of epidemics. For example, in the parish of Hampton Falls in New Hampshire the "sorethroat distemper" in 1735 nearly decimated the population. This epidemic, later identified as diphtheria, resulted in the deaths of 210 persons—or over one-sixth of the entire population of that parish. The outbreak of diphtheria caused fatalities particularly among young people— 95 percent of those who died in Hampton Falls were under the age of twenty. Nearly twenty families buried all of their children that year.[4]

Any person still skeptical of the existence of high mortality in early America would certainly be convinced by one of the few extant life tables for that period—the Wigglesworth Life Table of 1789. Edward Wigglesworth, Hollis Professor of Divinity at Harvard, became interested in life tables when he was advising the Massachusetts Congregational Charitable Society on how to establish an annuity fund for the widows of ministers. At that time there were no life tables available for the United States from which to estimate the life expectancies of the ministers and their wives. Therefore, Wigglesworth collected bills of mortality from various New England towns with the active cooperation of the newly established Academy of Arts and Sciences in Boston. From the sixty-two bills of mortality returned, Wigglesworth constructed a life table in 1789. He calculated that the average person in New England could expect to live only 35.5 years—thus reinforcing our grim image of health conditions in early America.[5]

Most writers have argued that death rates in seventeenth- and eighteenth-century New England were very high, and there is also a consensus that life expectancy improved significantly in the first half of the nineteenth century. This interpretation is based on a comparison of Wigglesworth's Life Table of 1789 and Elliott's table of 1855 for Massachusetts. On the basis of these two tables, it appears that the average person in the Commonwealth could expect to live an additional 4.3 years by 1855.[6]

Thus, the traditional picture of mortality in early America is one of high death rates in the seventeenth and eighteenth centuries followed by a marked improvement in the nineteenth century. A sociologist has recently summarized the extent of mortality in early America as follows:

> Although precise statistical evidence is lacking, the little that scientists have been able to compile from various anthropological and archaeological sources indicates that throughout most of his existence man has had to contend with an extremely high death rate. The brutally harsh conditions of life in the pre-industrial world made human survival very much a touch-and-go affair. A new born infant had no more than a fifty-fifty chance of surviving to adulthood; the average life expectancy of primitive man was probably not much in excess of twenty-five or thirty years. Even more significant, the survival situation was not a great deal better as recently as the middle of the eighteenth century. Early records for the state of Massachusetts, for example, indicate that average life expectancy in colonial America was still somewhat less than forty years.[7]

Most studies of Puritan attitudes toward death have accepted the notion that death rates in early New England were very high. In fact, the imminence of death in Puritan society is often used by historians to explain the preoccupation of early Americans with the process of dying.

This recent work in historical demography, however, raises serious questions about the validity of the traditional view of death in early America. During the last ten years historical demographers have used family reconstitution techniques to provide a very different interpretation of mortality levels in New England.[8]

This recent work verifies that death rates were very high in urban areas in colonial New England. Boston deaths averaged thirty to forty per thousand population during the years 1701 to 1774. Furthermore, there were large fluctuations in the death rates in Boston. Most of the sudden rises in the death rate in 1702, 1721, 1730, and 1752 were the result of epidemics that ravaged that busy seaport (see Figure 1).

The newer work also shows that death rates in urban areas such as Boston or Salem were not typical of the rest of the population. In most rural communities, the settlers who managed to survive the hardships of the early years could look forward to many more years of life in the New World. Though data on mortality levels are very scarce for the colonial period, historical demographers have been able to provide some estimates by relying on the reconstitution of families from the vital records of the community. On the basis of detailed investigations of Andover, Dedham, Hingham, Ipswich, and Plymouth, it now appears that life expectancy was much higher in rural New England than was previously believed. These communities experienced death rates of fifteen to twenty-five per thou-

**Figure 1**  NUMBER OF DEATHS PER THOUSAND POPULATION IN BOSTON, 1701- 1774

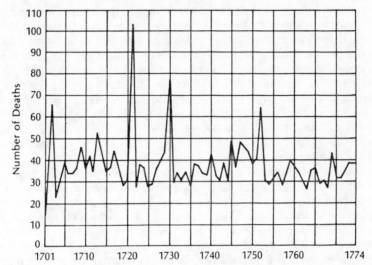

Source: John B. Blake, *Public Health in the Town of Boston* (Cambridge, Mass., 1959), pp. 247–49.

sand rather than the higher mortality rates in Boston or Salem. Since most people in America in the seventeenth and eighteenth centuries lived in small, rural communities, not unlike these five Massachusetts towns, it is likely that most Americans did not have the same frequent encounter with death that residents of commercial centers did.

Since most seventeenth- and eighteenth-century Americans were English or were at least influenced by an English heritage, it is useful to compare the death rates in the New and Old Worlds. Generally, death rates in America were lower than in Europe. Death rates for infants in Andover and Ipswich were significantly lower than those in Europe, while infant mortality rates in Salem were comparable to those in Europe. Similarly, death rates after the age of twenty were lower in most Massachusetts communities than in Europe.

These findings appear to be in direct contradiction to the expectation of life according to the Wigglesworth Life Table of 1789. A detailed examination of that life table, however, reveals serious methodological flaws in its construction and coverage. Wigglesworth's table is based only on the ages at death obtained from bills of mortality. Since he did not have data available on the population who were liable to die in that period, he was forced to assume that the age distribution of the deaths in the bills of mortality approximated the actual age distribution of the entire population. Though Wigglesworth realized that this crucial assumption was incorrect, his attempts to adjust his stationary population model must be viewed as intelligent guessing at best. Furthermore, his sample of towns was not representative of the entire region. Most of his data came from towns which were more urban than the area as a whole and consequently probably exaggerated the extent of colonial mortality. As a result, his estimate of life expectancy in colonial New England is probably too low and therefore does not invalidate the results from the family reconstitution studies.[9]

Another problem with many of the interpretations of living conditions in colonial America is that they are based on a faulty understanding of life tables. If the expectation of life at birth is 40.0 years, it means that the average person could expect to live that long. It does not mean, however, that once this average person had reached age twenty-one that he had only nineteen years remaining. When an individual had survived the perils of early childhood and the rigors of early adulthood, his or her chances of continuing to live were actually increased.[10] For example, the average male at age twenty-one in seventeenth-century Plymouth could expect another 48.2 years of life and the average female at the same age another 41.4 years (see Figure 2).

Most of the differences in life expectancy between colonial Americans and Americans of today are due to the much higher rate of infant and child mortality in the past. Adults in colonial New England often could anticipate lives almost as long as each one of us today—especially if they were male. The average male at age twenty-one in seventeenth-century Plymouth had a life expectancy only one year less than the typical American male today. The average female at age twenty-one in seventeenth-century Plymouth, however, could expect to live 14.6 years less than her counterpart today—in large measure because maternal mortality rates in colonial America were very high.

Death rates in early America did not remain constant. In the seventeenth century there were large rural-urban differences in mortality in

**Figure 2** LIFE EXPECTANCY OF ADULTS IN SEVENTEENTH-CENTURY PLYMOUTH

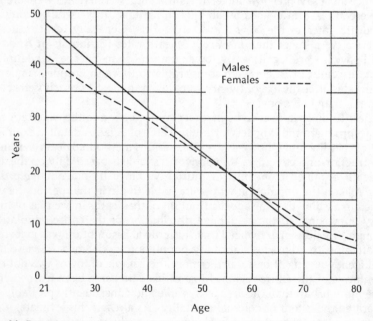

Source: John Demos, *A Little Commonwealth: Family Life in Plymouth Colony* (New York, 1970), p. 192.

Massachusetts since small agricultural communities such as Dedham, Plymouth, Andover, Hingham, and Ipswich had relatively high life expectancies whereas Boston and Salem had much lower ones. The eighteenth century witnessed the convergence of these rates as mortality rose slightly in some of the smaller towns while death rates fell in Salem. Boston continued to have very high death rates throughout the eighteenth century. In the early nineteenth century there was a further convergence as Boston death rates dropped to around twenty per thousand while mortality in rural areas remained fairly steady.[11]

In order to analyze the level of mortality in nineteenth-century America in more detail and to look especially at the rural-urban differences, life tables for various Massachusetts towns in 1860 have been calculated from the federal census and the state vital records. Since the only previous life table for this period that might be of use to us, Elliott's Life Table of 1855, is inadequate because of several methodological shortcomings, these tables provide an unusual opportunity to assess the presence of death in mid-nineteenth-century society.[12]

Life expectancy at birth in Massachusetts in 1860 was relatively high compared to most European countries. The average male at birth had a life expectancy of 46.4 years while the average female could look forward to 47.3 years of life (see Figure 3).

Contrary to the assertions of most other scholars, there was very little difference in mortality between rural and urban areas in Massachusetts. The major difference according to town size was between towns with populations under 10,000 and those with populations over 10,000. Furthermore, socioeconomic differences among these towns could not account for

**Figure 3**    LIFE EXPECTANCY AT BIRTH IN MASSACHUSETTS TOWNS IN 1860

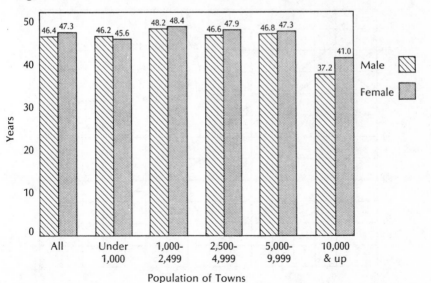

Source: Maris A. Vinovskis, 'Mortality Rates and Trends in Massachusetts before 1860,' *Journal of Economic History* 32 (1972): 211.

a large proportion of the differences in mortality. In a multiple regression analysis where the age-standardized death rate was the dependent variable and a variety of socioeconomic characteristics of those towns were the independent variables, the resultant equation for the state accounted for less than 15 percent of the variance in the death rates. Put more simply, our detailed statistical analysis of mortality levels among Massachusetts towns in 1860 displayed a remarkable similarity amongst themselves.[13]

Compared to England and Wales in 1838–1854, life expectancy in Massachusetts in 1860 was significantly higher for both males and females (see Figure 4). It is interesting to observe the generally similar pattern in life expectancy for both areas. If an American, English, or Welsh child survived the high levels of infant and child mortality, his life expectancy increased dramatically.

Though the overall level of mortality in colonial New England was probably much lower than previously estimated, it does not mean that death was not a serious problem—particularly for the young. Adults in rural New England could anticipate reasonably long lives, but their children faced much worse odds. Infant mortality rates in colonial America ranged from 115 per thousand births in seventeenth-century Andover to 313 per thousand for females and 202 per thousand for males in seventeenth-century Salem. In other words, 10 to 30 percent of the children never survived for the first year of life. In the United States in 1974, on the other hand, the infant mortality rate was 16.5 per thousand—or almost ten times less than that of the colonial period.

**Figure 4** LIFE EXPECTANCY IN MASSACHUSETTS IN 1860 AND IN ENGLAND AND WALES IN 1838–1854

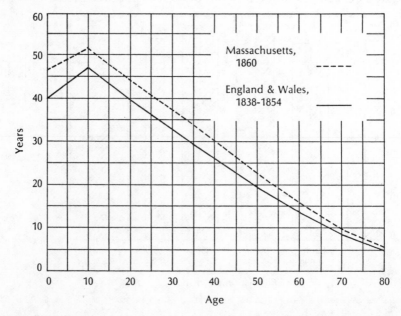

The higher mortality rate among children in the past can be illustrated by comparing the expectation of life for males in Massachusetts in 1860 with those of males in the United States in 1969 (see Figure 5). At the later ages the expectation of life for both groups is very similar, but there is a very substantial difference at birth. The average male child at birth today can expect to live to age 67.8; if he survives to age ten, he increases his total life expectation by only 1.8 years. On the other hand, the average male child in Massachusetts born in 1860 could anticipate 46.4 years of life; if he survived to age ten, his total life expectancy would increase by 16.6 years.

In addition, since the average family in colonial New England usually had three times as many children as we have today, there was a high probability that most families would experience the loss of at least one child during their lifetimes. The combination of high infant mortality rates and high birth rates increased the likelihood that the typical family in early America would have had to deal with the death of a member of their nuclear family.

Our analysis of mortality levels and trends in New England before 1860 suggests that most individuals, especially those who had survived the dangers of early childhood, could look forward to reasonably long lives. Therefore, we might expect that our Puritan ancestors would not have

**Figure 5**  LIFE EXPECTANCY IN MASSACHUSETTS IN 1860 AND IN U.S. IN 1969

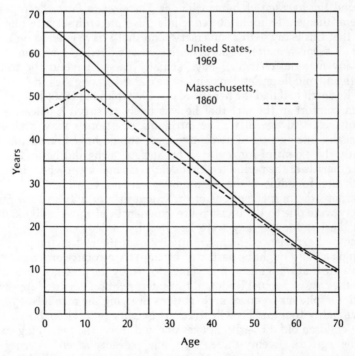

Sources: Maris A. Vinovskis, "Mortality Rates and Trends in Massachusetts before 1860," *Journal of Economic History* 32 (1972):211; U.S. Bureau of the Census, *The American Almanac: The U.S. Book of Facts, Statistics & Information*, 1973 (New York, 1973), p. 56.

been very concerned or worried about mortality—especially about deaths among adults. Yet New England society seemed obsessed with death despite the moderate mortality rates for that period. Even more astonishing is the fact that most people in those days greatly overestimated the extent of mortality in their society.

Some colonists, such as Edward Wigglewsworth, did realize that death rates in the New World were somewhat lower than in England. But even Wigglesworth, the foremost expert on colonial mortality, seriously underestimated the expectation of life in early New England. The general populace seemed convinced that death rates were very high. Anyone reading through the diaries of these people is immediately struck by the fascination and concern with death. The image of early American society one receives from these writings is that of a very unhealthy environment in which each individual anticipates his demise at any moment.[14]

For example, Samuel Rodman began to keep a diary at age twenty-nine in 1821. He was a very scientifically oriented man who collected weather data from 1812 to 1876 and was generally calm about discussions of death throughout his diary during the next thirty-eight years. But it is very interesting to observe how he misperceived the dangers to his life even well into the nineteenth century.

Rodman often mentions how he should devote more attention to his spiritual needs because he anticipates he may die at any moment. In 1838 he celebrates his birthday by noting in his diary that "this is the 46th anniversary of my birth. I have lived therefore already considerably beyond the average of human life."[15] Three years later, he repeats the general theme: "I should not conclude this note without attesting to the fact that this is my 49th anniversary, and that I have entered on my 50th year. It seems a matter of surprise that I have lived so long, and without yet any material change. I have actually passed beyond the period of youth and middle age and may justly be classed among the old."[16]

If Rodman had had the benefit of our life tables for 1860, he could have taken comfort in the fact that he was likely to survive at least another twenty years at age fifty. The intriguing question is why Rodman, an unusually intelligent and perceptive man, should have underestimated so greatly the extent of longevity in his society. Why did he and so many other diarists of the period feel that death was imminent when, in fact, the death rates for adults in the communities were not very high?

Perhaps the misperceptions of the extent of mortality in New England society were due to the unusual life experiences of those individuals who kept diaries. Maybe they were less healthy and/or came from families which had experienced higher mortality than the rest of the population. Keeping a diary might be part of an attempt to introduce order and stability in a life that was constantly overshadowed by the presence of death.

In the case of Samuel Rodman, this interpretation does not appear to be valid. Despite his frequent anticipations of dying, he managed to survive to age eighty-four and his wife lived to be eighty-two. Though two of their eight children did die early, at ages one and three, the remaining six lived to the ages of twenty-three, sixty-one, seventy-seven, seventy-eight, eighty-seven, and ninety-one. One might properly object that these figures are misleading because Samuel Rodman had no way of knowing how long he or his offspring would survive. Perhaps he was merely reacting to the much higher mortality of his parents and siblings. Yet his father lived to age eighty-two and his mother to age ninety-five. Furthermore, his sisters survived to the ages of thirty-one, sixty, seventy-eight, and eighty-one while his brothers died at ages twenty-four, sixty-eight, and eighty-one.[17] In other words, whatever indications of low life expectancy that Rodman had, they probably did not come mainly from the experiences of his immediate family.

Though our analysis of Rodman's own longevity suggests that his anticipation of imminent death probably was not based on his own physical frailty, we should be careful not to generalize about the relationship between personal health and preoccupation with death among diarists on the basis of just one individual. Kathryn Kish Sklar has coded data from published diaries of seventy-one American women who lived in the eighteenth and early nineteenth centuries. These data are of particular interest to us because many historians have remarked on the preoccupation of women with items about health and death in their diaries. We already know that women who kept diaries were more educated than the rest of the population and probably came from more affluent backgrounds. Using her data, it is possible to calculate age at death for forty of these women.[18] Therefore, one is now able to estimate the life expectancy of these women who kept diaries.

Of the forty women, the average age at death was 56.4 years. This compares very favorably with the expectation of life at birth for Massachusetts women in 1860 of 47.3 years. This is a very misleading comparison, however, because most women did not begin to keep diaries until they had already survived the perils of early childhood (see Figure 6).

Instead, we need to take into consideration the ages at which these

**Figure 6** DISTRIBUTION OF AGES AT WHICH WOMEN BEGAN TO KEEP THEIR DIARIES IN THE EIGHTEENTH AND NINETEENTH CENTURIES

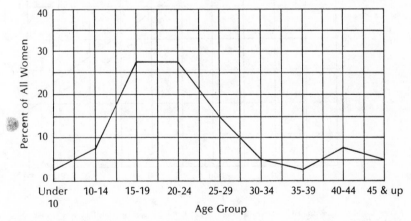

Source: Calculated from data on American diaries collected by Kathryn Kish Sklar of the University of California, Los Angeles.

women began their diaries before calculating their life expectancies. Now we can compare their expectation of life to that of women in the general public (see Figure 7).

The results indicate that women who kept diaries were, in fact, less healthy than Massachusetts women in 1860—particularly at ages twenty and thirty. Though this does reinforce the argument that unhealthy people were more likely to keep diaries, it is important to bear in mind that the average woman who kept a diary at age twenty could expect to live another 35.5 years. Thus, most women who kept these diaries were actually quite healthy and their own prospect of dying in the very near future was not very likely despite their utterances to the contrary in those diaries.

Since we cannot account for the misperceptions of the level of mortality in early New England in terms of the colonists' personal encounters with death, we need to look at the general context of life in that period to see what factors encouraged people to imagine such high death rates—especially among the adult population. Though death is a biological phenomenon, the reactions of people to it are largely defined by the manner in which society handles its dying. It is my contention that the great

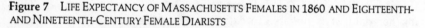

**Figure 7** LIFE EXPECTANCY OF MASSACHUSETTS FEMALES IN 1860 AND EIGHTEENTH-AND NINETEENTH-CENTURY FEMALE DIARISTS

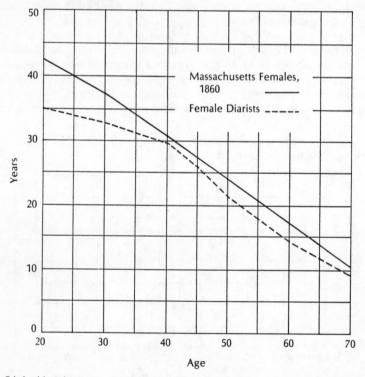

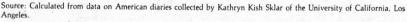

Source: Calculated from data on American diaries collected by Kathryn Kish Sklar of the University of California, Los Angeles.

emphasis placed on death in early New England led people to overestimate the extent of its occurrence in their communities and lives.

Americans today are remarkably unwilling to discuss death. Our society refuses to face the issue of death openly—thus, death has replaced sex as the major taboo. Geoffrey Gorer in a very insightful essay has argued that "In the 20th century there seems to have been an unremarked shift in prudery; whereas copulation has become more and more mentionable, particularly in the Anglo-Saxon societies, death has become more and more unmentionable as a natural process."[19]

Puritan society had a very different attitude toward death—there was a great fascination and interest in that subject, and people were encouraged to discuss it amongst themselves. Furthermore, the very process of dying in early New England forced people to come to terms with death rather than being able to pretend that death did not really exist.[20]

The location in which an individual dies is important because it determines the access his relatives and friends will have to him during that time. In addition, the place where a person dies also influences the amount of exposure the rest of society will have to the process of dying.

Today there is a debate over whether it is better to die at home or in a hospital. Some elderly actually prefer to die away from home in order to avoid becoming burdens to their families. Yet when one dies at home he or she is in familiar surroundings and among friends. A patient who is hospitalized is largely removed from the help and care of his family.

Public opinion in America has gradually shifted away from the idea of dying at home. Less than a third of the public now would prefer to have someone die at home. In 1968 a public opinion poll asked: "Do you feel that if an individual is dying and is beyond any available medical aid, that it is more desirable to remove the person to a hospital or other institution, rather than have them remain at home?" The replies were as follows:[21]

|  | N | Percent |
| --- | --- | --- |
| Yes, this is best for all concerned | 669 | 34.1 |
| No, death should be at home if at all possible | 553 | 28.2 |
| Undecided | 692 | 35.3 |
| No answer | 47 | 2.4 |

This change in attitudes has been accompanied by a shift in the actual location of dying. In 1963, 53 percent of all deaths occurred in a hospital and many others in nursing homes or as a result of accidents outside the home.[22] As a result, most Americans today do not often see the process of dying first hand. This isolation from death is compounded by the development of "retirement cities" in the United States where the elderly are in effect segregated from the rest of society. As Robert Fulton has so aptly put it, "Here for the first time modern man is able to avoid almost entirely the grief and anguish of death. By encouraging the aged members of the society to congregate in segregated communities, familial and friendship commitments are made fewer by time and distance, and emotional and social bonds are loosened. Physically and emotionally separated from those most likely to die, the modern individual is freed of the shock he would otherwise experience from their death. Herein may lie a form of man's "conquest of death."[23]

The colonists died mainly in their own homes since there were few hospitals or other institutions in which the aged could be placed. In the absence of a specialized nursing profession, relatives and neighbors attended to the needs of the dying—thus increasing the amount of contact between the living and the dying.

The homes of the early colonists were very small compared to today— especially those built in the early years of settlement. According to the probate inventories, the average number of rooms per house in rural Suffolk County, Massachusetts, rose from 4.3 in 1675–1699, to 5.7 in 1700–1719, and to 6.0 in 1750–1775.[24] Thus, there was relatively little privacy available in these homes to shield the dying person from the rest of the family even if the colonists had desired to isolate him.

Finally, since there were no funeral homes in the seventeenth and eighteenth centuries, the dead person remained in his own home where friends and neighbors could view him. As the art of embalming was still in its infancy in colonial America, very little effort was made to preserve or repair the dead body. People were forced to see the dead persons as they were rather than having them cosmetically preserved or improved to enhance their appearance in death.[25]

The funeral itself encouraged people to come into intimate contact with death. At first funerals in colonial America were simple affairs since there was an effort to avoid the excesses of English funeral practices. One contemporary observer of early colonial funerals described them: "At Burials nothing is read, nor any funeral sermon made, but all the neighborhood or a goodly company of them come together by tolling of the bell, and carry the dead solemnly to his grave, and then stand by him while he is buried. The ministers are most commonly present."[26]

Gradually funerals became more elaborate and expensive. The practice of distributing gifts of gloves, rings, or scarfs to participants at funerals was a custom brought over from England and which flourished in New England in the late seventeenth and eighteenth centuries. The practice quickly became excessive as the quality of the gifts distributed was supposed to reflect the social status of the deceased. At the funeral of Governor Belcher's wife in 1736, over 1,000 pairs of gloves were distributed. Ministers, who usually received gifts at all the funerals they attended, often accumulated large quantities of such items. For example, Andrew Eliot, minister of the North Church in Boston received 2,940 pairs of funeral gloves in his thirty-two years in the pulpit. Rather than allow such gifts to overwhelm his household, Reverend Eliot sold them to supplement his modest salary.[27]

As the costs of these funeral items rose, there were numerous attempts by the General Court as well as individual citizens to curtail funeral expenses. None of the proposed measures, however, succeeded because our colonial ancestors were just as determined to have extravagant funerals then as we are today.[28]

But these social aspects of funerals provided still greater encouragement for people to attend them. It was expected in the small rural communities of New England that everyone would attend the funerals of any of their townsmen. Given the death rate of that period, it was likely that in a small village of a thousand inhabitants, there would be at least ten to twenty-five funerals each year. Since most burials were handled by the neighbors and friends rather than by a professional undertaker, the significance of each funeral became even more important to the living. Thus, there was a constant reminder to the entire community of the presence of death whereas today most of us are not affected by the deaths of anyone except very close friends or relatives.

Finally, the practice of giving funeral sermons became established by the early eighteenth century. Ministers now used the occasion of the gathering at the grave to preach to the living the importance of coming to terms with the inevitability of death. Increasingly these sermons were published and distributed to the congregation as a remembrance of the departed and a reminder of the frailty of life.[29]

The awareness of death by an individual in colonial America did not end with the lowering of the body into the grave. The grave as well as the burial place continued to further the notion of the shortness of life on earth for the survivors. Scholars such as Harriette Forbes, Allan Ludwig, and Dickran and Ann Tashjian have already explored the artistic and symbolic implications of the early gravestones that are dotted throughout the countryside. Rather than simply repeat their insightful analyses of the meaning of these early artifacts, we will try only to reconstruct how these images of death might have influenced the perceptions of our ancestors about the extent of mortality in their communities.[30]

Before 1660, graveyards in New England were quite plain. Often people were buried in convenient locations near their homes rather than being interred in burial grounds near the churches. We can understand this casual attitude toward the burial site better if we recall that in England the common practice had been to bury many different individuals on the same plot of land. No effort was made to keep a separate spot for each person who died—rather bodies were buried with the expectation that someone else would share that same area as soon as the previous occupant had been decomposed sufficiently. Thus, the church of St. John the Baptist in Widford, Hertfordshire, buried nearly 5,000 people in a plot of less than half an acre in area. Usually these early English burials did not include even placing the deceased in a coffin.[31]

Gradually the burial places became more important to the Puritans as a reminder of the presence of death. As efforts were made to preserve the memory of those who had departed, gravestones were used to identify the bodily remains as well as to provide inspiration for the living. Partly for ornamental reasons but mainly for instructing the living, colonial gravestones began to depict the reality of death.

These symbolic illustrations of death were significant reminders of the frailty of life in a society in which many of its citizens were illiterate and therefore unable to read the messages about death from the inscriptions on the gravestones. These grim symbols of death were meant to remind the living that the day of judgment was coming and that all would be called upon to account for their lives.[32]

The symbolic messages of the early New England gravestones were usually simpler and plainer than those on the religious art works of Europe at that time. The Puritans were very anxious to avoid duplication of symbols that were commonly identified with the Roman Catholic Church. The imagery of the early New England gravestones ranged across a wide variety of themes—from emblems of death to symbols of resurrection. Furthermore, there was an evolution in gravestone imagery over time— from the vivid and often harsh depiction of death by the use of death's heads to the more cheerful and subtle representations of death by winged cherubs and weeping willows in the late eighteenth and early nineteenth centuries.[33]

Probably the single most important factor in reminding early New Englanders of the presence of death was their religion which placed such great emphasis on death and an afterlife for those who had been saved. Ministers preached with great frequency about death and the demise of any member of the congregation was seen as an opportunity to remind the living of the proper ways of serving God.[34]

Ministers tried to encourage everyone in their congregations to think about the meaning of death. Thus, Cotton Mather in his work *A Christian Funeral* advises the survivors that "when any Person known to me *Dies*, I would set my self particularly to consider; *What lesson of goodness or Wisdom I may learn from any thing that I may observe in the life of that Person.*"[35] And in his *Death Made Easie & Happy*, Mather implores his readers to remind themselves each day that "he is to die shortly. Let us look upon everything as a sort of Death's-Head set before us, with a *Memento mortis* written upon it."[36]

In the early decades of settlement, church leaders were relatively matter-of-fact about the presence and inevitablity of death. But as the children of the original settlers gradually turned away from the church, there was a widespread fear that their errand in the wilderness might fail. Ministers now seized upon the terrors of death to persuade their sinful townsmen to return to God's way. Thus, Solomon Stoddard in his *The Efficacy of the Fear of Hell to Restrain Men from Sin* wrote, "Many seem to be Incorrigible and Obstinate in their Pride and Luxury and Profaness . . . they are afraid of Poverty, and afraid of Sickness, but not afraid of Hell; that would restrain them from sinful Practices, Destruction from God would be a Terrour to them.[37]

Increasingly these ministers directed their message to young children. From a very early age, Puritan children were admonished to think of their impending doom in hell unless they were saved by God's grace.[38] This message can be seen in an anonymous broadside of that period:

> My Cry's to you, my Children . . .
> Be wise before it be too late.
> Think on your latter end.
> Though you are young and yet you must die,
> and hasten to the Pit.[39]

People were also encouraged to keep diaries in which they recorded their spiritual progress and failings. There seems to have been much emphasis on continually thinking about the shortness of one's own life. Therefore, it is not surprising that the death of anyone in the community often stimulated these diarists to reflect on their own precarious situation even though the actual conditions of life in that society were much healthier than they imagined.

Perhaps now we are in a better position to account for the misperceptions of early New Englanders of the level of mortality in their society. They came from England where mortality rates were very high. Their expectations of continued high mortality in the New World were reinforced by the difficulties of the early years of settlement, the uncertainty of life due to the presence of periodic epidemics, and the particularly high mortality of their children. Though their chances of survival in America were actually much better than those of their relatives and friends in the old country, they usually did not realize this fact because of the great emphasis that was placed on death by their religion. The continued reminder of the shortness of their lives whenever anyone died made it difficult for the average person to comprehend the changes in the overall mortality level that had occurred. Furthermore, their incessant preoccupation with death helps to explain why most scholars of colonial history thought that there was such a high death rate in the seventeenth and eighteenth centuries. Since most of these historians relied only on literary evidence, there was no reason for them to suspect that the colonists had incorrectly assessed the living conditions in early New England.

## NOTES

1. William Bradford, *Of Plymouth Plantation*, Harvey Wish, ed. (New York 1962), p. 70. For a more detailed discussion of the experiences of the Pilgrims, see George D. Langdon, Jr., *Pilgrim Colony: A History of New Plymouth, 1620-1691* (New Haven, 1966).

2. On the extent of mortality in Boston, see John B. Blake, *Public Health in the Town of Boston, 1630-1882* (Cambridge, Mass., 1952).

3. Blake *Public Health*, pp. 74-98; John Duffy, *Epidemics in Colonial America* (Baton Rouge, 1953), pp. 16-112.

4. Duffy, *Epidemics*, pp. 117-118; Ernest Caulfied, "A History of the Terrible Epidemic, Vulgarly Called the Throat Distemper, as It Occurred in His Majesty's New England Colonies between 1735 and 1740," *Yale Journal of Biology and Medicine* 11 (1938-1939), 219-272, 277-335.

5. Edward Wigglesworth, "A Table Shewing the Probability of the Duration, the Decrement, and the Expectation of Life, in the States of Massachusetts and New Hampshire, formed from sixty two Bills of Mortality on the files of the American Academy of Arts and Sciences, in the Year 1789," *Memoirs of the American Academy of Arts and Sciences*, 2, pt. 1 (1793): 131-135. For an analysis of the gathering of that data as well as its utilization, see Maris A. Vinovskis, "The 1789 Life Table of Edward Wigglesworth," *Journal of Economic History* 31 (1971) :570-590.

6. Warren S. Thompson and P. K. Whelpton, *Population Trends in the United States* (New York, 1933), pp. 228-240. A more recent interpretation of mortality trends by Yasukichi Yasuba argues that death rates probably were increasing just prior to the Civil War because of the increase in urbanization and industrialization. Yasukichi Yasuba, *Birth Rates of the White Population in the United States, 1800-1860: An Economic Study*, The Johns

Hopkins University Studies in Historical and Political Science, vol. 79, no. 2 (Baltimore, 1962), pp. 86–96.

7. Edward G. Stockwell, *Population and People* (Chicago, 1968), p. 26.

8. Philip Greven, Jr., *Four Generations: Population, Land, and Family in Colonial Andover, Massachusetts* (Ithaca, N.Y., 1970); John Demos, *A Little Commonwealth: Family Life in Plymouth Colony* (New York, 1970); Susan L. Norton, "Population Growth in Colonial America: A Study of Ipswich, Massachusetts," *Population Studies* 25 (1971): 433–452; Kenneth A. Lockridge, "The Population of Dedham, Massachusetts, 1636–1736," *Economic History Review*, 2d ser. 19(1966):318–344; Daniel Scott Smith, "The Demographic History of New England," *Journal of Economic History* 32 (1972):165–183; Maris A. Vinovskis, "American Historical Demography: A Review Essay" *Historical Methods Newsletter* 4(1971):141–148; Maris A. Vinovskis, "Mortality Rates and Trends in Massachusetts before 1860," *Journal of Economic History* 32(1972):184–213.

These generalizations only apply to the New England area. Mortality rates in the colonial South were considerably higher according to some of the recent work in that area. Irene Hecht, "The Virginia Muster of 1624/5 as a Source for Demographic History," *William and Mary Quarterly*, 3d ser. 30(1973):65–92; Lorena S. Walsh and Russell R. Menard, "Death in the Chesapeake: Two Life Tables for Men in Early Colonial Maryland," *Maryland Historical Magazine* 69(1974):211–227.

9. Vinovskis, "The 1789 Life Table of Edward Wigglesworth."

10. For an introduction to the use and interpretation of life tables, see Louis I. Dublin, Alfred J. Lotka, and Mortimer Spiegelman, *Length of Life: A Study of the Life Table* (New York, 1949).

11. Vinovskis, "Mortality Rates and Trends."

12. Ibid.

13. Ibid. The results of this regression analysis have not been published yet. However, the use of the 1860 standardized mortality in a regression analysis of fertility differentials in Massachusetts is reported in Maris A. Vinovskis, "A Multivariate Regression Analysis of Fertility Differentials among Massachusetts Towns and Regions in 1860," a paper presented at the Conference on Early Industrialization, Shifts in Fertility, and Changes in the Family Structure at Princeton University, June 18–July 10, 1972 (forthcoming in a volume of the conference proceedings to be edited by Charles Tilly).

14. Various scholars have commented on the preoccupation of early Americans with the issue of death in their writings. For example, see Charles Allen Shively, "A History of the Conception of Death in America, 1650–1860," (Ph.D. diss., Harvard University, 1969); Lewis O. Saum, "Death in the Popular Mind of Pre-Civil War America," *American Quarterly* 26 (1974):477–495.

15. Zepharriah Pease, ed., *The Diary of Samuel Rodman: A New Bedford Chronicle of Thirty-Seven Years:1821–1859* (New Bedford, Mass., 1927), p. 180.

16. Ibid., p. 218.

17. Ibid.

18. I am deeply indebted to Kathryn Kish Sklar of the University of California, Los Angeles, for allowing me to use her data for these calculations.

19. Geoffrey Gorer, *Death, Grief, and Mourning* (Garden City, N.Y., 1965), pp. 192–199.

20. For analyses of the reactions of Puritans to death, see David E. Stannard, "Death and Dying in Puritan New England," *American Historical Review* 78(1973):1305–1330; Shively, "History of the Conception of Death."

21. Glen M. Vernon, *Sociology of Death: An Analysis of Death-Related Behavior* (New York, 1970), p. 110. For a more general discussion of American attitudes toward death, see Richard G. Dumont and Dennis C. Foss, *The American View of Death: Acceptance or Denial?* (Cambridge, Mass., 1972).

22. Robert L. Fulton, "Death and the Self," *Journal of Religion and Health* 3(1964): 354.

23. Ibid., p. 367.

24. For a description of the development of embalming in America, see Robert W. Habenstein and William M. Lamers, *The History of American Funeral Directing* (Milwaukee, 1955).

25. David H. Flaherty, *Privacy in Colonial New England* (Charlottesville, Va., 1972), p. 39.

26. Thomas Lechford, *Plain Dealing or News from New England,* ed. J. Hammond Trumbull (Boston, 1867), pp. 17–88.

27. For a description of the extravagant expenditures on early funerals, see Alice Morse Earle, *Customs and Fashions in Old New England* (New York, 1894).

28. Though Jessica Mitford argues that the excesses in funeral expenditures are only a recent phenomena, there is ample evidence that often the colonists also spent large sums on their funerals. Jessica Mitford, *The American Way of Death,* paperback ed. (Greenwich, Conn., 1963).

29. On the evolution of Puritan attitudes and practices at funerals, see Shively, "History of the Conception of Death."

30. Harriette Merrifield Forbes, *Gravestones of Early New England and the Men Who Made Them, 1653-1800* (New York, 1927); Allan I. Ludwig, *Graven Images: New England Stonecarving and Its Symbols, 1650-1815* (Middletown, Conn., 1966); Dickran and Ann Tashjian, *Memorials for Children of Change: The Art of Early New England Stonecarving* (Middletown, Conn., 1974).

31. Habenstein and Lamers, *History of American Funeral Directing,* pp. 91–191.

32. On the extent of illiteracy in early New England, see Kenneth A. Lockridge, *Literacy in Colonial New England* (New York, 1974).

33. Ludwig, *Graven Images;* Tashjian, *Memorials for Children of Change.*

34. On the importance of religion during this period, see John Higham, "Hanging Together: Divergent Unities in American History," *Journal of American History* 61 (1974):5-29. For a very useful analysis of the role of liberal clergymen in emphasizing death in the mid-nineteenth century, see Ann Douglass, "Heaven Our Home: Consolation Literature in the Northern United States, 1830-1880," *American Quarterly* 26(1974):496-515.

35. Cotton Mather, *A Christian Funeral* (Boston, 1713), p. 27.

36. Cotton Mather, *Death Made Easie & Happy* (London, 1701), p. 94.

37. Solomon Stoddard, *The Efficacy of the Fear of Hell to Restrain Men from Sin* (Boston, 1713), p. 10.

38. The best account of death and young children in early American society is by David E. Stannard, "Death and the Puritan Child," *American Quarterly* 26(1974):456-476.

39. Quoted in Shively, "History of the Conception of Death," p. 52.

# SELECTED READINGS FOR PART SEVEN

BANKS, J. A. *Prosperity and Parenthood.* London: Routledge and Kegan Paul, 1954.

BEAVER, M. W. "Population, Infant Mortality and Milk." *Population Studies,* 27 (1973), 243–254.

BREEN, T. H., AND STEPHEN FOSTER. "Moving to the New World: The Character of Early Massachusetts Immigration." *William and Mary Quarterly,* 30 (1973), 189–222.

CALDWELL, JOHN C. "Toward a Restatement of Demographic Transition Theory." *Population and Development Review,* 2 (1976), 321–365.

CRAFTS, N. F. R. AND N. J. IRELAND. "Family Limitation and the English Demographic Revolution." *Journal of Economic History,* 36 (1976), 598–623.

EASTERLIN, RICHARD A. "Population Change and Farm Settlement in the Northern United States." *Journal of Economic History,* 36 (1976), 45–83.

HIMES, NORMAN E. *Medical History of Contraception.* 1936. Reprint. New York: Gamut Press 1963.

KNIGHTS, PETER R. "Population Turnover, Persistence, and Residential Mobility in Boston, 1830–1860." in *Nineteenth-Century Cities.* Ed. Stephan Thernstrom and Richard Sennett. New Haven: Yale University Press, 1969.

KNODEL, JOHN E. *The Decline of Fertility in Germany.* Princeton: Princeton University Press, 1974.

MCKEOWN, THOMAS. *The Modern Rise of Population.* New York: Academic Press, 1976.

SCHNUCKER, ROBERT V. "Elizabethan Birth Control and Puritan Attitudes." *Journal of Interdisciplinary History,* 4 (1975), 655–667.

SMITH, DANIEL SCOTT. "The Demographic History of Colonial New England." *Journal of Economic Research,* 32 (1972), 165–183.

———. "Family Limitation, Sexual Control and Domestic Feminism in Victorian America." *Feminist Studies,* 1 (1973), 40–57.

STANNARD, DAVID E., ed. *Death in America.* Philadelphia: University of Philadelphia Press, 1975.

———. *The Puritan Way of Death.* New York: Oxford University Press, 1977.

VAN DE WALLE, ETIENNE. *The Female Population of France in the Nineteenth Century.* Princeton: Princeton University Press, 1974.

VINOVSKIS, MARIS A. "Mortality Rates and Trends in Massachusetts Before 1860." *Journal of Economic History,* 32 (1972), 184–213.

WELLS, ROBERT V. *The Population of the British Colonies in America before 1776.* Princeton: Princeton University Press, 1975.

WESTOFF, CHARLES F. AND NORMAN B. RYDER. *The Contraceptive Revolution.* Princeton: Princeton University Press, 1977.

WRIGLEY E. A. *Population and History.* London: Weidenfeld and Nicholson, 1969.

# CONTRIBUTORS

MICHAEL ANDERSON (sociology), University of Edinburgh; G. J. BARKER-BENFIELD (history), State University of New York, Albany; LOIS GREEN CARR, St. Mary's City Commission, Annapolis, Maryland; MIRIAM COHEN (history), University of Michigan; NANCY F. COTT (American studies), Yale University; CARL N. DEGLER (history), Stanford University; JOHN DEMOS (history), Brandeis University; RICHARD A. EASTERLIN (economics), University of Pennsylvania; FRANK F. FURSTENBERG, JR. (sociology), University of Pennsylvania; PHILIP J. GREVEN, JR. (history), Rutgers University; HERBERT G. GUTMAN (history), Graduate Center, City University of New York; PETER D. HALL (history), Wesleyan University; TAMARA K. HAREVEN (history), Clark University; THEODORE HERSHBERG (history), University of Pennsylvania; JOSEPH F. KETT (history), University of Virginia; FRANCES E. KOBRIN (sociology), Brown University; ALLAN KULIKOFF (history), University of Illinois, Chicago; JOHN MODELL (history), University of Minnesota; EDMUND S. MORGAN (history), Yale University; ELIZABETH H. PLECK (history), University of Michigan; JOAN W. SCOTT (history), University of North Carolina; DANIEL S. SMITH (history), University of Illinois, Chicago; CARROLL SMITH-ROSENBERG (history), University of Pennsylvania; LOUISE A. TILLY (history), University of Michigan; MARIS A. VINOVSKIS (history), University of Michigan; LORENA S. WALSH, St. Mary's City Commission, Annapolis, Maryland; ROBERT V. WELLS (history), Union College; BARBARA WELTER (history), Hunter College.

# ACKNOWLEDGMENTS (continued from page iv)

## II  MARRIAGE: BEGINNINGS AND ENDINGS

"Parental Power and Marriage Patterns: An Analysis of Historical Trends in Hingham, Massachusetts" by Daniel Scott Smith. Reprinted from *Journal of Marriage and the Family*, 35 (August 1973), 419–428. Copyright 1973 by the National Council on Family Relations. Reprinted by permission.

"Marital Selection and Business in Massachusetts Merchant Families, 1800–1900" by Peter Dobkin Hall. Reprinted by permission of the author and publisher from *The Family and Its Structure and Functions*, ed. Rose Laub Coser. (New York: St. Martin's Press, 1974), pp. 226–242.

"Divorce and the Changing Status of Women in Eighteenth-Century Massachusetts" by Nancy F. Cott. Reprinted by permission of the author and publisher from the *William and Mary Quarterly*, 3rd Ser., 33 (October 1976), 586–614.

"Divorce in the Progressive Era" by William L. O'Neill. Reprinted by permission of the author and publisher from *American Quarterly*, Summer 1965, pp. 205–217. Copyright, 1965, Trustees of the University of Pennsylvania.

## III  STAGES OF LIFE

"Infancy and Childhood in the Plymouth Colony" by John Demos. From *A Little Commonwealth: Family Life in Plymouth Colony* by John Demos. Copyright © 1970 by Oxford University Press, Inc. Reprinted by permission.

"The Stages of Life" by Joseph F. Kett. Chapter I, "The Stages of Life," from *Rites of Passage: Adolescence in America, 1790 to the Present*, by Joseph F. Kett. © 1977 by Joseph F. Kett, Basic Books, Inc., Publishers, New York.

"Social Change and Transitions to Adulthood in Historical Perspective" by John Modell, Frank F. Furstenburg, Jr., and Theodore Hershberg. Reprinted from *Journal of Family History*, Autumn 1976, pp. 7–32. Copyright 1976 by the National Council on Family Relations. Reprinted by permission.

"Old Age in Early New England" by John Demos. Copyright 1975 by Case Western Reserve University. This is a revised version of a paper entitled "Old Age in Early New England" presented at a conference held at Case Western Reserve University, November 1975, on "Human Values and Aging: New Challenges to Research in the Humanities," a project funded by the National Endowment for the Humanities. The article is to be published in a volume, *Aging, Death and Completion of Being*, the University of Pennsylvania Press. Reprinted by permission of David D. Van Tassel, Project Director, and Case Western Reserve University

## IV  WOMEN: ROLES AND RELATIONSHIPS

"The Planter's Wife: The Experience of White Women in Seventeenth-Century Maryland" by Lois Green Carr and Lorena S. Walsh. Reprinted by permission of the authors and publisher from *William and Mary Quarterly*, 3rd Ser., 34 (1977) (forthcoming).

"Women's Work and European Fertility Patterns" by Louise Tilly, Joan W. Scott, and Miriam Cohen. Reprinted from *The Journal of Interdisciplinary History*, 6 (1976), 447–476, by permission of *The Journal of Interdisciplinary History* and the M.I.T. Press,

Cambridge, Massachusetts. Copyright 1976 by Massachusetts Institute of Technology and the editors of *The Journal of Interdisciplinary History*.

"The Cult of True Womanhood: 1820-1860" by Barbara Welter. Reprinted by permission of the author and publisher from the *American Quarterly*, Summer 1966, pp. 151-174. Copyright, 1966, Trustees of the University of Pennsylvania.

"The Female World of Love and Ritual: Relations Between Women in Nineteenth-Century America" by Carroll Smith-Rosenberg. Reprinted from *Signs*, 1 (Autumn 1975), 1-29, by permission of the author and the publisher, the University of Chicago Press. © 1975 by The University of Chicago. All rights reserved.

## V  SEX: BEHAVIOR AND IDEOLOGY

"The Puritans and Sex" by Edmund S. Morgan. Reprinted by permission of the author and publisher from the *New England Quarterly*, December 1942, pp. 591-607.

"The Spermatic Economy: A Nineteenth-Century View of Sexuality" by G. J. Barker-Benfield. Reprinted by permission of the author from *Feminist Studies*, 1, no. 1 (1972), 45-74. Copyright 1972 by G. J. Barker-Benfield.

"What Ought to Be and What Was: Woman's Sexuality in the Nineteenth Century" by Carl N. Degler. Reprinted by permission of the author from *American Historical Review*, 79 (December 1974) 1467-1490. By permission of Carl N. Degler, copyright holder.

"The Dating of the American Sexual Revolution: Evidence and Interpretation" by Daniel Scott Smith. Prepared especially for the first edition of this volume. Copyright © 1973 by Daniel Scott Smith. Reprinted by permission of the author.

## VI  ETHNICITY

"The Beginnings of the Afro-American Family in Maryland" by Allan Kulikoff. Reprinted from *Law, Society, and Politics in Early Maryland*, ed. A. C. Land, L. G. Carr, and E. C. Papenfuse (Baltimore: Johns Hopkins University Press, 1977). Reprinted by permission of the author and the publisher. Copyright 1977 by Hall of Records Commission of the State of Maryland.

"Persistent Myths About the Afro-American Family" by Herbert G. Gutman. Reprinted from *The Journal of Interdisciplinary History*, 6 (1975), 181-210, by permission of *The Journal of Interdisciplinary History* and the M.I.T. Press, Cambridge, Massachusetts. Copyright 1975 by Massachusetts Institute of Technology and the editors of *The Journal of Interdisciplinary History*.

"A Mother's Wages: Income Earning Among Italian And Black Women, 1896-1911" by Elizabeth H. Pleck. Previously published. By permission of the author.

## VII  DEMOGRAPHY: BIRTHS, DEATHS, AND MIGRATION

"Family History and Demographic Transition" by Robert V. Wells. Reprinted from the *Journal of Social History*, 9 (Fall 1975), 1-20, by permission of the editor.

"Factors in the Decline of Farm Family Fertility in the United States: Some Preliminary Research Results" by Richard A. Easterlin. Reprinted from the *Journal of American History*, 63 (December 1976), 600-614. By permission of The Organization of American Historians. Copyright 1976 by The Organization of American Historians.

"Angels' Heads and Weeping Willows: Death in Early America" by Maris A. Vinovskis. Reprinted by permission of the author and publisher from *Proceedings of the American Antiquarian Society*, 86, part 2 (1977), 273-302. Copyright 1977 by the American Antiquarian Society.

# INDEX